EUROPEAN CHALLENGES IN CONTEMPORARY FAMILY LAW

EUROPEAN CHALLENGES IN CONTEMPORARY FAMILY LAW

Edited by

Katharina Boele-Woelki
Tone Sverdrup

intersentia

Antwerp – Oxford – Portland

Distribution for the UK:
Hart Publishing Ltd.
16C Worcester Place
Oxford OX1 2JW
UK
Tel.: +44 1865 51 75 30
Fax: +44 1865 51 07 10

Distribution for Switzerland and Germany:
Stämpfli Verlag AG
Wölflistrasse 1
CH-3001 Bern
Switzerland
Tel.: +41 0 31 300 63 18
Fax: +41 0 31 300 66 88

Distribution for the USA and Canada:
International Specialized Book Services
920 NE 58th Ave Suite 300
Portland, OR 97213
USA
Tel.: +1 800 944 6190 (toll free)
Tel.: +1 503 287 3093
Fax: +1 503 280 8832
email: info@isbs.com

Distribution for other countries:
Intersentia Publishers
Groenstraat 31
BE-2640 Mortsel
Belgium
Tel.: +32 3 680 15 50
Fax: +32 3 658 71 21

European Challenges in Contemporary Family Law
Katharina Boele-Woelki and Tone Sverdrup (eds.)

ISBN 978-90-5095-692-5
D/2008/7849/8
NUR 822

PREFACE

What constitutes the European challenges in contemporary family law? The third CEFL Conference in Oslo from 7–9 June 2007 brought together more than 100 participants from 30 countries to provide answers to this question by addressing a wide range of issues that currently engage family lawyers in Europe. The conference was organised along the same lines as the two previous CEFL conferences held in Utrecht in 2002 and 2004. According to the CEFL, it is of the utmost importance that young researchers are invited to the general discussions concerning the process of the harmonisation of family law in Europe. Therefore, the CEFL has deliberately chosen two categories of presenters: recognized authorities on different aspects of family law on the one hand, and young researchers who have been selected after a call for papers, on the other. In this volume the reader will find their final written contributions.

The volume consists of five parts. Part one deals with THE HARMONISATION OF FAMILY LAW in Europe, especially the Nordic countries, and the United States. The general usage of the concepts of human rights, harmonisation and unification is among the subjects addressed in this part. Part two – CHILDREN AND THEIR PARENTS – deals with general aspects of the human rights of children, as well as specific questions arising from new family forms and the new technology of artificial fertilisation. This part relates to CEFL's second working field, and the Principles regarding parental responsibilities, which were published in no. 16 of this series, are presented. Part three contains contributions on IRREGULAR MARRIAGES AND THE INFLUENCE OF MULTICULTURALISM, especially Muslim traditions, in different areas of family law. The fourth part – (PROPERTY) RELATIONS BETWEEN SPOUSES AND COHABITANTS – deals with a broad range of key questions in connection with economic settlements upon the dissolution of marriage and cohabitation. Finally, the fifth part is dedicated to CROSS-BORDER FAMILY RELATIONSHIPS and the different legal instruments in this area of private international law.

These issues represent European challenges in contemporary family law and they are, in different ways, related to the remarkable change in family life that has taken place in Europe in the last three or four decades. Hardly any other field of law has experienced such profound and deep social and demographic changes as family law in this short period of time: an explosion in the divorce rates and extramarital cohabitation and the resulting increase in the number of children born out of wedlock; women joining the paid work force *en masse*, influencing, among other things, parental roles and property relations among partners; and – more recently – the growing social acceptance of same-sex relationships and new techniques of artificial insemination are just a few important features of this development. We are in the middle of a "silent revolution" in family life in Europe. And while these transformations take place, we experience a vast cross-border movement of people – both within Europe, and in the form of migration from other continents.

Some would maintain that it is impractical to develop principles of family law in such a period of transition. Others would argue that it is more important than ever to provide basic guidelines for a common legal framework for family life in Europe. As we know, different opinions exist on these and other questions of harmonisation. The contributions in this volume will, hopefully, enrich and inspire these discussions.

The 3rd CEFL conference was organised in co-operation with the Department of Private Law at the University of Oslo, and was largely financed by the Nordic Council of Ministers, the Norwegian Ministry of Justice and the Norwegian Ministry of Children and Equality. We would like to extend our heartfelt gratitude to all these four institutions for their substantial contributions.

Katharina Boele-Woelki and Tone Sverdrup
Utrecht and Oslo, December 2007

LIST OF AUTHORS

Maria Álvarez Torné
Research assistant at the Department of International Law and Economics, University of Barcelona

Anne-Florence Bock
PhD researcher and teaching assistant, University of Basel

Prof. Dr. Katharina Boele-Woelki
Professor of Private International Law, Comparative Law and Family Law at the Molengraaff Institute for Private Law, University of Utrecht

Prof. Dr. Ted M. de Boer
Professor of Private International Law and Comparative Law, University of Amsterdam

Prof. Dr. Dagmar Coester-Waltjen
Professor of Law, University of Munich

Dr. Mariel Dimsey
Associate at Lovells LLP, Frankfurt; former Research assistant at the University of Basel

Maebh Harding
NUI EJ Phelan Fellow of International Law and PhD Candidate at University College Dublin

Dr. Michael Hellner
Associate Professor of Private International Law, Uppsala University

David Hill
PhD researcher at the University of Dundee, Research assistant at Napier University

Anna Horínová
Postgraduate student (2nd degree), Masaryk University of Brno

Dr. Kathrin Kroll
Academic Assistant, Institute for German, European and International Family Law, University of Bonn

Dr. Göran Lind
Associate Professor, University of Uppsala, Manager of the Jura Law Institute

Prof. Dr. Peter Lødrup
Professor of Law, University of Oslo

Jo Miles
Fellow of Trinity College and University Lecturer in Law at the University of Cambridge

Mosa Sayed
PhD researcher, University of Uppsala

Prof. Dr. Lucy Smith
Professor of Law, University of Oslo

Dr. Balázs Somfai
Senior lecturer, University of Pécs

Prof. Dr. Tone Sverdrup
Professor of Law, University of Oslo

Dr. Aspasia Tsaoussis
Visiting Assistant Professor, ALBA Graduate Business School, Attorney-at-law, Athens

Dr. Machteld Vonk
Researcher/lecturer at the Molengraaff Institute for Private Law, University of Utrecht

Prof. Robin Fretwell Wilson
Professor of Law, Washington & Lee University School of Law

Dr. Eleni Zervogianni
Research Associate at the Faculty of International and European Studies of the University of Piraeus and at the Hellenic Institute of International and Foreign Law

TABLE OF CONTENTS

PART THREE. IRREGULAR MARRIAGES AND THE INFLUENCE OF MULTICULTURALISM

"TO AFFINITY AND BEYOND": A CRITICAL ANALYSIS OF THE LAW ON MARRIAGE WITHIN PROHIBITED DEGREES OF RELATIONSHIP

THE MUSLIM DOWER (*MAHR*) IN EUROPE – WITH SPECIAL REFERENCE TO SWEDEN

DIVIDING THE ASSETS UPON THE DISSOLUTION OF A MARRIAGE
A Comparison Between Legal Systems Which Apply a 'Hard and Fast Rule' and Systems with a Discretionary Approach to the Division of Assets

PROPERTY RELATIONS BETWEEN SPOUSES IN THE LEGISLATION OF THE CZECH REPUBLIC AND IN THAT OF SELECTED POST-COMMUNIST COUNTRIES

PART ONE
THE HARMONISATION OF FAMILY LAW

HUMAN RIGHTS AND THE HARMONIZATION OF FAMILY LAW IN EUROPE

DAGMAR COESTER-WALTJEN

1. THE PROBLEM

1.1. FAMILY LAW AND HUMAN RIGHTS

Of all the areas of the law, family law is perhaps the one where the need to respect human rights is the most important.[1] It seems evident that in a civilized society a right to marry and a right to found a family must be guaranteed. However, on a closer consideration of the issues, some doubts arise. What really constitutes a "marriage",[2] what are the elements of a "family"?[3] How can one describe "human

1 CARSTEN SMITH, "Human Rights as a Foundation of Society" in: LØDRUP/ MODVAR (Eds.), *Family Life and Human Rights*, 2004, pp. 15 ss.

2 PARKMAN, "To what "marriage" do we have a right?", in: LØDRUP/ MODVAR, op.cit., pp. 553 ss; ESTIN, ""Human Rights, Pluralism, and Family Law", in: LØDRUP/ MODVAR, op.cit., pp. 211 ss; ECHR October 9, 1979 Series A 32 Z. 33 "Airey"; ECHR December 18, 1986, EuGRZ 1987, 313 "Johnston"; ECHR December 18, 1987 Series A 128 No. 11329/85 EuGRZ 1993, 130 "F"; ECHR September 27, 1990. Series A 184, Z. 38 ss "Cossey"; ECHR July 11, 2002, RJD 2002 VI, Z. 71 "Goodwin"; ECHR October 17, 1986, Series A 106 Z. 37 "Rees".

3 SUMNER, "The Character of Fundamental Rights of the European Union and Sexual Orientation", in: LØDRUP/ MODVAR, op.cit., pp. 869, 876 s.; SCHEIWE, "Legal Provisions that allow women to give birth anonymously – apt to be exported from France to Germany?" in: LØDRUP/ MODVAR, op.cit., pp. 681, 687; MEULDERS-KLEIN, "Family Law, Human Rights and Judicial Review in Europe", in: LØDRUP/ MODVAR, op. cit., pp. 477, 486; BOOTH ""It's a wise man (sic) who knows his own father..." – Fatherhood's "Human Right" recognized: The unmarried Father and English Law", in: LØDRUP/ MODVAR, op.cit., p. 97; DEECH, "The Human Genome and Human Rights", in: LØDRUP/ MODVAR, op.cit., pp. 163, 171; TAMIKI, "Can One Choose One's Own Sex", in: LØDRUP/ MODVAR, op.cit., pp. 889, 898; ECHR October 27, 1994, A 297-C, Z. 30 "Kroon"; European Commission of May 19, 1992 no. 15666/89, Z. 1 "Kerkhofen"; ECHR May 26, 1994, EuGRZ 1995, 113 "Keegan"; ECHR June 13, 1979, EuGRZ 1979, 454 "Marckx"; ECHR April 22, 1997, RJD 1997 II, Z. 36 "X, Y, Z".

rights"?[4] Where do they come from?[5] Who is to interpret their meaning?[6] We may use the same words but they can have different meanings[7] and we may have different goals in using them.[8]

In preparing this speech, I reviewed the papers presented at the Oslo Conference of the International Society for Family Law[9] five years ago and concluded that there is a very broad range of ideas concerning the family, concerning marriage and concerning human rights as such.[10] There are different attitudes towards the very fundamental questions concerning family and marriage across time and across cultures. In the end I found myself "lost in definitions", unable to draw a sharp demarcation line between inalienable rights and indispensable rights concerning marriage and the family, and unable to define the "eternal truth" in these matters.

---

4 Eekelaar, "Personal Rights and Human Rights", in: Lødrup/ Modvar, op.cit., p. 179, 193; Palm-Risse, "Der völkerrechtliche Schutz der Ehe und Familie", 1990, pp. 30 ss.; Fahrenhorst, "Familienrecht und europäische Menschenrechtskonvention", 1994, pp. 13 ss., 94 ss.; Kopper-Reifenberg, "Kindschaftsrechtsreform und Schutz des Familienlebens nach Art. 8 EMRK", 2001; pp. 92 ss.; Meyer-Ladewig, "Handkommentar zur EMRK", Art. 1 no. 11; van Dijk/van Hoof, "Theory and Practice of the European Convention on Human Rights", 3rd ed. 1998 §2.2.

5 Finnis, "Natural Law and Natural Rights", 1980; Habermas, "Between Facts and Norms, Contributions to a Discourse Theory of Law and Democracy", 1996.

6 Critical with regard to the interpretation of the ECHR: Meulders-Klein, op.cit., pp. 477, 485; Antokolskaia, "Human Rights as a Basis of Harmonisation of Family Law?", in: Lødrup/ Modvar, op. cit., pp. 29, 38; for the evolving dynamic interpretation of the ECHR see (quite negatively) Hausheer, "Der Fall Burghartz oder: Vom bisweilen garstigen Geschäft der richterlichen Rechtsharmonisierung in internationalen Verhältnissen", EuGRZ 1995, 579, 580; Meulders-Klein, in: Lødrup/ Modvar, op.cit., pp. 477, 485; more positive, especially stressing the need to adapt to social change, is Limbach, "Lifestyles and the Development of the Family from the Point of View of Constitutional Law and Constitutional Policy", in: Mahoney/ Matscher/Petzold/Wildhaber (Eds.), *Protecting Human Rights: The European Perspective, Studies in Memory of Rolv Ryssdal*, 2000, pp. 763, 766 ss.

7 For example, the term marriage is already used in the Netherlands, Spain and Belgium for a union of homosexual persons as well as of heterosexual persons, whereas traditionally the meaning has been confined to the union between a man and a woman.

8 If we speak of human rights we might think of them as a postulate for protection or for non-interference, we might use the term merely to indicate value assessments within our society.

9 See the connection of papers presented at the 11th World Conference of the International Society of Family Law, edited by Lødrup and by Modvar, "Family Life and Human Rights"(as already cited above).

10 See, for example, Meulders-Klein, "Towards a European Civil Code on Family Law? Ends and Means", in: Boele-Woelki (Eds.), *Perspectives for the Unification and Harmonisation of Family Law in Europe*, 2003, pp. 105, 110, 112; Bradley, "A Family Law for Europe? Sovereignty, Political Economy and Legitimation", in: Boele-Woelki, *Perspectives*, op.cit., pp. 65, 103.

1.2. VALUES WITHIN A GIVEN TIME, A GIVEN SOCIETY OR CULTURE

However, this is not the end of the speech. It would be too easy to try to escape all responsibility by pointing at a possible and legitimate diversity of opinions in these matters. Every society has to try to define its own standards concerning fundamental issues for its own time. I want to avoid answering the question as to whether human rights exist *a priori*[11] or not. Even if they do exist, each society has to discover them, but may to a greater or lesser extent fail to do so. Thus, we can only ever speak of the values and standards which we recognize or accept for our society for the time being. But even with this general relativity of our judgments and classifications in mind, we have to realize that there is no homogenous body of universally accepted human rights that withstands change over a long period of time. The discussions on family law issues under the ECHR and the critical comments on decisions of the ECHR prove this conclusively. Therefore, I would like to draw a demarcation line between human rights as such and other value assessments. The latter may be embodied in international conventions, but they may be subject to evolving circumstances and to the spirit of the age.

Many different international instruments and the constitutions of our legal systems contain rules concerning marriage and the family.[12] I do not intend to go into technical details on the state of ratification of these Conventions,[13] their binding force[14] or the force and authority of court decisions on these

11 See Finnis, op.cit.; Dworkin, "Taking Rights Seriously", 1977, pp. 265.

12 Compare, for example, Carsten Smith, in: Lødrup/ Modvar, op.cit., p. 15; Agrawal, "Family Life and Human Rights", in: Lødrup/ Modvar, op.cit., p. 20; Palm-Risse, op.cit., p. 48; Seidel, "Handbuch der Grund- und Menschenrechte auf staatlicher, europäischer und universeller Ebene", 1996, pp. 48 ss (citing international conventions and the German Basic Law; Wittinger, "Familien und Frauen im regionalen Menschenrechtsschutz", 1999, pp. 31 ss. (comparing the ECHR with the African Charter of Human Rights); Estin, in Lødrup/ Modvar, op.cit., pp. 211, 212 ss.; Meulders-Klein, in: Lødrup/ Modvar, op.cit., p. 477, 481 (giving examples of national constitutions protecting marriage and the family). Compare also the overview of the national protection of the family and marriage in constitutions by Palm-Risse, "Der völkerrechtliche Schutz von Ehe und Familie", p. 45, who reviewed the constitutional framework in 168 states.

13 Estin, in: Lødrup/ Modvar, op.cit., pp. 210, 212 (with sources for the states of ratification).

14 For example the EU's European Charter on Human Rights does not have any binding force, but is only a political declaration, compare Schmitz, "Die EU-Grundrechte-Charta aus grundrechtsdogmatischer und grundrechtstheoretischer Sicht", JZ 2001, pp. 833, 835; C. Calliess, "Die Charta der Grundrechte der Europäischen Union – Fragen der Konzeption, Kompetenz und Verbindlichkeit", EuZW 2001, 261, 267; Altmaier, "Die Charta der Grundrechte der Europäischen Union", ZG 2001, 195, 204. Meulders-Klein, in: Lødrup/ Modvar, op.cit., p. 477, 489; Sumner, "The Character of Fundamental Rights of the European Union and Sexual Orientation", in: Lødrup/ Modvar, op.cit., p. 869, 884; Verschraegen, ""Family Members", The Right to Family Life and Family Reunification", in: Lødrup/ Modvar, op.cit., pp. 1919, 1920.

matters,[15] nor do I wish to point out the differences between the different states regarding the constitutional protection of marriage and the family.[16] Much has been said and written about these issues.[17] I do not wish to repeat what has been said about the effect of the provisions of the European Convention on Human Rights or which meaning has been given to these provisions in legal literature or by the Court of Strasbourg, because this has already been extensively discussed and – despite my original plans for this speech – I see no use in repeating these learned opinions or adding a slightly different one. And, further, I will not try to separate the "true" human rights in family matters from the mere value assessments. Instead I shall proceed on a rather abstract level and confine myself to the human rights aspects of the right to form an intimate, emotional partnership.

2. CHARACTERISTICS OF HUMAN RIGHTS

2.1. DIFFERENT DEGREES OF RIGHTS

2.1.1. The Inalienable

I think we can agree that there can be different degrees of human rights. There are some human rights which go to the very root of humanity like for example the protection of humans from slavery, genocide, racial discrimination, and – notwithstanding the current discussions in relation to terrorism, I dare say – from torture.[18] Those rights are guaranteed without any reservation or exception and without any margin of appreciation. Rights concerning marriage and the family

---

15 Compare with regard to the limited facts of the decisions of the ECHR: Binda, "Verkehrtes zum Verkehrsrecht", EuGRZ 2002, pp. 1 ss.; Cremer, "Zur Bindungswirkung von EGMR-Urteilen", EuGRZ 2004, 692, 693; Roller, "Die menschenrechts-konventionsgemäße Auslegung", DRiZ 2004, 337. Meulders-Klein, in: Lødrup/ Modvar, op.cit., pp. 477, 487.

16 Meulders-Klein, in: Lødrup/ Modvar, op.cit., pp. 477, 481.

17 Compare, for example, the whole volume of Lødrup/ Modvar, op.cit.; Wittinger, "Familien und Frauen im regionalen Menschenrechtsschutz", 1999; Palm-Risse, "Der völkerrechtliche Schutz von Ehe und Familie", 1990; Kopper-Reifenberg, "Kindschaftsrechtsreform und Schutz des Familienlebens nach Art. 8 EMRK", 2001; Fahrenhorst, "Familienrecht und europäische Menschenrechtskonvention", 1994; Seidel, "Handbuch der Grund- und Menschenrechte auf staatlicher, europäischer und universeller Ebene", 1996; Bradley, "Family Law for Europe? Sovereignty, Political Economy and Legitimation", in: Boele-Woelki (Eds.), op.cit., p. 65 ss.; Meulders-Klein, "Towards a European Civil Code on Family Law? Ends and Means", in Boele-Woelki (Eds.), op.cit., pp. 105 ss.; McGlynn, "Challenging the European Harmonisation of Family Law: Perspectives on "The Family"", in: Boele-Woelki (Eds.), op.cit., p. 219.

18 Palm-Risse, "Der völkerrechtliche Schutz von Ehe und Familie", p. 39; Frowein, "Verpflichtungen *erga omnes* im Völkerrecht und ihre Durchsetzung", in: *Festschrift für Hermann Mosler*, 1983, pp. 241, 243.

are normally not classified as belonging to this inner circle. They are regarded as subject to other rights and interests.[19]

Notwithstanding this weaker role which is attributed to the area we are talking about, I would like to propose here that, independent of any written rules, there is:

first, an inalienable and indispensable right of every human being to an intimate, emotional partnership with another human being of their free will, i.e. a partnership in the horizontal line,[20]

second – I mention this only in contrast to the first and I shall not have time to deliberate thereon – there is a human right of the same absolute category concerning the right to form a relationship from one generation to the next, i.e. a connection between human beings in the vertical line.

Before I move on to explain in detail what I mean by this first right and what conclusion we can draw in the context of the harmonization of family law in Europe, I would like to make some reservations.

2.1.2. Core and Periphery

First of all, I would like to distinguish between:

(a) The inalienable heart of a human right, the essential core which might be regarded as existing independently of cultural and temporal peculiarities or attitudes; an elementary component of humanity with a universalist basis; a right which pertains to everyone without exception and
(b) a kind of peripheral or border area around the core of the human right, where there is indeed room for cultural and social divergence.

2.1.3. Flexibility

I would also like to warn against precipitate classifications of rights as human rights and especially of rights which are characterized as lying at the heart of human rights. Not every right which we consider to be just and appropriate is to be attributed with the quality of a human right. Otherwise the system becomes too rigid and too exposed to changing attitudes in different societies at different times.

19 Palm-Risse, "Der völkerrechtliche Schutz von Ehe und Familie", op.cit., pp. 34 ss.
20 See for example on this "end-state": Eekelaar, in: Lødrup/ Modvar, op.cit., p. 191.

2.2. DIFFERENT FUNCTIONS

Further, the guarantee of human rights can have different intensity. A human right can be conceived as a right of the individual or of a group of individuals against the state, thus establishing a *negative obligation* on the state or society not to interfere with this right.[21] But a human right can also carry us one step further and oblige society *positively* to provide *access* to certain legal positions and to legally *recognize* certain relations or positions.[22] Another concept of a human right might include a positive obligation of the state or society to *protect* this right of the individual or group and to ensure effective observance of these rights.[23] The European Court of Human Rights on Strasbourg has applied every one of these aspects in different situations when dealing with the protection of marriage and the family.[24] Whether one or more aspects apply to a particular right or situation is dependant on the type of human right concerned and will be subject to more scrutiny later.

In addition to these three possible functions of human rights, given societies might want to express their absolute conviction as to certain values which they hold dear. These principles need not necessarily amount to human rights, because they might lack a universalist basis, but they can form valuable guidelines for lawmakers. However, such principles are more exposed to social change. Although, on the one hand, they allow more flexibility, on the other, the unanimity between societies achieved at one time may disappear at another time. Many of the international conventions have to deal with this special problem.

---

21 Meulders-Klein, in: Lødrup/ Modvar, op.cit., pp. 477, 485; Villinger, "Handbuch der Europäischen Menschenrechtskonvention", 1993, no. 160; Malinverni, "Les fonctions des droits fondamentaux dans la jurisprudence de la Commission et de la Cour Européene de Droit de L'Homme", in: Haller/Kölz/Müller/Thürer (Eds.), *Im Dienst an der Gemeinschaft, Festschrift für D. Schindler*, 1989, pp. 539, 540.

22 Malinverni, in: Haller/Kölz/Müller/Thürer, op.cit., pp. 539, 546.

23 Meulders-Klein, in: Lødrup/ Modvar, op.cit., p. 477, 485; Villinger, "Handbuch der Europäischen Menschenrechtskonvention", 1993, no. 160; Malinverni, "Les fonctions des droits fondamentaux dans la jurisprudence de la Commission et de la Cour Européene de Droit de L'Homme", in: Haller/Kölz/Müller/Thürer, op.cit., 1989, pp. 539, 540.

24 A right to no interference: ECHR July 13, 2000, RJD 2000-VII, Z. 43 "Elsholz"; ECHR July 23, 1963, Series A I B 6, EuGRZ 1975, 289 "Belgium Languages Case"; ECHR July 8, 1987 "W"; access and legal recognition: ECHR October 9, 1979, Series A 32 Z. 33, EuGRZ 1979, 626 "Airey"; ECHR May 26, 1994, A 290, EuGRZ 1995, 113 "Keegan"; protection and effective observance: ECHR May 26, 1994, A 290, EuGRZ 1995, 113 "Keegan"; ECHR June 13, 1979, A 31, EuGRZ 1979, 454 "Marckx".

2.3. POSSIBLE CONFLICTS

In the field of human rights under discussion, we have to bear in mind that there might be several human rights which could conflict with one another, restrict each other, or have to be brought into balance. Therefore, we have to be extremely careful when dealing with human rights in family law. This would be even more evident if we look at the right to found a family.

Having made these reservations and provided explanations for my understanding of human rights, I would now like to elaborate on my proposal concerning partnership.

3. A RIGHT TO AN INTIMATE, EMOTIONAL PARTNERSHIP FOR EVERY HUMAN BEING

3.1. TYPE OF PARTNERSHIP

3.1.1. Sex and Sexual Orientation

I would like to talk about the right of every human being to an intimate, emotional partnership with another human being of their free will. If we look at the history of mankind across our cultures, we cannot but agree that there is this need for an intimate and emotional relationship between one human being and another. Although this intimacy will very often involve sexual contact and relations, this is not an indispensable element of such partnerships. Thus, the right need not be confined to sexual relations only, but may also embrace other intimate emotional bonds. Further, although partnerships will be constituted in the majority of cases by persons of different sexes, one cannot deny the desire of an emotional bond for those human beings who long for a companion of the same sex. On a universalist basis no difference can be made with regard to sex or sexual orientation, because we are talking of a right arising from the status of being human.[25]

3.1.2. Free Will

The right of one human being must be limited by the rights of other human beings. Therefore, a right to such a partnership presupposes that the human beings concerned form this partnership of their own free will. Otherwise the

---

[25] Eekelaar, in: Lødrup/ Modvar, op.cit., pp. 179, 193.

rights of one human being would be sacrificed for the needs of another human being. This would be in conflict with human dignity and the principle of equality which is an inherent element insofar as we are considering the universalist basis.

From this, two further conclusions can be drawn. First, this right is not only the right of one individual but of the individuals forming this partnership and of the partnership itself. Second, the free will requirement pertaining to the human beings concerned presupposes the ability to form one's "free will". Thus, the right only pertains to persons who can be regarded as "masters of their own minds" concerning the issue in question.[26] Whether this means that they have to be of full age and have full mental capacity in all respects is another question. I do not think that there is an *a priori* answer of eternal validity to this question, but that across cultures, social circumstances and time, the limits may vary, and it is for each society to find the right balance between the right to an intimate emotional partnership, on the one hand, and the protection of the human beings involved by ensuring their free choice and assent, on the other. The prohibition on child marriages by the UN Convention on Consent to Marriage, Minimum Age, Former Marriage and Registration of Marriage[27] is justified and as far as the marital age is concerned, most European states consider the age of approximately 18 years to be appropriate.[28] But this is a question of balance which allows for a margin of appreciation.

3.1.3. The Number of Partners

A further question arises with regard to the number of persons possibly involved in such a partnership. There are societies and legal systems which allow polygamy or – to a lesser extent – polyandrous marriages.[29] Western society and especially European legal systems are more reluctant in this respect although they often recognize polygamous marriages if they have been validly entered into elsewhere and most of them accept the so-called subsequent or rotating polygamy. For the purpose of our considerations, however, I do not think that we have to go deeper into these matters, because these polygamous relationships can be split into the

---

26 ECHR January 1, 2003, no. 45 "S.L."; ECHR October 26, 1998, 142 "Norris"; ECHR October 22, 1981, A 45 "Dudgeon".

27 Convention of December 10, 1962, 521 UNTS 231.

28 Coester-Waltjen/Coester, "Formation of Marriage, International Encyclopedia of Comparative Law", vol. IV, ch. 3 no. 24–35; Palm-Risse, "Der völkerrechtliche Schutz von Ehe und Familie", p. 123 with regard to an inherent limitation on the national legislators with respect to the character of the relationship.

29 Coester-Waltjen/Coester, "Formation of Marriage, International Encyclopedia of Comparative Law", vol. IV, ch. 3 nos 40–48.

respective 'one to one' intimate and emotional bonds, each of which could enjoy the quality of a human right.

3.2. PROTECTION ATTRIBUTED

3.2.1. *"Protection"*

Let us now move to the more difficult question regarding the level of protection that should be attributed to this type of human right. Is it a mere right to be free from any state intervention, to be left alone from any interference (except the assurance of a free decision)? Does this human right require positive action in the sense of access to a legally recognized union or does this right oblige the state or the communities to positively secure its effective protection?

The human right we are talking about has been given a very broad definition and a very broad field of application. Therefore, the intensity of the obligations of society may vary and not all possible aspects of this right may generate the same level of protection.

3.2.2. *The Right to be Left Alone*

From what I have said before, it seems clear that the human right to form a partnership obliges the state not to interfere with this right, and – despite the former criminalization of homosexual activities in several legal systems – I think that this is no longer disputed.[30]

3.2.3. *The Right to Legal Recognition and Protection*

3.2.3.1. Marriages and Partnerships

It is a far more delicate issue to find an answer to the other two concepts. Are societies obliged to ensure access to a legally recognized institution for all intimate, emotional partnerships? With regard to marriage, there seems to be widespread agreement that there is this obligation. Thus, we find such institutional guarantees, for example, in Art. 12 of the European Convention on Human

30 I would like to stress the difference between this approach and the attitude of the ECHR in the Dudgeon (ECHR October 22, 1981, A 45) and Norris Cases (ECHR October 26, 1998, A 142), because I do not put weight on respect for the private life of the individual, but rather especially on the interaction with another human being.

Rights.[31] We find the same in Art. 9 of the European Charter[32] and in many state constitutions.[33] Due to these provisions a state cannot refrain from making available a legal framework for marriage although these provisions leave a wide margin of appreciation as to how to regulate the issue.[34] But does the above-described human right really oblige the state to do so[35] and does it have to do so for every form of partnership?

Having in mind the principles of equal treatment inherent to any human right, it seems that the need for the legal recognition and protection of intimate partnerships extends in principle to all partnerships. However, as only equal situations have to be treated equally, distinctions might be necessary. First of all, a line has to be drawn between long-term commitments and casual intimate relations. The latter seem to be outside the need for legal recognition and protection, it suffices that the state does not interfere with these companionships. But what about homosexual unions in the form of long-term commitments? One cannot escape the problem by defining marriage in such a way as to embrace all these kinds of partnerships, because this is definitively not the meaning of this term. Marriage, in contrast to intimate emotional partnerships, presupposes a kind of formalization and – though I know that many of you will initially object – marriage has always been confined to a heterosexual relationship.[36] One cannot give a different meaning to the term "marriage" just because other unions need the same recognition and protection. One would not call an old person who is unable to look after himself a child, although he might have the same needs as a child and corresponding rules should apply. Clear terminology and the open consideration of differences and problems further understanding and consensus. In addition, the right to individuality and human dignity infers the right to be different and to be accepted as being different. Therefore, I have a problem with covering homosexual unions under the umbrella of marriage.

---

31 See ECHR October 17, 1986, Series A, 106, Z. 37 "Rees", concerning transsexuals, later revised with regard to transsexuals by ECHR July 11, 202, no. 25680/94 Z. 51 "I"; RJD 2002 VI Z. 71 "Goodwin".

32 Art. 9 reads: Right to Marry and Right to found a Family. The right to marry and the right to found a family shall be guaranteed in accordance with the national law governing the exercise of these rights.

33 See, for example, the overview in Palm-Risse, "Der völkerrechtliche Schutz von Ehe und Familie", p. 45, footnote 76.

34 I cannot hereby agree with my learned colleague Meulders-Klein, in: Lødrup/ Modvar, op.cit., pp. 477, 484.

35 Positive for heterosexual partners: OLG Stuttgart, NJW 1963, 39 "Ehe – ewiges Naturrecht"; diff. View: KG, NJW 1961, 2209, 2211.

36 See ECHR October 17, 1986, Serie A, 106, Z. 37 "Rees", concerning transsexuals, later revised with regard to transsexuals by ECHR July 11, 2002, no. 25680/94 Z. 51 "I"; RJD 2002 VI Z. 71 "Goodwin"; EuGH May 31, 2001, Rs. C-122/99.

However, with regard to legal recognition and protection, I do not see any difference between heterosexual and homosexual unions. In particular, the inability of homosexual couples to jointly produce an offspring appears to be irrelevant, because heterosexual couples might also be unable or unwilling to procreate.[37] It would follow that the functional equivalence of homosexual and heterosexual partnerships consequently obliges the state to provide such partnerships with the same level of recognition, dignity and protection – either within one institution (which, however – for the reasons given above – I would not call marriage) or under a different heading.

It would initially seem that this consequence could only be denied if there are other compelling reasons to do so. Tradition alone and the religious beliefs of sections of society do not provide very convincing counter-arguments. On the other hand, we are within a wider concept of human rights and it may be argued that the question of access to and the recognition of intimate partnerships generates a less compelling human right than the negative obligation of non-interference. I do not think that there is even a human right to have legal rules concerning (heterosexual) marriage. The decision to do so, which many states have taken, is only a value assessment of the given society. Therefore, one may be reluctant to formulate an indispensable human right for the availability of, access to, and protection of a legally recognized homosexual partnership. It appears that this step is just a value adjustment of each society. For our time and our society it appears to be reasonable and consistent to offer a legally recognized and protected institution for homosexual as well as for heterosexual unions between two persons of sound mind, but I hesitate to embody this into a human rights obligation for the legislator. Thus, I would argue that the provisions of the Model Family Code by *Schwenzer*,[38] offering an institution as a legally recognized and protected partnership for both heterosexual and homosexual unions – although I would not call the latter a marriage – conforms to human rights principles, but is not compelled by a human right as such.

3.2.3.2. Informal Unions

A slightly different aspect is at issue if we look at the need for the protection of informal unions. If a formalized legally recognized and protected institution is available for the persons concerned, but the individuals decide not to formalize their union, the question arises whether they should be given access to other institutional protection. It may well be that a legislator offers different kinds of partnerships with different commitments – like a covenant marriage, normal

---

37 Compare with regard to transsexuals: ECHR July 7, 2002, no. 25680/94 Z. 51 "I".

38 Schwenzer/Dimsey, "Model Family Code from a Global Perspective", 2006.

marriages, freely dissoluble unions etc. – but this is not a human rights issue, it is rather a very important value assessment which any society may make for itself.

In contrast to this decision, the question of protection for the individuals of unions which are not legally recognized might very well be a human rights issue, because the particularities of emotional relationships generate the need to protect the rights of each individual from being sacrificed solely for the benefit of the other. There is, however, the question whether this protection of the partners in informal unions, which is in principle necessary, must have the same level of protection as that of formalized unions. Different commitments and different decisions on the part of the individuals may legitimate different solutions. The negative aspect of the human right to have intimate, emotional relationships free from state intervention may set limits to such protective activities. In this respect, the Model Family Code seems to go too far, for example, by establishing a mutual maintenance obligation (Art. 1.15) of the partners of all partnerships even those having nothing more in common than a common child (Art. 1.1 (2)(b)) or because one has made considerable contributions for the benefit of the other at one time (Art. 1.1 (2)(c)).

4. SUMMARY

Thus, I would like to summarize my humble thoughts on human rights and the harmonization of family law in Europe under the special aspect of the right to marry in the following way:

1. We should distinguish between human rights as elementary components of humanity with the universalist basis and value assessments which are absolute convictions about certain values held by a given society. The latter may be subject to change and to different views in the flux of time. The former should prove more stable and unchangeable. Not every rule which we agree to be a just and reasonable solution has a humanitarian root.

2. A human right may have different aspects. It may generate the negative obligation of the state and society not to interfere with the enjoyment of this right, but it can also generate the obligation of the state to take positive action to ensure access to a legally recognized relationship and/or to secure the protection of the relationship and the individuals concerned.

The negative obligation comes automatically with the recognition of the human right. If a right is elementary to humanity then it follows that it should not be interfered with. The question whether this right also generates the obligation to undertake positive action concerns another level and the answer may be subject to different value assessments within the realm of partnership and the family.

3. There is a human right of every human being to an intimate, emotional partnership with another human being of their free will. This means a partnership on the horizontal line in contrast to a relationship from one generation to the next, which is a completely different issue and which is not dealt with here. The human right to a partnership is independent of sexual relations and sex, but subject to the ability to give free and meaningful consent.

The state and society are under the negative obligation not to interfere with this right. With regard to the positive obligation, far greater caution is required. It seems that only long-term commitments, not casual relationships, would be embraced. But even then it seems doubtful whether the character of this human right requires positive action. For example, would a society that does not offer any rules concerning heterosexual marriage be in violation of an indispensable human right? I think not, although many societies – including most European states – make the value assessment that they do want to regulate heterosexual marriage. If they do, the principle of equal treatment requires a rational decision for the availability of similar positive treatment with regard to unions which fulfil functional equivalent purposes. But again, that is not a human rights issue. Protection is only required insofar as human beings have to be protected from becoming victims in the emotional relationship.

My main message is that it is dangerous to try to trace back all seemingly reasonable solutions to a human rights root. It is much better to openly admit that most of the rules we would like to propose are grounded on value assessments and that these values are open to discussion. These value assessments may evolve from international conventions, from the findings of the ECHR or from our discussions. They are essential for the success of all efforts to harmonize family law within Europe. Despite all social and cultural differences in our societies, we share at least some common values and some identical or at least similar goals, but there may also be fields where we cannot agree. It will be a cumbersome and time-consuming task to find agreement on all important issues, but we should not shirk from this challenge.

THE REHARMONISATION OF NORDIC FAMILY LAW

Peter Lødrup

1. HISTORICAL BACKGROUND

An analysis of the co-operation in legal matters between the Nordic countries cannot be understood without knowledge of certain historical facts. I will therefore provide a very short bird's-eye view of the history of these five countries: Denmark, Finland, Iceland, Norway and Sweden. This will explain, to a large extent, the common cultural heritage, the agreement on basic issues regarding the role of law in contemporary society and the common ideas behind the legislation in the field of family law for almost the last hundred years.

In the late Middle Ages the north-western part of Europe consisted of Denmark, Norway and Sweden; Iceland being a province of Norway and Finland being a province of Sweden. During the so-called Kalmar Union, the countries were ruled by the same monarch under a union ending formally in 1521. In the fourteenth century Denmark and Norway were united under one royal dynasty, a union which ended in 1814 as a result of the Napoleonic wars. In the peace treaty of Kiel, the Danish-Norwegian king ceded Norway to the king of Sweden – the latter having supported Napoleon's enemies, while Denmark-Norway had supported the French Emperor. Iceland did not follow the rest of Norway, and thus became a Danish province. Another result of the wars in Europe at that time was that Sweden had to give up Finland to the Russian Tsar. Swedish law was, however, still in force in Finland.

In the union with Sweden, Norway was independent with a constitution of its own, its own laws, currency and its own parliament. The only exception was foreign policy, where Sweden was the sole master. This union lasted until 1905; in 1917 Finland gained its independence from Russia, and Iceland finally became independent in 1942. This history reflects strong ties, even if the centuries had seen strong differences and many wars, which usually ended with Sweden conquering land from Denmark-Norway.

There we have the Nordic countries as they are today. It follows that Swedish and Finnish law have the same roots, as is the case for Iceland, Denmark and Norway. This is also reflected in family law, where one may talk about an east and west Scandinavian law with different characteristics in both principles and details.

2. FAMILY LAW – HARMONISATION AND UNIFICATION

Before I continue, however, it is necessary to clarify what is meant by family law in this context, and also what is meant by harmonisation.

When one talks about Nordic co-operation in the field of family law, this is mainly confined to the provisions on marriage, divorce, maintenance and matrimonial property. The relationship between parents and their children and the social and public aspects of the family law legislation have not been subject to any Nordic co-operation of any importance, and thus fall outside the scope of this presentation.[1]

Harmonisation in the words of Marie Therese Meulders-Klein "implies a concern to reconcile the preoccupations and the interests of the systems so as to avoid conflicts and clashes. This is the gentle approach involving neither coercion nor restraint, but rather goodwill and dialogue with due respect for all concerned and their specific positions, without any attempt to impose a uniform solution on all of them. Harmonisation is not unification".[2] In her book on the Harmonisation of Family Law in Europe, Masha Antokolskaia writes that harmonisation has also been defined "as every process that results in an increase in the degree of legal uniformity".[3] In other words, if harmonisation in this sense means that the goal is to present guidelines based on certain general principles that the different countries are invited to adopt, we are far away from the ambition and achievement of Nordic co-operation. Unification is a better term for the Nordic aims and results in the first phase covering the first half of the nineteenth century, where the co-operation produced texts which the different parliaments adopted with only minor amendments. The overall result was a legislation which was very close in both structure and wording. When one argues for or against harmonisation in

1 Marie-Therese Meulders-Klein, *Towards a European Civil Code on Family Law? Ends and Means in Perspectives for the Unification and Harmonisation of Family Law in Europe*, Ed. by Katharina Boele-Woelki 2003) p. 108 containing a much broader description of what is meant by family law.

2 Op.cit., p. 106.

3 P. 16.

the Nordic debate today, it is more of a discussion for or against a higher degree of unification. I think it is imperative to bear this in mind in order to understand what I will discuss in this paper and that my use of the term harmonisation may be narrower than one is possibly used to.

3. HOW IT BEGAN

Let me then briefly outline the background to Nordic co-operation towards unification in many fields of private law, including family law.

In the mid-19th century a wave of "Scandinavianism" hit Sweden, Denmark and Norway. (As I have said, Iceland was at that time a part of Denmark, and Finland a part of Russia). One of the main reasons was solidarity with Denmark in its war with Prussia and Austria in 1864. A result of this "Scandinavianism" was closer co-operation between the three countries in many fields. Of special interest to us is the initiative taken to arrange the so-called "Nordic Lawyers' Meetings", the first of which was held in Copenhagen in 1872. Even today it may be of interest to quote one sentence in the invitation to the meeting: "The general common view on basic legal issues between the Scandinavian countries, the common foundation on which our legal institutions are based, in spite of many differences, shows that the solutions in important issues should be developed in a uniform direction."

These meetings are still arranged every third year, and lawyers from all the five Nordic countries come together for four days of discussion on contemporary legal challenges. These meetings, with their reports and discussions, have represented an inspiration and a driving force for harmonised legislation in many different fields, of which family law is one of the most successful. A distinguished representative of the Finnish Ministry of Justice wrote in 1988 that "the Nordic co-operation in legislative matters is in many respects unique. It is unique with respect to its age. It is unique in the way the work has been done. The co-operation has no equal as regards the results achieved." Against this background it is not surprising that Nordic co-operation is mentioned in the founding document of the CEFL.

Let us look more closely at this statement in the context of family law development.

The first initiative was taken by Sweden in 1910 by inviting Nordic co-operation in drafting a modernised family law legislation. This resulted in uniform laws on separation and divorce and, a few years later, on matrimonial property. These Acts were enacted between 1917 and 1927. It is generally agreed that they were modern and well suited to meet the challenges of the next fifty years. The principles of no-fault divorce (with some exceptions) and equality between the spouses, including an exclusive right to dispose of his or her matrimonial property and protection against the creditors of the other spouse, were basic parts of this legislation. The experts (Supreme Court judges and law professors) worked very effectively in meetings which lasted up to four or five weeks. It may be suggested that one important reason for this success was that the politicians did not interfere – the drafts of the national committees were passed almost unchanged by the parliaments of the three countries.

The post-war period saw the establishment of the Nordic Council in 1952; an institution which has played an important role in Nordic co-operation. Its work is based on the so-called Helsinki Agreement of 1962. According to art. 4 "the countries shall continue the co-operation in order to achieve the greatest possible harmonisation in private law legislation". From 1972 the Nordic Council of Ministers played an important role, suggesting actions to the Nordic Council. Already in 1955, a year after the Nordic Lawyers' Meeting had discussed the issue, the Nordic Council had adopted a resolution recommending that the governments should consider the need for a revision of the legislation on matrimonial property, and that such a revision should have harmonised legislation as a goal.

When the national committees met, it was agreed that there was no need to start a general revision of the Nordic legislation. Representatives from the national committees held only short meetings, and the amendments to the different Acts proposed by each committee were not of such importance that unification was considered necessary. From a longer-term perspective, this revision was an episode in the years when family issues were not yet on the political agenda.

4. THE LAST FORTY YEARS

This situation did not last for very long. The Swedish Minister of Justice wrote in 1968 that the second phase of Nordic co-operation, which I have just mentioned, did not go far enough. The politicians also entered the arena in Denmark. National committees were set up in both countries, with a mutual goal of co-operation. A couple of years later, Norway, Iceland and Finland started to work on reform. From then on, we can witness the third phase of Nordic co-operation in the field of family law. It lasted for fifteen years. I had the privilege to be a member, and later the chairman, of the Norwegian committee, so the following remarks are also some personal reflections on the work on a Nordic basis during these years.

In international literature a great deal of attention has been paid to the so-called "guidelines" for the Swedish committee, presented by the Swedish Minister of Justice. But this attention does not accurately reflect their influence on reform. They have not been a milestone in the development of family law as this literature suggests. Masha Antokolskaia writes that Swedish reforms were "the most far-reaching and uncompromising in Europe",[4] and adds that David Bradley has rightly pointed out that it was felt that "legal rules and norms ... no longer reinforce(d) traditional values" and that "religion no longer had any ... influence on the civil law marriage".[5] This is, with due respect, not correct. In my opinion these remarks better characterise the reforms I have described in the first phase of Nordic co-operation than the reforms from the 1970s onward. The model law for the Nordic divorce acts from the beginning of the nineteenth century was the Norwegian Divorce Act from 1909. Its basis was an unconditional secularisation of divorce law. In the explanatory notes to the Norwegian Parliament it is said that the divorce law "must be based on what is considered to be the needs of society and the individual, without paying attention to clerical or theological views on this matter".[6]

The Nordic co-operation during this third period did not have uniform texts as its goal. Politicians were represented in all national committees. The Swedish committee was chaired by a lawyer, with six politicians as members. On the other hand, the Norwegian committee had a majority of lawyers, and several politicians left the committee after a few years. In Denmark, lawyers and politicians were equally represented. Two or three members from each national committee usually met once a year for a two-day exchange of views; none of the politicians participated in these meetings. The Swedish attitude was that the unification of Nordic family law legislation was no longer realistic. The Swedish Parliament expressly said that Nordic unification was not a goal in itself; new ideas should not wait for Nordic unity to be legislated. This view dominated the Nordic meetings, in spite of the clear opinions from Denmark, Iceland and Norway that it would be worth while trying to achieve unification in certain matters. The Swedish representatives showed no interest at all. Here we see how the past casts its shadow – the west Scandinavian countries were in agreement on many questions. Let me add that all the meetings were held in a very friendly atmosphere.

---

4 Antokolskaia, *Harmonisation of Family Law in Europe: A Historical Perspective*, 2006, p. 288.

5 Op.cit. 289–290, Bradley, *Family Law and Political Culture*, 1996 p. 66.

6 Ot. prp. nr. 8 (1909) p. 20. It was also stated (p. 21) that obtaining a divorce cannot be conditional on fault.

It is however surprising that the flow of resolutions from the Nordic Council during the 1970s, emphasising the need for harmonisation and even unification, did not have any impact at all – even if the members of that council were also politicians.

There are without doubt more differences in Nordic family law today than forty years ago. Although Denmark has amended the old legislation, the other four countries have legislation which was introduced in the 1980s and 90s. But, in my opinion, these differences are not of a fundamental character touching upon what we might call the basic framework which was shaped during and shortly after the First World War. We still have a Nordic model based on the same ideas on the institution of marriage, divorce, maintenance and matrimonial property. I think that we here have a good example of what can be described as harmonisation through convergence.

5. COMPARATIVE STUDIES OF NORDIC FAMILY LAW AND THE LAW OF SUCCESSION

The increasing differences were noted in political forums and the Nordic Council of Ministers decided, in 1998, to establish a project group to study the current situation of Nordic family law. The terms of reference for the group were to:

- describe the most important differences in the legislation regarding presentation, use and purpose,
- clarify the extent to which differences can cause problems, for example when families move between the countries, and the extent of such problems,
- analyse the issues on which, from a practical point of view, it is preferable to legislate through Acts based upon Nordic co-operation,
- draw a picture of which issues in the present legislation might be appropriate for harmonisation from a short, medium and long-term perspective.

The task of the project group was thus to discuss all major issues in family law: the requirements to establish a valid marriage; divorce; maintenance; matrimonial property; and also the relationship between parents and children. Even if Nordic co-operation on succession and wills had been very superficial, the close relationship between matrimonial property law and the position of the surviving spouse presented issues of importance for spouses. Consequently, the law of succession was included in the project.

The group's work resulted in four volumes, each of which is almost 500 pages in length, published by the Nordic Council of Ministers in 2003. Anders Agell of Sweden wrote the volume on divorce and matrimonial property; my responsibility was the second volume on inheritance and wills; Anna Singer, from Sweden, analysed the financial responsibilities of parents towards their children and I wrote on fatherhood and motherhood in the third volume. In the fourth volume Svend Danielsen, from Denmark, discussed parental responsibility and related issues. We met for discussion and critical comments on our drafts on fifteen occasions, each meeting lasting at least two days. Urpo Kangas participated to advise on Finnish law; Icelandic law was also included. Our method was to look at the different factual issues and to compare the legal solutions in each country. At the end of each chapter we analysed and concluded which issues could be a basis for harmonisation. We had no illusion that these conclusions would meet with general approval. Our aim, and ambition, was that the material we presented would be a sufficient basis for further discussions on the need for harmonisation, its forms, and a possible debate on the quality of different options. It should be added that when the word harmonisation is used in these books, it is closer to unification than harmonisation in the sense of how I have described these concepts.

We learned, in spite of the many similarities in legal traditions and in the substantive law, how extremely difficult it was to write correctly about the legal system of another country. We also learned, when we discussed the need for harmonisation in search of the best possible answer to a question, how deep-rooted the ties were between our opinions and our own national rules. It took us considerable time to learn not to defend our own system, but to look objectively for the best solution.

6. HOW FAR IS NORDIC FAMILY LAW HARMONISED TODAY?

Let us look a little further into some of the differences we now have in Nordic law. I will argue that we still have, with very few exceptions, a harmonised family law in the Nordic countries. The legislation from the 1920s was in this respect more of a unification, by which I mean the Acts in different countries have to a large extent the same wording and are based on common principles and values.

1. *Divorce.* My first example is divorce. In Denmark, Norway and Iceland a period of separation is conditional for divorce. This period is one year, although in Denmark and Iceland this is only six months if the spouses agree to divorce. In Sweden and Finland a divorce may only be granted after six months' "reflection

time", unless the spouses have no children and agree to divorce. In all five countries either spouse can obtain a divorce on demand, following a period of two years living apart.

Here we meet the following question: Is the divorce law of the Nordic countries harmonised? We have a no-fault system which can be triggered by either spouse, and the waiting period for a divorce is nowhere longer than one year. My answer is: Yes, it is harmonised, but not uniform. The rules are based on the same ideas and, for the spouses, the practical aspects of any of the differences are negligible. In Finland and Sweden all the so-called "divorce grounds" have been repealed, while Denmark, Iceland and Norway have retained one, namely family violence.[7] I may add that if the Norwegian and Danish committees had recommended joining the Swedish "waiting period" system, which we seriously considered, a uniform law would have been the result. Practical considerations motivated our opinion and we did not feel that the Swedish view could in any way be called "radical", breaking with traditional values.

2. *Maintenance.* The rules on maintenance may be characterised in the same way. The basic principle is that one spouse does not have any duty to pay maintenance to the other after separation or divorce. The requisite exceptions have some variations in their scope of application.

3. *Matrimonial property.* As regards matrimonial property, it is Norway that has deviated from the Nordic harmony. In 1975 the Supreme Court stated that domestic work in the home and raising children could be a relevant factor when deciding on ownership of the matrimonial home. Consequently, one may say that in the majority of marriages the home is regarded as being jointly owned by the spouses – a rule that normally benefits the wife, of course. In the other four countries, such work is regarded as irrelevant in this respect. Secondly, the Norwegian Act from 1991 broke with the other countries regarding assets which a spouse had at the date of the marriage and had acquired by a gift or inheritance during the marriage. In Norway these are exceptions to the main rule of an equal division of property. These exceptions also apply in Denmark and Iceland, but are limited to cases where the marriage has lasted for only a short period of up to five years, while in Finland and Sweden they will only apply if an equal division would be highly unreasonable. With these two exceptions, the structure of the Acts on matrimonial property is to a large extent harmonised; many paragraphs are almost identical.

---

7 In 2007 a new ground for a direct divorce was adopted in Norway, namely for a spouse who had been forced to marry by an unlawful act.

On the other hand, there are many paragraphs which differ in detail, either in the words used or concerning an intentional choice for a different rule. One may of course ask if there should be a goal to attain identical rules for all the different problems, as long as harmonisation is attained concerning the main principles. The general opinion seems to be that differences in detail are acceptable. On the other hand, one may ask: when agreement is reached on the main issues, why should details differ? There is nothing in Nordic traditions, culture or a general sense of justice which can explain such a development. Neither ordinary people nor politicians have views on these details. The explanation for the present situation is in my opinion quite simple: When the representatives from the different countries disagree during the Nordic committee meetings, the personal opinions of these individuals have a strong tendency to survive the passage of the Act through the parliaments. Let me put it simply: if the Danish and Norwegian representatives, the latter being myself, had followed the Swedish points of view on many minor questions, I am convinced that these alternatives would also have been accepted in our countries.

7. SOME CONCLUSIONS

What conclusion can be drawn from the presentation in this paper?

- Nordic co-operation in the field of family law, as in other private law matters, is still a high priority challenge to both Nordic politicians and in legal circles
- We still have a Nordic model regarding the aspects of family law described above
- Even if the differences after the reforms in the 1980s and 1990s are greater than previously, it is still correct to say that the family law of the Nordic countries is harmonised in the sense of how harmonisation is described above. Many texts are still almost identical, examples of unification in the true sense of the word.[8]
- There are different opinions on the need for a more unified legislation.
- The basic cultural and legal traditions are still common – the divergences do not follow national borders but are found in all the countries.
- The present Nordic legislation, even though it is no more than fifteen to twenty years old, should in my opinion now be evaluated. It is evident that such an evaluation should be done in close Nordic co-operation. If we agree, as we do, on the basic principles and values, I think it is contradictory that different

8 When Meulders-Klein op.cit. p. 109 includes Nordic countries among examples of countries where "national differences create clear dividing lines", I cannot agree with her.

solutions should prevail on issues which may be said to be of minor importance.

Thus my last words will be that Nordic co-operation will also in the future play an important part in the reform work in family law. The form of co-operation and its goals will depend upon a case by case evaluation. The days of harmonisation and even unification are not over, but, of course, European integration will add an uncertain element in considering the future.

THE HARMONISATION OF FAMILY LAW IN THE UNITED STATES

Robin Fretwell Wilson*

In the United States, family law is in deep flux, with large swaths of family law that were once established now being reassessed. Questions about divorce, cohabitation, same-sex relationships, and the nature of parenthood and parenting dominate the headlines of newspapers across the U.S. and provide fodder for editorialists, television talk show hosts, and sometimes legislators – almost always at the state level. This debate is fueled by the different approaches to family law that arise out of the American federalist system, which allows individual states to define everything from who may marry, to when they can divorce.

Federal law sometimes plays a role in shaping family law, usually in providing a constitutional brake on state action.[1] For example, at one time, some states severely limited the rights of non-marital fathers to establish relationships with their children, in violation of federal constitutional principles.[2] But federal law tends to be a relatively small part of our body of family law in the U.S. Thus, states in the U.S. can have deep rifts and differences over some very fundamental questions: Who is a parent? Should individuals be able to walk away from the promises made at marriage, and if so under what circumstances? Who should be able to marry at all?

This Chapter addresses three areas in which such divisions occur: the role of fault in dissolving a marriage; whether de facto parents should receive custody or

---

* I am grateful to the Commission on European Family Law ("CEFL") and the Department of Private Law, University of Oslo, for the opportunity to give this keynote address at the Third Conference of the CEFL on European Challenges in Contemporary Family Law.

1 See Harry D. Krause, "Comparative Family Law: Past Traditions Battle Future Trends—and Vice Versa", in *The Oxford Handbook of Comparative Law 1099* (Mathias Reimann & Reinhard Zimmermann eds., Oxford University Press 2006) ("[T]he United States Supreme Court has imposed federal constitutional mandates on topics ranging from illegitimacy to abortion and marital privacy, thereby 'unifying' often divergent state laws.").

2 See *Lehr v. Robertson*, 463 U.S. 248, 261 (1983) (stating that "[w]hen an unwed father demonstrates a full commitment to the responsibilities of parenthood by 'coming forward to participate in the rearing of his child,' his interest in personal contact with his child acquires substantial protection under the due process clause") (quoting Caban v. Mohammed, 441 U.S. 380, 414 (1979)).

visitation with a child after the adults break up; and whether lesbians and gays should be able to marry or receive other protection for their relationships. Using these three examples, this Chapter reviews important methods in the U.S. for harmonizing the very different approaches taken by various states. These methods include uniform acts which can close differences in state laws; state and national law reform commissions which can urge legislative changes; and legal challenges based on the federal constitution, which can force a common understanding among the states.

1. UNIFORM ACTS & DIVORCE SHOPPING

The fact that we are a mobile society and that Americans can easily pass from one geographic area to another raises the question of how and whether to harmonize very different regimes for regulating families from state to state. It also raises a possibility that Europe is struggling with now: divorce shopping or the rush by one spouse to file with the court of a particular jurisdiction in order to exploit that jurisdiction's advantageous laws.[3] With twenty-seven countries in the European Union ("EU") and sixteen percent of Europe's 875,000 divorces annually involving "international" couples[4] – where the parties can file in more than one country – a lot of strategic maneuvering can occur.

The jurisdiction in which a party files sometimes can mean a great difference for one party or the other in the effect or favorability of the law. For example, last year a Polish businessman who left Poland to work in Finland later filed for divorce in Finland because he knew that a divorce in Poland would be a difficult, protracted affair – while one in Finland would be much quicker and easier to obtain.[5] Such forum shopping also occurs in the United States. [6] States in the U.S. largely resolve the question about which jurisdiction will decide a divorce through divorce recognition acts – that is, legislation that determines when a state will recognize a divorce from another jurisdiction or will instead decide the question itself. Usually,

3 See Stephen Castle, "EU Plans Legal Reforms to End 'Divorce Shopping'", July 19, 2006 ("The European Commission has unveiled plans to end the widespread practice of 'divorce shopping,' where one separating spouse rushes to court before the other to exploit advantageous laws in a particular European country.").

4 *Id.* (estimating that 170,000 couples annually can file in more than one EU country).

5 See *id.* (recounting a Polish man's decision to seek a divorce in Finland because he knew "that the process in his native country would be long and drawn out").

6 Thomas Oldham, "Marital Property Rights of Mobile Spouses at Divorce", *Abstract for International Society of Family Law North American Regional Conference*, Vancouver, B.C., June 18–20, 2007 (observing that it is a fairly common occurrence in the U.S. for couples to have multiple jurisdictions in which they can file for divorce "since 1.2 million couples move from one state near the time of divorce").

a state jealously guards its prerogatives to decide a divorce when both parties live there or when the property that will be divided is principally in that state.[7]

2. STATE LAW REFORM COMMISSIONS & NO-FAULT DIVORCE

In the U.S., deep divisions often occur among geographic neighbors.[8] For instance, states in the U.S. continue to take different approaches even to questions of exit from marriage. The majority of states allow divorce for reasons of fault: principally, desertion for more than one year, adultery, physical cruelty or domestic violence, and habitual drunkenness or drug use.[9] In the U.S., all but two states also recognize unilateral "no-fault" grounds for divorce – meaning that one party can unilaterally exit the marriage without the other party's consent. The two exceptions are New York and Mississippi – interestingly, two very different states politically. In both New York and Mississippi, spouses can divorce in the absence of fault if they mutually agree or do not contest the divorce, and satisfy a waiting period, but they cannot divorce if one person opposes the divorce.[10]

The chief justice of New York's highest court, Chief Judge Judith Kaye, recently formed a Matrimonial Commission to study family law reform, one recommen-

---

7 For instance, the Uniform Divorce Recognition Act "provides that a divorce obtained in another jurisdiction is of no force or effect in the enacting state if both parties to the marriage were domiciled in [the] enacting state at the time the proceeding for divorce was commenced." 24A Am. Jur. 2d Divorce and Separation §1154 (2007).

8 Other deep divisions exist between states, as well, and may lead to forum shopping. For instance, states differ in how they classify the way property is held during a marriage. There are two property systems recognized in the U.S.: the community property system and the common law property system. Angela M. Vallario, "Spousal Election: Suggested Equitable Reform for the Division of Property at Death", *52 Cath. U. L. Rev. 519*, 522 (2003). Under a common law property system, the husband and wife can separately own the property that each individual acquires in his or her own name during the marriage, while under a community property system, the property accumulated during the marriage is held collectively by the couple. *Id.* at 524–25. Upon dissolution, both systems disregard how an asset is titled when apportioning the couple's marital property and use equitable principles in making the division. *Id.* at 523–24. But the two systems differ in how they divide property upon the death of one spouse. Under a common law property system, a spouse at death can dispose of only that property titled in her own name. *Id.* In contrast, under a community property system, a spouse can dispose of one-half of the community property at death, with the surviving spouse entitled to the remaining half. *Id.* at 524.

9 See Lynn D. Wardle, "Beyond Fault and No-Fault in the Reform of Marital Dissolution Law", in *Reconceiving the Family 9*, 20 (Robin Fretwell Wilson ed., 2006).

10 See McKinney's DRL §170 ("The husband and wife have lived separate and apart pursuant to a written agreement of separation... for a period of one or more years...."); Miss Ann. Code §93-5-2 ("Divorce from the bonds of matrimony may be granted on the ground of irreconcilable differences, but only upon the joint complaint of the husband and wife....").

dation of which was that New York should have unilateral, no-fault divorce. [11] A case recently dismissed by the New York Court of Appeals illustrates just why the Commission and Chief Judge Kaye[12] believes that New Yorkers need access to unilateral, no-fault divorce. In March 2007, a New York court refused to grant a divorce to Simon and Chana Taub, who had been married for 21 years.[13] While the divorce was pending, Chana asked for exclusive use of the residence, which the court denied.[14] But recognizing the strife between them, the judge ordered Simon to erect a wall in their residence to provide for separate living accommodations.[15]

Despite this extraordinary measure, the strife in the marriage did not qualify for a fault divorce because the spouses' acts did not rise to the level of "cruel and inhuman treatment."[16] At trial, Chana testified that her husband had attacked her with everything from a telephone to a treadmill during their "hellish" twenty-one-year marriage.[17] Their four children also testified against him.[18] After five hours of deliberations, however, the jury rejected Chana's grounds for divorce, leaving the couple stunned, speechless, and still married.[19] Both spouses now assert that the other will resort to murder to end the marriage.[20] Simon rushed to court the following day to get a protective order.[21] One is hard pressed to find a better story to make Chief Judge Kaye's point: even though the trial judge found that the couple's marriage had deteriorated so significantly that they needed to

---

11 Chief Judge Kaye established the Matrimonial Commission in January 2004 to "examine every facet of the divorce and custody determination process and recommend reforms to reduce trauma, delay and cost to parents and children so personally impacted by the system." State of New York Unified Court System, Matrimonial Commission, Report to the Chief Judge of the State of New York, at vi (2006), available at http://www.nycourts.gov/reports/matrimonial-commissionreport.pdf (last accessed Aug. 15, 2007).

12 Chief Judge Kaye endorsed the committee's recommendation for unilateral, no-fault divorce. See Judith S. Kaye, "The State of the Judiciary 2007" (New York State Unified Court System 2007) at 10, available at http://www.courts.state.ny.us/admin/stateofjudiciary/soj2007.pdf (last accessed Aug. 15, 2007) ("I continue to support no-fault divorce, urged by the [Matrimonial] Commission.").

13 Nancy L. Katz et al, "Sentenced Till Death! Warring Couple Wanted Split, but Jury Sez No", *N.Y. Daily News*, Mar. 29, 2007, at 7.

14 *Taub v. Taub*, 33 A.D.3d 612, 612 (NY Ct. App. 2006). The wife did not meet her burden of proving that the removal of her husband from the marital residence was necessary to ensure her safety. See *id.* ("[Her] only allegations of actual violence were incredible, and the alleged threats made by the husband were uncorroborated.").

15 *Id.*

16 Katz, supra note 16, at 7

17 *Id.*

18 *Id.*

19 *Id.*

20 See *id.* (reporting that Simon was scared that Chana would hire a hit man and that Chana expressed fear because Simon told people that he is going to "get rid" of her).

21 *Id.*

build a wall in their house to separate them, the couple was still not able to get a divorce.[22]

Despite such bizarre results under current New York law, Chief Judge Kaye's efforts for legislative reform went nowhere. The New York Times reported last year that "[t]he state Senate and Assembly went home … without having made any real progress toward a divorce law overhaul,"[23] and the legislature did no better this year.[24]

But where New York failed, New Jersey succeeded. New legislation in New Jersey will make divorce much easier to obtain. In January of this year, the New Jersey Governor Jon Corzine signed into law a bill that changes immediately the waiting period for a no-fault divorce from 18 months to 6 months.[25] It does this by adding irreconcilable differences as a basis for divorce, which has a much shorter waiting period.

But there is certainly nothing close to unanimity about the virtues of easy exit. Last year, Louisiana lengthened the waiting period for no-fault divorce from 6 months to one year when couples have children, but otherwise left childless couples to the faster track.[26] This two-track system essentially follows an approach taken in Sweden.[27] Louisiana was careful to provide prompter exits in instances of domestic violence or child abuse – responding in part to the hardships that result when divorce is too hard to obtain.[28]

What accounts for pockets of resistance to no-fault divorce? Reasons include the growing social science evidence that divorce often hurts children;[29] renewed

---

22 The Taubs could have secured a bilateral no-fault divorce if they lived separately for one year and entered into a financial settlement agreement. See N.Y. Dom. Rel. Law §170(6) (McKinney 2003) (outlining requirements for an uncontested divorce in New York).

23 "The Politics of Exploding Houses", *The New York Times*, July 13, 2006, at A22.

24 A.B. 6978, 230th Leg. Sess., 2007–2008 Reg. Sess. (N.Y. 2007).

25 N.J. Stat. Ann. §2A:34–2 (2007).

26 La. Civ. C. Art. §103.1 (2007). Virginia has used a two-track system since 1982, which allows couples without children to receive a divorce decree after six months of separation, while couples with children must wait a year. See Virginia Code §20–91(9) (2007). No other states in the U.S. use this scheme.

27 Maarit Jänterä-Jareborg, "Grounds for Divorce and Maintenance Between Former Spouses: Sweden, National Reports, Commission on European Family Law", available at http://www2.law.uu.nl/priv/cefl/ (noting that spouses have an immediate right of divorce except when "there is a child under sixteen years of age, making it obligatory to first go through a reconsideration period of six months").

28 La. Civ. C. Art. 102, 103.1 (providing for quicker exit upon a "finding by the court… that the other spouse has physically or sexually abused the spouse seeking divorce or a child of one of the spouses").

29 See Robin Fretwell Wilson, "Evaluating Marriage: Does Marriage Matter to the Nurturing of Children", *42 San Diego L. Rev. 847*, 851 n.14 (2005) (discussing two studies that conclude

recognition of the importance of legally protecting mothers who stay at home to raise children;[30] and, better, newer evidence that legal rules do affect behavior – in this case, that easier access to divorce in the U.S. and elsewhere increased divorce rates.

Consider just two studies on the last point. The first, by Professor Leora Friedberg, appeared The American Economic Review in 1998 and examined the divorce rates in from 1968 to 1988.[31] Friedberg concluded if those states that switched to unilateral divorce after 1968 had not adopted unilateral exit rules, the divorce rate would have been about six percent lower in 1988.[32] Friedberg's study also indicated that the type of unilateral divorce a state adopted mattered.[33] The purest unilateral divorce states – where there are no separation requirements or fault does not affect property division – experienced a 11.9 percent increase in the divorce rate.[34]

A separate study by Professor Jonathan Gruber and published in the Journal of Labor Economics in 2004 also concluded that "unilateral divorce regulations do significantly increase the incidence of divorce."[35] Gruber showed that unilateral divorce raised the odds of divorce for women and men by 11.6 percent.[36]

Concededly, these studies are controversial. Not everyone agrees with how the individual states were "coded," and therefore how much weight to give the findings.[37] Nonetheless, of twenty-four studies conducted in the past decade

---

"that marriage matters to how children thrive and to the extent to which their parents are willing to invest in them"); JUDITH S. WALLERSTEIN et al., "The Unexpected Legacy of Divorce: A 25 Year Landmark Study (2000)".

30 See MARCIA PAPPAS, "Divorce New York Style", *The Legislative Gazette*, July 5, 2005 ("The problem with unilateral no-fault divorce is that it hurts women by removing the incentive for the moneyed spouse (who is usually the husband) to make a settlement. Instead of negotiating with a dependent spouse—whose only leverage for avoiding an impoverished post-divorce life for herself and her children may be her assent, or lack of it, to divorce—the husband can simply go to court and obtain an uncontested divorce.").

31 LEORA FRIEDBERG, "Did Unilateral Divorce Raise Divorce Rates? Evidence from Panel Data", 88 *The American Economic Rev.* 608–27 (1998).

32 *Id* at 608..

33 See *id.* at 620 (finding that "[s]eparation requirements proved more of a constraint on divorce behavior than fault-based property division did").

34 *Id.*

35 JONATHAN GRUBER, "Is Making Divorce Easier Bad for Children? The Long-Run Implications of Unilateral Divorce", *22 J. of Labor Economics* 799, 799 (2004).

36 *Id.* at 812 ("[F]or women, unilateral divorce being in place raises the odds of divorce by... 11.6%. For men the increase is... 11.6%.").

37 See DOUGLAS W. ALLEN, "Does Divorce Law Affect the Divorce Rate? Empirical Research", 1995–2006, *iMAPP Policy Brief*, at 3, Apr. 25, 2007 (Inst. For Marriage and Pub. Pol'y) ("[S]cholars have not always agreed even on the basics, such as what cluster of legal changes constitutes a "no-fault" divorce law, and when a particular state has moved to a no-fault divorce system.").

examining whether divorce reform accelerated the rate of divorce, seventeen have concluded that it did.[38] The clearest evidence of this impact occurred outside the United States in countries where grounds for divorce are uniform across the nation, as in Great Britain.[39]

Easy exit raises concerns for children, of course, but also for adults. A study by professors Matouschek and Rasul forthcoming in the Journal of Law and Economics[40] observes "that divorce costs can be 'too low' and that when they are too low, the very purpose of the marriage contract is undermined."[41] Said another way, when a contract can be easily exited, the value of entering the contract drops off.

3. THE ROLE OF NATIONAL LAW REFORM BODIES

The fact that states in the U.S. have very different rules about the same thing raises deep discomfort in many of us. This in turn has stimulated efforts by national law reform bodies in the U.S. to harmonize the law of the 50 states. The most prestigious of these bodies is the American Law Institute ("ALI"). Composed of judges, lawyers, and academics, the ALI seeks "to promote the clarification and simplification of the law and its better adaptation to social needs."[42] The ALI has been tremendously influential in the development of American law through its publications and Restatements of Law.[43]

---

38 *Id.*

39 See *id.* at 5 ("The international studies generally find a large and statistically significant positive effect of no-fault divorce on the divorce rate. For example, one study by Binner and Dnes found that no-fault divorce increased the divorce rate in Great Britain by 0.8 divorces per 1000 people. Considering the average divorce rate is 1.84 divorces per 1000 people in a given year, this is quite a substantial effect (about a 43% increase).").
Importantly, these same studies have found that the effect of eased access to divorce on the divorce rate disappears after approximately a decade because the couples who marry are better matched and less divorce prone. See id. at 4 ("A number of recent studies... found that the increase in the overall divorce rate under no-fault, while sustained for a number of years eventually fades and the divorce rate moves back to trend.... Thus the lowering of divorce rates from the peak in the early 1980s may be partially explained by more better-matched, more intrinsically stable couples choosing to marry."). Couples who are less well matched and who would have chosen to marry in past decades, choose instead to cohabit—with the result that eased access to divorce drives more fragile couples out of marriage entirely. *See id.* at 4 ("As the law retreats from enforcing marriage contracts, some couples respond by searching longer, delaying marriage and (sometimes) avoiding it altogether.").

40 Niko Matouschek & Imran Rasul, "The Economies of the Marriage Contract: Theories and Evidence", Forthcoming, 2007, *J. of Law & Economics.*

41 *Id.* at 5.

42 Robin Fretwell Wilson, "Introduction to Reconceiving the Family", 1, 1 (Robin Fretwell Wilson ed., *Cambridge University Press 2006*).

43 Carl S. Schneider, "Afterword: Elite Principles: The ALI Proposals and the Politics of Law Reform", in *Reconceiving the Family 489*, 491 (Robin Fretwell Wilson ed., Cambridge Univ. Press 2006).

The ALI took up the deep divisions in state family law in the early 1990s. In 2002, after 11 years of work, it published its ideas for harmonisation in a massive 1187 page volume entitled PRINCIPLES OF THE LAW OF FAMILY DISSOLUTION: ANALYSIS AND RECOMMENDATIONS ("PRINCIPLES").[44] The PRINCIPLES, if enacted, would leave few areas of family law untouched. They address fault, the division of property, alimony payments, child custody, child support, domestic partnerships, and private agreements between adults who cohabit or marry. Many of the proposals contained in the PRINCIPLES would change current law dramatically; many are extremely controversial.[45] This Part discusses only two proposals – how to treat fault in the dissolution of the marriage and how to treat functional or "de facto" parents after the adults break up.

3.1. THE ROLE OF FAULT IN DIVORCE

The ALI believes that states should uniformly remove fault from the laws of divorce so it does not matter as a grounds for divorce, in determinations of alimony, or in how marital property is divided.[46] In fact, the ALI is so distrustful of fault that they would not permit a couple to privately agree that fault would matter to their relationship.[47]

Despite the ALI's proposals, five years later, not a single state has passed new legislation to eliminate fault entirely in family law, although some had already diminished the importance of fault.[48] Quite the contrary, as of 2006, thirty states considered fault in property or alimony awards.[49] A number of scholars across the spectrum are also now questioning the wisdom of removing fault entirely.[50]

44 American Law Institute, "Principles of the Law of Family Dissolution: Analysis and Recommendations" (2002) [hereinafter Principles].

45 ROBIN FRETWELL WILSON, "Introduction to Reconceiving the Family", 1, 1 (ROBIN FRETWELL WILSON ed., Cambridge University Press 2006).

46 See Principles §1, Topic 2, at 43.

47 Principles §7.08(1), at 1004 (providing that such agreements would be unenforceable).

48 See, e.g., ROBIN FRETWELL WILSON, "Don't Let Divorce Off The Hook, Opinion-Editorial", *New York Times* (October 1, 2006); Cal. Fam. Code §2335 (1993) (eliminating consideration of fault altogether by providing that "in a pleading or proceeding for dissolution of marriage or legal separation of the parties... evidence of specific acts of misconduct is improper and inadmissible").

49 LYNN D. WARDLE, "Beyond Fault and No-Fault in the Reform of Marital Dissolution Law", in *Reconceiving the Family 9*, 15 (ROBIN FRETWELL WILSON ed., 2006).

50 See, e.g., *id.*; KATHARINE B. SILBAUGH, "Money as Emotion in the Distribution of Wealth at Divorce", in *Reconceiving the Family 234*, 236 (ROBIN FRETWELL WILSON ed., 2006) ("The sidelining of nonfinancial matters is also expressed in the drafters' decision not to account for contributions to a marriage in dividing assets, and not to consider fault either as a ground for divorce or in financial settlements.").

The ALI's distrust of fault stems in part from its belief that the better remedy in cases of bad acts is to sue in tort for the harm.[51] The question of whether tort or family law is the better remedy arose recently in the high-profile divorce of former New Jersey Governor James McGreevey and his wife, Dina Matos McGreevey. In 2004, then-governor McGreevey announced that he was "a gay American" and having an extramarital affair with a male aide. Several months after the announcement, McGreevey resigned as governor and separated from his wife.[52]

Litigation over the divorce is still pending, with an impassioned fight over custody of their five-year-old daughter and heated allegations about who knew what, when.[53] Dina alleges that McGreevey knew he was bisexual when he proposed to her during his run for governor, but that he married her to gain political cover.[54] McGreevey claims that Dina knew he was homosexual and that her attempts to "rewrite history" now constitute "homophobia in its worst form"[55] and is nothing more than hype for her new book.[56]

Meanwhile, Dina filed a personal injury suit against McGreevey, alleging fraud, infliction of emotional distress, and two counts of libel along with requests for punitive and compensatory damages – all of which Dina included in her divorce papers as well.[57] She charges that McGreevey fraudulently induced her to marry him and, as a result of his fraud, she has suffered significant emotional and financial damage.[58]

It is not clear what the success of Dina's personal injury suit will be. A jury may decide that Dina knew that McGreevey was gay and came to the situation knowingly, or a court may dismiss the tort suit on the basis that Dina will be made whole in the divorce.[59]

---

51 See Principles §1, Topic 2, at 43 ("[T]he rationale for excluding fault from the dissolution law has been strengthened since adoption of the [Uniform Marriage and Divorce Act] by changes in the tort law, which in most states now recognizes claims between former spouses that might once have been excluded by blanket rules of spousal immunity.").

52 "McGreevey Files Suit for Custody of Daughter; Change in Divorce Case Also Seeks Support from Matos", *The Record* (Bergen County, N.J.), Mar. 14, 2007, at A4.

53 *Id.*

54 Jeane MacIntosh, "McGay Bashing – Ex-Gov Labels Wife a 'Homophobe'", *N.Y. Post*, Apr. 24, 2007, at 5.

55 *Id.*

56 Judith Lucas, "McGreevey Says Wife's Exploiting Daughter for Publicity", *Star-Ledger*, April 13, 2007, at 24.

57 Jeane MacIntosh, "MCG is 'Cruel Fraud'; Wife's Divorce Claim", *N.Y. Post*, May 8, 2007, at 9.

58 Chris Newmarker, "Dina Claims Extreme Cruelty", *Associated Press*, May 8, 2007.

59 Principles ch. 1, Topic 2, III, at 49.

3.2. WHAT IS A PARENT?

One area in the U.S. that is ripe for harmonisation is the treatment of heterosexual and homosexual partners of a child's biological parent, in particular whether such partners will receive parental rights. In this area, the ALI has been quite influential. The ALI has proposed a test for "de facto" parents which is invariably cited by courts. Massachusetts adopted the ALI's concept of a de facto parent, until confronted recently with the grim reality of that test for some children.[60]

The ALI test confers parental rights on ex live-in partners who share caretaking responsibility for their partner's child for as little as two years.[61] This proposal significantly constrains the ability of mothers to decide who has access to their children – with some potentially devastating repercussions for at least some of the children involved.[62] The PRINCIPLES can urge such seismic shifts because they are directed at legislators, who have the option to write on a blank slate. [63] In a sense, the ALI is urging legislators to fashion new rules from whole cloth to standardize these decisions and take away from judges the discretion they have historically enjoyed in deciding these cases.[64]

It is helpful to consider the ALI's test for de facto parenthood within the ALI's larger scheme for custody law reform. The ALI's custody proposals (for all kinds of parents, including de facto parents) would scrap nearly all the tools traditionally employed by courts in custody determinations:

(1) The best interests test, set aside for a new standard that uses "past caretaking" to determine shared parenting arrangements after divorce;[65]
(2) Doctrines of standing that historically have precluded unrelated third parties from seeking custody; [66] and

60 See Part III.B.2 infra.
61 See Principles §2.03 cmt. c, at 119 ("The individual must have lived with the child for a significant period of time (not less than two years)").
62 See Part III.B.2 infra.
63 IRA MARK ELLMAN, "Chief Reporter's Forward", in *Principles,* at xvii (noting that some sections of the Principles "are addressed to rulemakers rather than decisionmakers").
64 Principles §2.02(1)(f), at 96 (describing as the primary objective of Chapter 2 the "expeditious, predictable decisionmaking and the avoidance of prolonged uncertainty respecting arrangements for the child's care and custody"); Principles §2.08 cmt. b, at 182 ("The allocation of custodial responsibility presumed in [the past caretaking standard] yields more predictable and more easily adjudicated results, thereby advancing the best interests of children in most cases without infringing parental autonomy.").
65 PATRICK PARKINSON, "The Past Caretaking Standard in Comparative Perspective", in *Reconceiving the Family 446*, 446 (ROBIN FRETWELL WILSON ed., Cambridge Univ. Press 2006) (describing the past caretaking standard as a "bold new direction in the law of parenting after separation").
66 See Principles §2.04, Reporter's Notes, cmt. d, at 140 (noting the "traditional rule... that a nonparent cannot file an action for custody or visitation without a showing that the parents are

(3) Doctrines in the law giving biological and adoptive parents (together, "legal parents") exclusive say in caretaking matters, at least when abuse and neglect are not present.[67]

The ALI replaces these doctrines with a highly technical test – one that had never before been adopted in the United States prior to the PRINCIPLES' publication – that uses multiple factors and a pre-determined range of results to constrain the discretion of judges.[68]

3.2.1. The ALI Rationale

In many ways, the ALI is engaged in an admirable undertaking: providing children with enduring contact with, in the ALI's words, the "only father [a] child ha[d] known"[69] – that is, the mother's married partner or co-resident boyfriend. The ALI believes that giving parental rights to these "de facto parents" is necessary to conform to the lived experience of many children and that these relationships are "critically important to the child's welfare."[70] Further, disregarding these relationships at break-up "ignores child-parent relationships that may be fundamental to the child's sense of stability."[71]

The ALI proposes a three-part test for de facto parent that requires residency, caretaking, and agreement. The residency prong is satisfied when a parent's partner lives with the child and the parent for as little as two years.[72] The caretaking prong is satisfied when the partner has performed at least half of the caretaking functions for the child,[73] such as taking the child to the doctor, reading to the child, and arranging for education.[74] Finally, the child's parent must agree to

---

unfit or unavailable").

67 See DOUGLAS E. ABRAMS & SARAH H. RAMSEY, "Children and the Law: Doctrine, Policy and Practice" (3d ed. 2007) ("Parents have a substantive due process right to raise their children as they see fit without unreasonable state interference, but the state may limit this right where necessary to protect children's health or safety.").

68 See PARKINSON, supra note 67, at 446 (arguing that the "Principles advocate a radical new approach to determining parenting arrangements after separation").

69 See Principles §2.03 cmt. b, at 129 (discussing equitable-parent cases).

70 Principles ch. 1, Topic 1.I(d), at 5.

71 Principles ch. 1, Topic 1.I(d), at 5–6.

72 Principles §2.03 cmt. c, at 119.

73 Principles §2.03 cmt. c, at 119.

74 Section 2.03(5) defines "caretaking functions" as "tasks that involve interaction with the child or that direct, arrange, and supervise the interaction and care provided by others." Principles §2.03(5) at 108.Section 2.03(5) sets forth a non-exclusive list of caretaking functions including "satisfying the nutritional needs of the child," "directing the child's various developmental needs," "providing discipline," "supervising chores," "performing other tasks that attend to the child's needs for behavioral control and self-restraint," "arranging for the child's education," "providing moral and ethical guidance," and a host of other specified functions). Principles §2.03(5)(a)-(h), at 109.

allow the partner to perform an equal share of the child's caretaking.[75] Because agreement can be implied, this prong can easily be satisfied when a parent acquiesces to the partner's behavior – behavior that virtually any parent would welcome in her partner, such as making dinner for the family.[76]

The ALI not only recognizes these de facto parents, it ties their share of time with the child to a new test for custody after the break-up, the past caretaking standard.[77] The standard essentially works as a time in/time out test. In other words, a person who performs half of the caretaking for a child presumptively receives as much as half the time with the child after the adults break up.[78]

Some initial observations are in order before examining this test in depth. First, as with any right, handing out new parental rights is a zero-sum game. Where a right for one person is enlarged, it is necessarily diminished for another. In this equation, someone winds up with less discretion in their parenting choices at the end. Whose parental prerogatives are being overridden here? This will be mothers disproportionately because most non-marital children live with their mothers, as do huge numbers of children after divorce.[79]

---

75 Principles §2.03 cmt. c, at 119.

76 Principles §2.03 cmt. c (iii), at 121; Principles §2.03, illus. 22, at 122 (providing the following illustration of implied agreement: "For the past four years, seven-year-old Lindsay has lived with her mother, Annis, and her stepfather, Ralph. During that period, Ralph and Annis both worked outside the home, and divided responsibility for Lindsay's care roughly equally between them. ...Annis's sharing of responsibility for Lindsay's care with Ralph constitutes an implied agreement by her to the role assumed by Ralph.").

77 Elizabeth S. Scott, "Domestic Partnerships, Implied Contracts, and Law Reform", in *Reconceiving the Family* 9 (Robin Fretwell Wilson ed., 2006).

78 See Principles §2.08 (stating that "the proportion of time the child spends with each parent [approximates] the proportion of time each parent spent performing caretaking functions for the child prior to the parents' separation," unless an exception applies); but see Parkinson, supra note 67, at 450 ("Even if the past caretaking standard does promote greater predictability, this is only likely to occur when it is the rule itself, rather than one of the exceptions, that is the major issue at trial. Arguably, the exceptions to the standard are so many that they threaten to swallow up the rule.").

79 Of the children who live with either their mother or father only, 83% live with a mother. U.S. Census Bureau, America's Families and Living Arrangements: 2003, tbl.C2 (2004), available at http://www.census.gov/population/socdemo/hh-fam/cps2003/tabC2-all.pdf (last accessed Aug. 16, 2007)(reporting that approximately 16.8 million children live with their mother only compared to approximately 3.3 million children who live with their father only). Among divorced and separated couples with children, mothers maintain over four times as many households as fathers. U.S. Census Bureau, America's Families and Living Arrangements: 2003, tbl.FG6 (2004), http://www.census.gov/population/socdemo/hh-fam/cps2003/tabFG6-all-1.pdf (last accessed Aug. 16, 2007) (reporting that approximately 1.3 million households are maintained by fathers compared to approximately 5.3 million households maintained by mothers).
Minority women may have their parental prerogatives overridden more often than white women. See Sarah H. Ramsey, "Constructing Parenthood for Stepparents: Parents by Estop-

Second, the ALI's test encroaches on the parenting decisions of mothers in several ways. De facto parents receive standing to press a claim unilaterally[80] – an option that is unavailable in many states[81] and would be unnecessary if the mother simply agreed that her ex-partner should see the child. De facto parents are also generally placed on par with legal parents, i.e., the mother, for physical custody rights and receive a share of time that approximates their prior relationship with the child.[82] Thus, presumptively, the de facto parent is awarded half the time with the child.[83] And because the de facto parent is receiving the same physical custody rights as the legal parent, this time could encompass overnight stays and unsupervised weekends – all over the objection of the mother.[84]

Third, with rights usually come obligations. But the ALI includes one key limit on the obligations of de facto parents: they do not have to pay child support for the child in whom they are receiving parental rights, unlike every other category of parent recognized in the *Principles*.[85]

---

pel and De Facto Parents Under the American Law Institute's Principles of the Law of Family Dissolution", *8 Duke J. Gender L. & Pol'y 285*, 287 (2001) (recognizing that family formation patterns often differ by race).

80 Section 2.04 gives standing and notice rights to a de facto parent who "resided with the child within the six-month period prior to the filing of the action or who has consistently maintained or attempted to maintain the parental relationship since residing with the child." Principles §2.04 (1)(c), at 134. The six-month window is waived if the de facto parent "consistently maintained or attempted to maintain the parental relationship since no longer sharing the same residence." Id. §2.04 cmt. d, at 136. This waiver "eliminate[s] the advantages of uncooperative or strategic behavior by the custodial parent." Id.

81 Very few states permit unmarried cohabitants to initiate actions for custody or visitation See, e.g., *Engel v. Kenner*, 926 S.W.2d 472 (Mo. Ct. App. 1996) (denying joint custody to boyfriend of mother who lived with mother and child for five months and helped support child for three years thereafter)..

82 See supra note 80 and accompanying text.

83 This presumption arises because to qualify as a de facto parent in the first place, the individual must have performed the majority of the caretaking functions or at least performed a share equal to or greater than the share assumed by the legal parent to satisfy the caretaking prong. Principles §2.03 cmt. c, at 119. Thus, in conjunction with the approximation standard, which seeks to mirror the previous arrangement in terms of time spent, the de facto parent receives at least half the time with the child. *See* supra note 71.

84 Principles §2.05, illus. 2., at 149 (reserving supervised visitation for instances when protecting the child or the child's parent is warranted, as when the courts finds "credible evidence of domestic violence").

85 See Katharine K. Baker, "Asymmetric Parenthood", in *Reconceiving the Family 121*, 133 (Robin Fretwell Wilson ed., Cambridge Univ. Press 2006) (analyzing the Principles' child support provisions and teasing out "precisely the kind of scenario in which someone is likely to have custody or visitation rights as de facto parent under [the ALI's custody proposal], but not have financial responsibility for a child under [its child support proposals]. Fred, a widowed father of two, cohabited with Allen for five years before separating. During their cohabitation Fred and Allen shared their earnings and the children benefited from the increased household income. Assume also that Fred and Allen shared caretaking responsibilities with Allen doing as much as Fred. Allen would have custodial rights as a de facto parent but, absent affirmative

In short, the ALI would not allow mothers to exercise their judgment about who should see their child. The ALI assumes that she cannot evaluate as well as the PRINCIPLES can when continuing contact will be a good thing for her child and when it will not. In addition to usurping traditional parental prerogatives, the ALI's test raises other, deeper concerns that flow from an established body of social science research, to which this Chapter now turns.

3.2.2. Critiquing the ALI Test

A convincing case must be made that children on the whole will be made better off before policymakers remove children from the exclusive custody of their legal parents (here, their mothers) and place trust for their well-being in the hands of ex-boyfriends. But in their zealousness to provide continuing contact with good father-figures, whose relationship society has an interest in preserving, the ALI has latched on to an easily administrable caretaking test, a test that fails to screen out even the worst risks to a child.

Caretaking functions consist of the chores necessary for the "direct delivery of day-to-day care and supervision to the child."[86] They include "physical supervision, feeding, grooming, discipline, transportation, direction of the child's intellectual and emotional development, and arrangement of the child's peer activities, medical care, and education,"[87] as Figure 1 illustrates. The ALI places this emphasis on caretaking functions because these functions, in their own words, "involve tasks relating directly to a child's care and upbringing, [and so these tasks] are likely to have a special bearing on the strength and quality of the adult's relationship with the child."[88]

While the ALI assumes that caretaking responsibilities mirror a loving and bonded relationship, those same activities can indicate a very different type of relationship: child molestation. As Figure 1 illustrates, child molesters groom children by engaging in conduct that most of us would find heart-warming. Child molesters read to children. Child molesters bathe children. Child molesters shower children with attention and assure them that what they are doing is "right." Thus, the ALI's test not only fails to screen out bad risks, it gives the worst men an "A+" based on the very behaviors that should sometimes raise red flags.

conduct indicating ... an agreement to assume a parental support obligation and even then only in exception circumstances, Allen would not be responsible for any child support") (internal quotations and citations omitted).

86 Principles §2.03 cmt. g, at 125.

87 Principles §2.03 cmt. g, at 125.

88 Principles §2.03 cmt. g, at 125.

Figure 1: A Comparison of ALI Caretaking Functions and Grooming of Child Victims

ALI Caretaking Functions	**Grooming Behaviors**
Grooming[1]	Bathing[3,4]
Washing[1]	Bathing[3,4]
Dressing[1]	Dressing[3,4]
Toilet Training[1]	Bathroom Behavior[3]
Playing with child[1]	Attention;[2,3,6] Affection [2,6]
Bedtime and Wakeup[1]	Being around child at bedtime[6]
Satisfying Nutrition Needs[1]	
Protecting child's safety[1]	
Providing transportation[1]	
Directing development[1]	
Discipline[1]	Discipline[6]
Arranging for education[1]	
Helping to develop relations[1]	
Arranging for health care[1]	
Providing moral guidance[1]	Assure child of rightness;[3] telling child that acts would not hurt them[3]
Arranging alternate care for child[1]	
	Bribes[2,3,5,6]
	Trust [2,3,6]
	Alienating child from peers and family[3,6]
	Secrecy[3,4,6]
	Sexually Explicit and Vulgar Conversation [3,6]

Sources:
1) *Principles* §2.03 cmt. g., at 125.
2) David Finkelhor, *Child Sexual Abuse: New Theory and Research* (1984).
3) John R. Christiansen & Reed H. Blake, The Grooming Process in Father-Daughter Incest, in *The Incest Perpetrator: A Family Member No One Wants to Treat* (Anne L. Horton et al. eds., 1990).
4) Patricia Bell, Factors Contributing to a Mother's Ability to Recognise Incestuous Abuse of Her Child, 25 *Women's Stud. Int'l F.* 347 (2002).
5) Jon R. Conte, The Nature of Sexual Offenses Against Children, in *Clinical Approaches to Sex Offenders and Their Victims* (Clive R. Hollin & Kevin Howells eds., 1991).
6) Jon R. Conte et al., What Sexual Offenders Tell Us About Prevention Strategies, 13 *Child Abuse & Neglect* 293 (1989).

While the test for de facto parenthood is itself problematic, the ALI also fails to address other potential downsides of granting parental rights to male co-residents. For instance, it might be appropriate to encourage continuing contact in the form of dinners every other week. But embracing overnight stays[89] and allotting presumptively half the time with the child is an entirely different matter since the risk of physical and sexual abuse soars when mothers are not present.[90]

It is well-established that the risk of physical abuse soars when a child lives with an unrelated male.[91] A study published in 2005 in Pediatrics by Schnitzer and Ewigman[92] examined the household composition of all children in Missouri under the age of five who died between January 1, 1992 and December 31, 1999, and compared the household structure for children who died due to inflicted injury death with those who died by natural causes.[93] Inflicted injury death includes death resulting from intentional abuse, but not neglect (unlike maltreatment death, which would include both). The study identified 149 inflicted-injury deaths in its population. The study found that the "majority of perpetrators were male (71.2%), and most were the child's father (34.9%) or the boyfriend of the child's mother (24.2%)."[94] Because so few children in the study lived with their mother's boyfriend, however, "[c]hildren residing in households with unrelated adults were nearly 50 times as likely to die of inflicted injuries than children residing with 2 biological parents."

Perhaps child death is an extreme example; we might expect lesser forms of child maltreatment would follow different patterns. Yet the over-representation of unrelated males appears with lesser forms of physical abuse as well, as shown in studies of maltreatment death (that is, death that occurs due to intentional injury

89 See supra note 84 (discussing when supervised visitation is warranted).

90 For instance, the mere absence of a girl's mother heightens her risk for sexual exploitation. Robin Fretwell Wilson, "Undeserved Trust: Reflections on the American Law Institute's Treatment of De Facto Parents", in *Reconceiving the Family* 90, 112 (Robin Fretwell Wilson, ed., Cambridge University Press, 2006). Researchers have compared girls who lived without their mother before the age of sixteen to those who remained with their mother throughout childhood. The sexual vulnerability of the estranged girls was nearly 200 percent greater than that of other girls, leading one researcher to conclude that "missing a mother is the most damaging kind of disruption." *Id.* This pattern of a girl's heightened vulnerability in mother-absent households is repeated in multiple studies. *Id.*

91 See Rebecca M. Bolen, "Predicting Risk to Be Sexually Abused: A Comparison of Logistic Regression to Event History Analysis", 3 *Child Maltreatment* 157 (1998) ("[C]hildren living with males in the household after separation [of their parents] were more than seven times more likely to be abused... [than] children living with only females after separation.").

92 Patricia G. Schnitzer & Bernard G. Ewigman, "Child Deaths Resulting from Inflicted Injuries: Household Risk Factors and Perpetrator Characteristics", 11(5) *Pediatrics* 687–693 (2005).

93 *Id.* at 691.

94 *Id.* at 687.

and as a result of neglect),[95] as well as in all reports of child maltreatment,[96] and studies of the risk of physical abuse.[97]

The ALI's failure to consider such social science research is part of a broader blind spot exhibited throughout the PRINCIPLES. Professor Marsha Garrison, for example, questions the basis for treating unmarried cohabitants as if they are married, especially since cohabitants do not see their relationships in the same way and would never expect this result.[98] How could the ALI have missed the extensive empirical literature on a range of questions? Professor Harry Krause believes the ALI Principles "may be ahead of our time."[99] This likely occurred because, as Professor Carl Schneider argues, the ALI radically departed in the PRINCIPLES from its founding mission: the restatement of the law.[100] Professor Schneider explains:

> The ambition of ALI programs has expanded impressively over the years. The founders rather modestly thought that the law's uncertainty and complexity had produced a "general dissatisfaction with the administration of justice." They rather modestly assumed that those problems could be ameliorated if experts collaborated to solve essentially technical problems in interpreting the law. ... At their heart was an attempt to understand a body of law in light of the complexities time had produced in it and to rationalize its doctrines cogently and acutely. This is the kind of work lawyers are trained to do, it is work skillful lawyers do better than mediocre lawyers, and it raises relatively few concerns about how elites exercise their powers.

---

95 MICHAEL N. STIFFMAN et al., "Household Composition and Risk of Fatal Child Maltreatment", *109 Pediatrics* 615, 616 (2002).

96 See ARUNA RADHAKRISHNA et al., "Are Father Surrogates a Risk Factor for Child Maltreatment?", *6(4) Child Maltreatment* 281 (November 2001) (discussing all forms of child maltreatment and finding that "[c]hildren who had a father surrogate living in the home were twice as likely to be reported for maltreatment after his entry into the home than those with either a biological father... or no father figure in the home").

97 See ROBERT WHELAN, "Broken Homes and Battered Children: A Study of the Relationship Between Child Abuse and Family Type", *tbls. 12 & 14* (1994) (reporting a risk of physical abuse for children living with two natural married parents of 0.23, compared to a risk of 7.65 for children living with their natural mother and a cohabitee and a risk of fatal abuse for children living with both natural, married parents of 0.31, compared to a risk of fatal abuse of 22.9 for children living with their natural mother and a cohabitee).

98 See MARSHA GARRISON, "Marriage Matters: What's Wrong with the ALI's Domestic Partnership Proposal", in *Reconceiving the Family 305* (ROBIN FRETWELL WILSON ed., Cambridge Univ. Press 2006).

99 HARRY D. KRAUSE, "Comparative Family Law: Past Traditions Battle Future Trends—and Vice Versa," *The Oxford Handbook of Comparative Law* 1099 (MATHIAS REIMANN & REINHARD ZIMMERMANN eds., Oxford University Press 2006).

100 CARL S. SCHNEIDER, "Afterword: Elite Princples: The ALI Proposals and the Politics of Law Reform", in *Reconceiving the Family* 491 (ROBIN FRETWELL WILSON ed., Cambridge Univ. Press 2006) (noting that "[t]he ALI has wielded influence beyond the fantasies of its founders. The Model Penal Code and the Restatements are as close to binding precedent as nongovernmental authority can be,...").

> But ... [t]he ALI has long since ceased to regard itself as just a source of technical proficiency in the law and has come to value itself as a source of social policy.[101]

There are certainly problems that arise with any attempt at standardization.[102] But if the ALI seeks to standardize the law, it should at least structure the presumption in a way that responds to good social science research. It has not done that with its proposals for de facto parents. The ALI makes no inquiry into why a mother will not voluntarily allow access to her child[103] – maybe she senses the man is dangerous to her child and separates from him for that reason. Moreover, the ALI makes no inquiry into how the child will fare as a result of continuing contact or because the child loses that contact; instead, it simply assumes that the loss of contact will be detrimental to the child. But the impact on the child from loss of contact, a fact-specific determination, cannot be assessed because the ALI's test does not even ask the question.[104]

These concerns are not merely speculative or academic. In 2005, eleven-year-old Haleigh Poutre was rushed to Noble Hospital in Westfield, Massachusetts with "both old and new bruises, old and new open cuts, several apparent weeping burns, and ... a subdural hematoma."[105] She was in a coma. The Massachusetts Department of Social Services ("DSS") believes that her stepfather, Jason Strickland, bludgeoned her with a baseball bat. The beating was only the most severe in a series of fourteen abuse incidents reported to Massachusetts DSS.[106]

The state charged Strickland and Haleigh's mother with assault and battery.[107] Soon thereafter, Haleigh's mother committed suicide, leaving Haleigh without a legal guardian and in the sole custody of DSS.[108] Strickland then asserted his "right" as Haleigh's de facto father to make medical decisions on her behalf. He

101 *Id.*

102 See e.g., Patrick Parkinson, "The Past Caretaking Standard in Comparative Perspective", in *Reconceiving the Family* 446, (Robin Fretwell Wilson ed., Cambridge Univ. Press 2006) (explaining how the past caretaker standard is "prejudicial to the primary earning parent in role-divided marriages").

103 Cf. infra notes 120–123 and accompanying text.

104 Cf. infra note 124 and accompanying text.

105 Patricia Wen, "Accused Stepfather Fights to Keep Girl Alive", *The Boston Globe*, Nov. 6, 2005, available at http://www.boston.com/news/local/massachusetts/articles/2005/11/06/accused_stepfather_fights_to_keep_girl_alive (last accessed June 20, 2007).

106 Patricia Wen, "Accused Stepfather Fights to Keep Girl Alive", *The Boston Globe*, Nov. 6, 2005.

107 *Id.*

108 See In Re Care and Protection of Sharlene, 840 N.E.2d 918, 927 (Mass. 2006) (ruling that decisions on Haleigh's medical status rested with DSS as she was in their custody).

wanted to avoid a potential murder charge, so he insisted that she not be removed from life support, despite the doctors' belief that she was brain dead.[109]

While Haleigh lay in the hospital, her case wound its way to the Supreme Judicial Court of Massachusetts.[110] That Court had to perform doctrinal back flips in order to deny Strickland the right to prolong her ordeal because it had already "expressly adopted the [ALI's] concept of 'de facto' parenthood."[111] Faced with Strickland's claim, the Court concluded that "to recognize [Strickland] as a [de facto parent], in order that he may participate in medical decisionmaking for [Haleigh] is unthinkable in [these] circumstances and would amount to an illogical and unprincipled perversion of the doctrine."[112] Although "our cases," the Court said, "have focused exclusively on the existence of a significant preexisting relationship ..." that "... standard ... presumes that the bond between a child and a de facto parent will be, above all, loving and nurturing."[113] Reading new, additional requirements into the ALI test was necessary because the ALI's test looks at time spent with the child and chores done, not at the quality of a de facto parent's relationship with the child.[114] The existence of a loving relationship is precisely the kind of qualitative test that the ALI expressly rejected in favor of a more easily administrable test that focuses on chores and time.[115]

Of course, none of this suggests that male cohabitants should never be treated as de facto parents. But Haleigh's experience drives home the fact that the gravamen

---

109 Patricia Wen, "Bid to End Life Support Was Quick", *The Boston Globe*, Feb. 7, 2006 (reporting that the DSS brief to withhold life support stated that Haleigh had "no meaningful hope of recovery" and that she had the "least amount of brain function that a person can have and still be considered alive").

110 840 N.E.2d 918.

111 *Id. at* 926 (noting that the court adopted the concept in 1999 and later, in 2003, it "noted, without adopting, further refinements to the concept that a de facto parent must live with the child for not less than two years and the caretaking relationship have been established for reasons primarily other than financial compensation and with the agreement of a legal parent to form a parent-child relationship or as a result of a complete failure or inability of any legal parent to perform caretaking functions")(internal quotations omitted).
See also E.N.O. v. L.M.M., 711 N.E.2d 886, 891 (Mass. 1999) ("A de facto parent is one who has no biological relation to the child, but has participated in the child's life as a member of the child's family. The de facto parent resides with the child and, with the consent and encouragement of the legal parent, performs a share of caretaking functions at least as great as the legal parent.... The de facto parent shapes the child's daily routine, addresses his developmental needs, disciplines the child, provides for his education and medical care, and serves as a moral guide.") (citing Principles). The Massachusetts court employed the ALI's definition of a de facto parent in a more recent case, as well. See A.H. v. M.P., 857 N.E.2d 1061, 1069–70 (Mass. 2006) (citing *id.*).

112 *Id.* at 927

113 *Id.* at 926

114 *Id.* at 926

115 See Principles, supra note 63, and accompanying text.

of the relationship – a loving, bonded, dependent relationship – should be of paramount importance. Taking love into account and not just the performing chores will help ensure a significant upside for children and mitigate concerns about any potential downside.

Alternatives to the ALI's test exist. Several states have enacted thoughtful and protective tests. Wisconsin and Oregon, for instance, emphasize the bond between the child and the former partner.

Oregon requires physical residence with the child,[116] as does the ALI. In addition, Oregon, like the ALI, considers whether the de facto parent provided for the child's physical needs.[117] But Oregon also looks for a crucial piece missing from the PRINCIPLES: the de facto parent must fulfill the child's psychological needs for a parent and be seen by the child as a parent.[118] Moreover, there is a second aspect of the Oregon test that is entirely absent from the ALI: Oregon defers to the mother's judgment. Once a de facto parent meets the threshold standard, he or she must also overcome the presumption that the child's biological parent is acting in the best interests of the child by denying access. Additionally, that person has to show that ending the child's ongoing relationship with the de-facto parent would affirmatively injure the child.[119]

Other states have experimented with different formulations for deciding which bonds between a child and an adult should not be disrupted. Wisconsin asks whether there is a bonded, dependent relationship of a parental nature between the child and the adult.[120] And Kentucky awards rights to a de facto custodian – someone who has been the primary caregiver for a financial support of a child, usually for more than a year – when doing so serves a child's best interests.[121] In Kentucky, a de facto custodian literally "stands in the place of a natural parent"[122] – meaning that the child cannot have more than two legal parents, unlike movements in New Zealand and elsewhere to recognize multiple legal parents.[123]

116 Or. Rev. Stat. §109.119 (2003).

117 *Id.*

118 *Id.*

119 *Id.*

120 In re Custody of H.S.H.-K. v. Knott, 533 N.W.2d 419 (1995).

121 Ky. Rev. Stat. Ann §405.020 (West 2006).

122 *Boone v. Ballinger*, 2007 WL 1300713 (Ky. App. May 4, 2007).

123 See New Zealand Law Commission, New Issues in Legal Parenthood (Report 88) 68 (Apr. 2005), available at http://www.austlii.edu.au/nz/other/nzlc/report/R88/R88.pdf (last accessed Aug. 16, 2007) (recommending New Zealand amend the Status of Children Act 1969 to allow couples to appoint a donor as a third parent); *Jacob v. Schultz-Jacob*, 923 A.2d 473, 482 (Pa. Super. Ct. 2007) (affirming various full and partial custody awards to the three adults, thereby recognizing that a minor can have more than two parents).

3.2.3. *The Essential Role of the Constitution*

The fact that these definitions of parenting are so different does pose some difficulties in the United States, in particular when families move from place to place. Unfortunately, this type of collision is unlikely to be resolved by means other than the federal courts interpreting the U.S. Constitution.[124] For example, in 2004, Oklahoma amended a statute governing foreign adoptions[125] to provide that Oklahoma will "not recognize an adoption by more than one individual of the same sex from any other state or foreign jurisdiction."[126] Oklahoma took this bold move despite the fact that twenty-five jurisdictions now allow adoptions by same-sex couples.[127] Three same-sex couples who moved to Oklahoma from California, New Jersey, and Washington where they adopted children challenged the constitutionality of Oklahoma's statute.[128] The United States Court of Appeals for the Tenth Circuit, affirming the lower court, concluded that the Full Faith and Credit Clause of the United States Constitution required Oklahoma courts to recognize the adoption decree from another state.[129]

---

124 See Ronald J. Krotoszynski, Jr., "Navigating Dangerous Constitutional Straits: A Prolegomenon the Federal Marriage Amendment and the Disenfranchisement of Sexual Minorities", *76 U. Colo. L. Rev 599*, 607 2005) (explaining that one of the characteristics of federalism is that "different states will reach different outcomes on various questions of public and private morality"); J. Harvie Wilkinson III, "Hands Off Constitutions: This Isn't the Way to Ban Same-Sex Marriage", *Washington Post*, Sep. 5, 2006, available at 2006 WLNR 15452019 ("State constitutional bans on same-sex marriages vary considerably in their wording, particularly with respect to civil unions.").

125 10 Okl. Stat. Ann. §7502–1.4 (1996).

126 10 Okl. Stat. Ann. §7502–1.4(A) (1996).

127 "Relationship Recognition for Same-Sex Couples in the U.S.", *National Gay and Lesbian Task Force*, available at http://www.thetaskforce.org/downloads/reports/issue_maps/2nd_parent_adoption_5_07.pdf (last visited July 18, 2007) (noting that in 15 of those states, only the state trial court level has granted second- parent adoption).

128 *Finstuen v. Edmondson, Finstuen v. Crutcher*, No. 06–6213 (10th Cir. August 3, 2007).

129 See *Id.* (finding that "final adoption orders and decrees are judgments that are entitled to recognition by all other states under the Full Faith and Credit Clause.
The U.S. District Court also found that the Amendment violated the Equal Protection Clause. See *Finstuen v. Edmondson*, No. CIV-04-1152-C, 2006 WL 1445354, 8 (W.D. Okla. May 19, 2006) ("[B]ecause the Amendment attempts to strip away the parental status of at least one of the adult [p]laintiffs from each family unit, it violates the Equal Protection clause and must be struck down."). In reaching that conclusion, the court also stated that the Amendment violated the Equal Protection Clause because it had a "disparate impact on homosexual individuals seeking recognition of out-of-state adoptions." *Id.* at 12. The Tenth Circuit did "not reach the issues of whether the adoption amendment infringes on the Due Process or Equal Protection Clauses" because it affirmed on other grounds. *Finstuen v. Edmondson, Finstuen v. Crutcher*, No. 06–6213 (10th Cir. August 3, 2007).

4. STATE APPROACHES TO SAME-SEX MARRIAGE

Questions across state boundaries are popping up in the area of same-sex marriage as well. In 2003, the Massachusetts Supreme Court in Goodridge v. Department of Public Health[130] held that the State may not "deny the protections, benefits, and obligations conferred by civil marriage to two individuals of the same sex who wish to marry."[131] As a result of Goodridge, Massachusetts became the first state, and remains the only state, to recognize same-sex marriage.[132]

A staggering number of states in the U.S. have since explicitly rejected same-sex marriage.[133] Other states are simply silent.[134] As a result of this divergence, a number of issues arise across jurisdictional boundaries. For instance, what happens when a same-sex couple marries in Massachusetts and then seeks a divorce or the benefits of marriage in a state that has not condoned same-sex marriage?[135] This occurred recently in Rhode Island, where a lesbian couple, married in Massachusetts, is now seeking a divorce.[136] U.S. academics are split about how the courts will resolve these collisions.[137] In our federalist scheme, we are likely not to have a good answer to this question until the United States Supreme Court resolves it.

---

130 *Goodridge v. Dept. of Pub. Health*, 798 N.E.2d 941, 948 (Mass. 2003) (holding that there exists no adequate reason under the Massachusetts Constitution to deny civil marriage to same-sex couples).

131 *Id.*

132 "Relationship Recognition for Same-Sex Couples in the U.S.", *National Gay and Lesbian Task Force*, available at http://www.thetaskforce.org/downloads/reports/issue_maps/relationship_recognition_7_07.pdf (last visited July 18, 2007)

133 See "State Prohibitions on Marriage for Same-Sex Couples", *Human Rights Campaign*, available at http://hrc.org/Template.cfm?Section=Center&CONTENTID=28225&TEMPLATE=/ContentManagement/ContentDisplay.cfm (last accessed July 20, 2007) (showing 26 states that have passed constitutional amendments to define marriage as between one man and one woman).

134 Kate Bramson, "More Info Sought on Gay Divorce Case", *Providence Journal Bulletin*, Jan. 18, 2007, at B1.

135 *Chambers v. Ormiston*, 916 A.2d 758, 758 (R.I. 2007) (remanding the case to the trial court to determine, among other things, whether each party resided in Rhode Island prior to filing an application for marriage in Massachusetts, and where the parties were residing at the time of solemnization).

136 Kate Bramson, "More Info Sought on Gay Divorce Case", *Providence Journal Bulletin*, Jan. 18, 2007, at B1.

137 Compare Gary J. Simson, "Beyond Interstate Recognition in the Same-Sex Marriage Debate", *U.C. Davis L. Rev. 313*, 383 (2006) (arguing that courts will have to recognize same-sex marriages from other states because not doing so violates the constitutional principles of due process, equal protection, and nonestablishment of religion) with Mark D. Rosen, "Why the Defense of Marriage Act is not (Yet?) Unconstitutional: Lawrence, Full Faith and Credit, and the Many Societal Actors that Determine what the Constitution Requires", *Minn L. Rev. 915*, 999–1001 (concluding that the Defense of Marriage Act is constitutional and therefore courts can deny recognition).

The backlash against same-sex marriage places a premium on state law approaches to recognizing in another way the relationships between lesbians and gays, as well as between heterosexual cohabitants. A number of states have extended marital rights to same-sex couples without the title of marriage. Hawaii, for example, has recognized a "reciprocal beneficiary relationship."[138] While not granting a couple all the rights and obligations conferred through marriage,[139] it does give same-sex couples additional rights with regards to third parties.[140] New Jersey follows much the same approach in its Domestic Partnership Act: limited protections for domestic partners.[141] Four states, California,[142] Washington,[143] Vermont,[144] and New Hampshire[145] place same-sex partners in the same position as spouses, affording them "all the same benefits protections and responsibilities under law, ... as are granted to spouses in a marriage."[146]

5. CONCLUSION

In the United States' federalist system, state laws governing family relations can differ dramatically, even between geographic neighbors. During our 200 years of experience with a federalist system, a number of mechanisms have evolved to bring some measure of harmony, although not uniformity, to the treatment of family law by the various states. These include top-down approaches, in which the U.S. Supreme Court resolves differences when constitutional principles are implicated – as well as bottom-up approaches, in which state law reform commissions and national law reform bodies attempt to close gaps between the laws of the states. Despite these mechanisms, deep divisions remain over such fundamental questions as who is a parent.

138 Haw. Rev. Stat. §572C-4 (2006).

139 Haw. Rev. Stat. §572C-6 (2006).

140 Haw. Rev. Stat. §572C-2 (2006).

141 N.J. Stat. Ann. §26:8A-2(d) (West 2007). Oregon places domestic partners in the same position as spouses only with regards to children and tax liability. Oregon House of Representatives Bill 2007 (2007).

142 California Fam. Code §297.5 (West 2007)

143 2007 Wash. Sess. Laws Ch. 156 §8 (2007).

144 Vt. Stat. Ann. tit. 15 §1504 (2007).

145 N.H. Rev. Stat. Ann. §457-A:6 (West 2007)

146 Vt. Stat. Ann. tit. 15 §1504 (2007).

PART TWO
CHILDREN AND THEIR PARENTS

RECENT DEVELOPMENTS IN CHILD LAW

LUCY SMITH

1. INTRODUCTION

I am honoured to be invited to deliver this key-note speech to this distinguished Commission on European Family Law that I have heard so much about from my colleagues here at the Faculty. Child Law encompasses both private and public law. Even though CEFL is about family law, I do hope that I will be forgiven for drifting outside the usual concept of family law.

I have had some problems with what can be characterized as *recent developments*; for example, I have noticed that what I find to be recent times, my grandchildren would characterise as the Stone Age. But I suppose I will be allowed to use my own definition. Not exactly back to the Stone Age, but the last few decades. Medical majority is a concept in several European countries, and it will generally be lower than the age of majority.

First, a few words about history. If you search for *Child Law* on Google today, you will get around 120 million results. *Family Law* gives you 260 million, but I still think the number of results for Child law is a good illustration of what has happened in the field of Child law in recent times. Of course I have no numbers from earlier years to compare with, but I think it could be said that before 1980 Child Law was not a field of law at all, or a discipline. At least I had heard of no other law faculties having courses on Child law when the University of Oslo started with these in around 1980.

The most *striking* development lately may be the emerging jurisprudence on the new methods of procreation. But in my opinion the most important development as regards child law in the last few decades is certainly the growing recognition of the fact that children are the subjects of rights. We see this all over the world, although more in legislation than in real life. One of the reasons for the strong emphasis on Children's rights in recent years is of course the Convention on the Rights of the Child (CRC). The CRC has led to great changes in the legislation of many countries, to the greatest extent in developing countries. But also in most of the European countries there has been some new legislation, most of it regarding the right to be heard, the best interest of the child, legislation on a children's ombudsman and the juvenile justice system.

The Convention has also attracted much interest from scholars; more from child law scholars than from human rights scholars. The CRC is mentioned by national courts to a certain extent, but is more often pleaded by the lawyers than being referred to by the courts. To what extent the Convention is applicable in the national courts will of course depend on the status of international conventions in the respective countries, but even in countries with a monistic system, national law will often be preferred because it is more detailed and precise than the convention. Quite often, lawyers use the convention uncritically, instead of referring to more precise national legislation.

I started my personal work with children's rights in the 1970s after having studied several Supreme Court cases on custody and visitation rights, and finding that the child as a person tended to disappear in these cases, and that it was the parental rights that dominated. In cases of taking into care, the rights of the parents were in focus, which resulted in a weaker protection for the child. So I started writing about the child as a subject of law, and children's right to be heard in important decisions affecting them.

Questions of custody and visitation rights when the parents split up are in my opinion no longer an acute *legal* problem. The case law has been developed and refined during the last few decades, and the right of the child to be heard is solidly established in most national legislations. The hottest issue in custody questions is now whether joint physical custody should be the main rule or whether it should only be possible when it is the wish of both parents, and there are different solutions in different countries. The question of joint physical custody is not first and foremost a legal question, but more an issue for child behaviour specialists. The custody question and visitation rights have now, at least in my country, become the playing field for politicians, with new legislation almost every year, often media-driven, and I for one have withdrawn from the discussion. And so has the Norwegian Supreme Court; it is now quite seldom that a traditional custody case is heard by the Supreme Court in Norway, as the disputes now hardly raise questions which are of interest. But with many parents with different nationalities, international private law is becoming very topical. The application of the Hague Convention on the Civil Aspects of International Child Abduction especially raises many difficult and interesting questions, and is widely discussed all over the world, and there is a large body of case law. The jurisprudence on the right to be heard and to gradually attain autonomy in certain areas is still developing in most countries. Here the CRC has played an important role, and I will discuss some of the questions related to article 12 and children's participation rights.

2. INTERPRETATION OF THE CONVENTION

First, I will make some general remarks about the interpretation of the Convention. Many of the articles in the convention are vague with wide-ranging wording, and are thus difficult to interpret. Partly because of this, several of the articles are not self-executing, and are therefore not directly applicable in the national courts in countries with a dualistic system. There is no individual complaints procedure, which adds to the interpretation problems.

In my opinion, the travaux préparatoire are not of any great assistance. The drafters were an open-ended working group, there were different opinions on many important issues, and the final draft in many ways represented a compromise. This implies that the individual statements of the delegates in the working group are of less interest, and that it is first and foremost the text as it stands that must be the basis for the Committee in its work.

However, the CRC Committee has published ten so-called General Comments, the last in 2007 on corporal punishment. For the moment the Committee is working on two general comments, one on article 12, and another on indigenous children. The general comments from all the treaty bodies (the expert committees of the UN human rights conventions) are first and foremost interpretations of the convention regarding special thematic issues. The interpretations will among other things be based on experiences which the committees have gathered through the State Party reports, the dialogue with the State Parties and UN organisations and NGOs. The conventions with an individual complaints procedure will usually have developed more jurisprudence than the others, and will thus have a broader basis for their interpretation. But behind the publishing of General Comments from the CRC is a broad and participatory process, with many experts, institutions and organisations taking part (but not the State Parties). It could be said, though, that most of the persons involved in the drafting process will no doubt usually give preference to a wide interpretation of human rights. It is also a fact that lawyers are not in the majority among the Committee members. However, the Committee must base its Comments as well as its concluding remarks on the Convention. If the Committee goes outside the strict meaning of the Convention, it should use the words "encourage" or "recommend".

The General Comments are not legally binding. Assessments of the Comments vary. The general opinion is, however, that they are of importance as guiding texts and interpretative tools. They will without doubt contribute to a certain dynamism in the interpretation of the conventions, and sometimes they might even establish a basis for customary human rights law.

Taking into consideration the often vague and open-ended character of the articles, and the difficulties involved in amending the conventions, it is in my view necessary to a certain degree to regard the Convention as a living instrument, as is the case with the European Human Rights Convention. One of the arguments *against* a dynamic interpretation is that the Convention is relatively young. On the other hand, in the field of child rights much has happened since the Convention was adopted in 1989. The Committee must find a balance between a static interpretation and the boldest interpretation, sometimes described as "legislation by Committee". The interpretation must at least be in accordance with the general development in society. Several of the General Comments published by the Committee demonstrate that the Convention in the opinion of the Committee is considered to be a living instrument. One example is General Comment no. 8 on corporal punishment, where the Committee states that any sort of corporal punishment is in conflict with the CRC. Another example is the adolescent's right to autonomy in certain health issues. I will come back to that in a moment.

3. PARTICIPATION RIGHTS AND ARTICLE 12

The most controversial – and innovative – parts of the CRC have been article 12 on the right of the child to be heard and to have his/her views taken into consideration, and, in addition, the civil and political rights of the child expressed in articles 13 to 16. The expression "participation rights" is often used to imply all these articles. But "participation rights" is a concept without a clear definition. It has been defined as the right to take part in decision-making processes affecting one's life and the life of the community in which one lives. The right to participation is not used in any of the articles of the CRC, except for article 23 about the disabled child's active participation in the community. But it is obvious that articles 13 to 16 on civil and political rights are about the participation of the child in society.

The most important part of the concept of participation is however expressed in article 12, which concerns the right of the child to express his or her own views in all matters affecting him or her, the views of the child being given due weight in accordance with the age and maturity of the child. In what follows I will discuss some aspects of this article. The first paragraph concerns the right to be heard in general, the second highlights the right to be heard in judicial and administrative proceedings affecting the child.

There is a discussion on how to interpret the wording "*affecting the child*". Many scholars maintain that this implies a wide understanding – very few matters do not concern the child, either directly or indirectly. Apart from those affecting the child directly like custody cases, medical decisions, issues in the family, school, it certainly applies to decisions that are more general, and include more than one child, typically school decisions about the curriculum and working methods. In the widest sense, almost all political decisions will affect a child, typical environmental issues and road security, budget allocations. I believe that this wide interpretation was not the intention of the drafters. The interpretation of the Committee is not exactly clear. What is certain, however, is that it is a widespread opinion that article 12 is not only about matters that affect one individual directly, but also rights that affect children as a group, and in political processes. However, the problem is still how exactly to interpret the word *affect*.

For me article 12 concerns, first and foremost, the right of the individual child to be heard in all decisions affecting him or her, within the family, in preschool as well as in school – here also through representative forums like school councils, in medical decisions, in child institutions, and in judicial and court procedures as catered for in part 2 of article 12. However, I see the importance of children as a group taking part in the political processes, especially in the municipalities regarding issues like city planning, playgrounds etc., and environmental issues. In many countries young children are now represented in the governing bodies of municipalities, or they are involved in the consultative procedures. If this was not the intention of the drafters, it could at least be maintained that it follows from a dynamic interpretation of article 12. The participation of children on the local level will certainly be recommended by the Committee as good practice, although I would hesitate to say that it is in conflict with the Convention not to have children heard in connection with decisions in the municipalities.

In many countries a child will have the right to self-determination in special areas, for example medical issues, religious issues and education, before they reach the age of majority. In my opinion it is a weakness of the CRC that it does not give mature children the right to self-determination in some areas when they reach a certain age. This is especially so as regards medical issues. Medical majority is a concept in several European countries, and it will be lower than the age of majority. Medical issues are extremely personal, and it is difficult to accept that parents shall have the final say as regards medical treatment, reproductive health and other medical issues regarding adolescents. Under Norwegian law children as a main rule have full autonomy concerning health issues from 16 years of age, in some other countries from the age of 14, or when they are judged to be of sufficient maturity. The CRC General comment on adolescent health, states the following:

> 31. …"However, if the adolescent is of sufficient maturity, informed consent shall be obtained from the adolescent her/himself, while informing the parents if that is in the "best interest of the child" (art. 3).
>
> 32. With regard to privacy and confidentiality, and the related issue of informed consent to treatment, States parties should (a) enact laws or regulations to ensure that confidential advice concerning treatment is provided to adolescents so that they can give their informed consent. Such laws or regulations should stipulate an age for this process, or refer to the evolving capacity of the child; and (b) provide training for health personnel on the rights of adolescents to privacy and confidentiality, to be informed about planned treatment and to give their informed consent to treatment.

The relationship between article 12 and article 13 on freedom of expression is unclear. It helps to bear in mind that article 13 is a copy of articles on freedom of expression in other human rights instruments, while article 12 is specifically tailored for children in matters that affect them and subjects the State Parties to a positive obligation to provide the mechanisms which are necessary to facilitate active participation. Article 13, on the other hand, does not subject the State Party to any obligation, but it follows from the article that the State Party must not interfere with the child's right to expression concerning all matters, with some exceptions mentioned in 13(2). The contested issues in this area most often concern school papers and demonstrations in school areas. There are several cases in the US which have been raised by organisations on behalf of children, but I know of no such cases in the Nordic countries.

4. THE EUROPEAN COURT OF HUMAN RIGHTS (ECHR)

Time does not allow me to delve deeply into the case law of the ECHR. As is well known and documented, this Court has not been strong on children's rights, first of all because the Convention does not explicitly mention child rights. But there does seem to be a development in the Court concerning child rights, and the CRC is referred to in some cases. One of the decisions that provides the clearest evidence of this is the case of *Z and others v. the UK* from 2001, where 4 siblings were awarded compensation for psychological and physical damage resulting from the abuse and neglect by their parents over a period of more than four years. The breach of Article 3 concerned the failure of the local authority to take reasonable steps which were available to them to protect the children from harm. The Court found that there was therefore a direct causal link between the breach and the damage suffered by the children, and they were awarded both pecuniary and non-pecuniary damages.

The case of *C v. Finland* from 2006 concerned, among other things, the relationship between the child's right to have his views heard and the parents' rights. And again it shows that parental rights have a strong position in the ECHR. The Court stated:

> "Article 8 requires that the domestic authorities should strike a fair balance between the interests of the child and those of parents and that, in the balancing process, particular importance should be attached to the best interest of the child which, depending on their nature and seriousness, may override those of the parents. In particular, a parent cannot be entitled under article 8 of the Convention to have measures taken as would harm the child's health and development..."

This is a sentence which is often cited in the Court. This case concerned two children who, after their parents' divorce, had been living with their mother and her female partner in Finland. When the mother died, both the partner and the father, who lived in Switzerland, requested custody. The Supreme Court in Finland overturned the decisions by the lower courts that awarded custody to the father, and decided that the children should stay with the female partner of their deceased mother, in the home they had lived in for many years, first with their mother and her partner, and after the death of their mother, with the partner alone. The European Court stated that:

> "The Supreme Court ... placed exclusive weight on the views expressed by the children, then 12 and 14, without considering any other factor, in particular the applicant's rights as a father, effectively giving the children ... an unconditional veto power..."

The Court concluded that the decision-making procedure failed to strike a proper balance between the respective interests and that there had been a violation of Article 8 of the Convention in this respect. The father was awarded non-pecuniary damages because he had suffered a real loss of opportunity in addition to anxiety, stress and feelings of injustice. One could ask, however, whether the children would not have suffered the same anxiety, stress and feelings of injustice had the Supreme Court reached a different result.

The problem with this decision is that the European Court does not really discuss what would be in the best interest of the child, but bases its conclusion on the fact that the Finnish Supreme Court did not consider the rights of the father. At least in the Norwegian courts the opinions of the children will be weighed against the best interest of the child, and not against the interests of the parents. The result may, however, be partly explained by the fact that this case was about the award of damages, and not about the placement of the children. There were also many special circumstances here, a biological father versus a non-biological female partner of the mother. On the other hand, the father was Swiss, and if he had been awarded custody, the children would have had to move to a foreign country with a language which was unfamiliar to them. Here, the best interest of the child, and the right to be heard, lost in the conflict with the father's interest.

5. THE BEST INTEREST OF THE CHILD

A few words about the *best interest principle,* although too much has probably been said and written about this principle. Again and again the best interest principle has been criticized for its indeterminacy, that it is vague, abstract, worthless, saying nothing about what is in the best interest of the child. On my part, I have always been saying that the point of the best interest principle is not to say anything about what is the best interest, but to emphasise that the best interest principle must always be evaluated and taken into consideration, and must always be given great weight compared to other interests, as has been said by John Tobin:

> "It does, however, operate to recalibrate the balancing process and make visible the interests of children which historically have been subsumed with those of adults, ignored or devaluated." [1]

And as such the principle is extremely important.

I think that in many ways I have been proved right. It is gratifying to see how the principle has been incorporated in legislation around the world. But, some would say, this does not mean anything. Yes, it does! It means that legislators, judges and municipalities are reminded of the fact that the interests of children should be given paramount consideration by the courts and in administrative practice. It is extremely interesting when a judge from the US writes:

---

1 John Tobin, "Children's Health Needs", in *International Journal of Children's Rights,* (2006) p. 287.

> "The best interest principle is not so novel as to be considered outside the bonds of what is customary international law... Given its widespread acceptance, to the extent that it acts to codify longstanding, widely-accepted principles of law, the CRC should be read as customary international law."[2]

As is well known, the best interest of the child is not *the*, but *a* primary consideration, which means that other interests can also be taken into consideration. One example is when there is a question of giving a family with small children a residence permit for humanitarian reasons. This problem, which most rich countries in the West struggle with, constitutes a real challenge for the immigration authorities. International law does not recognize the right of aliens to enter or reside in the territory of a foreign state, and it is in principle a matter for the State who it will admit to its territory. This is a fundamental right for all States. Article 22 of the CRC is in accordance with this, and gives protection to asylum-seeking children only when they are in the country. For children it will therefore first and foremost be the best interest principle that will decide whether they will be given a residence permit if they do not fall within one of the categories for the protection of refugees.

6. REPRODUCTIVE TECHNOLOGIES

In my abstract I mentioned that the legal problems resulting from *new technologies regarding artificial conception* are numerous, and will certainly increase in the future. Bone marrow donations and creating saviour children are examples of questions that several legislators now struggle with, and also the courts where the legislators have not managed to keep up with the science and reproductive technologies. There is no time to speak about this exciting emerging jurisprudence, and I will confine myself to one single issue: There is a widespread belief that article 7 of the CRC gives the child a right to information about its biological parents. The relevant wording in the first paragraph is the following:

> "... and shall have the right from birth to a name, the right to acquire a nationality and, as far as possible, the right to know and be cared for by his or her parents."

It is reasonably clear that it was not the intention of the drafters to say anything about the identity of the biological father in cases of sperm donation. The wording does not support such an understanding. I am personally against the anonymity of the donor, but I do not think that this is an issue of child rights, but more a

2 From Jane MacAdam, "Asylum under the Convention on the Rights of the Child", *International Journal of Children's Rights,* (2006) p. 268: A case for Complementary Protection.

question of human rights. I am not so sure, either, that it would be in the best interest of the child to receive this information early, or at all, before the age of majority.

It is important to know the genetic heritage for medical reasons, and many persons feel a great need to know about "my roots". I am therefore pleased to see that a right to genetic truth is developing regarding this issue. I agree with Sally Sheldon that this should not be a source of concern, as knowledge concerning the biological father "may not disrupt one's relationship with one's social father; that social and genetic ties can coexist harmoniously".[3]

7. SOME FINAL REMARKS

When I read some of the English cases concerning the Human Fertilisation and Embryology Act, I sometimes feel like a wide-eyed child entering a brave new world. Amel Alghrani writes: "The reproductive evolution, it seems, is leading on rapidly to an area enhanced by reproductive liberty, and rightly so." [4] I am not there yet. And maybe this will never be a natural place for a professor beyond the age of 70 and engaged in child rights. But at least I have more sympathy for a child who needs a donor in order to survive, than an unmarried man whose ex-partner initially sought and participated in treatment with him, but successfully conceived with an embryo fertilized by his donor sperm and implanted only after they had separated.

In any case, I will study these issues – as with all issues that affect children – from the standpoint of the child, and will allow the interest of the child to be the primary consideration.

---

3 Susan Sheldon, "Fragmenting Fatherhood: The regulation of Reproductive Technologies", *Modern Law Review*, 2005, p. 523–553 (p. 550).

4 Amel Alghrani: "Suitable to be a saviour: R (Quintavalle) v Human Fertilisation and Embryology Authority", in *Child and Family Law Quarterly* (2006) no.3, p. 422.

THE CEFL PRINCIPLES REGARDING PARENTAL RESPONSIBILITIES: PREDOMINANCE OF THE COMMON CORE

Katharina Boele-Woelki

1. A NEW SET OF PRINCIPLES

At its third international conference on European family law the CEFL presented a new set of Principles. These Principles address parental responsibilities.[1] They were published in March 2007 and – three years earlier – were preceded by CEFL's first set of Principles which deal with divorce and maintenance between former spouses.[2] Before focussing on the content of the Parental Responsibilities Principles, it should be mentioned that their publication, including the preceding materials,[3] are the result of teamwork in which 26 legal experts in the field of comparative family law are currently contributing.[4] This joint effort is one of the major characteristics of the CEFL.

This contribution contains the following parts: First, a brief overview of the structure of the Principles will be provided. Then CEFL's concept of parental responsibilities will be briefly explained. Additionally and more extensively, the question whether and to what extent the drafters have built on convergence and coped with divergence will be dealt with. Are the Principles on Parental Responsibilities common core-based or has a better law approach been applied? This is an essential part of any introduction concerning common Principles which are aimed at harmonising family law in Europe. At the end a concise comparison between the different sets of Principles is provided.

---

1 Boele-Woelki, K./Ferrand, F./González Beilfuss, C./Jänterä-Jareborg, M./Lowe, N./Martiny, D./Pintens, W., *Principles of European Family Law Regarding Parental Responsibilities*, European Family Law Series no. 16 (2007).

2 Boele-Woelki, K./Ferrand, F./González Beilfuss, C./Jänterä-Jareborg, M./Lowe, N./Martiny, D./Pintens, W., *Principles of European Family Law Regarding Divorce and Maintenance Between Former Spouses*, European Family Law Series no. 7 (2004).

3 Boele-Woelki, K./Braat, B./Curry-Sumner, I. (eds.), *European Family Law in Action, Volume III: Parental Responsibilities*, European Family Law Series no. 9 (2005).

4 Boele-Woelki, K., 'The Working Method of the Commission on European Family Law', in: Boele-Woelki, K. (ed.), *Common Core and Better Law in European Family Law*, European Family Law Series no. 10 (2005), p. 15–38.

2. STRUCTURE OF THE PRINCIPLES ON PARENTAL RESPONSIBILITIES

The CEFL Principles contain a Preamble and 39 Principles split between eight chapters.[5] Each section containing a Principle consists of four parts. The text of the Principle itself (1)[6] is followed by an overview of the relevant international and/or European provisions regarding the issue addressed in the Principle (2) in order to recall the international commitments that have previously been achieved. The international obligations built the framework along which the Principles have been drafted. The comparative overviews (3) and the comments (4) do not only refer to the twenty-two national reports by the CEFL experts, but include, in addition, the related international and/or European instruments. All four parts belong together. Referring only to the black-letter text of the Principles might lead to misunderstandings which should be avoided.

Preamble	III **Parental Responsibilities of Parents and Third Persons** *3 Principles*	VI **Termination of Parental Responsibilities** *2 Principles*
I **Definitions** *2 Principles*	IV **Exercise of Parental Responsibilities** A: Parents *6 Principles* B: Third Persons *2 Principles*	VII **Discharge and Restoration of Parental Responsibilities** *3 Principles*
II **Rights of the Child** *5 Principles*	V **Contents of Parental Responsibilities** A: The Child's Person and Property *6 Principles* B: Maintenance of Personal Relationships *5 Principles*	VIII **Procedure** *5 Principles*

Which issues are addressed? Essentially, a distinction is made between three different areas. Chapters I, II and VIII contain general rules. To these general rules

5 Boele-Woelki, K./Martiny, D., 'The CEFL and its Principles of European Family Law Regarding Parental Responsibilities', ERA Forum, 2007, p. 125–143.

6 Enclosed in the Appendix at the end of this contribution.

belong four different parts: first, the Preamble, second, two Principles which define, first, the concept of parental responsibilities and, second, the holders of parental responsibilities. The choice for a broad concept of parental responsibilities necessitates indicating who can be attributed with parental responsibilities and can exercise its rights and duties. CEFL's concept explicitly makes a distinction between parents and third persons. Primarily parents are in charge of exercising parental responsibilities. However, persons other than parents as well as public bodies can also have parental responsibilities. The relevant international and European human rights instruments have profoundly marked Chapter II which is devoted to the rights of the child. With its five Principles this Chapter forms the main general part of the CEFL Principles. The rights of the child are always to be taken into account in all matters of parental responsibilities. They constitute the principal point of departure along which all other issues should be addressed. Also the procedural aspects are of a general nature. Chapters III, IV and V address three aspects: the position of parents and third persons, the exercise of parental responsibilities and their content. Chapters VI and VII, finally, deal with the termination of parental responsibilities and being discharged therefrom.

3. CEFL'S CONCEPT OF PARENTAL RESPONSIBILITIES

What are parental responsibilities and who are its holders? Two definitions are provided in the first Chapter. In accordance with international and European instruments the CEFL opted for a broad concept of parental responsibilities consisting of a collection of rights and duties that embody the concept of taking care of the child's person and property (Principle 3:1). Concepts like guardianship and custody that are still used in national systems have been abandoned. CEFL's concept of parental responsibilities applies to children from the moment of their birth until they have reached the age of majority. A difference between younger and adolescent children has been recognized, although the indication of an age limit has intentionally been avoided. It not only depends on the child's age but also upon his/her maturity whether his/her opinion should be taken into account.

The Principles refer to the rather long-winded term "holders of parental responsibilities". Normally, the child has two parents who are the holders of parental responsibilities. However, also a person other than a parent, who has no legal ties with the child, can be attributed with and exercise parental responsibilities. Principle 3:2 clarifies this distinction. Primarily, the parents are in charge of the exercise of parental responsibilities. However, physical persons other than the parents as well as public bodies can also have parental responsibilities. According to the CEFL Principles it is thus possible that there might be even more than two holders of parental responsibilities.

4. CEFL'S APPROACH IN DRAFTING THE PRINCIPLES: COMMON CORE AND/OR BETTER LAW

The establishment of the CEFL and its drafting of common Principles have led to a widespread and intensive debate among family law comparatists about the working method to be applied. Similarities and differences, convergence and divergence, common law and/or better law are the key expressions which are discussed in the process of indicating the various findings. The main questions boil down to the following: When and why should we build on similarities, convergence and, finally, the common core and how can we cope with differences and divergence as well as when and why do we opt for the better law approach? In drafting the Principles of Parental Responsibilities these questions were repeatedly posed and finally answered for each specific subject. In contrast to some aspects of the Divorce and Maintenance Principles it was this time less difficult to agree on the drafting of the Principles and to justify their content because many similarities, a great deal of converging tendencies and a common core regarding numerous issues could be detected.

4.1. HARMONISATION THROUGH INTERNATIONAL AND EUROPEAN INSTRUMENTS

In my work-in-progress report, which I delivered in 2004 at the 2nd CEFL conference which was held shortly after we had received all the national reports from the CEFL experts, I came to the preliminary conclusion that with regard to the great majority of aspects compared, common solutions could be found.[7] At that point, I was inclined to predict that also with regard to the other questions the practical results will often be very similar.[8] This prediction, which is far from unexpected, has turned out to be true and realistic. In the field of parental responsibilities the differences among the European systems are considerably less strong than in

7 Boele-Woelki, K., 'Parental Responsibilities – CEFL's Initial Results', in Boele-Woelki, K., *ibid.*, note 4, p. 141–168.

8 This presumption of similarity (*praesumptio similitudinis*) is a generally accepted working rule in comparative law. It also applies to parental responsibilities which, as part of family law, no longer belong to those topics which are "heavily impressed by moral views and values." In this sense see Zweigert, K./ Kötz, H., *Introduction to Comparative Law*, 1998, p. 40.

other fields of family law. Hence, in the majority of issues CEFL's Principles only restate the common solutions that are generally applied. This does not come as a real surprise. It is generally acknowledged that the harmonisation of the law regarding parental responsibilities within Europe has gradually taken place through the many international and European instruments. In drafting the Principles on Parental Responsibilities we took into account 16 conventions by respectively the United Nations,[9] the Hague Conference on Private International Law, the Council of Europe and the European Union, 1 EU Regulation, 4 Declarations of the United Nations, 13 Recommendations and, additionally, the White Paper of the Council of Europe. Although each of these instruments only addresses some specific aspects of the law regarding parental responsibilities, they collectively built the general framework which to a considerable extent has also determined the national systems in Europe. Parenthetically, a compilation of the texts of all the instruments could be a publication of considerable length in itself. Besides, in no other field of family law have so many agreements between states been drafted, concluded, adopted and have become binding. This development which started some 50 years ago and which culminated in 1989 with the adoption of the Convention on the Rights of the Child can be classified as a spontaneous harmonisation of the law regarding the parent-child relationship. It forms the very foundation on which the CEFL Principles were drafted.

4.2. CATEGORISATION OF THE APPLIED METHODS REGARDING EACH SPECIFIC ISSUE

In the following an attempt is made to indicate which approach the drafters of the Principles applied. Where was it possible to detect a common core? Was this common core selected as the best solution? In respect of which aspects was it not possible to find a common core? When was a better law solution selected? Which issues were left to national law? Below an overview[10] is provided regarding the different subjects which were selected upon the basis of the comparative material. In conformity with the CEFL Principles regarding Divorce and Maintenance between Former Spouses[11] the following five different approaches are to be differentiated:

9 The international legal context of parenting and childhood is dominated by the UN Convention on the Rights of the Child. This Convention provides a first stage democratic experience for every individual member, including children – an experience shaped by mutual respect and one that strengthens the child's capacity for informed participation in the decision process. See Council of Europe, *Parenting in contemporary Europe: a positive approach*, 2007, p.27

10 I would like to thank Kathrin Spangenberg (Hamburg) for the preparation of the tables. She worked in October and November 2007 as an intern with the CEFL.

11 Boele-Woelki, K., *ibid.*, note 4., p. 33–35.

1. The common core was found and selected as the best solution.[12]
2. The common core was found, but a better solution was selected.[13]
3. The common core was found, but the solution was left to national law.
4. No common core was found and the best solution was selected.
5. No common core was found and the solution was left to national law.

The overview below, which addresses the subjects of each chapter separately, confirms that only in respect of a small number of aspects could no common core be identified. In the comments concerning each Principle the selected approach has been explicitly specified and more importantly justified. The brief explanations provided under each table[14] are restricted to the main features which are apparent in the Principles belonging to each Chapter.

Chapter I: Definitions

Principle	Aspect	Applied method	Number method
P 3:1	Concept of PR	Common core was found and selected as the best solution	1.
	Content of PR	Common core was found and selected as the best solution	1.
P 3:2	Parents as holders of PR	Common core was found and selected as the best solution	1.
	Third persons as holders of PR	Common core was found and selected as the best solution	1.

The first two Principles are clearly based on the common core. Only the terminology, 'parental responsibilities', on the one hand, and 'holders of parental responsibilities', on the other, has been slightly changed and adapted to international and European instruments. However, both the content of parental responsibilities and the definition of the persons who can hold them are common core-based.

Chapter II: Rights of the Child

Principle	Aspect	Applied method	Number method
P 3:3	Best interests of the child as the primary consideration	Common core was found and selected as the best solution	1.

12 The common core and the selected solution are thus identical.
13 The common core and the selected (better) solution can be compared.
14 In the tables the following abbreviations are used: PR = parental responsibilities; CA = competent authority.

Principle	Aspect	Applied method	Number method
P 3:4	Autonomy of the child	Common core was found and selected as the best solution	1.
	Consideration given to the child's developing abilities	Common core was found and selected as the best solution	1.
P 3:5	Non-discrimination of the child	Common core was found and selected as the best solution	1.
	No difference regarding the relationship of the holders of PR	No common core was found and the best solution was selected	4.
P 3:6	Child's right to be heard in all matters concerning him/herself	No common core was found and the best solution was selected	4.
	Consideration given to the child's age and maturity	Common core was found and selected as the best solution	1.
	Child's right is obligatory	Common core was found and selected as the best solution	1.
P 3:7	Protection of the interest of the child in case of conflict with the interests of the holders of PR	Common core was found and selected as the best solution	1.

> "Children are vested with the full range of human rights. It is, however, vital that children's rights be recognised as a self-standing set of concerns and not simply subsumed into wider efforts to mainstream human rights in general. This is appropriate since certain rights have an exclusive or particular application to children, for example the right to education and the right to maintain relations with both parents."[15]

This quotation is taken from the European Commission's recent Communication entitled "Towards an EU Strategy on the Rights of the Child". It perfectly echoes CEFL's ideas and intentions as to how the position of the child should be improved. Chapter II on the Rights of the Child contains five rights of the child which its drafters considered to be of essence, particularly in the field of parental responsibilities. Evidently, all these rights are well-established principles, rules and notions and by and large they are applied in various legal fields. Why was it then deemed to be necessary to recall these rights in the CEFL Principles? The reasons are twofold: First, it is useful to identify and bring together all children's rights which are of specific importance in relation to parental responsibilities. In the national family law systems these rights are laid down in different legal sources, either in binding conventions, in the national constitution, in the national legislation or have devel-

15 COM (2006) 367 final, p. 3.

oped in the national case law. Accordingly, the CEFL compiled these rights and addressed them at the beginning of the Principles because they should respectively be taken into account in all the following Principles. Actually, this is a commonly applied method of drafting a set of rules in a specific area. Secondly, the drafters wanted to recall the international obligations and commitments which exist in the field of child law, but which in practice are very often not applied or not taken into account. Moreover, in drafting the CEFL Principles, the child's perspective was the point of departure. Therefore, it was necessary to exemplify this perspective by indicating its content. Finally, it should be noted that in their entirety, the rights of the child in Chapter II cannot be found in any national codification of the law on parental responsibilities. In this respect a new approach has been chosen.

Also in Chapter II the common core is the most often applied approach. In this area international and European instruments play a fundamental role. The rights of children are generally acknowledged in all jurisdictions surveyed. In respect of two aspects where no common core could be detected the CEFL Principles go further in prohibiting discrimination against children. It is to be regretted that in the majority of jurisdictions represented in the CEFL differences in the treatment of children still apply, in particular depending on whether the parents of the child are or have been married to each other. Furthermore, in many countries a person's homosexuality disqualifies him or her from becoming a holder of parental responsibilities. Consequently, the legal position of children differs.[16] Principle 3:5 opts for equality among all children. This is considered to be the best solution which also applies in respect of the second aspect. The child's right to be heard is an obligatory point of departure and should not be at the discretion of the competent authority or the holders of parental responsibilities.

Chapter III: Parental Responsibilities of Parents and Third Persons

Principle	Aspect	Applied method	Number method
P 3:8	Parents: only the legal relationship with the child is relevant, not the relationship between the parents	Common core was found and selected as the best solution	1.
	Establishment of parentage	No common core was found and the solution was left to national law	5.

16 Vonk, M., *Children and Their Parents, A Comparative Study of the Legal Position of Children with Regard to Their Intentional and Biological Parents in English and Dutch Law*, European Family Law Series no. 20, 2007.

Principle	Aspect	Applied method	Number method
P 3:9	Third persons can hold PR in whole or in part	Common core was found and selected as the best solution	1.
	How and on what conditions may a third person be attributed with PR	No common core was found and the solution was left to national law	5.
	Effect of agreements regarding the attribution of PR to third persons	No common core was found and the solution was left to national law	5.
P 3:10	The dissolution of a marriage/ separation has no effect on PR	Common core was found and selected as the best solution	1.

The three Principles of Chapter III on Parental Responsibilities of Parents and Third Persons follow significant common-core solutions. In accordance with the non-discrimination Principle 3:5 only the relationship between parents and their children is a relevant constituent element for legal parenthood and parental responsibilities. This is the general approach in the majority of the legal systems. The establishment and contesting of a parent-child relationship (legal parenthood) has consequently been referred to national law due to the fact that these Principles only address parental responsibilities. Also the rights and responsibilities of third persons, in particular the parent's partner, have been gradually recognised in the majority of jurisdictions. This positive development has been supported in Principle 3:9. However, issues as to how and under which circumstances third persons may hold parental responsibilities in whole or in part are also left to national law. Finally and as a consequence of Principle 3:8, neither the dissolution of the parents' relationship nor the separation of the parents whether legal or factual has any effect on parental responsibilities. This is the commonly adopted approach in the great majority of the family systems in Europe.

Chapter IV: Exercise of Parental Responsibilities

Principle	Aspect	Applied method	Number method
P 3:11	Holders of PR jointly exercise PR	Common core was found and selected as the best solution	1.
P 3:12(1)	Parent with joint PR can act alone in daily matters	No common core was found and the best solution was selected	4.

Principle	Aspect	Applied method	Number method
P 3:12(2)	Important decisions should be taken jointly	Common core was found and selected as the best solution	1.
	Parent can act alone in urgent cases	Common core was found and selected as the best solution	1.
	Other parent has to be informed immediately	No common core was found and the best solution was selected	4.
P 3:13(1)	Agreements on the exercise of PR are possible between holders of joint PR	Common core was found and selected as the best solution	1.
P 3:13(2)	The CA can scrutinize the agreement	Common core was found and selected as the best solution	1.
	How the agreement is to be scrutinized	No common core was found and the best solution was selected	4.
P 3:14(1)	In case of disagreement parents with joint PR can apply to the CA	Common core was found and selected as the best solution	1.
P 3:14(2)	CA promotes an agreement between the parents	Common core was found and selected as the best solution	1.
P 3:14(3)	In case of disagreement the CA decides the dispute or authorises one of the parents	No common core was found and the best solution was selected	4.
P 3:15	One parent with joint PR can exercise them alone upon a decision of the CA	Common core was found and selected as the best solution	1.
	One parent with joint PR can exercise them alone upon agreement	No common core was found and the best solution was selected	4.
P 3:16	One parent with sole PR can exercise them alone	Common core was found and selected as the best solution	1.
P 3:17	Third persons can exercise some/all PR	No common core was found and the best solution was selected	4.
	Procedure and grounds for the exercise of PR by third persons	No common core was found and the solution was left to national law	5.
	Choice of person(s) to exercise PR besides/instead of the parents	No common core was found and the solution was left to national law	5.
P 3:18	The parent's partner may take decisions in	Common core was found and selected as the best solution	1.

The majority of Principles which belong to Chapter IV regarding the Exercise of Parental Responsibilities are based on the common core which can be found in both the national systems and the international and European instruments. These general rules to be applied were selected as the best solutions. In respect of a few, but important, aspects it was not possible to discover a common approach. Regarding these aspects a solution was selected which is applied in only a few countries. They are practicable and in line with CEFL's objectives in creating a flexible and efficient system which is also based on equality. This applies to the power of the parents having joint parental responsibilities to act alone in daily matters (Principles 3:12 (1)), the obligation of the parent who acted in urgent cases to inform the other parent without undue delay (Principles 3:12(2)), the competence of the competent authority to decide a dispute or to authorize one of the parents having joint parental responsibilities in case of disagreement between them (Principles 3:14(3)), the exercise of parental responsibilities by one parent if both parents made an agreement to that end (Principle 3(15)) and the recognition that parental responsibilities may be exercised by third persons in addition to or instead of the parents (Principle 3:17). The aspects which are referred to national law address some specific procedural issues.

Chapter V: Content of Parental Responsibilities

Section A: The Child's Person and Property

Principle	Aspect	Applied method	Number method
P 3:19(1)	Concept of PR: care, protection, education, religious upbringing, medical treatment	Common core was found and selected as the best solution	1.
	Medical treatment: child can decide alone or additional consent of the holders of PR is required	No common core was found and the solution was left to national law	5.
P 3:19(2)	No corporal punishment/humiliating treatment	No common core was found and the best solution was selected	4.
P 3:20(1)	In case of living apart holders of joint PR should agree on the child's residence	No common core was found and the best solution was selected	4.
P 3:20(2)	An alternating residence is possible upon agreement or decision	No common core was found and the best solution was selected	4.
	Procedure to gain an alternating residence	No common core was found and the solution was left to national law	5.

Principle	Aspect	Applied method	Number method
P 3:21(1)	Relocation requires consent of both holders of PR	Common core was found and selected as the best solution	1.
	Information of the other holder of PR	No common core was found and the best solution was selected	4.
	Manner of information	No common core was found and the solution was left to national law	5.
P 3:21(2)	In case of disagreement concerning the relocation the CA can be requested to decide	No common core was found and the best solution was selected	4.
P 3:21(3)	Factors to be considered by the CA	No common core was found and the best solution was selected	4.
P 3:22(1)	The CA takes appropriate measures if the child's property is in jeopardy	Common core was found and selected as the best solution	1.
	Administration of the child's property in the best interest of the child and with due care and diligence	Common core was found and selected as the best solution	1.
P 3:22(2)	Gifts allowed if they are made under a moral obligation	Common core was found and selected as the best solution	1.
P 3:22(3)	Income derived from the child's property may be used for the needs of the family	Common core was found and selected as the best solution	1.
P 3:23(1)	No unrestricted administration of the child's property	Common core was found and selected as the best solution	1.
P 3:23(2)	Income of the child is excluded from administration by the holder of PR unless the child is not of sufficient age and maturity	Common core was found and selected as the best solution	1.
P 3:23(3)	Authorisation by the CA is needed for transactions carried out on behalf of the child	Common core was found and selected as the best solution	1.
P 3:24(1)	Legal representation of the child in matters concerning his or her person or property	Common core was found and selected as the best solution	1.
P 3:24(2)	No legal representation in case of conflict of interests between the child and among the holders of PR	Common core was found and selected as the best solution	1.

Principle	Aspect	Applied method	Number method
P 3:24(3)	Child's right to self-representation in legal proceedings concerning personal matters	No common core was found and the best solution was selected	4.
	Additional consent of the holders of PR is required	No common core was found and the solution was left to national law	5.

Almost all Principles of Section A on the Child's Person and Property which forms part of Chapter V on the Content of Parental Responsibilities follow common solutions which could be identified in the jurisdictions surveyed. There are, however, a few exceptions. One of them, for instance, is addressed in Principle 3:19(2). It concerns the prohibition of corporal punishment and any treatment that is unreasonable and detrimental to the welfare of the child. It is surprising that such a prohibition does not yet reflect the common core in Europe whereas all countries surveyed are contracting states to the Convention on the Rights of the Child of 1989 which provides in its Article 19 para. 1 that the States Parties shall take all appropriate measures to protect children against ill-treatment and violence.

Another issue which falls under the exception that no common core could be found relates to the child's residence. The lack of a common core regarding this aspect is due to the fact that, on the one hand, we are witnessing a greater mobility of persons not only within Europe but all around the globe, and, on the other hand, that joint parental responsibilities increasingly lead to equal parenting which eventually results in an alternating residence of the child. These developments are new and are approached differently in the systems surveyed. Legislation is exceptional and judicial decisions differ to a great extent. In this area, the CEFL Principles provide new solutions which to a certain extent are based on the legal practice of some countries. These solutions may function as guidelines not only for legislatures but primarily for the courts and other administrative bodies which are requested to decide on disputes concerning the child's residence. First, in the case of living apart the holders of joint parental responsibilities should agree on the child's residence (Principle 3:20(1)); second, the alternating residence of the child should be based either upon an agreement between the holders of parental responsibilities or upon a decision of the competent authority (Principle 3:20(2)); third, before a parent wishes to change the child's residence either within or outside the jurisdiction he or she should inform the other parent (Principle 3:21(1)); fourth, in the case of disagreement concerning the change of the child's residence a decision by the competent authority may be requested by each holder of parental responsibilities; and finally and most importantly, a non-exhaustive list of factors is provided in Principle 3:21(3) which the competent authority should take into account in deciding relocation disputes. In addition to these innovative clarifications a few aspects have been referred to national law. They primarily concern the way in which the other parent should be informed (Principle 3:21(1)), the issue whether an alternating residence has to be requested by at least one of the holders of parental responsibilities or whether the competent authority may decide of its own motion (Principle 3:20(2)) and whether, in addition to the consent of the child, the holders of parental responsibilities should consent to certain acts (Principles 3:19(1), 3:24(3)).

Chapter V: Content of Parental Responsibilities
Section B: Maintenance of Personal Relationships

Principle	Aspect	Applied method	Number method
P 3:25(1)	Child has a right of contact with parents	Common core was found and selected as the best solution	1.
P 3:25(2)	Child has a right of contact with close relatives	Common core was found and selected as the best solution	1.
	Right of close relatives to see the child against the will of the holders of PR	No common core was found and the solution was left to national law	5.
P 3:25(3)	Contact between the child and a third person due to close personal relations	No common core was found and the best solution was selected	4.
	Right of third persons to see the child against the will of the holders of PR	No common core was found and the solution was left to national law	5.
P 3:26(1)	Content of contact	Common core was found and selected as the best solution	1.
P 3:26(2)	Contact only in the best interests of the child	Common core was found and selected as the best solution	1.
P 3:27(1)	Parents can agree on contact	Common core was found and selected as the best solution	1.
	Third persons who hold PR can agree on contact	No common core was found and the best solution was selected	4.
P 3:27(2)	CA may scrutinize the agreement	No common core was found and the best solution was selected	4.
P 3:28	CA may restrict or terminate contact	Common core was found and selected as the best solution	1.
	Procedure for restriction or termination	No common core was found and the solution was left to national law	5.

Principle	Aspect	Applied method	Number method
P 3:29	Informing the other holder of PR about the personal situation of the child	Common core was found and selected as the best solution	1.
	Informing third persons	No common core was found and the solution was left to national law	5.

Also in respect of Section B on the Maintenance of Personal Relationships in Chapter V the solutions selected can only be classified into three approaches. First, a common core was found and selected as the best solution. This applies to the right of the child to have contact with his or her parents and with close relatives (Principle 3:25(1)(2)); the content of contact (Principle 3:26(1)) and the general premise that contact should only take place if it is in the best interest of the child (Principle 3:26(2)); the freedom of parents to agree on contact (Principle 3:27(1)); the power of the competent authority to restrict or terminate contact (Principle 3:28) and, finally, the obligation of parents to inform the other parent about the personal situation of the child (Principle 3:29). Second, no common core was found and the best solution was selected. Three issues fall under this category: Contact between the child and a third person due to close personal relations should be possible (Principle 3:25(3)); also third persons who are holders of parental responsibilities may agree on contact (Principle 3:27(1)); and, finally, all agreements on contact may be scrutinized by the competent authority (Principle 3:27(2)). At last, the third category: no common core was found and the solution was left to national law. Four aspects are not addressed by the CEFL Principles: the right of close relatives and third persons to see the child against the will of the holders of parental responsibilities (Principle 3:25(2)(3)), how parental responsibilities might be restricted or terminated (the procedure) (Principle 3:28) and informing third persons about the child's personal situation.

Chapter VI: Termination of Parental Responsibilities

Principle	Aspect	Applied method	Number method
P 3:30(1)	*Ex lege* termination of PR	Common core was found and selected as the best solution	1.
P 3:30(2)	Adoption by a parent's partner only terminates the PR of the other parent	No common core was found and the best solution was selected	4.
P 3:31(1)	PR belong *ex lege* to the surviving parent if PR are exercised jointly	Common core was found and selected as the best solution	1.

Principle	Aspect	Applied method	Number method
P 3:31(2)	CA decides whether surviving parent or third person becomes holder of PR if the parent, who held PR alone, dies	Common core was found, but a better solution was selected	2.
P 3:31(3)	Protective measures to be taken by the CA regarding the person and property of the child in case of death of both parents	No common core was found and the best solution was selected	4.
	Kind of measures to be taken	No common core was found and the solution was left to national law	5.
	Possibility for the parents to appoint a new holder of PR	No common core was found and the solution was left to national law	5.

Only in Chapter VI on the Termination of Parental Responsibilities has the CEFL opted for a better solution despite the fact that a common core could be discovered. What should happen if the parent, who is the sole holder of parental responsibilities, dies? Should the surviving parent or a third person, e.g. the deceased parent's partner, become a holder of parental responsibilities by operation of law? Although most legal systems make no distinction between the surviving parent who does or does not hold parental responsibilities and consequently determine that in particular the parent who is not a holder of parental responsibilities automatically obtains this position, the CEFL opted for a solution which it considers to correspond better with the best interests of the child. This implies that the competent authority should take a decision about who should be attributed with parental responsibilities if the parent holding sole parental responsibilities dies (Principle 3:31(2)). This guarantees that the concrete circumstances of the case are reflected and only the interests of the child are finally decisive. A general rule attributing parental responsibilities to the parent who either never held parental responsibilities or whose parental responsibilities had been terminated would not be in harmony with the general concern about the welfare of the child. If, however, parental responsibilities were held jointly and one of the parents dies the common core was followed (Principle 3:31(1)). Moreover, the circumstances which in almost all jurisdictions lead to the termination of parental responsibilities by operation of law (majority, entering into a formal relationship, being adopted and death) are adopted as the absolute common core in Principle 3:30(1). If the parent's partner adopts the child of the parent, however, Principle 3:30(2) favours the rule that the parental responsibilities in relation to the other parent should be terminated. In respect of this issue the solutions in the countries represented in the CEFL differ and a common core was not evident. The same applies when both parents die. In this situation, Principle 3:31(3) proposes that the competent authority should take protective measures regarding the child's person and property. However, what kind of measures may be taken and whether parents should have the possibility to appoint a new holder of parental responsibilities in advance have been left to national law (Principle 3:31(3)).

Chapter VII: Discharge and Restoration of Parental Responsibilities

Principle	Aspect	Applied method	Number method
P 3:32	General clause in the case of being discharged from PR	Common core was found and selected as the best solution	1.
P 3:33(1)	Discharge may be requested by the parent with PR or any institution protecting the child's interest	Common core was found and selected as the best solution	1.
	The child may request the discharge	No common core was found and the best solution was selected	4.
	Procedural implementation	No common core was found and the solution was left to national law	5.
P 3:33(2)	CA may act on its own motion	Common core was found and selected as the best solution	1.
P 3:34	Restoration of PR if the circumstances have changed	Common core was found and selected as the best solution	1.

In the Principles of Chapter VII on the Discharge and Restoration of Parental Responsibilities the common core dominates. According to the CEFL the solutions provided in the majority of the systems reflect the best solutions. Principle 3:33(1), however, not only allows any parent having parental responsibilities and any institution protecting the interests of the child to request the discharge, but also extends this possibility to the child. This might further strengthen his or her position. Only the procedural implementation of the discharge has not been dealt with and as a result has been referred to national law.

Chapter VIII: Procedure

Principle	Aspect	Applied method	Number method
P 3:35(1)	CA can be a judicial body	Common core was found and selected as the best solution	1.
	CA can be an administrative body	No common core was found and the best solution was selected	4.
	Decision of the CA may be modified if there is a change of circumstances	Common core was found and selected as the best solution	1.

Principle	Aspect	Applied method	Number method
P 3:35(2)	Appointment of a suitable person to investigate the child's circumstances	Common core was found and selected as the best solution	1.
	Only in case of necessity	No common core was found and the best solution was selected	4.
P 3:36	Increased awareness of ADR mechanisms	Common core was found and selected as the best solution	1.
	Compulsory alternative dispute resolution	No common core was found and the solution was left to national law	5.
P 3:37(1)	CA hears the child in all proceedings concerning PR	Common core was found and selected as the best solution	1.
	CA has to give reasons for refusing to hear the child	No common core was found and the best solution was selected	4.
	Stage of proceeding at which the child should be heard	No common core was found and the solution was left to national law	5.
P 3:37(2)	Hearing can take place directly or indirectly	No common core was found and the best solution was selected	4.
P 3:37(3)	Hearing in an appropriate manner concerning the child's age and maturity	Common core was found and selected as the best solution	1.
	Method and place of hearing	No common core was found and the solution was left to national law	5.
	Presence of other persons during the hearing	No common core was found and the solution was left to national law	5.
P 3:38	Appointment of a special representative if the child's interests conflict with those of the holders of PR	Common core was found and selected as the best solution	1.
	Appointment of a special representative when the welfare of the child is otherwise at risk	No common core was found and the best solution was selected	4.
P 3:39(1)	Enforcement of the decision of the CA and of an agreement between the holders of PR	Common core was found and selected as the best solution	1.
P 3:39(2)	Refusal of enforcement due to the child's best interests	Common core was found and selected as the best solution	1.

The content of the final Chapter is dedicated to Procedure. In 2004, at the 2nd CEFL conference, Frédérique Ferrand forcefully persuaded the CEFL to also deal to a certain extent with procedural law. The CEFL should not be afraid to include subjects other than substantive law in their Principles because it is now something of a myth to maintain that procedural law cannot and should not be harmonised.[17] This time we have convincingly followed her advice and drafted five Principles. All five Principles are based on the common core. These concern the following issues: It is generally acknowledged and practised that in deciding on or intervening in matters of parental responsibilities the situation of the child should be investigated. To that end, the competent authority which, according to Principle 3:35, can either be a judicial or an administrative body, should, where necessary, appoint any suitable person or body in order to obtain a clear view of the child's situation. In addition to this more traditional approach the increasing importance of alternative dispute resolution, which is being recognised by all national laws,[18] is also acknowledged by the Principles. Also in this field the common core is apparent. Consequently, in all disputes regarding parental responsibilities alternative dispute resolution mechanisms should be available (Principle 3:36). Principle 3:37(1) stresses that the child should be heard in the context of proceedings. It is recognised, however, that there are situations where such a hearing could do more harm than good. If the authority decides not to hear the child it should give specific reasons for this. In this respect a common core is not available therefore the best solution was selected instead. There is no uniform approach in the national systems as to whether the hearing of the child should take place directly before the competent authority or indirectly before a person or body appointed by the competent authority. The Principles prefer a direct hearing; the court should use the knowledge of experts but should form its own impression. Additionally, the child should be heard in a manner which is appropriate to his or her age and maturity (Principle 3:37 (3)). No specific age limit is given. It is the common core of the majority of the 22 jurisdictions represented in the CEFL that the child should have a special representative appointed in all cases in which the child's interest could be in conflict with those of the holders of PR or in which the welfare of the child is otherwise at risk. This guarantee is provided in Principle 3:38. The appointment of a special representative should take place ex officio by an order of the competent authority or may be requested by the child subject to the condition that he or she has sufficient understanding. Finally, the principle of the speedy and effective enforcement of a decision by the competent authority or an agreement concerning parental responsibilities is approved in Principle 3:39. This is the main rule. Exceptionally, the enforcement may not take place if it is obviously irreconcilable with the child's best interests. Consequently, and subject to

17 Ferrand, F., 'Divorce and Spousal Agreements', in: Boele-Woelki, K., *ibid.*, note 4, p. 71–82 (81).

18 Boele-Woelki, K./Braat, B./Curry-Sumner, I., *ibid.*, note 3, p. 741 ff.

the condition that the child has sufficient understanding, a residence or contact order, for instance, should not be enforced against the wishes of the child.

5. BRIEF COMPARISON OF THE DIFFERENT CEFL SETS OF PRINCIPLES

A brief comparison between CEFL Principles reveals the following findings. The Principles on Parental Responsibilities contain 39 Principles whereas the first set regarding Divorce and Maintenance between Former Spouses has only 20 Principles. This indicates the complexity of the law of parental responsibilities. More importantly, international and European instruments are dominant in the field of parental responsibilities, whereas they do not exist in the field of divorce and maintenance between former spouses as far as substantive law is concerned. Regarding private international instruments in these areas the situation is different.[19] Nevertheless, the CEFL only referred to the Brussels II bis Regulation in the introduction to the first CEFL Principles and not to this or any other international instrument in the comparative overviews or comments under the specific Principles. The existence of so many international and European instruments addressing the parent-child relationship forced the drafters of the principles in this field to carefully study these instruments and to put all of them into the right place. On the one hand, this made it easier to deal with specific issues. On the other hand, it was sometimes more difficult because, in addition to the extensive national reports, we had to take these international and European standards into account.

Another difference between the two 'yellow books' concerns procedural issues. Five principles are included in the last chapter of the Parental Responsibilities Principles. In that sense progress has been made.

In respect of the approaches applied the general conclusion is that the great majority of subjects in the field of parental responsibilities represent common core solutions. In the field of divorce and maintenance between former spouses the common core is also present but is not as overwhelmingly dominant as in the field of parental responsibilities. However, also a long list of aspects of the law on divorce and maintenance, with respect to which the CEFL was able to detect a common core as well as converging tendencies, has been compiled.[20] Generally, it can be

19 Boele-Woelki, K., 'The European Agenda: an Overview of the Current Situation in the Field of Private International Law and Substantive law', *IFL* 2006, p. 149–154 (149–151).

20 Boele-Woelki, K., 'Building on Convergence and Coping with Divergence in the CEFL Principles of European Family Law', in: Antokolskaia, M., *Convergence and Divergence of Family Law in Europe*, European Family Law Series no. 18, p. 253–269.

concluded that in drafting the CEFL Principles it was discovered that more countries now take the same approach and, within a certain approach, the differences are becoming less pronounced. After evaluating their effectiveness and suitability, the common solutions were considered to be the best solutions. As a result we opted for a better law solution less frequently in the field of parental responsibilities. Furthermore, it is striking that the third methodological approach (a common core was found but the solution was left to national law) was not applied in the Principles of Parental Responsibilities whereas, in contrast, in respect of a few aspects this approach was adopted in the Principles of Divorce and Maintenance. Finally and more importantly, it should be stressed that the Parental Responsibilities Principles, in contrast to the first set, also address completely new aspects which in most national systems are either not possible or rarely occur in practice whereas in others the concepts have only recently been (re)introduced. Specifically, the Principles on alternating residence and relocation, for instance, provide an answer to new developments.

6. COMING TO A CLOSE

By and large, the Divorce/Maintenance and the Parental Responsibilities Principles form a frame of reference which is useful for any legislator. Comparative research has been carried out in the respective fields, the material is easily accessible and widely disseminated, similarities and differences are determined, explanations are provided and, finally, while evaluating the solutions common Principles are proposed. They are based on the comparative findings.

The whole project is a long-term, time-consuming and ambitious enterprise. Throughout the past six years, however, the cooperation among the CEFL experts has proven to be highly fruitful, motivating, supportive and reliable and extremely enjoyable. We are continually learning from each other's jurisdictions, we are becoming more open towards new and different solutions and we are trying to solve functional problems from a European perspective. There is sufficient reason to be confident that CEFL's teamwork will also be a success during our next endeavour, namely the property relationship between spouses which constitutes CEFL's third working field.

Apart from the current and future activities it may be noted that it took the CEFL three years to complete the Principles on Parental Responsibilities. During ten meetings of the Organising Committee and one meeting of the Expert Group the huge amount of comparative material was researched and studied, the Principles were drafted and discussed, amended and improved. It should be considered to be of importance that in the end the final result will acquire a decent standing within the plethora of international and European instruments addressing the parent-child relationship. Then CEFL's final goal will have been achieved. Only by the empirical testing of the Principles in a number of legal systems can one demonstrate whether they are indeed acceptable and/or are regarded as an improvement on existing national laws. This has been done by Esin Örücü and Jane Mair in respect of the Divorce and Maintenance between Former Spouses Principles.[21] They have recently announced that they will embark on a similar project in relation to the Principles on Parental Responsibilities. With great interest the CEFL is looking forward to reading their comparative assessment.

APPENDIX
PRINCIPLES OF EUROPEAN FAMILY LAW REGARDING PARENTAL RESPONSIBILITIES

PREAMBLE

Recognising that, notwithstanding the existing diversities of national family law systems, there is nevertheless a growing convergence of laws;

Recognising that the free movement of persons within Europe is hindered by the remaining differences;

Desiring to contribute to common European values regarding the child's rights and welfare;

Desiring to contribute to the harmonisation of family law in Europe and to further facilitate the free movement of persons within Europe;

The Commission on European Family Law recommends the following Principles:

CHAPTER I: DEFINITIONS

Principle 3:1 Concept of parental responsibilities

Parental responsibilities are a collection of rights and duties aimed at promoting and safeguarding the welfare of the child. They encompass in particular:

(a) care, protection and education;
(b) maintenance of personal relationships;
(c) determination of residence;
(d) administration of property, and
(e) legal representation.

21 Örücü, E./Mair, J. (eds), *Juxtaposing Legal Systems and the Principles of European Family Law on Divorce and Maintenance*, European Family Law Series no. 17, 2007.

Principle 3:2 Holder of parental responsibilities

(1) A holder of parental responsibilities is any person having the rights and duties listed in Principle 3:1 either in whole or in part.

(2) Subject to the following Principles, holders of parental responsibilities are:
   (a) the child's parents, as well as
   (b) persons other than the child's parents having parental responsibilities in addition to or instead of the parents.

CHAPTER II: RIGHTS OF THE CHILD

Principle 3:3 Best interests of the child

In all matters concerning parental responsibilities the best interests of the child should be the primary consideration.

Principle 3:4 Autonomy of the child

The child's autonomy should be respected in accordance with the developing ability and need of the child to act independently.

Principle 3:5 Non-discrimination of the child

Children should not be discriminated on grounds such as sex, race, colour, language, religion, political or other opinion, national, ethnic or social origin, sexual orientation, disability, property, birth or other status, irrespective of whether these grounds refer to the child or to the holders of parental responsibilities.

Principle 3:6 Child's right to be heard

Having regard to the child's age and maturity, the child should have the right to be informed, consulted and to express his or her opinion in all matters concerning the child, with due weight given to the views expressed by him or her.

Principle 3:7 Conflict of interests

The interests of the child should be protected whenever they may be in conflict with the interests of the holders of parental responsibilities.

CHAPTER III: PARENTAL RESPONSIBILITIES OF PARENTS AND THIRD PERSONS

Principle 3:8 Parents

Parents, whose legal parentage has been established, should have parental responsibilities for the child.

Principle 3:9 Third persons
Parental responsibilities may in whole or in part also be attributed to a person other than a parent.

Principle 3:10 Effect of dissolution and separation
Parental responsibilities should neither be affected by the dissolution or annulment of the marriage or other formal relationship nor by the legal or factual separation between the parents.

CHAPTER IV: EXERCISE OF PARENTAL RESPONSIBILITIES

SECTION A: PARENTS

Principle 3:11 Joint exercise
Parents having parental responsibilities should have an equal right and duty to exercise such responsibilities and whenever possible they should exercise them jointly.

Principle 3:12 Daily matters, important and urgent decisions
(1) Parents having joint parental responsibilities should have the right to act alone with respect to daily matters.
(2) Important decisions concerning matters such as education, medical treatment, the child's residence, or the administration of his or her property should be taken jointly. In urgent cases a parent should have the right to act alone. The other parent should be informed without undue delay.

Principle 3:13 Agreement on exercise
(1) Subject to the best interests of the child, parents having joint parental responsibilities may agree on the exercise of parental responsibilities.
(2) The competent authority may scrutinize the agreement.

Principle 3:14 Disagreement on exercise
(1) Where parents having joint parental responsibilities cannot agree on an important matter they may apply to the competent authority.
(2) The competent authority should promote agreement between the parents.
(3) Where agreement cannot be reached the competent authority should divide the exercise of parental responsibilities between the parents or decide the dispute. Nigel: do we have to insert a comma after reached?

Principle 3:15 Sole exercise upon agreement or decision
Subject to the best interests of the child a parent may exercise parental responsibilities alone

(a) upon agreement between the parents according to Principle 3:13, or
(b) upon a decision of the competent authority.

Principle 3:16 Sole exercise by one parent
If only one parent has parental responsibilities he or she should exercise them alone.

SECTION B: THIRD PERSONS

Principle 3:17 Exercise in addition to or instead of the parents
A person other than a parent may exercise some or all parental responsibilities in addition to or instead of the parents.

Principle 3:18 Decisions in daily matters
The parent's partner living with the child may take part in decisions with respect to daily matters unless the other parent having parental responsibilities objects.

CHAPTER V: CONTENT OF PARENTAL RESPONSIBILITIES

SECTION A: THE CHILD'S PERSON AND PROPERTY

Principle 3:19 Care, protection and education

(1) The holders of parental responsibilities should provide the child with care, protection and education in accordance with the child's distinctive character and developmental needs.
(2) The child should not be subjected to corporal punishment or any other humiliating treatment.

Principle 3:20 Residence

(1) If parental responsibilities are exercised jointly the holders of parental responsibilities who are living apart should agree upon with whom the child resides.
(2) The child may reside on an alternate basis with the holders of parental responsibilities upon either an agreement approved by a competent authority or a decision by a competent authority. The competent authority should take into consideration factors such as:
    (a) the age and opinion of the child;

(b) the ability and willingness of the holders of parental responsibilities to cooperate with each other in matters concerning the child, as well as their personal situation;
(c) the distance between the residences of the holders of the parental responsibilities and to the child's school.

Principle 3:21 Relocation
(1) If parental responsibilities are exercised jointly and one of the holders of parental responsibilities wishes to change the child's residence within or outside the jurisdiction, he or she should inform the other holder of parental responsibilities thereof in advance.
(2) If the other holder of parental responsibilities objects to the change of the child's residence, each of them may apply to the competent authority for a decision.
(3) The competent authority should take into consideration factors such as:
  (a) the age and opinion of the child;
  (b) the right of the child to maintain personal relationships with the other holders of parental responsibilities;
  (c) the ability and willingness of the holders of parental responsibilities to cooperate with each other;
  (d) the personal situation of the holders of personal responsibilities;
  (e) the geographical distance and accessibility;
  (f) the free movement of persons.

Principle 3:22 Administration of the child's property
(1) The holders of parental responsibilities should administer the child's property with due care and diligence in order to preserve and where possible increase the value of the property.
(2) In administering the child's property the holders of parental responsibilities should not make gifts unless the gifts are deemed to be made under a moral obligation.
(3) The income derived from the child's property which is not needed for the proper management of the property or for the maintenance and education of the child may, where necessary, be used for the needs of the family.

Principle 3:23 Restrictions
(1) The holders of parental responsibilities should not administer property acquired by a child through a testamentary disposition or a gift, if the testator or the donor so instructed.
(2) Similarly the earnings by the child should not be administered by the holders of parental responsibilities unless the child is not of sufficient age and maturity to decide himself or herself.

(3) Where transactions can have significant financial consequences for the child the authorisation of the competent authority should be necessary.

Principle 3:24 Legal representation

(1) The holders of parental responsibilities should legally represent the child in matters concerning the child's person or property.
(2) Legal representation should not take place where there is a conflict of interest between the child and the holders of parental responsibilities.
(3) Having regard to the child's age and maturity, the child should have the right to self-representation in legal proceedings concerning himself or herself.

SECTION B: MAINTENANCE OF PERSONAL RELATIONSHIPS

Principle 3:25 Contact with parents and other persons

(1) The child and the parents should have the right to obtain and maintain regular contact with each other.
(2) Contact should be established between the child and his or her close relatives.
(3) Contact may be established between the child and persons with whom the child has close personal relations.

Principle 3:26 Content of contact

(1) Contact comprises the child staying for a limited period of time with or meeting a parent or person other than a parent with whom he or she is not usually living; and any form of communication between the child and such person.
(2) Such contact should be in the best interests of the child.

Principle 3:27 Agreement

(1) Subject to the best interests of the child, the parents and the other persons identified under Principle 3:25(2) and (3) may agree on contact.
(2) The competent authority may scrutinize the agreement.

Principle 3:28 Restrictions

Contact may be restricted, terminated or made subject to conditions by the competent authority if the best interests of the child so require.

Principle 3:29 Information to parents

A parent should have the right to be informed about matters concerning the personal situation of the child.

CHAPTER VI: TERMINATION OF PARENTAL RESPONSIBILITIES

Principle 3:30 Termination

(1) Parental responsibilities should be terminated in the case of the child:
  (a) reaching majority;
  (b) entering into a marriage or registered partnership;
  (c) being adopted;
  (d) dying.

(2) If a parent's partner adopts the child of the parent the parental responsibilities in relation to the other parent should be terminated.

Principle 3:31 Death of the parents

(1) If parents have joint parental responsibilities and one of them dies the parental responsibilities should belong to the surviving parent.

(2) If a parent having sole parental responsibilities dies, responsibilities should be attributed to the surviving parent or a third person upon a decision by the competent authority.

(3) On the death of both parents, of whom at least one parent had parental responsibilities, the competent authority should take protective measures in respect of the person and the property of the child.

CHAPTER VII: DISCHARGE AND RESTORATION OF PARENTAL RESPONSIBILITIES

Principle 3:32 Discharge of parental responsibilities

The competent authority should discharge the holder of parental responsibilities, wholly or in part, where his or her behaviour or neglect causes a serious risk to the person or the property of the child

Principle 3:33 Request for discharge of parental responsibilities

(1) The discharge of parental responsibilities may be requested by:
  (a) any parent having parental responsibilities;
  (b) the child, and
  (c) any institution protecting the interests of the child.

(2) The competent authority may also order the discharge of parental responsibilities of its own motion.

Principle 3:34 Restoration of parental responsibilities

Having regard to the best interests of the child, the competent authority may restore parental responsibilities if the circumstances that led to the discharge no longer exist.

CHAPTER VIII: PROCEDURE

Principle 3:35 Competent authority

(1) All decisions on parental responsibilities should be taken by the competent authority which can either be a judicial or an administrative body.
(2) Where necessary, the competent authority should appoint any suitable person or body to investigate the child's circumstances.

Principle 3:36 Alternative dispute resolution

In all disputes regarding parental responsibilities alternative dispute resolution mechanisms should be available.

Principle 3:37 Hearing of the child

(1) Subject to Principle 3:6, the competent authority should hear the child in all proceedings concerning parental responsibilities but if it decides not to hear the child it should give specific reasons.
(2) The hearing of the child should take place either directly before the competent authority or indirectly before a person or body appointed by the competent authority.
(3) The child should be heard in a manner appropriate to his or her age and maturity.

Principle 3:38 Appointment of a special representative for the child

In proceedings concerning parental responsibilities in which there could either be a serious conflict of interests between the child and the holders of parental responsibilities or in which the welfare of the child is otherwise at risk, the competent authority should appoint a special representative for the child.

Principle 3:39 Enforcement

(1) Failing voluntary compliance, a decision by the competent authority and an enforceable agreement concerning parental responsibilities should be enforced without delay.
(2) Enforcement should not take place if it is manifestly contrary to the best interests of the child.

THE RIGHT OF THE CHILD TO PARENTAGE (DESCENT)

Balázs Somfai

1. INTRODUCTION

The title of this paper sounds perhaps somewhat strange at first and needs some explanation. What does the "right of the child to parentage (descent)" actually mean? We are aware of the right of the child to know about his or her parentage from the Child Protection Act,[1] and we can also read about it in the different articles of the Convention on the Rights of the Child[2] (hereinafter, the Convention). We know that the child has the right to know who his or her parents are, if possible, and to have them care for him or her.[3] We also know that when it has been justified to separate the child from his/her parents if this was in the best interest of the child, the State Party shall, upon request, provide information on the parents to the child (or vice versa), except if this would be detrimental to the welfare of the child.[4]

---

1 Act XXXI of 1997 on the protection of the child and on guardianship administration Article 7 paragraph (4): Unless the law provides otherwise, in case of the discontinuation of the parental rights of the parents, the child has the right to know his or her biological parentage, and to keep in contact with them if the biological family gives its consent.

2 Act LXIV of 1991 on the promulgation of the Convention on the Rights of the Child signed in new York on 20 November, 1989 a Gyermek jogairól szóló, New Yorkban.

3 Article 7 of the Convention.
1. The child shall be registered immediately after birth and shall have the right from birth to a name, the right to acquire a nationality and. as far as possible, the right to know and be cared for by his or her parents.
2. States Parties shall ensure the implementation of these rights in accordance with their national law and their obligations under the relevant international instruments in this field, in particular where the child would otherwise be stateless.

4 Article 9 of the Convention
1. States Parties shall ensure that a child shall not be separated from his or her parents against their will, except when competent authorities subject to judicial review determine, in accordance with applicable law and procedures, that such separation is necessary for the best interests of the child. Such determination may be necessary in a particular case such as one involving abuse or neglect of the child by the parents, or one where the parents are living separately and a decision must be made as to the child's place of residence.
2. In any proceedings pursuant to paragraph 1 of the present article, all interested parties shall be given an opportunity to participate in the proceedings and make their views known.

It is worth mentioning that the Convention lists the family relations of the child among the child's elements of personal identity, which allows us to conclude that the Convention refers especially to the importance of the child's connections with his/her parents, relatives and friends which are determining factors in the identity of the child.[5]

From all this it seems that the range of the rights of the child was defined in the Convention based on the theoretical and practical situation that the child descends from his/her parents – from a mother and a father. Based on this presumption, the most important rights of the child were listed as:

- the right to know his/her parents,
- the right to be cared for by the parents,
- the right to family relations and contacts.

Looking at this from another angle we can see that the Convention consistently mentions parents – and not just one parent, either a mother or a father – when it lists the rights of the child to family relations:

- the right of the child to know his or her parents,
- the right not to be separated from his/her parents,
- the right to maintain relations with both parents.

The Convention uses the plural also in connection with its provisions regarding the child's relationship with his/her parents, just as when it stipulates certain obligations of the parents regarding their children:

---

3. States Parties shall respect the right of the child who is separated from one or both parents to maintain personal relations and direct contact with both parents on a regular basis, except if it is contrary to the child's best interests.

4. Where such separation results from any action initiated by a State Party, such as the detention, imprisonment, exile, deportation or death (including death arising from any cause while the person is in the custody of the State) of one or both parents or of the child, that State Party shall, upon request, provide the parents, the child or, if appropriate, another member of the family with the essential information concerning the whereabouts of the absent member(s) of the family unless the provision of the information would be detrimental to the well-being of the child. States Parties shall further ensure that the submission of such a request shall of itself entail no adverse consequences for the person(s) concerned.

5 Article 8 of the Convention.

1. States Parties undertake to respect the right of the child to preserve his or her identity, including nationality, name and family relations as recognized by law without unlawful interference.

2. Where a child is illegally deprived of some or all of the elements of his or her identity, States Parties shall provide appropriate assistance and protection, with a view to re-establishing speedily his or her identity.

- the parents are equally responsible for the upbringing and development of the child,
- it is primarily the parents' responsibility to provide the necessary living conditions for the development of the child.

Finally, the State Party[6] shall provide assistance to the parents in exercising their duties in the upbringing of their children.[7]

Based on the above, it is evident, in my opinion, that the spirit of the Convention is to presume the child's descent from his/her parents, that is from a mother and a father. Considering this presumption, it defines certain rights and names those who are eligible for these rights and those who have certain duties.

It follows from all this that the person who is the primary target of the Convention and who is institutionally empowered by the Convention to make use of these rights – the child – is given certain rights and therefore opportunities that the State Party – regarding certain rights – can only restrict if certain circumstances defined in the Convention are present, and even then only when this is in the best interests of the child.

---

6 By State Party we mean the Country that is a Party to the Convention.

7 Article 18 of the Convention
1. States Parties shall use their best efforts to ensure recognition of the principle that both parents have common responsibilities for the upbringing and development of the child. Parents or, as the case may be, legal guardians, have the primary responsibility for the upbringing and development of the child. The best interests of the child will be their basic concern
2. For the purpose of guaranteeing and promoting the rights set forth in the present Convention, States Parties shall render appropriate assistance to parents and legal guardians in the performance of their child-rearing responsibilities and shall ensure the development of institutions, facilities and services for the care of children.
3. States Parties shall take all appropriate measures to ensure that children of working parents have the right to benefit from child-care services and facilities for which they are eligible.
Article 27
1. States Parties recognize the right of every child to a standard of living adequate for the child's physical, mental, spiritual, moral and social development.
2. The parent(s) or others responsible for the child have the primary responsibility to secure, within their abilities and financial capacities, the conditions of living necessary for the child's development.
3. States Parties, in accordance with national conditions and within their means, shall take appropriate measures to assist parents and others responsible for the child to implement this right and shall in case of need provide material assistance and support programmes, particularly with regard to nutrition, clothing and housing.
4. States Parties shall take all appropriate measures to secure the recovery of maintenance for the child from the parents or other persons having financial responsibility for the child, both within the State Party and from abroad. In particular, where the person having financial responsibility for the child lives in a State different from that of the child, States Parties shall promote the accession to international agreements or the conclusion of such agreements, as well as the making of other appropriate arrangements.

I have made this brief overview because the provisions of Articles 11 and 12 of Act CLXXXI of 2005 amending the 1997 Act on Health Care (hereinafter, the Health Act) entered into force on 1 July 2006. The amendment of the Health Act provides assistance not only to those couples who cannot have children in a natural way, but it offers this assistance to single women as well. With these changes that have taken effect last summer, the reproduction process can start not only at the request of common law couples (a man and a woman) and married couples (a husband and wife), but also of single women. Thus the title of this paper is now beginning to make some sense. I wish to investigate here how this amendment will concern, or may concern, the rights of the child; do children have the right to know their parentage, to their descent, to a mother and a father, at least at the moment of conception.

2. LEGISLATION IN FORCE

According to the provisions of the Health Act in force before 1 July 2006, fertilization can be carried out in the course of assisted reproduction in the case of a married couple or a different-sex couple living in a common law relationship if any health reason (infertility) in the case of either of the partners prevents the couple, with a high degree of probability, from having healthy children in the natural way. In the case of unmarried couples living in a common law relationship, this procedure can only be carried out if neither of the parties are married. (Health Act, Article 167 paragraph)

Fifteen years ago the Hungarian Constitutional Court already rejected a motion to declare the Ordinance of the Ministry of Health 12/1981(IX.29)[8] unconstitutional. This Ordinance makes artificial fertilization possible, but it ties it to marriage and an age limit.[9]

The following arguments were taken into consideration in the ruling of the Constitutional Court:

> "No fundamental human or civil right is attached to artificial fertilization that is a right given to everyone without discrimination. This form of fertilization is an institutional medical remedy, whose purpose is to assist those people to have offspring who are, with a high degree of probability, unable to conceive children within their marriage in the natural way. Artificial fertilization, as a health care service, can be tied to certain conditions if such conditions comply with the basic principles of the Constitution.

8 Abrogated as: 30/1998 (VI.24.) NM Ordinance.

9 I refrain from examining the issue of the age limit. 750/B1990. AB (Constitutional Court) ruling and 18/2001. (VI. 1.) AB ruling tackle the issue of the age limit.

> Article 15 of the Constitution provides that the Republic of Hungary protects the institutions of marriage and the family. The assistance provided artificially when a couple cannot have children in the natural way enhances the institution of marriage, and makes the starting of an actual family (couples with children) possible. It is desirable for children to be born within complete families if possible, since not only maternal care, but also the person of the father and the upbringing by the father are extremely important for the development of the child."10

What has changed in the past fifteen years?

3. SINGLE PERSONS

Structural changes became general all over Europe and the reasons were mostly due to shifts in mentality and values. These changes started at the beginning and in the middle of the 1980s, and they started to increase dynamically in the 1990s. This means that the family as a lifestyle started to change in Hungary, just as it did in a number of countries in Europe. Clearly the spreading of common law relationships is one of the reasons for this. The media give the impression that a single person is 25–35 years old, with a rising career, who is basically balanced, who does not simply accept his or her situation, but who is absolutely satisfied with it.

While agreeing with the above, I still feel that this circle must be enlarged and we should try to find an answer to how a single woman of today can become pregnant, and this is perhaps not a sociological, a legislative or a judicial/law enforcement task. Let us leave it to everyone's fantasy, and consider it as a private matter. But providing information on the legal possibilities of having a child – meaning artificial fertilization, adoption, or even foster parenting – is, however, a state duty.

4. BACKGROUND AND IMPACTS OF THE AMENDMENT

Artificial fertilization was permitted for single people in Denmark in 2006.[11] "Evidently with the birth of the European Union, family law and human rights measures introduced in one Member State will influence people living in other

10 750/B1990. AB ruling.

11 Act no. 535 of 8 June 2006. For further information, see "Assisted Reproduction in the Nordic Countries. A comparative study of policies and regulation", TemaNord 2006:505. See also http://www.norden.org/pub/sk/showpub.asp?pubnr=2006:505&lang=1.

Member State as well. In France the regulation of artificial fertilization has been an issue for a long time, but practice has been "Union" for years already: single or lesbian women awaiting fertilization go to Brussels where it is possible to undergo this routine operation without much ado."[12]

One can often hear the argument of why should we be so afraid of this because thousands of children live in single-parent families or with single foster parents. Many children do not know their fathers and live as semi-orphans throughout their lives, and there are children who are abandoned and neglected. True, the necessary conditions for the best interests of the child are often lacking. The "only" difference is that here we are consciously creating a fatherless situation and, on the other hand, circumstances may develop in this direction in spite of the state having done everything it could to comply with its duties so that, if possible, the child should grow up with his or her parents at his or her side.

Helping a child awaiting adoption, supporting a mother to give birth to and bring up a baby even though she is single, or to use all the possibilities that medical science provides us with in order to allow a child to be conceived against nature without a parent, without a father (paternal protection) and to grow up in these circumstances are not the same categories at all.

In my opinion the amendment created a schizophrenic situation for the state and its bodies. On the one hand, they stress the best interest and the rights of the child standing above all else, while, on the other, in citing discrimination-free measures they discriminate against children without weighing any of the necessary interests.

The already quoted ruling of the Constitutional Court clearly states that the restrictive measures protect the rights of the child to be born out of artificial fertilization since the child has the right to the protection and care of the state and of society which is necessary for the physical, intellectual and moral development of the child (Article 67 of the Constitution).

According to Directive 17 of the Supreme Court both the parents and the child will have to make efforts to maintain parent-child relations because it is in the best interest of the child to know that both his or her parents are supporting him or her, and especially at the pivotal points of life to be able to count on their support when deciding, for example, on certain studies or preparing for life in general.

---

12 http://gaycenter.freeweb.hu/Mas/2005/egynemuszulok.htm.

I feel that the role of the parent in the life of the child and the importance of the parent's relationship with the child cannot be questioned. But it is only worth discussing it and doing something about it if that parent actually exists!

Object loss in psychology means that a person loses something that is important to him or her. This can be something other than a real physical object; it could be a loved person, for example. Accordingly, object loss can also have different levels, and the more important role the lost object has played in the life of the given person, the more stress it might induce. The loss of close relatives is already a very significant feeling of loss.[13]

I am not saying that we should draw a parallel between the loss when placing a child for adoption or losing a father and the situation of a child who has no father to begin with, but there is something in common regarding the consequences: the missing parent.

5. PATERNAL PRESUMPTION IN THE CASE OF INFERTILE COUPLES

The provisions of the Family Act stipulate the presumption of the paternity of the man taking part in the reproduction procedure unless the mother is married. The reproduction procedure can be carried out at the joint request of married couples or unmarried couples in common law relationship, which is to be laid down in a substantiating private document.[14] By this act they both accept that the legal family status of the child to be born after insemination will be absolutely equal to that of a biological child.[15]

---

13 "Psychology and psychopathology for lawyers", Mária Fekete – Dr. András Grád, *HVG-ORAC*, 2002. Budapest, p. 425.

14 Health Act, Article 168 paragraph (1): The reproduction procedure – in the case of a single woman the continuation thereof – can be carried out in the absence of the joint statement of the married (common law) couple, or the statement of exclusion as per Article 167 paragraph (2), and within the framework of the right of disposal of the deposited embryo – at the written request of the single woman. The request must be laid down in a substantiating private document. A common law couple shall make a statement based on the effect of their common law relationship in a public document.

15 Family Act, Article 36: If the mother was not married from the beginning of conception until the birth of the child, the following person is to be considered as the father:
a) the man who recognized the child as his in a fully effective statement, or
b) the person who was declared to be the father of the child in a binding court ruling, or
c) in case the conditions of the present Act prevail, the man who married the mother after the child is born, or

If descent is the result of the reproduction procedure, the ground for contesting it is not that biological descent is other than the legal one, it can only be contested if the mother's husband or common law partner does not consent to the procedure. (Family Act, Article 43 paragraph (1). In the case of a reproduction procedure, contesting on the ground of other presumptions can be explained by the fact that in such cases the spouse or the partner in the relationship has to give his consent to become a father as a result of a procedure in which the biological relationship is unknown and cannot be found. Since all the above circumstances are known to the parents when they make such decisions, and if they do make use of this possibility, the parent cannot, retrospectively, strip the child of his or her right to have a legal father, considering especially that finding the biological father and establishing paternity are ruled out.[16] We can see that the provisions of the Family Act, with regard to the provisions of the Health Act, have included the presumption of the paternity of the partner (husband, common law partner) who took part in the reproduction procedure as an applicant among the presumptions of paternity. The prohibition of searching for the biological father is understandable in connection with the above presumption.

6. FINAL REMARK

Certainly there will be those who consider my position "old-fashioned" or conservative even. I have to disappoint them: basically there are liberal attitudes behind my thoughts. Nevertheless, I feel that all amendments of similar importance must be assessed from all possible aspects before too hastily waiving everything aside and calling the former regulation "discriminatory". This brief overview does not wish to express any opposition to those who think differently. I only wished to analyse, in a wider context, the possible relationship between the amendment concerning children and the rights and/or best interests of the child.

---

d) the man who participated in the special procedure aimed at human reproduction with the mother as under the provisions of the law, and the descent of the child is the result of the reproduction procedure.

16 "Explanation of the Family Act", Sári Péterné Vass Margit, ed. *KJK*, 2002. Budapest, pp. 749, 750.

MULTI-PARENT FAMILIES IN THE 21ST CENTURY

Mariel Dimsey*

1. INTRODUCTION

The impulse to discuss this issue was prompted by the recent decision of the Ontario Court of Appeal in the case of *A.A. v. B.B.* 2007 ONCA 2. In this case, two lesbian partners had enlisted a male friend to conceive a child. The biological mother and father were registered as the child's parents, despite the fact that the biological mother's lesbian partner was for all intents and purposes a mother of the child. All three adults had a decisive and significant role in the child's life, and the partner of the biological mother sought, by bringing this case, to have her legal parentage declared in addition to that of the biological parents. In this truly landmark decision, in declaring the lesbian partner as one of three legal parents of the child, the court recognized the importance, and indeed the best interests of the child concerned, in having both his mothers, namely the biological mother and her long-term partner, as well as the biological father, who had played a significant role in the child's upbringing, all recognized as parents of the child.

Currently, this decision constitutes the tip of the iceberg in a long line of developments at both domestic and international levels that increasingly seek to recognize and pay heed to the concept of "social parentage",[1] efforts which are long overdue in light of the widespread recognition and acceptance of relationships going far beyond the traditional, very outdated portrayal of a heterosexual husband and wife couple, focusing instead on the best interests of the child as the sole criterion.

Indeed, same-sex relationships enjoy increasing recognition in the western world nowadays, with several countries in Europe, Canada, select US states, Australia,

---

* I am greatly indebted to my former boss, Professor Dr. Ingeborg Schwenzer, LL.M., University of Basel, for her help and support in preparing this paper.

1 Cf. generally Schwenzer, 'Convergence and Divergence in the Law on Same-sex Partnerships', in Antokolskaia (ed.), 'Convergence and Divergence of Family Law in Europe', Antwerp/Oxford 2007, p. 145–157.

England and New Zealand offering legal institutions to same-sex couples.[2] These unions range from full marriage on equal level with the traditional "heterosexual" model[3] to really just a mere "term" as a means for partners to recognize their relationship, to which no, or limited, legal consequences are attached.[4] However, what may be described now as the beginnings of establishing some sort of legal "commonality"[5] for same sex relationships at an international level does not, unfortunately, extend to the legal recognition of parentage in the same way.

The status of children in same-sex relationships has been a bit of a Pandora's box for many years. It has long been accepted – even required – in most jurisdictions that a child must have a mother and a father. But two mothers? Two fathers? Two

---

2 Cf. fn. 3, 4 below, also for Denmark: Act no. 372 of 7 June 1989 on registered partnership with effect from 1 October 1989; Sweden: Lag om registerat partnerskap (Registered Partnership Act), Act 1994:1117 of 23 June 1994, in force as of 1 January 1995; Finland: Registered Partnership Act, Act 950/2001, in force as of 1 March 2002; Norway: Lov om registreret partnerskap, No. 40/1993 of 20 April 1993, in force as of 1 August 2003; Iceland: Act on registered Partnership, No. 87 of 12 June 1996, in force as of 27 June 1996; Germany: Lebenspartnerschaftsgesetz (LPartG) of 16 February 2001, BGBl I 266, in force as of 1 August 2001, modified by the Law of 6 February 2005, BGBl I 203 with effect from 1 January 2005; England: Civil Partnership Act 2004, in force as of 5 December 2005; Czech Republic: Civil Partnership Law, in force as of 1 July 2006; Slovenia: Law on Registered Partnership, in force as of 23 July 2006; Switzerland: Partnerschaftsgesetz (PartG) of 18 June 2004, SR 211.231, in force as of 1 January 2006.

3 Cf. for the Netherlands: Art. 1:30(1) Dutch Civil Code, inserted by the Act Opening Marriage to Same-Sex Couples of 21 December 2000, in force as of 1 April 2001, Staatsblad 2001, No. 9; for South Africa: In *Lesbian and Gay Equality Project and Eighteen Others v. Minister of Home Affairs and Others,* Constitutional Court of South Africa, CCT 10/05, 1 December 2005 and in *Minister of Home Affairs and Another v. Fourie and Another,* Constitutional Court of South Africa, CCT 60/04, 1 December 2005, the court has declared s 30(1) Marriage Act 25 of 1961 and the commom law definition of marriage inconsistent with the Constitution. It has, however, suspended the declaration of invalidity for twelve months in order to allow the parliament to correct the defects by assigning to same-sex couples the same status, entitlements and responsibilities as marriage law accords to heterosexual couples. The Chair of the South African Parliamentary Committee on Home Affairs has recently announced that same-sex marriage will be legalized by way of amendments to the Marriage Act 1961 rather than by constitutional amendment, see British Institute of International and Comparative Law, 16 BLD 2006; for Canada: Art. 2 Civil Marriage Act, in force as of 20 July 2005; for Belgium: Art. 143 Code civil; for Spain: Art. 44 Código civil, Ley 13/2005, de 1 de julio, por la que se modificó el Código civil en materia de derecho a contraer matrimonio (BOE núm. 157 de 2 de julio de 2005), see also GONZÁLES BEILFUSS, 'Gleichgeschlechtliche Ehen und Blitzscheidung im neuen spanischen Familienrecht', *Die Praxis des Familienrechts (FamPra.ch)* 2006, 878–885. Cf. generally BOELE-WOELKI/FUCHS, 'Legal Recognition of Same-Sex Couples in Europe', Antwerp/Oxford/New York 2003, 13 et seq.

4 Cf. France: Loi relative au pacte civil de solidarité, loi no. 99–944 of 15 November 1999, inserting Arts. 515–1 to 515–7 in the Code civil; Portugal: Lei no. 7/01 of 11 May 2005, Adopta medidas de protecção das uniões de facto, DR Série I-A, 2797; Luxemburg: Loi du 9 juillet 2004 relative aux effets légaux de certains partenariats, published in Mémorial A, no. 143 on 6 August 2004, 2020, in force as of 1 November 2004.

5 Cf. SCHWENZER in SCHWENZER (ed.), 'Tensions between Legal, Biological and Social Conceptions of Parentage', Antwerp/Oxford 2007, p. 2.

fathers AND a mother? So progressive they ain't. But perhaps they should be. Because up until now, it appears that, beyond accepting the *existence* of same-sex relationships, perhaps even giving them a name, the approach to children of one or both of the partners has almost been dealt with coincidentally through other legal mechanisms that, in a way, avoid the status of the parties AS parents, indeed intended parents, altogether.[6] Thereby, a child may, in fact, have more than two parents, but due to the haphazard mechanisms for recognizing parentage in these situations, at least one intentional parent may well be left out in the cold.

What the Canadian decision does is give *express* regard to this constellation, signifying a departure, hopefully, from the shadowy legal regulation concerning multi-parent families that has prevailed up until now. It needs to be stated here, at the outset, that the issue of multi-parent families is not confined to homosexual relationships of course; this also arises in the context of patchwork families where only heterosexual parties are involved.[7] However, I find the developments in the context of same-sex partnerships especially interesting because they also have an impact on and are reflective of other legal developments in this dynamic area.

2. CURRENT APPROACH TO SAME-SEX PARENTING

In looking at the current approach to same-sex parenting, some fundamental differences can be observed in the approaches taken. A very rough means of division is to classify the approaches as the "Common Law" and the "Civil Law" approaches. Whilst the common law legal systems of Canada, New Zealand, Australia, England and select US states, as well as some Scandinavian countries, now allow same-sex partners of biological parents to be recognized as parents of a child through various mechanisms, the Germanic and Roman legal systems of continental Europe lag behind in this area and seem to have trouble overcoming the traditional concept of the two-parent heterosexual family.

---

6 In limited legal systems, through the attribution of parental responsibility in others through certain rights concerning the day-to-day upbringing of the child, see below 3.

7 Cf. generally SCHWENZER, 'Elterliche Verantwortung in und nach Auflösung von Patchwork-Familien', *FamZ* 2007, 15–20.

3. LEGAL RECOGNITION OF SOCIAL PARENTAGE OF SAME-SEX PARTNERS

As I mentioned, a number of legal systems do already recognize the possibility of parentage being legally granted to the same-sex partner of a biological parent, either through intentional parentage by use of reproductive medicine, or by adoption.

3.1. REPRODUCTIVE MEDICINE

Current possibilities in reproductive medicine have contributed much to the abolishment of old notions of parentage. The old legal maxims of *mater sempe certe est* and *pater est quem nuptiae demonstrant* simply do not apply with the same force these days.[8] The possibilities of egg and embryo donation now mean that the person giving birth to a child is not necessarily also the genetic mother. However, what is still more often used as a means for same-sex couples to have children is artificial insemination. Whilst initially used as means for infertile heterosexual couples to have children, whether through homological or heterological insemination, this possibility is increasingly used by lesbian partners looking to conceive. Out of those countries that have established legal institutions for same-sex couples, the "common law"-shaped select US states,[9] Canada,[10]

---

8 Although both are still relied on in e.g. Austria: Art. 138(1) ABGB; Belgium: Art. 315 Code civil; Croatia: Art. 54 Family Act; Germany: §1592 BGB; Greece: Art. 1465 Civil Code; Japan: Art. 772(1) Civil Code; Switzerland: Art. 225(1) ZGB.

9 E.g. Massachusetts: Mass. Gen. Laws Ann. 46 §4B; California: Cal. Fam. Code §297.5(d) and §7613(a), cf. also the UPA-Provision on presumed parents in Cal. Fam. Code §7611(d); Vermont: 15 V.S.A. §1204(f) (2006) and 15 V.S.A. §308(4); Connecticut: Conn. Gen. Stat. §46b-38nn (2006) and Conn. Gen. Stat. §45a-774 (2006); New Jersey: *In the matter of the Parentage of the child of Kimberly Robinson*, Superior Court of New Jersey, Chancery Division 2005, 383 N.J. Super. 165, 890 A.2d 1036; see also JOSLIN, 'The Legal Parentage of Children Born to Same-Sex Couples: Developments in the Law', 39 *Fam. L. Q.* (2005), 683, 684 et seq; ELROD/SPECTOR, 'A Review of the Year in Family Law: Parentage and Assisted Reproduction Problems Take Center Stage', 39 *Family Law Quarterly* (2006), 879, 887 et seq.; FRELICH APPLETON, 'The Public and Private Faces of Family Law: Adoption in the Age of Reproductive Technology', *The University of Chicago Legal Forum* 2004, 393, 414 et seq.; FORMAN, 'Married with Kids and Moving: Achieving Recognition for Same-Sex Parents under the Uniform Parentage Act', 4 *Whittier Journal of Child and Family Advocacy* (2005), 241, 252 et seq. Cf. generally CHAMBERS, 'What if – The Legal Consequences of Marriage and the Legal Needs of Lesbian and Gay Male Couples', 95 *Michigan Law Review* (1996), 447, 466.

10 Art. 2(e) Assisted Human Reproduction Act 2004, c. 2. Cf. also Alberta: *Fraess v. Alberta*, Alberta Court of Queen's Bench, [2005] A.J. No. 1665 Q.B.; British Columbia: *Gill and Maher, Murray and Popoff v. Ministry of Health*, British Columbia Human Rights Tribunal, 2001 BCHRT 34; Ontario: *M.D.R. v. Ontario*, Ontario Superior Court of Justice, [2006] O.J. No. 2268; Quebec: Art. 538.1 Civil Code.

England,[11] Australia,[12] New Zealand[13] and South Africa,[14] as well as a new wave of civil law legal systems including Sweden,[15] The Netherlands,[16] and Spain,[17] now make the possibility of artificial insemination available to lesbian couples. Of these countries, a few are still inconsistent in their refusal to then grant legal parentage to the lesbian partner of the birth mother, namely the Netherlands and Spain and notably England, which is yet to amend its laws governing reproductive medicine to align them with the Civil Partnership Act 2004.

What is interesting is that, even in the absence of legal recognition, many lesbian couples do, in practice, use artificial insemination as a means of having children anyway. This is due to the fact that, of those legal systems that allow artificial insemination, some do allow single women to receive it.[18] So, providing that you are not in a marriage or registered partnership, ostensibly "single" women can bear children through artificial insemination and raise them with a partner de facto, without legal recognition. However, this is not a satisfactory solution, as this method fails to vest the non-birth mother with any legal capacity regarding the child.

Obviously, these legal rules cannot apply in the case of gay men, who are dependent on surrogacy arrangements. At this stage, I believe that only South Africa, in

---

11 Cf. ALMACK, 'Seeking Sperm: Accounts of lesbian couples' reproductive decision making and understandings of the needs of the child', 20 *International Journal of Law, Policy and the Family* (2006), 1, 3 et seq.

12 Australian Capital Territory: sec. 11(4) Parentage Act 2004; Northern Territory: sec. 15DA Status of Children Act; Tasmania: sec. 10C(1) Status of Children Act 1974; Western Australia: sec. 6A Artificial Conception Act 1985. Cf. generally BEEM, 'Where Does a Man Stand on Issues of Assisted Reproduction, Surrogacy, Artificial Insemination within Lesbian Relationships and Posthumous Conception?', 18 *Australian Journal of Family Law* (2004), 41, 45 et seq.

13 Sec. 18 Status of Children Act 1969, modified by sec. 14 Status of Children Amendment Act 2004.

14 In *J and B v. Director General: Department of Home Affairs and Others*, Constitutional Court of South Africa, CCT 46/02, 28 March 2003, the court held that sec. 5 Children's Status Act was inconsistent with the Constitution and ordered that it should be read to provide the same status to children born from artificial insemination to same-sex permanent life partners as it currently provides to such children born to heterosexual married couples.

15 Cf. Prop. 2004/05:137, Asisterad befruktning och föraldraskap (= Governmental Bill on Artificial Fertilisation and Parenthood); see also BURRELL, 'Assisted Reproduction in the Nordic Countries – a Comparative Study of Policies and Regulation, Nordic Council of Ministers', Copenhagen 2006, 15.

16 Cf. DETHLOFF, 'Registrierte Partnerschaften in Europa', *Zeitschrift für Europäisches Privatrecht* 2004, 59, 64.

17 Art. 6 Ley 14/2006 de 26 mayo sobre técnicas de reproducción humana asistida, BOE núm 126, 19950, expressly states that any woman, regardless of her sexual orientation, can have access to medically-assisted reproduction technology.

18 Cf. e.g. Denmark: sec. 3 Artificial Reproduction Act.

its new Children's Act 2005, has rules in this respect, where a valid surrogate motherhood has the effect that, for all purposes, the commissioning parents are the child's legal parents, thus including two gay men within this spectrum.[19] In all other legal systems, if surrogacy is allowed at all – and even if it's unenforceable –, a change of parentage may only be effected by way of adoption.[20]

3.2. ADOPTION

Current trends show that the attitude to adoption in Western legal systems is extending beyond the traditional, heterosexual married couple model nowadays. Firstly, a number of common law countries have gone so far as to do away with any questions of status at all in allowing persons to adopt.[21] Thus, adoption has been extended to non-married, "merely" cohabiting partners. Although this was initially confined to persons of different sex, so the heterosexual de facto relationships, the modern abandonment of status issues has led to the "general principle", if you like, being extended to same-sex partners.

In the USA, where marriage between persons of the same sex is, to a large extent, not yet allowed, several states nevertheless allow same-sex couples to adopt, for example, New York, California and the District of Columbia;[22] this, however, is usually a matter settled by case law rather than being enshrined in legislation. Canada[23] and Australia[24] show a similar trend, with this issue being left to the

19 §297(1)(a) Children Act 2005 (no. 38 of 2005).
20 Cf. Schwenzer (fn. 5), p. 10.
21 Cf. Schwenzer (fn. 5), p. 21.
22 See generally Liberty Counsel, Same-Sex Adoption Laws by State, available online at: http://www.lc.org/ProFamily/samesex_adoption_by_state.pdf, last accessed 8 October 2007.
23 Joint and step-parent adoption possible in British Columbia: sec. 5 Adoption Act [R.S.B.C. 1996] ch. 5; Manitoba: The Charter Compliance Act [S.M. 2002], c. 24; Newfoundland & Labrador: sec. 20 Adoption Act [S.N.L. 1999] c. A-2.1 as amended by sec. 10 An Act to amend the Adoption Act [S.N.L. 2002] c. 13; Northwest Territories: sec. 1(1), 5(1)(b) and 5(1)(c) Adoption Act [S.N.W.T. 1998] c. 9 as amended by sec. 1 [S.N.W.T. 2002] c. 6; Nova Scotia: Re M (S.C.) (2001), 194 N.S.R. (2d) 362, 202 D.L.R. (4th) 172 [S.C.(Fam.Div.)]; Ontario: sec. 146 Child and Family Services Act [R.S.O. 1990] c. 11 and sec 10(1) Human Rights Code [R.S.O. 1990] c. H19; Quebec: Art. 546 Civil Code; Saskatchewan: sec. 16(2)(c) Adoption Act [S.S.) ch. 5.2; see also Fisher, 'Outlaws or In-laws?: Successes and Challenges in the Struggle for LGBT Equality', 49 *McGill Law Journal* (2004), 1183, para. 14; Wintemute, 'Sexual Orientation and the Charter: The Achievement of Formal Legal Equality (1985–2005) and Its Limits', 29 *McGill Law Journal* (2004), 1143, para. 28; Casswell, 'Any two Persons in Canada's Lotusland, British Columbia', in: Wintemute/Andenæs, 'Legal Recognition of Same-Sex Partnerships, A Study of National, European and International Law', Oxford/Portland Oregon 2001, 215, 228.
24 Joint Adoption: e.g. Australian Capital Territory: sec. 18(1)(b) Adoption Act 1993; Western Australia: sec. 39(1)(d) Adoption Act 1994; step-parent Adoption: Tasmania: sec. 20(2A)(a) Adoption Act 1988; see also Cooper, For Richer for Poorer, in Sickness and in Health: Should Australia Embrace Same-Sex Marriage?, 19 *Australian Journal of Family Law* (2005), 153, 161.

states and provinces, with the consequence that a large degree of divergence in approach is still apparent. New Zealand provides an interesting example of inconsistency in the legislative approach: whilst a lesbian partner of the birth mother is able to obtain legal recognition of her parentage, adoption by same-sex partners is still in the pipeline.[25] England offers a very sweeping approach now with the Adoption and Children Act 2002, whereby adoption is simply open to two people, without any mention of sex.[26] In South Africa, the same position has been established by case law.[27]

Where questions of status do play a role, they are usually based upon the legal institutions available to same-sex partners in the legal system in question. For example, where actual same-sex *marriage* is allowed, adoption, being open to married partners, is also allowed by those partners,[28] with the notable exception of Belgium. Where a registered partnership is provided for, a divergence of approaches exists.

Whilst select few legal systems, such as Sweden,[29] genuinely place homosexual registered partners on the same footing as heterosexual married partners regarding the law on adoption, a number of European countries, including Norway[30] and Germany[31], now provide for stepparent adoption by the registered partner of

---

25 New Zealand Parliamentary Debates (Hansard) Vol. 622, 17423, 7 December 2004. Cf. also Law Commission of New Zealand, Report 65, Adoption and its Alternatives, A Different Approach and a New Framework, Wellington 2000, para. 350 et seq.; Law Commission of New Zealand, Preliminary Paper 38, Adoption: Options for Reform, Wellington 1999, para. 179 et seq.

26 Sec. 49(1)(a) Adoption and Children Act 2002. The term "couple" is defined in sec. 144 (4)(aa) and (b) as "two people who are civil partners of each other" (aa) or as "two people (whether of different sexes of the same sex) living as partners in an enduring family relationship". Cf. also Harper/Landells, 'The Civil Partnership Act 2004 in Force', 39 *Family Law* (2005), 963, 969; Washington/Alexander, 'Civil Partnership Made Easy', 39 *Family Law* (2005), 243, 245.

27 *Du Toit and Another v. The Minister for Welfare and Population Development and Others*, South Africa Constitutional Court, CCT 40/01, 10 September 2002.

28 Cf. e.g. for Spain: joint adoption: Art. 176(4) Código Civil; step-parent adoption: Arts. 176 and 178(1) Código Civil; García Cantero, 'Family Law Reform in Differing Directions', in: Bainham (ed.), The International Survey of Family Law, 2006 Edition, Bristol 2006, 435, 437.

29 On 1 February 2003, ch. 3 §2 of the Law on Registered Partnership was rescinded (SFS 2002:603); now registered couples have the same right to adopt as married couples. See Jäntera-Jareborg/Sörgjerd, 'The Experiences with Registered Partnership in Scandinavia', *Die Praxis des Familienrechts (Fam.Pra.ch)* 2004, 577, 581; Saldeen, 'The Children's Ombudsman, Adoption by Homosexual Partners and Assisted Reproduction', in: Bainham (ed.), The International Survey of Family Law 2004, 439, 440 et seq.

30 §5a(2) Act on Adoption (Adoptionsloven).

31 §9(7) LPartG, BGBl 2001 I, 3396, in force as of 1 January 2005; Dethloff/Kroll, 'The Constitutional Court as Driver of Reforms in German Family Law', in: Bainham (ed.), fn. 28, 217, 223; Siegfried, 'Kinder vom anderen Ufer', *Familie Partnerschaft Recht* 2005, 120, 121; Wellenhofer, 'Das neue Recht für eingetragene Lebenspartnerschaften', *Neue Juristische Wochen-*

the "parent" of the child. However, this is really only a valid solution where there is no other legal parent in the picture, since stepparent adoption would then deprive that parent of their legal parentage. In contrast, a number of legal systems, however, offer only a half-baked solution: whilst *prima facie* allowing registered partnerships, no provision for adoption by these partners is made. Switzerland counts among the countries following such an approach.[32]

The legal systems outlined above allow *legal* recognition of what has come to be termed as *intentional parentage* in the context of same-sex couples. As mentioned earlier, a lot of these approaches also of course hold true for non-marital different-sex couples.

Where legal systems do not grant intentional parentage, recognition of at least some form may be gained by the attribution of parental responsibility.

4. "SOCIAL" RECOGNITION – PARENTAL RESPONSIBILITY

A "weaker" right and duty, so to say, than actual parentage, is that of parental responsibility. There are indeed an isolated number of legal systems that do, in their approach to this issue, make the possibility of multi-parent families seem a quite plausible reality.

Nonetheless, the general rule remains that the two persons that are recognized as the legal parents of the child are also the persons who have parental responsibility for him or her. In the greatest majority of cases, this joint responsibility also survives divorce or separation.[33] With regard to third, non-parental parties gaining parental responsibility, two distinctions need to be made, particularly in the continental European context.

Firstly, there are cases where the non-parent in the partnership, including same-sex partnerships, is entitled to mini-custody, the *kleines Sorgerecht* in Switzerland and Germany, which basically allows that person to take part in the day-to-day

schrift 2005, 705, 706; PÄTZOLD, 'Die gemeinschaftliche Adoption Minderjähriger durch eingetragene Lebenspartner', *Familie Partnerschaft Recht* 2005, 269 et seq.

32 Art. 28 PartG; COTTIER, 'Registered Partnerships for Same-Sex Couples in Switzerland: Constructing a New Model of Family Relationships', in: MACLEAN (ed.), Family Law and Family Values, Oxford 2005, 181, 195; SCHWENZER, 'Registrierte Partnerschaft: Der Schweizer Weg', *Die Praxis des Familienrechts (Fam.Pra.ch)* 2002, 223, 231 et seq. Cf. also Finland: Art. 9(2) Registered Partnership Act.

33 Cf. SCHWENZER, fn. 5., 13.

upbringing of the child.[34] This right, however, ends upon divorce or separation; under "normal" circumstances, parental responsibility reverts to the biological parent.[35] The second case concerns the strict Swedish approach, where only two people are entitled to exercise parental responsibility.[36]

A liberal approach is taken in many common law systems, which simply allow parental responsibility by agreement, without regard for the numbers of holders of parental responsibility, or their sex.[37] In some cases, this is also possible by court order in adversarial cases.[38] In most common law systems, the dissolution of the partnership or marriage between the holders of parental responsibility has no impact on its attribution; joint parental responsibility continues to exist.[39]

The most modern approach is taken by the Netherlands, which allows the spouse or partner of the birth mother at the time of the birth of the child to automatically obtain joint parental responsibility, even if this person is not recognized as the legal parent of the child.[40] If a second legal parent already exists, attribution to a third person is possible by joint application, thus essentially by agreement.[41]

5. MULTI-PARENT?

Thus, as you can see, whilst Ontario is, as yet, the first system to allow unreservedly the attribution of *parentage* to more than two persons

34 Cf. Germany: §9(1) LPartG; DETHLOFF, "Parental Rights and Responsibilities in Germany", 39 *Family Law Quarterly* (2005), 315, 325; SCHWAB, 'Die eingetragene Lebenspartnerschaft', Bielefeld 2002, 171 et seq. Switzerland: Art. 27(1) PartG; GRÜTTER/SUMMERMATTER, 'Das Partnerschaftsgesetz', *Die Praxis des Familienrechts (Fam.Pra.ch)* 2004, 449, 463 et seq. Cf. generally SCHWENZER, fn. 7, 16–18.

35 Cf. Germany: §1687b(4) BGB; Switzerland: Art. 299 ZGB; SCHWENZER, fn. 7, 17, 18.

36 Cf. Ch. 6 Föräldrabalken.

37 E.g. England: secs. 2(6), 4A Children Act 1989; sec. 75(2) Civil Partnership Act 2004. Australia: secs. 61D(2), 63C, 64C 65C Family Law Act 1975. In RE MARK: AN APPLICATION RELATING TO PARENTAL RESPONSIBILITIES, [2003] FamCA 822, 23 August 2003, the Australian Family court issued a parenting order to the male same-sex partner of the biological father of a child conceived pursuant to a surrogacy agreement; cf. also DICKEY, Family Law, Sydney 2002, 362 et seq. New Zealand: according to sec. 23 Care of Children Act 2004, step parents (by civil union or de facto partners) can be appointed as additional guardians by consent of the child's parents; ATKIN, 'New Zealand, Landmark Legislation', in: BAINHAM (ed.), fn. 28, 305, 311.

38 Cf. England: sec. 14(1) Child Custody and the Right of Access Act; sec. 10(5A) Children Act 1989.

39 Cf. Australia: secs. 64C, 65C Family Law Act 1975; Denmark: §11(2) Lov om forældremyndighed og samvær; England: sec. 4A Children Act 1989; Canada: §601 Civil Code (Quebec), Part III Children's Law Reform Act (Ontario); New Zealand: sec. 23 Care of Children Act 2004.

40 Art. 253aa Dutch Civil Code (Burgerlijk Wetboek); BOELE-WOELKI, 'Registered Partnership and Same-Sex Marriage in The Netherlands', in: BOELE-WOELKI/FUCHS, fn. 3, 46.

41 Art. 253t Dutch Civil Code (Burgerlijk Wetboek).

simultaneously, other legal systems, particularly those of Anglo-American background, and, to a lesser extent, western and northern Europe, have adopted a milder version of this approach, with *parental responsibility*, if not quite *parentage*, allocable to persons outside the biological and status-oriented sphere.

6. OUTLOOK

With respect to future developments, it is probably fair to say that it is likely to be other common law countries that will be the first to follow in the footsteps of Ontario. This view is held partly due to the flexible judicial law-making by case law available in those systems, but also because the current approach of countries like Australia and England makes it seem a necessary next step. The lack of status issues coming into play in the area of multiple parental responsibility should make multiple parentage a not insurmountable hurdle in the near future.

For the sake of completeness, the question that perhaps should be asked here is whether recognition of multiple legal parentage is actually necessary. This hinges on the scope of rights that are granted to holders of parental responsibility without parentage. At the moment, being a "mere" holder of parental responsibility has serious detrimental effects. In the case of A.A. v. B.B., the judge referred to a long list of matters and rights from which the lesbian partner of the birth mother would be excluded were she not recognized as a parent.[42] If a holder of parental responsibility were to be vested with more rights and duties, would there even need to be recognition of social or intentional parentage? These kinds of arguments echo the arguments used in discussing whether marriage should be done away with – do we even need it in a world free of status?

In the case of parentage, we most definitely still do. Being a "parent" is something to be proud of – people want this title, it defines who they are, shows an emotional bond. The solution is not to make parental responsibility for non-parents more extensive. That also appears to be an insult for both the intentional parent and the child. There is hope now that, in the mid-term, the concept of "parentage" as being confined to only two persons may go down the same path as many other status-oriented notions have done and might give way to acceptance and recognition of multi-parent families, where all parties who have assumed a caring role for a child are given due recognition, without being confined to archaic limitations on number and sex. When the lawmakers catch up with what as been the case for a long time and start calling it what it is, instead of what it once was – only four in

---

42 *A.A. v. B.B.* para. 14.

ten families now fit the traditional nuclear mould –,[43] finally appropriate regard will be had to the modern reality of intentional parentage and the best interests of the child.

43 Cf. http://www.familyhelper.net/news/070109threeparents.html, last accessed 8 October 2007, quoting the Vanier Institute of the Family, based in Ottawa, Canada.

THE RECOGNITION OF HOMOSEXUAL PARENTS IN THE UNITED KINGDOM

David Hill

1. INTRODUCTION

This paper considers how the parental qualities of homosexual individuals and couples are recognised within the United Kingdom. It will begin with an overview of how such individuals and couples were treated in the recent past and an identification of how these attitudes have now changed. It will then move on to consider *why* these attitudes have changed and suggest three factors which have had, or could reasonably be suggested to have had, a substantial impact upon the increasing recognition of homosexual parents.

2. HOMOSEXUAL PARENTS – A BRIEF HISTORY

It is one of the fundamental tenets of child law in the United Kingdom that parents do not have absolute rights over their children but are only entitled to exercise such rights in order to fulfil their parental responsibilities when to do so would be in the interests of the child.[1] This view forms part of the wider concept of the 'welfare principle' which demands that, in any case involving a child, the welfare and best interests of the child should always be the paramount consideration.[2] However, what is seen to be in the best interests of a child is subject to different determinations at differing times, something particularly evidenced when considering the recognition of homosexual parents.

Initially, as male homosexual conduct was classified as a criminal offence,[3] this criminal character of a gay lifestyle was reason alone for it to be superfluous even

1 For instance, see the Children (Scotland) Act 1995, s 2(1).

2 See the Children (Scotland) Act 1995, s 11(7)(a), the Children Act 1989, s 1(1) and the United Nations Convention on the Rights of the Child, Article 3(1).

3 Although no doubt subjected to the same social disapproval, female homosexual acts were never classified as criminal in the United Kingdom due to it being inconceivable to male Victorian legislators that women could behave in such a way. See, for instance, the gender specific language of the Criminal Law Amendment Act 1885. This can be contrasted with

to consider the possibility of such people being recognised as acceptable and capable parents. Further, as the implications of a person being open about their sexual orientation could result in a high degree of stigmatisation, persecution or even prosecution,[4] homosexual individuals generally lived in secrecy and thus did not allow their sexuality to become a live issue for consideration in any circumstances.

Decriminalisation occurred in England and Wales in 1967[5] and in Scotland in 1980,[6] thus preceding the decision in *Dudgeon v United Kingdom*[7] which deemed a total prohibition on homosexual activity as an unjustifiable interference with a person's private life under the European Convention for the Protection of Human Rights and Fundamental Freedoms 1950[8] and resulted in decriminalisation in Northern Ireland in 1982.[9] These developments allowed homosexual individuals and couples to become gradually more visible in society. This increasing social visibility, and eventually acceptance,[10] helped provide people with a new sense of courage to be open about their sexuality without fear of detrimental effects on themselves or their relationships, either with other adults or with their children. Moreover, the establishment and growth of gay rights groups has led to an increased awareness of the problems that homosexual individuals and couples

homosexual sodomy legislation in certain jurisdictions of the United States where sodomy was defined as any sexual activity outside of the penile penetration of the vagina. These various laws prohibiting homosexual sexual activity, however defined, have now been invalidated by the decision in *Lawrence v Texas* 539 US 558 (2003).

4 For discussion of one such high profile prosecution see Cretney S., *Same-Sex Relationships: From 'Odious Crime' to 'Gay Marriage'* (Oxford University Press, Oxford, 2006) pp. 1–2.

5 As a result of the Report of the Committee on Homosexual Offences and Prostitution, commonly known as 'The Wolfenden Report' after its chair Sir John Wolfenden (Cmnd. 247, 1957) most consensual homosexual acts between adult men in private were decriminalised in England and Wales by the Sexual Offences Act 1967, s 1.

6 The Criminal Justice (Scotland) Act 1980, s 80 decriminalised homosexual acts between men provided they took place in private, were consensual, and both parties were over the age of 21. The age of consent was reduced further to 18 by the Criminal Justice and Public Order Act 1994, s 145, whilst s 80 of the 1980 Act was replaced by the Criminal Law (Consolidation) (Scotland) Act 1995, s 13, as amended by the Sexual Offences (Amendment) Act 2000, s 1(3) (reducing the lawful age of consent to 16 years) and the Convention Rights (Compliance) (Scotland) Act 2001, s 10, which removes the prohibition on homosexual activity in the presence of more than two people.

7 *(No 1)* (1981) 3 EHRR 40 and *(No 2)* (1982) 4 EHRR 149.

8 (1981) 3 EHRR 40, paras. 97 and 115.

9 See the Homosexual Offences (Northern Ireland) Order 1982 (S.I. 1982/1536 (N.I. 19)).

10 According to the British Social Attitudes Survey of 1987 only 10.8 per cent of people believed sexual relations between two adults of the same sex to be 'not at all wrong'. By the 2000 survey this figure had more than trebled to 34.1 per cent.

face in their desire to become parents and have provided forums to facilitate claims for equality and legal recognition.[11]

With this decriminalisation of homosexual acts, and therefore homosexuality itself, it was no longer possible for the claims of homosexual parents to be ignored in totality, without further justification, on the basis of the inherent moral wrongness or illegality of the homosexual individual and their actions. Instead, when considering a homosexual person's claims to fulfil a parental role, specific reasons were required to justify the negative views towards, and a rejection of, homosexual parenting. As a result, arguments were volunteered that gay parents subjected their children to disproportionate risks on two distinct bases. Firstly, it was suggested that children would be 'contaminated' or 'corrupted' by homosexuality, such as by being more likely to suffer confusion over their gender and sexual identities, leading to an increased 'risk' of becoming homosexual themselves; that homosexual parents were more sexually promiscuous and, as a result, more likely to molest their own children; that children are more likely to lose a homosexual parent to AIDS, substance abuse or suicide, and to suffer a greater risk of depression and emotional difficulties, or that homosexual couples themselves were more unstable than their heterosexual counterparts and likely to separate, something which would undoubtedly cause upset for the child.[12] Secondly, it has also been argued that children of homosexual parents would face an increased risk of suffering from stigmatisation, bullying and social ostracism on the basis of the sexuality of their parents.[13]

The influence of these negative attitudes can be identified in a number of decisions in which the sexual orientation of a parent, or potential parent, became a matter for consideration. Thus, in *Re D (An Infant) (Adoption) (Parent's Consent)*[14] there was discussion as to whether a child was likely to be placed in danger if his

---

11 For instance, see the Stonewall parenting 'information bank': http://www.stonewall.org.uk/information_bank/parenting/default.asp and the work of the International Lesbian and Gay Association (Europe) http://www.ilga-europe.org.

12 For an example of a particularly negative view towards homosexual parenting see Wardle L., "The Potential Impact of Homosexual Parenting on Children", *University of Illinois Law Review*, 1997, 833.

13 See Reece H., "Subverting the Stigmatisation Argument", 23 *Journal of Law and Society*, 1996, 484 and Norrie K. McK., "Sexual Orientation and Family Law", in Scoular J. (ed), *Family Dynamics: Contemporary Issues in Family Law* (Butterworths, Edinburgh, 2001) pp. 154–159. In Sweden, an official Commission published a report in 1984 (Commission Report, Homosexuals and Society (SOU 1984:63)) which rejected the argument that children could be 'contaminated' by homosexuality but still argued against homosexual adoption and joint custody on the basis that children living in same-sex households may regard themselves as deviant because of public perceptions (p. 274). Cited from Bradley D., *Family Law and Political Culture* (Sweet and Maxwell, London, 1996) p. 102.

14 [1977] AC 602.

homosexual father was allowed contact with him and what safeguards would be needed to protect said child from this perceived danger.[15] Further, it was stated that, regardless of decriminalisation and increasing public tolerance, the courts still had to consider, with 'vigilance and severity', the risks to children presented by a homosexual parent which could cause 'severance from normal society' and 'psychological stresses and unhappiness and possibly even to physical experience which may scar them for life'.[16]

More recently, attitudes were still generally negative when, in *Re P (A Minor) (Custody)*[17] a court spoke about homosexual orientation as a 'sexual deviance' and stated that it faced 'serious consternation' before being 'driven to the conclusion' that children should be allowed to live with their lesbian mother. Further, in *Early v Early*[18] a boy was removed from the care of a lesbian mother, with custody given to the father (who had never looked after him and had two convictions for child neglect), on the basis of fears over taunting at school with regards to his domestic situation if he continued living with his mother. These fears were accepted even though there was no actual evidence of taunting or indeed any likelihood of there being so in the future.[19] In *B v B (Minors) (Custody, Care and Control)* a mother in a lesbian relationship was granted custody of her child from a previous heterosexual relationship, a course of action which was justified, in part, on the basis that the mother was a kind of lesbian who 'was a private person and did not believe in advertising their lesbianism' as opposed to those who were classified as 'militant lesbians who try to convert others to their way of life'.[20]

A fundamental shift in attitudes and policy considerations is evident in the case of *T Petitioner*[21] where an adoption was granted in favour of a homosexual applicant who expressly intended to share the upbringing of the child with his same-

15 Ibid. at 608–609 per Orr LJ.

16 Ibid. at 629 per Lord Wilberforce. On the basis of these concerns it was concluded that a homosexual father who was acting reasonably would consent to the adoption of their child as, although this would mean the father would never see them again, the adoption would protect his son from these negative effects of his and his gay associates' sexual orientation.

17 (1983) 4 FLR 401.

18 1990 SLT 221.

19 Norrie K. McK., op cit (fn 13) has suggested how, although the judges in this case denied the mother's sexual orientation was a decisive factor, it is somewhat revealing to compare the minimal time that was spent worrying about the father's convictions with the time allocated to a consideration of the mother's lesbianism: p. 157, n. 3.

20 [1991] 1 FLR 402.

21 1997 SLT 724. For comment see "Case and Comment: Another Unfounded Assumption Laid to Rest?", *Juridical Review*, 1997, 373; Norrie K. McK., "Parental Pride: Adoption and the Gay Man", *Scots Law Times (News)*, 1996, 321; Ross M., "Attitudes to Sexual Orientation in Adoption Law", 1 *Edinburgh Law Review*, 1997, 370 and Thomson J., "Family Law: Homosexuality, Adoption and the Welfare Principle", 65 *Scottish Law Gazette*, 1997, 24.

sex cohabitant. In its rejection of the suggestion that it a fundamental question of principle whether the adoption process should ever entertain applications from people of a homosexual orientation[22], this decision re-established, in relation to cases involving homosexual parents, the principle that the welfare of the child is paramount.[23] It has been suggested that this approach must be correct as a general prohibition preventing homosexual individuals from adopting would be inconsistent with the true fundamental principle in adoption law as it would elevate a political or moral decision regarding the worth of homosexuality beyond the welfare of a particular child.[24] Thus, if a child's best interests will be served by having contact with a parent, or being adopted by a person, who happens to be homosexual and perhaps even cohabiting with their same-sex partner, this should not play a significant role in the determination over whether an order should, or should not, be granted.

This decision marked the beginning of a decade of rapidly changing attitudes towards, and the treatment of, homosexual parents both judicially and also legislatively. It is now clear that whenever a court is asked to consider a dispute regarding children the same legal principles should apply to children regardless of the sexual orientation of their parent(s).[25] Moreover, whereas homosexuality was previously seen as, if not entirely determinative,[26] certainly a weighty factor to be taken into account, the sexual orientation of a parent is now considered to be no more than background information with no adverse inferences to be drawn from it.[27] Unequivocal support for homosexual parenting has also been forthcoming from the legislature. The Civil Partnership Act 2004 extends to a civil partner similar opportunities to access rights and responsibilities in relation to children as would apply to a step-parent in an opposite-sex marriage. Additionally, whereas the adoption process had previously been limited to married couples or individual applicants, thereby excluding a same-sex couple by definition, recent reforms, which took place in England and Wales in 2002 and Scotland in 2007 have provided for joint adoption by a couple whether they be married, civil partners or

---

22 1997 SLT 724 at 731–732.

23 This decision had already been reached previously in an Ontario court in the case of *Re K and B* (1995) 125 DLR (4th) 653. Equivalent decisions were subsequently given in England in *Re W (A Minor) (Adoption: Homosexual Adopter)* [1997] 3 All ER 620 and in Northern Ireland in *Re M (Adoption: Joint Residence Order: Same Sex Couple)* [2004] NI 241.

24 Norrie K. McK., op cit (fn 21) p. 323.

25 *Re G (Children) (Residence: Same Sex Partner)* [2006] 1 WLR 2305, per Baroness Hale of Richmond at 2308.

26 For instance, see *Re D (An Infant) (Adoption) (Parent's Consent)* [1977] AC 602 where it was stated that there was 'no general principle of dispensing with a parent's consent on the ground of homosexual conduct alone', at 629 per Lord Wilberforce. This proposition was also made by Viscount Dilhorne at 633, Lord Simon of Glaisdale at 640, Lord Kilbrandon at 641 and Lord Edmund-Davies at 647.

27 G v F (Shared Residence: Parental Responsibility) [1998] 2 F.L.R. 799, per Bracewell J at 805.

simply two people living in an enduring family relationship, regardless of their gender mix.[28]

Thus, great advances have be made following the decriminalisation of homosexual activity, which acted as the catalyst for subsequent developments in the recognition of homosexual parents through bringing such issues to the public and judicial conscience. Initially, such recognition was curtailed by fears over the perceived risks of contamination and stigmatisation which a child with a homosexual parent may suffer. However, after social and psychological research[29] disproved these theories, and it was highlighted how the use of the stigmatisation argument simply allowed one discriminatory act (homophobia in the community) to justify another (depriving homosexuals of parental rights),[30] the significance of these fears has dramatically diminished.

Alongside these developments, the social visibility of homosexual parents has also been aided by medical advances in assisted parenthood meaning that same-sex couples now have the opportunity not only to raise children from a previous relationship or to adopt a child but may also now plan to have children specifically within the context of their relationship.[31] Thus, lesbian couples have the option of one partner undergoing artificial insemination by donor[32] or they may even opt

---

28 See the Adoption and Children Act 2002, s 144(4) and the Adoption and Children (Scotland) Act 2007, s 29(3). Joint adoption is still restricted to married couples in Northern Ireland: see the Adoption (Northern Ireland) Order 1987 (S.I. 1987/2203 (N.I. 22)), ss 14–15. However, the 1987 Order does not preclude an individual adoption by a person living in a same-sex relationship and there is nothing in the Order which prevents a mother applying to adopt a child whilst also applying for a joint residence order along with their lesbian partner: see *Re M (Adoption: Joint Residence Order: Same Sex Couple)* [2004] NI 241.

29 For summaries of a number of different pieces of research in this field see, amongst others, McNeill K., "The (Lack of) Differences between Gay/Lesbian and Heterosexual Parents: A Review of the Literature", 4(1) *National Journal of Sexual Orientation Law*, 1998, available from http://www.ibiblio.org/gaylaw/; Murray C., "Same-Sex Families: Outcomes for Children and Parents", 34 *Family Law*, 2004, 136; Reece H., op cit (fn 13) and Tasker F. And Bellamy C., "Reviewing Lesbian and Gay Adoption and Foster Care: The Developmental Outcomes for Children", 37 *Family Law*, 2007, 524. However, see Stacey J. and Biblarz T.J., "(How) Does the Sexual Orientation of Parents Matter?", 66 *American Sociological Review*, 2001, 159 who, whilst agreeing that there are no substantial differences between the children of hetero- and homosexual parents, suggest previous studies have conceptual, methodological and theoretical limitations and suffer as a result of the charged political atmosphere, especially in the United States, in which they take place.

30 Boyd S., "What is a "Normal" Family?", 55 *Modern Law Review*, 1992, 269 at p. 274.

31 A similar pattern of development has also been identified as occurring in the United States, beginning in San Francisco, from the late 1970s onwards: see Polikoff N.D., "Recognising Partners but Not Parents/Recognising Parents but Not Partners: Gay and Lesbian Family Law in Europe and the United States", 17 *New York Law School Journal of Human Rights*, 2000, 711 at pp. 730–731.

32 For an example of such an occurrence, and the problems that may arise where the donor is known to the couple, see *Re D (Contact and Parental Responsibility: Lesbian Mothers and*

for *in vitro* fertilisation where the egg of one partner is fertilised outside the womb and then implanted into the other partner making the former the genetic mother and the latter the gestational mother of any child born through this technique. Alternatively, a gay couple may enlist the help of a surrogate in order to realise their desire to raise a child. However, homosexual couples still face many difficulties in this area including the fact that a provider of licensed infertility services is required to take account of the child's need for a father,[33] an obviously problematic requirement for a lesbian couple,[34] and the option of surrogacy is, by its nature, a heavily regulated, complicated and emotive area.[35]

3. CHANGING RECOGNITION AND ATTITUDES

Whilst decriminalisation and the resultant increase in the visibility and acceptability of homosexual parents goes some way towards explaining how these issues first came to be considered, they do not sufficiently explain *why* there has been such a pronounced ideological shift in a relatively short period of time. This change of attitudes and treatment is even more prominent in that it has occurred in an area as politically and emotionally sensitive as family law where change is often a long, laborious and drawn-out process.[36]

It has been stated that there is a 'network of social norms which is formally independent of the legal system, but which is in constant interaction with it'[37] although 'it is probably not now possible to separate out legal changes and social changes

Known Father) (No 2) [2006] 1 FCR 556. For discussion over a similar case in the Netherlands see Vonk M., "One, Two or Three Parents? Lesbian Co-Mothers and a Known Donor with 'Family Life' Under Dutch Law", 18 *International Journal of Law, Policy and the Family*, 2004, 103.

33 Human Fertilisation and Embryology Act 1990, s 13(5).

34 Whether this requirement should place a male same-sex couple in an advantageous position as the child will therefore have two fathers is not addressed by the legislation. See Wallbank J., "Reconstructing the HFEA 1990: Is Blood Really Thicker Than Water?", 16 *Child and Family Law Quarterly*, 2004, 387.

35 For instance, see the comprehensive review of United Kingdom surrogacy regulation: Brazier M., *Surrogacy: Review of Current Arrangements for Payment and Regulation* (Cmnd. 4068, 1998).

36 For example, compare the pace of change here with the length of time taken to modernise the law of divorce where reform was first suggested in England and Wales in 1990 (*Family Law: The Ground for Divorce*, (Law Com No 192, 1990)) and is still yet to be implemented and in Scotland in 1989 (*Report on Reform of the Grounds of Divorce*, (Scot Law Com No 116, 1989)) and then again in 1999 (*Improving Scottish Family Law*, Part II, pages 3–7 (Scottish Office, March 1999)) before the law was eventually changed by the Family Law (Scotland) Act 2006, ss 11–15.

37 Eekelaar J., "Uncovering Social Obligations: Family Law and the Responsible Citizen", in Maclean M. (ed), *Making Law for Families* (Hart Publishing, Oxford, 2000) 9 at p. 16.

and to identify one as leading the other – rather it is likely that they fed off and justified each other'.[38] However, it is suggested that there are three influences which could be argued as having a more significant impact in this area than most; firstly, the European Convention for the Protection of Human Rights and Fundamental Freedoms 1950[39], secondly, the changing structure and move from a status-based to a more functional definition of the family and, finally, the financial considerations which may underpin many of these seemingly altruistic developments of increasing recognition.

3.1. THE EUROPEAN CONVENTION OF HUMAN RIGHTS

The ECHR was signed and ratified by the United Kingdom in 1951 and incorporated into domestic law by the Human Rights Act 1998.[40] Section 3(1) of the 1998 Act requires all primary and subordinate legislation to 'be read and given effect in a way which is compatible with the Convention rights', 'so far as it is possible to do so'. Since these interpretational requirements were introduced they have had an unquestionable effect in a multitude of different areas with the influence within family law particularly evidenced by two cases concerned with succession to tenancies by a same-sex partner of the deceased tenant.

In *Fitzpatrick v Sterling Housing Association Ltd*[41] a same-sex partner of a deceased man tried to succeed to a protected tenancy under the Rent Act 1977. The Act provides that when a protected tenant dies the tenancy will be transferred to either his 'spouse' or a 'member of his family'.[42] The surviving partner claimed entitlement under both heads, failing under the former, as it was held that the word is necessarily limited to a partner of the opposite sex[43], but eventually succeeding (by a majority) under the latter.

Following this decision, in the case of *Ghaidan v Mendoza*,[44] it was held that 'living together as his wife or her husband' under Paragraph 2(2) of Schedule 1 of

38 Norrie K. McK., op cit (fn 13) p. 165.
39 Hereinafter, the 'ECHR'.
40 Hereinafter, the '1998 Act'.
41 [2001] 1 AC 27.
42 Rent Act 1977, Schedule 1, paras. 2 and 3 (as amended by the Housing Act 1988). There is a technical difference between the two claims in that a 'spouse' would succeed to statutory tenancy whilst a 'member of the family' would succeed to an assured tenancy, the former having a number of advantages over the latter. These provisions have now been amended to include surviving civil partners: see the Civil Partnership Act 2004, Schedule 8, para. 13(4).
43 [2001] 1 AC 27, per Lord Slynn of Hadley at 34, Lord Nicholls of Birkenhead at 43, Lord Clyde at 47, Lord Hutton at 57 and Lord Hobhouse of Woodborough at 69.
44 [2004] 3 All ER 411.

the Rent Act 1977 was to include the survivor of a same-sex relationship, something that the same court in *Fitzpatrick* had felt unable to do just three years earlier. It seems highly probable that this change in interpretation, in such a short period of time, can be attributed almost exclusively to the interpretational requirements of the 1998 Act, which were not applicable in the *Fitzpatrick* case.[45] Indeed, due to the interpretational flexibility provided by section 3(1), the court in *Fitzpatrick* felt it impossible to define same-sex partners as spouses, whereas Lord Rodger saw this recognition as only a 'modest extension' of the concept of a spouse.[46]

Conversely, whilst the above is an impressive example of the impact that the ECHR and the 1998 Act can have, its influence should not be overestimated, particularly in relation to the recognition of homosexual parents. For example, as long ago as 1977, even though attitudes towards homosexuality were decidedly negative, it was still explicitly stated that a natural parent would not be discriminated against in a decision affecting their child on the ground of their homosexual conduct alone.[47] In contrast, it was not until 2001 and the decision of *Salgueiro Da Silva Mouta v Portugal*[48] that similar principles were espoused by the European Court of Human Rights when it recognised that natural parents could not be discriminated against in residence disputes on the grounds of sexual orientation alone.

Moreover, the decision in *T, Petitioner*[49] rejecting discrimination against applicants on the grounds of their sexual orientation alone in the adoption process, coupled with the recent reforms to adoption legislation, have put the majority of the United Kingdom's constituent territorial units into the vanguard in the recognition of homosexual parents through the adoption process. These changes have been implemented without any recourse to ECHR jurisprudence where the European Court of Human Rights recently considered it 'quite natural' that 'the national authorities ... should enjoy a wide margin of appreciation when they are asked to make rulings' about the suitability of a single homosexual man – in contrast with a single heterosexual – to adopt a child.[50] The Court believed that in this context, 'delicate' issues were involved, that there was little common ground among the signatory states, and that the law appeared to be in a transitional stage when it came to adoption.[51]

45 Although the decision was given in 2001 the original tenant at the centre of the case had died in 1994.

46 [2004] 3 All ER 411 at 457. For a discussion of the application of the section 3 interpretational requirements in this case see Tomlinson E., "Same-Sex Relationships: Going with the Grain or Judicial Vandalism?", 63 *Cambridge Law Journal*, 2004, 577.

47 Re D (An Infant) (Adoption) (Parent's Consent) [1977] AC 602, see note 26 above.

48 (2001) 31 EHRR 47.

49 1997 SLT 724.

50 *Fretté v France* (Application No 36515/97) [2003] 2 FLR 9, at para. 41.

51 ibid. at paras. 41–42.

It is therefore apparent that, whilst the ECHR has played an important role in compelling the United Kingdom to take action in those areas in which, for whatever reason, it has lagged behind many other signatory states,[52] this is not the case in the recognition of homosexual parents. Whilst the ECHR guarantees a *minimum* level of protection for homosexual parents, the United Kingdom has by far surpassed these standards. Instead, the importance of the ECHR and the interpretational requirements of the 1998 Act is to be found in the flexibility it gives to the judiciary to interpret statutory provisions liberally, something they were previously constrained from doing. Thus, if the ECHR cannot solely be described as an explanation for changing attitudes in this area then attention must turn to the domestic law to consider what wider changes at a domestic level could have aided the recognition of homosexual parents.

3.2. CHANGING FAMILY STRUCTURE

Historically, the only family form accepted by society and recognised by the legal system was that founded upon a heterosexual marriage in which procreation of the biological children of both parties could be effected.[53] Only a man and woman who were lawfully married to one another as husband and wife had legally enforceable rights against and obligations towards the other.[54] Children born into these relationships were classed as legitimate and received preferential treatment whilst the hegemony of this marriage-centric approach was preserved through the law ignoring any other family forms in existence.[55]

In contrast to these traditional views there has been, in recent times, a steep decline in the number of people who choose to marry[56] along with a

52 Such as, for example, in relation to the recognition of the right of transsexual persons to marry in their acquired gender: see *Goodwin v United Kingdom* (Application No 28957/95) (2002) 35 EHRR 447 and the Gender Recognition Act 2004.

53 It has been said that 'marriage effectively served to define the family, since it was the fact that a child's parents were married which conferred on the child the status of legitimacy – in effect, recognition of the child's family relationship'. See Cretney S., Masson J. and Bailey-Harris R., *Principles of Family Law*, (Sweet and Maxwell, London, 2002) 7th Edition, p. 1.

54 In *The Ampthill Peerage* [1977] AC 547, Lord Simon of Glaisdale, at 577, described marriage as being 'the condition of belonging to a class in society to which the law ascribes peculiar rights and duties, capacities and incapacities'.

55 For example, see the comments of Lord Fraser that 'it is the policy of the law to discourage every other connection than that of marriage, by not acknowledging, as to any legal effect, the relations which spring from connections unsanctioned by marriage. The rights and privileges of husband and wife, of parent and child, it reserves for those who are known to the law in these relationships' in *The Law of Scotland Relative to Parent and Child and Guardian and Ward*, (W. Green, Edinburgh, 1906) 3rd Edition, p. 144.

56 In 2005 there was a total of 283,730 weddings in the United Kingdom which equated to a fall of nearly 10 per cent since 2004 when there were 313,550 weddings and substantially lower

corresponding increase in couples, either with or without children, who prefer to cohabit.[57] Furthermore, for those who do marry, there has been a substantial increase in the number of divorces[58] which has led to a preponderance of reconstituted families where children are primarily raised by someone other than their biological parent(s).[59] These factors have all resulted in a dramatic shift in attitudes, both social and legal, towards defining which social groupings can be classified as a family and what individuals can be recognised as fulfilling parental roles and have challenged the traditional view of the family to such an extent that it is no longer sustainable in modern discourse.

If a legal system, in light of these changing social patterns, continued to adhere rigidly to an outdated view of family law then it would quickly become irrelevant and unsuitable for reacting to and regulating the varied domestic arrangements in which people are now living. Instead, it would be nothing more than a punitive system which punished those, through the withholding of recognition, who did not meet its highly exclusive criteria. Thus, it is no longer justified to refuse to recognise new family forms in order to protect the 'traditional' family, whose legal standing and recognition will be unaffected by extending these same rights and responsibilities to others in similar situations.[60] As a result, there is now a more functionalist, rather than formalist, approach to family law which focuses upon how a relationship operates in reality rather than its precise legal status.[61] If there is evidence of love, affection, commitment and support then this will, regardless of the formal label attached to the relationship, provide clear evidence of a family unit.[62]

than in 1940 when there were 426,100 first-partner marriages in England and Wales alone: National Statistics Online, 21 February 2007, available at http://www.statistics.gov.uk/.

57 According to the General Household Survey 2005 the proportion of non-married women aged 18–49 who were cohabiting at the time of interview has increased from 11 per cent in 1979 to 29 per cent in 2005. Among single women, the proportion cohabiting had almost quadrupled from 8 per cent in 1979 to 31 per cent in 2005. These figures refer only to women as questions on marriage and cohabitation in the General Household Surveys were initially solely aimed at women meaning that only this group can be used to identify long term trends.

58 Although between 2005 and 2006 there was a decrease of 4.5 per cent in the number of divorces granted to 148,141 from 155,052 this number is still significantly higher than in 1961 when 27,200 divorces were issued in Great Britain: National Statistics Online, 30 August 2007, available at http://www.statistics.gov.uk/.

59 According to Social Trends 37 (2007), in 2005 there were 136,000 children under sixteen whose parents divorced in England and Wales and more than 10 per cent of all families with dependent children in Great Britain were step families.

60 Although the court in *Karner v Austria* (Application Number 40016/98) (2004) 38 EHRR 24 did accept that the protection of the traditional family was still a legitimate and weighty reason this was with the caveat that any differential treatment must be proportional and justified.

61 See Minow M.L., "Redefining Families: Who's In and Who's Out?", 62 *University of Colorado Law Review*, 1991, 269.

62 Fitzpatrick v Sterling Housing Association Ltd [2001] 1 AC 27, per Lord Nicholls at 44.

In juxtaposition to this increasing acknowledgement and appreciation of a variety of family forms, there has been a reconsideration of what the term 'parent' encompasses, what this status entails, and which individuals are suitable to be defined as such. Along with it being no longer sustainable to focus exclusively on the traditional family it has also become necessary to abandon the limited view of a parent in purely biological terms. Instead, an adherence to a strict legal and biological definition has been replaced with a need to understand which people actual fulfil vital roles in relation to children within modern families.[63] Along with the genetic parents, it is now acknowledged that social, psychological and gestational parents may play an equally, or even more, prominent role in the life of a child. Although there still remains some bias in favour of the natural parent, such as the need for compelling reasons before a child will be removed from the primary care of his or her biological parents, this is no longer the weighty presumption that it once was.[64] Instead, it is now much more important to understand how a child actually lives, who they consider to be important figures in their life, and to allocate parental status, rights and responsibilities accordingly.

These changing attitudes and definitions have been of particular importance in the claims for recognition by homosexual couples raising children as one partner will always, by definition, fail any strict biological test of parenthood. Moreover, even if such recognition was not forthcoming, it is unlikely that this would discourage homosexual parents from raising children. However, it would prevent such children from enjoying the security of a legally recognised relationship, and the associated benefits of such relationship, with their de facto parent, who may be a much more important figure in their life than a biological parent. Aside from psychological and emotional support, which will be present regardless of legal recognition, such recognition will place upon a parent a responsibility economically to support a child and this highlights the third factor relevant in this area: the financial considerations underpinning the changing nature of family law and the increasing recognition of homosexual parents.

3.3. FINANCIAL CONSIDERATIONS

As has been explored, the acceptance of which social groupings can constitute a family has changed markedly over time from a marriage-monopolistic position towards a more inclusive approach. However, before this family label can be applied, there are still a number of factors which are seen as integral to its very nature. These include such things as love, care, commitment, the sharing of

63 See Bainham A., "Who or What is a Parent?", 66 *Cambridge Law Journal*, 2007, 30.

64 *Re G (Children) (Residence: Same Sex Partner)* [2006] 1 WLR 2305.

responsibilities, emotional support and, perhaps most importantly, the idea that a family will form a single economic unit with a pooling of financial resources in which the members will financially provide for and support one another. Further, where there are children of the family, their parents, however defined, will both be expected to support the child, emotionally and economically.

Whilst the family unit and its constituent members coexist happily this economic support, much like its emotional counterpart, will usually be taken for granted and enjoyed without reservation. Once the relationship comes to an end, however, it will be the loss of this economic support which may well cause the greatest long-term problems for at least one of the now ex-partners. These problems are particularly acute in relation to children, who are unavoidably dependent upon those who have assumed a parental role in their life until they reach adulthood and are capable of supporting themselves. For the child, this reliance will not be dependent upon whether an individual is biologically related to them, what status they are ascribed by the law, or what relationship this person has with another parent.

In light of this, it is generally accepted that, when considering continuing economic support for children, those who have previously fulfilled a parental role in the child's life should continue to provide such support. If they neglect to provide this support then the state will be justified in adopting measures to enforce their personal responsibilities and to compel them to adhere to their familial commitments. As the determination of what constitutes a 'family' and who can be identified as a 'parent' is often determined through the principles of family law this means that family law definitions regularly act as the gatekeeper for apportioning rights and responsibilities, including those of a financial nature, in relation to children.

If family law persevered with a traditional view of the family, and an undue emphasis on biological parenthood alone, this approach would ignore the large number of partners who had formed less traditional familial relationships and also any parent who had brought up children other than their genetic offspring. Homosexual parents would be immune to claims for aliment from the children they had raised with their partner, and also free of any other legal constraints enforcing continuing financial responsibility, if the law refused to recognise them as a parent in the context of a same-sex relationship.[65] The significance of this potential lack of financial liability would be that, if a child or ex-partner did require continuing economic assistance, it is likely that this claim would have to be redirected towards the state and the public purse.

---

65 See Norrie K. McK., "We Are Family (Sometimes): Legal Recognition of Same-Sex Relationships After", *Fitzpatrick*, 4 *Edinburgh Law Review*, 2000, 256.

Thus, whilst the expansion of familial concepts and parental definitions has evidenced a growing recognition for same-sex families and homosexual parents these changes have also resulted in a large expansion in the number of people who fall within the ambit of some of the key terms for determining financial responsibility. By furnishing homosexual parents with familial and parental recognition the state is not only reacting to social changes but also increasing the number of people who can be relied upon to provide private financial support if and when necessary. In other words, individual aspirations of homosexual parents to receive full legal recognition have become increasingly congruent with the state's desire to privatise economic dependency.[66]

Such an approach is not a new phenomenon. For example, the Child Support Act 1991 removed decisions in relation to maintenance from the compass of judicial discretion as judges were considered to be too lenient in their awards. Moreover, in a large number of cases these awards were either completely ignored or the aliment was paid erratically. Instead, in order to enforce more efficiently private financial responsibilities towards children, a Government agency took charge and facilitated the administrative application of a fixed formula to calculate maintenance payments.[67] Although in hindsight it is clear that this system has disintegrated into an inefficient failure[68] the specific policy underlying its introduction, namely a desire to enforce personal responsibilities, reduce social security spending and protect the public purse, remains as influential today as it was in the past.

A consideration of the recognition of homosexual parents also highlights the influence of such financial considerations. Thus, in *Re P (A Minor) (Custody)*,[69] where a lesbian mother was granted custody of her child as a final alternative before the child was placed in local authority care (the father's preferred course of action), what could have influenced the ranking of a lesbian household, for which

66 As Norrie has pointed out, these developments provide a strange irony in that the law is adhering to a right-wing model of society, where the role of the state is limited in light of an emphasis on individual responsibility, but the means of achieving this are to reject the right-wing adherence to the notion of the traditional family and embrace more left-wing philosophies of functional families and the recognition of homosexuals: see Norrie K. McK., op cit (fn 13) p. 169.

67 For a discussion on the policy background to the 1991 Act see Maclean M., "The Making of the Child Support Act of 1991: Policy Making at the Intersection of Law and Social Policy", 21 *Journal of Law and Society*, 1994, 505.

68 The Child Support Agency, which was formed following the Child Support Act 1991 to trace the non-resident parent, to assess how much s/he should pay in maintenance, to provide a collection service if required and to enforce payment if necessary, has recently been heavily criticised in a damning report in which it was described as one of the greatest public administration disasters of recent times: House of Commons, Committee of Public Accounts, Child Support Agency: Implementation of the Child Support Reforms, 37th Report, HC 812.

69 (1983) 4 FLR 401.

the judge had an obvious disdain, above that of state care? It is suggested that, no matter the negative view of homosexuality still prevalent in both society and the legal system, the enforcement of a lesbian mother's responsibilities towards her child was still regarded as a more worthy cause than the condemnation of homosexuality and would also prevent the care of the child falling upon the state.[70]

Furthermore, the decision of *T, Petitioner*[71] in its rejection that it was a fundamental question of principle whether homosexual individuals should ever be able to access the adoption system had the additional consequence of confirming the homosexual community as abundant pool of adopters, recognition of whom would help remove responsibility for the caring of children away from state supported institutions. These financial considerations may have had a particularly strong influence in this case as the child in question had a number of special needs and required a high (and expensive) level of care and attention, something the applicant in question was ideally suited to provide. Thus, in light of these circumstances, any concerns over the sexual orientation of the adopter and his living arrangements were significantly outweighed by the special circumstances of the case and the financial benefits of finding the child a home outwith local authority care.

Financial motivations influencing the adoption process can also be identified in the United States, which has generally evidenced a more receptive attitude to homosexual parents adopting children than in other countries.[72] For example, the first adoption of a child by a natural parent's same-sex partner occurred in Alaska in 1985 when the United Kingdom judiciary was concurrently grappling with issues over whether a lesbian mother should even be allowed to care for their natural child following the breakdown of her relationship with the father.[73]

---

70 In the New South Wales case of *W v G* (1996) 20 Fam L. R. 49 (NSW) a former lesbian partner refused to continue to provide financial support for a child born to her ex-partner through donor insemination during their relationship. The court was able to enforce her financial responsibilities through the utilisation of a common law doctrine: discussed in Millbank J. and Sant K., "A Bride in Her Everyday Clothes: Same-Sex Relationship Recognition in NSW", 22 *Sydney Law Review*, 181, pp. 209–210. Similarly, the protection of the public purse was held to be an important consideration by the Canadian courts in the lesbian spousal support case of *M v H* (1999) 171 DLR (4th) 577.

71 1997 SLT 724.

72 For a comparison between the approach of the United States to that of Europe see generally Polikoff, op cit (fn 31) and for a specific comparison between the Netherlands and the United States see Maxwell N.G, Mattijssen A.A.M and Smith C., "Legal Protection For All Children: Dutch-United States Comparison Of Lesbian And Gay Parent Adoptions", 17 *Arizona J. Int. & Comp. L.*, 2000, 309 (also available in the *Electronic Journal of Comparative Law*, vol. 3.1 (August 1999)).

73 Compare *In re* A.O.L. No. 1JU-85-25-P/A (Alaska 1st Jud. Dist. July 23, 1985) (cited from Maxwell N.G. et al, ibid. p. 315) and *Re P (A Minor) (Custody)* (1983) 4 FLR 401.

Such financial considerations are immediately apparent when considering adoptions by homosexual parents, whether individually or as a couple. Within the United States, where health care and support is primarily private and there is far less public assistance than in the United Kingdom, the adoption of a child will provide a number of significant economic consequences including social security benefits and coverage under a parent's private health insurance policy.[74] Therefore, the recognition of homosexual parents aids the public interest in permitting such a person to be accountable for the child's financial support instead of dependence falling upon government funding. Further, financial repercussions can also be identified when it is considered that, in many states, if a person is not a legal parent then that person is treated, in the eyes of the law, as a stranger to the child.[75] Unlike in the United Kingdom where parental rights and responsibilities may be granted to a variety of persons other than parents,[76] adoption has become the primary means in the United States by which to ensure a de facto parent will be financially responsible for a child, thereby reducing the chances that the state will have to supplement the upbringing of a child in economic terms.[77]

Once gay men and lesbians are recognised in individual adoptions it then becomes difficult, if not impossible, to maintain a categorical position against homosexual parents in the adoption process at a more general level. Thus, when considering the adoption process on a more macro-level, the influence of financial considerations can again be seen. Due to the problems of a shortage of adoptive parents in relation to the large number of children in the foster care system[78] there is now an appreciation that homosexual parents can go some way to address this shortfall and that, in this context, entirely to exclude any group of people from adopting would be a financially undesirable prospect. Indeed, the financial disincentive to enforce moral attitudes towards homosexual parents in the adoption process is particularly emphasised by a recent report which suggested that a country wide ban on homosexual foster care in the United States could cost between $87 and $130 million.[79] These financial implications are even more pessimistic as it is

74 In the Matter of Jacob 660 N.E.2d 397 at 399.

75 See Maxwell N.G. et al, op cit (fn 72) pp. 343–344.

76 For example, in Scotland an application in relation to parental responsibilities, parental rights, guardianship or the administration of the child's property may be made by any person claiming an 'interest': see the Children (Scotland) Act 1995, ss 11(3)(a)(i) and (ii).

77 See Maxwell N.G. et al, op cit (fn 72) pp. 344–348.

78 For example, on 30 September 2005 it is estimated that there were 513,000 children in foster care, 114,000 of these were waiting to be adopted with 24,395 of this figure having been in continuous foster care for five years or more: see the Adoption and Foster Care Reporting and Analysis System, *Preliminary Estimates for FY 2005 as of September 2006*, AFCARS Report No. 13.

79 See Gates G., Badgett L.M.V., Macomber J.E. and Chambers K., *Adoption and Foster Care by Lesbian and Gay Parents in the United States*, The Urban Institute (Research Report), March 2007.

believed that homosexual parents are particularly likely to care for children with special needs or those who have been particularly difficult to place in the past.

Accordingly, through a combination of changing social and legal attitudes, and the more mundane influence of financial necessity, concepts of 'family' and 'parent' have been reconsidered with the result that homosexual parents are now recognised within the United Kingdom without any negative assumptions made about their sexuality. Whilst the identification of financial considerations as an important aspect in this recognition may seem unduly cynical in a family law context, such motivations are perhaps not as questionable as one may first presume. Thus, family law is generally a system of redistributing property and protecting individuals within the family unit, whether this be on breakdown of the relationship or the death of one of the partners. Consequently, equality is advanced by assimilating same-sex partners and parents to the same onerous economic responsibilities to each other and their children as their opposite-sex counterparts, even if this does benefit the public purse whilst placing increased economic responsibility upon private individuals. As one writer has commented, equality requires taking the rough with the smooth.[80]

4. CONCLUSIONS

When considering the recognition of homosexual parents and the position of children in same-sex families it is imperative that such a child receives the same level of protection, whether this be emotional, legal, financial, or otherwise, as children in other family forms are entitled to. To deny, as a class, children of homosexual parents the security of a legally recognised relationship with their parents cannot be justified and serves no legitimate public interest. Further, if social prejudice were grounds for restricting the right to be a parent generally, and not just in relation to homosexual parents, then an extremely limited pool of adults would be able to qualify as parents. Moreover, if the legal system were to deprive a child of any of these protections due to the sexual orientation of their parent(s), or the lack of a biological relationship between them, then this would undoubtedly contravene the welfare principle and the approach that the best interests of the child should always be the paramount consideration.

It is vital that the legal protection provided to a child reflects the reality of their life and, therefore, if a homosexual person is carrying out a parental role then the legal system should acknowledge this. Only through the legal recognition of the child's emotional and social reality will their best interests be respected. Even if

80 Norrie K. McK., op cit (fn 13) 170.

recognition were withheld this would not act as deterrent against the existence of same-sex families but would place a child in a seriously disadvantaged position, both emotionally and financially, in relation to their parent(s). In addition, granting legal rights and respect to gay parents and their children should help lessen the remaining stigma that it has some opponents suggests they currently suffer from, send a strong message of acceptance to society and also help remove any other problems it has been argued are associated with being raised by homosexual parents.

Whilst much focus has been placed upon the increasing liberal interpretation of what constitutes a family, something influenced by financial implications, the limits to this approach must also be emphasised. Thus, the redefining of familial and parental concepts should only go as far as is necessary to reflect the changes which have occurred in society. The state should not be allowed to provide over inclusive definitions simply to shift burdens onto private individuals where such regulation does not accurately and fairly reflect how people live their lives, a point which is of equal relevance to both opposite- and same-sex couples. In all circumstances there needs to be a legitimate and rational connection between the responsibilities imposed and the reality of the parent-child relationship.

Within the United Kingdom homosexual parents have now achieved almost total equality with their heterosexual counterparts. Now that this position has been reached the next challenge in this area will be for the law to decide whether positive steps could or should be taken to assist gay and lesbian men and woman in their desire to become parents. Movements can already be seen in this area with the Government's refusal, despite strong opposition, to allow Catholic adoption agencies an exemption from anti-discrimination laws[81] when considering applications from homosexual adopters. Further, in consideration of the fact that homosexual parents are disadvantaged in being unable naturally to procreate, should there be a reconsideration of the law in relation to artificial insemination and surrogacy in order to make access to such treatments and arrangements easier for same-sex couples who want to start a family?

However the law develops from this point onwards it is evident that the United Kingdom presently provides much more expansive recognition for homosexual parents and protections for their children than many other countries, both within Europe and around the world. Nonetheless, there is still room for further recognition and it seems likely that financial implications will have some role to play in these developments.

81 See the Equality Act 2006.

TOWARDS A NEW CONCEPT OF PARENTHOOD: PROCREATIONAL RESPONSIBILITY

Machteld Vonk

1. INTRODUCTION

This paper focuses on the legal position of children born into families where only one of the parents is genetically or biologically related to the child. This includes children born into same-sex families as well as children born into different-sex families.[1] The subject is approached from a comparative legal perspective and covers two jurisdictions: England[2] and The Netherlands. The paper aims to answer the question of what are the implications for children *born into* these families if their current legal position is assessed on the basis of the notion that

- a child's family situation deserves legal protection;[3] and
- a child should have the possibility to acquire two legal parents.[4]

---

1 This paper is an adaptation of the final chapter of the author's PhD thesis *Children and their parents: a comparative study of the legal position of children with regard to their intentional and biological parents under English and Dutch law*, Antwerp - Oxford: Intersentia, 2007. For more detail on the subject-matter discussed in section 2 of this paper refer to Chapters 3 to 6 of the aforementioned book.

2 English law is a formal 'term of art' that describes the law in force in England and Wales. See the England and Wales Interpretation Act 1978, Schedule 1. Hereinafter, references to England will mean England and Wales.

3 The ECtHR has established that there may be family life between a child and a non-biological parent *X.Y.Z. v. United Kingdom*; it is however unclear what the exact position of the ECtHR is concerning the relationship between same-sex parents with regard to family life. In *Karner v. Austria* the court stated that "Where the Contracting States' margin of appreciation was narrow, [...] the principle of proportionality between the means employed and the aim sought to be realized did not merely require the measure chosen to be suitable for realising the aim; it also had to be shown that it was necessary to exclude homosexual couples from the scope of the legislation in order to achieve that aim." See M v. Secretary of State for Work and Pensions [2006] UKHL 11 and Wikeley (2006) p. 542–547 for the position under English law. See Forder (2002) p. 992–995 for a discussion of Dutch case law on the question whether there can be family life between same-sex partners and their children. Also Forder & Saarloos (2007) p. 65–74.

4 This is inherent in both legal systems. A child may not always automatically acquire two legal parents, but in both jurisdictions there is the possibility to have the legal parenthood of a

These two notions are derived from the presumption that it is inherent in the legal systems of the two jurisdictions that children in so-called typical families with a biological mother and a biological father *do* have the opportunity to acquire two legal parents (legal parenthood) and that their family situation *is* adequately protected (parental responsibility). In both jurisdictions the law is in a transition from a parent-centred family law to a child-centred family law. In line with this transition the focus must shift from the differences between the parents to the equivalent nature of the needs and rights of the child. In this context it may be relevant to consider the following quote from NUSSBAUM:

> "Human beings have a dignity that deserves respect from laws and social institutions. This idea has many origins in many traditions; by now it is the core of modern liberal democratic thought and practice all over the world. The idea of human dignity is usually taken to involve an idea of equal worth: rich and poor, rural and urban, female and male, all are equally deserving of respect, just in virtue of being human, and this respect should not be abridged on account of a characteristic that is distributed by whims of fortune. Often, too, this idea of equal worth is connected to an idea of liberty: to respect the equal worth of persons is, among other things, to promote their ability to fashion a life in accordance with their own view of what is deepest and most important."[5]

It is in essence the dignity of the child, in this case the child born into an atypical family that deserves respect.[6] This respect is best expressed in the law not by stressing the fact that the child's legal position vis-à-vis his or her parents cannot be the same as that of the overall majority of children because his or her parents are not the same as those of the overall majority of children, but by departing from the notion that all children should have the most favourable legal position in life.[7]

This paper will answer the above question with regard to the legal position of children in a family with one biological and one non-biological parent (section 2). First, the child's options to acquire two legal parents will be discussed (section 2.1) and then the child's legal position in his or her family (section 2.2). In section

---

biological parent established. This notion is confirmed in the Children's Convention in article 7 which concerns the child's right to know and be cared for by his or her parents.

5 NUSSBAUM (1999), p. 5.

6 In this paper a typical family consists of two biological (and genetic) parents and their child(ren); an atypical family is a family with one biological and one non-biological parent or a family with two non-biological parents.

7 RAWLS (1971) p. 302. In Rawls' theory of justice social and economic inequalities are to be arranged so that they are to the greatest benefit of the least advantaged, See for the implications of Rawls' theory of justice in parent-child relationships DWYER (2006) p. 106–122 for the theoretical underpinnings of relationship rights for adults and p. 123–169 for the relationship rights of children.

2.3 a possible explanation for the differences and similarities between the two jurisdictions will be provided and section 2.4 will briefly introduce the proposals made in the two jurisdictions with regard to same-sex parenthood. Section 3 will introduce a new concept of legal parenthood: *procreational responsibility*. In order to provide the framework for this concept the three legal dimensions of the child's family circle are explained in section 3.1. Subsequently, the notion of *procreational responsibility* is expanded upon in order to seek a solution to the deficiencies encountered in the law in this area (section 3.2). The new concept will then be applied to the legal position of children in families with one biological and one non-biological parent and to surrogate families (section 4). The paper will close with some recommendations on how to proceed in amending existing legislation in this field (section 5).

The majority of this paper is concerned with children born into different-sex families and female same-sex families, simply because children cannot be born *into* male same-sex families. The male couple will have to engage a surrogate mother to conceive and give birth to a child which is genetically related to one of the male partners. The position of children in surrogate families will be summarily discussed in section 3.3.3. However, where relevant, reference will be made to the position of children in male same-sex families. In both jurisdictions the legal position of children in same-sex families is at present subject to (advanced) legislative activity, where relevant proposals in this field will be discussed.[8]

2. THE LEGAL POSITION OF CHILDREN IN A FAMILY WITH ONE BIOLOGICAL PARENT AND ONE NON-BIOLOGICAL PARENT

2.1. THE CHILD'S OPTIONS TO ACQUIRE TWO LEGAL PARENTS

Children in different-sex and female same-sex families

In both legal systems, children will in general have the possibility to acquire two legal parents. In some cases they will acquire them automatically and in some

8 In England the HFE Bill which contains far-reaching amendments to the present HFEA 1990 was introduced in the House of Lords on 8 November 2007. In The Netherlands the Commission on lesbian parenthood and international adoption (Commissie Kalsbeek) published its report on lesbian parenthood on 31 October 2007. The government will consider the recommendation of the Committee and possibly introduce a Bill on this topic in parliament.

cases they acquire one automatically and may acquire another.[9] The systems in the two jurisdictions are largely in accordance with the following notion expressed in the Council of Europe's White Paper on principles concerning the establishment and legal consequences of parentage: "It should be underlined that it is in the best interests of the child, first of all, to establish *parentage* as from the moment of the birth and, secondly, to give stability over time to the established *parentage*."[10] Hence the White Paper leaves room for social factors to prevail over biological factors: "The law may opt not to allow the *parentage* to be established on the basis of biological affiliation, for instance in cases of medically assisted procreation with an anonymous donor of sperm."

That having been said, how about the possibilities for children with one biological parent and one non-biological parent to acquire two legal parents? The system in England with regard to this question is clear-cut. In principle all children have the possibility to acquire two legal parents. Children born into a marriage will have two legal parents by operation of law; children born outside marriage may have the legal parenthood of their biological or HFEA parent[11] established by means of a declaration of parentage.[12]

The one exception to this rule is the child conceived with donor sperm in accordance with the HFEA 1990 by a single mother or a mother in a same-sex relationship.[13] In the first case there is no other legal parent available because the biological father is a sperm donor in accordance with the HFEA 1990 and is thus protected from any claims by children conceived with his sperm. In the second case the child can neither establish the legal parenthood of the sperm donor nor the legal parenthood of the intentional non-biological second parent, because this parent is also a woman. This means that the child is entirely dependent on the willingness of the co-mother to adopt. If the co-mother does not adopt there is no possibility for the child to establish the parenthood of this co-mother, despite her role in planning the conception and her implicit or explicit consent.

---

9 Vonk (2007) p. 39–90.

10 *Report on principles concerning the establishment and legal consequences of parentage – "The White Paper"* as adopted on 11–14 May 2004 by the CDJD.

11 An HFEA parent is a parent who is to be treated as the child's legal parent pursuant to the parenthood provisions in the HFEA 1990.

12 Vonk (2007) p. 147–206.

13 This is also true for a child conceived by means of post-mortal procreation. The name of the child's father may be registered on the birth certificate, but this has no legal consequences (HFEA 1990 s. 29(3B)(a) and (b)). In effect such a child has only one legal parent. The HFE Bill does not propose to change this situation.

In The Netherlands the situation is less clear.[14] This is due to the distinction that is made in Dutch law between *begetters* and *sperm donors* which is based on the question whether or not the biological father has had sexual intercourse with the birth mother. Children born into a different-sex marriage will have two legal parents by operation of law. Children born into any other kind of relationship will *not* have two legal parents by operation of law. Children may establish the legal parenthood of a *begetter*, a man who has had sexual intercourse with their mother. If there is no *begetter* the child may establish the legal parenthood of his or her mother's life partner if this partner consented to an act that may have resulted in the conception of the child. The legal parenthood of a sperm donor cannot be established by the child, unless he was the mother's consenting life partner.

The child conceived with donated sperm outside of a different-sex marriage may establish the legal parenthood of his or her mother's partner, if this partner is a man and he consented to the conception with donated sperm. If the partner is a woman her legal parenthood cannot be established regardless of her consent to the conception and her relationship with the child's mother. If there is no consenting male life partner, and the sperm donor did not have sexual intercourse with the child's mother, the child cannot establish the legal parenthood of a second parent. On the other hand, where the conception occurred outside marriage through intercourse with a third party with the consent of the mother's male life partner, the child has a choice whose legal parenthood he may establish, provided of course that the legal parenthood of the biological father has not already been established.

This means that in The Netherlands where a single woman or a woman in a relationship with another woman (whether married, in a registered partnership or in a non-formalised relationship) makes use of sperm donation (without sexual intercourse) the child cannot establish the legal parenthood of a second parent. The only means by which the birth mother's female partner can become the child's legal parent is through adoption. However, if the co-mother is unwilling to adopt the child, the child cannot make her a legal parent against her will.

In conclusion, with regard to the legal position of children in families with one biological parent and one non-biological parent, one can say that almost all children in different-sex families have the possibility of acquiring two legal parents, whereas this is not true for children in same-sex families.

---

[14] Vonk (2007) p. 147–206.

Children in male same-sex families

Since children in male same-sex families are born into another family, they have at least one legal parent outside their family. Their legal position within their resident family can only be secured by the transfer of legal parenthood from the family of their birth to the family in which they are being raised. This is an issue that is covered by the provisions on surrogate families and adoption and will not be discussed here.

2.2. PROTECTION OF THE CHILD'S POSITION IN HIS OR HER FAMILY

Children in different-sex and female same-sex families

The protection of these children in their families has two sides. On the one hand, it concerns the recognition of the fact that the child has a biological parent outside his or her resident family, and, on the other hand, the legal protection of the child's position in his or her *resident* family. This protection entails that the child's resident parents have the rights and duties to take care of the child on a daily basis; in practice this means that they will have parental responsibility.[15] On the basis of the study carried out in this book and the subsequent analysis, the question may be answered whether such protection exists in the two jurisdictions at present.

With regard to the first issue: both jurisdictions have introduced legislation which ensures that children conceived with donor sperm during assisted conception services have a right to information concerning the person and the identity of the donor of the genetic material. A register has been set up in both jurisdictions to store this information. Furthermore, both jurisdictions also recognise that a child has a right to know his or her biological/genetic history outside the context of assisted conception services. However, there is no register where such information is collected and children very much depend on what their parents tell them.

---

15 It will be attempted to find a solution with the concepts that operate within the present system of the law. Creating in-between statuses may lead to first-class and second-class parents. As has been established in English case law with regard to unmarried fathers, it is important for the child that this parent is given a seal of approval. See for instance *Re S (Parental Responsibility)* [1995] 2 FLR 648; *Re H (Parental responsibility)* [1998] 1 FLR 855 and *Re C and V (parental responsibility)* [1998] 1 FLR 392, CA (a parental responsibility order is independent from a contact order).

The second part of the question concerns the legal protection of the child's resident family. There is a distinction between children born in a formalised relationship and children born in a non-formalised relationship. In The Netherlands all married parents and parents who have entered into a registered partnership will have parental responsibility with regard to the children born into their relationship, unless the child already has a legal parent outside the marriage or the registered partnership. Children born in non-formalised relationships will have one parent with parental responsibility ex-lege: namely their birth mother. The birth mother's partner may acquire parental responsibility, but the complexity of this process depends on his or her sex. A male partner may recognise the birth mother's child and subsequently register joint parental responsibility in the parental responsibilities register with the birth mother. A female partner may only acquire parental responsibility with regard to the child by court order on her joint request with the birth mother, or by means of adoption.

In England a child born into a marriage will have two parents with parental responsibility. A child born into a civil partnership or in a non-formalised relationship will not automatically have two resident parents with parental responsibility. The non-biological parent in the child's resident family may acquire parental responsibility, but how this may be done depends on the sex of this parent and the status of his or her relationship with the mother and the child. The birth mother's male partner (provided he is an HFEA father) may register on the child's birth certificate with the mother's consent and will subsequently acquire parental responsibility. Alternatively, he may also enter into a parental responsibility agreement with the child's mother or apply for a parental responsibility or a residence order. The birth mother's female partner, provided she has entered into a civil partnership with the child's mother, may enter into a parental responsibility agreement with the child's mother and apply for a parental responsibility order or a residence order. A female partner who has not entered into a formalised relationship with the child's mother may apply for a residence order with maternal consent or without consent if she has lived with the child for three years or if the court gives her leave to do so.

In both jurisdictions the parental responsibility acquired by the non-biological parent does not cease upon separation. It may be terminated by court order (except in England if the non-biological parent is a legal parent and in both jurisdictions in the case of adoption), but only subject to the child's interests.

In conclusion, one may say that the position of the child in a family with one biological parent and one non-biological parent is well protected in The Netherlands in those cases where the child is born into a formalised relationship. Furthermore, children born into non-formalised different-sex families receive a higher measure of protection than children in non-formalised same-sex families. In both cases the parents need to undertake certain action to acquire parental responsibility, but this is more complex for same-sex parents than it is for different-sex parents. This is partially due to the fact that the male partner of the child's mother has access to the status of legal parent on the basis of his sex whereas a female partner has no access to the status of a legal parent outside the possibility of adoption.

In England there is only parental responsibility by operation of law for children born into marriage. With regard to all other children, also those born into a civil partnership, the parents need to undertake certain action to acquire parental responsibility with regard to the children born into their relationship. The nature of the action that needs to be undertaken depends on whether the mother's birth partner is a legal parent, a same-sex parent in a formalised relationship or a same-sex parent in a non-formalised relationship. The first two kinds of parents may acquire parental responsibility without court intervention, the last kind of parent cannot.

Children in male same-sex families

In England male same-sex partners who have entered into a civil partnership may jointly acquire parental responsibility with regard to the children they raise in their family by entering into a parental responsibility agreement with the child's birthmother, provided one of the men is the child's biological father.[16] Furthermore, they may acquire parental responsibility on the basis of the fact that the child has been living with them for a certain period of time. In The Netherlands male same-sex partners who have entered into a formalised relationship (either marriage or a registered partnership) will not automatically acquire parental responsibility over the children they raise in their family, since the child always has a legal parent outside the relationship of the male couple, namely the birth mother. Moreover, it is not possible for them to acquire joint parental responsibility as long as the child's mother holds parental responsibility.

16 This is a two-step process: the biological father will first enter into a parental responsibility agreement with the birth mother (s. 4 CA 1989). Subsequently, the biological father's male partner may enter into a parental responsibility agreement with the birth mother and the biological father (s. 4A CA 1989).

2.3. POSSIBLE EXPLANATION FOR THE DIFFERENCES AND SIMILARITIES BETWEEN THE JURISDICTIONS

When trying to explain the differences in the approach taken in the two jurisdictions towards securing the legal position of the child, the differences between common law and civil law play an important role in the case of *legal parenthood*. Traditionally, legal parenthood is in both jurisdictions based on biology. In the approach taken by the English system this basis remains more or less intact because legal parenthood not based on biology is regulated in a specific piece of legislation. Due to the lack of statutory interference in the field of legal parenthood, the English legislature was able to provide for a completely enclosed statutory framework to operate alongside, and instead of, the existing common law rules. In The Netherlands adaptations to developments in society in this area have to be made within the existing framework of the Dutch Civil Code. This means that legal parenthood for non-biological parents is regulated in the same Title in the DCC that also regulates legal parenthood for biological parents. Amendments in this area touch upon the very heart of the Dutch law on legal parenthood.

The differences in the field of *parental responsibility* are less likely to be explained by the common law-civil law dichotomy. It is far more likely that an explanation is to be found with the fact that both jurisdictions are in the middle of a process of transforming from the traditional parent-centred approach to a child-centred approach. An element of this process is the recognition of non-legal parents who have a child in their care. This has resulted in a loosening of the connection between legal parenthood and parental responsibility.[17] Such parents may not become legal parents but they may be attributed with parental responsibility. How and at what pace the transition from a system that assigns children to parents to a system that assigns parents to children is made may in part be determined by the legal system, but also by politics, pressure groups and other factors.[18]

Both jurisdictions are striving to give greater recognition to intentional parents and other social parents; however, the aim and underlying considerations of legislative changes, and thus the results, may differ. A prominent example in the

---

17 With regard to English law, for instance, Woelke (2006) p. 100 who states that with the introduction of the Children Act 1989 "the question of parents' status or relationship has become secondary and the welfare of the child has become paramount in questions surrounding all aspects of what was once called custody. As a result the law in England has to some extent been flexible enough to adapt to changing family structures."

18 See for instance Antokolskaia (2006) p. 452: "At the same time, neither can the diversity of present-day filiation laws be regarded as merely being diverse in the technical aspect of the chosen solution. That is to say, this diversity is based on dissimilar political choices made with regard to the position of the parents, rather than merely a matter of dissimilar legal means to reach similar ends."

field of parental responsibility is the fact that in The Netherlands registered partners acquire parental responsibility with regard to a child born into their relationship and civil partners in England do not. This difference is a consequence of the fact that in England no distinction has been made between children born during the civil partnership and children born in a relationship prior to the current civil partnership. Since in the latter case the child may very well have a legal parent with parental responsibility outside this civil partnership, an automatic attribution of parental responsibility to the parent's civil partner is not advisable.

Despite the fact that both jurisdictions are in the process of moving from a parent-based to a more child-oriented system, it has become obvious from section 2.1 and 2.2 that the legal position of children in a number of families with one biological parent and one non-biological parent is still far from optimal, in particular where children in same-sex families are concerned. They have no possibilities to acquire a second legal parent and their parents will not always be able to acquire parental responsibility. Is it just that a child, through no actions or choices of his or her own, is from the moment of his or her birth in a position which is less favourable than the majority of his or her peers? With regard to children born outside marriage this question has been answered in the negative,[19] but with regard to children born into same-sex relationships the answer has not been unequivocally negative.

The argument against legal parenthood by operation of law for a consensual non-biological mother is that such automatic parenthood fails to take into account the possible parenting intentions of the biological father.[20] This is in itself a reasonable argument and indeed the parenting intentions of the biological father, if they exist, need to be considered; but only in those cases where such intentions do exist. Nevertheless, when considering the intentions of the biological father and the means by which they may be taken into account, it should be kept in mind that article 3(1) of the Children's Convention requires the interests of the child to be the primary consideration in *any* actions undertaken, including those undertaken by legislative bodies.

2.4. BILLS AND PROPOSALS REGARDING SAME-SEX PARENTHOOD

In both jurisdictions serious attempts are being made to enhance the legal position of same-sex parents with regard to the children they raise in their family. In England these attempts are at a very advanced stage and concern the legal posi-

19 See ANTOKOLSKAIA (2006) p. 443–453.

20 For example for The Netherlands *Dutch Second Chamber* 26 672/26 673 no. 15 p. 7.

tion of children being raised in female same-sex families and of children being raised in male same-sex families. On 8 November 2007 the HFE Bill which contains numerous amendments to the present HFEA 1990, including provisions that would grant the birth mother's female partner the status of legal parent by operation of law given that a number of requirements are met, was introduced in the House of Lords. If the female couple have entered into a civil partnership, the female partner will be attributed with the status of legal parent by operation of law provided that use has been made of assisted conception services.[21]

Furthermore, clause 43 of the HFE Bill proposes to grant female partners who have *not* entered into a civil partnership the same position as different-sex partners in a non-formalised relationship who make use of assisted conception services, by introducing so-called 'agreed female parenthood conditions'. These conditions require both the prospective mother and her female partner to notify the 'person responsible'[22] in writing of their consent to the female partner being treated as the child's legal parent. Furthermore, the conditions require that neither party has withdrawn consent at the time the embryo, the sperm and eggs, or sperm are placed in the woman, nor has the woman indicated that she wishes another person (male or female) to be regarded as the child's legal parent.[23] The woman and the female partner may not be within the prohibited degrees of consanguinity in relation to each other. If either of the parties withdraws consent, the other party must be informed. Withdrawal of consent, either by the woman or the female partner, will not prevent the woman from continuing the treatment.

The HFE Bill which seeks to amend the status provisions of the HFEA 1990 to provide for legal parenthood for the mother's female partner by operation of law also includes amendments to the parental responsibility provisions in the CA 1989. The mother's (female) civil partner will acquire parental responsibility if the civil partner is to be treated as a parent by virtue of c. 42 of the HFE Bill. Furthermore, where the child was born before the couple entered into a civil partnership and the mother's female partner was at that time regarded as the child's parent pursuant to c. 43 of the HFE Bill, the female partner will be attributed with parental responsibility upon entering into a civil partnership with the mother.[24]

The HFE Bill contains provisions with regard to the attribution of parental responsibility to female couples who have not entered into a formalised

21 Cl. 42 HFE Bill.

22 The 'person responsible' is the person under whose supervision licensed activities are carried out. See the Explanatory Note attached to the HFE Bill, p. 30.

23 Cl. 44–45 HFE Bill.

24 Section (2)1A(a) and (b) CA 1989 to be inserted after section 2(1) if the HFE Bill is accepted. In practice this is equivalent to the legitimacy provisions in relation to marriage.

relationship. The female partner who is to be treated as a parent pursuant to c. 43 of the HFE Bill will be granted the same possibilities with regard to the acquisition of parental responsibility as an unmarried father: i.e. automatic parental responsibility upon registration on the birth certificate; entering into a parental responsibility agreement with the birth mother or applying for a court order.[25] Furthermore, where a residence order is made in favour of such a female partner, the court will also make a parental responsibility order pursuant to the proposed section 4ZA if the female partner does not already have parental responsibility.[26]

Furthermore, the HFE Bill proposes to amend the provisions for the transfer of parental rights after a surrogacy arrangement, the parental order of s. 30 of the HFEA 1990, in such a manner as to make male and female same-sex couples and cohabiting couples eligible for a parental order, provided one of the partners of the commissioning couple is genetically related to the child and all the other conditions have been met.[27]

In The Netherlands proposals to strengthen the legal position of children in same-sex families are restricted to the position of children growing up in female same-sex families and have not yet resulted in a Bill being introduced in parliament. In May 2007 the government set up a Commission on lesbian parenthood and international adoption which has to investigate how the legal position of co-mothers with regard to their partner's children can be improved outside the realm of adoption. The committee recommended in its report of 31 October 2007[28] that co-mothers be granted more or less the same legal position with regard to the children born during their relationship with the birth mother as an unmarried consensual non-biological father. In practice this means that a co-mother will not become a legal parent by operation of law, whatever the status of her relationship with the birth mother, but that she may become the child's legal parent by means of recognition if the birth mother consents. Furthermore, the child and the birth mother will be granted the possibility to have the legal parenthood of the co-mother established by court.

---

25 S. 4ZA CA 1989, to be inserted after section 4 if the HFE Bill is accepted.

26 S. 12(1A) CA 1989 to be inserted after s. 12(1) if the HFE Bill is accepted.

27 Cl. 54 HFE Bill.

28 Commissie Kalsbeek (2007).

3. PROCREATIONAL RESPONSIBILITY

In order to conceive of a system that takes into account the child's interests in a solid legal position on the one hand, and the possible parenting intentions of both the consensual parent and the biological father on the other, the notion of *procreational responsibility* may be used. In order to establish the framework in which this notion may function, it is necessary to first introduce the three legal dimensions of the child's family circle.

3.1. THE LEGAL DIMENSIONS OF THE CHILD'S FAMILY CIRCLE

It is relevant at this point to take a closer look at the three legal dimensions of the child's family circle, namely: *biological parenthood*, *legal parenthood* and *parental responsibility.*

I. The first dimension concerns the biological and/or genetic parenthood of the child. In the overall majority of cases this dimension will contain two parents: a biological father and a birthmother, but since the introduction of IVF this dimension may contain an additional mother, namely a genetic mother.
II. The second dimension: *legal parenthood* may only contain two parents in both England and The Netherlands; these parents may or may not be the child's biological or genetic parents.
III. The third dimension: parental responsibility may consist of only two parents in The Netherlands and more than two parents in England; these parents may be legal parents or non-legal parents.

Taking into account the role played by these dimensions in the present provisions on parent-child relationships and subsequently expanding on them somewhat, the following functions may be assigned to the different dimensions. Dimension I on genetic/biological parenthood (*afstamming*) is concerned with safeguarding and registering the child's biological/genetic history. This dimension will in principle give access to the dimension of legal parenthood, unless the law provides otherwise, for instance in the case of egg donation and some forms of sperm donation. Dimension II on legal parenthood (*ouderschap*) is concerned with assigning legal parents to children. Legal parenthood, among other things, has consequences for the child's financial position in life, for his or her nationality and for his or her position with regard to inheritance law. This dimension is no longer exclusively reserved for genetic and biological parents.[29] Dimension III on parental responsibility is concerned with ensuring that the parents who are caring for the child have the rights and duties associated with this task.[30]

The separation of the three dimensions makes it possible to recognise the role played by different parents in the child's life. The child's biological/genetic history can be protected because the non-biological legal parent and the donating biological parent will both be present in the child's family. Whether this presence is limited to the fact that the person-identifying information of this biological parent is accessible to the child at a later date, depends on the intentions of the parents involved and the child's interests. Furthermore, the separation of the three dimensions also allows for the possibility to increase the number of persons who may hold parental responsibility with regard to a child, since parental responsibility is not necessarily connected with legal parenthood.[31]

The recommendations made in this paper are based on the 'two legal parent model', since this model has for a long time had a satisfactory application for the overall majority of children.[32] This means that where there are tensions between biological and consensual non-biological parenthood, choices have to be made between possible legal parents. Depending on the circumstances and the interests of the child either the biological parent or the intentional parent will be the child's legal parent. The point of departure should be, however, that the child's position in his or her resident family will be protected, and third parties outside this resident family will be recognised in such a manner that the interest of the child is best served.

---

29 As Bainham (1999) p. 44, concludes on this issue: "It could have been exceptionally neat and tidy to say that those with a proven genetic connection are the parents and everyone else gets parental responsibility and no more. But this is not the course we have followed in England and it is too late to turn back now."

30 See CEFL reports on England Lowe (2005) and The Netherlands Boele-Woelki, Schrama & Vonk (2005), for the specific content of parental responsibility in the two countries and the CEFL principles with regard to a common approach Boele-Woelki et al. (2007b).

31 In The Netherlands the two dimensions have been partially disconnected but this has not resulted in changes in the number of persons who may have parental responsibility. In England more than two persons may have parental responsibility with regard to a child.

32 Recently Schwenzer has proposed a system in which a child would only acquire one legal parent by operation of law, namely the birth mother. The legal parenthood of the other parent may be established with maternal consent or by court order, subject to the child's interest. Schwenzer (2006) articles 3.4 to 3.10.

3.2. EXPLANATION OF THE NEW CONCEPT OF PROCREATIONAL RESPONSIBILITY

Having made a distinction between genetic/biological parenthood *(afstamming)* and legal parenthood *(ouderschap)*, the question must be asked what is the exact delineation between biology-genetic parenthood and legal parenthood on the one hand, and intentional parenthood and legal parenthood on the other. In order to answer this question it will be useful to take a closer look at the concept of *procreational responsibility*. This responsibility has two sides: responsibility before conception and responsibility after conception.

Procreational responsibility before conception is concerned with the personal integrity of the child to be conceived. This entails ensuring that the child's genetic/biological history is available for the child at a later date, and being aware of the fact that the story surrounding his or her conception and birth must be accessible and acceptable to the child. Furthermore, this responsibility before the child's conception involves considering who will have what position in the child's life when a known donor is used. Not everything can be foreseen, but these things need to be thought through beforehand.

Procreational responsibility after conception concerns the responsibility for the child during its life and is the basis for attributing legal parenthood to a parent. It is based on the idea that those persons who are responsible for the conception of the child, either because they are a biological parent or because they planned and arranged for the conception of the child, should be responsible for the child during his or her life. The child must be able to depend on the fact that this responsibility may become operational in practice. This means that it must be possible to establish a legal relationship between the child and the parent on the basis of the parent's responsibility by giving this parent the status of a legal parent. Whether this attribution is automatic and how possible conflicts between biological parents and intentional parents should be resolved will be discussed in the next section.

When applying the concept of *procreational responsibility* to the contemporary regulations, it becomes obvious that the beginnings of this system are already present in both jurisdictions. However, as was concluded earlier there are a number of situations in both jurisdictions where only the *procreational responsibility* of the birth mother is recognised and other parents, be they biological or intentional, are safeguarded from responsibility in the form of legal parenthood. Intentional parents who are willing to take on this responsibility may do so under certain circumstances, with the consent of the birth mother, but the child him or herself cannot establish the legal parenthood of these parents.[33] Can this problem be solved through bringing the law into line with the idea of *procreational responsibility*? This is the topic of the next section on the legal position of children in families with one biological parent and one non-biological parent.

4. APPLICATION OF THE CONCEPT OF PROCREATIONAL RESPONSIBILITY

4.1. CHILDREN BORN INTO RELATIONSHIPS WITH ONE BIOLOGICAL PARENT AND ONE NON-BIOLOGICAL PARENT

If the concept of *procreational responsibility* is applied in the law on legal parenthood there are in principle three parents available to fill the two legal parent slots: the birth mother,[34] the biological father and the intentional parent. The law determines or should determine which two parents will fill these two slots.[35]

In the contemporary English system a distinction has been made between donations and assisted conception treatment covered by the HFEA 1990 and donations outside the scope of the HFEA 1990. Under the HFEA 1990, the donor's intention *not* to parent and the consensual parent's intention to parent result in the status of a legal parent being attributed to the consensual parent. In all cases not covered by the HFEA 1990, the biological father is the child's (potential) legal father. The result of this system is that the child may always acquire two legal parents, except where fertility treatment in accordance with the HFEA 1990 has been provided to a single woman.

In the light of the concept of *procreational responsibility* it may be questioned whether assigning the status of a legal parent to a party outside the child's resident family, who may or may not have parenting intentions, is the most appropriate

33 To use the words of Archard (1995) p. 104: "The developments I mentioned at the outset – in household forms and in reproductive technology – mean that we need to be much clearer than we presently are about the principles which should inform the formation of families. If blood does not matter, or matters far less than is presumed, it is crucial that we can agree what should matter." Apparently blood in these cases does not matter, but an alternative has not been sought.

34 It has to be noted that the birth mother need not be a genetic parent but she is a biological parent by dint of giving birth.

35 A birth mother is automatically a legal parent even if she is not the child's genetic mother. Unless otherwise indicated, the following sections concern the position of a sperm donor.

choice. However, this is a question to be answered by the English legislature. Assigning legal parenthood to non-biological parents outside the scope of the HFEA 1990 would mean a radical break with the aims of the HFEA 1990.

In addition to further developments in this field in England, it may be worthwhile to adopt the approach taken in The Netherlands and to strengthen the position of children in same-sex families by attributing joint parental responsibility to civil partners with regard to the children born during their civil partnership. Furthermore, it may be made easier for unmarried same-sex couples to acquire joint parental responsibility with regard to the children born during their relationship. Proposals to this end have been made in the HFE Bill with regard to co-mothers who are to be treated as legal parents pursuant to cl. 42 or 43 of the Bill.

The Dutch system is far less clear-cut. If each child is to have the possibility of acquiring two legal parents, there are two options. Firstly, a system akin to the English system could be adopted. This would mean that a clear distinction is made between a donor from a clinic, who may for instance be referred to as a *genetic* father, and non-clinic donors, who will fall into the larger group of *biological* fathers. Only the donors who donate to a clinic would be exempted from any rights and duties with regard to the child. All non-clinic donors would be regarded as biological fathers whose legal parenthood may be established by the child. Secondly, the notion of intentional parenthood that is already present in the law where different-sex couples are concerned, could be expanded to include same-sex parents. The system under the second course of action could take two forms based on whether the donor's intentions are taken into account.

4.1.1. Legal parenthood for intentional parents without evaluating the donor's intentions

Attribution *without* regard to the intentions of the donor is the course followed in Dutch law at present where married different sex-couples are concerned. Extending this presumption of parentage in all formalised relationships would result in a simple, clear provision on the legal parenthood of children born into any kind of formalised relationship regardless of the sex of the parents. [36] With regard to children born outside a formalised relationship, the position of the intentional parent (male or female) with regard to legal parenthood should be the same as

36 This has been proposed by Henstra (2002) with regard to married same-sex couples and by Wortmann (1998) for same-sex couples in a registered partnership. See also Rosato (2006) p. 74–86 on the United States who argues that children in same-sex families "deserve the security blanket of the parentage presumption."

that of a biological father.[37] This means that either the child, the intentional parent or the child's birth mother can establish his or her legal parenthood.

However, a disadvantage of such a system would be that it leaves no room for the evaluation of the donor's intentions with regard to the child. Furthermore, such automatic attribution does not provide an opportunity to ensure that any person-identifying information about the donor is available for the child at a later date.

4.1.2. *Legal parenthood for the intentional parents with regard to the intentions of the donor*

The second option concerns a system which makes it possible to evaluate the intentions of the donor. Three different scenarios need to be considered with regard to the intentions of the donor:

1. Double consent in a clinical setting; this means that the donor has consented to the use of his or her genetic material by third parties and the mother's partner has consented to the use of this material for the conception of a child by his or her partner. [38] This consent has been given in a clinical setting, which means that DIY donation and insemination at home are not included.
2. The known sperm donor has consented to the use of his sperm and will relinquish his parental right to the non-biological parent. The non-biological parent has consented to the use of this genetic material by his or her partner to conceive a child. This concerns cases of DIY donation and insemination at home.
3. There is the consent of the partner of the non-biological parent to the use of third party genetic material by his or her partner for the conception of a child. However, there is no clarity about the donor's intentions with regard to the child's legal parenthood, either because the donor is not known (e.g. sperm has been purchased on the internet) or because the donor is unwilling to relinquish his parental rights to the non-biological parent.

The distinction made between situations 1 and 2 is the distinction already made under English law between an HFEA donor[39] and a DIY donor (who is a legal father in terms of common law). This distinction as such is not made in Dutch law.[40] The position of the donor may be clarified in Dutch law if the sperm donor

37 Henstra (2002) p. 180–181 proposed automatic parenthood for the same-sex partner married to the birth mother, and recognition for the unmarried same-sex partner.

38 With regard to egg donation and the consent of the egg donor only the first situation is relevant, since egg donation always takes place in a clinical setting.

39 Schedule 3 HFEA 1990.

40 However, in a Bill concerning adoption that is currently before the Dutch parliament a beginning is made by distinguishing between known and unknown donors. It is proposed in this

who donates to a sperm bank is referred to as a genetic father and the other kinds of donors are given a position akin to a *begetter*.

If there is double consent, either because the donation and treatment have taken place in a hospital (situation 1),[41] or the biological and intentional parents have agreed that the child to be conceived will grow up in the family of the birth mother and her partner (situation 2), the birth mother and the intentional parent will be the child's legal parents.[42] In such a system it is vital that there is proof of the parents' intentions and the donor's consent, to be produced when the child's birth is registered.[43] Such proof may for instance consist of consent forms signed at the clinic[44] or a contract drawn up between the parties involved.[45] In case of conflict or in case there is no proof of the donor's intention, the intervention of a court may be required to decide on the legal parenthood of the child involved. Such a procedure need *not* be an adoption procedure but may be a new kind of procedure aimed at establishing the legal parenthood of the child in line with the child's best interests. It is not necessarily in the child's interest that the legal parenthood of the biological parent is established, although this may be the case under certain circumstances.[46] It is also very important to consider the child's position in his or

Bill that a co-mother who produces a declaration by the Donor Data Foundation stating that use has been made of the sperm of an unknown donor, may in principle adopt her partner's child. *Dutch Second Chamber* 2006–2007, 30 551 1–7.

41 Wortmann (2001) p. 235–236 stated that adoption was not appropriate in same-sex relationship if use had been made of an unknown donor.

42 The status of the consent given is a subject for further research. Consent given in a hospital after being informed of the consequences of such consent (informed consent) is not the same as consent given outside a clinical setting. This latter consent may or may not be informed consent.

43 The Civil Code of Québec (CCQ) makes it possible for a non-biological parent, either male or female, to acquire the status of a legal parent if the parties have entered into a so-called 'parental project' for assisted conception, which is defined as the situation "when one person, or spouses by mutual consent, decide to conceive by relying on genetic material donated by a third party." Campbell (2007) p. 254.

44 In The Netherlands proof of the consent of the donor could take the shape of a declaration by the Donor Data Foundation that the child concerned was conceived with the sperm of an unknown donor. In a proposal concerning adoption that is currently before the Dutch parliament such a declaration is also mentioned with regard to the adoption of a child by the birth mother's female partner. *Dutch Second Chamber* 2006–2007, 30 551, no. 1–8.

45 Further research into the status of contracts regarding parent-child relationships is required, in particular the standing of such a contract in case of conflict. Donor contracts or consent forms are sometimes used by courts in adoption proceedings to obtain clarity about the donor's intention. See, for instance, Rechtbank Utrecht, 13 December 2006, *LJN*: AZ7383 or Rechtbank Utrecht, 13 December 2006, *LJN*: AZ7379. For an example of the use of donor contracts by an Australian court see Dempsey (2004) p. 76–102.

46 Shanley (2001) p. 146 "Providing children with stability and care is among the most pressing needs of contemporary [...] society. The primary source (although not the only one) of such stability and care is a child's family."

her resident family and the wider family circle of the two resident parents.[47] Recognition by the law of the child's family situation may facilitate the child's integration into his or her wider family and into society itself.

An advantage of this system is the fact that the donor's intention may be taken into account. Moreover, it makes it possible to require that the person-identifying information is made available upon registering the birth so that this information can be stored for instance in the donor data register for the child's future use.

Whatever choice is made, the point of departure should be that if there are three persons responsible for the conception of a child: the birth mother, the biological father and the female partner of the birth mother, it cannot be that the child can only have one legal parent. It should be possible to establish the legal parenthood of one of the two other responsible parents, either the biological father or the intentional mother. If the law shields the biological parent from responsibility in any form with regard to the child, it cannot at the same time prevent the intentional parent from becoming the child's legal parent. It cannot be so that both are excluded from legal parenthood because of the existence of the other. Furthermore, as is stated in article 7 of the Children's convention, a child has a right to be raised and be cared for by his or her parents. If one accepts that on the basis of the notion of *procreational responsibility* parents are not only biological parents, but may also be intentional parents, one must conclude that the law is obliged to make it possible for a child to acquire two legal parents.

4.2. CHILDREN IN SURROGATE FAMILIES

The notion of *procreational responsibility* may also play a role in the context of surrogate parenthood. First of all, because *procreational responsibility* before conception requires the parties to consider the consequences of the arrangements about to be made. With regard to responsibility after the child is born there is a major difference between surrogacy and the assisted conception with donor sperm discussed in the previous sections. In the latter case it is the intention that the child remains in the family into which it was born, whereas in the case of surrogacy the intention is that the child will be transferred from the family of its birth to another family. The intention of the commissioning parents and the sur-

47 Archard (1995) p. 105 "It is important to be clear that natural parents have a claim to bring up their own children only because such an arrangement is optimal. It is not the case that the arrangement is thought best because natural parents have a prior claim to rear their own. This is the crucial point. For, when there is a dispute over who should rear a child, the claim of the natural parent to have custody over her own does not carry weight simply in virtue of the existence of the biological relation. Blood as such does not matter."

rogate parents plus the question of who is genetically related to the child may play a part.

With regard to surrogacy a distinction should be made between three types of surrogacy:

1. surrogacy arrangements where the commissioning parents are both genetically related to the child carried by the surrogate mother (gestational surrogacy);
2. arrangements where one of the commissioning parents is genetically related to the child carried by the surrogate mother (gestational or traditional surrogacy depending on whether the egg is provided by the surrogate mother);
3. and cases where neither of the commissioning parents are genetically related to the child carried by the surrogate mother (gestational or traditional surrogacy depending on whether the egg is provided by the surrogate mother).

In the first case, the surrogate mother is not genetically related to the child, but in the second and third case she may be, but need not be if use is made of a donated egg. This means that if the concept of *procreational responsibility* is applied with regard to the attribution of legal parenthood, the concept needs to accommodate a third variable besides biology and intention, namely genetic parenthood. In cases where the commissioning mother's egg is used, she is the genetic and intentional mother whereas the surrogate mother is the biological mother.

In England the commissioning parents in situations 1 and 2 can become the child's legal parents by means of a parental order if a number of conditions are met, one of these being that the surrogate parents consent to the transfer of parental rights. In the recently published HFE Bill it is proposed to expand the group of commissioning parents who are eligible for a parental order to include female and male same-sex couples and co-habiting couples.[48] In The Netherlands there are no provisions specifically designed for the transfer of full parental status in surrogacy cases. Since surrogacy is allowed under certain conditions, a provision akin to a parental order may be considered, in particular in cases where both the commissioning parents are genetically related to the child. At present such surrogacy arrangements are allowed under supervision after extensive screening, but the commissioning parents are left completely in the dark with regard to their possibility of becoming the child's legal parents.

Nevertheless, the most difficult cases are those in which conflicts arise with regard to the child. In those circumstances the concept of *procreational responsibility*

48 Cl. 54 HFE Bill.

may play a role in that it allows for intention to be a fundament for assigning legal parenthood.[49] A commissioning couple who are both genetically related and the intention to become the child's parent may from this point of view have a stronger claim than a surrogate mother who is not genetically related to the child.

5. HOW TO PROCEED?

The situation in England, if the changes to the HFEA 1990 proposed in the HFE Bill become law, would protect the position of children born into families with one biological and one non-biological parent in those cases where the parents have made use of assisted conception services in accordance with the HFEA 1990. Whether the proposed cl. 42, which concerns the legal position of the birth mother's civil partner, also covers the situation where use was made of sperm donated *outside* the ambit of the HFEA is not entirely clear. It is advisable that this is made clear during the remainder of the legislative course of the HFE Bill. Where a female couple who have *not* entered into a formalised relationship make use of sperm donated outside the ambit of the HFEA 1990, the situation is clear: cl. 43 of the HFE Bill does not apply. In those cases the common law rules will be applicable. Co-mothers who are to be treated as legal parents pursuant to cl. 42 or 43 will obtain joint parental responsibility either *ex lege* or upon registration on the birth certificate.

Changes in the legal position of children conceived with donor sperm outside the context of the HFEA 1990 may be slow to come. It may require legislation outside the context of fertility treatment. Nevertheless, other changes may be made to enhance the child's legal position where the intentional parent is not recognised as a legal parent. For instance, by extending the applicability of the 'child of the family' provisions to couples in an enduring family relationship.[50] Thus, after the breakdown of the relationship the intentional parent who is not a legal parent may still be liable for child maintenance.

In The Netherlands changes are required to the Dutch Civil Code if it is to be brought into line with the notion of *procreational responsibility*. This may be done by further integrating new regulations with regard to children conceived with third party genetic material in the already existing provision. However, for the sake of clarity it may be advisable to regulate the legal position of these children separately.

---

[49] Steinbock (2006) p. 108–115.

[50] S. 105(1) CA 1989.

First of all, Title 11 of Book 1 of the Dutch Civil Code which is currently entitled '*parentage*' (*afstamming*) should be renamed 'legal parenthood' *(juridisch ouderschap)*.[51] Subsequently, a new Title, Title 11a, should be inserted which regulates legal parenthood with regard to children conceived with third party genetic material. This new title would include provisions based on the same concepts as are used in Title 11, such as recognition, judicial establishment of legal parenthood and denial of legal parenthood. Furthermore, it should also contain provisions on issues such as consent to the conception of the child and the donor's consent to the use of his genetic material by a third party. It may contain a new definition of the concepts of sperm donor (*genetic father*) and biological father as suggested earlier on in this paper. And last but not least, it should contain a provision which ensures that a child has the right of have access to his or her genetic/biological history.

If intentional parents become legal parents with the cooperation of the child's birth mother they should be attributed with parental responsibility.[52] However, where the intentional and biological parent becomes a legal parent without the cooperation of the birth mother, such a parent will have to apply to a court to be attributed with parental responsibility.

Moreover, it may also include provisions on the transfer of parental status pursuant to surrogacy arrangements, where one or both of the commissioning parents are genetically related to the child concerned. It may in this context be advisable for the legislature to make an inventory of developments taking place in England, but also in Sweden,[53] New Zealand[54] and Canada[55] and possibly other counties that have or are in the process of introducing similar legislation in this field.

The recommendations of the Commission on lesbian parenthood[56] are a step in the right direction but do not meet all the criteria set out above. The advantage of *not* opting for automatic legal parenthood for the co-mother is that it will remain possible for lesbian couples to share parenthood with the child's biological father. However, in the present proposals there is virtually no room to take the intentions of the biological father/donor into account where these are not the same as the intentions of the mother(s). Furthermore, little to no effort has been made to

---

51 In Dutch: Titel 11: Juridisch ouderschap; Titel 11a: Juridisch ouderschap bij gebruik van genetisch materiaal van derden.

52 The CEFL suggest that legal parents should have parental responsibility, Boele-Woelki et al. (2007b) principle 3:5.

53 See for instance Jänterä-Jareborg (2006) for the present situation in Sweden.

54 See for instance Atkin (2006) p. 311–317 on the situation in New Zealand.

55 See Campbell (2007) p. 242–273 for the situation in Quebec.

56 Commissie Kalsbeek (2007).

ensure that the child will have access to his or her biological/genetic history once he or she has reached the age of majority.

In conclusion, it may be said that despite the fact that serious efforts are made to enhance the legal position of children in same-sex families in both jurisdictions, the proposals are not entirely compliant with the concept of *procreational responsibility*. In England the position of children born after DIY donation in a non-formalised female same-sex relationship remains unchanged. Furthermore, the legal position of children born after DIY donation in a civil partnership needs further clarification. In The Netherlands the recommendations made only concern children born into female same-sex families and do not consider the legal position of children growing up in male same-sex families. If legislative reform in this area is approached with the underlying notion in mind that a child deserves the most favourable legal position in life and in his or her family, it may be so in the near future that the family is truly made to fit the child and not the child to suit the family.

BIBLIOGRAPHY

Antokolskaia (2006): M. Antokolskaia, *Harmonisation of Family Law in Europe: A historical perspective, A tale of two millennia*, Antwerp – Oxford: Intersentia.

Archard (1995): D. Archard, What's blood got to do with it? The significance of natural parenthood, *Res Publica*, vol 1.1. p. 91–106.

Bainham (1999): A. Bainham, 'Parentage, Parenthood and Parental Responsibility: Subtle, Elusive Yet Important Distinctions', in Bainham, Sclater & Richards (eds) (1999), *What is a parent? A socio-Legal Analysis*, Oxford: Hart Publishing, p. 25–46.

Atkin (2006): B. Atkin, 'Landmark family legislation in New Zealand', in A. Bainham, *International survey of family law 2006 edition*, p. 305–320.

Boele-Woelki, Schrama & Vonk (2005): K. Boele-Woelki, W.M. Schrama, & M.J. Vonk in: Boele-Woelki, K., Braat, B. & Curry-Sumner, I., *European family law in action Volume III: Parental responsibilities*. Antwerp: Intersentia.

Boele-Woelki et al. (2007b): K. Boele-Woelki, F. Ferrand, C. González Beilfuss, M. Jänterä-Jareborg, N. Lowe, D. Martiny & W. Pintens, *Principles of European family law regarding parental responsibilities*, Antwerp: Intersentia.

Campbell (2007): A. Campbell, Conceiving parents through law, *International Journal of Law, Policy and the Family*, vol. 21. p. 242–273.

COMMISSIE KALSBEEK (2007) COMMISSIE LESBISCH OUDERSCHAP EN INTERNATIONALE ADOPTIE, *Lesbisch ouderschap.*

DEMPSEY (2004): D. DEMPSEY, Donor, father or parent? Conceiving paternity in the Australian Family Court, *International Journal of Law, Policy and the Family*, vol, 18, p. 76–102.

DWYER (2006): J.G. DWYER: *The relationship rights of children*, Cambridge: Cambridge University Press.

FORDER (2002): C.J. FORDER: Het mensenrechtelijke hart van het familierecht: overzicht van de ontwikkelingen 1995–2002 (Deel I), *NJCM,-Bulletin*, vol 27, nr. 8, p. 992–1011.

FORDER & SAARLOOS (2007), C.J. FORDER & K. SAARLOOS, 'The establishment of parenthood: a story of successful convergence?' In ANTOKOLSKAIA (ed) (2007), *Convergence and divergence of Family Law in Europe*, Antwerp – Oxford: Intersentia, 169–235.

HENSTRA (2002): A.E. HENSTRA, *Van afstammingsrecht naar ouderschapsrecht. Een beschouwing over de positie van sociale en biologische ouders in het familierecht*, (thesis), Den Haag: Boom Juridische Uitgevers.

JÄNTERÄ-JAREBORG (2006): M. JÄNTERÄ-JAREBORG, 'Parenthood for same-sex couples: Challenges for private international law from a Scandinavian perspective' in ERAUW, TOMLJENOVIĆ & VOLKEN (2006), *Liber Memorialis Petar Šarčević: Universalism, Tradition and the Individual*, München: Sellier European Law Publishers, p. 75–91.

LOWE (2005): N. LOWE in BOELE-WOELKI, K., BRAAT, B. & CURRY-SUMNER, I. *European Family Law in Action Volume III: Parental Responsibilities*. Antwerp: Intersentia.

NUSSBAUM (1999): M. NUSSBAUM, *Sex & social justice*, New York – Oxford: Oxford University Press.

RAWLS (1971): J. RAWLS, *A theory of justice* (original edition), Cambridge: Harvard University Press.

SCHWENZER (2006): I. SCHWENZER, *Model Family Code from a global perspective*, Antwerp – Oxford: Intersentia.

SHANLEY (2001): M.L. SHANLEY, *Making babies, making families: What matters most in an age of reproductive technologies, surrogacy, adoption and same-sex and unwed parents*, Boston: Beacon Press.

STEINBOCK (2006): B. STEINBOCK, 'Defining parenthood', in: SPENCER & DU BOIS-PEDAIN (2006): JR. SPENCER & A. DU BOIS PEDAIN, *Freedom and responsibility in reproductive choice*, Oxford and Portland Oregon: Hart Publishing, p. 107–128.

VONK (2007): M. VONK, *Children and their parents: a comparative study of the legal position of children with regard to their intentional and biological parents under English and Dutch law*, Antwerp – Oxford: Intersentia

WIKELEY (2006): N.J. WICKELEY, Same sex couples, family life and child support, *Law Quarterly Review*, vol. 122, p. 542–547.
WOELKE (2006): A. WOELKE, *Civil partnership: law and practice*, London: The Law Society.
WORTMANN (1998): S.F.M. WORTMANN, *Als een eigen kind*, inaugural speech at the University of Groningen.
WORTMANN (2001): S.F.M. WORTMANN, Sekseneutraal afstammingsrecht?, *Tijdschrift voor familie- en jeugdrecht*, p. 231–236.

PART THREE
IRREGULAR MARRIAGES AND THE INFLUENCE OF MULTICULTURALISM

"TO AFFINITY AND BEYOND": A CRITICAL ANALYSIS OF THE LAW ON MARRIAGE WITHIN PROHIBITED DEGREES OF RELATIONSHIP

MAEBH HARDING

1. INTRODUCTION

Since antiquity marriage has been prohibited between persons related by marriage or blood ties. As the right to marry becomes a stronger and more established concept in international law, the restriction on marriage have become increasingly scrutinised. The article will look at the origin of the prohibited degrees of relationship as a restriction to marriage in Ireland, England and Wales and France. It will examine to what extent the rules have become distanced from the modern idea of kinship. The article will also question the purpose of such restrictions and query whether the pursuit of these goals justifies the non-recognition of irregular marriages celebrated by those within the prohibited degrees.

2. HISTORICAL BEGINNINGS OF THE PROHIBITED DEGREES OF RELATIONSHIP

Canon law laid down prohibitions to marriage if the parties were too closely related to each other. These prohibitions to marriage were based on consanguinity and affinity. The prohibitions based on consanguinity forbade marriage between parties related by blood, while the prohibitions on affinity forbade marriage between people related by legal or spiritual ties.[1] These restrictions on marriage were based on Leviticus xviii 7–13 and xx 17, 19 which prohibited marriage or sexual relations between and man and his mother, granddaughter, aunt by

[1] When a couple married they were considered to be 'of one flesh' by canon law. Thus a wife's blood relatives were considered from then on to be a related to the husband as his own blood relatives. Marriage to any of these affinal relatives was governed by the same rules as for blood relatives. In addition, it was not permitted for a person to marry their godparents or any blood relatives of their godparents. See A. SERIAUX, *Droit Canonique*, PUF 1996, n228.

blood on either side, sister or half sister. Parties who married within these degrees were subject to ecclesiastical censure and their marriages were declared void.

The scope of the canon law prohibition on marriage changed over the centuries.[2] A system of dispensations developed to allow those who had converted to Christianity to remain married even though their marriages were not necessarily in compliance with canon law. Under current canon law, marriage within the degrees of consanguinity is invalid in the direct line and up to the fourth degree in the collateral line.[3] What this means is that man cannot marry his parent, grandparent and so on in ascending order. Nor can a man marry his child, grandchild and so on in descending order. This is the direct line. The collateral line concerns those who have a common ancestor such as a man's sister, aunt or cousins. What is prohibited under this impediment is marriage between those who are first cousins or more closely related. Dispensations can be granted for marriages between first cousins and for marriages between an uncle and niece or aunt and nephew but only for very grave reasons.[4]

The scope of the prohibition based on affinity has also changed in the history of the Church. Originally affinity could be created by sexual intercourse alone. However, the 1917 Code of Canon law changed the basis of the impediment to a valid, ratified marriage even if the marriage was not consummated. This meant that one's spouse's relatives became equivalent to blood relatives by marriage alone. Since the introduction of the 1983 code of Canon law, marriage is only prohibited between those related by affinity in the direct line.[5]

Marriage law in Europe was originally governed entirely by the canon law[6] and when the secular law in this area emerged it was heavily influenced by its canon law roots.

2 For example In 732 AD, a canon by Gregory III forbade marriage among Germans to the seventh degree of consanguinity, seemingly to encourage the newly converted Franks and other Germans to marry outside their tribal groups and strengthen the control of the Church. By the Fourth Lateran Council in 1215, Pope Innocent III, limited the application of the restriction to affinity and consanguinity up to the fourth degree. This barred marriage between first cousins and the spouses of cousins. According to the computation style of the canon law, brother and sister are related in the second degree, niece and uncle in the third, and first cousins in the fourth degree. See generally: A. Esmein, *Le mariage en droit canonique*, 1891, Paris.

3 Canon 1091 of the 1983 Code of Canon Law.

4 G. Garrett, 'Nullity and Dissolution of Marriage in the Law of the Catholic Church', [2001] 3 *Irish Journal of Family Law*, p.12; J. Mc Areavey, *The Canon Law of Marriage and the Family*, 1997, Four Courts Press, Dublin, p. 92–93.

5 i.e. between father-in-law and daughter-in-law. See Canon 1092 of the 1983 Code of Canon Law.

6 See further: J. Mc Areavey, *The Canon Law of Marriage and the Family*, 1997, Four Courts Press, Dublin; A. Esmein, *Le mariage en droit canonique*, 1891, Paris.

2.1. THE BREAKAWAY FROM CANON LAW IN IRELAND AND ENGLAND

The law in Ireland and England[7] was identical until the reign of King Henry VIII and was based entirely on canon law. While some European countries, including France, have rules prohibiting marriage between relatives subject to the possibility of dispensation; the influence of Henry VIII meant that Ireland and England developed a series of absolute laws with no exceptions to the general rule.[8]

The reason for state involvement in marriage law at this time, was because the canon law prevented King Henry from getting out of his marriage to Catherine of Aragon in order to have a legitimate male heir to the throne.[9] Three statutes were passed to try and redefine the law in the area to the King's advantage.[10] These statutes had a lasting effect on the matrimonial law of the common law world.

The first relevant act was laid down by Henry in 1535.[11] Section 2 outlined the degrees prohibited by God's law[12] and declared all marriages within these degrees void. The statute invalidated all dispensations granted by the Church as a usurpation of God's law. The absence of dispensations in English and Irish Law can be traced back to this act.

---

7 See generally: *Wing v Tayor* (1861) 2 Siv and Tr 278; Law Reform Commission, 'Report on Nullity of Marriage' (LRC 9–1984); *O'Shea v Ireland* Unreported Judgment, High Court, Laffoy J, 17/10/2006 [2003 No 13349 P]; S. Cretney, *Family Law in the 20th Century: A History*, 2003, OUP, Oxford.

8 Except for the procedure of a Personal Bill which will be discussed below.

9 For a detailed description of the ups and downs of King Henry VIII's personal life see: J. J. Scarisbrick, *Henry VIII*, London, Eyre & Spottiswood 1968.

10 25 Hen VIII c22 1534, s 9 and 10, 28 Hen VIII c7 1537 and 32 Hen VIII c38 1540.

11 25 Hen VIII c22 entitled "An Act concerning the King's Succession". The purpose of the act was to declare Henry's marriage with Catherine of Aragon null and void in order to ratify his marriage to Queen Anne.

12 God's Law appears to be Leviticus although this is not expressly stated:
And furthermore, since many inconveniences have fallen, as well within this realm as in others, by reason of marrying within the degrees prohibited by God's laws, that is to say, the son to marry the mother or the stepmother, or the son to marry the daughter of his father procreate and borne by his stepmother, or the son to marry his aunt, being his father's or mother's sister, or to marry his uncle's wife, or the father to marry his son's wife, or the brother to marry his brother's wife, or any man to marry his wife's daughter, or his wife's son's daughter, or his wife's daughter 's daughter or his wife's sister.

The second act, passed by Henry in 1537,[13] repealed the first. The same degrees of affinity were outlined as before.[14] In the same session, Henry passed an act[15] stating that all dispensations obtained from Rome would be void henceforth. The effect of these acts was to reduce the prohibited degrees of relationship that had been extended by canon law[16] back to the smaller category of people outlined in Leviticus. All marriages outside Leviticus were now valid regardless of their status in canon law but there was no dispensation within the Levitical degrees. The Acts were extended to Ireland and still govern the prohibited degrees of relationship for the purpose of marriage.[17]

However the full scope of relatives precluded from marrying in English and Irish law was not limited to those expressly laid down in the 1537 Marriage Act. As marriage in the British Isles was governed by the Ecclesiastical courts until 1857[18] the interpretation of the relatives prohibited by Leviticus used was that laid down by canon 99 of the ecclesiastical law of the Church of England.[19] This was referred to as Archbishop Parker's Table. In *R v Chadwick* the temporal Courts decided as a matter of statutory interpretation that the phrase 'Levitican degrees' could not be confined literally to the classes of relatives named in Leviticus but should be taken to include all the relatives laid down in Archbishop Parker's table. Thus the

---

13 28 Hen VIII c7 "Touching the succession of the Crown."

14 Furthermore, with many inconveniences have fallen as well within this realm as in others, by reason of marrying within the degrees of marriage prohibited by God's laws, that is to say the son to marry the mother or the stepmother carnally known by his father, the brother the sister, the father the son's daughter, or his daughter's daughter, or the son to marry his aunt, being his father's or mother's sister, or to marry his uncle's wife carnally know by his uncle, or the father to marry his son's wife carnally known by his son, or the brother to marry his brother's wife carnally known by his brother, or any man marriage and carnally knowing his wife to marry his wife's daughter or this wife's son's daughter, or his wife's daughter's daughter or this wife's sister.
And furthermore, to dilate and declare the meaning of these prohibitions, it is to be understood that if it chance any man to know carnally any woman, that then all and singular persons, being in any degree of consanguinity or affinity as is above written to any of the parties so carnally offending, shall be deemed and adjudged to be within the cases and limits of the said prohibitions of marriage.

15 28 Hen VIII c16.

16 Leviticus only expressly prohibits marriage to the third degree of consanguinity. It does not include first cousins.

17 28–29 Henry VIII c2 (Ir) Thact if succession of the king and queane Anne, 28–29 Henry VIII c17 (Ir) 'Thacte of succession betwixt the kyng and queane Jane', 33 Henry VIII c6 (Ir) 'An Act for Marriages'. The new act Civil Registration Act 2004 states that 'For the purposes of this Act there is an impediment to marriage if… the marriage would be void by virtue of the Marriage Act 1835 as amended by the marriage (Prohibited Degrees of Relationship) Act 1907 and 1921'. (Pt 1 S2). The Marriage Act 1835 refers to the degrees of relationship prohibited by law which has been interpreted to encompass the 1537 Marriage Act.

18 The Matrimonial Causes Act 1857 transferred the jurisdiction to the Temporal Courts.

19 4 Burn's Ecc. L.659, 9th ed. (appendix II).

Church of England's interpretation of the bible became the law in Ireland and England until the end of the 20th century.

2.2. THE BREAKAWAY FROM THE CANON LAW IN FRANCE

In France[20] the prohibited degrees of relationship are laid down in the civil code of 1804. Although at that time France viewed marriage as a purely civil contract the rules governing the prohibited degrees of relationship show echoes of the canon law regime both in the scope of relationships that were prohibited and the types of dispensation that could be granted.

During the French Revolution the law was very liberal in comparison to the canon law previously in force. The draftsmen of the code civil brought the law back towards canon law and placed an impediment on marriage between members of the same household, whose ties of affection should not be troubled by sexual pressures.[21] Thus prohibitions were extended to all blood relations in the direct line. The previous impediment on marriage between cousins was abandoned as it was felt that households were no longer composed of extended families and thus there was no justification for a prohibition.

As regards prohibitions based on affinity, it was felt that the increases in divorce rates since the revolution were partly caused by the fact that marriages between brothers-in-law and sisters-in-law were no longer forbidden by revolutionary legislation. To prevent brothers and sisters from breaking up their siblings' marriages, an impediment on marriage between those related by affinity was reintroduced in the *Code Civil*.[22] Since 1804, the general trend has be the abolition of certain categories of restriction altogether and dispensations have been more widely granted.

No text in the code civil directly outlaws incest as such.[23] Its condemnation is drawn from a two prohibitions, firstly that marriage cannot be celebrated by a

---

20 See generally: P. Courbe, *Droit de la famille*, 4 ed, 2005, Armand Colin Paris; Appendix to the Interdepartmental Committee on Reform of Marriage Law, 'Discussion Paper No.5' (2005) available online <http://www.groireland.ie/docs/marriagelaw_discussion_paper_no5.pdf> access date 27/2/2006; P.A. Fenet, *Exposé des Motifs* cited by F. Swennen, 'The evolving marriage concept', www.ua.ac.be/frederik.swennen.

21 P.A. Fenet, *Exposé des motifs by Portalis before the Corps Législatif*, p. 149.

22 P.A. Fenet, *Portalis in Discussion with the Conseil d'Etat*, p. 23–25.

23 F. Dekeuwer-Défossez, 'Les qualités et conditions requises pour contracter un mariage', in J. Mestre (ed), *Lamy: Droit des personnes et de la famille*, Collection Lamy Droit civil, Lamy, 2005. [307–17]

state official if incest exists and secondly, that it is impossible to establish legal parentage for a child born of such relations.[24]

The prohibitions to marriage based on consanguinity are as follows: Article 161 of the Code civil prohibits marriage between ascendants and descendents both legitimate and illegitimate. Article 162 prohibits marriage between brother and sister. Article 163 prohibits it between uncle/niece and aunt/nephew.[25] The prohibition under Article 163 was extended to prohibit marriage between a granduncle and his great niece.[26] However Art 164 allows the Président de la République to lift the prohibitions of Art 163 in extreme circumstances.

Originally in the old Art 162 and 161 of the Napoleonic code marriage was forbidden between all persons related by affinity,[27] even after the dissolution of the first marriage by death or divorce. Today the impediment on marriage between a brother-in-law and a sister-in-law has been abolished. In 1938, the *loi de 10 mars* introduced a possibility of dispensation in the case of marriage between a sister-in-law and brother-in-law. This dispensation was granted in most cases. In 1975, the moral views had changed to a degree so as to allow complete abolition of the impediment between brothers-in-law and sisters-in-law. This was put into place by the *loi du 11 juillet 1975*. This law also abolished adultery as a basis for divorce.

However a prohibition on marriage between those related by affinity in the direct line remains (Article 161).[28] Art 164 allows those related by affinity to marry if the person creating the affinity has died and a dispensation has also been granted by the *Président de la République*.[29] However dispensation cannot be granted after a divorce rather than a death.[30]

---

24 Article 334–10 C.c. Where there exists between the father and mother of the illegitimate child one of the impediments to marriage provided for by Articles 161 and 162 above by reason of kinship, if parentage is already established with regard to the one, it is forbidden to establish parentage with regard to the other.

25 S. Bigot de la Touranne (ed), *Guide Juridique Dalloz Tome IV*, Guide Juridique Dalloz, Paris 2006, 345–3.

26 Req. 28 nov 1877: DP 1878. 1. 209; *Ca Rouen, 23 february 1982, Dalloz,* 1982 IR p.211.

27 Article 161 Cc. (anc) En ligne directe, le mariage est prohibe entre tous les ascendans et decendans légitimes ou naturels, et les allies dans la même ligne.
Article 162 Cc. (anc) En ligne collatérale, le mariage est prohibé entre le frère et la sœur légitimes ou naturels, et les alliés au même degré.

28 I.E. a father-in-law cannot marry his daughter-in-law nor a mother-in-law her son-in-law.

29 Article 164 Cc.

30 P. Malaurie & H. Fulchiron, *La Famille,* 2nd edn, Defrénois, Paris, 2006, p.345–3.

Dispensation to any of the prohibitions is not given lightly, only for *des causes graves*.[31] The interest of children is the most commonly held reason but economic reasons are also taken into consideration. Applicants are usually required to wait a year before marrying if one is widowed. The dispensation is usually refused if there is a huge age gap between the applicants. The dispensation is accorded by a decree of the President of the Republic. It cannot be appealed as the decision is sovereign.

3. THE GENERAL TREND TOWARDS AN EROSION OF THE PROHIBITED DEGREES

It has been suggested[32] that as the considerations of public interest which supported state intervention in marriage have changed, the rationale for any limitation on marriage must meet higher requirements. Thus every impediment to marriage must, as a limitation of the right to marry, be rationally justified by considerations of public interest, relevant to the nature and purpose of marriage.

Swennen argues that there has been a convergent trend of erosion of impediments to marriage between relatives within Europe because of this change.[33] His argument is supported since Belgium, the Netherlands and Germany have passed legislation to relax the categories of people who are restricted from marrying by virtue of consanguinity or affinity.[34] In France a trend towards the erosion of the prohibited degrees can be seen from the complete abolition of the impediment between brothers and sisters in law in 1975 and the extension of dispensations.

The common law countries of England and Ireland appear to fit with this trend to a certain extent. The action of the ECHR seems to suggest that the trend towards total abolition of prohibitions on marriage between people related by affinity is likely to continue supported by the right to marry under the European Convention on Human Rights.

---

31 Article 164 and Article 366 Cc.

32 F. Swennen, 'The evolving marriage concept', www.ua.ac.be/frederik.swennen.

33 He examined the laws of Belgium, France, Germany and the Netherlands.

34 For example Swennen describes how in the Netherlands, the impediment to marriage between step-parents and step-children and parents-in-law and children-in-law was abolished in 1983 on the ground of a change in moral views and the interest of children. In Germany the impediment was abolished in 1998.

3.1. THE LEGISLATIVE EROSION OF THE PROHIBITED DEGREES IN ENGLAND

In England the strict system of absolute bars to marriage between anyone related in the degrees outlined in Archbishop Parkers table often conflicted with the social reality of marriage.[35]

Although such marriages came to be considered to be voidable[36] rather than void *ab initio*, Lord Lyndhurst's Act[37] in 1835 restored the status of void upon such marriages.[38] This restored the rigidity of the system at a time when many churches and other countries were relaxing their rules by dispensations.[39] The justification for such a move was stated in the preamble to the act: '[It is] unreasonable that the state and condition of children of marriages between persons within the prohibited degrees of affinity should remain unsettled during so long a period" i.e. until avoided by the Ecclesiastical Court. This Act was also the law of Ireland.[40]

Although Section 2 of the Act states, "All marriages which shall hereafter be celebrated between persons within the prohibited degrees of consanguinity or affinity shall be absolutely null and void to all intents and purposes whatsoever," the prohibited degrees were not defined in the act itself. This meant that the exact extent of the degrees in England was unclear while in Ireland the accepted

35 When a wife died leaving children behind, the wife's sister would often move in with the family to look after the children. Marriage was usually the next step.. For many years such couples lived in ope that no one would institute proceedings to invalidate their marriage or took limited protective action By instituting a suit against his spouse in the Ecclesiastical courts. It was not possible for anyone to institute a second suit while the first was pending. Thus the parties could make their marriage safe during their lifetime: S. Cretney, *Family Law in the 20th Century: A History*, 2003, OUP, Oxford, p. 43.

36 Until 1857 the Ecclesiastical Courts had exclusive jurisdiction to declare a marriage void. However, in certain circumstances the common law courts would prevent the Ecclesiastical courts from impeaching a marriage when either party had died. Marriage within the prohibited degrees of affinity was one of these areas and such marriages became considered to be voidable rather than void. Blackstone, *Commentaries on the Laws of England*, 4th Ed, 1770, vol 1, p. 434.

37 The Marriage Act 1835 5 & 6 Will. 4 c. 54.

38 It did not work retrospectively and declared marriages already celebrated within the degrees to be valid.

39 Other countries within Europe such as Denmark and Germany had laxer prohibited degrees and in particular permitted marriage of a deceased wife's sister. Australians who had married in Australia under law permitting marriage with a deceased wife's sister came to England and they were not regarded as lawfully married and their children were considered illegitimate. Although in fact as Cretney points (S. Cretney, *Family Law in the 20th Century: A History*, 2003, OUP, Oxford, p. 46 n59) this reflected a misunderstanding in the law as if both parties were domiciled in Australia at the time of the marriage, it should have been recognized in England.

40 From 1800 to 1922 Ireland was part of the United Kingdom of Great Britain and Ireland.

position by the courts was that the act of 1537 remained the standard of the prohibited degrees.

Lord Lynhurst's Act was not well received. Many people acted as if it was never passed[41] while others sought to circumvent it by getting married abroad.[42] Many bills for reform were presented to Parliament but the Ecclesiastical Lords in the House of Lords blocked every bill. The justification was that sexual attractions within the intimate family circle would confuse the feelings of familial love, disrupt the family and in turn unsettle the whole basis of society.

In 1907, the Deceased Wife's Sister Act was passed, allowing a man to marry his wife's sister on the occasion of his wife's death. The Deceased Wife's Sister Act was unsatisfactory as it only dealt with the single case of the deceased wife's sister. For example, a woman was not allowed to marry her deceased husband's brother. This offended the feminist movement in the UK[43] and caused problems in the aftermath of World War I when the male population was decimated and women wished to marry their choice of men.

The Deceased Brother's Widow's Marriage Act of 1921 brought equality of treatment. The 1907 act allowed a man to marry his wife's sister, not the sister's daughter (i.e. his niece) who was arguably a less likely candidate to cause family disruption. Many unsuccessful bills were introduced to remove the anomalies in the system.[44] In 1931, the Marriage (Prohibited Degrees of Relationship) Act allowed men and women to marry a nephew or niece related to them by marriage. The 1949 Marriage Act confirmed the previous three acts and specifically included half- blood relatives.

In Ireland the 1537 act was effectively amended by the Deceased Wife's Sister's Marriage Act of 1907 and the Deceased Brother's Widow's Marriage Act of 1921 but these were the last of the British reforms to touch Irish Law.

Although the combination of these acts made it possible for a man to marry his deceased wife's sister and his deceased brother's widow, subsection 2 of s3 of the

---

41 The 1848 Royal Commission reported that in the decade after the enactment of the act, 1, 364 'marriages' had been solemnized in areas covered by the Commission's survey.

42 The 1848 Royal commission also heard evidence that it was common for couples to go to Denmark to marry under the inaccurate belief that such a marriage would be valid in England. In *Brook v Brook* (1861) 9 HLC 193 the House of Lords held that the legal capacity of someone domiciled in England to contract a marriage remained governed by English law in spite of the whereabouts of the marriage ceremony.

43 The Southport Women's Liberal Association had protested against the idea as early as 1888. S. Cretney, *Family Law in the 20th Century: A History*, 2003, OUP, Oxford, p. 48.

44 Ten bills between 1922 and 1931.

1921 act expressly stated that it was not lawful for a man to marry the sister of his divorced wife or the divorced former wife of his brother. Therefore the former spouse would have to die before marriage to his/her sibling was permitted. This was a deliberate decision by the legislature in England as divorce had already been introduced in 1857. The question did not really arise in Ireland until the introduction of divorce in 1996.[45] The prohibited degrees of relationship were not again revisited in Ireland until 2006.

In 1947, Ray Stevenson sought to introduce a personal bill to enable him to marry his divorced brother's wife during his brother's lifetime. The personal act effectively exempts the individuals from the application of a statutory prohibition on marriage.[46] Stevenson argued that it would be in the interest of the child of the divorced couple to be part of a stable marital family and that it was the policy of the 1857 Divorce Act that after divorce, it should be lawful for the parties to marry again as if the prior marriage had been dissolved by death.[47] The Personal Bills committee felt that the circumstances of the case were not exceptional enough to warrant giving one individual the right to contract a marriage which would still be forbidden to other citizens.

The case caused a review of the prohibited degrees of marriage to be included in the terms of reference of the 1956 *Royal Commission on Marriage and Divorce*. The commission concluded that the prohibition on marriage merely because the last marriage had ended in divorce and not death was unwarranted. They doubted that the legal prohibition influenced the matter to any extent.

The resulting Marriage (Enabling) Act 1960 provided that no marriage between a man and the sister, aunt or niece of a former wife of his 'whether living or not' should be held voidable as being within the prohibited degrees. The equivalent provision for women was also inserted. However, marriage was still barred between a man and his mother-in-law or daughter-in-law.

Pressure to abolish all prohibitions on marriage between affines continued in England although there was unease about allowing marriage between step-parent

45 Although it could have been an issue in the exceptional case of Irish recognition of a foreign divorce.

46 Such an act is passed at the discretion of the Parliament. There were no established criteria for the granting of a personal Act of Parliament in order to permit a marriage otherwise prohibited by the 1949 act. Although the procedure is still available in the UK, no such acts have been passed since 1987. For example, the Valerie Mary Hill and Alan Monk (Marriage Enabling) Act 1985 permitted the marriage between Valerie Hill (the mother of Alan Monk's first wife) and Mr Monk at a time when there was an absolute prohibition on marriage between parents-in-law and children-in-law.

47 Matrimonial Causes Act 1857 s57.

and step-children as potentially exposing the child to abuse. A review group appointed by the Archbishop of Canterbury, including members of the House of Lords, on the question of the prohibition of marriages on the grounds of affinity was set up in 1984. [48]

The Marriage (Prohibited Degrees of Relationship) Act 1986 was introduced to reflect the agreed changes of the committee. The bill adopted represented the common ground between the majority and minority views, removing the impediment for step relations where both parties were over 18 and the younger party had never been treated as a child of the family. In the case of parent-in-law and child-in-law such marriages could only take place if the former spouses of the parent-in-law and the child-in-law were dead and both parties had attained the age of 21.

The act reflected the realization that hard and fast rules regarding the marriage of parent-in-law and child-in-law are not always appropriate. Today extended families do not generally live under the same roof and it is possible that a father might never even meet his daughter-in-law until after her marriage to his son had ended. Instead of bringing in a dispensation, marriage was permitted in certain circumstances to avoid family rivalry. If the son and the father's wife had died, marriage could be permitted but while they remained alive no marriage was possible. This rule did not achieve its end and instead provided a motive for double murder. It was still possible that a father could break up his son's marriage and cohabit with his daughter-in-law until the death of his son and former wife while a father who met his daughter-in-law after the end of her marriage to his son could not marry. In contrast, a divorcee could marry the child of their former spouse under any circumstance as long as the child had never lived as a child of the family.

Cretney pointed out that at the end of the century there was, "no evidence that the change in law has encouraged men more frequently to look on their mothers-in-law with lustful eyes nor was there any evidence of pressure to follow the example set in Australia to abolish all legal restrictions on marriage between in-laws."[49] However the UK had gone from a strong system of prohibited categories to a system of arbitrary subcategories. The pressure to change was to come from the ECHR.

---

48 Group Appointed by the Archbishop Of Canterbury, 'No Just Cause', CIO Publishing London 1984.

49 S. Cretney, *Family Law in the 20th Century: A History*, 2003, OUP, Oxford, p. 56.

3.2. THE INTERVENTION OF THE ECHR

The issue of prohibited degrees of affinity as a restriction on the right to marry under was addressed by the ECHR in *B and L v UK*[50] in September of 2005. The applicants were father-in-law (B) and daughter- in-law (L). They had been cohabiting since 1996 with the daughter-in-law's son (W) who was the father-in-law's grandson. The applicants planned to adopt the child and this was permitted by English adoption law.

The applicants were informed by the Superintendent Registrar of Deaths and Marriages that they would not be allowed to marry until both their former spouses had died. The basis for the decision was section 1 of the Marriage Act of 1949 as amended by the Marriage (Prohibited Degrees of Relationship) Act 1986.[51] By virtue of section 1(3) of the 1949 Act (as amended), marriages between former step-parents and step-children are not void if both parties have attained the age of 21 and the younger party was never a 'child of the family' in relation to the other party. The applicants claimed that their right to marry under Article 12 of the European Convention of Human Rights[52] had been infringed. The applicants submitted that the restriction denied them the *very essence* of the right to marry as they were absolutely prevented from exercising that right at that time and for the foreseeable future. In order for them to marry, the father would have to outlive his son or the couple would have to apply for a personal Act of Parliament. The applicants claimed that there were no sensible or coherent distinctions between their situation and that of other categories of persons who were permitted to marry (step-father and step-child etc). They suggested that there could be no claim of sexual rivalry in their case as both relationships with their previous partners had finished before they commenced their relationship with each other. Nor was there any ground for objection on behalf of the son, as he wanted to be part

50 36536/02 [2005] ECHR 584 (13 September 2005) available online < http://www.worldlii.org/eu/cases/ECHR/2005/584.html> access date 21/2/2007.

51 (4) Subject to subsection (5) of this section, a marriage solemnized between a man and any of the persons mention in the first column of Part III of the First Schedule to this Act or between a woman and any of the persons mentioned in the second column of the said Part III shall be void.
(5) Any such marriage as is mentioned in subsection (4) of this section shall not be void by reason only of affinity if both parties to the marriage have attained the age of twenty-one at the time of the marriage and the marriage is solemnized –
(b)In the case of a marriage between a man and the former wife of his son, after the death of both his son and the mother of his son;
(c) In the case of a marriage between a woman and the father of a former husband of hers, after the death of both the former husband and the mother of the former husband.

52 Men and women of marriageable age have the right to marry and to found a family, according to the national laws governing the exercise of this right.

of a 'normal' family and actively supported their marriage. The prohibition only prevented the recognition of what was already *de facto* reality.

The Court held that while Article 12 was subject to the national laws of the contracting states, the limitations thereby introduced must not restrict or reduce the right in such a way that the very essence of the right is impaired. The Court stated that as Article 12 provided expressly for the regulation of marriage by national law, the Court must not rush to substitute its own judgment in the place of the authorities who were best placed to assess and respond to the needs of society. It also noted the large number of contracting states which had concerns about allowing marriages of this degree of affinity.[53]

In *B and L* the Court felt that the applicants' right to marry had indeed been impaired and that the fact that the applicants could marry if both their former spouses died did not remove the impairment of the essence of that right, nor did the possibility of applying to Parliament. Thus the Court acknowledged that the rules regarding marriage within the prohibited degrees are a restriction on the right to marry under the Convention and must be justified and proportionate.

The Court also addressed the coherence of the prohibited degrees of relationship with the rest of British law. The purpose of such restriction was to prevent turmoil in families and protect vulnerable people from sexual pressure from their relatives. However, the British bar on marriage did not prevent relationships occurring. In addition, there were no incest laws or other criminal laws to prevent extra-martial relationships between parents-in-law and children-in-law. Therefore the law did not prevent any alleged confusion to the second applicant's son as any confusion would also occur from the cohabitation of the parties which was not forbidden by law.

The Court also found that by having an arbitrary exception to the rule in the form of a personal Act of Parliament, the UK had conceded that the law was unjustified. This would seem to suggest that the European countries such as France which operate a dispensation system have already conceded that marriage is permissible in certain circumstances barred by statute. However, the British system had two exceptions to the rule that father-in-law and daughter-in-law could not marry. The first was the statutory exception outlined in the 1986 act that governed in all cases and allowed the couple to marry if both former spouses were dead. The second was the arbitrary personal Act of Parliament. The personal Act of Parliament did not seem to entail any proper enquiry into the circumstances to ensure

53 Most states had at some time restricted marriage between relationships of affinity and 21 Contracting States still maintained either conditional or absolute prohibitions.

they were exceptional and personal acts were generally obtained.[54] The Court concluded that this failure to distinguish a reason why the rule should apply to the general public but not to those who applied for a personal bill showed that the rule was unjustified and there had been violation of Article 12 of the Convention.

Under the British Human Rights Act 1998, a declaration of the ECHR that a provision is incompatible with a Convention right does not affect the validity, continuing operation or enforcement of the provision in question but the provision can be changed by ministerial order.[55] The Marriage Act 1949 (Remedial) Order 2006 proposed to repeal the provisions of the Marriage Act 1949 governing marriage between in-laws.[56] It also exempted any Church of England or Church of Wales clergyman from having to solemnize such a marriage.[57]

The Church of England's Archbishop's council opposed the order and questioned whether the Lord Chancellor had the requisite power to remove the age restriction on marriage between parent-in-law and children-in-law as the ECHR had not directly considered the age restriction.[58] The Government considered it necessary to remove the restriction in order to remove the incompatibility with Article 12 ECHR across the board.[59] The second draft order was approved by the House of Lords on the 25 of January 2007.

The judgment in *B and L v United Kingdom* has already been implemented by Scotland in the Family Law (Scotland) Act 2006, which amended Section 2 and Schedule 1 of the Marriage (Scotland) Act 1977 and came into effect on 4 May 2006; and by Northern Ireland in the Law Reform (Miscellaneous Provisions) (Northern Ireland) Order 2006, which came into force on 19 September 2006.

The remaining restrictions in UK law based on affinity are outlined in Section 1 (2) of the Marriage Act 1949 and Part II of the first Schedule to that act. A marriage

54 Since the 1980s, all three bills put forward had been passed.
55 (s4) if a Minister considers that there are compelling reasons for proceeding he may by order make such amendments to the legislation as he considers necessary to remove the incompatibility.
56 Marriage Act 1949 s 1(4) to (8) and Part 3 of Schedule 1.
57 Generally, such clergymen have a legal obligation to solemnize the marriage of a person resident in his parish or entered on the church electoral roll of his parish. However, when the 1949 act was amended in 1986, a conscience clause was inserted to exempt any clergymen from this obligation where people proposing to marry would have been, before the 1986 Act, within the prohibited degrees of affinity to each other. The order merely extended this exemption.
58 The age restriction was not directly an issue in *B and L* as both parties were over 21.
59 The Government felt that there would be very few cases involving a party under 21 because the younger individual must have been 16 or over to enter into their first marriage, and then could not divorce for at least one year afterwards, and secondly because very few couples marry at so young an age.

between an individual and his or her stepchild, step-parent step-grandparent or step-grandchild is void. Section 1(3) states that such marriages will be valid if both parties are 21 the younger party was not the child of the family in relation to the older party while under the age of 18. A person is considered a child of the family if he/she lived in the same household and was treated by that person as a child of the family.[60] As the personal act of parliament system is still valid in the UK these rules would seem to be subject to challenge under the European Convention of Human Rights.

3.3. THE EROSION OF THE PROHIBITED DEGREES BY THE COURTS IN IRELAND

At the beginning of the 21st century the prohibited degrees in Ireland were governed by ss. 2 and 9 of the1537 act and the relevant provisions of the 1542 act. The Statute Law Revision (Pre-Union Irish Statutes) Act of 1962 deleted references to marrying a sister or brother in law from section 2 and thus brought the act into line with the 1907 and 1921 acts.

Prior to 1922, marriage within the prohibited degrees was not absolutely outlawed because it was possible to obtain an exception to the statute by a private Act of Parliament. The point is debatable whether the 1922 parliament had such a power[61] but there is no such power under the 1937 Constitution. Although the laws relating to marriage within the prohibited degrees of relationship had been criticised for years[62] and there had even been suggestions that they were unconstitutional[63] no changes were made.

In 2006 two plaintiffs brought proceedings to declare the legislation governing degrees of affinity unconstitutional.[64] The first plaintiff wished to marry the second plaintiff, the brother of her former husband whom she divorced in 2000. The couple were informed by the General Register Office that they were prohibited from marrying by the provisions of the Deceased Wife's Sister's Marriage Act 1907 and the Deceased Brother's Widow's Marriage Act 1921.

---

60 G. Rhys, 'The law relating to Affinity After B and L v UK', *Fam LJ*, 35 (955).

61 G. Hogan/G. Whyte (Eds), *JM Kelly: The Irish Constitution*, 4 ed, 2003, Tottel, para 7.6.97.

62 A. Shatter, *Shatter's Family Law*, 4 ed, 1997 Butterworths, Dublin; J.P. Casey, *Constitutional Law in Ireland,* 3 Ed, 2000, Roundhall, Dublin; Law Reform Commission, 'Report on Nullity of marriage' (LRC 9–1984); Law Society Law Reform Committee, 'Nullity of Marriage: The Case for Reform' (2001) available online at <http://www.lawsociety.ie/documents/committees/lawreform/nullity2.pdf> access date 27/2/2007.

63 J.P. Casey, *Constitutional Law in Ireland*, 3 Ed, 2000, Roundhall, Dublin.

64 *O'Shea v Ireland*, Unreported Judgment, High Court, Laffoy J, 17/10/2006 [2003 No 13349 P] p. 8.

The plaintiffs claimed that the relevant acts were rendered void by the operation of Article 50 of the Irish constitution[65] and were no longer in force. They pleaded that such provisions violated their rights to marry, to freely associate with persons of their choice and to form an established marital family. Although this case occurred after *B and L* the plaintiffs initiated proceedings which predated the coming into operation of the European Convention on Human Rights Act 2003.[66] The plaintiffs did not invoke convention rights but they did rely on the jurisprudence of the Court as persuasive authority.

Laffoy J concluded that the 1537 act and the relevant part of the 1542 were still in force in Ireland. The plaintiffs' problem lay in the subsection 2 of s3 of the 1907 act as amended by 1921.[67] While there was no prohibition on such a marriage after the death of the woman's husband while the former spouses remained alive such a marriage was *void ab initio*. As an Interdepartmental Report noted years before[68] the introduction of divorce had created an anomaly in the law. If a marriage was terminated by divorce as opposed to the spouse's death the prohibition on a woman marrying her deceased husband's brother still remained. Laffoy J interpreted Article 50 to mean that acts inconsistent with the constitution as it stood at that time. The issue was whether s3(2) was inconsistent with the Constitution as amended in 1996[69] to provide for dissolution of marriage in certain specified circumstances.[70] The burden on the plaintiff was to prove that the impugned

65 Subject to this Constitution and the extent to which they are not inconsistent therewith, the laws in force in Saorstát Éireann immediately prior to the date of the coming into operation of this constitution shall continue to be of full force and effect until the same or any of them shall have been repealed or amended by enactment of the Oireachtas.

66 The European Convention on Human Rights Act 2003 gave effect to the European Convention on Human Rights in Irish Law. The act was a significant improvement on the European Convention on Human Rights Bill 2001 which only allowed for the ECHR to be used as an interpretative guide in Irish law but the act was not applicable to *O'Shea v Ireland*.

67 Notwithstanding anything contained in the Act or the Matrimonial Causes Act 1857, it shall not be lawful for a man to marry the sister of his divorced wife or his wife by whom he has been divorced, during the lifetime of such wife or the divorced wife or the wife of his brother who has divorced his brother during the lifetime of such a brother.

68 Interdepartmental Committee on Reform of Marriage Law, 'Discussion Paper No.5' (2005) available online <http://www.groireland.ie/docs/marriagelaw_discussion_paper_no5.pdf> access date 27/2/2006 5.33.

69 Art 41.2- A Court designated by law may grant a dissolution of marriage where, but only where, it is satisfied that
  i. at the date of the institution of the proceedings, the spouses have lived apart from one another for a period of, or periods amounting to, at least four years during the five years,
  ii. there is no reasonable prospect of a reconciliation between the spouses,
  iii. such provision as the Court considers proper having regard to the circumstances exists or will be made for the spouses, any children of either or both of them and any other person prescribed by law, and
  iv. any further conditions prescribed by law are complied with.

70 *O'Shea v Ireland*, Unreported Judgment, High Court, Laffoy J, 17/10/2006 [2003 No 13349 P] p. 12.

provision infringed one or more of their constitutional rights and that such an infringement was irrational or disproportionate.[71] This was a similar test to that used in *B and L v UK*.

The only real issue for the Court to decide was whether s3(2) was inconsistent with the Constitution as an unjustified restriction on the right to marry. The only precedent for this decision was a High Court order by Justice Smyth in 2001 declaring a marriage between a woman and her deceased aunt's husband to be valid.[72] This order was noted in the Law Society's report. At that time judgment was withheld although the report felt that it would reveal that the 1537 act was unconstitutional. No such judgment was ever produced leaving the 1537 Act in an insecure position.[73]

The defendants stated that the provision was founded on two constitutional imperatives the State's obligation to promote the common good and the State's guarantee to protect the family and to guard with special care the institution of marriage as provided for in Article 41. This argument addressed a perceived danger to the institution of marriage by permitting marriage within the close degrees of affinity. The argument was not advanced that these rules were part of the institution of marriage itself. Marriage between the spouse and a sibling would undermine the stability of the marital unit based on the assertion that a person who marries into a family adopts as his or her own the siblings of the other spouse.

Laffoy J did not give much credence to the idea that the prohibition prevented affections forming between a wife and her husband's brother: 'I doubt if it is sound at a time when the stigma which formerly attached to cohabitation outside marriage is disappearing'.[74] The evidence was that the plaintiffs cohabited for twenty years and felt no stigma. As the ECHR had pointed out in B and L the bar on marriage did not prevent a *de facto* relationship from forming.

The defendants also claimed that children of the first marriage would suffer confusion and hurt from such a relationship. Laffoy J felt that this was not a issue upon which the Court could or should make an assumption. There was considerable evidence that the brother in law had successfully reared his brother's children without subjecting them to confusion and hurt. This argument is also subject to

---

71 Ibid p 14.

72 Irish times 'Marriage case judgment reserved' 26 May 2001; Irish Times 'Woman told her marriage 29 years ago was lawful' 28 June 2001.

73 Laffoy J mentioned in her judgment that the Smyth judgment was not available.

74 *O'Shea v Irelanda*, Unreported Judgment, High Court, Laffoy J, 17/10/2006 [2003 No 13349 P] p. 28.

the criticism that it does not take into account the rights of any children born in the second relationship to be part of a stable, legally recognised, marital family.

Laffoy J held that the prohibition contained in s.3(2) was a restriction on the constitutional right of each of the plaintiffs to marry because it prevented each marrying his or her chosen partner. She also held that the plaintiffs had established that the restriction was not justified in support of the constitutional protection of the family and the institution of marriage.[75] The question of proportionality did not arise as the judge could find no basis to conclude that there was any benefit conferred by the existence of the restriction nor any basis for concluding that there was any rational justification for the existence of the right. It is clear that Laffoy J did not feel that the restriction on marriage within the prohibited degrees formed part of the institution of marriage.

By holding that the impugned provision was inconsistent with the plaintiff's right to marry under Article 40.3.1 of the Irish constitution, Laffoy J went further than the Court in *B and L*. In the UK the problem with the affinity rule in question was that it was not applicable to all and was subject to arbitrary exception. In Ireland under s.3(2) no one was allowed to marry within the prohibited degrees in question until their former spouse died. It is arguable that arguments of rational justification and proportionality used by Laffoy J to declare s.3(2) invalid could be applied to any of the existing rules prohibiting marriage between people related by affinity. While Laffoy J did not rule on the constitutionality of the 1537 act it would seem that many of the prohibitions included could also be found to be unconstitutional.

S3(2) of the 1907 Act as amended by s1(2)(b) of the Act of 1921 was declared inconsistent with the constitution by Laffoy J and is no longer in effect.[76] The current prohibited degrees are governed by the 1537 act although marriage between brother and sister in law is now permitted as is marriage between a man and his uncle's wife and a woman and her aunt's husband.[77] As can be seen Ireland still

---

75 Ibid p. 29.

76 *O'Shea v Ireland* Unreported Judgment, High Court, Laffoy J, 17/10/2006 [2003 No 13349 P] p. 12.

77 The current prohibited degrees in Ireland appear to be as follows:
A man may not marry his:
Grandmother, mother, father's sister, mother's sister, sister, father's daughter, mother's daughter, daughter, son's daughter, daughter's daughter, brother's daughter' sister's daughter. Grandfather's wife father's wife, father's brother's wife, son's Wife, son's son's wife, daughter's son's wife, brother's son's wife, sister's son's wife, wife's grandmother, wife's mother, wife's father's sister, wife's mother's sister, wife's daughter, wife's son's daughter, wife's daughter's daughter, wife's brother's daughter, wife's sister's daughter.
A woman may not marry:

has a much greater range of prohibited degrees of relationship than either France or England and Wales.

4. QUESTIONING THE RATIONALE BEHIND THE PROHIBITED DEGREES OF RELATIONSHIP

Although Lévi-Strauss stressed the universal nature of prohibitions based on blood ties or family connections,[78] the range of the prohibitions has always differed from society to society depending on the cultural definition of kinship. Although the laws on prohibited degrees of relationship in the Western world have evolved in different ways[79] they have all been influenced to a lesser or greater extent by the canon law. In the era of a more multi-cultural Europe, in an age where divorce has become more common and family ties more fleeting it must be considered whether or not these restrictions can be rationally justified or whether they are merely a remnant of an ancient taboo. It the right to marry is to be taken seriously then any restrictions upon that right must be proportionate and relevant to the protection of marriage.

In his submission to the 1940 Commission on Kindred and Affinity as Impediments to marriage, Prof Malinowski summed up the reasons for marriage prohibitions as follows.[80] The main sociological reason for marriage taboos and prohibited degrees was the elimination of sexual pressure on relations within the family. In these situations sexual approaches act as a competitive and disruptive force incompatible with the stability of family life. However he recommended that the State restrict the prohibited degrees to a well-considered minimum. As to the range of relations that should be forbidden he had the following to say:

> ...it is clear that the number and nature of prohibited degrees depends on the character of the family, or the joint-family, and on the importance of extended kinship in any

---

Grandfather, father, father's brother, mother's brother, brother, father's son, mother's son, son, son's son, daughter's son, son, son's son, daughter's son, brother's son, sister's son.
Grandmother's husband, mother's husband, father's sister's husband, daughter's husband, son's daughter's husband, daughter's daughter's husband, sister's daughter's husband, husbands grandfather, husband's father, husband's father's brother, husband's mother's brother, husband's son, husband's son's son, husband's daughter's son, husband's brother's son, husband's sister's son.

78 C. Levi-Strauss, *The elementary structures of Kinship*, 1949. In this work he puts forward the assumption that the incest taboo was the foundation of all human social behaviour.

79 The most notable difference being that marriage to cousins is forbidden in many states in America but in no country in Europe.

80 B. Malinkowski, 'A sociological analysis of the rationale of the prohibited degrees in marriage' Appendix 3 to *Commission on Kindred and Affinity as Impediments to Marriage* (1940).

given type of society. It also depends on the general nature of relations between men and women; on the degree in which their associations and possibilities of easy friendship are strictly determined by the bonds of kinship and affinity, or else, can be formed irrespective of such bonds.[81]

The Irish Law Reform Commission[82] noted that legislation should not place unnecessary obstacles in the path of persons who wish to marry and that religious or cultural mores from the 19th century would not justify such legislation.

In France it is more readily acknowledged that the prohibited degrees of relationship are dependent on social mores. For example Malaurie does classify exogamy as an essential element of marriage but rather classifies it as a condition dependent on social morality. Such a condition does not touch the essence of marriage as much as the others but is more dependent on the mores of society and more open to change.[83]

It is submitted that prohibitions on marriage based on affinity are out of touch with the idea of kinship in modern Europe. Both the Irish Law Reform Commission and the Law Society Law Reform Committee[84] recommended that the prohibited degrees based on affinity be abolished. Their reasoning was threefold: First that the idea of kinship had changed over times and people related by the degrees of affinity often had no real familial ties to each other. In such cases the prohibition on marriage could not be justified as no familial links were severed. Secondly even in the case where familial links existed between in-laws the disruption to the family was the same in the case of a relationship whether or not the parties actually married. Thirdly the commission felt that it would be too difficult to draft a law that would be appropriate in all cases.

4.1. CULTURAL DIFFERENCE IGNORED BY THE PROHIBITED DEGREES OF RELATIONSHIP

Both prohibitions based on blood ties and affinity prohibitions can be considered to be out of sync with the idea of kinship amongst some minority cultures in Europe. The prohibited degrees in Europe, although eroded from the full set in canon law, are based on Christian values and do not take into account the ideas of kinship in other cultures. These other ideas of ideas of kinship can come from a

81 Reproduced in Group Appointed by the Archbishop Of Canterbury, 'No Just Cause', CIO Publishing London 1984, p. 136.

82 Law Reform Commission Report on 'Nullity of marriage' (LRC 9–1984).

83 P. Malaurie/H. Fulchiron, *La Famille*, 2nd edn, Defrénois, Paris, 2006, p. 95.

84 Law Reform Commission Report on 'Nullity of marriage' (LRC 9–1984) p. 71.

different religious another interpretation of the bible[85] or can have developed over the years for cultural reasons.

For example in Ireland the Irish Travelling Community feel under pressure to marry within the community. In *Becoming Conspicuous: Irish Travellers, Society and the State 1922–70*[86] Bhreatnach describes how over the years the Travelling Community have tend to marry within their own cultural group for a variety of reasons. In *Irish Travellers: Racism and the Politics of Culture*[87] Helleiner investigated the marriage practices in the Travelling community in Cork in the 1980s. At that time close kinship ties were maintained in the travelling community The most common reason offered by Travellers for arranged marriages was the avoidance of marriages with non-Travellers. Such marriages were feel to be extremely risky with the risk of the marriage dissolving. Studies such as Helleiner's one found that first cousin marriage was common. Marriage was seen as an important opportunity to create of strengthen ties between family groups. Helleiner suggest that Traveller close-kin marriage is part of a strategy to create stable household unit and a wide ranging social network.[88]

Most studies on Traveller marriage have focused on first cousin marriage but marriages within the legal prohibited degrees are not unknown and there are documented cases of uncle-niece marriage, aunt-nephew marriage.[89] The significance of ties between women is often masked as the society is patrilineal and the use of surnames often makes the link invisible to the outsider.

In *Travellers: Citizens of Ireland*[90] it is suggested that the role of the extended family in the traveller community is changing and there has been a growing number of separation and marital problems. Even so, there are a number of marriages that slip through the General Registrar's net in Ireland every year and are contracted between parties within the prohibited degrees of relationship such marriages are

---

85 Such as that of the Jewish faith which has interpreted Leviticus as permitting avuncular marriage. Indeed in Rhode Island in the USA Jews are exempt from the prohibition on marriage between an uncle and a niece. See M. Ottenheimer, *Forbidden Relatives*, 1996 University of Illinois Press, p. 19.

86 E. Bhreathnach, *Becoming Conspicuous: Irish Travellers, Society and the State 1922–70*, UCD press Dublin 2006.

87 J.L. Helleiner, *Irish Travellers: Racism and the Politics of Culture*, University of Toronto Press 2000.

88 J.L. Helleiner, 'The Tinker's Wedding' Revisited: Irish Traveller Marriage' in *100 years of Gypsy Studies* (The Gypsy Lore Society 1990 Maryland).

89 S. Gmelch, *The Irish Tinkers: The Urbanization of an Itinerant People*, California: Cummings Publishing Company 1977.

90 E. Mc Donagh, 'Family, Marriage and the Faith: Changing Times in the Traveller Community' in E. Sheehan (ed), *Travellers citizens of Ireland: Our challenge to an Intercultural Irish Society in the 21st Century*, Dublin 2001.

void under Irish law. These people find themselves in a very irregular situation and have no legal protection if such a 'marriage' breaks down.

Any benefits of the laws of prohibited degrees must be weighed up against the negative effect they have on individual from other cultures who identify with a different system of kinship.

4.2. THE SOCIAL CONCERNS ADDRESSED BY THE PROHIBITED DEGREES

The prohibited degrees of affinity in marriage have been justified for two social reasons: preventing inappropriate sexual influences within extended families and a confusion of roles. Under this theory family life creates strict bonds between its members and marriage and the confusion of family roles could create disorder.[91] This justification dates from a time where sexual conduct was only tolerated within marriage. The idea that this prohibition prevents the confusion of family roles relies on the assumption that the only reason for making advances to a relative such as a nephew's wife would be because the goal of eventually want to marrying her.

However it is difficult to believe that the fact that any future marriage would be void would provide much of a deterrent those who feel inappropriate sexual urges towards other members of their family. Arguably this concern is better served by incest legislation and child protection statutes. However if we compare the scope of the prohibited degrees of relationship to incest laws we see that in general the incest laws prohibit a much narrower class of relationships. While it is consistent that unions banned by incest legislation should also be void under marriage law there does not really seem to be any justification under this ground for the bar on affinity marriages.

In Ireland the crime of incest only applies to relationships traced through blood not affinity.[92] The Punishment of Incest Act of 1908 includes grand-daughter, daughter, sister, or mother, grandfather, father, brother or son. Age is irrelevant although a female under 17 cannot be prosecuted under the act.[93] Consent is also irrelevant. The 1995 Act increased the maximum penalty to life imprisonment for a male while a female over 17 is liable only to a maximum of 7 years imprison-

91 P. Malaurie/H. Fulchiron, *La Famille*, 2nd edn, Defrénois, Paris, 2006, p. 119.

92 Nor is it against the current British incest laws: the crime of 'sex with an adult relative' under s65 of the Sexual Offences Act 2003 (which replaced incest unders 10 and 11 of the Sexual Offences Act 21956) is not committed under these circumstances.

93 s2 Incest Act 1908.

ment[94]as originally the male participant was guilty of a felony and the female a misdemeanour. The incest scope is further narrowed by the fact that no criminal offence is committed if the accused was unaware to the familial connection whereas any marriage between affines is void *ab initio* regardless of the knowledge of the spouses.[95]

In France no criminal proceedings follow unless the matter can be dealt with under the prohibition on abuse of authority.[96]

In America the prohibited degrees of relationships and the incest statutes overlap to a greater extent. Marriages are prohibited on the basis of being incestuous in 11 states and 9 of those states punish the attempted marriages criminally this includes certain step -relatives and in-laws. The states generally treat marriage regulation and criminal non-marital sexual activity separately. Although the Uniform Marriage and Divorce Act eliminated all relationships by affinity[97] this has not been widely adopted.

Apart from preventing the confusing of roles another social justification for the prohibited degrees is that they protect children from abusive relationships. This is not really a strong argument as both parties are punished by having their marriage declared void.[98] This punishes the former child by removing any legal protection they might have on the breakdown of such a relationship and this interest is better served by the relevant child protection legislation such as the English Sexual Offences Act 2003 which prohibits sexual relations while the child is under 18[99] but no crime is committed if the parties enter into a sexual relationship after the child has reached 18.[100] Although the prevention of sexual abuse of children is clearly a legitimate aim to pursue, it appears that the restriction on marriage does not actually achieve that aim. In addition it seems paternalistic to blanket ban unrelated people from marrying no matter what their age because it is possible that one may have unduly influenced the other. Surely if this actually were to happen the marriage would be void anyway due to lack of consent.

94 S2 Incest Act 1908.

95 C. Barton, 'Incest and the Prohibited Degrees – Present Position', *NLJ*, Vol 137 No. 6307 p. 502.

96 Ibid.

97 Uniform Marriage & Divorce Act s 207 cmt (1998) as cited in Ch. McNiece Metteer, 'Some "Incest" is Harmless Incest: Determining the Fundamental Right to Marry of Adults Related by Affinity without Resorting to State Incest Statutes' Heinonline *10 Kan J.Land Pub Policy* 262 2000.

98 As indeed they are under incest legislation.

99 S25 -sexual activity with a child family member.

100 S65 does not prohibit sexual relationships between persons related through marriage.

4.3. GENETIC CONCERNS

Marriage between those related by blood ties is forbidden for physiological or eugenic considerations that the offspring of unions related by blood would have health problems.[101] Although genetics is now put forward as the strongest reasons for the retention of prohibited degrees in marriage it was not originally a strongest concern. Most arguments before the discovery of classical genetics were based on morality and bible interpretation as can be seen in the heated debate in the UK concerning marriage with a dead wife's sister in the 19th century. With the discovery of inheritable characteristics genetic concerns became a major concern in the USA in the marriage statutes of new states joining the Union.

No state in the Union before 1860 prevented the marriage of first cousins and most forbade marriage of people related by affinity. After 1861 the opposite became the norm. This coincided with the evolution of classical genetics and the work of Gregor Mendel and Thomas Hunt Morgan.[102]

Since this time the United States has given less weight to affinity as grounds for prohibiting marriage but there has been increasing emphasis on regulating consanguinity within marriage. During this time many of the older states changed their laws to forbid first cousin marriage and to eliminate their prohibition against marriage within the degrees of affinity. Today only 12 states maintain prohibitions based on affinity: Alabama, Georgia, Maryland, Massachusetts, Mississippi, New Hampshire, Oklahoma, Rhode Island, South Carolina, Tennessee, South Dakota and Texas. In contrast since the middle of the nineteenth century there has been an increase in legislation forbidding first cousins from marrying and some even include first cousins once removed. This is main difference between the laws there and in Europe and reflects a prioritisation of genetic concerns over more tradition moral issues.[103]

However the goal of the law in protecting potential offspring from genetic harm can be compromised where the law does not recognised what is in fact a close blood tie. For example due to the need for affiliation proceedings in French law to establish legal paternity, there is controversy as to whether a father can marry his natural daughter if no official affiliation proceedings have ever taken place.

This problem has been made greater by scientific developments such as IVF which can make it harder than ever to establish genetic ties in law. In the UK the Human

101 P. Malaurie/H. Fulchiron, *La Famille,* 2nd edn, Defrénois, Paris, 2006, p. 119.
102 M. Ottenheimer, *Forbidden Relatives*, 1996 University of Illinois Press, p.79.
103 Ibid p.85.

Fertilisation and Embryology Act 1990 which defines a mother as the person who carries the child means that it would be no crime for a man to have sex with his genetic mother.

This conflict between protecting vulnerable parties from pressure from within the legally recognised family unit and allowing those who are genetically unrelated to marry is again demonstrated in the inconsistent treatment of adopted people throughout Europe. On one hand we have the concern that adopted people should not be allowed to marry their blood relatives for genetic reasons and on the other we have the concern that they should not be allowed marry their adopted relatives in order to protect them from undue influences. The result is an uncertain and sometimes impossible position for adopted people.

In France prohibitions on marriage between an adopted child and members of their adopted family are absolute in the case of formal adoption as if the adopted family were blood relatives. This principle is not outlined in the code but can be deduced from the wording of article 354[104] and article 358.[105] In the case of informal adoption, marriage is prohibited between the adoptive parents and the adoptee and their descendants.[106] By the same article marriage is allowed between the adoptee and the ascendants of the adoptive parents. In simple adoption the same prohibitions apply to the blood family as the original legal links are maintained. The same applies with full adoption for genetic reasons.[107] Again Courbe points out that the application of these prohibitions is impossible as formally adopted people do not have any information as to the identity of their blood relatives. Thus adopted people find themselves barred from marrying a greater number of people than anyone else and to top it off it is impossible for them to identify half of them.

In Ireland the issue of marriage between persons related by adoption has not be addressed under statute or common law. Section 24 of the Adoption Act 1952 provides that upon an adoption order being made, the adopted child:

Shall be considered with regard to the rights and duties of parents and children in relation to each other as their child of an adopter or adopters, born to him, he or them in lawful wedlock.

---

104 'L'adoption confère a l'enfant une filiation qui se substitue a sa filiation d'origine'.

105 'L'adopté a dans la famille de l'adoptant, les mêmes droits et les mêmes obligations qu'un enfant légitime.'

106 Article 366 C.c.

107 Article 356 al. 1 C.c.

Shatter notes that it is doubtful whether the adoption act could be interpreted so as to prohibit a marriage between an adopted child and such child's adoptive brother and sister.[108] The Law Reform Commission recommended that statutory prohibition apply to marriage between a parent and his/her adoptive child and between adoptive siblings even in cases where an adoption order ceases to exist.[109] The Commission also considered the question of informal adoption and decided that on balance it would be too difficult to draft legislation for such a case.

As regards adoption in the UK, the 1926 act reflected the view that it would be abhorrent to allow a purely artificial relationship to operate as a bar to marriage and there was no provision to about the effect of adoption on the prohibited degrees. It was only in 1949 that the Adoption of Children Act 1975 barred marriage between a child and his or her adopted parents. No legislation in the UK bars marriage between an adopted child and their adopted brothers and sisters.

It would appear when it comes to adoption that the genetic argument for justifying the affinity laws and the undue influence argument are in conflict. While the genetic argument may seem paramount it is not carried over to other areas of the law. While it is admirable for the law to prevent harm to potential offspring of a relationship it is doubtful that this interest is really served in situations by punishing parties to a marriage when they do not know that they are genetically related. Arguable a better policy would be to make such marriages void only in the situation where the parties married in wilful knowledge of the genetic relationship.

4.4. THE PROHIBITED DEGREES OF RELATIONSHIP IN OTHER FORMS OF REGISTERED PARTNERSHIP AND *DE FACTO* RELATIONSHIPS

The *de facto* argument advanced in both *B and L* and *O'Shea* was that regardless of the justification for the rules prohibiting marriage within the prohibited relationships the reality is that the rules do not prevent such relationships from actually happening. The point has been made that there cannot be unlimited rights to marry as the law regards the relationship as one of legal significance and so the conferring of legal consequences on a relationship gives the law the rights to state who may enter into that relationship.[110] It is clear from the prohibited degrees that relationships between those related by legal ties are to be discouraged but not to

108 A.J. Shatter, *Shatter's Family Law*, 4 ed, 1997 Butterworths, Dublin, p. 156.

109 Law Reform Commission Report on 'Nullity of marriage' (LRC 9–1984).

110 K. McK. Norrie, 'Incest and the Forbidden Degrees of Marriage in Scots Law', *Journal of the Law Society of Scotland*, 1992 Vol 37 No 6, p. 216.

the extent that the law interferes with the de facto equivalent of such relationships. The question remains as to whether the prohibited degrees of affinity should then apply to registered partnerships. Does the legislature although admitting that affinity laws cannot prevent such relationships in fact occurring, disapprove of them so much that no legal significance should be given to people in these relationships?

As other forms of formal relationship developed in Europe the question arose as to whether the same prohibitions should apply to civil unions and other registered partnerships. To extend the prohibitions would show that such relationships were still unacceptable but would be contrary to public policy as it would prevent such couples from availing of the protection of a registered partnership. The traditional impediments to marriage have been copied into the French PACS,[111]and the British Civil Partnership Act. The prohibitions in the French PACS are actually stricter than those for marriage as they are not subject to dispensation.[112]

The British Civil Partnership Act 2004 has equivalent prohibitions to those in the Marriage Act 1949 as the policy was that the law of marriage and of civil partnership should be as similar as possible[113] This meant that the prohibited degrees were copied into the act for no better reason than they remain part of the marriage legislation.

Although Ireland currently has no legal framework for relationships outside marriage, recent bills on the subject have included the traditional prohibited degrees of relationship. Section 23 of the 2006 Civil Union Bill[114] prohibited a union between a person and their ascendants, descendents or siblings. At first glance it did not seem to include those related by affinity however Section 43 of the Act stated that says that for the purpose of any enactment the expressions brother-in-law, daughter-in-law etc. include relationships arising by virtue of a civil union. Presumably this would include the 1537 act as amended and preclude those related by affinity from entering into a civil union.

As the purpose of registered partnerships is generally to give legal recognition to those who do not have the capacity to marry, it is submitted that there is no social justification for denying those related by affinity from such recognition.

---

111 Art 515-2 Cc.

112 P. Malaurie/H. Fulchiron, *La Famille*, 2nd edn, Defrénois, Paris, 2006 [217].

113 The 16th Report of the Joint Committee on Human Rights "Proposal for a Draft Marriage Act 1949 (Remedial) Order 2006", HL Paper 154 HC 1022.

114 A person has no capacity to enter into a civil union with–
a lineal ancestor or descendant
a sibling, or
a sibling of a lineal ancestor or descendant·

5. CONCLUSION

Australia,[115] Norway and Sweden[116] have abolished all bars on marriage based on affinity. The ECHR in *B and L* established that arbitrary prohibitions on the right to marry are contrary to the convention. It is clear that the prohibitions on marriage between those related by affinity have changed from being a universally understood element of marriage itself to being a restriction on marriage. This change is yet another example of how the right to marry is growing stronger and the restrictions on the right to marry are constantly being eroded.

It is not this author's contention that we should throw away all rules restricting marriage particularly between those related by blood ties. However the law must reflect on the purpose of invalidating marriages between those related by affinity or where the parties are not at fault. As family ties become ever looser we should wonder as to why we prevent people from forming stable legally recognised relationships because of perceived kinship ties that are not universally recognised by society at large.

115 S. Parker et al., *Australian Family Law in Context. Commentary and Material*, Sweet and Maxwell, 1994.

116 D. Bradley, *Family Law and Political Culture – Scandinavian Laws in Comparative Perspective*, Sweet and Maxwell, 1996.

THE MUSLIM DOWER (*MAHR*) IN EUROPE – WITH SPECIAL REFERENCE TO SWEDEN

Mosa Sayed*

1. INTRODUCTION

During the last three decades Sweden has experienced, through immigration, a considerable enlargement of the Muslim population in the country. As a result Swedish courts and other authorities more frequently have had to deal with Muslim family law and to make decisions in questions origination from Muslim legal orders. One of the most frequently arising issues has been how Swedish courts should respond to demands on *mahr* – the Muslim dower – by Muslim wives. Today, there are several cases decided by Swedish courts relating to *mahr*.[1] Such claims have been made both in situations where the legal relationship, due to its foreign connections, falls with in the ambit of the Swedish private international law rules and in situations where the case is purely internal (domestic). Since a legal construction similar to *mahr* does not exist in the Swedish legal system, it has turned out to be challenging how to assess claims like these.

The *mahr*[2] is an agreement where the husband-to-be promises or gives property to his future wife as a result of the forthcoming marriage. It can be money or anything of economic value. The *mahr* is compulsory for the Muslim husband-to-be irrespective of whether he is marrying a Muslim woman or a woman with

* I would like to thank Professor Maarit Jänterä-Jareborg at the University of Uppsala for reading and commenting on several drafts of this article. Throughout the discussions with Professor Jänterä-Jareborg I have drafted the most central parts of the paper.

1 RH 1993:116 (decision by a court of appeal), RH 2005:66 (decision by a court of appeal), Case no. T 10083–04 (unpublished decision by a court of appeal), Case no. T 3289–02 (decision by the district court of Uppsala), Case no. T 3391–05 (conciliation by the district court of Falun) and Case no. T 1069106 (an ongoing case in the district court of Gothenburg).

2 The Koran uses different words for *mahr*. One expression is sadaq (chapter 4 verse 4) which in its basic form comes from the root of to be sincere or to speak the truth. Another word that the Koran uses for *mahr* is *farida* (chapter 2 verses 236 and 237). *Farida* is the term used to describe a religious obligation. A third Koranic word for *mahr* is ajr (chapter 5 verse 5). The meaning of ajr is a (religious) reward without any consideration.

another religion (chapter 5 verse 5 Koran) and whether the marriage is concluded in a country with a Muslim legal order or not.

Decisions by the Swedish courts show that the Muslim dower is handled with great difficulties by the Swedish authorities. The *mahr* has turned out to be a complicated legal institution from the point of view of Swedish private international law as well as Swedish substantive law. At the same time the majority of Muslims – in Sweden and abroad – consider the *mahr* to be an integrated part of the Muslim marriage and as an institution manifesting a tradition closely connected to a religious practice. For these reasons, but also for the sake of safeguarding the interests of Muslim women in Sweden, it is of importance that we seek clarity in how to deal with the Muslim dower.

2. *MAHR* IN SWEDEN – PRESENTATION OF TYPICAL CASES

Questions relating to *mahr* occur in Sweden in both private international law cases and in purely internal cases where the agreement is domestic. The difference between situations of an international and an internal nature will be illustrated below through five different examples concerning situations where an agreement on *mahr* (or the conclusion of the marriage) may be made:

1. The agreement is concluded by foreign citizens in a foreign country with a Muslim legal order (where the spouses were also living at the time of the marriage).
2. The agreement is concluded abroad by two persons, where one (irrespective of citizenship) was living in Sweden and the other, a foreign citizen, was living in the foreign country where the agreement was concluded.
3. The agreement is concluded abroad by parties who both live in Sweden.
4. The agreement is concluded in Sweden by persons living in Sweden at the time of the marriage and at least one of them was a foreign citizen.
5. The agreement is concluded in Sweden among two Swedish citizens living in Sweden.

These situations give rise to different legal questions. Situations 1–4 qualify as private international law cases since the legal relationship in these cases has connections with a foreign legal order (either by way of residence in a foreign country or by the parties′ foreign citizenship or by the foreign marriage/*mahr* contract). In the last case, the spouses are Swedish citizens living in Sweden. Because of these reasons and since the legal relationship lacks any relevant connecting factors to a foreign legal order, the case qualifies as an internal (domestic) case and will not, in contrast to cases 1–4, raise questions of private international law. Private international law questions relate to issues of the courts′ jurisdiction, the applicable law and issues on how and when a domestic court should apply foreign law. The last case, on the contrary, is in all circumstances governed by appropriate (substantive) rules in Swedish law, since there is no foreign connection.

3. *MAHR* AGREEMENTS AMONG MUSLIMS IN SWEDEN

Many Muslim spouses who conclude a marriage in Sweden agree on *mahr*. A survey which I carried out at the Uppsala mosque shows, however, that the terms in the *mahr* agreements differ greatly. This survey covered 46 marriages celebrated at the Uppsala mosque during 1996–2000. [3] The amount of the agreed *mahr*, how it is paid and when it is paid (that is to say if it is prompt or deferred) differed among the studied contracts. Although in the majority of the studied cases the spouses-to-be had agreed on *mahr*, the content of the agreement appeared to be dependent on the spouses' country of origin, but also on the parties' personal characteristics. In cases where one of the spouses was of Swedish origin and had converted to Islam the spouses agreed upon a prompt dower (payable at the time of signing the marriage agreement) of symbolic value.

In the majority of the studied cases the parties had divided the *mahr* into two parts, i.e. the first part payable at the time of signing the marriage contract (the so-called prompt dower) and the other part being deferred. None of the contracts stipulate when the deferred part is payable, probably at the time of divorce since this is the custom when there is a lack of a specific agreement. The prompt part of the dower was often composed of a symbolic value (from 0 to 9,000 euro). [4] In some cases it consisted of a flower, a Koran or an item of jewellery (a ring, necklace or bracelet). The deferred part, on the other hand, could represent a considerable sum of money. In one case the parties had agreed on 25,000 euro being deferred (in this case the prompt part was also 25,000 euro). Another couple had agreed upon 10,000 euro as a deferred part. In two cases the deferred part of the *mahr* was a house (in the first case a house in Algeria and in the other a house in

---

3 I thank Sayed Osman and the mosque in Uppsala for allowing me to use the files containing marriage contracts concluded under the authority of the mosque. In Sweden certain religious communities are authorised to officiate at legally binding marriages, which includes the mosque in Uppsala (certain Imams there).

4 Only 1 out of 46 studied contracts had stipulated a *mahr* with a zero amount.

Sweden). In eight cases the deferred dower amounted to a value of between 3,000–6,000 euro.

My moderate survey shows that in the absolute majority of marriage contracts the couples had agreed on *mahr*. The parties in most cases had a strong connection with Sweden (out of 92 persons, 43 were Swedish citizens). Only in a few cases did the parties agree to a *mahr* with a very high value (10,000 euro or more). It was also evident that in cases where one of the parties was of Swedish origin the *mahr* consisted of a symbolic object with a limited value or money which was of symbolic value. On the other hand, the agreements with the highest value where among the cases where both parties originated from a country with a Muslim legal order. The *mahr* was often divided into two parts, where the deferred part was considerably more than the prompt part. This implies that the parties, in accordance with the traditions of the country of origin, wished to use the *mahr* as an institution closely connected to divorce, rather than to circumstances prevailing at the time of signing the marriage contract (or to marriage itself).

4. *MAHR* BEFORE THE ADVENT OF ISLAM

An understanding of the essence of the *mahr* in the Muslim legal system[5] requires some knowledge of how the pre-Islamic rules relating to *mahr* were constructed in the area where the Islamic message was announced. Statements regarding the pre-Islamic society are in this text simplified and presented briefly. It is important to note that the tribal pre-Islamic society was not a homogeneous society and that the evidence concerning the pre-Islamic situation is sometimes fragmentary.[6] Mecka, for example, was a developed commercial town where women to some extent were allowed to own property. As an example we could refer to the Prophet's first wife Khadija bint Khuwaylid. Khadija was an independent businesswoman who owned trade caravans.

It is however generally accepted that the Koran resulted in vast legal reforms.[7] Many of the rules in the Koran were a reaction to the rules of the pre-Islamic

5 Discrepancies do sometimes exist between the law and practice in some Muslim communities. It is important to bear in mind that the theory of *mahr* is not always the same as how the people practise the institution.

6 Watt, Muhammad at Medina p. 283. According to Watt, for example, "it may be that Islam merely consolidated a social trend that was already dominant" in the pre-Islamic society. However, by allowing women to personally receive the *mahr* paid by the bridegroom, it is, according Watt, notable that Islam came to treat the woman as an individual, Muhammad at Medina p. 283.

7 Roberts, *The Social Laws of the Qoran*.

society. The Koran prohibited, reformed, or sometimes merely adopted customs with some modification governing life in the Arabic peninsula at the time of the revelation.[8] The *mahr*, as we see it today in the Muslim legal systems, has many other legal institutions as its origin in the pre-Islamic society. The rules in the Koran radically transformed the institution of *mahr*. The Koranic form of *mahr* is constructed with the ambition of improving the financial and legal position of women.

In the pre-Islamic society the *mahr* was an essential part of the marriage contract and a marriage without a *mahr* was regarded as shameful and looked upon as concubinage.[9] The *mahr* was given to the guardian (the *wali*) of the bride and it was equivalent to a purchase price.[10] Through the *mahr* arrangement the bride became the property of the husband. The husband's heir (such as sons from an earlier relationship and brothers) could at the time of his death inherit the wife in the same way as other inheritable property. This meant that they could marry the wife without paying a *mahr* since the *mahr* had already been paid by the deceased husband. Marital rights were in the pre-Islamic society equivalent to rights of property which could be inherited and which the heir could sell if he pleased. These customs were forbidden by the Koran.

5. *MAHR* ACCORDING TO THE KORAN

The Koran states explicitly that it is forbidden to inherit women against their will (chapter 4 verse 19). The rules in the Koran – by way of the revised *mahr* – raised the woman to the same legal level as the man in the negotiations preceding a marriage. According to the Koran, to pay the *mahr* is an obligation for every Muslim man who intends to enter into a marriage. The Koran states that lawful wives are those to whom the dower has been paid (chapter 33 verse 50) and Muslims should give to women their dower (upon marriage) as a free gift (chapter 4 verse 4). In accordance with these rules, the *mahr* became a gift given by the husband *directly* to the wife. The dower belongs to the woman and no one else. The relevant verse namely speaks about the *mahr* as belonging to the wife, in contrast to the custom in the pre-Islamic society. It is only when the wife remits part of the *mahr* voluntarily that her husband can share it or take part therein (chapter 4 verse 4). The

8 The situations where the Koran retains legal solutions (with more or less modifications) originating from the pre-Islamic time is not limited to *mahr*. For example, the Muslim law of inheritance is a combination of new Koranic rules and the prevailing pre-Islamic customs relating to this field. In this legal field the Koran only introduced radical changes to the pre-Islamic situation.

9 *The Encyclopedia of Islam* (edited by Bosworth, Donzel, Lewis and Pellat 1991) p. 78–80.

10 Robertson Smith, *Kinship & marriage in early Arabia* (1885 new impression 1990) p. 111.

dower is given to the woman as a gift without consideration. The Koranic dower differs from the pre-Islamic customs since a marriage combined with *mahr* was no longer seen as a purchase, thereby obtaining ownership over a woman which is inheritable by the heirs of the deceased.

6. *MAHR* IN CONTEMPORARY MUSLIM LEGAL ORDERS

Statutory provisions in contemporary Muslim legal orders have followed the basic rules established in the Koran. On a detail level there exist differences caused by the fact that different Muslim legal orders follow different schools of law.[11] The differences are the result of legal schools' different interpretations of the legal sources (the Koran and the Prophetical traditions, e.g. the *Sunna* of the Prophet).

Another major impact on how the *mahr* is constructed are the customs prevailing in the society in question. Since Muslim law was fashioned in close connection to prevailing local customary law and practice, the law could take different forms depending on the society. In some Muslim communities, old customs are also given preference before the Muslim Sharia. And in some of them, a great discrepancy exists between the law and its practice among the people. Among the *Kabyles*, who belong to the Berbers of Algeria, marriage is still a form of purchase in which the dower is paid by the husband to the father of the bride.[12] In Egypt a marital financial system called *Shabka* exists parallel to *mahr*. The *Shabka* (gold jewellery), which becomes the property of the wife, is given by the husband in close relation to the conclusion of a marriage.

The *mahr* often takes two forms called *mahr musamma*, a specified dower, or *mahr al-mithl*, which can best be translated as "a dower and the like" which means a dower appropriate to the status of the woman. The *mahr al-mithl* is required where a marriage contract lacks an agreement on *mahr* or the agreed *mahr* is invalid. An example of a *mahr* that is invalid is when the agreement concerns a prohibited item or where the husband, as an alternative to a material *mahr*, prom-

---

11 In Islamic jurisprudence there are two major directions called Sunni and Shia. The majority of Muslims adhere to one of the Sunni schools of law. Today there exist four Sunni schools of law called Hanafi, Maliki, Shafii and Hanbali. According to the majority of Muslim scholars these schools have the same value. Among the Shia there is one dominant school of law called the Jafari school of law or Ithna asharia (the twelvers). In Iran the Jafari is the official school of law (article 12 of the Iranian constitution).

12 Anderson, *Law Reform in the Muslim World* p. 11.

ises his wife an undertaking such as a divorce from his former wife. [13] *Mahr al-mithl* is considered to be a *mahr* of a woman who is the wife's equal (a close relative on the paternal side, such as her sisters, paternal aunt, paternal cousins and so on). It is also based on circumstances relating to the woman's personal qualities, such as her age, beauty, virginity, education, character, social status and other such considerations. The *mahr musamma* is specified in the marriage contract. Further, a specified dower is often, but not always, divided into *mahr muqaddam* (in advance) and *muákhar* (deferred). Another way of settling the payment of *mahr* is to stipulate in the contract that the deferred *mahr* is to be paid upon the request of the woman (*'inda mutalib*). The prompt dower is paid in connection with the signing of the marriage contract and before the consummation of the marriage by sexual intercourse. The deferred dower is in general payable upon divorce (if the spouses have not agreed anything else). The payment of *mahr* in advance, upon divorce or at the request of the woman is merely a traditional way of fixing the agreement. These conditions do not affect the *mahr* itself. It becomes the property of the woman by the agreement, and if she dies her heirs may claim it as part of her estate.[14]

In traditional Muslim law as well in contemporary legislation in Muslim legal orders, the agreed *mahr* is in practice only payable when the spouses have consummated the marriage by sexual intercourse. In cases where a divorce occurs on the initiative of the husband, without the marriage being consummated, the wife is entitled to receive only half of the agreed *mahr* (chapter 2 verse 237 Koran). If the divorce occurs before consummation, without there being an agreement on *mahr*, the wife is, according to the Koran, entitled to a gift but not to a *mahr* (chapter 2 verse 236).[15] In theory, the rules indicate that the payment of *mahr* is closely linked to the act of consummation.[16] In practice this is not the case as questions relating to *mahr* and its payment in most cases occur when there is a divorce.

7. THE FUNCTIONS OF *MAHR*

When it comes to analyzing the functions of *mahr*, it is important to emphasize the religious dimensions of the institution. For many Muslims, independent of

13 Tyabji, *Muhammadan Law* p. 172.

14 El Alami, *The Marriage Contract in Islamic Law* p. 110.

15 This also means that a marriage contract is valid without an agreement on the *mahr*, since a divorce can only occur after a valid marriage.

16 The wife has the right to refuse her husband's conjugal rights until the fulfilment of the agreement. This means, in cases where the husband has fulfilled his obligation to give the *mahr* or in cases where the spouses have agreed on a deferred dower, that the wife cannot refuse her husband's conjugal rights.

whether they live in a country with a Muslim legal order or not, the *mahr* is a religious practice with important and far-reaching legal consequences, since it is a practice which is prescribed in the Koran. Because of this, agreements on *mahr* are often carried out as part of the religious practice.

It is often said that the *mahr* is stipulated to underline the prestige of the marriage and to stress its importance.[17] The *mahr* is given, according to this reasoning, as a mark of respect for the wife and also as a sign of the husband's seriousness concerning the marriage.[18]

In practice, the *mahr* will have different functions depending on the conditions prevalent in a country. Of relevance is how the rules relating to family relations are construed in the current country (for example, the grade of the patriarchal structure and how divorce rules are construed), the financial and social status of the spouses-to-be and their personal qualifications such as education. It is not unusual that customs relating to *mahr* differ among people in the same country, depending, for example, on whether it is a marriage in a rural or an urban part of the country.

7.1. *MAHR* AS AN INSTRUMENT FOR THE TRANSFER OF PROPERTY

The *mahr* has financial implications when property is transferred from the husband to the wife. If the spouses have agreed on a prompt dower, it will increase the wife's property in marriage. Since in a Muslim legal order marriage does not result in any community of property between the spouses, the wife will independently control the property obtained as *mahr*. Since a maintenance obligation is a duty for the husband, the wife does not need the *mahr* for maintenance but can dispose of it as she pleases. In cases where the *mahr* is deferred, it means a financial safety net for the wife in case of divorce, subject to the condition that it is large enough.

7.2. *MAHR* AS A SAFEGUARD FOR WOMEN IN MARRIAGE

The customs and rules relating to *mahr* show that women develop strategies to manage and survive in patriarchal systems with rigid rules relating to family rela-

---

17 Nasir, *The Islamic Law of Personal Status*, p. 83.

18 Sayyid Sabiq, *Fiqh us-Sunnah*, Vol. 3 p. 31 (it can be found in translation by Amira Zrein Matraji).

tions. *Mahr* can, to some extent, be used as a counterbalance to family rules that manifest strict traditional views and in relation to men who use these structures to their advantage in marriage. Even if the financial implications of *mahr* can play a roll, these are often of minor importance in legal orders with a rigid family system. In these cases *mahr* will play its most important role in creating family stability. Additionally, it will not only safeguard the rights of women in marriage and create family stability, but in many cases it will also be used as the only instrument for ending an unwanted marriage.

Iran provides an illustrating example of how family law rules affect the decisions and conduct relating to how *mahr* is used. Before the Islamic revolution in 1979 it was not unusual for couples to stipulate a symbolic *mahr* with a minimum value, e.g. a gold coin or a Koran.[19] Among educated couples the *mahr* was often viewed as "an outdated institution, indicative of the purchase of women through marriage".[20] Since the Iranian law at this time gave women and men equal rights in matters of divorce and custody, women felt that they no longer needed a substantial *mahr* as a safeguard. However, when men's traditional right to divorce and polygamy were reintroduced, as a result of the Islamic revolution, the importance and value of the agreed *mahr* increased. One major reason for this, according to Mir-Hosseini, is that a *mahr* with a high value functions as a safeguard for women in marriage. Regarding Iran, Mir-Hosseini`s study shows that the value of the agreed *mahr* is always beyond the immediate financial means of the groom.[21] This is essential in order to ensure the role of the *mahr* as a safeguard for women in marriage. It will be costly for the husband to divorce his wife and costly to take several wives since the first could force him to pay the *mahr* if she disagrees with the second marriage. Since the payment of the *mahr* in Iran in predominant cases is made upon the request of the wife, the *mahr* will not only safeguard the interests of the wife in the marriage, but it can also be used as a bargaining instrument by the wife to end an unwanted marriage.[22]

---

19 It is interesting that the survey relating to *mahr* agreements concluded in Uppsala also shows that in many cases where the couple or one of them had his or her origins in Iran the contract stipulated only a Koran or a finite amount of money, although there are examples of the opposite among parties originating from Iran. This could be a sign of the fact that couples relate their agreement on *mahr* to the legal, social and financial conditions prevailing in Sweden, in the same way as the *mahr* agreement in Iran before 1979 was a reflection of the legal and financial conditions of the country.

20 Mir-Hosseini, *Marriage on Trial – Islamic Family Law in Iran and Morocco,* p. 75.

21 Mir-Hosseini, *Marriage on Trial – Islamic Family Law in Iran and Morocco,* p. 73.

22 Over 50 per cent of all divorces in Teheran (Iran) were so-called khul' divorces, Mir-Hosseini p. 82. Khul' is the termination of the marriage at the request of the wife by returning property to the husband. Usually the wife gives up her right to *mahr* or returns property amounting to the value of a received *mahr.*

A *mahr* with elevated value will perhaps prevent the husband from divorcing his wife impulsively. However, customs that presuppose a high *mahr* will also have certain negative consequences. A high *mahr* can become an obstacle to marrying. In urban Egypt it has become a normal situation that people do not marry because they cannot afford the marriage gifts (the Shabka) and the *mahr*. At the same time marriage is regarded as an essential part of religious practice. Since extramarital relations are considered to be a disgrace, the situation has become frustrating for young people without the financial means to marry.

In the same way as in societies with a mainly Muslim legal order, *mahr* can create family stability in Muslim marriages in Sweden. The typical case for litigation in the Swedish courts concerning *mahr* has turned out to be the case where a man, often a Swedish citizen, originating from a country with a Muslim legal order, marries a woman who at the time of the marriage still lives in the couples's country of origin. In certain cases, the woman has received a temporary residence permit in Sweden and moves to Sweden. A short time after her arrival, the husband announces that he wishes to terminate the marriage by divorce. A woman in this situation is, for explainable reasons, in a weak, inferior position and a divorce will place her in a precarious situation, since the residence permit is temporary and conditional upon the existence of the marriage. When the divorce becomes definitive, the woman will only have the option either to return to her country of origin or to stay illegally in Sweden. A return to her country of origin is, presumably, connected with shame. And to illegally stay in Sweden and risk deportation is connected with strong psychological pressure and insecurity.

A liability to fulfil an agreement on *mahr* in these cases would not, in all certainty, change the prevailing situation. But knowledge of the fact that a divorce is linked to a considerable *mahr* obligation would most likely have a preventive effect. As a result, a divorce would be preceded by careful thought and consideration, and this in turn could control impulsive pledges for divorce. Another aspect, concerning the fact that a marriage in these cases can give rise to a liability to pay a considerable *mahr*, is that it will force people (men) to reflect before entering into a marriage. The reason is that a liability to pay *mahr* could also prevent inconsiderate, impulsive decisions to enter into a marriage, since a divorce can have considerable financial consequences for the husband. This could in the long run consequently improve marriage and family stability.

7.3. *MAHR* AS WOMEN'S BARGAINING TOOL FOR ACHIEVING A DIVORCE

Divorce laws in some Muslim legal orders, such as Iran and some other Muslim states, unilaterally favour men. Traditionally, men can divorce their wives without providing any grounds, whereas women, at best, can obtain a divorce from a court only upon establishing certain grave reasons often stipulated in the marriage contract.[23] If such grounds are not established, it is difficult, if not impossible, for women to obtain a divorce. In these cases the wife has to rely on the husband's goodwill, since a divorce is formally established at the initiative of the husband. *Mahr* can be of decisive importance as a bargaining tool in achieving a divorce from the husband. One can say that the wife, by giving up her right to *mahr*, will purchase the divorce from her husband.

These divorce rules have to some extent been compensated by the Khul′ institution which allows the wife to obtain a divorce by returning or giving some property to the husband.[24] However, in traditional Muslim law the Khul′ divorce is meant to be applied in situations where the marriage leads to harm to one of the parties. Further, a khul′ in its traditional form is only established by the consent of the husband.[25] The property which the wife has to return to the husband is a

---

23 All schools of Muslim law allow the wife to initiate a judicial divorce. However, there is a divergence of opinion among the schools concerning the grounds for the court to dissolve a marriage. The Hanafi school of law, predominant in South East Asia, in some Middle Eastern countries and Egypt, is the most restrictive. Shii law is only slightly more generous concerning the grounds on which it permits a wife to petition for divorce, see Caroll, Quran 2 229 "A Charter Granted to the Wife"? Judicial Khul′ in Pakistan, Islamic Law and Society, Vol. 3, No. 1, 1996. To widen women's options with regard to divorce, Egypt has taken most of its rulings from the more liberal Maliki school of law (by way of *takhayyur*, the legal method where Muslims can choose among the laws in the different legal schools). The Hanafi school of law is generally regarded as sensitive to changes and developments, see WELCHMAN, *Womens Rights & Islamic Law – Perspectives on Reform*, p. 32.

24 Khul′ is often defined as al-Talaq bil′wad, a divorce by giving something in return, Doi, Sharia, The Islamic Law p. 192. There are several verses in the Koran that have been interpreted as legitimizing the khul′ institution. Chapter 4 verse 128 says that if a wife fears cruelty or desertion on the part of her husband, there is no blame if they reach an amicable settlement. Further, chapter 2 verse 229 states that if you (judges and the court) fear that they (the spouses) would be unable to keep the limits ordained by God, there is no blame on either of them if she gives something for her freedom. In the Prophetical traditions it is narrated that the wife of Thabit bin Qais came to the Prophet saying "O Allah's Messenger! I do not blame Thabit for defects in his character or his religion, but I, being a Muslim, dislike behaving in an un-Islamic manner (if I remain with him)." The Prophet answered, "Will you give back the garden which your husband has given you (as *mahr*)?" She answered "yes". The Prophet ordered Thabit to divorce her, as narrated in AL-BUKHARI, Vol 7 (*Kitab talaq, The book of divorce*) hadith no. 5273–5277, it can be found In the translation by MUHSIN KHAN.

25 For example, when Doi is speaking about Khul′ he says that the wife "can release herself from the tie, by giving up the whole or some of the property in return, in consideration of which the

matter for the spouses to decide, although in most cases the wife returns the *mahr* or other value amounting to the *mahr*. In cases where the agreement stipulates a deferred dower, she will simply give up her right to thereto.

In 2000 the Egyptian legislator enacted a controversial law,[26] whose original draft had attracted severe criticism from the religious establishment.[27] One of the most criticised and discussed parts of the new law was the wife's right to obtain a khul′ divorce from the court in return for giving up all her Sharia financial rights and returning the dower (Article 20).[28] The most sensational part of this is that the wife can petition and obtain a divorce by a court order without establishing grounds or proving injury even cases where the husband refuses to agree to a divorce. However, she must explicitly state that "she detests her life with her husband, that there is no way that their marital life can continue, and that she fears that she will fail to abide by the limits of God by reason of the hatred she has".[29]

In the debate concerning the draft it was alleged that such rules "would open the door to in particular wealthy women to flee their marital responsibilities and to break up their families" (The Islamic Studies Academy). According to the religious scholars of al-Azhar the proposed Khul′ provision was an explicit violation of the rulings in Sharia, and extremely dangerous for the integrity of the family since it gave the final decision to the judge and overrode the will of the husband. Opponents of the law attacked it on social, religious and political grounds. It was claimed that poor women could not resort to the law since they are not able to return the *mahr*, that the provision is a direct violation of the Sharia and a result of a Zionist conspiracy, initiated by foreign parties.

Regarding *mahr* as a tool for divorce for Muslim women Muslims in Sweden often seek a divorce decision by the religious leaders in the new country, i.e. Sweden. This, informal, religious divorce is demanded side by side with the formal divorce decision announced by a Swedish court. There are several reasons for this conduct. The most important one is that marriages concluded in a Muslim legal order (the spouses' country of origin) or concluded abroad but registered and

husband is to give her a "Khul′" and when they have done this, an irreversible divorce would take place with the consent of each other", Sharia, *The Islamic Law*, p. 193.

26 Law no. 1 of 2000 Concerning Certain Situations and Procedures of Litigation in Personal Status Matters.

27 The views and criticism brought forward in the debate by different Egyptian organization is summarized in Welchman, Womens Rights and Islamic Law – Perspectives on Reform p. 58–68.

28 The wife loses all her financial rights if she applies for a Khul′ divorce. This means that she has to return not only the *mahr*, but also other gifts (the Shabka) given in connection with the marriage, and also her right to maintenance under the waiting period for divorce.

29 Welchman, p. 68.

recognized in the country of origin can often be dissolved only if the divorce corresponds to the rules in the Islamic Sharia. This means that there is a risk that the authorities in the country of origin will not recognize a divorce announced by a Swedish court, since the divorce grounds do not correspond with the Muslim rules in the country in question. The consequence could therefore be a so-called "limping marriage/limping divorce". The spouses are divorced under Swedish law, but at the same time they are still married in the view of the law of the country of origin. This has of course far reaching consequences for the spouses and in particular for the wife. In the view of the country of origin, guardianship over the wife and the children is still with the husband. This means that the (divorced) wife needs the husband's permission for making decisions that affect the family. For example, if she visits her country of origin she will, in the view of the prevailing law in that country, need permission from the husband to leave the country, since she is regarded as a married woman. This situation can be solved by the assistance of Muslim authorities' in the mosques of Sweden. The mosques may issue a "Muslim" divorce certificate written in Arabic corresponding to the Swedish court decree. But experience has shown that in some cases mosques have refused such a request with reference to the fact that the wife lacked Sharia grounds for divorce. In these cases, the *mahr* can play an important role in the divorce negotiations, since a divorce based on the rules in the Sharia presuppose the consent of the husband or that the spouses′ are in agreement.

8. *MAHR* IN CASES WITH FOREIGN CONNECTING FACTORS

In the majority of the *mahr* cases heard by the Swedish courts, there was a strong legal relationship with a country with a Muslim legal order. The spouses had namely entered into the marriage abroad in such a country where also the agreement on *mahr* had been made. I will use two cases as examples, RH 1993:116 and RH 2005:66 decided by two different Swedish courts of appeal (the second instance in the Swedish court hierarchy) to illustrate the problems that may rise when dealing with claims relating to the *mahr* in the Swedish courts. The cases are international in character and raise a multitude of questions. These questions relate to how to qualify the institution, the jurisdiction of the Swedish courts, the choice of the applicable law, *lis pendens* (since the issue at stake is often raised in the courts in more than one country), public policy and so on. All these questions will not be discussed. Instead this paper will focus on questions directly connected to the essence and legal nature of *mahr*.

Considering the outcomes in these cases, the qualification of *mahr* has turned out to be problematic. Since the classification of the institution varies in these cases, it is of major interest to present and discuss the argumentation by the courts concerning this issue in more detail. The qualification issue is decisive in how to decide on the applicable law. Questions relating to public policy will not be discussed in this paper, since this aspect has not been at stake in these cases.[30]

8.1. RH 1993:116 – GENERAL DESCRIPTION

In this case two Israeli citizens of the Muslim faith and of Palestinian origin had entered into a marriage in August 1987 in Israel, in accordance with the family law rules applicable to Muslims in Israel. Immediately after the marriage the husband returned to Sweden, where he was already habitually resident at the time of the marriage. The wife was granted a residence permit in Sweden where she arrived in March 1988. The marriage contract between the spouses was subsequently registered in the religious Sharia court in Nazareth in Israel. The contract stipulated a *mahr* amounting to 15,000 Israeli shekels (at the time of the agreement equivalent to the value of around 4,500 euro).[31]

The spouses lived together in Sweden for a period of five months. The wife returned to Israel in August 1988. In October 1988, the husband applied for divorce in a Swedish court. After a period of reconsideration the wife approved the husband's divorce application, asking the district court to oblige him to pay her maintenance and to fulfil the agreement on *mahr.* According to the court of appeal, as regards maintenance, the applicable law should be the law in the country where the person entitled to maintenance has his or her habitual residence. And "in regard to what has been disclosed about *mohar*" (= *mahr*), the question relating to the applicable law should, in the view of the court of appeal, be treated in the same way as the maintenance issue. The applicable law should consequently follow the law in the country where the wife (as the one entitled to *mahr*) is habitually resident. Since the wife at the time of the decision was resident in Israel, the dispute relating to *mahr* was decided in accordance with relevant (Muslim) rules in Israel.

---

30 Public policy questions could of course arise. Assume that the husband grants half of the *mahr* but no more, claiming that the spouses have not consummated the marriage. Can a Swedish court approve this objection or does it contravene Swedish public policy? If a claim concerning the *mahr* is governed by the rules in a Muslim legal order, could a husband object to such a claim by saying that the fault for the breakdown of the marriage is to be attributed to the wife. This question was raised by Bogdan in "Islamisk brudpenning (*mahr*) inför svensk domstol", SvJT 1993 p. 600. Questions related to Swedish public policy could be raised in these and similar situations.

31 The *mahr* in this case was termed *mohar.* The term *mohar* is the Hebraic expression for *mahr*, *The Encyclopedia of Islam*, Vol VI p. 79 (Editors: Bosworth, Donzel, Lewis and Pellat).

The court obliged the former husband to fulfil the *mahr* agreement in accordance with the wife's request wife.

The court did not expressly raise the qualification issue and it did not explain its conclusions as to how it qualified the institution of *mahr*. Instead, it seems as if the court followed the opinion and the decision taken at first instance (= the district court). The expression "in regard to what has been disclosed about *mohar*" seems to refer to the district court's decision since nothing has been disclosed in the court of appeal relating to *mahr*. It is the district court that in its decision discussed, to some extent, the essence and the nature of *mahr*.

If we analyse the result with regard to statements in the district court's decision, the court seems to have focused on *one* aspect of *mahr*. Since *mahr*, when it is payable upon divorce (i.e. it is a deferred *mahr*), can have a function similar to that of maintenance paid as a lump sum upon divorce, the court equated it with maintenance. In the statements of the district court, a view that the court of appeal also seems to have shared, it is said that *mahr* "serves for the woman as insurance for the upholding of the marriage, since the husband at the time of divorce is compelled to fulfil his liability at once. In circumstances of divorce, on the other hand, the dower will function as the wife's maintenance and financial security."[32] The reasoning is based, according to the district court, on the fact that in Muslim family law mutual rights and obligations between the spouses come to an end upon divorce. When the marriage contract stipulates that the *mahr* is payable upon divorce it will, according to the court, function as maintenance.

8.2. QUALIFICATION OF *MAHR* AS A MAINTENANCE OBLIGATION

In RH 1993:116 the court of appeal stated that according to the rules applicable to the Muslim population in Israel, rights and obligations between the spouses are terminated upon divorce. The wife's right to maintenance and the (husband's) obligation to support is therefore a matter of rights and duties *within* marriage. In a situation where the spouses agree that the *mahr* is to be fulfilled in the case of divorce, the *mahr* will have the same function as maintenance. When the wife's right to maintenance ends by divorce, the *mahr* will replace the loss of the right of maintenance originating from the marriage. The approach taken by the courts

32 "Morgongåvan, vars storlek oftast fastställs i äktenskapskontraktet, fungerar för kvinnan som säkerhet för äktenskapets bestånd, eftersom mannen vid äktenskapsskillnad omedelbart måste uppfylla sin betalningsförpliktelse. Vid en eventuell äktenskapsskillnad kommer morgongåvan istället att fungera som hustruns underhåll och hennes finansiella skydd".

seems to be based on aspects of coherence; the *mahr* is interpreted in relation to how the maintenance obligation in marriage is constructed.

It is easy to understand the reason for the court's decision. It is uncomplicated to declare that the agreement on *mahr* will have the same result as a maintenance obligation. The spouse in need of maintenance (the wife) was also the receiver of the *mahr*. However, if the qualification of *mahr* as a maintenance right was to be seen as a general principle applicable in all cases, then this kind of qualification becomes problematic since it leads to uncertainty and sometimes to a loss of justice for Muslim women. Suppose that the husband was the one who lived in the Muslim legal order and the wife in Sweden (a situation which is quite normal in practical life among Muslims in Sweden) and the marriage contract stipulated a deferred *mahr*. According to the choice of law rule created by the court in RH 1993:116, the applicable law should follow the rules of the country where the spouse entitled to maintenance had his or her habitual residence. If the wife has had her habitual residence in Sweden, the applicable law would accordingly be Swedish law since it is the wife who is entitled to the *mahr* (to maintenance as the *mahr* was qualified in the case). Imagine, further, that the wife in this situation is the one with most wealth and income, since the standard of living, wages and possibilities to earn money are higher in Sweden than, for example, in Israel for the Palestinian population. Can a maintenance obligation for the husband, in relation to the decision in RH 1993:116, ever be possible? Can we speak about *mahr* as a maintenance obligation under such circumstances?

Characteristic of maintenance is, according to the Swedish concept, that it aims to meet the receiver's needs complementing or replacing the lack of income. A maintenance obligation is based on the fact that the supplier has the possibilities to provide it and that the receiver is in need of maintenance. If these conditions are not fulfilled, we cannot conclude that the *mahr* forms part of the maintenance institution. At least not in the sense that maintenance is understood under Swedish law!

Another problematic consequence of the qualification made in RH 1993:116 is that Swedish law will in this case be applied irrespective of the fact that the legal relationship has a stronger connection with the foreign legal order than it has with Sweden. Remember that the marriage in most of these cases had been concluded in the Muslim legal order from where the *mahr* agreement originated as the spouses or one of them often have a strong relationship with that legal order through the family, culture, citizenship or/and habitual residence. In view of fundamental private international law principles it is not reasonable to select the rules in one country in spite of the fact that the legal relationship is more strongly linked to another country.

Another aspect of the qualification of *mahr* made in RH 1993:116 is how to view agreements concluded in Sweden among Swedish Muslims, i.e. a situation where private international connecting factors pointing to a foreign legal order are lacking. Should these agreements, in accordance with RH 1993:116, be seen as (or placed on the same footing as) maintenance settlements between the spouses? Can spouses, before entering into a marriage, settle their maintenance relationship independent of future occurrences? Can spouses act in this way with the result of achieving a binding maintenance agreement, irrespective of the spouses' financial position at the time when the agreement is realized?

The Swedish substantive law rules relating to maintenance are generally seen as compulsory for the spouses. An agreement where a spouse gives up his or her right to maintenance in the future will for that reason not bind that spouse (RH 2004:42). Consequently, an agreement on maintenance obligations that has to be realized in the future cannot be binding if the circumstances in the case, at the time of realization, are not in line with the provisions of the maintenance rules. Since a spouse cannot give up the right to maintenance this means that a spouse cannot be obliged to pay maintenance in the future irrespective of the circumstances. If a stipulation on *mahr* is seen as a maintenance agreement it would follow that it would only be binding if a parallel responsibility to support is established by the maintenance rules in the relevant law.

Another issue is how to respond to cases where the agreement has to be fulfilled upon request. Let us say that the wife, in accordance with the agreement, demands that the husband fulfils the agreement at the time of the marriage. Is such a claim legally valid and enforceable if *mahr* is qualified as a maintenance obligation?

8.3. RH 2005:66 – GENERAL DESCRIPTION

The actual circumstances in this case are similar to those in RH 1993:116. In this case the marriage had been concluded in Iran between a man habitually resident in Sweden (with both Swedish and Iranian citizenship) and an Iranian woman habitually resident in Iran. Since the man could not return to Iran (for political or similar reasons) he entered into the marriage through a representative (the mother of the wife-to-be), i.e. marriage by proxy. In connection with the marriage agreement the spouses-to-be (the husband through the representative) settled a *mahr* amounting to 500 Bahar Azadi coins (representing a value of 25,000 euro), due to be paid at the request of the wife. The wife was granted a temporary residence permit in Sweden, and three days after her arrival in Sweden her husband explained that he wished to terminate the marriage. In connection with the divorce proceedings the wife demanded that the court should oblige the husband to fulfil the agreement on *mahr*, as was stipulated in the marriage contract.

In RH 1993:116 the court had qualified *mahr* as a maintenance obligation. In this case the court of appeal qualified *mahr* as an arrangement forming part of the spouses' matrimonial property relations. The court of appeal referred to the decision of the district court where the *mahr* was regarded as an institution that "adjusts the property relations between the spouses".[33] An adjustment of this kind, according to the court of appeal, falls within the ambit of spouses' matrimonial property relations regulated in the Act (1990:272) on questions of international character relating to spouses' and cohabitees' (matrimonial) property relations (LIMF) .[34] This kind of qualification seems to emanate from the reasoning of the lower court. Since the spouses had not obtained a habitual residence in the same country, the court had to find the law which had the strongest connection to the legal relationship. Since both spouses were citizens of Iran, the wife was also habitually resident in Iran at the time of the marriage and both parties had relatives in Iran, the court considered Iranian law to have the strongest connection with the legal relationship. Subsequently, the husband was obliged to fulfil the *mahr* agreement.

The district court's argumentation is based on some comments made in the preparatory works (the travaux préparatoires) to the 1990 law. According to these works, problems of demarcation can arise between lump-sum maintenance payments and the spouses' matrimonial property rights. The problem is whether to regard this lump sum as maintenance (and to follow the private international law rules relating to maintenance) or to regard the lump sum as an adjustment of the property relations between the spouses (and consequently regulated by the private international law rules relating to spouses' matrimonial property regimes). Characteristic of maintenance is, according to the preparatory works, that it aims to meet the daily needs of the receiver by complementing or replacing the lack of an income. On the other hand, a payment relating to the field of matrimonial property regimes seeks to bring about a (financial) adjustment between the spouses. In these cases the supporting aspect is typically of minor importance.

---

33 "I likhet med tingsrätten finner hovrätten att *mahr* skall anses vara en sådan utjämning av makars förmögenhetsförhållanden som faller under LIMF".

34 (Lag (1990:272) om internationella frågor rörande makars och sambos förmögenhetsförhållanden).

According to the preparatory works the court should in every given case come to a decision by considering the purpose of the payment and the circumstances under which it is made. These principles should guide the court independently of how the spouses have chosen to call their arrangement. Since *mahr* (in accordance with the Iranian provisions) becomes the property of the wife immediately upon the marriage ceremony and the wife from this moment has full disposal rights over the property, the court considered the *mahr* to be an arrangement forming part of the spouses′ matrimonial property relations.

8.4. *MAHR* AS PART OF THE SPOUSES' MATRIMONIAL PROPERTY

In RH 2005:66 the court qualified *mahr* as an institution within the area of spouses' matrimonial property relations. This means that in the case of litigation, the applicable law will be decided in accordance with the provisions in the 1990 law. According to §3 LIMF the spouses are able, with some restrictions provided in the law, to choose the applicable law concerning their matrimonial property relations.[35] If the spouses have not used the freedom to choose the applicable law, any litigation relating to the spouses′ matrimonial property should be decided in accordance with the law of the country where the spouses acquired habitual residence at the time of the marriage (§4 LIMF). In situations where the spouses did not acquire a common habitual residence, the case should, according to statements in the travaux préparatoires, be decided in accordance with the law of the country most closely connected to the legal relationship.

The chosen qualification of *mahr* in RH 2005:66 is in many cases well balanced and useful as a general principle.[36] It is functional in private international law cases as well as in cases where Swedish Muslims, without connecting factors pointing to a foreign legal order, agree on *mahr* in Sweden. In cases where we are dealing with an agreement that has to be decided in accordance with Swedish law, problems will of course arise when deciding on the exact rules to be applied. But this is an issue that falls outside the ambit of this article.

In my opinion many aspects make this qualification more appropriate than the one made in RH 1993:116. *Mahr* is an agreement that the spouses conclude before their marriage or in close connection thereto. The agreement can take several

35 The question whether one could regard a *mahr* agreement as a choice of law is not discussed in this paper.

36 A qualification of *mahr* as forming part of the spouses' matrimonial property regime is also recommended by Wolfgang Wurmnest in "Die Mär von der *mahr* – Zur Qualifikation von Ansprüchen aus Brautgabevereinbarungen", *Rabels Zeitschrift* 2007.

different forms. Depending on the context the results of the agreement will be different. In RH 2005:66 the *mahr* was due for payment at any time, provided that the wife requested the husband to perform his obligation. Since the wife had (already) had the *mahr* from the time of the marriage, the agreement could be seen as an agreement that adjusted the property relations between the spouses, an institution used to distribute assets between men and women in relation to a marriage. Depending on the outcome of the agreement, the agreed amount of *mahr* and the spouses' financial circumstances the *mahr* can be compared to a division of property, made in advance, between the husband and wife.

The approach taken in RH 2005:66 is furthermore useful in cases where property is transformed from the husband to the wife, that is to say in cases where the main part of the *mahr* is payable at the time of signing the marriage contract.

A reason against a qualification of *mahr* as part of the spouses' matrimonial property regime is that *mahr* agreements can take different forms depending on the parties′ interests and the social standards current in the country where the agreement is concluded. *Mahr* can be payable immediately at the time of signing the contract, deferred and payable upon divorce or other stipulated event. The *mahr* can be of symbolic or extensive value, comprising of money or objects. In cases where the *mahr* is deferred and payable upon divorce (in the majority of *mahr* agreements) it is, in the view of Swedish law, difficult to qualify *mahr* as forming part of the property regimes in cases where property has not been transferred from one spouse to the other. In addition, as the section relating to the functions of *mahr* shows, deferred *mahr* – especially in cases where the settlement is made in a Muslim legal order – often has other purposes than regulating the property regimes. The *mahr* is often used as a safeguard and as a bargaining tool for women who wish to end an undesired marriage. Further, a *mahr* agreement in its deferred form, payable upon divorce, is in reality not meant to regulate the spouses′ property rights since the agreement is meant to be implemented after the marriage (when the marriage is terminated). It is difficult to believe that the spouses at the time of agreeing on deferred *mahr* are of the opinion that the *mahr* is to be paid within the lifetime of both the spouses (in that case that would mean in practical terms that the marriage is temporary since the *mahr* is payable upon divorce).

In my opinion, it is more appropriate to take a third approach regarding how to qualify the *mahr*, namely that *mahr* should be considered as a special form of agreement or i.e. an agreement of its own, separated from both maintenance and the field of spouses' matrimonial property relations.

9. *MAHR* AS AN INSTITUTION OF ITS OWN – CONCLUSIONS

An agreement on *mahr* has characteristics which are similar to both maintenance and to dispositions which fall within the field of spouses′ matrimonial property rights. Even if *mahr* occasionally has functions similar to maintenance, and sometimes similar to spouses' property rights, it is important to emphasize that it is an institution within its own right.

When the applicable choice of law rule needs to be selected it is more suitable to regard the *mahr* as a special form of contract to be governed in accordance with the rules of the country where the agreement was concluded. So, the law applicable to the contract on *mahr* should be the law of the country where the agreement was concluded. If an agreement is made in, for example, Iran it is, according to my view, appropriate to govern the agreement by the application of Iranian law.

This approach has several benefits. First of all, it is an approach which functions as a general principle since it is easy to apply. And secondly, this approach is supposedly in line with the spouses' intention on the matter of the applicable law at the time of signing the contract. If a marriage contract is concluded in, say, Iran, the spouses-to-be must have had Iranian customs, practices and law in mind when they agreed on *mahr*. We can assume that their intention, at the time of the agreement, was that the *mahr* was binding upon them in accordance with the provisions in Iranian law. Thirdly, this approach would better fulfil the objectives of the *mahr* agreement in every specific case. Since the functions of *mahr* differ depending on the country where the agreement is concluded, the qualification approach taken will create a choice of law that corresponds with the purpose of the *mahr* agreement. One weakness in this reasoning is those cases where the spouses change residence, for example from the country of origin (a Muslim legal order) to Sweden, and live in the new country for a long period of time. The original purpose of *mahr*, e.g. as a safeguard within marriage or against divorce may not be enforceable (or meaningful) after a long residence in the new country. But in situations where an application of the law of the country where the contract was concluded would lead to consequences that could be regarded as unlawful the court may refuse to apply the foreign rules with reference to Swedish public policy.

BIBLIOGRAPHY

Anderson, Norman, *Law Reform in the Muslim World* (1976)

Bogdan, Michael, *Islamisk brudpenning (mahr) inför svensk domstol,* SvJT (1993 p. 597–600)

Carrol, *Quran 2 229 "A Charter Granted to the Wife"? Judicial Khul' in Pakistan,* Islamic Law and Society (Vol. 3, No. 1, 1996)

C.E Bosworth., E. van Donzel, B. Lewis, CH. Pellat, W.P. and Heinrichs, *The Encyclopedia of Islam,* (Vol. VI, MAHK-MID, 1991)

Doi, Abdur Rahman I., *Sharia: The Islamic Law* (1984)

El Alami, Dawoud Sudqi, *The Marriage Contract in Islamic Law, in the Shariah and Personal Status Laws in Egypt and Morocco* (1992)

Mir-Hosseini, Ziba, *Marriage on Trial, A study of Islamic Family Law* (2000)

Nasir, Jamal J., *The Islamic Law of Personal Status* (2002)

Roberts, Robert, *The Social Laws of the Quran* (1925)

Robertson Smith, W., *Kinship and Marriage in Early Arabia* (1885)

Summarized Sahih Al-Bukhari (Arabic-English), Vol. 7 (Kitab talaq, The book of divorce), Translation Muhsin Khan, Muhammad (1994)

Tyabji, Faiz Badruddin, *Muhammadan Law* (1940)

Watt, Montgomery, *Muhammad at Medina,* (1956)

Welchman (editor), Lynn, *Women's Rights &Islamic Family Law, Perspectives on Reform* (2004)

Wurmnest, Wolfgang, "Die Mär von der mahr – Zur Qualifikation von Ansprüchen aus Brautgabevereinbarungen", *Rabels Zeitschrift* (2007)

MULTICULTURALISM AND FAMILY LAW: THE CASE OF GREEK MUSLIMS

ASPASIA TSAOUSSI* and ELENI ZERVOGIANNI**

The law is a site of struggle within the more encompassing terrain of the state upon which many groups contest over institutions such as the family.[1]

1. INTRODUCTION

Multiculturalism calls for the recognition of the distinct norms and values of minority communities. Nevertheless, the accommodation of cultural differences may be incompatible with the traditional values of Western societies, especially in the area of family law. This is evident when it comes to institutions such as polygamy, Muslim divorce proceedings and the marriage of minors as well as the rules on the attribution of parental responsibilities for minors in case of divorce.

The examination of the Greek case is particularly interesting since sacred Islamic law (the Shari'a) may be applied on two different occasions: The *first* one, not surprisingly, is in the context of private international law, when conflict rules lead to the application of a foreign law governing family relations that may be religious. The *second* occasion is Greek-specific: As a consequence of a series of international conventions signed by Greece and Turkey dating back to 1881, the Mufti, who is the religious leader of the Muslims in Greece, has been granted the power by law to decide on issues pertaining to the personal status of Greek Muslims. This is still the case of the Muslim minority of Western Thrace, a geographic area in north-eastern Greece. Thus, Islamic Law is actually a special part of the national Greek legal order, whose scope of application is however restricted to some 100,000 Greek citizens.

* Author of sections 3 and 4 of the paper.

** Author of sections 1 and 2 of the paper.

1 M. ALBERTSON FINEMAN, "The Neutered Mother, the Sexual Family and Other Twentieth Century Tragedies" (New York: Routledge, 1995) p. 15.

The aim of this paper is twofold: *first*, to illustrate the scope of application of Islamic family law in Greece and the problems arising therefrom; and *second*, to seek ways of reconciling respect for cultural diversity and the protection of human rights. These issues are treated in an interdisciplinary manner: Our inquiry departs from the conflict of legal frameworks. More concretely, in *section 2* we elaborate on the scope of application of Islamic law in Greece, by referring to the jurisdiction of the Mufti and the law he applies, as well as to the controversial way in which Greek civil courts deal with the application of Islamic law. We then comment on the coexistence of secular and religious jurisdiction and suggest that a single secular jurisdiction is the only regime that can lead to results compatible with the values of Western democracy. In *section 3*, we proceed to a more in-depth analysis of competing value systems at the level of the social norms permeating family life and propose the use of alternative dispute resolution mechanisms as a unifying framework that is predicated on the values and beliefs shared by the majority and the minority in Muslim Thrace. Finally, because Islamic social systems both culturally and politically have been experienced by many as oppressive towards women, we discuss the positive impact of human rights education for Muslim women. In the last part of the paper (*section 4*) we evaluate the results and implications of our analysis.

2. ON THE APPLICATION OF ISLAMIC LAW IN GREECE

2.1. THE MUFTI JURISDICTION

The History – The first provision on Muslim religious courts is to be found in the Convention of Istanbul of 1881, signed by Greece and Turkey.[2] By means of this Convention the Greek territory expanded, as Turkey ceded most of Thessaly (which is now central Greece) to Greece. In this Convention it was provided that the Muslim population living in the new territories of the Greek State would enjoy freedom of religion and that religious courts would have competence to decide on religious issues. Religious issues comprised those relating to the personal status of Muslims, namely family and succession law.[3]

---

2 See Art. 8 of the Convention, which Greece ratified by Law ΠΛΖ/1882.

3 See, however, I. Ktistakis, "Sacred Islamic Law and Greek Muslims" [in Greek] (Athens-Thessaloniki: Sakkoulas Publishers, 2006), p. 90, who refers to the jurisprudence of the Greek Court of Cassation (Areios Pagos – *hereinafter*: AP) at the time and mentions that the term "personal status" was initially interpreted in such a narrow manner that cases of succession law would not fall within the scope of the jurisdiction of the Mufti.

The next relevant Convention is the Athens Treaty of Peace of 1913, signed by Greece and Turkey at the end of the first Balkan war.[4] The Convention included provisions for the protection of the Muslims living in the areas conquered by Greece, mainly in Macedonia and Epirus. It was provided that the Mufti would have competence over certain family and succession law cases of those populations.[5] In any case, in order to enforce the abovementioned obligation the Greek Government passed Law 147/1914, which is still in force, and Law 2345/1920, which remained in force until 1991 when it was repealed by Law 1920/1991.

The most crucial convention which is still binding for Greece and Turkey is the Convention of Lausanne of 1923.[6] According to this Convention, which applies to the entire Greek state, with the exception of the Dodecanese islands,[7] Turkey and Greece ought to adopt measures so as to ensure that all matters pertaining to the personal status of the minorities would be resolved in accordance with their religious customs. In the Convention no explicit reference is made to religious courts. Moreover, no provision restricts the possibility of a future different regulation of those issues, provided that the relevant decisions would be taken by special commissions, in which the minority would be represented. In case no consensus could be reached, the issue would be decided by a European arbitrator.[8] Indeed in 1926 Turkey made use of this provision and did away with religious law: The minorities consented to the repeal of their special status and the family and succession law

---

4 Greece ratified this Treaty by Law ΔΣΙΓ/1913.

5 See Art. 11 of the Athens Treaty of Peace. At this point it is worth noting that the attribution of judicial powers to the Mufti constitutes a deviation from Islamic law, since traditionally the Mufti is a spiritual leader with powers of a consultative nature. The judge of religious courts is the Qadi. On this issue, see specifically I. Ktistakis, *supra* note 3, p. 32. *Cf.* S. Minaides, "The Religious Freedom of Muslims in the Greek Legal Order" [in Greek] (Athens-Komotini: Ant. N. Sakkoulas Publishers, 1990) [in Greek], pp. 351–352, who argues that already at the time of the Ottoman Empire the Mufti was granted judicial powers.

6 The Convention of Lausanne was ratified by the Legislative Decree of 25.8.1923. Previously Greece and Turkey had signed the Convention of Sèvres of 1920, which was ratified by the Legislative Decree of 29.9.1923. As regards the law that was applicable to the Muslim minority, the Convention of Sèvres is of limited interest, since the same provisions are repeated in the Convention of Lausanne. On this issue, see in more detail I. Ktistakis, *supra* note 3, p. 96.

7 This matter is nevertheless highly disputed. In any case the interpretation of the Paris Treaty of Peace of 1947, by means of which the Dodecanese islands were annexed to the Greek State, is crucial. For the exception of the Dodecanese, see I. Ktistakis, *supra* note 3, p. 108–110; Z. Papassiopi-Passia, "Problems Referring to the Field of Application of Interpersonal Law in Greece and to the Jurisdictional Competence of the Mufti" [in Greek with an English summary], *Koinodikion* (Law Journal) 2001/7.B, pp. 391 *et seq.*, esp. p. 399; S. Minaides, *supra* note 5, pp. 122–124; AP (Full Bench) 738/1967, *Nomiko Vima* (Law Journal- *hereinafter*: NoV) 1967, p. 975. *Cf.* A. Kotzambasi, "The Scope of Application of the Sacred Islamic Law on the Family Relations of Greek Muslims" [in Greek], *Elliniki Dikaiosini* (Law Journal, *hereinafter*: EllDni) 2003, pp. 56 *et seq.*, esp. p. 64. *Contra* see K. Tsitselikis, "The Competence of the Mufti as a Religious Judge" [in Greek], *NoV* 2001, pp. 583 *et seq.*, esp. p. 586.

8 See Art. 42 of the Convention of Lausanne.

of the Turkish Civil Code, which was inspired by its Swiss counterpart, entered into force for the Turkish population in its entirety.[9]

The international law questions which arise out of the abovementioned Conventions are numerous and still unresolved. According to the Greek Court of Cassation (*Areios Pagos*) Greece is internationally bound by the Conventions of Istanbul (1881) and Athens (1913) to maintain the jurisdiction of the Mufti. This opinion is also shared by the National Commission on Human Rights.[10] The Highest Administrative Court of Greece, on the other hand, has repeatedly ruled that the Convention of Lausanne is the only binding Convention for Greece, since it was meant to repeal the previous conventions.[11] If this opinion is adopted, Greece has no international obligation to maintain the jurisdiction of the Mufti.[12]

The current legal framework – The special legal regime provided for the Muslim minority by the abovementioned international Conventions is still maintained, so issues of personal status are resolved by religious courts. According to Article 4 of Law 147/1914 which is still in force,[13] issues pertaining to the formation and the dissolution of marriage, the personal relations between spouses, as well as the kinship of Greek Muslims are governed by religious law. Furthermore, Article 5 para. 2 of Law 1920/1991 stipulates the jurisdiction of the Mufti in *exclusively enumerated* issues. In addition to those mentioned in Article 4 of Law 146/1914, Article 5 para. 2 of Law 1920/1991 refers to maintenance, custody and guardianship, and the emancipation of minors, to Islamic wills as well as to the intestate succession of *Greek Muslim citizens who* reside *within the district of the Mufti*, provided that Islamic law is applicable. The decision of the Mufti cannot be

9 See I. Ktistakis, *supra* note 3, p. 104. *Cf.* however A. Bedermacher-Gerousis, "The Interpersonal Law in Greece, particularly in Thrace" [in Greek], *Armenopoulos* (Law Journal – *hereinafter*: *Arm.*) 1977, pp. 628 *et seq.*, p. 630 claiming that the consent of the minority was null and void and thus Turkey acted in violation of the international obligation arising out of the Convention of Lausanne.

10 See the decision of the Commission on the marriage of minors, Point A1, in: http://www.nchr.gr/media/word/moufti_31_03_2005.doc.

11 See Decisions 1333/2001, *Arm.* 2001, p. 1263 and 466/2003, *Intrasoft-Nomos Databank*, of the Highest Administrative Court. See also S. Minaides, *supra* note 5, p. 355; S. Georgoulis, "The Institution of the Mufti in the Greek and Foreign Legal Order" [in Greek] (Athens-Komotini: Ant. N. Sakkoulas Publishers, 1993), pp. 32 *et seq.*, esp. p. 36.

12 In favour of this opinion, see G. Koumantos, "Family Law I" [in Greek] (Athens: Sakkoulas Publishers, 1988), p. 245; I. Ktistakis, *supra* note 3, p. 115 "The Mufti, the Shari'a and Human Rights" [in Greek], *NoV* 2007, pp. 228 *et seq.*, esp. p. 236.

13 According to Art. 6 of the Introductory Law to the Greek Civil Code, Law 147/1914 has been repealed only as regards the religious jurisdiction of the Greek Israelites. On this issue see, among others, A. Kotzambasi, "The Scope of Application of the Sacred Islamic Law on the Family Relations of Greek Muslims" [in Greek], *Elliniki Dikaiosini* (Law Journal, *hereinafter*: EllDni) 2003, pp. 56 *et seq.*, esp. pp. 62–63. *Contra*: G. Koumantos, *supra* note 12, p. 245.

revised, since there is no appellate religious court.[14] According to recent jurisprudence, when Muslims abstain from entering into a religious marriage, they opt out of the jurisdiction of the Mufti.[15]

As regards the abovementioned provisions, two points must be elaborated: *First*, taking into account that the enumeration of the issues on which the Mufti may decide is exclusive, no expansion of his jurisdiction is possible by analogy. Thus, according to the case law, neither the proprietary effects of marriage[16] nor adoption fall within the Mufti's jurisdiction.[17] It is disputed whether the contact of the parent with the child after divorce falls within his jurisdiction.[18] *Second*, according to the prevailing opinion, the Mufti only has jurisdiction over Greek Muslims residing in his district. Given that nowadays three religious courts are operating in Greece, all of them in Thrace,[19] only Greek Muslims residing in Thrace can, according to the prevailing opinion, bring their case before the Mufti.[20] Nevertheless, this opinion is criticized as being incompatible with the international obligations of Greece.[21]

According to Article 5 para. 3 of Law 1920/1991, the decisions of the Mufti do not constitute final judgments unless they are declared enforceable by the competent Court of First Instance. Court review, however, is restricted: it may only be

---

14 Law 2345/1920 provided for the existence of an Arch-Mufti. This provision, which has never been materialized, was not repeated in Law 1920/1991.

15 See Decision 1623/2003 of the one-member Court of First Instance of Xanthi, *Arm.* 2004, p. 366 annotated by A. Kotzambasi. See also Z. Papassiopi-passia, *supra* note 7, p. 403.

16 See Decision 119/2006 of the Appeal Court of Thrace, *Arm.* 2006, p. 1565; Decision of the one-member Court of First Instance of Xanthi 251/1982, *Arm.* 1982, p. 740.

17 See Decision 356/1995 of the Appeal Court of Thrace, *Arm.* 1996, p. 41. See also G. Mpekiaridis, "Muftis as Religious Leaders of the Muslims in their District and as Public Authorities" [in Greek], *Arm.* 1973, esp. p. 894.

18 See Decision 1057/2000 of the one-member Court of First Instance of Chalkis, *Intrasoft-Nomos Databank*, which accepted the jurisdiction of the Mufti on this issue. *Contra*: Decision 7/2001 of the Appeal Court of Thrace, *Arm.* 2001, p. 692. *Cf.* A. Kotzambasi, *supra* note 13, p. 70, who questions whether issues of parental responsibility in general fall within the jurisdiction of the Mufti.

19 Religious Courts operate in Xanthi, Komotini and Didymoteixo.

20 See Z. Papassiopi-Passia, *supra* note 7, p. 403, S. Minaides, *supra* note 5, p. 354; S. Georgoulis, *supra* note 11, p. 37; A. Kotzambasi, *supra* note 13 p. 65; Opinion 347/2003 of the (Greek) Council of the State [in Greek], available at: http://www.nsk.gr/gnompdf/2003/3472003.pdf. *Contra*: Ch. Fragistas, in: *Ermineia Astikou Kodikos* [in Greek] (Athens, 1963) Art 6 of the Introductory Law to the Greek Civil Code, n. 27; K. Tsitselikis, *supra* note 7, p. 586; A. Bedermacher-Gerousis, *supra* note 9, p. 630; I. Ktistakis, *supra* note 3, p. 39 who claim that religious law is applicable to all Greek Muslim citizens (apart from the citizens of the Dodecanese – see *supra* note 7). *Cf.* also Decision AP 1723/1980, *EEN* 1981, 725. Nevertheless, it is worth noting that in quite some instances the Muftis have acted in excess of their jurisdiction by deciding on cases where the parties were either not both Greek Muslim citizens, or were not residing in Greece. On this issue, ee I. Ktistakis, *supra* note 3, pp. 43–46.

21 Explicitly so I. Ktistakis, *supra* note 3, p. 37.

examined whether the Mufti remained within his field of competence and whether the law applied contravenes the Constitution.[22] The last provision constitutes probably the most important feature of the new law; in the previous legal regime the control of unconstitutionality was not a prerequisite for the ratification of the judgments of the Mufti.[23]

Finally, it is disputed whether the competence of the Mufti is exclusive, meaning that the Greek Muslims may only bring their case before the Mufti,[24] or concurrently, meaning that they may bring their case before the Greek civil courts if they wish to do so.[25] The latter interpretation is the only one which is compatible with the Constitution: The subordination of Greek Muslims exclusively to the jurisdiction of the Mufti would be contradictory to religious freedom, as the parties would always have to state their religion before the Courts, in order to found their right of judicial protection.[26] Moreover, only civil courts provide the guarantees for fair trial and efficient legal protection.[27] In any case, the jurisdiction of the Mufti is recognised as a form of minority protection and, as such, it cannot be imposed on the members of the minority against their will.[28]

---

22 This provision was inserted for the first time by Law 1920/1991 – no such control was required according to Law 2345/1920.

23 See Z. Papassiopi-Passia, in: A. Grammatikaki-Alexiou/Z. Papassiopi-Passia- E. Vassilakakis, *Private International Law* [in Greek], 3rd ed. (Athens-Thessaloniki: Sakkoulas Publishers, 2002), p. 48.

24 See Decision AP 1723/1980, *EEN* 1981, 725; Decision 1057/2000 of the one-member Court of First Instance of Chalkis, *Intrasoft-Nomos Databank*. *Cf.* also K. Beis, Case note on Decision 405/2000 of the one-member Court of First Instance of Thebes [in Greek], *Dike* (Law Journal) 2001, p. 1098 *et seq.*, esp. p. 1099. *Cf.* Decision AP 1041/2000, *EllDni* 2001, p. 429.

25 See S. Minaides, *supra* note 5, p. 357; Z. Papassiopi-Passia, *supra* note 7, p. 406 and *supra* note 23, p. 48; I. Ktistakis, *supra* note 3, pp. 43–46; Decision 405/2000 of the one-member Court of First Instance of Thebes, *NoV* 2001, p. 661.

26 See K. Tsitselikis, *supra* note 7, p. 592. *Cf.* G.P. Arvanitis, "The Optional Character of Religious Laws in Greece" [in Greek], *EllDni* 1979, pp. 113–114; I. Ktistakis, *supra* note 3, p. 155; A. Kotzambasi, *supra* note 7, p. 65.

27 On this issue, see *infra,* under section 2.4. *Cf.* E. Roucounas, "Jurisprudence hellénique – Droit international privé: Compétence du Moufti pour connaître des matières qui relèvent du statut personnel des ressortissants Grecs de religion musulmane", *Revue hellénique de Droit International (RHDI)* 1981, pp. 151 *et seq.*, esp. p. 154, who claims that the right of the Greek Muftis to bring their case before the Greek Courts is based on Art. 8 para. 1, according to which no person shall be deprived against his will of the judge assigned to him by law. Of the same opinion, S. Minaides, *supra* note 5, p. 357. According to Decision AP 1723/1980, *EEN* 1981, 725 there is no such problem, since the Mufti is a judge in the sense of Art. 8 para. 1. On this issue see also I. Ktistakis, "The Mufti, the Shari'a and Human Rights" [in Greek], *NoV* 2007, pp. 228 *et seq.*, [in Greek], esp. p. 230, who claims that the Mufti lacks the constitutional prerequisites for the office of a judge.

28 See K. Tsitselikis, *supra* note 7, p. 593. *Cf.* also G.P. Arvanitis, *supra* note 26, pp. 113–114.

2.2. THE SHARI'A AS APPLIED IN WESTERN THRACE

Introductory Remarks – The Mufti judges the cases brought before him according to the Shari'a, which is the body of Islamic law based mainly on the Qur'an and Islamic tradition. The interpretation and application of the Shari'a is not uniform among the different Islamic legal schools of thought. The Muslims of Western Thrace are not homogenous, neither ethnically (50% Turkish origin, 35% Pomaks and 15% Roma)[29] nor religiously (nearly 90% are Sunnis, whereas the rest are Sufi, and more particularly Bektashi).[30] Although there exist considerable differences among the Muslim population of western Thrace there is little dispute concerning the substantial Islamic law that is applicable as regards their personal status,[31] which is namely Hanafi law as applied in the Ottoman Empire.[32]

The main areas of conflict between the Shari'a family law provisions and fundamental principles of the Greek (and international) legal order pertain to the well-established (in Western legal orders) principle of equality of the sexes[33] and the concern for the best interest of the child.[34] Throughout the analysis, it is also evident that because of the content of substantive Islamic law in the issues examined, the requirements of fair trial cannot be met.[35] In what follows we refer to selected issues in order to illustrate the conflict between Muslim family law and human rights.

---

29 See "The Education System in Greece", in: Eury Base, The information database on the education Systems in Europe, 2004–2005, p. 12, available at: http://www.eurydice.org/ressources/Eurydice/pdf/eurybase/2006_DNEL_EL.pdf, p. 12; Ministry of Foreign Affairs (of the Hellenic Republic), Information Service, "The Muslim Minority of Thrace" available at: http://www.hri.org/MFA/foreign/musmingr.htm.

30 See E. Zegkinis, "Religious Freedom and Religiousness of the Muslims of Western Thrace" [in Greek], available at http://lyk-limnis.eyv.sch.gr/komotini/arthromeion2.htm; S. Georgoulis, *supra* note 11, p. 40.

31 See E. Zegkinis, *supra* note 30.

32 *Cf.* Minaides, *supra* note 5, p. 57· S. Georgoulis, *supra* note 11, p. 17.

33 See, among other texts, Art. 4 para. 2 of the Greek Constitution (*hereinafter*: GC), according to which Greek men and women have equal rights and equal obligations, as well as Art 14 of the European Convention on Human Rights, according to which the enjoyment of the rights and freedoms set forth in this Convention shall be secured without discrimination on any ground such as sex, race, colour, language, religion, political or other opinion, national or social origin, association with a national minority, property, birth or other status.

34 See, among other texts, Art. 21 para. 1 GC, according to which the family, as the foundation of the preservation and advancement of the Nation, as well as marriage, motherhood and childhood, shall be under the protection of the State, Art. 21 para. 3 GC, according to which the State shall care for the health of its citizens and shall adopt special measures for the protection of its youth, as well as the UN Convention on the Rights of the Child.

35 See I. Ktistakis, *supra* note 3, p. 157, who mentions that even if the parties appear in the proceedings, they may still not be able to defend themselves, since there are no books on the law applied by the Mufti and the decision is written using the Ottoman alphabet (which is a version of the Arabic alphabet). See also *infra*, under section 2.4.

Equality of the Sexes – The unequal treatment of the sexes is demonstrated by the Islamic law on divorce and polygamy. More concretely, the Shari'a contains three distinct provisions on divorce:

The first form of *divorce* proceeding is that of the repudiation of the wife by the husband (*talāq*). In such a case the man may unilaterally state that he does not wish the continuation of the marriage. According to a recent study on judgments of the Greek religious courts,[36] the following conclusions may be derived: The repudiation of the wife is no longer commonplace. In any case, the repudiation must take place before the Mufti and not privately. Usually the husband invokes a reason for divorce, however the Mufti does not really look into the facts of the case.[37] The wife has no right to be heard in this procedure. In any case the wife keeps the dower (*mahr*) she received upon marriage.[38] She may also receive maintenance (*nafaquah*), which however, according to Islamic law, does not exceed the period of waiting that is imposed upon a woman who has been divorced or whose husband has died, after which a new marriage is permissible (*iddat*).[39] Moreover, the man may have to compensate the wife for the dissolution of the marriage, if such an agreement had been concluded in the marriage contract.[40] This agreement, especially if the amount in question is of considerable value, serves in practice as a mechanism in order to prevent the husband from thoughtlessly exercising his right of repudiation. However, it should be noted that it is disputable whether such claims may be brought before the Mufti or if this matter exceeds his jurisdiction, because it refers to the property relations of the spouses.[41]

The second relevant provision is divorce by consent (*khul*). In such a case both spouses appear before the Mufti and state their will to obtain a divorce. In practice, this is the most common form of divorce. Nevertheless, this kind of divorce is substantially different from the divorce by mutual consent as it is perceived in Western legal orders. In fact, under Islamic law the wife must compensate her husband for the termination of the marriage.[42] In a way she has to buy herself out

36 See I. Ktistakis, *supra* note 3, pp. 64–66.

37 See I. Ktistakis, *ibid.*

38 On this issue, see M. Sayed, "The Muslim dower (mahr) in Europe – with special reference to Sweden", this volume, pp. 187–208.

39 In the case of *Talaq*, *Iddat* lasts until the completion of the wife's subsequent three normal menstrual periods (and in the case of missed periods, for three months and ten days). The *Iddat* of a pregnant woman lasts until the baby is delivered. During the waiting period, the spouses should refrain from sex but if they engage in sex or decide on rapprochement, they can do so and they are again husband and wife. This is called *Rujat*. See also I. Ktistakis, *supra* note 3, pp. 67–68.

40 See A. Kotzambasi, *supra* note 7, p. 69. *Cf.* M. Sayed, *supra* note 38.

41 See I. Ktistakis, *supra* note 3, p. 67.

42 See A. Kotzambasi, *supra* note 7, p. 69, I. Ktistakis, *supra* note 3, pp. 60–61.

of the marriage, usually by returning the dower (*mahr*) she had received for the formation of the marriage,[43] by waiving her right to alimony or even her right to the custody of the children.[44]

If the husband does not agree to the divorce, the wife can only achieve the termination of the marriage on important reasons pertaining to the fault of the husband. The Greek Muftis have accepted that such fault-based reasons include the desertion of the wife, adultery, a change of religion, the non-performance of the obligation to maintain, bigamy or the violent behaviour of the husband, and in general the breakdown of the marriage due to the behaviour of the husband. Nevertheless, it has been reported that the Mufti often rejects divorce applications filed by women, who thus remain trapped in non-functioning marriages.[45]

As far as polygamy is concerned, it is allowed by the Qur'an. Nevertheless, in Thrace this possibility is practically no longer relevant.[46] The Muftis in principle do not grant permission to a man to marry a second wife.[47] Even if such permission is granted, the conclusion of a second marriage on the part of the husband not only constitutes legal grounds for divorce in favour of the first wife,[48] but is also a criminal offence.[49]

Best Interests of the Child – The rules of Islamic law which are not consistent with the rights of the child as declared in the relevant UN Convention pertain to the marriage of minors as well as to the way post-divorce child custody is awarded.

As far as the attribution of *parental responsibilities* after the dissolution of marriage is concerned, according to Islamic law the only relevant parameter is the age of the child; following Hanafi law, the mother obtains custody of boys until the age of seven and of girls until the age of nine. Thereafter, the parental rights are attributed to the father. This rule is followed by a significant number of decisions

---

43 See M. Sayed, *supra* note 38.

44 See A. Kotzambasi, *supra* note 7, p. 69, I. Ktistakis, *supra* note 3, pp. 60–61, who cites numerous decisions of religious courts.

45 See E. Tsoukalas, "The Family and Succession Law of the Muslims of our Thrace" [in Greek] *EllDni* 2002, pp. 1305 *et seq.*, esp. p. 1306 and "The competence of the Muftis" [in Greek], *EllDni* 1988, p. 1655.

46 See Decision of 31.3.2005 of the National Commission on Human Rights, available at: http://www.nchr.gr/media/word/moufti_31_03_2005.doc.

47 See I. Ktistakis, *supra* note 3, p. 55.

48 See I. Ktistakis, *supra* note 3, p. 63; S. Aldeeb/A. Bonomi (Eds.), "Le droit musulman de la famille et des successions á l'épreuve des ordres juridiques occidentaux" (Zurich: Schulthess, 1999), p. 97.

49 See Art. 356 of the Greek Penal Code. The landmark Decision on this issue is Ruling 89/1995 of the Council of the Court of Appeal, *Yperaspisi* (Law Journal) 1998, p. 78, annotated by S. Pavlou.

of the Mufti in Thrace.[50] Nevertheless, it is noted that there are a large number of exceptions to this rule.[51] The factors which are taken into account in the case of those deviations refer to the fault grounds for divorce. Moreover, as mentioned above, in some cases women have to give up their right to have custody of their children as the only way to buy themselves out of a non-functioning marriage. In any case, little doubt may exist as to the fact that the examination of the best interests of the child does not seem to be the main concern when taking the decision.[52]

As regards the *marriage of minors*, the Qur'an does not explicitly prohibit the marriage of young children.[53] According to Hanafi law, however, a person has the capacity to marry only once (s)he has reached puberty.[54] It is presumed that puberty is reached at the age of fifteen.[55] However, it can be proved that younger persons have attained this stage of maturity.[56] In the latter case, however, the marriage may only be entered into if parental consent (meaning paternal consent)[57] is granted. In Thrace the Mufti has agreed to the marriage of girls as young as eleven years old.[58] Marriages involving minors are relatively frequent due to the very conservative mentality of the small society of the Thrace minority. It is worth noting that the Greek Civil Code does not set an absolute minimum age for marriage, but grants the judge the power to give permission for the marriage of a minor, if this is justified by a special reason.[59] The social circumstances

50 See I. Ktistakis, *supra* note 3, p. 70.

51 *Ibid.*

52 See I. Ktistakis, *supra* note 3, p. 72.

53 See S. Aldeeb/A. Bonomi (Eds), *supra* note 48, p. 68.

54 See I. Ktistakis, *supra* note 3, p. 52.

55 See D. Pearl/W. Menski, "Muslim Family Law", 3rd ed. (London: Sweet & Maxwell, 1998) p. 141.

56 According to Hanafi law, the absolute minimum age for marriage is nine years old for girls and twelve for boys. See D. Pearl/W. Menski, *supra* note 55. *Cf.* I. Ktistakis in Report of 3.2.2005 for the National Commission of Human Rights, (available at: http://www.nchr.gr/media/word/moufti_31_03_2005.doc), who refers to the prohibition on contracting a marriage under the age of twelve.

57 See K. Tsitselikis, *supra* note 7, pp. 589–590; S. Georgoulis, *supra* note 11, p. 116. It is worth mentioning that if the person who had parental responsibilities, and thus consented to the marriage, was not the father of the minor of a paternal grandfather, the child may exercise his "option of puberty" once he reaches the age of fifteen, which can lead to the dissolution of the marriage. See A. Demosthenous, "Women and Islam" (Athens: Akritas Publications, 2005) pp. 186–187.

58 See A. Giotopoulou-Maragopoulou, Report of 21.3.2005 for the National Commission of Human Rights, section II (available at: http://www.nchr.gr/media/word/moufti_31_03_2005.doc); see also I. Ktistakis *supra* note 3, p. 53, referring to the marriage of thirteen year old girls.

59 See Art. 1350 of the Greek Civil Code. Lately there have been proposals to amend this provision so that a marriage involving minors will no longer be possible. On this issue, see the Decision of the National Commission of Human Rights on 31.3.2005, *supra* note 46.

of the society in which the minor resides is taken into account when deciding on this issue.[60] Thus in some cases the minors would have been able to marry also according to secular law. However, there remains a crucial difference between the decision of the civil courts and the decisions of the Mufti on the marriage of minors, which pertains, namely, to the degree to which the best interests of the child are taken into account.

General Remarks on the Islamic Law Applied in Western Thrace – The Muftis in Thrace seem to apply a relatively mild version of Islamic law. Even under these conditions, the inequality between men and women as well as the divergence from the pursuit of the best interests of the child can hardly be disputed. Moreover, due to the fact that the law applied is not written, legal uncertainty cannot be avoided. The solutions provided depend largely on the personality of the Mufti. This also provides an explanation for the differences between the decisions of the three religious courts of Greece.[61]

2.3. THE RECEPTION OF MUSLIM LAW BY THE GREEK COURTS – COMPARATIVE REMARKS

The way in which the Greek civil courts deal with Islamic law is controversial: On the one hand, the decisions of the Mufti are routinely declared enforceable by the Greek Courts, while on the other hand in cases of conflict of laws the judges deny the application of Islamic law, or even the recognition of court rulings based on Islamic law, as being incompatible with the "public order". "Public order" is defined as the fundamental moral, ethical, social, legal or economic principles[62] and, according to the prevailing opinion, is crystallised in the light of the constitution.[63]

More concretely, as far as the Muslims of Thrace are concerned, according to recent statistical data, over the last fifteen years (*i.e.* since law 1920/1991 entered into force) the civil courts, which are supposed to examine whether the decision of the Mufti is incompatible with the Constitution, denied enforceability in only

---

60 See, *inter alia*, E. Kounougeri-Manoledaki, "Family Law I", 3rd ed. [in Greek] (Athens-Thessaloniki: Sakkoulas Publishers, 2002), pp. 66–70, esp. p. 69.

61 See *supra* note 19.

62 See Decision AP (full bench) 17/1999, *EllDni* 1999, p. 1288; Decision AP (full bench) 9/1990, *Epitheorisi Nautikou Dikaiou* (Law Journal) 1991, p. 1; Decision AP 335/2006, *Chronika Idiotikou Dikaiou* (Law Journal) 2006, p. 622.

63 See S. Minaides, *supra* note 5, p. 152.

11 cases out of 2,679.[64] In view of the content of Islamic law on family law issues, and particularly in view of the specific decisions which have been declared enforceable, it is obvious that Greek judges do not really look into the substance of the decisions in order to decide on their unconstitutionality.

However, Greek Muslims who do not reside in Thrace or nationals of a foreign country where personal law issues would be decided according to Islamic law may not bring their case before the Mufti, even if conflict rules would lead to the application of Islamic law (*e.g.* in the case of a Pakistani couple residing in Greece).[65] In the same context, the civil courts may deny the application of foreign law if, in the specific case, this would contravene the Greek public order.[66] Non-discrimination on the basis of sex, the pursuit of the best interests of the child and the principles of fair trial are indisputable elements of the public order. Hence, if civil courts were called upon to apply Islamic law, there can be little doubt that they would abstain from this. This conclusion is reinforced by the fact that Greek civil courts have refused to recognize foreign decisions issued on the basis of Islamic law.[67] This has been repeatedly the case when it comes to the recognition of divorce by repudiation.[68]

The judicial control of whether the judgment of the Mufti contravenes the Constitution is not identical to controlling whether the judgment contravenes the public order.[69] Nevertheless, there is no doubt that the abovementioned Islamic family law provisions contravene both.[70] Hence, the practice of the courts is inconsistent in two ways: *First*, the same law which civil courts refuse to apply to foreign nationals as being contrary to the Greek legal order is applied to Greek Muslims by the Mufti, whose decisions are then routinely ratified by a Greek judge. *Second*, not all Muslims, not even all Greek Muslims, may bring their case before the

---

64 See I. Ktistakis, *supra* note 3, p. 158. *Cf.* S. Manos, Proceeds of the parliamentary sitting of 30.3.2006, Discussion on the legislative proposal concerning the "regulation of the relations between the Church and the state and the protection of religious freedom", which mentions that, over the last 15 years, only 1 out of 1071 decisions has recently been found to be unconstitutional.

65 See *supra* note 20.

66 See Art. 33 of the Greek Civil Code.

67 See Art. 323 n. 5 (and 905 para. 4) of the Greek Code of Civil Procedure.

68 See Decisions 10719/1995 of the Athens Court of Appeal, *EllDni* 1997, p. 638, annotated by M.P. Margaritis and 3020/1997 of the one-member Court of First Instance of Athens, *Arm.* 1997, p. 206, both denying the recognition of such a divorce issued by a Jordan religious court. *Cf.*, however, Decision 10159/1998 of the one-member Court of First Instance of Thessaloniki, *Arm.* 1999, p. 717.

69 *Cf.*, however, K. Tsitselikis, *supra* note 7, p. 590, who argues that when the Courts review a judgment by the Mufti, they should examine whether this contravenes public order.

70 See Z. Papassiopi-Passia, *supra* note 23, p. 48. *Cf.* however M.P. Margaritis, Case note on Decision 10719/1995 of the Court of Appeals of Athens, *EllDni* 1997, pp. 638–639.

Mufti, but only those Greek Muslims who happen to reside in Thrace may do so. Thus, similar cases are treated in quite dissimilar ways, without convincing (or with hardly any) justification.

2.4. EVALUATION OF THE LEGAL REGIME OF MUSLIMS IN GREECE: IS "CONCURRENT JURISDICTION" A SOLUTION?

The current regime fails to protect the interest of the weaker members of the minority, namely women and children. Despite the provision of Law 1920/1991 according to which civil courts ought to control the unconstitutionality of the Mufti decisions before ratifying them, courts abstain from such a control. If they were to actually carry out this control, most of the decisions of the Mufti would not be enforceable.[71]

The concurrent jurisdiction between the civil and the religious courts is often considered as means to overcome this problem.[72] Nevertheless, concurrent jurisdiction is not enough to protect the abovementioned categories of the population for practical reasons:

First, the choice of jurisdiction is made by the plaintiff. It is questionable whether the Mufti would refuse to adjudicate a case because the defendant does not consent to his jurisdiction. Even worse, if the defendant happens to be a woman, she may not even be given an opportunity to consent to this jurisdiction since it is often the case that she does not take part in the proceedings. A Mufti decision issued under these circumstances cannot be reviewed by a second-degree religious court, while the civil courts do not really look at the substance of the decision. Thus, in practice, there is no guarantee that the rights of the weaker party will be respected.

Second, due to strong social pressures in their confined religious society, the vast majority of cases are brought before the Mufti, even when the plaintiff is the weaker party.[73] This also explains why the number of civil marriages among

71 Explicitly so Z. Papassiopi-Passia, *supra* note 7, p. 410.

72 See above section 2.1.

73 See S. Minaides, *supra* note 5, p. 362.

Muslims remains low,[74] although this might ascertain the opting out from the religious jurisdiction.[75]

No defence of the current situation may be based on compliance with international conventions signed by Greece and Turkey.[76] This is due to the fact that since 1923 both Greece and Turkey have signed and ratified numerous conventions on human rights, such as the International Covenant on Civil and Political Rights, the Convention on the Elimination of all Forms of Discrimination against Women (CEDAW), and the UN Convention on the Rights of Children.[77] Hence, according to Art. 30 of the Vienna Convention on the Law of Treaties of 1969, which codified principles of customary international law, in the case of successive treaties, the provisions of an earlier treaty only apply to the extent that they are compatible with the new, special one.[78] In any case, irrespective of all the above considerations, the application of Islamic law cannot be accepted when it leads to results that are contrary to the Constitution, which ranks above international conventions.[79]

Furthermore, the application of Islamic law is not necessary for the protection of minorities. Islamic law is not applied in any other European country. At this point it is worth noting that according to point I. 5 of the 1993 Resolution of the Vienna World Conference on Human Rights, "While the significance of national and regional particularities and various historical, cultural and religious backgrounds must be borne in mind, it is the duty of States, regardless of their political, economic and cultural systems, to promote and protect all human rights and fundamental freedoms."[80]

It is indisputable that the application of religious law to the Muslims of Western Thrace has its roots in political circumstances. Likewise, the continuation of the

---

74 Especially when it comes to marriages involving minors, since the parties would often be unable to enter into the marriage according to the provisions of the Greek Civil Code (see *supra* section 2.2.).

75 See *supra* note 15.

76 See *infra*, under section 2.1.

77 See Status of Ratifications of the Principal International Human Right Treaties of the Office of the United Nations High Commissioner for Human Rights (as of 9.6.2004), available at: http://www.unhchr.ch/pdf/report.pdf.

78 See A. Giotopoulou-Maragopoulou, *supra* note 58.

79 See E. Roucounas, *supra* note 27, pp. 154–155. *Cf.* Report of A. Manitakis of 10.2.2005 for the National Commission of Human Rights, (available at: http://www.nchr.gr/media/word/moufti_31_03_2005.doc), who claims that, because of its institutional autonomy, the minority may apply rules which deviate from the Greek Constitution, insofar as these deviations do not manifestly contradict fundamental principles and values of European civilization.

80 See A. Kotzambasi, *supra* note 7, p. 71. The Resolution is available at: http://www.unhchr.ch/huridocda/huridoca.nsf/(Symbol)/A.CONF.157.23.En? OpenDocument. See also I. Ktistakis, *supra* note 3, p. 156.

application of Islamic law is due to the high political costs associated with any change to this regime. From a legal perspective, however, we suggest that a single jurisdiction of the state courts is the only regime which could lead to results which are compatible with the values of Western democracy. Deviations from state family law in order to comply with Muslim culture may only be permissible if they rely on the unbiased consent of all parties and do not contradict fundamental human values. Such solutions may indeed emerge though mediation. However, the existence of a single jurisdiction system is a prerequisite for such a possibility to arise.

3. ALTERNATIVE DISPUTE RESOLUTION PROCESSES (ADR) IN THE CONTEXT OF A SINGLE JURISDICTION SYSTEM

In this section of the paper we will show that the current system of "concurrent jurisdiction" places Muslim women in a disadvantageous position compared to Muslim men. The Mufti's decisions fail to address their legitimate interests as family members who enjoy equality under the law. We suggest that there is a better alternative and propose that Greek citizens, regardless of their religion, should turn to mediation to settle their family disputes. Parallel and alternative legal mechanisms may help to enhance the protection of the fundamental human rights of the Muslim minority. Such mechanisms need to function in concert with formal legal systems and in cooperation with government authorities to ensure full compliance with international human rights standards. In the analysis that follows, we aim to illustrate that the core principles of mediation satisfy the deeper moral and religious concerns of both communities in bicultural Western Thrace. Thus, they serve and accommodate the shared values of the two competing and coexisting systems.

In any case, we should point out that this is a *de lege ferenda* proposal: the law introducing the out-of-court settlement of certain disputes involving private law which took effect in September 2000[81] has limited applicability: it cannot be applied to cases of divorce, the annulment of marriages, or in labour law disputes. But it may be used to settle cases of property law and inheritance law, and also cases involving the division of marital property under article 1400 of the Greek Civil Code.

---

[81] The out-of-court settlement of certain types of disputes was introduced to the Greek legal order in 1997, more particularly under article 6 of L. 2479/1997 and article 18 of L. 2743/1999 which amended article 214A of the Code of Civil Procedure, in alignment with the Council of Europe's Recommendation R (86) 12 (of 16-12-1986). Under the new provisions, the attempt to settle out of court has become a necessary stage of the pre-trial process.

3.1. COMPETING VALUE SYSTEMS IN THE FAMILY SETTING

The family is a social institution that shares many common patterns of structure and functions across cultures. Family arrangements are rarely unique because of the influences of various socially learned expectations, attitudes, and forms of behaviour.[82] Circumstances outside individual families have a powerful impact in shaping family life. The economic resources which people bring to the families they form and the existing legal institutions are characteristic examples of powerful outside influences. Legal changes are even more significant in their impact, as they have been shown to affect patterns of behaviour within families and the variation in family forms. In fact, this transformative or educative function of the law is usually one of the primary stated goals of any legal reform.

Underlying the conflict at the level of legal systems and the administration of justice is the tension between different social and religious norms. Normative systems always reflect the dominant cultural and social ideologies. In this sense, the dominant societal values of non-Muslims prevail and are further embedded on a doctrinal level, through the implementation of family law.

Different societies have different moral beliefs and practices. But in any given society, morals are "encoded" in the behaviour of its members. Social actors express their moral beliefs through their preferences, their choices, and their way of life. It is these preferences that sociologists observe and record, and lawmakers take into account when they aim to introduce new legal rules.

When drafting legal rules to regulate family life, lawmakers assign values to different kinds of behaviour. On the level of legal terminology, these values or ideals are theoretical abstractions that serve the specific classification purposes of a particular legal system. On another level, however, these "values embodied in legal rules" are an expression of the moral values that are generally accepted in a given society at the time of legislative change.[83]

Lifestyle choices reveal the moral attitudes and inclinations of social actors. The varying degrees of approval or disapproval of generally accepted patterns of life

82 See L. Kramer, "The Sociology of Gender: A Brief Introduction" (Los Angeles: Roxbury Publishing Company, 2001) p. 88.

83 M.A. Glendon begins her comparative study among the family law systems of four industrialized countries by pointing to the differences "between the institutions imagined, described, and elaborated in the law, and marriage and family behaviour as imagined and lived in a given society." See M. A. Glendon "The Transformation of Family Law: State, Law, and Family in the United States and Western Europe" (Chicago: University of Chicago Press, 1989) p. 6.

express the variations in the preferences of social actors. The body of norms regulating social behaviour also guides informal, everyday behaviour in small groups (*e.g.* families). Hence, the behaviour of small groups is generally ritualized and treated as strictly normative. Legal sociology has given convincing explanations about the reactions of small groups to exogenous change. When presented with a new social situation (a change in their environment), these small groups first respond according to the established patterns generated by their own social experience. But if these groups (or members thereof) ultimately recognize that these pre-existing patterns are inadequate, then they react (after several adjustments to their behaviour) by generating new patterns of behaviour.[84]

3.2. WOMEN AS A DISADVANTAGED GROUP DURING AND AFTER MARRIAGE

Greek Muslims living in Thrace are members of a religious subculture. As a result, the family life of Greek Muslims is imbued by the values of traditionalism and religionism. Practices such as homosexual relationships, unmarried cohabitation, adultery and fornication are generally frowned upon.

The Orthodox Greeks who comprise the dominant cultural group have decidedly moved in the direction of individualist social values in the last twenty years. The principal value configurations within Greek culture (in stark similarity to other societies of the West) include the attachment of high significance to individuality and progress, achievement and success, work and activity, efficiency and rationality, material comfort and patriotism.[85]

So at first blush it seems that the family values of Greek Muslims as a minority are sharply at odds with the family values of the majority of Greeks. Yet this is not so, because Greek family life has maintained many elements of traditionalism, when compared to family life in other Western nations. The social perceptions of Orthodox Greeks about marriage and the family indicate that Greeks have more

---

84 An important mechanism by which state laws affect the behaviour of social actors is the internalization of values. Through the process of internalization, social actors evaluate laws relative to their moral standards and support laws that conform to these standards. In fact, under a rational, self-interested theory of the internalization of values, people change their preferences to increase their opportunities for cooperation with others (See R. Cooter, "Do Good Laws Make Good Citizens? An Economic Analysis of Internalized Norms," *Virginia Law Review* 86 (2000), pp. 1577–1601, 1579).

85 See A. Tsaoussis-Hatzis, "The Greek Divorce Law Reform of 1983 and Its Impact on Homemakers: A Social and Economic Analysis" (Athens-Komotini: Ant. N. Sakkoulas Publishers, 2003) p. 39.

faith in traditional family forms than other Europeans do.[86] Also, a significant proportion of Greeks think it is best for children to be raised in a household by two parents who are married to each other.

Another shared element of traditionalism is the universal rule of homemaking that applies in both communities. Research indicates that Greek married women (fully employed or not) typically perform most of the daily care duties involving the home and the children.[87] Therefore, the universal norm of homemaking retains its force despite the steady increase in the number of financially independent married women. The Muslim family is traditional and gender-differentiated. In this family, the male breadwinner generally enjoys high status and increased bargaining power, while the female homemaker as a rule has low status and diminished bargaining power, both during and after marriage.

Both Christian and Muslim homemakers provide domestic unpaid labour that is undervalued. Homemakers are particularly vulnerable under the current no-fault divorce regime. The primary reason is that the advent of no-fault divorce has pressed all marriages toward a particular mould: one in which both parties are independent, self-supporting, and free to go without a finding of culpable action.[88] Predominantly house-working wives are exposed to high risks of marital opportunism on the part of their husbands because their contributions during marriage are asymmetric in relation to the contributions of their husbands.[89] The primary child-rearing obligations assumed by wives most often occur before the peak earnings period of the husbands. Since they have specialized in domestic labour

---

86 In a Eurostat survey measuring the attitudes of EU residents regarding marriage as a precondition for having children, Greeks displayed a greater commitment to marriage (or perhaps a greater conservatism) than any other nation. More specifically, the question "Do you believe that couples who want to have children should get married?" was answered affirmatively by 57 percent of the Greeks, 46 percent of the Portuguese, 33 percent of the Irish, 28 percent of the Italians, 24 percent of the Spanish, and so on. [Source: Eurostat, *Demographic Statistics* 1996].

87 This unequal division of household labour is a cultural norm that is firmly embedded in contemporary societies, despite the dramatic changes in women's economic roles over the last few decades. In a 1991 report, the OECD (1991) notes that the main reason for the prevalence of this norm is that life in our Western societies is organized according to an implicit social contract with two components: (a) a gender contract which assumes that women do most of the domestic work and men earn most of the money, and (b) a labour contract that reinforces this gender contract by defining the employee in terms of a money earner who works full-time throughout his entire working career.

88 See K. Abrams, "Choice, Dependence, and the Reinvigoration of the Traditional Family", *Indiana Law Journal* 73 (1998), pp. 517–534, 517.

89 See especially L. Cohen, "Marriage, Divorce, and Quasi Rents; or, 'I Gave Him the Best Years of My Life'", *Journal of Legal Studies* 16 (1987), pp. 267–303.

during the marriage, the dissolution of the marriage often means an end to their occupation as homemakers.[90]

Reduced bargaining power upon divorce leads to lower alimony and child-support payments,[91] as well as to unsatisfactory and unfair financial settlements for women.[92] These settlements usually consist of a return of any separate property and an equal division of the marital property -generally ignoring the largest source of the couple's wealth, which is human capital.

All these problems are exacerbated in the Muslim subculture. In every society where family affairs are regulated according to instructions derived from the Shari'a or Islamic law, women are disadvantaged. The injustices these women are exposed to in the name of Islam vary from extreme cruelty (forced marriages; imprisonment or death after rape) to grossly unfair treatment in matters of marriage, divorce and inheritance.[93] These social problems which reflect institutionalized and pervasive gender discrimination assume particular significance when seen in the light of international human rights developments, and in particular, the *International Convention on the Elimination of All Forms of Discrimination Against Women.*[94]

3.3. WHY MEDIATION IS THE BEST APPROACH

Methods of alternative dispute resolution like negotiation and mediation have the potential of helping women by giving them better stakes in the outcomes. ADR methods can also potentially broaden access to justice for socially disadvantaged groups. Generally speaking, alternative dispute resolution methods are more

90 This occupation, though invaluable to the welfare of the national economy, accrues no health, retirement, or unemployment benefits. Displaced homemakers find it difficult to get employment after divorce, because of their lack of vocational skills, their lack of experience and their age.

91 See E. Peters, "Marriage and Divorce: Informational Constraints and Private Contracting", *American Economic Review* 76 (1986), pp. 437–454.

92 See P.E. Bryan, "The Coercion of Women in Divorce Settlement Negotiations", *Denver University Law Review* 74 (1997), pp. 931–940.

93 For divorce proceedings see *supra*, under section 2.2. As regards inheritance law, according to the Shari'a, wives will only receive a small portion of the property of their husbands and a sister will get half of what her brother receives.

94 U.N.G.A. Res. 34/180, G.A.O.R. 34th Sess., Supp. 46, p. 193, 19 I.L.M. 33. Article 3 of the Convention mentions that the states shall take all appropriate (and legislative) measures to ensure the advancement of women in all fields (political, social, economic and cultural). Article 4(1) provides: "Adoption by States Parties of temporary special measures *aimed at accelerating de facto equality* between men and women shall not be considered discrimination as defined in the present Convention, but shall in no way entail as a consequence the maintenance of unequal or separate standards; these measures shall be discontinued when the objectives of equality of opportunity and treatment have been achieved".

open and responsive to the needs of the parties. The settlements reached by the parties are voluntary and the parties usually have better information than judges do. With information and volition, the parties have the control to satisfy their legitimate interests to a greater extent than under litigation.[95]

In mediation, the parties agree to take part in a structured settlement negotiation through the guidance of an independent, neutral expert. By participating in this process, the parties do not agree that they will actually settle and the mediator does not have the authority to impose such a settlement. Mediation is a type of intervention in which the disputants accept the offer of a third party to recommend a solution for their dispute—whereas arbitration is a judicial procedure, with all its manifested shortcomings. Compared to arbitration, mediation has clear advantages: it has proven to be far less expensive in terms of procedural costs, a lot quicker[96] and more satisfactory for the parties.[97] Whereas arbitration imposes solutions, mediation helps the parties to resolve their own disputes. According to the theory of procedural justice[98] disputants prefer procedures that provide them with a voice, control over the outcome, and fair treatment by the third party. Mediation gets higher marks than arbitration on all of these characteristics.

A specially trained mediator, especially one who has a legal education,[99] can help the parties to understand the strengths and weaknesses of their positions within the current legal regime. The mediator's functions vary depending on the personalities and wishes of the disputants, the nature of the issues, and the skills of the mediator. Mediators can play many roles: getting the participants to talk to each other, setting the agenda, helping disputants understand their problems, and suggesting possible solutions.[100] However, 'lawyers turned mediators' can be more

95 See generally R. Fisher/W. Ury, "Getting to Yes: Negotiating Agreement Without Giving In" (New York: Penguin, 1991) and G.R. Shell, "Bargaining for Advantage: Negotiation Strategies for Reasonable People" (New York: Penguin, 1999).

96 J.M. Brett/Z.I. Barsness/S.B. Goldberg, "The Effectiveness of Mediation: An Independent Analysis of Cases Handled by Four Major Service Providers", *Negotiation Journal* 12 (1996), pp. 259–269.

97 D. Shapiro & J.M. Brett have demonstrated that parties are more satisfied with the mediation process than with arbitration. See D. Shapiro/J.M. Brett, "Comparing Three Processes Underlying Judgements of Procedural Justice: A Field Study of Mediation and Arbitration", *Journal of Personality Social Psychology* 65 (1993), pp. 1167–1177.

98 See J. Thibaut/L. Walker, "Procedural Justice: A Psychological Analysis" (Hillsdale, NJ: Erlbaum, 1975).

99 In the U.S more than 40 of the 94 district courts and almost all the circuit courts have mediation programmes using judges or lawyers as mediators. Mediation programmes are also under way in more than one-third of the state courts and in many bankruptcy courts.

100 T.B. Carver/A.A. Vondra, "Alternative Dispute Resolution: Why It Doesn't Work and Why It Does." In *Harvard Business Review on Negotiation and Conflict Resolution* (Boston, MA: Harvard Business School Press, 2000) pp. 189–213, p. 209.

effective in their evaluative function, when studying the relevant documents submitted by the parties, such as pleadings, depositions, reports and briefs. They are also better in predicting court outcomes and can thus urge the parties to settle or to accept a particular settlement proposal.[101]

The Greek state should establish and encourage mediation as the best alternative to the costly and time-consuming adversarial proceedings. In cases of family and divorce disputes, mediation enables couples to regulate their post-divorce affairs (both personal and financial) more effectively. Furthermore, mediation allows couples to avoid the emotional stress, frustration and trauma of litigation. The informality of mediation and its potential for privacy make the parties feel more comfortable—and this is particularly advantageous for female participants.

More importantly, the mediation process ensures that the interests of both parties are satisfied to the greatest extent possible: the mediator (as the facilitator) is ethically obliged to steer the parties to identify the disputed issues and to generate options that help them to reach a mutually satisfactory resolution. Any settlement reached should have the agreement of both/all parties. This is in stark contrast to the law of arbitration, built upon the foundation of standard contract law, which recognizes that agreements will sometimes be entered into where a power imbalance exists between the parties. Therefore, the arbitration of family law disputes could result in the definition of legal rights by the powerful rather than by the application of fundamental societal values reflected in the rule of law.[102]

In the context of mediation and with the help of specially trained legal counsel, Muslim women could negotiate better agreements for themselves, safeguarding their interests in matters of post-divorce spousal maintenance, the distribution of marital assets,[103] child custody[104] and visitation

---

101 L.L. Riskin/J.E. Westbrook, "Dispute Resolution and Lawyers", 2d ed. (St. Paul, MN: West 1997) pp. 321–322.

102 J. Aslam, "Judicial Oversight of Islamic Family Law Arbitration in Ontario: Ensuring Meaningful Consent and Promoting Multicultural Citizenship", *International Law and Politics* 38(2006), pp. 841–876, esp. pp. 873–874.

103 A common experience among women in Shari'a divorce proceedings in the U.S. and Canada is that men dominate the proceedings and that men benefit the most when it comes to tangible marital property. Both parties may sign a document during the Shari'a divorce proceedings that is subsequently merged into a binding separation agreement to be made part of the record of a civil divorce case. When the female party retains counsel to represent her in the civil divorce proceedings, she often finds out for the first time that she may have been entitled to a greater share of the marital property if she had sought relief in the civil system instead.

104 Joint custody is a popular option among conciliatory spouses who have opted for mediation after divorce. However, child custody remains a frequent battleground for less than conciliatory spouses.

rights.[105] As more disputants enter into mediated settlements and as more attorneys become prominent as mediators, the Greek legal system will be ripe for the next move, which is the enhancement of private ordering in family law. The legislator could allow the spouses to enter into legally enforceable marital agreements that would restrict the grounds for divorce or penalize the divorcing spouse. Precommitment devices such as premarital contracts indirectly promote cooperative behaviour[106] and reduce conflict during marriage by reducing the likelihood that divorce will be considered.[107] Directly adding to the cost of seeking a divorce has been shown to promote marital stability. When divorce is not readily available, spouses are induced to behave less selfishly during marriage. Premarital agreements also protect against the risks of marital opportunism. Even if a couple did not start out from positions of equal outside options and equal extramarital welfare, the ability to negotiate a binding antenuptial agreement would still have salutary effects, because it would arrest the bargaining squeeze and eliminate the potential for opportunism that it presents.[108]

Therefore, it is safe to conclude that there are areas where the societal values of Christian Orthodox Greeks and Greek Muslims do not compete, but overlap.[109] The shared beliefs that lie at the core of these two religious subcultures find their

105 In the U.S., Muslim male clients generally do not contest the physical custody of young children and, most often, will give sole custody to the wife until the children reach the age of puberty in keeping with the majority opinion of Muslim scholars. However, the non-custodial father usually wants to be involved in all the decisions relating to the children. Muslim fathers who do contest physical custody are usually those married to women who have never converted to Islam. The main concern at the time of the divorce is that the child will lack an Islamic upbringing if the mother has sole physical custody (see http://www.aals.org/am2004/islamiclaw/conflictresolution.htm).

106 Haas introduces a game theoretic model to understand marriage in terms of cooperative or selfish behaviour. He applies a standard prisoner's dilemma-type matrix to conceive of marriage as a game in which each player (partner) chooses to act either cooperatively or selfishly, cooperation being defined as acting to maximize group welfare and selfishness being defined as seeking to maximize one's own welfare without concern for one's spouse. There are different versions to the game. In the more attractive version, each partner derives utility not only from his or her own welfare, but also from the welfare of the other. See T.F. Haas, "The Rationality and Enforceability of Contractual Restrictions on Divorce", *North Carolina Law Review* 66 (1988), pp. 879–930, p. 886).

107 E.S. Scott, "Rational Decision Making about Marriage and Divorce", *Virginia Law Review* 76 (1) (1990), pp. 9–94, esp. pp. 44–46.

108 A.L. Wax, "Bargaining in the Shadow of the Market: Is There a Future for Egalitarian Marriage?", *Virginia Law Review* 84 (1998), pp. 509–672, 629.

109 However, we need to determine the degree of acculturation of Greek Muslims in Greek society before making any conclusions about the assimilation of social values. See J. Georgas/ J.W. Berry/A. Shaw/S. Christakopoulou/K. Mylonas, "Acculturation of Greek Family Values", *Journal of Cross-Cultural Psychology* 27 (1996), pp. 329–338, for an excellent cross-cultural study of the change in family values held by Greeks that undergo the experience of acculturation in different host societies (more specifically, in Canada, where integration is the policy, and in European countries where assimilation is more heavily emphasized).

apt expression in the basic tenets of the Alternative Dispute Resolution paradigm: tolerance, fairness, empathy, understanding the concerns and needs of others, adopting fundamental and universal principles such as equality and non-discrimination. With its emphasis on the amicable resolution of conflict, it provides a unifying framework for the regulation of family life in both communities.

This normative framework can adequately protect the rights of disadvantaged parties. The Muslim women of Thrace have all the characteristics of a disenfranchised social minority. When minority members cannot claim their just rights, they become the victims of prolonged discrimination. In a single-jurisdiction system, mediation can orient Muslim women towards agreements that are tailored to accommodate their cultural and religious beliefs. For example, the Mufti of the French island of Mayotte (in the Pacific Ocean) relinquished all his judicial powers by Law 2001–616 of July 11, 2001 and was assigned the duties of a mediator.[110] However, to achieve a lasting resolution of family-related conflicts, the state should go one step further and enhance human rights education to the benefit of all Greek citizens. Human rights education could be made a core curriculum subject in universal primary education. Both minority and majority groups can be taught to respect human rights and appreciate cultural diversity that enriches society as a whole.[111]

With the widespread use of mediation to settle family disputes, the Muslim community will reinforce its commitment to the ethical and spiritual principles that lie at the heart of their religious belief system. The peaceful and amicable resolution of differences is central to the Muslim world. The Quranic solution to divorce provides the most characteristic example. In Islam, divorce is permissible only when serious differences arise which cannot be resolved through reconciliation. Divorce has to be the last resort, since the Prophet (*Pbuh*) has described divorce as the most detestable of all lawful things in the sight of God. Therefore, the Qur'an exhorts the parties to make a serious attempt at reconciliation in the following order: (1) The parties must try to settle their disputes and solve their problems between themselves; (2) If they fail, two arbitrators, one from the husband's

---

110 See the Report by I. Ktistakis of 3.2.2005 for the National Commission of Human Rights, (available at: http://www.nchr.gr/media/word/moufti_31_03_2005.doc).

111 On December 10, 2004 the General Assembly of the United Nations proclaimed the World Programme for Human Rights Education to advance the implementation of human rights education programmes in all sectors. The Plan of Action was adopted by all Member States of the UN General Assembly on 14 July 2005 (see http://www.ohchr.org/english/issues/education/training/docs/planaction-inbrief.pdf). Greater emphasis should be placed on the need to train teachers in anti-racism and human rights, appreciation of world cultures, and inter-cultural communications and sensitivity. An education oriented towards human rights also ensures that children are not denied the right to education on the basis of cultural practices (see *e.g.* http://www.hrea.org/lists/wcar/flowers.html).

side and the other from the wife's side, should be commissioned so that the differences between the two can be settled.[112] (3) If the arbitrators' efforts also fail, divorce may be applied.[113] A legal order that would permit ADR methods in matters of family law would provide Muslims with a way of doing things that reflects fundamental aspects of their sense of justice. Mediation would allow participants to settle their disputes in an informal religious setting, with fair and impartial proceedings.

Practising the peaceful resolution of family problems can imbue the members of the Muslim minority with a consciousness as to their reciprocal moral responsibilities as fellow human beings. At the same time, the sense of responsibility and compassion towards all people is one of the cornerstones of Christian ethics. Therefore, the civilizing virtues that are cultivated as parties attempt to resolve their differences out of court constitute an important area of common ground between these two religious populations. Negotiation and mediation procedures also satisfy the state's persistent concern for the "enforcement of morals".[114] The cultivation of communal morality can sustain a "community of observance".[115]

Muslim communities can respond well to conflict resolution processes, as they have recently subjected age-old practices to a critical eye. It is characteristic that in India Sunni leaders like Maulana Abdul Haq have opposed the practice of "talāq divorce"[116] saying that it is against the teachings of Islam, and welcomed the "nikahnama" model drawn up by Shia leaders to give women of the community the right to initiate divorce.[117] In the Arab Republic of Egypt, case law has in recent years restricted the scope of talāq.[118] In France and more recently in Brit-

---

112 Allah's command is as follows: "If you fear a breach between the couple, then appoint an arbiter from the man's family and an arbiter from the woman's family. If the two [man & wife] desire to reach a settlement, God will effect a reconciliation between them." [Qur'an 4:35]

113 The limits of the arbitrators' authority have been debated among Muslim jurists. The prevailing opinion is that the arbitrator has legal powers tantamount to those of the Qadi. However, this applies only if the husband agrees to their absolute power. If he questions it, the arbitrators do not have the authority to dissolve the marriage on their own. See A. Demosthenous, "Woman and Islam" (Athens: Akritas Publications, 2005) pp. 109–110.

114 *Cf.* P. Devlin, "The Enforcement of Morals" (London: Oxford University Press, 1959).

115 In this context, group identity is defined by a common adherence to a detailed code of conduct that sharply separates members from outsiders and serves as a continuing affirmation of loyalty and solidarity. See P. Nonet/P. Selznick, *Law and Society in Transition: Toward Responsive Law* (New Brunswick, NJ: Transaction Publishers, 2001).

116 On this issue, see *supra*, under section 2.2.

117 See http://www.indianmuslims.info/news/2006/december/01/indian_muslim/ islamic_family_values_stressed_on_worlds_aids_day.html for a report on "Islamic Family Values stressed on World's AIDS day".

118 Some characteristic examples follow: *Talāq* expressed indirectly, while intoxicated or under coercion, or conditionally with coercive intent is ineffective; repudiation to which a number is added verbally or by gesture is effective only as a single revocable *talāq* (except third of three);

ain, there have been both political and social concerns surrounding the political decisions and debates on the *Hijab* (headscarf) and the *Niqab* (veil) worn by Muslim women. The development of Islamic feminism is crucial to deconstructing traditional views of Islam and essential to developing and contributing to universal values of humanity and justice.[119]

Finally, our proposal is well aligned with the two most important global developments in the area of marriage and divorce: (a) the liberalization of moral values (the rise of moral relativism) and (b) the increasing focus of family law on individuals rather than groups. These two trends have been widely documented in the literature on both sides of the Atlantic over the last half century and have become more prominent in Western states.[120]

3.4. SOME CAVEATS: MEDIATION AND THE LIMITS OF "FREE CHOICE"

Given the nature of promises exchanged before or during marriage, and the context in which they are made, it is very likely that many of them will never materialize. The environment created by a failed marriage is conducive to the deployment of all kinds of pressure tactics on the part of the more powerful party (a refusal to negotiate, extreme or escalating demands, calculated delays and "take it or leave it" ultimatums). Although it is conceivable that in extreme circumstances, concessions can be gained under the explicit threat of immediate physical harm, in most marriages coercion is likely to be more subtle. In marriages characterized by a sharp division of labour, husbands can opportunistically threaten not to perform their obligations under the implicit marriage agreement – obligations that wives cannot effectively enforce.[121] Even well-meaning spouses who make

written and notarized certification of *talāq* must be obtained within 30 days of repudiation and the notary must forward a copy of the certificate to the wife; certain financial effects of *talāq* suspended on her knowledge if the husband is found to have concealed this (http://www.law.emory.edu/IFL/legal/egypt.htm).

119 S. Dewan, "The Development of Islamic Feminism: Emancipation of Women; Opportunities towards the development of Democracy and Universal Human Rights", Paper presented at the 8th Annual Conference of the Center for the Study of Islam and Democracy entitled "The Rights of Women in Islam and Muslim Societies", 2007. Abstract available at: http://www.csidonline.org/index.php?option=content&task=view&id=384.

120 J.A. Aycock, "Contracting Out of the Culture Wars: How the Law Should Enforce and Communities of Faith Should Encourage More Enduring Marital Commitments", *Harvard Journal of Law and Public Policy* 30 (2006), pp. 231–281, 237.

121 The legal challenge in traditional marriages is that "it will often be difficult for an external observer to be able to infer with confidence whether the economically dependent spouse is acting out of fear or love, and if the latter whether it is excessively unconditional or non-self-reflective" See M. Trebilcock/S. Elliott, "The Scope and Limits of Legal Paternalism: Intra-

promises that they intend to keep cannot be bound to perform, given the intimate nature of the relationship.

Furthermore, the actual price of this consent is likely to be low for the paying spouse, if his main bargaining strategy has been based on lies (ranging from deliberate deception to misrepresentation about facts or intentions), psychological abuse or positional pressure tactics. The employment of dirty tricks infects the negotiation climate. If, during a given negotiation, one party bluffs and lies about his underlying interests and preferences, the other party who has been open and has honestly disclosed her preference (*e.g.* for custody of the children) will be disadvantaged concerning the distributive aspect of the negotiation and will receive a smaller piece of the pie.

Because of all these asymmetries, it has been shown that mediation procedures cannot eliminate all bargaining problems for divorcing women.[122] These problems are exacerbated for divorcing mothers: mediation poses some risks of coercion and intimidation insofar as it enhances the opportunity for the stronger parent to exploit the vulnerabilities of the weaker one. As noted by the National Center on Women and Family Law, wives in divorce cases are not in a position to assert equal bargaining power in informal settings without representation by counsel.[123] After all, mediation is a process that rests on the free and voluntary exchange of information. The success of any mediation process depends on certain criteria—one of them is that the legitimate interests of both parties will be satisfied to the greatest extent possible. This presupposes that the parties have symmetrical bargaining power. Mediation is likely to fail if the parties depart from positions of gross asymmetry in financial, political or social power. In such cases, the most powerful disputant will most likely walk away from the mediation forum and take the dispute to court. But this is a general problem that pervades all cultures and all legal systems.[124] One way to overcome it is to direct parties to mediation as a mandatory stage of pre-trial proceedings; in other words, the state

---

Familial Financial Arrangements and Gatekeeper Responsibilities", University of Toronto, Law and Economics Working Paper Series No. 64 (1996), p. 22. This is an argument that applies *a fortiori* to Muslim marriages.

122 See especially M. Shaffer, "Divorce Mediation: A Feminist Perspective", *University of Toronto Faculty of Law Review* 46 (1988), pp. 162–200; W.A. Wiegers, "Economic Analysis of Law and 'Private Ordering': A Feminist Critique," *University of Toronto Law Journal* 42 (1992), pp. 170–206.

123 C. Lefcourt, "Women, Mediation, and Family Law", *Clearinghouse Review* 18 (1984), pp. 266–269.

124 Discussing unequal power between prospective spouses in the context of premarital agreements, B. Bix, "Bargaining in the Shadow of Love: The Enforcement of Premarital Agreements and How We Think About Marriage," *William and Mary Law Review* 40 (1998), pp. 145–207, 205 points out that in all parts of life, and not just in relationships between men and women, "people enter substantively unfair agreements because their relative lack of power leaves them

could require litigants to use mediation.[125] Therefore, if the powerful disputant exits the mediation, the failure to reach agreement can then be taken into due consideration by the divorce court.[126]

Another problem is that the ADR movement in Greece is at an embryonic stage. Out-of-court settlement is still relatively uncommon, since the law regulating negotiation as a distinct substantive process is relatively recent. The legislation enacted recently in Greece sets the "*mutually acceptable resolution of the dispute*" as a basic requirement of the negotiation process. The new provisions (see art. 214A para. 4 of the Code of Civil Procedure) also call for the presence of a mediator who cannot later be called to testify as a witness or expert witness. However, Greek lawyers remain unfamiliar with ADR processes, as they lack the necessary knowledge or expertise to engage successfully in the mediator role.[127]

The Greek State needs to take bold initiatives in the direction of expanding the scope of the existing provisions and injecting Greek legal culture with the much needed elements of the ADR paradigm. However, society is likely to once again lag behind the law: the inequalities stemming from socially embedded gender hierarchies will not be easily uprooted. Even in legal systems with strong ADR traditions (like the U.S.), women have willingly "bargained away" their rights in

---

little or no other choice." This is likely to be the case in the Muslim family, characterized by the wife's dependence on the husband.

125 If ADR processes were more firmly established as a parallel system, court mediation programmes could involve referral by the court to outside ADR programmes run by bar associations, non-profit groups, other local courts, or private ADR providers.

126 Reviewing a number of studies dealing with women's tendency to be more risk averse and more altruistic than men, M. Brinig, "Does Mediation Systematically Disadvantage Women?" *William and Mary Journal of Women and the Law* 2 (1995), 1–34, 34 concludes that congested courts cannot justify mandatory mediation in cases where one spouse holds a monopoly on marital power. "No one should order mediation when there has been abuse within the family, substance abuse, or systematic hiding of assets." (*ibid*). See in a similar vein P.E. Bryan, "Killing Us Softly: Divorce Mediation and the Politics of Power", *Buffalo Law Review* 40 (1992), pp. 441–523 and C. Bohmer & M.L. Ray, "Effects of Different Dispute Resolution Methods on Women and Children After Divorce", *Family Law Quarterly* 28 (1994), 223–245.

127 Every indication demonstrates that attorneys have made very limited use of this new institution. The main reason behind the law's ineffectiveness has to do with the unfamiliarity of Greek lawyers with ADR methods and their lack of specialized knowledge. Another reason is a flaw inherent in the law itself, which does not provide attorneys with sufficient incentives to engage in negotiations with their adversaries. There are no sanctions/disincentives for negotiation deadlock, so attorneys simply "go through the motions": they arrange the meeting between opposing counsel required by the law but they do not prepare to negotiate. Instead, they are fully determined to proceed with litigation, so they hold the meeting only to sign the "no agreement reached" section of the relevant minutes (see A. Tsaoussis, "Female Lawyers as Pragmatic Problem Solvers: Negotiation and Gender Roles in Greek Legal Practice" (2007) Forthcoming in *International Negotiation Journal* [available at http://papers.ssrn.com/sol3/cf_dev/AbsByAuth.cfm?per_id=327973]).

order to get custody of their children and at the same time to avoid litigation.[128] Moreover, women do not seem to be very successful in negotiations regarding their property.

Several explanations have been offered about women's tendency to accumulate less property than men. For example, Rose has used game theory and the assumption that women have a greater "taste for cooperation" to account for this phenomenon.[129] Grillo argues that because women (more than men) seek connection through relationships, they systematically fare worse because they trade their financial or custodial property to strengthen the relationship with their former spouses.[130] Another strand of studies explains power asymmetries by suggesting that the family can be studied as a non-cooperative game.[131]

Finally, culture-specific and religion-specific complications may arise as Muslim women enter into mediation agreements. The Ontario Arbitration Act in Canada provides an illustrative example. The government had some desire to use the 1991 Arbitration Act and (more specifically voluntary arbitration) to help clear up the log-jam in the Ontario Courts. Some Muslim groups (most notably the Canadian Islamic Congress and the Islamic Institute for Civil Justice) had proposed that it would be a good idea to permit family law matters to be resolved by applying Shari'a on a *voluntary* arbitration basis.[132] Other Muslim groups (most notably the Muslim Canadian Congress) had vociferously opposed this proposal and pointed out that this so-called voluntary participation would in fact be coerced – that women would be blacklisted in their communities if they did not go along with Muslim law.[133]

---

128 J.W. Ellis, "Surveying the Terrain: A Review of Divorce Reform at the Crossroads", *Stanford Law Review* 44 (1992), pp. 471–508 has suggested that women are likely to trade custody for money to avoid litigation because they are more risk averse than their husbands. J.B. Singer/ W.L. Reynolds, "A Dissent on Joint Custody", *Maryland Law Review* 47 (1988), pp. 497–523, esp. pp. 515–518 have shown that women commonly enter into a range of financially disadvantageous property settlements in order to prevent challenges to the custody of their children.

129 C.M. Rose, "Women and Property: Gaining and Losing Ground", *Virginia Law Review* 78 (1992), pp. 421–459.

130 T. Grillo, "The Mediation Alternative: Process Dangers for Women", *Yale Law Journal* 100 (1991), pp. 1545–1610.

131 S. Lundberg/R.A. Pollak, "Separate Spheres Bargaining and the Marriage Market", *Journal of Political Economy* 101 (1993), pp. 988–1010 and S. Lundberg/R.A. Pollak, "Noncooperative Bargaining Models of Marriage", *American Economic Review, Papers and Proceedings* 84 (1994), pp. 132–137. Under this approach, the decision-making processes within a family may lead to inefficient allocations of resources.

132 The "Muslim Marriage Mediation and Arbitration Service" was one of the groups advocating the application of mediation for resolving Muslim marital disputes. For an illuminating synopsis of their arguments, see their position paper online (at http://www.muslim-canada.org/brochure.htm).

133 See especially http://www.eagle.ca/~roda/RodMerArts/UnderstandingIslam/Shariah.html.

Muslim women's arguments were that "free choice" is relative when you are psychologically, financially and socially dependent on your family, clan or religious group.[134] International human rights groups like *Amnesty International* also opposed the passage of the Act, expressing concerns over the fact that processes applying religious laws are often significantly discriminatory towards women even when they are part of the formal legal system.[135] On December 20, 2004, Marion Boyd (the former attorney general in the Rae government and appointed by Premier McGuinty to report on this issue) issued her report "Dispute Resolution in Family Law: Protecting Choice, Promoting Inclusion". In February 2006, Ontario's legislature passed the "*Family Statute Law Amendment Act*", codifying McGuinty's decision by mandating that only Canadian law may be applied to family law arbitrations in Ontario.

To sum up, mediation may incur some process dangers for women,[136] but on the whole it remains a superior alternative to litigation. It is more empowering for women and its virtues are accentuated when it applies to women who are already subordinated in a given society. Mediation processes have been shown to produce more equitable results for women.[137] Finally, divorcing couples who used mediation to settle all their divorce issues were more satisfied with its process and outcomes than couples using a traditional "adversary" process with two lawyers.[138]

4. CONCLUSION

Women in Islamic countries have been relinquished to play secondary social roles in both the private and public sphere. They are obliged to follow a strict dress code and are denied fundamental human rights safeguarded by international conventions. Their life cycle is defined by their isolation and segregation from the general society. In the West, freedom of religion does not conflict with women's civil

---

134 A.H. Ali, "Unfree Under Islam: Sharia Endangers Women's Rights from Iraq to Canada", *Wall Street Journal*, August 16, 2005.

135 See http://www.amnesty.ca/take_action/actions/canada_ont_arbitration_act.php.

136 The process dangers that arise because of power imbalances can effectively be dealt with by a well-trained divorce mediator: see especially D. Neumann, "How Mediation Can Effectively Address the Male-Female Power Imbalance in Divorce", *Mediation Quarterly* 9 (1992), pp. 227–239.

137 See especially J. Pearson, "The Equity of Mediated Divorce Agreements," *Mediation Quarterly* 7 (1991), pp. 347–363.

138 See J. Kelly, "Mediated and Adversarial Divorce: Respondents' Perceptions of Their Processes and Outcomes," *Mediation Quarterly* 24 (1989), pp. 71–88, but especially J. Kelly, "Mediated and Adversarial Divorce Resolution Processes: An Analysis of Post-Divorce Outcomes" (Washington, D.C.: *Fund of Research in Dispute Resolution*, 1990). See also J.D. Rosenberg, "In Defense of Mediation", *Arizona Law Review* 33 (1991), pp. 467–507.

rights. However, in Islamic subcultures living in countries of the West, freedom of religion has become the legitimate excuse for Muslim women's inferior legal and social status relative to men. Multiculturalism is a very clever word to use when trying to explain religious and cultural differences—but it does not hold up very well when trying to account for weak or non-existent rights. Muslim women living in Greece are twice disadvantaged: once as members of a religious minority (as Muslims) and twice as members of a social minority (as women). If they were free to choose, they would no doubt choose the legal system that would offer them greater guarantees for the protection of their rights. Because they are not free to choose, the State must choose for them and secure their access to any and all mechanisms of legal redress.

Women's civil liberties are threatened in political regimes that are heavily influenced by religion.[139] The empowerment of women in the family can bolster their equality and empowerment in all social arenas, both in Islamic and non-Islamic societies. Especially mediation, but also other alternative dispute resolution policies provide additional safeguards for conflict prevention, resolution and management. As they enhance trust building and commitment, they also have the potential of fostering social cohesion within communities.

The above analysis clearly illustrates that the existing system of "concurrent jurisdiction" is contradictory and problematic. It is also unfair, as it legitimizes the decisions of a religious court that fails to take into account the legitimate interests of the weaker parties. The experience of Greek Muslims calls for a careful approach on the part of policymakers, legislators and local administrators. Bicultural communities pose special challenges as they seek to promote peace and prosperity. The stability of the region is of special importance to the Greek state for many

139 In countries marked by political instability there is a strong threat that Islamic-oriented governments will increase the influence of religion. Democracy and non-secularism go hand-in-hand for educated women in these countries. Turkey provides an illustrative example: Turkey has one of the strongest women's movements in the world - some 40 per cent of its top university academics are female. Over the past decade, women have won a host of civil rights, including the amendment of the country's penal code that, until very recently, sided with those who committed honour killings. Despite these victories, their representation in parliament is 4.4 per cent, lower than it was in Atatürk's day. See H. Smith, "Women on the streets", *The New Statesman*, 21 May 2007, available at: http://www.newstatesman.com/200705210018). Physical appearance was of central importance for Ataturk, who discouraged the wearing of the Islamic veil and sought to make women the symbols of his new Turkey: unveiled, Western-dressed, and educated. This narrative continues to hold great weight in Turkish society. Many condemn Islamic influences in the public sphere, and view the veil as the greatest symbol of women's oppression. See N. Razavi, "Reclaiming their Rights through Islam: Islamist Feminism in Turkey", Paper presented at the 8th Annual Conference of the Center for the Study of Islam and Democracy entitled *The Rights of Women in Islam and Muslim Societies*, 2007. An abstract is available at: http://www.csidonline.org/index.php?option=content&task=view&id=384).

reasons, geopolitical, economic and cultural. Therefore, in times when communities are more sensitized to issues of multiculturalism and pluralism, it is expedient to give minority problems higher priority on the political agenda.

To meet the demands of successful legal implementation in a multicultural community, the legal system needs to provide options that are realistic, flexible and viable. The proposed regimes should also provide room for future change based on possible cultural shifts. Thus, the relativism of moral values should be adopted as the main philosophy underlying legal principles. Equality, individual freedom, tolerance and equity should be understood and interpreted in this light.[140] Members of religious communities should be encouraged and empowered to make their own long-term choices for their families.

140 "Pluralism dictates that involvement by communities of faith should be respected alongside marriages officiated by civil authorities." See J.A. Aycock, *supra* note 120, p. 280.

PART FOUR
(PROPERTY) RELATIONS BETWEEN SPOUSES AND COHABITANTS

LEGISLATION FOR THE SURVIVING COHABITANT FROM A COMPARATIVE PERSPECTIVE

Göran Lind

1. INTRODUCTION

Let me announce that a "war" is going on and the battlefield is today Italy, where this spring the Italian government proposed new legislation for same-sex and unmarried heterosexual couples.[1] The law, referred to as DICO ("*Diritti di coppie conviventi*") has been attacked by Pope Benedict the XVIth, who has stated that this is "the mother of all battles".[2] On the other side, the terrorist group "The Red Brigade" has warned a bishop, threatening that if he stops the law, "he will die."[3]

After this glimpse from the front, let me say to this presumably more peaceful audience that the objective of my presentation is to highlight the legal status of surviving cohabitants from a comparative perspective. This presentation is limited to family law regulations in which the parties' cohabitation constitutes the legal basis for their rights and obligations. Outside of this framework any legislation is based on registration. It would also be stretching it too far here to take into consideration property law solutions outside of family law as well as public law legislation, even if these are significant complements or alternatives to family law.

It is my intent to present the different types of legal constructions that have been chosen in the Western World and the reasons given for the regulations. This entails that I will also analyze arguments for and against cohabitation legislation.

1 Disegno Di Legge, Senato Della Republica, XV Legislatura N. 1339 (2007).
2 La Chiesa sul DICO: Sí o No?, Whispering in the Loggia, Monday, February 19, 2007.
3 Vatican Fears Gay Marriage in Italy, Ohmy News International, 2007-04 12.

2. DIFFERENT LEGAL CONSTRUCTIONS

2.1. COMPLETELY IDENTICAL RULES AS FOR MARRIAGE

First, there is a group of regulations that posit completely identical rules as for marriage. This is the most far-reaching protection for a surviving cohabitant and is offered by eleven American jurisdictions recognizing the old doctrine of common law marriage. The legal effects of such a marriage are the same as for an official marriage, for example with regard to the division of property, spousal maintenance, inheritance, tort claims, social benefits, insurance rights, the legitimacy of children born to the couple, etc.[4]

For example, according to *Texas* law in cases of death an informal relationship has the same legal effects as marriage if the parties (1) had the legal capacity to enter into a marriage, (2) had formed a marriage agreement, (3) had cohabited together, and (4) had held themselves out as a married couple. The agreement need not to be express, but can be inferred from the parties' cohabitation and conduct. A certain period of time is not required for the cohabitation. If the parties have lived together as a married couple and held themselves out as such, then the surviving party will have the same rights as a surviving spouse.

If the parties have no children all community property,[5] real or personal, is taken by the surviving common law partner. As to the decedent's separate real estate 1/2 is taken by his or her parents or brothers and sisters if the parents are dead, and 1/2 by the surviving common law partner. All other separate property is taken by the surviving common law partner.

If the parties have mutual children the surviving party inherits all the community property of the decedent and 1/3 of the separate property and if the children are not children of both parties the surviving party and the children take 1/2 each of the community property. The surviving party takes 1/3 of any separate property. The division can be changed by will and by community property survivorship agreements.[6]

4 See Göran Lind, 'Common Law Marriage. A Legal Institution for Cohabitation', 2008, Oxford University Press. Already present at the net.

5 Texas applies a community property system, which distinguishes between community property that is accumulated during the common law marriage through the efforts of either party, and separate property that is accumulated before the marriage or during the marriage by gift or inheritance. See J. Thomas Oldham, *Texas Marital Property Rights* 465 (4th ed. 2003).

6 Tex. Prob. Code §§37 and 45 (Vernon 2007); Oldham, *id.*

2.2. IDENTICAL RULES AS FOR MARRIAGE AS TO THE DIVISION OF PROPERTY

2.2.1. *Identical Rules for Cohabitants and for Spouses through Joint Legislation*

A *second* group comprises jurisdictions that have gone considerably far in the direction towards common law marriage by granting identical rules as for marriage, but only as to the division of property and inheritance. For example, New South Wales in *Australia*, and *New Zealand*, have enacted legislation equating a "de facto relationship" (both heterosexual and homosexual) with marriage in 1999[7] and 2002,[8] respectively, regarding issues as significant as the equal division of property acquired during the relationship, inheritance and maintenance.

The requirement for these legal effects to arise in Australia is two years of cohabitation and in New Zealand three years. The extensive nature of these reforms can also be seen from the fact that the concepts and terminology have changed. As the

7 Regarding *New South Wales*, Australia, see Property (Relationships) Act (1984), which for the purpose *inter alia* of also including homosexual couples has been changed by the Property (Relationships) Amendment Act (1999). Within the concept of a "domestic relationship" falls not only "de facto relationships", but also a "close personal relationship" that is not a marriage, or a "de facto relationship" between two adult persons who live together, regardless of whether they are related to each other or not, in which the one or both without compensation provides the other with domestic support and personal care. Similar legislation in a number of legal areas has been enacted for Australia's other jurisdictions. For more on this, *see* DOROTHY KOVACS, "De Facto Property Proceedings in Australia" (1998); LINDA WILMOTT et al., "De facto Relationships Property Adjustment Law – A National Direction", *17 Aust. J. Fam. L. 1* (2003); REG GRAYCAR & JENNI MILLBANK, "The Bride Wore Pink... to the Property (Relationships) Legislation Amendment 1999: Relationship Law Reform in New South Wales", *17 Can. Fam. J. L. 227* (2000); REBECCA BAILEY-HARRIS, "A decade of reforms in Australia", *9 IJLF 233* (1995); "Law and unmarried couples – oppression or liberation", *8 Child Fam. L.Q. 137* (1996).

8 Property (Relationships) Act (1976), amended by law in 2001, which came into force on 1 February 2002. See Property (Relationships) Amendment Act, 2001. In order to give cohabiting unmarried persons also the right to maintenance and inheritance, amendments were made at the same time to the Family Protection Act of 1955, the Administration Act of 1969 and the Family Proceedings Act of 1980. Regarding the development in New Zealand, see BILL ATKIN, "The Challenge of Unmarried Cohabitation – The New Zealand Response", *37 Fam. L.Q. 303* (2003); M. HENAGHAN AND B. ATKIN, "Family Law Policy in New Zealand" (2nd ed. 2002); VIRGINIA GRAINER, "What's Yours is Mine: Reform of the Property Division Regime for Unmarried Couples in New Zealand", *11 Pac. Rim. L. & Pol'y. J. 287* (2002); NICKY RICHARDSON, "The New Property (Relationships) Act in Practise", *Int. Fam. L.J. 221* (2003); BILL ATKIN AND WENDY PARKER, "Relationship Property in New Zealand" (2001); BILL ATKIN, "Reforming Property Division in New Zealand: From Marriage to Relationships", *3 E.J.L.R. 349* (2001); WENDY PARKER, "New Zealand's property rights legislation: A changing landscape", *57 Fam. Matt.* 62 (2000).

law no longer only applies to married couples, the term "matrimonial property" has been replaced by the term "relationship property".[9]

The same development can be seen in *Canada*. For example, in the province of *Manitoba*,[10] all regulations concerning married persons' property rights became applicable through new legislation in 2002 to "common-law partners".[11] Upon separation, the parties are entitled to half the value of the property that they acquired during the cohabitation. If a party dies, the surviving party receives all, or the majority of, the deceased party's property.[12] If a will exists leaving the property to another party, the surviving common-law partner is still entitled to a "fair share" of the couple's "family property", a new term that has replaced the term "marital property" also with respect to formally married couples.

The Canadian legislation applies to persons who are deemed to be "common law partners", which means persons (homosexual or heterosexual) who have either registered the "common-law relationship" or who have cohabited in a "conjugal relationship" during a period of at least three years. In many of the Canadian laws, for example with respect to maintenance and inheritance, at least one year's cohabitation is sufficient if the parties have mutual children.

2.3. IDENTICAL RULES FOR COHABITANTS AS FOR SPOUSES APPLIED BY ANALOGY

Without any new legislation, the Supreme Court in the *State of Washington*, in the United States, has made the community property system for spouses analogously applicable to unmarried cohabitation (both same sex and heterosexual)[13] and

9 Through amendments in 2001, which came into force on February 1, 2002, to New Zealand's Matrimonial Property Act of 1976, several exceptions were made to the regulations concerning the division of a marital estate between spouses, making it applicable to heterosexual as well as homosexual cohabiting unmarried couples. Because of this, the law was renamed the Property (Relationships) Act of 1976.

10 The constitutional basis was laid down by Canada's Supreme Court in *M. v. H.*, (1999) D.L.R. 577 and was followed by *Barbeau v. British Columbia (Attorney General)*, (2003) BCCA 406 (BC Court of Appeals 2003) and *Halpern v. Canada (A.G.)*, (2003) O.J. No. 2268 (Ontario Court of Appeal 2003).

11 The Common-Law Partner's Property and Related Amendments Act, S.M. 2002, c. 48 (in force June 30, 2004).

12 The Intestate Succession Act, C.C.S.M. C. 185, 13(2).

13 *Vasquez v. Hawthorne*, 99 Wash.App. 363 (2000), 145 Wash.2d 103, 107 (2001). The court did not decide the case finally but rather remanded it for decision as to whether the relationship was sufficiently "stable". Thomas Andrews has found that the case has set out two principles: "First, equitable division of property under Connell is available at the end of a same-sex relationship in Washington if it is sufficiently long-term and stable to justify such equitable treatment. Second, equitable division of property is available under Connell regardless of whether

despite the fact that the Court had already refused to recognize common law marriages at the end of the 1800s.[14] Community property, upon separation or death, is to be divided in a fair and equitable distribution and property acquired during the cohabitation is presumed to be owned by both parties.[15] The court's requirement for this right is that the parties live in a "stable, marital-like relationship where both parties cohabit."[16]

3. PARTIAL RIGHTS FOR COHABITANTS

A *third* group of regulations gives rise to partial rights for cohabitants, which can be limited in different ways.

3.1. PROTECTION ONLY UPON DEATH

An old legal system granting cohabitants legal protection only upon the death of one of the parties is *New Hampshire* in the United States, where the surviving party is granted all rights that accrue to a surviving spouse if the parties have lived together during the *last three years* prior to the death of one of the parties. On the other hand, the law does not include any protection upon separation.[17]

---

the relationship ends during the life of both partners, or at the death of one", see THOMAS ANDREWS, "Property Rights of Domestic Partners in the United States and Scandinavia: A Comparative Study" 37–38 (2003) (unpublished paper, University of Washington). The community property laws were applied by analogy upon death also in *Olver v. Fowler*, 131 Wash. App. 135, 126 P.3d 69 (2006). Compare *Peffley-Warner v. Bowen*, 113 Wash.2d 243, 778 P.2d 1022 (1989), in which a cohabiting person did not receive the status of a surviving spouse.

14 *In re McLaughlin's Estate*, 4 Wash. 570, 30 P. 651 (1892). See LIND, *supra* note 4, at 184.

15 See *In re Marriage of Pennington*, 142 Wash.2d 592, 14 P.3d 764, 770 (2000); *Connell v. Francisco*, 127 Wash.2d 339, 351, 898 P.2d 831 (1995).

16 *Connell v. Francisco*, 127 Wash.2d 339, 346, 898 P.2d 831 (1995). The case is commented upon in GAVIN M. PARR, "What is a "Meretricious relationship"? - An Analysis of Cohabitant Property Rights Under Connell v. Francisco", *74 Wash. L. Rev. 1243* (1999).

17 The applicable legal regulation speaks of persons "cohabiting and acknowledging each other as husband and wife, and generally reputed to be such, for the period of 3 years, and until the death of one of them…", see N.H. Rev. Stat. Ann. 457:39 (West 2003). The legislation has old roots, see already RS 149:11 (1842); *Joan S. v. John S.*, 121 N.H. 96, 427 A.2d 498 (1981). From the beginning, acommon law marriage was completely recognized in New Hampshire, see *DeLisle v. Smalley*, 63 A.2d 240 (N.H. 1949) and See LIND, *supra* note 4, at 150. A majority of all cohabiting persons in the United States, both homosexual and heterosexual, prefer that a part of their estate be distributed to their surviving cohabiting partner, see MARY LOUISE FELLOWS, et. al., "Committed Partners and Inheritance: An Empirical Study", *16 Law & Inequality 1*, 9 (1998). Approximately 30% of heterosexual couples and approximately 60% of homosexual couples draft wills, see JENNIFER K. ROBBENHOLT and MONICA KIRKPATRICK JOHNSON, "Legal Planning for Unmarried Committed Partners: Empirical Lessons for a Preventive and Therapeutic Approach", *41 Ariz. L. Rev. 417*, 441 (1999).

Another example is a *Norwegian* proposal submitted in January 2007 (høringsnotat) also limited to cases of death in which a right of inheritance for the surviving party would be established if the parties have, had or expect a mutual child or children, or have lived together in a marriage-like relationship for at least five years prior to the death of one of the parties. The surviving party then receives the right to a minimal inheritance, this year comparable to NOK 250,000 (four times the basic amount as established in the public insurance system), as well as a right for the party to retain the estate undistributed.[18]

Also in *Denmark* a proposal was made by a parliamentary committee in 2006 as to a right of inheritance (for the surviving party) if the parties have, had or expect a mutual child or children and have lived together for at least two years. According to this proposal, the surviving party would be granted a right to one-fourth of the estate after the demise, but with a maximum of DKR 500,000, however.[19] The Danish Minister of Justice has rejected the proposal as to a legal right of inheritance, but has proposed a right for a party through a will to receive the same inheritance rights as spouses. In addition, a right to take over the mutual residence has been proposed.[20]

Very limited protection exists in *England & Wales*, where the surviving party has the right to maintenance from the estate, assuming that the parties have lived together as husband and wife for two years before the death. The English attitude to reform has long been characterized by hesitancy and cautious accommodation. Later this year the Law Commision will present a proposal concerning cohabitation.[21]

3.2. PROTECTION ONLY UPON SEPARATION

Other proposed systems provide no protection upon death, only upon separation. Thus the *American Law Institute* ("ALI") in 2002 recommended legislation con-

18 See Høringsnotat, January 2007. Snr.200405522EP.

19 See Betaenkning no. 1473, 2006.

20 See L 100. Forslag til arvelov Dec. 6, 2006., para. 15.3.1.

21 See Law Reform (Succession) Act 1995 Sh. 2, which amended the Inheritance (Provision for Family and Dependents) Act 1975 Sh. 25. With respect to the English stance, see STEPHEN CRETNEY, "Family Law in the Twentieth Century, A History 520" (2003), who finds that the attitudes to the reform are characterized by "hesitancy and uncertainty". See also DAVID BRADLEY, "Regulation of Unmarried Cohabitation in West-European Jurisdictions – Determinants of Legal Policy", *15 IJLPH 22* (2001); JOHN M. EEKELAAR, "The Family Law Bill – The Politics of Family Law", *26 Fam. L. 45* (1996); S.M. CRETNEY AND J.M. MASSON, "Principles of Family Law" 243 (1997); *Law Commission 44* (1995); MARY ANN GLENDON, "The Transformation of Family Law" 268 (1989), who speaks of a politics of "cautious accommodation".

cerning the division of property when the relationship of "domestic partners", both homosexual and heterosexual couples, is dissolved through separation.[22] The "domestic partnership property" is distributed between the partners, which would have corresponded to "marital property" if the parties had been formally married.[23] The principle that is recommended is a presumptive equal division of property acquired during the relationship, which is supplemented with several exceptions. In contrast with Washington case law, no regulations on the dissolution of the relationship by death are proposed. On the other hand, a domestic partner is also entitled to compensatory payments on the same basis as spouses.[24] The parties have the opportunity through a contract to avoid an application of the regulations concerning the division of property.[25] In contrast to a common law marriage, the principles do not create any rights in relation to third parties or in public law. The appropriateness of the ALI Principles is still being debated.[26]

3.3. LIMITED PROTECTION UPON SEPARATION AND DEATH

There are also jurisdictions providing a more limited protection upon both separation and death. For example *Sweden*, which since the 1960s until 2004 had the lowest frequency of marriage and the highest number of unmarried cohabiting couples in the Western world, has legislation intended to give the parties a minimum degree of protection.[27] According to the act, which was replaced in 2003, the parties in the case of separation or death have a right to an equal share only of the residence and household goods that they have acquired during the cohabitation, upon death to a value of at least SEK 80,000. The party in greatest need also has the right to take over the residence, which occurs if it has an economic value in exchange for financial compensation. The surviving party does not have any

22 See the American Law Institute (ALI), Principles of the Law of Family Dissolution: Analysis and Recommendations (2002), particularly Chapter 6, Domestic Partners and Chapter 4.

23 *Id.* §6.04 and §4.09.

24 *Id.* §6.06.

25 *Id.* §6.01. In David Westfall, "Forcing Incidents of Marriage on Unmarried Cohabitants: The American Law Institute's Principles of Family Dissolution", *76 Notre Dame L. Rev.* 1467, 1480 (2001), the author carries out an exhaustive critical analysis of the possibilities and difficulties for the parties to contract out of the domestic partnership status.

26 For a critical discussion, see, e.g., Reconceiving the Family. Critique on the American Law Institute's Principles of the Law of Family Dissolution (Robin Fretwell Wilson ed., 2006), and Lind, *supra* note 4, at 958–1029.

27 Cohabitees Act (2003:376); Legislative Bill 2002/03:80, Ny Sambolag, at 25. In Sweden, legislation (SFS 1987:232) was enacted in 1987 that gives couples who live together under marriage-like conditions the right *inter alia* to a division of the residence and its belongings which the parties acquired during the cohabitation. The law was also applicable to homosexual couples (SFS 1987:813). These laws were replaced in 2003 by a new Act.

inheritance rights, but the parties can bequeath property to each other. Couples wishing to have a more extensive financial community are recommended to enter into a formal marriage.[28]

A prerequisite for these rights is that the parties (of the same or different sexes) have lived together continuously as a couple with a mutual household.[29]

Limited legislation was also enacted in *Scotland* in 2006 for couples "living together as if they were husband and wife". According to the new regulations, the parties are presumed to have a right to an "equal share" of "household goods" that are acquired during the cohabitation and to monies and property that are tied to their mutual household expenses. The residence is not included in the property. Upon death, the surviving cohabitant can receive "a capital sum" from the decedent's estate.[30]

In *Spain,* cohabitation legislation has been enacted in several regions in recent years. In *Catalonia,* a law was adopted in 1998 (*d'unions estables de parella*) for cohabitants who have lived together in marriage-like conditions during a period of two years or who have mutual children.[31] In cases of death, the surviving party has the right to continue to live in the residence for one year as well as the right to the household goods that belonged to the common residence.

An example of a very limited family law regulation is the existing system in *Norway* (Huslejeloven 1991). This legislation is applicable not only to men and women who live together, but also to two or several unmarried persons who have lived in a common household for at least *two years* or have mutual children. The legal

28 See Legislative Bill 2002/03:80, Ny Sambolag, p. 25.

29 Section 1 of the Cohabitees Act (2003:376). As there is no time requirement, in certain cases it has been sufficient with only a few months of cohabitation, RH 2005:34. Couples not wishing to be included within this system have the possibility to contract out of the regulations concerning the division of the estate (§9).

30 The Family Law (Scotland) Act (2006).

31 Ley 10/1998, de 15 de Julio, d'unions estables de parella (DOGC num. 2687, 23.07.1998). Thereafter, similar legislation was enacted in three additional regions that have the authority to legislate within civil law. Regarding *Aragonia*, see LAY 6/1999, de 26 de marzo, relativa a parejas estables no casados (BOE num. 112, 10.05.2001). Regarding *Navarra*, see LEY FORAL 6/2000, de 3 de julio, para la igualdad juridica las parejas estables (BOE num. 214, 6.09.2000). Regarding the*Balearic Islands*, see LEY 18/2001, de 19 de diciembre, de Parejas Estables (BOE num. 14, 16.01.2002). See *also* a number of autonomous areas. Regarding *Valencia*, see LEY 1/2001, de 6 de abril, por la que see refgulan las uniones de hecho (BOE num. 112, 10.05.2001). Regarding *Madrid*, see LEY 11/2001, de 19 de diciembre, de Uniones de Hecho de la Communidad de Madrid (BOE num. 55,.05.03.2002). Regarding *Asturien*, see LEY 4/2002, de 23 de mayo, de Parejas Estables (BOE num. 157, 02.07.2002). For more on this, see MIQUEL MARTÍN-CASALS, "Same-Sex Partnerships in the Legislation of Spanish Autonomous Communities, EU ERA Conference", unpublished paper, Uppsala 19–20 (September 2002) at 2.

effect is limited to a right to the residence and household goods. If the assets have a value, compensation must be paid therefore. The law gives no right to a division of the estate, inheritance or maintenance.[32]

As mentioned above, the latest proposal comes from *Italy*, where this spring the Italian government proposed new legislation for same-sex and unmarried heterosexual couples.[33] The law, referred to as DICO ("*Diritti di coppie conviventi*"), would, inter alia, upon separation give the parties maintenance rights after three years of cohabitation and, upon death, the surviving cohabitant inheritance rights after nine years of cohabitation. The surviving party inherits 1/3 if there is only one child and 1/4 if there are two or more children. If the deceased only has parents or siblings, 1/2 is taken by the cohabitant. If there are no children, parents or siblings the surviving party takes 2/3 and if there are no relatives closer than the third degree (second cousins) the surviving cohabitant takes the whole inheritance. Art. 1 of the proposed law requires parties to be united by mutual emotional bonds and to cohabit continuously and give each other support and solidarity, materially as well as morally. Cohabiting partners will have to go to the registry office to declare their de facto union.

4. ARGUMENTS FOR COHABITATION LEGISLATION

4.1. PROTECTION FOR THE VULNERABLE PARTY

One of the strongest motives behind a common law marriage and all the legislation for unmarried cohabiting couples which has been promulgated during the last 30 years is that it provides protection for the more vulnerable party during the cohabitation as well as upon its dissolution through separation or death. As it is the woman who most often has been the more vulnerable party, at least financially, a common law marriage has come to constitute a certain degree of protection for her.[34] This has given rise to feminist proposals as to the reinstatement of

---

32 Lag No. 45, 4 July 1991. *See* Peter Lødrup, "Family law in Norway", in *Family Law in Europe 353* (Carolyn Hamilton et al. eds., 1995). A proposal has been presented that gives couples who have children or who have lived together for two years a stronger degree of protection. Complete equality with spouses has not been sought, however, due to the freedom of choice. See NOU 1999:25, Samboerne og samfunnet. For the latest proposal for an inheritance right for the surviving cohabitant, see Høringsnotat, January 2007. Snr.200405522EP, *supra* note 15.

33 Disegno Di Legge, *supra* note 1. The law would also allow the surviving party to make decisions as to funeral arrangements and organ donations. If they have cohabited for three years or have mutual children they will have a right to take over a lease.

34 Ariela R. Dubler, "Wifely Behavior: A Legal History of Acting Married", *100 Colum. L. Rev. 957*, 964 (2000), maintains that the common law marriage during the 1800s "took as its premise

the common law marriage in those American states where it has been abolished.[35]

As to cohabitation law, the regulations, for example in *Sweden*,[36] *Australia*[37] and *New Zealand*,[38] primarily purport to provide protection upon separation and in cases of death. The principles as proposed by the *American Law Institute* (ALI) are also based on the idea that the relations "closely resemble marriages in function and therefore pose the same social and legal issues as does the dissolution of a

---

that the law should protect innocent women from the whims and contrivances of irresponsible or rakish men." The same author states: "For over a century in New York, common law marriage essentially functioned to protect women plaintiffs who came to court in search of economic support. In recognizing common law marriage, courts sought to protect innocent women from abandonment and poverty." (*Id.* at 1002). Women earn less than men, see Lynne M. Casper & Suzanne M. Bianchi, "Continuity and Change in the American Family 53" (2002).

35 See, e.g., Cynthia Grant Bowman, "A Feminist Proposal to Bring Back Common Law Marriage", *75 Or. L. Rev. 709*, 779 (1996), who maintains that common law marriage "protects the interests of women, especially poor women and women of color…" and who maintains that non-recognition of common law marriage "often results in what appears to be substantial injustices to women who are especially vulnerable" (at 755). The author also notes the possibility for a marital divorce with a division of the estate and maintenance, as common law marriage offers women who are victims of abuse a means for "seeking to escape an abusive marriage" (at 760). According to Ellen *Kandoian, women in the nearest predictable future will be the most economically vulnerable party in a cohabitation relationship. See* "Cohabitation, Common Law Marriage, and the Possibility of a Shared Moral Life", *75* Geo. L.J. 1829, 1859 note 132 (1987). See also Lind, *supra* note 4, at 928–932.

36 One of the reasons behind the Swedish law was to give protection to the more vulnerable party in the event of separation and/or death. In addition to this, the legislator wished to offer a practical possibility to divide the home they have built up together. *See* Legislative Bill 1986/87:1, pp. 105, 106 and 108. In SOU 1980:81, p. 622, the Commission stated: "What is needed is to find solutions to practical problems and, in particular, to protect the weaker part upon the dissolution of cohabitation". Also Kathleen Kiernan mentions, concerning the developments in Europe, the "protection of weaker and vulnerable family members" as a justification for regulations relating to cohabitation, see "Redrawing the Boundaries of Marriage", *66 J. Mar. and Fam. 980,* 983 (2001).

37 See, e.g., Linda Wilmott et al., "De facto Relationships Property Adjustment Law – A National Direction", *17 Aust. J. Fam. L. 1,* 9 (2003), who contends that "individuals in de facto relationships possess interests identical to (those of) married couples" and who argues that the whole marital legal system should be extended to de facto couples in Australia. Associate Minister of Justice Margaret Wilson has stated that de facto relationships "have a right to the same legal protection" as married couples, *see* Property (Relationship) Amendment Bill: Third Reading (March 29, 2001).

38 Reasons that were the basis for the new legislation in New Zealand, *supra* note 7, were stated to be *inter alia* the need for protection for women, who for a period leave their careers and take care of children, but with "changing work patterns" also for men, see Bill Atkin, "The Rights of Married and Unmarried Couples in New Zealand: Radical New Laws on Property and Succession, International Society of Family Law World Conference", unpublished paper, Copenhagen/Oslo, (August 2002), at 3. Virginia Grainer, "What's Yours is Mine: Reform of the Property Division Regime for Unmarried Couples in New Zealand", *11 P.R.L.P. 287,* 300 (2002), holds that the reform was based on the fact that "the property situations of persons in de facto relationships were identical to those in marriages" and that they deserved the same treatment.

marriage."[39] Even in *Canada* the protection of the vulnerable party is generally the justification for the state's interference in private relationships, such as the imposition of obligations on a former "common law partner" when the relationship breaks down.[40] Even behind the new legislation in *Scotland* in 2006 for couples "living together as if they were husband and wife" the motive is "to protect vulnerable people either on breakdown of the relationship or when a partner dies".[41] The same motives can also be seen behind the *Norwegian* proposal this year concerning a minimum inheritance right and a right to keep the estate undivided for surviving cohabitants.[42]

If one only looks at the need for protection, one can question why so many jurisdictions have stopped at regulations more limited than formal marriage. Why does the *American Law Institute* propose the same rules for "domestic partners" only upon separation, but not upon cases of death?[43] And why do the *New Hampshire* legislation and the *Danish* and *Norwegian* proposals only care about protection upon death, but not upon separation?[44] It must be difficult for many couples to understand that they are cohabitants in one situation but not in another. And why does the system in *Sweden* only concern the residence and its belongings, but

---

39 See the ALI Principles, *supra* note 22, at Chapter 6, Domestic Partners, §6.02 (1). Comment: a. The basis of this Chapter; GRACE BLUMBERG, who contributed to the drafting of the principles, has argued that the principles which are applied to spouses are "equally pertinent at the end of a stable nonmarital cohabitation of substantial duration, whether same-sex or opposite-sex," see "The Regularization of Nonmarital Cohabitation: Rights and Responsibilities in the American Welfare State", *76 Notre Dame L. Rev. 1265*, 1295 (2001). The goal of providing partners in long-term unions with more effective means of enforcing financial obligations between themselves has been held "laudable", *see* ELIZABETH S. SCOTT, "Domestic Partnerships, Implied Contracts, and Law Reform", in *Reconceiving the Family, Critique on the American Law Institute's Principles of the Law of Family Dissolution* 331 and 339–340 (ROBIN FRETWELL WILSON ed., 2006).

40 Law Commission of Canada (Personal Relationships) (1999), II A., states that "most Canadians accept that economically vulnerable partners should not be left destitute at the end of a relationship..."; MARGUERITE TRUSSLER & ELLEN VANDERGRIFT, "Changing Relationships: How the Law and Governments Have Accommodated Them. A Canadian Perspective, June 1 2001, Court of Queen's Bench of Alberta; Winifred Holland, Intimate Relationships in the New Millennium: The Assimilation of Marriage and Cohabitation?", *17 Can. J. Fam. L. 114*, 128 (2000).

41 See the Family Law (Scotland) Act 2006; Family Law (Scotland) Bill, SP Bill 36B, 18, Session (2005), sections 18–22; Policy Memorandum, Family Law (Scotland) Bill (SP Bill 36)(2005) at

42 See HØRINGSNOTAT, January 2007. Snr. 200405522 EP at 11.

43 See the ALI Principles, *supra* note 22, Chapter 6. Domestic partners. By assuming that cohabitation and marriage were similar, but only legislating for the limited purpose of dissolution, it has been held that the principles create a default rule that few would want, see MARGARET F. BRINIG, "Domestic Partnership and Default Rules", in *Reconceiving the Family. Critique on the American Law Institute's Principles of the Law of Family Dissolution* 269 (ROBIN FRETWELL WILSON ED., 2006).

44 N.H. REV. STAT. ANN. 457:39 (West 2003). See also the Norwegian proposal, *id.*

not, in principle, all the property as for spouses?[45] Long-term cohabitation and the creation of a family as between unmarried persons commonly in social aspects are identical with marriage and create the same needs for protection during the relationship and upon its dissolution.

A relevant objection may be that the factual situation for cohabitants widely defined is actually not the same as for married couples. Many relationships are brief and less stable.[46] But also concerning long-term and very marriage-like cohabitation there are answers to the question which are to be found on another level than the need for protection, and which also considers the intentions of the parties. Perhaps everyone does not desire a system of protection and the obligations that the state imposes upon them.

4.2. COMPENSATION FOR CONTRIBUTIONS AND SACRIFICES

There are also cases where the surviving cohabitant's rights cannot be justified by the need for protection, for example if she or he has a large fortune. In such cases, on the other hand, the rights can be justified by the surviving party's contributions to the deceased's fortune and to the family's economy as a whole and by the sacrifice, for example, of a professional career in order to take care of the children, etc.[47] It should be observed that the arguments of contribution and sacrifice are often used as legal grounds for property rights outside family law, but here they are the justification behind the legislation, where the ground is cohabitation. The argument of contributions is more relevant with regard to property acquired during the relationship than with regard to separate property that the deceased has acquired before or during the cohabitation by gift or inheritance.

4.3. ETHNIC, CULTURAL AND SOCIAL REASONS

The endeavour in American law has historically been to place marriage at the disposal of population groups whose traditions do not necessarily include cere-

45 According to the Swedish Cohabitees Act (2003:376); Legislative Bill 2002/03:80, Ny Sambolag, at 25, the main purpose is merely to provide minimum protection.

46 Garrison, *supra* note 38, at 839 and 845, who criticizes the equivalence claim, contends that "cohabitants typically behave and describe their relationships very differently than married couples. Even more importantly, it shows that cohabitants rarely make marital commitments or engage in sharing behavior that might induce dependency."

47 The need for protection in New Zealand has been considered especially significant for those who sacrifice a part of their professional career in order to take care of the children, see supra note 3 As to Swedish law, see legislative bill 1986/87:1, p. 105.

monial marriage. Through this tolerant attitude, traditions among Native Americans, African Americans[48] and European Americans from poorer segments of society could be recognized as common law marriage.

Formless cohabitation has also been extensive among peoples of Spanish and Mexican descent.[49] Long-standing cohabitation has been more frequent among lower economic classes.[50] It has therefore been said that cohabitation still operates

---

48 Steven G. Brown, Comment, "Pennsylvania Common Law Marriage and Annulment: Present Law and Proposals for Reform", *15 Vill L. Rev. 134*, 140 (1969). See also Nancy Rebecca Shaw, Note, "Common Law Marriage and Unmarried Cohabitation: An old Solution to a New Problem", *39 U. Pitt. L. Rev. 579*, 586 (1977), in which the author states: "[I]t may be noted that Pennsylvania is a state in which a wide variety of ethnic groups, cultural backgrounds and lifestyles find representation. Marital customs vary among these diverse groups and Pennsylvania's protection of the marital status extends to all of them by means of the common law tradition." The reluctance in Florida during the 1950s to repeal the common law marriage appears to a great extent to have depended upon considerations concerning the African American population. In 1957, the proposal to repeal was rejected, *see* H.B. No. 41, 36th Regular Session, Florida (1957). See Daniel E. Murray, "Domestic Relations", 12 U. *Miami L. Rev. 428*, 429 (1958); Skolnick, "The Social Contexts of Cohabitation", *29 Am. J. Comp. L. 339*, 341 (1981); William A. Reppy, Jr., "Property and Support Rights of Unmarried Cohabitants: A Proposal for Creating a New Legal Status", *44 La. L. Rev. 1677*, 1679 (1984). For more on this, see Lind, *supra* note 4, at 923.

49 Cynthia Bowman, who has researched the consequences of the non-recognition of common law marriage in individual cases, draws the conclusion that it "clearly has a disparate impact upon different races and ethnic groups as well, falling particularly hard upon African Americans, Mexican Americans, and Native Americans", see Bowman, *supra* note 35, at 744, 747, 767–770. See also Jacobus TenBroek, "California's Dual System of Family Law: Its Origin, Development, and Present Status", *17 Stan. L. Rev.* 614, 618 (1965), who researched families in California. Another study, which was limited to Santa Clara County, California, demonstrated that among Mexican American women, 27.7% of the marriages were common law and 72.3% formal marriages. The comparable amount among Anglo-American women was 6.2% common law marriages and 93.8% formal marriages, see Woodrow Borah & Sherburne F. Cook, "Marriage and Legitimacy in Mexican Culture: Mexico and California", *54 Cal. L. Rev. 946*, 987–988 (1966). Homer Clark, who has recommended the retention of common law marriage, states: "Without it there would be more injustice and suffering in the world than there is with it. This is particularly true among those social and economic classes who have not accepted middle class standards of marriage. Certainly American marriage law should tolerate this much cultural diversity," see Homer H. Clark, Jr., "The Law of Domestic Relations in the United States I", 122 (2nd ed. 1987). See also Kathryn S. Vaughn, Comment, "The Recent Changes to the Texas Informal Marriage Statute: Limitation or Abolition of Common-law Marriage?" *28 Hous. L. Rev. 1131*, 1147 (1991), maintains that, considering ethnic and cultural groups that do not use formal marriage, "states should not force these groups to comply with the white middle-class conception of a 'proper' marriage."

50 Walter Weyrauch maintained in 1960 with respect to the formless marriage that "it may aid and protect the poor and the ignorant in their family relations", see Walter O. Weyrauch, "Informal and formal marriage – an appraisal of trends in family organization", *28 U. Chi. L. Rev. 88*, 101 (1960). See also John R Williams, "Solemnization of Marriage: The common law marriage - never solemn and no longer common – will it remain law?" *13 U. Miami L. Rev. 447*, 453 (1959); Martha L. Fineman, "Law and Changing Patterns of Behaviour: Sanctions on Non-Marital Cohabitation", *Wis. L. Rev. 275*, 322 note 189 (1981); and Thomas Clifford

as "a poor man's marriage."[51] Historically, it is easy to determine that many couples lacked the economic possibilities to enter into a ceremonial marriage. The social requirements of an expensive wedding in some circles ought to constitute an impediment even today.[52] However, it should be noted that formless cohabitation during the last twenty years has expanded to all classes of society.[53]

Billig and James Phillip Lynch, "Common-Law Marriage in Minnesota, A Problem in Social Security", *22 Minn. L. Rev. 177,* 178 (1938). See also TenBroek, *supra* note 42, at 617: "[C]eremonial marriage is often expensive and may not be a part of the cultural mores of various minority groups." Compare José E. Arraros, "Concubinage in Latin America", *3 J. Fam. L. 330,* 333 (1963), which states that concubinage is accepted among the poor, who develop their own norms, values and attitudes. See also Meyer F. Nimkoff, "Marriage and the Family" 219 (1947) and John Sirjamaki, "The American Family in the Twentieth Century", 69 (1953) (Common law marriage is common among groups with lower socio-economic status). Even if there is a correlation between social class and race and ethnicity, with whites being the most privileged economically, see Wendy D. Manning & Pamela J. Smock, "Living Together Unmarried in the United States: Demographic Perspectives and Implications for Family Policy", *26 Law & Policy 87,* 98 (2004), it should be observed that many white couples are not privileged.

51 Manning & Smock, *id.*, at 100.

52 A clear testimony as to the fact that economic impediments can exist can be found in *Elliot v. Industrial Accident Board,* 101 Mont. 246, 53 P.2d 451, 452–453 (1936), in which the woman testified as to the conversation she had had with the man: "Ed. where are we going to get married?' to which he replied, 'Dell, it costs 2.00 dollars for a marriage license and 5.00 dollars for a justice of the peace to marry us, and I have not got a cent and you have very little. If we agree to get married and if we agree that we are married and go ahead and live together as man and wife, it will be a common law marriage...it will be just as good.'" In the case of *In re Hines's Estate,* 10 Pa.Super. 124, 126 (1894), the woman testified at trial that the man had said: "I will take you for my wife; and asked me if I was satisfied, and I said, 'yes', and he said he would have a ceremony performed, but he did not have any money at that time; he was in bad circumstances at that time." *Compare Trammell v. Trammell,* 196 S.W.2d 209 (Tex.Civ.App. 1946), in which the parties lived together in a common law marriage, but in which they intended sometime in the future, when their economic situation would permit it and from a practical viewpoint it would be appropriate, to solemnize their relationship.

53 Manning & Smock, *supra* note 50, at 97–98, hold that "whites, blacks and Hispanics report similar *levels* of cohabitation experience" and that "cohabitation is commonplace in all these groups". According to the authors, children are more likely to be present in black and Hispanic cohabiting couple households than in white cohabiting households. See further *Vaughn, supra* note 49, at 1142: (cohabitation has recently become common concerning middle and upper-class couples). See also Mary Ann Glendon, "The Transformation of Family Law" 277 (1989), who maintained that cohabitation is spread among different social groups and notes that it also concerns "upper-middle-class cohabitation." Compare Bowman, *supra* note 35, at 766, who even in 1996 maintained that "informal unions are simply more frequent among lower income groups than among middle class". Compare also Reppy, *supra* note 48, at 1681; Barbara Freedman Wand, "The Relevance of Premarital Cohabitation to Property Division Awards in Divorce Proceedings: An Evaluation of Present Trends and a Proposal for Legislative Reform", *63 B.U.L. Rev. 105,* 106 (1983); Leonore Weitzman, "The Marriage Contract" 361–363 (1981); and Skolnick, *supra* note 48, at 399.

4.4. FULFILMENT OF THE PARTIES' GOOD FAITH EXPECTATIONS

A considerably more limited reason behind common law marriage and cohabitation law has been to fulfil the parties' expectations to be united in marriage and thereby *to avoid unjust results.* A special method for this in some American states is the putative marriage doctrine which is applied when the parties have entered into a ceremonial marriage that is invalid on the basis of a mistake in form or an impediment and a party has entered into the invalid marriage in good faith. Compared with common law marriage, the putative marriage is more limited with respect to its legal effects.[54]

4.5. THE STATE'S INTEREST IN CAPTURING 'THE LOST SHEEP'

One reason behind common law marriage is the legislator's interest in capturing 'the lost sheep' and imposing obligations upon them. This strategy was already used in Medieval Canon law, within the marital law system, trying to capture, so to speak, men and women who informally lived together.[55] The same strategy can be traced in common law marriage in American law, albeit not as tangibly.[56] This method includes a further ideological dimension. By placing upon individuals in a family certain economic obligations as against each other, the state can free

54 See LIND, *supra* note 4, at 940–951.

55 *See* LIND, *id.*, at 107 and 954–958.

56 *Stump v. Stump,* 111 Pa. Super. 541, 546 (1934); *Schurler v. Industrial Comm'n,* 86 Utah 284, 43 P.2d 696, 698–699 (1935). The same reason can be traced in older case law, see e.g. *People v. Spencer,* 199 Mich. 395, 165 N.W. 921, 923 (1917); *Bishop v. Brittain Invest. Co.*, 229 Mo. 699, 129 S.W. 668 (1910); *Ingersol v. McWillie*, 9 Tex.Civ.App. 543, 30 S.W. 56, 60 (1895); *Askew v. Dupree*, 30 Ga. 173, 188 (1860); *Londonderry v. Chester,* 2 N.H. 268, 281, 9 Am.Dec. 61 (1820). See in modern case law, *e.,g.*, *Laws v. Griep,* 332 N.W.2d 339, 340–341 (Iowa 1983), which held that the policy favouring marriage would be subverted if persons could gain marital legal rights without accepting "correlative marital legal responsibilities." See also in the literature, WARREN D. HARRIS, "The Essentials of a Valid Marriage in Virginia", *6 Va. L. Reg. 437,* 443 (1900). ARIELA R. DUBLER, "Governing Through Contract: Common Law Marriage in the Nineteenth Century", *107 Yale L.J. 1885*, 1886 (1998). Compare NANCY F. COTT, "Giving Character to Our Whole Civil Policy: Marriage and the Public Order in the Late Nineteenth Century", in *U.S. History as Women's History: New Feminist Essays* 107 (LINDA K. KERBER et al. eds., 1995); JAMES SCHOULER, "A Treatise on Husband and Wife" 47 (1882), states that the formless marriage rests upon the idea that "an institution of such fundamental importance to our race ought to be good independently of, and prior to, the formal requirements which human government imposes at an advanced stage of society". See also JAMES SCHOULER, "Marriage, Divorce, Separation & Domestic Relations" I, 42 (6th ed. 1921).

itself from responsibility for social welfare. This reason appears to be the case in the United States.[57]

If the marriage rate continues to decrease in the Western world, it cannot be ruled out that the attitudes to cohabitation law will become entirely reversed. Conservatively tinged states, protective of the family and marriage and which desire to place upon the parties different obligations, can introduce cohabitation legislation for the purpose of capturing these 'lost sheep'. Common law marriages can then appear as "an old solution to a new problem".[58]

5. ARGUMENTS AGAINST COHABITATION LEGISLATION

5.1. LIMITING THE FREEDOM OF THE PARTIES

An ideological argument against cohabitation legislation in general is that such systems can be forced upon the parties without the couple having chosen them by marriage, registration, contract or their own free will.[59] The fact that they actually

57 This reason appears behind the reinstatement of the common law marriage in Utah and behind the ALI Principles with respect to the dissolution of "domestic partnerships". A secondary objective for the principles regarding the dissolution of relationships between "domestic partners" is said to be the "protection of society from social-welfare burdens that should be borne, in whole or in part, by individuals". See the ALI Principles, *supra* note 22, at §6.02, (2), Comment: B) The Objectives of this Chapter. See Lind, *id.*, at 956.

58 Shaw, *supra* note 48, at 579.

59 Reppy, *supra* note 48, at 1713 ("The writer cannot see how morality is advanced by the law's telling a couple that it will treat them as married even though they do not want to be"); M. Freeman, & C. Lyon, "Cohabitation Without Marriage" 51–54, 183–185 (1983); Marjorie Maguire Schultz, "Contractual Ordering of Marriage: A New Model for State Policy", *70 Cal. L. Rev. 204*, 287 (1982). Fineman, *supra* note 50, at 325, states: "The choice of cohabitation is, after all, a choice not to marry and it would seem incongruous to attach to it identical consequences"; H. A. Finlay, "The Informal Marriage in Anglo-Australian Law", in *Marriage and Cohabitation in Contemporary Societies 156*, 166 (John M. Eekelaar, Sanford N. Katz eds., 1980); Walter O. Weyrauch, "Metamorphoses of Marriage: Formal and Informal Marriages in the United States", in *Marriage and Cohabitation in Contemporary Societies 265*, 266 (John M. Eekelaar, Sanford N. Katz eds., 1980); Simitian, "Property Rights and the Unmarried Homemaker: Marvin v. Marvin, and the California Experience", *5 Com. Prop. J. 3*, 7, 10 (1978); Christina M. Fernández, Note, "Beyond Marvin: A Proposal for Quasi-Spousal Support", *30 Stan. L. Rev. 359*, 370 (1978). Homer H. Clark, Jr., "The New Marriage", 12 *Willamette L.J. 441*, 452 (1976), appears to assume that couples who refrain from formally marrying make a legal choice. Compare, on the other hand, the same author in "The Law of Domestic Relations in the United States" 57 (1968), in which he argues that the choice between formal marriage and common law marriages is not a conscious choice; John R. Valeri, "Informal Marriages and Other Curative Devices", *17 How. L.J. 558* (1972). See also, Marsha Garrison, "Marriage Matters: What's Wrong with the ALI's Domestic Partnership Proposal", in *Reconceiving the Family, Critique on the American Law Institute's Principles of the Law of Family Dissolution 322*

live together in practice already triggers a system of rights and obligations that becomes applicable to their relationship. This liberal attitude, which places the freedom of the individual in the foreground, stands in direct contrast to the strategy that the law should capture the 'lost sheep'. The liberal philosopher *John Stuart Mill* stated: "'If a person possesses any tolerable amount of common sense and experience, his own mode of laying out his existence is the best, not because it is the best in itself, but because it is his own mode. Human beings are not like sheep..."[60]

The freedom to choose and personal autonomy in matters of family life are values that are guaranteed, for example in *American* and *Canadian* constitutional doctrine.[61] This dilemma is also clearly illustrated by the development in *Scotland*, in which the legislator has pronounced: "Where families are strong and functioning well, the Executive considers the state should play little or no role. Family life should, wherever possible be an issue for families themselves." However, this

(ROBIN FRETWELL WILSON ed., 2006), who holds that the ALI Proposal as to domestic partnership based on cohabitation "diminishes personal liberty and privacy; individuals are forced into a marital mold whether or not that family form comports with their own goals and personal choices".

60 JOHN STUART MILL, On Liberty 82–83 (London, Longman, Roberts & Green Co., 1859).

61 With respect to American doctrine, see, e.g., GARRISON, *id.* at 320, referring to the Fourteenth Amendment and the case of *Planned Parenthood v. Casey*, 505 U.S. 833, 851 (1992). See *also Santosky v. Kramer*, 455 U.S. 745, 753 (1982); *Zablocki v. Redhail*, 434 U.S. 374 (1978); *Loving v. Virginia*, 381 U.S. 1, 12 (1967). See with respect to Canadian doctrine, *R. v. Salituro* (1991) 3 S.C.R. 654, 674. The Law Commission of Canada has stated: "The freedom to choose whether and with whom to form close personal relationships is a fundamental value in free and democratic societies", see Law Commission of Canada (2001), *Beyond Conjugality* at 17. Ottawa: Law Commission of Canada. The reluctance in the province of Quebec to provide the same regulations for cohabitation as for marriage has been based on respect for freedom of choice, see CÉLINE LE BOURDAIS and ÉVELYNE LAPIERRE-ADAMCYK, "Changes in conjugal life in Canada: Is cohabitation progressively replacing marriage?", *66 J. Mar. & Fam. 929–942 (2004)*. See also Kenneth KARST, "The Freedom of Intimate Association", *89 Yale L.J. 637* (1980). When the Canadian legislators hesitated in extending the application of the marital division of property rules to unmarried cohabitants, this was justified by the argument that the cohabitants did not give their consent thereto. Quebec's Minister of Justice Serge Ménard has stated: "S'il s'est abstenu de le faire, c'est par respect pour la volonté des conjoints : quand ils ne se marient pas, c'est qu'ils ne veulent pas se soumettre au régime légal du mariage". See National Assembly *Debates of the National Assembly.* June 18, Bill 84 (1998). *See also* Martha Baily, *Regulation of Cohabitation and Marriage in Canada,* 26 LAW & POLICY 153, 155 (2004). When the Supreme Court of Canada, in a decision from 2002, found that it was not unconstitutional to exclude unmarried cohabitants from the application of the same rules, the court held that spouses have freely accepted the rights and obligations of marriage and that a decision not to marry should be respected. See *Attorney General of Nova Scotia v. Walsh*, 4 S.C.R. 325 (2000). TRUSSLER and VANDERGRIFT, *supra* note 40, at 15, state on the conjugal cohabitation-based approach: "The disadvantage is that it imposes obligations on those that may have chosen not to marry for the express purpose of avoiding those sorts of obligations". See also MARTHA BAILY, "Regulation of Cohabitation and Marriage in Canada", *26 Law & Policy 153*, 155–156 (2004). Compare the dissenting opinion by Justice L'Heureux-Dubé.

policy declaration did not impede the law giving rights to all couples living together as if they were husband and wife.[62]

The same arguments also appear in the Nordic countries. In *Denmark*, a proposal in 1968 concerning "common law marriage" with all incidents of marriage for couples having lived together for three years was rejected by parliament with reference to the parties' freedom to choose, and, in 2006, the Ministry of Justice rejected the proposal concerning legal inheritance rights for surviving cohabitants, inter alia, with reference to the same arguments.[63] Similar concerns as to autonomy and choice caused *Norway* to abstain from placing cohabitation on an equal footing with marriage in 1999.[64]

The argument that cohabitation law limits freedom naturally appears most clearly in cases in which the parties have chosen not to formally marry simply in order to avoid the legal effects of marriage so as to be more independent or for the sake of children from a previous marriage.[65] Against this argument it should be noted

62 See The Family Law (Scotland) Act 2006; Family Law (Scotland) Bill, SP Bill 36B, 18, Session 2 (2005); Policy Memorandum, Family Law (Scotland) Bill (SP Bill 36), at 1.

63 In 1968, the Minister of Justice, Knud Thestrup, justified the decision with reference to the parties' freedom to choose. *See* the parliamentary debates (folketingets forhandlinger), 24th of May 1968, at 3628–3650. Since then, no cohabitation legislation between the parties has been enacted in Denmark. One of the reasons has been that the parties have the option to marry and that legislation would be a manifestation of a 'Big Brother' attitude. *See* Betænkning 8, Aegdeskab, Samliv uden ægdeskab I, 50 (nr. 915/1980). As to the rejection of the proposal concerning legal inheritance rights in 2006, see L 100. Forslag til arvelov. Dec. 6, 2006, para. 15.3.1.

64 See NOU 1999:25, para. 2.4. On the other hand, it should be noted that in January 2007, the Norwegian Ministry of Justice sent a proposal to different institutions so as to obtain feedback concerning a proposed minimum inheritance right and a right to keep the estate undivided as to residence and household goods for surviving cohabitants. See Høringsnotat, January 2007, Snr. 200405522 EP. As for Finland, see Caroline Forder, "European Models of Domestic Partnership Laws: The Field of Choice", *17 Can. J. Fam. L. 371*, 381 (2000). The Finnish Ministry of Justice has rejected inheritance rights for surviving cohabitants with reference to the possibility to make a will, see Bet. 2004:6.

65 This argument is raised from time to time. See, e.g., Brinig, *supra* note 43, at 269, who holds that "parties who did not want to get married but wanted to cohabit would find themselves with a set of responsibilities on dissolution that they did not want to assume; if they had wanted these responsibilities, they would have married"; Forder, *id.* at 452, who holds: "The possibility of avoiding assimilation with spouses is important, as many unmarried couples have deliberately chosen not to marry and do not wish for assimilation to married couples." The author recommends the Swedish regulation, which creates a "middle way" between being unmarried and being married. See also Martha Bailey, "Marriage and Marriage-Like Relationships" (Ottawa: Law Commission of Canada, 1999) at 31, who held that "some object to this as an unjustified interference with the autonomy of parties who may have chosen not to marry in order to avoid responsibility to their partners". See also Howard O., Hunter, "An Essay on Contract and Status: Race, Marriage and the Meretricious Spouse", *64 Va. L. Rev. 1039*, 1094–1095 (1978), who says that "two people who choose to live together without marriage

that the parties generally have the possibility to contract out of the systems.[66] This possibility assumes, however, that they are aware of and in agreement as to this.[67]

With regard to inheritance, it should be observed that the rights can normally be changed by a will and that state coercion exists irrespective of who the heirs are under the law.[68]

It ought also to be added that the parties in many cohabitations might not have any decided intentions of a legal nature at all, either as to avoiding the marital legal effects or receiving them.[69] The Swedish sociologist Jan Trost stated during the 1970s that "couples do not choose to cohabit instead of to marry. They just cohabit".[70]

5.2. COHABITATION LEGISLATION UNDERMINES MARRIAGE, THE FAMILY AND THE COMMUNITY

A second traditional argument against common law marriage during the first part of the 1900s is that it undermines marriage, the family and the entire

often may be seeking to avoid that status obligations of marriage itself…" *Compare* Note, *The Decline and Fall of Common-law Marriage in Pennsylvania*, 18 *Temp. L.Q.* 264, 265 (1944).

66 See, e.g., the ALI Principles, *supra* note 22, §6.01 (2), the parties have the right to contract away the system as to the division of an estate as between "domestic partners". Compare the Swedish scheme according to which the parties have the right to contract out of the system as to the division of an estate in accordance with the Cohabitees Act (2003:376) §9, but, on the other hand, not the right for a cohabiting partner to take over the other's residential apartment (§22).

67 See also The Law Commission of Canada (2001). *Beyond Conjugality*, at 116. Ottawa: Law Commission of Canada, which holds that treating cohabitants as if they were married "infringes upon the value of autonomy. Although people may opt out of certain statutory provisions governing their relationships, they are not always aware of this possibility".

68 The possibility to negate, by will, the other party's right to inherit by statute can come as a surprise to the latter. In order to avoid this, in Norway it has been proposed that there should be a duty to inform for the party wishing to terminate the statutory right of inheritance by will. *See* Høringsnotat, January 2007. Snr.200405522EP, at 22–23.

69 See *Kandoian, supra note 35, at 1858*. Compare Homer H. Clark, Jr., "The Law of Domestic Relations in the United States" 57 (1968) (not a conscious choice, drift into); Carol S. Bruch, "Property Rights of De Facto Spouses Including Thoughts on the Value of Homemakers' services", *10 Fam. L.Q. 101*, 135 (1976), maintains that the majority probably choose to live together as unmarried "either 1. In ignorance of the legal consequences of either marriage or non-marriage (perhaps the majority of non-lawyers believe that common law marriage exists in all jurisdictions and that protection is granted to stable nonmarital relationships), 2. under the assumption that some legal protections are available, or 3. with absolutely no thought given to the legal consequences of their relationship". *Compare* Atkin, *supra* note 38, at 4, who maintains that "de facto couples" do not make vows in the same manner as spouses, but that they "do make a choice to live together".

70 Jan Trost, "Unmarried Cohabitation" 186 (1979).

community.[71] Objections, however, can be raised against these somewhat sweeping arguments. It should be observed that this marriage entails the same legal effects as formal marriage. The spouses in a common law marriage are consequently subjected to the same morally-coloured obligations as formally married spouses, even the regulations concerning marital divorce. Further, it should be observed that the requirements for such a marriage to be established ordinarily mean that the parties must live together and outwardly appear and receive a reputation as spouses. Thus, a marriage-like common law marriage in actual fact must be more marriage-like than a marriage itself needs to be in order for the legal effects to arise!

However, what about cohabitation legislation, which generally has more limited legal effects than common law marriage, does it entail a threat to marriage, the family and the community? A pervasive feature in the cohabitation legislation is merely that it ordinarily contains rights with respect to an economic resolution upon separation or death, but no regulations as to divorce. Despite a gradual retreat during the past 30 years from state-defined grounds for divorce to the benefit of no fault divorces, the majority of states still show an interest in safeguarding the stability of families not in the least for the sake of children. While common law marriage maintains this interest through the regulations concerning marital divorce, cohabitation legislation can be characterized as capitulation to this goal. Safeguarding the stability of families must therefore for many states be an argument against cohabitation legislation lacking divorce regulations.[72]

In the spring of this year Pope Benedict the XVIth came out against the Italian proposal: "No man-made law can subvert one made by the Creator without society being dramatically damaged in its very foundation."[73] The Pope, however, seems not to have listened carefully enough to the Creator, because the Holy Scriptures do not say anything with regard to forms of marriage. Therefore Popes before the Council of Trent in 1563 recognized cohabitation as informal marriage. But Benedict has a point as long as cohabitation law does not have the same legal effects as formal marriage and, of course, as to cohabitation legislation for same-sex partners.

This raises the question of whether cohabitation legislation affects the marriage rate and thereby undermines marriage in that the parties and the families do not fall within the more extensive legal protection and the divorce regulations which

---

71 Lind, *supra* note 4, at 983–986.

72 *Id.* at 996.

73 *See Whispering in the Loggia*, *supra* note 2.

formal marriage offers. Even if this hypothesis appears to be reasonable,[74] I have found that marriage habits in common law marriage states, where the cohabiting parties have all the rights of marriage, appear to be fairly independent of the existence of common law marriage. The marriage rate there is just as high as in other states.[75]

5.3. THE LACK OF THE FORM'S FUNCTIONS

A third argument against common law marriage as well as cohabitation law is that they lack several of the form's functions that marriage and registered relationships fulfil,[76] for example, (a) *the protective function* in the sense that they protect the parties concerned from hasty actions. This function must be seen as material when two parties are facing the choice of cohabitation form, perhaps one of the most important decisions in their life. The ceremonial marriage's form requirements, and to some extent the registered forms of cohabitation, fulfil this function in that they provide a reason for reflection and serious consideration concerning the significance of the planned relationship.

The absence of form with the establishment of a common law marriage or a formless cohabitation is a deficiency in this respect. For couples who simply drift into a relationship and who do not make any legal assessments or make any actual decisions concerning their cohabitation but rather merely cohabit, there is not the same protection against hasty actions.

The observance of a certain form also has a (b) *clarifying function* in the sense that the legal status is clarified for the parties. However, the observance of the formalities ought to be an expression of the parties' intent to subject themselves to the legal effects that the state offers them when they have been given a marital status.

The absence of the protective and clarifying functions in the formless systems naturally constitutes a serious deficiency from the perspective of legal certainty.

---

74 *Anders Agell*, with respect to the Swedish development, has expressed such concern, stating: "In my view, it is possible, or even likely, that the decrease in the marriage rate and the weakening of the nuclear family in Sweden has been unintentionally promoted by legislation...The expansion of laws regulating cohabitation is in itself an incentive to cohabitation instead of marriage". See ANDERS AGELL, "Should and Can Family Law Influence Social Behaviour?", in *The Changing Family 125*, 136 (JOHN EEKELAAR and THANDABANTU NHLAPO eds. 1998).

75 LIND, *supra* note 4, at 983–986.

76 For more on the form functions, see LIND *id.*, at 987–998.

A third form function is (c) *the initial control of legal capacity* to prevent unsuitable relationships. One of the state's most important instruments of power in influencing the creation of families and in preventing unsuitable relationships has been to determine which persons are to be given the legal capacity to enter into a marriage with each other. With respect to ceremonial marriages and registered partnerships, the state controls beforehand that the conditions are fulfilled. It therefore appears as somewhat paradoxical that the legislator at the same time accepts that other long-term family relationships, such as common law marriage or cohabitation, are established without the same requirements as to the parties' legal capacity being checked beforehand.

The state's control function also clearly appears through the formal (d) *regulations concerning marital divorce*, which, inter alia, purport to safeguard the stability of families, particularly families with children. Despite a gradual retreat during the past 30 years from state-defined grounds for divorce towards the benefit of no fault divorces, the majority of states still show an interest in safeguarding the stability of families, not in the least for the sake of children. While common law marriage states maintain their interest, through the regulations concerning marital divorce, with respect to the stability of families in such marriages, cohabitation legislation to a great extent can be characterized as capitulation to this goal.

The form requirements for the commencement of a marriage also have a (e) *publicity function*. Through the wedding ceremony and the ensuing registration of the marriage, third parties who enter into legal obligations with one of the parties can obtain information concerning his/her marital status and the need for the other spouse's consent for different transactions. The registration contributes to creating order.

No comparable registration is ordinarily required concerning a common law marriage or cohabitation. A transfer of real estate can therefore be invalid if it is carried out by one party in a common law marriage without the consent of the other party. For a modern community in need of statistical information with respect to formless relationships, the absence of a registration thereof is a considerable inconvenience.

5.4. FRAUDULENT BEHAVIOUR AND OTHER ABUSE

A fourth historically forceful objection against common law marriage has emphasised that the doctrine could give rise to perjury, fraudulent behaviour and other abuse. The courts in several cases have, often with moral indignation, complained of the risk that one party, ordinarily the "gold-digging woman", through baseless allegations as to the existence of a common law marriage, seeks to obtain the man's property. Particularly during the first part of the 1900s, this argument was taken up in the academic legal literature, which formed a crusade against common law marriage and came to contribute to many states repealing the institution.[77]

Let me say that my own investigation of more than 1,000 cases, however, does not support any finding that perjury and fraudulent behaviour have been so extensive as claimed, even if one cannot disregard that such a risk always exists, especially with respect to claims directed against a deceased's estate. However, the requirements of long "cohabitation" and "holding out" as spouses as well as strong evidentiary requirements are dedicated to preventing these problems.

5.5. APPLICATION PROBLEMS

A fifth argument against cohabitation legislation is the application problem. Despite all efforts in many countries to define the concept of cohabitation and to identify relevant factors as supporting the interpretation, it must be stressed that application problems are difficult to avoid. Questions always arise, for example, as to when the cohabitation commenced if the parties were merely friends from the very beginning, or if they cohabited on a trial basis without any final intention to live together for a long time. Is it cohabitation if the parties do not later, due to work in different places, studies or military service, share a household or residence the entire time? Perhaps one party may have had a relationship with someone else on a certain occasion, etc. Was the cohabitation really sufficiently marriage-like? And when was the relationship definitively dissolved if it subsequently ended? Was it dissolved before one of the parties died? Well, there are no certain answers to these questions and this results in considerable legal uncertainty.[78]

A requirement of cohabitation for a certain time, for example 2–3 years, does not avoid these problems. When did it commence and when did it end and was it marriage-like during the whole period? It would further cut through a large segment of the cohabiting population, making it difficult to materially justify why all couples who live together one week longer than others are granted all rights while the latter fall entirely outside the system of regulation. The parties in a shorter relationship had perhaps decided and planned for a long life together before one

77 *Id.* at 967–976.
78 *Id.* at 967–976.

of the parties died. A possibility of capturing such cases within the scope of the legislation would be to employ a contract requirement, which common law marriage uses and modern cohabitation legislation lacks.

Further, legal regulations that require investigations into the parties' personal relationships also constitute a threat to *personal integrity*. Especially sensitive, of course, are investigations with respect to the parties' sexual relationship.[79] One method to limit the problems could possibly be to use presumptions based on the existence of objective facts which do not have such a personal character. However, the opposing party will in many cases attempt to rebut the presumption by citing personal circumstances. We were just friends! A more certain method in order to avoid the problem is to make parties' sexual relationship legally irrelevant or to forbid the investigation thereof. Such a solution, however, will expand the circle to whom the regulations apply, for example friendships, cohabitation between relatives, boarders etc., which are ordinarily not intended. It seems difficult to avoid that the sexual relationship is considered to be a cornerstone in what we call a marriage, a marriage-like or a couple relationship. Furthermore, it is not easy to interpret the concept of "friendship".

The application problems are nothing new. From history we have learned that informal marriages were already abolished primarily because of these problems in Ancient Roman law, later in Canon Law in 1563, later in England through Lord Hardwick's Act in 1753 and in many American States during the 1900s. There is perhaps a good reason to learn from history![80]

6. CONCLUSIONS

From this presentation it can be seen that there are strong reasons for as well as against cohabitation legislation. *On the one side*, there are probably many legislators who find it well justified to give protection to the more vulnerable party and to the children in a formless relationship or to fulfil their expectations in good faith. This is so particularly within ethnic and social groups in which the marriage rate is low. On the other side, there are probably legislators who, faced with a strongly decreasing marriage rate, see the legislative advantages of capturing the 'lost sheep' within the obligations which the law creates.

79 Case law is full of cases where the sexual relationship has been the object of evidence. It has also occurred that a party, during the hearing, has introduced video evidence showing the parties' sexual activities, see *Bar-Mordecai v. Rotman & others* (2000) NSW CA 123. See further, LIND *id.* at 998–1005.

80 LIND, *supra* note 4, at 1005–1015.

On the other side, few legislators ought to be able to disregard the problems which such legislation entails with respect to the limitations of the parties' freedom to determine for themselves whether they are to be seen as married persons or cohabitants. Some legislators will presumably consider such legislation to be a threat to the family and the community. Others ought to perceive the difficulties for the state in controlling the parties' legal capacity to enter into relationships and dissolve them. Also no legislator should disregard the risks of fraudulent behaviour, insufficient legal uncertainty, investigations which violate personal integrity, application difficulties, disputes and costs.

A plausible *compromise* between the need for protection on the one side, and the freedom of the parties to choose, on the other, could be legislation that only provides basic minimum protection and that the parties, in order to attain more extensive protection, must themselves actively take legal measures by entering into a contract, drafting a will or marrying. A disadvantage of such compromises is naturally that neither side is satisfied.

Another solution could be some kind of *registration system*.[81] A simple registration ought not to be seen as being too burdensome for a couple wishing to create a family and to establish a lifelong or, in any case, an abiding marital relationship. Many of the problems I have mentioned would thereby be avoided or reduced, such as the evidentiary difficulties, the violations of personal integrity and the problems relating to the freedom to choose. The parties would not be forced into a system which they have not chosen. Through registration they would be conscious of whether and when the legal relationship between them has arisen. Registration promotes legal certainty!

However, what about those who do not register? In order to avoid unjust results, there can be a need for protective regulations of a purely exceptional nature. Such a need could be met through, e.g., "the putative marriage doctrine", which purports to fulfil the parties' expectations, in good faith, as to being married or otherwise legally protected.[82] Another need for protection exists in those cases in which one party has given the other promises or expectations as to marriage or

81 Registration systems for same-sex partners have been enacted in Denmark 1989, Norway 1993, Sweden 1994, Iceland 1996, Finland 2001, Germany 2004, England & Wales 2004, and in the United States in Vermont 2000, Connecticut 2005 and New Jersey 2006. Registration systems even for heterosexual partners were enacted in the Netherlands 1997, Belgium 1998, France 1999, the region of Catalonia in Spain 1998, California 2003, the Canadian provinces of Nova Scotia 2001, Quebec and Manitoba 2004, New Zealand 2004, and with restricted legal effects in the District of Columbia, Hawaii and Maine in the United States, as well as in Italy, according to the 2007 proposal, *Disegno Di Legge*, *supra* note 1. See further LIND, *supra* note 4, at 821–832.

82 LIND, *supra* note 4, at 940–948 and 1043.

registration, but these have never been kept. There can also be a need for providing certain protection in order to avoid unjust results in other particularly exceptional situations, for example when one party after a very long-term cohabitation, perhaps 25–30 years, risks being left with nothing.[83] Therefore registration, completed with special exceptions, should to be a laudable solution for many legislators in the 21st Century.

Let me *finally* return to Pope Benedict the XVIth, where I commenced, and his battle of today, and to give you my prediction that, if the marriage rate continues to radically decrease, the Pope will probably change his mind and, in accordance with his Medieval predecessors, will accept legislation on cohabiting men and women with all the rights and obligations of marriage, in order to catch the 'lost sheep' and to force them to be covered by marital regulation.

83 Compare TRUSSLER and VANDERGRIFT, *supra* note 40, at 17, who with respect to "the registration-based approach" argue: "The disadvantage is that it may not adequately protect a person who is stuck in a relationship and cannot force her partner to register the relationship, any more than she should force her partner to get married". See also CYNTHIA GRANT BOWMAN, "Legal Treatment of Cohabitation in the United States", 26 *Law & Policy 119,* 126 (2004), who believes that there are women who do not have the fortitude to insist on marriage or common ownership of property. See further LIND, *supra* note 4, at 1043.

FINANCIAL RELIEF BETWEEN COHABITANTS ON SEPARATION: OPTIONS FOR EUROPEAN JURISDICTIONS

Jo Miles*

1. INTRODUCTION: THE SOCIAL AND POLITICAL CONTEXT

Cohabitation – the relationship between couples who live together outside marriage[1] – is one of the challenges faced by family law throughout Europe at the start of the twenty-first century. Different jurisdictions have taken different approaches to whether and how such relationships should be recognized by law, and what legal consequences should flow from that recognition.[2] This paper explores some of the basic questions that arise for the law-maker who wishes to legislate in this field, focusing on the issue of financial rights and remedies in the event of relationship breakdown. It begins by setting the social and political scene.

1.1. THE DEMOGRAPHIC EVIDENCE

As is well known, since the latter decades of the twentieth century, there have been significant changes in family demography throughout much of Europe.[3] In

* The author was seconded to the Law Commission for England and Wales in 2005–07 to work on the Cohabitation project, which reported in July 2007: *Cohabitation: The Financial Consequences of Relationship Breakdown* (2007) Law Com No 307, www.lawcom.gov.uk/cohabitation.htm. All views expressed in this article are the author's own, and should not be taken to represent the views of the Law Commission. I am grateful to Jens Scherpe for comments on a draft of this article.

1 Other types of formalised relationship are discussed below.

2 On this topic generally, see contributions by Aeschlimann, Schrama, Scherpe, Asland, Medina, Erdös and Sörgjerd in *Common Core and Better Law in European Family Law*, K. Boele-Woelki (ed.), (2005); and *Die Rechtsstellung nichtehelicher Lebensgemeinschaften / The Legal Recognition of Cohabitants*, J. Scherpe and N. Yassari (eds) (2005).

3 See K. Kiernan, "The Rise of Cohabitation and Childbearing Outside Marriage in Western Europe" (2001) 15 *International Journal of Law, Policy and the Family* 1; and "Unmarried Cohabitation and Parenthood in Britain and Europe" (2004) 26 *Law and Policy* 33.

many jurisdictions, marriage rates have declined, divorce rates have risen, an increasing proportion of children are born to unmarried parents, and many couples (whether parents or not) are living together without marrying. The intensity of this change varies considerably in different countries,[4] broadly speaking, between north and south, the Mediterranean countries retaining a much stronger tradition of marriage than many others, particularly the Scandinavian countries. But the change is evident nevertheless, particularly amongst younger cohorts of the population.

In the case of England and Wales,[5] the last Census recorded more than 2 million cohabiting couples, over 740,000 of which had dependent children living with them, and over 1.25 million children who were dependent on such couples.[6] It is expected that by 2031, the number of cohabiting couples will have increased to 3.8 million, or, put another way, that one in four couples will be cohabiting rather than married.[7] Over 40 per cent of children are now born outside marriage, and three-quarters of those are born to parents living at the same address.[8] It appears that many cohabiting relationships are relatively short-lived, the parties either marrying each other or separating after only a few years. But the average length of cohabiting relationships is rising, and researchers have found many examples of long, "marriage-like" cohabitations.[9]

It seems clear that these social changes are here to stay. But what should be the legal and policy response?

1.2. POLITICAL CONTROVERSY: PROTECTING TRADITIONAL FAMILY LIFE AND MARRIAGE

The social phenomenon of cohabitation and proposals for its greater legal recognition have both attracted strong opposition in many jurisdictions, on both faith-

4 On the importance of policy-makers having regard to the findings of demographic and sociological research about cohabitation (in all its diverse forms) in their particular jurisdiction, see W. Schrama, "General Lessons for Europe Based on a Comparison of the Legal Status of Non-Marital Cohabitants in the Netherlands and Germany", op. cit. n 2.

5 For a general survey of demographic and other data relating to cohabitation in that jurisdiction, see Law Commission For England And Wales, *Cohabitation: The Financial Consequences of Relationship Breakdown* (2006) Law Com CP 179, especially Part 2.

6 Office For National Statistics, *Census 2001*.

7 Figures calculated by the Government Actuary's Department: www.gad.gov.uk.

8 Office For National Statistics, *Social Trends 36* (2006) and *Birth Statistics* Series FM1 no 33 (2005).

9 See data discussed by the Law Commission, op. cit. n 5, from para. 2.30.

based and secular grounds.[10] Most recently, for example, Italian proposals for a new form of partnership registration have generated considerable controversy.[11] Often, opponents' concerns focus specifically the recognition of relationships between of same-sex partners. But the recognition of relationships between opposite-sex couples who cohabit together outside marriage may also be controversial. Many opponents of reform are concerned about what they view as a further erosion of the moral basis of family life. They seek to promote traditional values of family, commitment and stability, which they associate exclusively with heterosexual marriage, and argue that the recognition of other couple-relationships would serve to undermine that institution. Promoters of marriage often point to research identifying correlations between marriage and positive outcomes such as family stability, good educational attainment and behaviour by children, material wealth and good health. They therefore oppose legal changes which might induce couples to cohabit rather than marry.

Proponents of reform respond that the good outcomes associated with marriage are in large part the product of a "selection effect", i.e. that individuals who choose to marry already exhibit these characteristics. It is not marriage that makes them committed, stable, wealthy, and so on, but their inherent attributes. Australian data, and indirect evidence from some European jurisdictions, suggest that the legal framework may have little if any impact on people's decisions about their personal relationships: no correlation has been found between trends in marriage rates and the legal recognition of cohabitants.[12] The family in contemporary society is increasingly diverse, and many consider that the law should respond to that reality, rather than seek to dictate the form in which individuals live their family life by confining family law to the married state.[13]

In light of such discussions, it is interesting to observe that even some jurisdictions with constitutional protection for marriage have moved to provide some level of legal protection both for cohabiting couples and for their children. For example, Article 41 of the Irish Constitution recognizes family based on marriage as "the natural primary and fundamental unit group of society", and the State is bound to "guard with special care the institution of marriage... and to protect it

---

10 For full discussion of the arguments made by opponents of reform in England and Wales, see Law Commission For England And Wales, *Cohabitation: The Financial Consequences of Relationship Breakdown* (2007) Law Com No 307, from para. 2.26.

11 Originally, the *dirriti di coppie conviventi* ("DICO"), since superseded by a revised Bill which would create the *contratti di unione solidale* ("CUS").

12 See K. Kiernan, A. Barlow and R. Merlo, "Cohabitation Law Reform and its Impact on Marriage: Evidence from Australia and Europe" (2007) *International Family Law* 71.

13 See for example S. Aeschlimann and W. Schrama, op. cit. n 2; A. Barlow, S. Duncan, G. James and A. Park, *Cohabitation, Marriage and the Law* (2005).

against attack".[14] Notwithstanding the special constitutional status of marriage, however, the parliamentary Committee on the Constitution concluded that legislation protecting families outside marriage could be enacted without any amendment to the Constitution,[15] and the Irish Law Reform Commission has recently published recommendations for the enhancement of various legal rights and duties of cohabitants.[16]

On another tack, opponents of reform for cohabitants (specifically) point to other familial relationships outside marriage which are said to be equally, if not more, deserving of special legal protection. The recent English case of the elderly Burden sisters provides a powerful case study.[17] The sisters have lived together and supported each other for all their adult life in the same home, neither having ever married. When the first sister dies, the survivor will be liable to pay tax on the value of the deceased sister's estate,[18] including her share in the value of their home. This may necessitate the sale of the property. Were the sisters able to marry or form a civil partnership they could secure exemption from that tax (which is available only to spouses and civil partners) and so the survivor would be spared the loss of the home. But being closely related, they are disqualified from doing so.[19] They are complaining to the European Court of Human Rights that English law's failure to recognize their relationship for these purposes violates their rights under Article 14, in conjunction with Article 1 to the First Protocol.

Cohabitants may be said to have a choice to marry or form a civil partnership, and so to ameliorate their legal position, in a way that is simply not open to the Burden sisters. So, it is argued, the case for new legal measures is stronger in the latter case, and recognition of such relationships would pose no threat to the institution of marriage. Some jurisdictions have provided avenues for the legal recognition of such relationships, either by providing a registration scheme or simply by refer-

14 Bunreacht Na hÉireann / Irish Constitution, Art 41.1.1 and 41.3.1.

15 All-Party Oireachtas Committee on the Constitution, *Tenth Progress Report: The Family* (2006).

16 *Rights and Duties of Cohabitants* LRC 82–2006. Contrast the current position in Germany, discussed by W. Schrama, op. cit. n 2; though note potential implications of Article 6(5) and recent decision of Constitutional Court for cases involving children: Bundesverfassungsgericht of 28.2.2007 (1 BvL 9/04) printed in FamRZ 2007, 965 (with comment by Born at p. 973).

17 *Burden and Burden v United Kingdom* (2007) 44 E.H.R.R. 51, currently on appeal to the Grand Chamber: Application No. 13378/05.

18 Above the value to which a nil tax rate applies.

19 Since marriage in English law remains an opposite-sex institution, they would have to form a civil partnership, but are barred by the prohibited degrees rules (identical for marriage and civil partnership) from doing so: Civil Partnership Act 2004, s. 3(1)(d) and Sch. 1, Part 1.

ence to the de facto existence of the parties' relationship.[20] But an increasing number of states have also, or instead, provided for cohabiting couples,[21] or are considering whether they should do so, and it is on these cases that the remainder of this paper focuses.

One last introductory point. Cohabitation is not yet an area in which the European Convention on Human Rights has provided particular impetus for reform in relation to the legal relationship between the adult parties.[22] Even assuming that a cohabiting couple is regarded as having a "family life" for the purposes of Article 8, no violation has been found where states have, for example, declined to confer on cohabitants a private law right to be maintained by their partner or to inherit on intestacy.[23] Complaints brought under Article 14 (in relation to tax and welfare law, as well as financial remedies on separation) have also failed, the European judicial bodies upholding states' different treatment of spouses and cohabitants in these areas as legitimate measures designed to promote the traditional concept of family based on marriage.[24] This is not to say that the Convention, as a living instrument, might not one day be found to require states to adopt a more accommodating stance towards cohabitation. But for the time being, it would seem that the legal regulation of cohabitation remains largely a matter for individual states to determine for themselves.

2. DIFFERENT EUROPEAN RESPONSES TO COHABITATION

Before turning to the particular question of financial relief between cohabitants, it is necessary to set out the family law context in which the treatment of cohabitation has to be evaluated. Different European states have adopted different approaches to cohabitation, to some extent reflecting the particular legal traditions of those jurisdictions. The first question is the format whereby any legal

20 E.g. Belgian "legal cohabitation" (*la cohabitation légale,* Law of 23 November 1998) is open to related pairs; likewise the Tasmanian "caring relationships": Relationships Act 2003.

21 In some cases, as in Belgium and Tasmania, cohabitants are covered by the same legal instrument that recognises relationships such as that of the Burden sisters.

22 Contrast the treatment of children of cohabitants: e.g. *Johnson v Ireland* (1987) Series A No 112. Cf. recent decision of German Constitutional Court on impact on children of laws regarding maintenance for unmarried mothers: Bundesverfassungsgericht of 28 February 2007 (1 BvL 9/04) printed in *FamRZ* 2007, 965 (with comment by Born at p. 973.).

23 E.g. *Johnston v Ireland* (1987) Series A No 112; *Saucedo Gomez v Spain* App No 37784/97, Commission decision of 26 January 1999 (unreported); cf. in relation to a same-sex couple, *Mata Estevez v Spain* ECHR 2001-VI.

24 E.g. *Saucedo Gomez v Spain* App No 37784/97, Commission decision of 26 January 1999 (unreported); *Quintana Zapata v Spain* (1998) 92 D&R 139.

recognition should be granted: should it be based on an "opt-in" model (registration scheme) or an "opt-out" model (de facto recognition by default, but – for at least some purposes[25] – with liberty for parties to opt out by agreement)?[26] Secondly, it may be desirable for the model of financial relief adopted for cohabitants to fit, at least in broad terms, with the prevailing model of financial relief on divorce in the relevant jurisdiction. We shall therefore also need briefly to examine the profound differences in the way common law and other European jurisdictions deal with the property and income of spouses on divorce.

2.1. REGISTRATION OR DEFAULT SCHEME: "OPT-IN" OR "OPT-OUT"?

The first question is the format for granting legal recognition, commonly posed in the following terms: opt-in or opt-out?

2.1.1. Opt-In Schemes: Partnership Registration

Often, the nature of the legal response to cohabitation has been affected by the dual purposes of the legislator: (1) to recognise relationships between cohabiting couples; and (2) specifically, to provide a form of relationship recognition and status for same-sex couples in jurisdictions where they – unlike opposite-sex couples – are not entitled to marry. That second purpose has often propelled the legislator to adopt registration or "opt in" schemes.

For so long as marriage is (or was[27]) confined to couples of the opposite sex, gay and lesbian couples may have no means of obtaining legal recognition from the state, certainly not in a manner or of a degree comparable to that enjoyed by spouses. Many jurisdictions have responded to the situation of same-sex couples by creating a new legal regime which couples can opt into by registering their relationship.

25 The state might have reasons to deny the option to opt out in relation to certain matters, such as welfare benefits and taxation rules.

26 See J. Scherpe, op. cit. n 2 and "Protection of Partners of Informal Long-term Relationships" *International Law FORUM du droit international* (Journal of the International Law Association) 7:207–213 (2005).

27 The Netherlands, Spain, Belgium, Canada, Massachusetts and South Africa have all now opened marriage to same-sex couples.

In some jurisdictions, such as the United Kingdom,[28] that new form of relationship has been confined to same-sex couples. The UK's "civil partnership" confers almost all of the legal rights and responsibilities of civil marriage[29] and is subject to very similar conditions for creation and dissolution.[30] So opposite-sex couples may now marry and same-sex couples may become civil partners. Couples who do not take whichever step is open to them enjoy only the legal consequences attaching to informal cohabitation.[31]

But in other jurisdictions, such as the Netherlands and France, the new model of relationship has been made available to opposite-sex couples too. This model has provided opposite-sex couples with a choice – to marry or become registered partners (or *pacsés*); and, at least until marriage is opened up to same-sex couples, as it has been in the Netherlands, has given same-sex couples access to a form of legal recognition.

Whether open to same-sex couples only, or to both same-sex and opposite-sex, the legislator can attach various legal consequences to this new form of registered relationship. Those consequences may be broadly the same those attaching to marriage, or different, and they may include some measure of financial relief or property regime in case of separation.[32]

The introduction of opt-in schemes has been profoundly important in many European states, particularly for same-sex couples. But this model of legal

---

28 The Civil Partnership Act 2004 extends to all parts of the United Kingdom, but the particular legal consequences vary between England and Wales, Northern Ireland and Scotland, in line with the particular legal consequences of marriage within each jurisdiction.

29 Only a very few, specifically gendered rules relating to marriage have not been extended to civil partners: e.g. Married Women's Property Act 1964, s. 1.

30 The principal differences are the omission from the grounds for nullity and dissolution of non-consummation and adultery, and the prohibition on registering a civil partnership in a religious ceremony or in religious premises. Overseas same-sex marriages and same-sex (but not opposite-sex) registered partnerships are recognised by UK law as civil partnerships: Civil Partnership Act 2004, Sch 6, unsuccessfully challenged in *Wilkinson v. Kitzinger* [2006] EWHC 2022. On the non-recognition of overseas opposite-sex partnership registrations, see J. Scherpe "Neue Entwicklungen im Englischen Familienrecht", *FamRZ* 2007, 1496, 1498 f. and J. Scherpe, "Legal Recognition of Foreign Formalised Same-Sex Relationships in the United Kingdom", *International Family Law* (2007), 198.

31 Provided, in many contexts, that they are "living together as husband and wife" or "as if civil partners".

32 For comparison of legal regimes for same-sex couples in Europe, see I Curry-Sumner, *All's well that ends registered?* (2005); K. Boele-Woelki/A. Fuchs (eds), *Legal Recognition of Same-sex Couples in Europe* (2003); and K. Waaldijk, with J. Asland et al., *More or less together: Levels of legal consequences of marriage, cohabitation and registered partnerships for different-sex and same-sex partners: A comparative study of nine European countries* (2005), www.same-sex.ined.fr/publica_doc125.htm.

recognition has its problems and limitations. It may be opposed by those concerned that, at least for opposite-sex partners, a registration scheme may create a rival status for marriage. Moreover, self-evidently, it does nothing to protect those couples who do not take the formal step of opting in, and take-up rates for opt-in schemes which do not confer the same status and legal consequences as marriage have not been high.[33]

Opt-in systems depend for their effectiveness on the population being aware of the legal options available to them and on individuals taking proactive steps to secure the protection that only opting in will bring.

Both of these have proved problematic in the UK context. The British public is curiously affected by what is known as "the common law marriage myth": the (legally erroneous) belief that, simply by virtue of living together (and perhaps after the passage of particular period of time), cohabiting couples enjoy the same legal status as formally married couples. The British Social Attitudes survey in 2000 found that 56% of the adult population believed that this was true, and that 59% of cohabitants did so.[34] Couples labouring under this misapprehension are unlikely to take steps to protect their relationships, since they already think that they have that protection.[35]

But even armed with the correct information, research indicates that many individuals in the UK are slow to take legal action regarding their personal relationships, particularly in order to protect their position in anticipation of a possible future separation, for example, by making a "living together agreement" with their partner, seeking to regulate their affairs by contract.[36] Many are either too embarrassed to raise the issue, or find it (understandably) somewhat unromantic to do so, or simply live in the contented belief that their relationship, unlike those of a large proportion of the rest of the population, will not breakdown.[37]

All this is not necessarily a conclusive argument against the opt-in model. For many, the appropriate response to these problems is not legal reform, but public education. It is said that the state should work harder to ensure that the public is better informed about the legal treatment of different types of relationship (for example, that marriage and civil partnership confer various rights and duties

33 See data reported at Law Commission, op. cit. n 5, p. 106.

34 A. Barlow, S. Duncan, G. James and A. Park, "Just a piece of paper? Marriage and cohabitation", in A Park et al. (eds.), *British Social Attitudes: the 18th Report* (2001).

35 C. Sörgjerd, op. cit. n 2 discusses a similar problem of public misunderstanding of the law in Sweden, at p. 345.

36 The legal status of such contracts in English law is not entirely certain: see Law Commission, op. cit. n 5, from para. 3.15.

37 See research discussed by Law Commission, op. cit. n 5, Part 5.

which cohabitation does not). If people then fail to act on that information, it may be argued that that is their right as autonomous adults and that there is no justification for the state to interfere.[38]

2.1.2. Opt-Out Schemes: Protection by Default

By contrast with the foregoing discussion, the alternative model for recognizing cohabiting relationships, found in many common law jurisdictions and elsewhere,[39] gives greater weight to protection of those in potentially vulnerable situations. The "opt-out" approach entails automatic legal recognition of couples whose relationship, as a matter of fact, falls within eligibility criteria set out by the governing legislation. Those criteria might require, for example, that the parties have cohabited for a given number of years, or that they have cohabited and had children together. The default position, therefore, is one of protection.

But it may also be felt important to recognise the diversity of the cohabiting population. There are many cohabitants who may be ignorant of the relative lack of legal recognition of their relationship, who assume that the law does recognise their relationship, and so who would benefit from reform providing default protection. But some others may deliberately have declined to marry in order to avoid the legal consequences attaching to marriage. These latter couples may wish to preserve the legal privacy of their relationship, and so are likely to object to reform which would encroach on that freedom.

The solution to this dilemma – providing much needed protection, whilst still respecting party autonomy – may lie in entitling couples who wish to do so to "opt out" of the default regime by reaching alternative agreement. This model has been adopted within Europe, for example, by Sweden[40] and Scotland,[41] and has recently been recommended for Ireland[42] and for England and Wales.[43]

The opt-out model is arguably the better option in the particular context of financial relief on relationship breakdown. Proponents of opt-in reform for cohabitants are often concerned to enhance the recognition of cohabitants' relationship vis-à-

---

38 See the views discussed by Law Commission, op. cit. n 10, from para. 2.46.

39 Notably, in all Australian states, several Canadian provinces and territories, Scotland, Sweden and New Zealand.

40 Cohabitees Act 2003. For discussion of the "neutrality" theory underpinning this approach, see C. Sörgjerd, "Neutrality: The Death or the Revival of the Traditional Family", op. cit. n 2.

41 Family Law (Scotland) Act 2006.

42 See Irish Law Reform Commission, op. cit. n 16.

43 See Law Commission, op. cit. n 10.

vis the state, for example to gain taxation, retirement pension and other public benefits. Many registered partnership schemes across Europe accordingly provide a wide range of public law consequences for those who opt in. But where the only issue at stake is the rights and duties of the private parties to the relationship *inter se*, it is perhaps not obvious that the opt-in model is appropriate, requiring as it does the co-operation of both parties in order for the legal protections to apply.

Take the extreme example of domestic violence: there is clearly a very strong argument to say that victims of abuse perpetrated within their own homes ought to be able to access special legal remedies designed to deal with that problem regardless of whether the victim and perpetrator had married or otherwise registered their relationship. Abusive relationships are precisely those in which an imbalance of power may mean that the party who would benefit from legal protection will be unable to persuade the other partner to confer that protection by consenting to opt into the relevant legal regime.

The same might also be said of access to financial remedies on relationship breakdown, since, in crude and simplistic terms, these may appear to benefit one party at the expense of the other in the event of separation. The party who has the greater financial resources is likely to be the one who would be required to provide financial support in the event of separation. Following recent high profile and high value divorce cases in England, there is anecdotal evidence of many men (and some affluent women) saying that they will no longer marry because the perceived financial risks of divorce are too high. It is not immediately obvious why such a person would opt into some other legal regime for cohabitants if the only consequence of opting in were that he (or she) would stand to lose out financially on separation.

But just as there may be felt to be a considerable public interest in securing protection for victims of physical abuse, so too may there be a strong public interest in securing a measure of financial protection for those who find themselves in an economically vulnerable situation at the end of a cohabiting relationship. This public interest may be felt to be particularly strong where there are children involved, as the financial standing of the primary carer of those children following separation is likely to affect the children's standard of living, despite the availability of child support and other remedies which may exist for the benefit of the children in their own right. In the absence of any special family law regime, the financial and property disputes of cohabiting couples are resolved by the general law. It is the failure of that general law to provide adequately for economically vulnerable parties in these cases which has provided particular impetus for reform in many jurisdictions.[44]

3. THE NATURE OF THE FINANCIAL REGIME OR REMEDY

Having determined whether legal protection is to arise (1) following registration of the relationship, or (2) by default on satisfaction of prescribed eligibility criteria, the next issue is the basic nature of the financial and property regime or remedies that should flow from recognition. Three inter-related sets of questions need to be addressed here. First, should cohabitants simply be subject to the same laws as spouses in the relevant jurisdiction? If not, what sort of regime or remedy should be adopted for cohabitants? Here, of course, in relation to marriage and divorce, there is a significant divergence within Europe, in which (broadly speaking) the jurisdictions within the UK and of the Republic of Ireland stand apart from the rest. And finally, on what principles should that regime or remedy be based?

3.1. ASSIMILATION WITH SPOUSES OR DIFFERENT TREATMENT?

Assuming that the legislator has decided, notwithstanding the concerns of those opposed to any legal recognition of cohabitants, that there should be reform, there is one further important basic question to be addressed. Should cohabitants have access to the same property regime or financial remedies as spouses, or should they receive different treatment? That single question in fact raises two quite different issues. First, *as a matter of principle*, ought spouses and cohabitants to be treated identically by the law in this area (or generally), whatever that law might entail? Second, is the law that currently applies to spouses suitable for extension to cohabitants?

Like the basic question about whether there should be reform at all, these are not pure legal questions, but raise issues of social policy and so of politics, and the answers to them vary between jurisdictions. Those who are in principle opposed to *any* reform are, of course, likely to want any reform that is pursued to confer on cohabitants a "lesser" degree of legal protection than that enjoyed by spouses, in order to preserve for marriage a unique and "superior" status. But such opponents

44 In the case of the law of England and Wales, see the criticisms of the current law made by the Law Commission, op. cit. n 5 and n 10.

may not represent the majority view. Data from the British Social Attitudes survey shows that there is strong public opinion in England and Wales in favour of treating spouses and cohabitants in the same way in a variety of legal contexts, including financial remedies on separation, particularly where the couple have had children together or lived together for some time.[45] Some advocates of reform accordingly strongly promote an assimilationist approach, arguing that the situations of spouses and cohabitants are functionally similar, that is to say, their experience of day-to-day life is similar, and they experience the same sorts of practical problems on separation which merit the same legal response.[46] Reflecting this approach, some jurisdictions, notably New Zealand,[47] Western Australia,[48] Croatia[49] and Slovenia[50] have extended to cohabitants broadly the same financial regime that applies in those jurisdictions between spouses on divorce.

Other supporters of reform might take the view that, without making any value judgement about the relative "superiority" or otherwise of marriage and cohabitation, there are nevertheless tangible differences between those categories which merit distinctive treatment. Others again might answer the first question in favour of assimilation, but have reservations about applying the relevant jurisdiction's matrimonial law to cohabitants.

Those advocating different treatment on either basis just identified may be swayed by various considerations. Particularly if the chosen model of reform is "opt-out" rather than "opt-in", it may be felt appropriate to attach some meaningful weight to the fact that cohabitants have not made any formal commitment, and so not positively elected to bring themselves within the scope of the applicable law. It is also important for the legislator to have regard to any local social science data and what they indicate about the nature of marital and cohabiting relationships in that jurisdiction.[51] If (as is likely) the cohabiting population is a diverse body, composed of couples who (at one end of the scale) are "marriage-like" in their behaviour and commitment[52] and much more "casual" relationships (at the other

---

45 For the most recent data, see A. PARK et al., *British Social Attitudes: the 24th Report* (forthcoming, 2008).

46 In the English context, see for example A. BARLOW, S. DUNCAN, G. JAMES and A. PARK, *Cohabitation, Marriage and the Law* (2005).

47 Property (Relationships) Act 2001 (NZ). See B. ATKIN, "The rights of married and unmarried couples in New Zealand – radical new laws on property and succession" (2003) *Child and Family Law Quarterly* 15: 173.

48 Family Court Act 1997 (WA). See generally O. JESSEP, "Australia and New Zealand", in *Die Rechtsstellung nichtehelicher Lebensgemeinschaften*, J. SCHERPE and N. YASSARI (eds) (2005).

49 See D. HRABAR, "Kroatien", ibid.

50 See V. RIJAVEC and S. KRALJIĆ, "Slowenien", ibid.

51 See also W. SCHRAMA, op. cit. n 4.

52 Data comparing the property-holding and money management arrangements adopted by spouses and cohabitants may be particularly useful here, though researchers have cautioned

end of the scale), it may not be felt appropriate to subject cohabitants as a class to matrimonial laws.[53] A number of jurisdictions which have legislated for cohabitants (such as Sweden and Scotland) have, for one or other reason, therefore adopted a different approach for cohabitants. This is also the approach recently recommended by the Law Commission in England and Wales and by the Irish Law Reform Commission.[54]

3.2. A PROPERTY REGIME OR REMEDIAL APPROACH?

In most European jurisdictions, marriage brings with it a matrimonial property regime of some sort, either imposed by default by the law or agreed by the parties. Ordinarily, it entails the option of some form of community of property, which may either operate during marriage as well as on divorce, or simply determine the division of assets in the event of divorce. The only "remedial" issue that may arise on divorce in such systems is the question of regular maintenance, which is dealt with separately from the property division dictated by the relevant matrimonial regime.

The jurisdictions within the British and Irish islands have a very different tradition, which makes them awkward companions for the rest of Europe in attempts to harmonise law in this area.[55] They have no concept of "matrimonial property". During marriage, spouses (like cohabitants and others) operate independently, each entitled to own their own property. The fact of marriage does not entitle either spouse to a share in the ownership of the other's assets or require them to assume liability for each other's debts.[56] However, while English lawyers say that each spouse owns his or her "separate property" that does not mean, in European terminology, that English law has a "regime" of separate property in the event of divorce. That would create serious hardship in many cases, particularly where one

against drawing quick and simple conclusions from this data, as couples' behaviour in these respects may not be deliberate and considered, or determined by the sort of considerations thought by the legislator to be significant: see discussion in LAW COMMISSION, op. cit. n 10, App C.

53 This might be felt to hold true even if the scope of the proposed default regime has been narrowed via eligibility criteria based on the presence of children or duration of the relationship.

54 Op. cit. nn 10 and 16.

55 For discussion of this issue, see J SCHERPE, "Matrimonial Causes for Concern? A comparative analysis of *Miller v Miller; McFarlane v McFarlane* ...' *Kings Law Journal* 18: 348. See also the EU Commission Green Paper on Conflict of Laws in Matters concerning Matrimonial Property Regimes, including the Question of Jurisdiction and Mutual Recognition, COM (2006) 400 final (SEC (2006)) 952), in which the discussion is predicated on matrimonial property regimes which are alien to the common law jurisdictions.

56 This strict separation is mitigated by certain rights of support: e.g. the mutual duties of maintenance, and occupation rights relating to the family home.

spouse had forgone paid employment during all or part of the marriage in order to remain at home caring for children and so was unable to accumulate any "separate property" for him- or herself.

English law therefore takes a remedial approach. In broad terms, when spouses divorce, all of the financial resources that each of them owns may be redistributed between the parties, regardless of technical questions of ownership. All forms of property are included – land, money, goods, retirement pension funds, investments, and so on – along with the parties' incomes and earning capacities. The court[57] exercises a wide statutory discretion to achieve a result which is "fair"[58] in light of all the circumstances, giving first consideration to the welfare of minor children of the family.[59] In pursuit of "fairness", the court is able to order transfers and settlements of property and money, share pension funds and order periodical payments, commonly for the purposes of maintenance.[60] English law does not formally separate the issue of maintenance from property division; it is all part of the same exercise. So, for example, occupation of the matrimonial home following divorce, and the allocation of its value, may be determined in large part by the relative needs of the parties and any dependent children.

3.3. WHAT GOVERNING PRINCIPLES?

Particularly if a "remedial" approach is to be adopted for cohabitants, rather than some form of community of property regime, it is highly desirable to identify the basis on which those remedies should be granted.[61] While there is no framework of principles on the face of the English legislation governing financial relief on

---

57 The vast majority of cases are settled without application to court, save in order to obtain a consent order enshrining an agreement reached by the parties.

58 That word does not appear in the legislation, but is implicit: *White v White* [2001] AC 596.

59 The statute enumerates a number of specific factors to which the court should have regard, including the spouses' financial resources, needs and obligations, their ages and the duration of the marriage, their contributions to the welfare of the family, and so on: Matrimonial Causes Act 1973, s. 25. The court is also required to consider whether a "clean break" can be achieved, bringing to an end the parties' financial obligations to each other (principally, by declining to order periodical payments, or limiting such payments to a finite period): s. 25A.

60 The governing statutory provisions are found in the Matrimonial Causes Act 1973, Part II and the Civil Partnership Act 2004, Sch 5.

61 See LAW COMMISSION, op. cit. n 10, from para 4.15.

divorce,[62] recent judicial decisions have identified three principles to guide the court's assessment of what is "fair" on divorce:[63]

(i) sharing or partnership;
(ii) compensation for economic disadvantage which has arisen as a result of the parties' contributions to the relationship, for example, as a result of one spouse giving up paid employment in order to care for children; and
(iii) the needs of both parties.

These principles provide a useful menu to consider when devising a new scheme for cohabitants in all European jurisdictions. Indeed, the choice between a "regime" or a remedial system demands a similar inquiry: is the sharing entailed in community of property appropriate for cohabitants?

3.3.1. Community of Property and Other "Sharing" Schemes

A remedial scheme based, in full or in part, on a "sharing" principle may (more or less loosely) be regarded as equivalent in some respects to deferred community of property,[64] so we shall discuss these together. Evidently, such a regime (immediate or deferred) or principle may cover a wider or narrower range of assets.[65] On this model, cohabitants who are eligible under the particular scheme (whether as a result of having opted in or by virtue of satisfying de facto eligibility criteria) are taken to have entered into an economic partnership which justifies sharing wealth equally on separation.

New Zealand and Sweden, have both adopted sharing regimes for cohabitants. New Zealand has taken an assimilationist approach, so the regime of deferred community of property applicable to eligible cohabitants largely mirrors that which applies between spouses, though equal sharing may be modified by compensatory adjustment of property division and needs-based maintenance.[66] By

---

62 Contrast the principles set out in the Family Law (Scotland) Act 1985, ss. 9–11. Ireland's Family Law (Divorce) Act 1996, Part III is similar to the English legislation, setting out a checklist of factors to which the court is to have regard but no dispositive principles, thus granting the courts a wide discretion.

63 *White v. White* [2001] AC 596; *Miller v. Miller; McFarlane v. McFarlane* [2006] UKHL 24. See also *Charman v Charman* [2007] EWCA Civ 503.

64 See S. Cretney, "Community of Property Imposed by Judicial Discretion?" (2003) *Law Quarterly Review* 119: 349; albeit that, in the context of financial provision on divorce in England and Wales, it is accompanied by further principles of need and compensation.

65 In English divorce cases, this ordinarily warrants an equal sharing of property acquired during the marriage (otherwise than by gift or inheritance from a third party), and the matrimonial home, but may extend to other assets.

66 Property (Relationships) Act 1976.

contrast, the Swedish Cohabitees Act 2003 sets up a sharing regime which is more restrictive than that which applies between spouses in Sweden, sharing being confined to a relatively narrow pool of property.[67] The Swedish approach also differs from that in New Zealand in so far as maintenance is not payable in any circumstances, and the Swedish exceptions to equal sharing between cohabitants are not designed to favour the needier party, but instead enable the property owner to retain more of his or her own property in certain circumstances.

The more or less automatic sharing of property (and, in some cases, of debts) required by such schemes may be thought to require careful justification. The party who would otherwise be entitled as a matter of property law to retain the bulk of the assets following separation may ask why he or she is required to give some of it up to the other party. Where the scheme applies only to couples who have opted in by registering their relationship, the consent of each party to registration readily provides that justification. But if the regime applies by default to all couples unless they have taken the step of opting out by agreement, the case for justification based on consent may be felt to be somewhat less strong.

It is important to bear in mind the diversity which often exists within a cohabiting population. As mentioned earlier, in England and Wales "cohabitation" covers a wide range of relationships, from long-term, strongly committed couples with children who are, functionally, indistinguishable from spouses, through to more or less temporary arrangements of convenience between young couples, who may only live together for a relatively short period. Some cohabitants live together as a form of trial marriage, and their commitment to each other is perhaps therefore by definition less than that of spouses, since they have consciously not yet taken the step of marrying; indeed, one member of the couple may be more committed to the relationship than the other. Others have actively rejected marriage (perhaps following a divorce) and are seeking to base a new relationship on different foundations; they may wish to remain economically independent on each other. Social science data about how spouses and cohabitants arrange their domestic economies may also be instructive. If cohabitants, as a class, typically pool their resources and elect to own their property in joint names, sharing on separation may be entirely appropriate. By contrast, if cohabitants are significantly less likely than spouses to own property jointly or to pool their incomes, that may indicate that the sharing paradigm of marriage cannot appropriately be applied to cohabitants.[68]

---

67 See C. Sörgjerd, op. cit. n 2; E. Ryrstedt, "Sweden", in J. Scherpe/N. Yassari (eds), op. cit. n 248.

68 But see n 52 above.

It may be argued that this diversity amongst cohabitants can be accommodated by providing couples who wish to do so to opt out of the applicable regime by agreement, and by drawing up restrictive eligibility criteria intended (however crudely) to exclude couples for whom a sharing regime may be particularly inappropriate. But it might alternatively be felt that such measures can have only limited success in ensuring that most relationships falling within the scheme are suited to a sharing principle, and that the potential financial and other costs of opting-out to which those who would want to avoid a sharing principle would be subject are too great to justify applying that principle by default to cohabitants as a class.

3.3.2. Needs-Based and Contribution-Based Remedies

If a sharing principle or community regime is not judged suitable for cohabitants, it may be preferable to find a basis for financial relief which can be more closely responsive to the particular situation of each couple and the economic position in which the individuals find themselves at the end of their relationship.[69] It may therefore be appropriate relief to be based on need, or on the economic impact of contributions made by each party to the relationship. Examples of both approaches can be found within Europe and beyond.

Several Canadian jurisdictions have declined to extend their matrimonial property regimes to cohabitants, but have applied their laws of spousal support to them.[70] The Irish Law Reform Commission has recently recommended that relief between cohabitants be granted on the basis of economic dependency.[71] On this model, cohabitants who satisfy the prescribed eligibility requirements[72] are taken to assume responsibility for each other's needs. In assessing the case for needs-based remedies, various questions may be posed. Whether and when is it appropriate to infer that such responsibility has been assumed, or should be imposed, between cohabiting couples? Does it matter that the parties have not made any formal commitment to each other? Does the fact that the parties have cohabited for a given number of years provide a satisfactory basis on which to require one party to relieve the other's needs? Does it matter what the cause of the applicant's

69 In the vast majority of cases following divorce in England and Wales, where the parties' needs cannot be met (or can only just be met) by available assets, this principle in practice dictates how resources are to be distributed.

70 See W. Holland, "Canada", in J. Scherpe and N. Yassari, op. cit. n 2.

71 Op. cit. n 16.

72 Under the Irish recommendations, unusually, cohabitants with children would also ordinarily be required to satisfy a minimum duration requirement (of two years, cf. the three-year requirement for those without children), unless "serious injustice" would be caused by denying them the right to apply for financial relief.

particular needs is, i.e. whether they arise from the relationship or from extraneous causes, such as illness or unemployment?

Scotland has taken different approach, similar to the scheme subsequently recommended by the Law Commission for England and Wales.[73] Like the Canadian jurisdictions, the Scottish Parliament declined to extend to cohabitants the fair (generally equal) sharing principle that applies between spouses on divorce.[74] Nor may relief be granted, as it may be on divorce, simply on the basis of dependency or hardship.[75] Instead, the new legislation takes a more compensatory/restitutionary route, basing relief on the "economic advantage" and "economic disadvantage" arising to the parties from their contributions to the cohabiting relationship, and the economic burden of child care. To some extent, this approach may overlap with needs-based relief, as need experienced on separation may often be a symptom of economic disadvantage arising, typically, from sacrificing paid employment in order to care for home and family. The "economic advantage" principle, meanwhile, enables individuals to recover the positive value of contributions, often financial, to the parties' relationship.

As New Zealand's legislation and English case law on divorce demonstrate, the legislator could elect to combine several of these principles within one regime. Thus, in New Zealand, "relationship property" is initially divided equally, but those shares may be adjusted in light of any economic disparity that exists between the parties on separation, arising from the division of functions between the parties during their relationship; and needs-based maintenance payments may also be ordered.[76]

4. SUMMARY

It is clear that there is a wide range of options for the law reformer contemplating the introduction of financial relief between cohabiting couples on separation. The legislator needs to select a model that will "fit": with the legal traditions of its particular jurisdiction; with prevailing social norms; with the wider context of state support and the nature of the employment market (particularly for parents); and

73 Family Law (Scotland) Act 2006, s 28; contrast Law Commission, op. cit. n 10.

74 Though see limited presumptions of joint ownership created by s 27, ibid.

75 See Family Law (Scotland) Act 1985, s 9.

76 For discussion, see J. Miles, "Financial Provision and Property Division on Relationship Breakdown: A Theoretical Analysis of the NZ Legislation" (2004) *New Zealand Universities Law Review* 268; and "Principle or Pragmatism in Ancillary Relief: The Virtues of Flirting with Academic Theories and Other Jurisdictions" (2005) *International Journal of Law, Policy and the Family* 242.

with the nature of cohabiting relationships in that jurisdiction. But within those constraints, there may be as many options for financial relief between cohabitants as there are different matrimonial regimes and remedies. That diversity is reflected in the different regimes that have already been adopted or recommended in several jurisdictions worldwide.

This is an issue which more jurisdictions will need to address and then revisit as the demographic development continues. But for all jurisdictions, the basic questions are the same:

1 Should cohabitants be given increased recognition in law at all?
2 If so, should that recognition be based upon registration of the relationship, or by default on satisfying de facto eligibility criteria?
3 On what basis should the financial resources of couples be distributed when they separate?

While an increasing number of jurisdictions are providing a positive answer to the first question, it is likely that responses to the second and, in particular, the third questions will continue to vary considerably between jurisdictions within Europe and beyond.

DIVIDING THE ASSETS UPON THE DISSOLUTION OF A MARRIAGE

A Comparison Between Legal Systems Which Apply a 'Hard and Fast Rule' and Systems with a Discretionary Approach to the Division of Assets

Anne-Florence Bock

1. POLICY REASONS UNDERLYING MATRIMONIAL PROPERTY LAW

Before examining any system of financial adjustment upon divorce – be it maintenance, matrimonial property law or pension sharing, it is useful to recollect the policy reasons that should underlie any financial relief at the end of marriage. Clearly, the result should be a fair adjustment of benefits and detriments due to marriage.[1] In many legal systems there is also general agreement that the following principles should apply to the process of financial adjustment: not to discriminate between gender roles,[2] to recognize the respective contributions,[3] to protect

---

1 Cf. R. Bailey-Harris, "Dividing the Assets on Breakdown of Relationships outside Marriage: Challenges for Reformers", in: R. Bailey-Harris (Ed.), *Dividing the Assets on Family Breakdown*, Bristol 1998, p. 73; I. Schwenzer, *Model Family Code*, Antwerp/Oxford 2006, p. 46 et seq.; I. Schwenzer, "Grundlinien eines modernen Familienrechts aus rechtsvergleichender Sicht", *Rabels Zeitschrift für ausländisches und internationales Privatrecht*, 71, p. 705 et seq.

2 Cf. M. Antokolskaia, *Harmonisation of Family Law in Europe: A Historical Perspective*, Antwerp/Oxford 2006, p. 475; cf. M. A. Glendon, *Introduction: Family Law in a Time of Turbulence*, in: M. A. Glendon (Ed.), *International Encyclopedia of Comparative Law*, Volume IV, Family and Persons, Tübingen et al. 2006, p. 6; cf. M. Rheinstein/M. A. Glendon, *Interspousal Relations*, in: A. Chloros (Ed.), *International Encyclopedia of Comparative Law*, Volume IV, Persons and Family, Tübingen/Alphen a.d. Rijn 1980, p. 169; I. Schwenzer, "Familienrecht im Umbruch", *Zeitschrift des Bernischen Juristenvereins 1993*, p. 257; see also Botschaft über die Änderung des Schweizerischen Zivilgesetzbuches (Wirkungen der Ehe im allgemeinen, Ehegüterrecht und Erbrecht), *Bundesblatt 131 (1979)*, p. 1191 et seq., p. 1236 and p. 1207 et seq.

3 Cf. J. Eekelaar, "Should Section 25 be Reformed?", *Family Law 1998*, p. 470 et seq.; cf. R. Bailey-Harris, "Dividing the Assets on Family Breakdown: The Content of Fairness", *54*

legitimate interests,[4] as well as to assume responsibility.[5] With regard to the result, the desirability of a 'clean break' is recognized.[6] Also, there is an immediate appeal to the notion that assets should be allocated in a way which preserves their value, and that they should be placed in the hands of the party who values them most and will put them to their most efficient use. Finally, the process through which a financial adjustment is accomplished should be both predictable and efficient.[7]

Although the underlying policy and the aims of matrimonial property are likely to be similar in most European countries, the legal techniques used to achieve fair compensation are widely different.[8] The most striking difference[9] can be found between countries following a 'discretionary approach'[10] and countries which apply 'hard' and seemingly mathematically precise rules, which govern in detail to whom which asset belongs, and how benefits acquired during marriage and an eventual surplus value of property are to be split.[11] Consequently, two systems, whose property adjustment systems are diametrically different, shall be comparatively examined.

Current Legal Problems 2001, p. 533 et seq., p. 535. See also Art. 25(2)(f) Matrimonial Causes Act 1973.

4 This idea is *inter alia* reflected in the provisions affording special protection to the matrimonial home, which can be found in many legal systems. Cf. for Switzerland A. Büchler/R. Vetterli, *Ehe Partnerschaft Kinder*, Basel 2007, p. 111. For a comparative overview see D. Henrich/D. Schwab, *Der Schutz der Familienwohnung in Europäischen Rechtsordnungen*, Bielefeld 1995.

5 This is evidenced by, e.g., section 25 (1) Matrimonial Causes Act 1973 which directs the Court to primarily consider the needs of any minor child. This idea is also reflected in the concept of maintenance, which focuses inter alia on the adjustment of marriage-related detriments, see Th. Sutter/D. Freiburghaus, *Kommentar zum neuen Scheidungsrecht*, Zürich 1999, Vorb. zu Art. 125–132, para. 4 et seq. See also *Miller v Miller*; *McFarlane v McFarlane*, [2006] UKHL 24, para. 138 per Baroness Hale; *Rossi v Rossi*, [2006] EWHC 1482 (Fam) at para. 91.8. Cf. also American Law Institute, *Principles of the Law of Family Dissolution: Analysis and Recommendations* (hereafter cited as "ALI Principles), 2002, §5.01(3) with comment on p. 788 et seq.

6 I. Schwenzer, "Das Clean Break-Prinzip im nachehelichen Vermögensrecht", *Praxis des Familienrechts 2000*, p. 609 et seq., p. 611. Specifically for England & Wales: section 25A (1) Matrimonial Causes Act 1973. For Switzerland see H. Hausheer/Th. Geiser/R. Aebi-Müller, *Das Familienrecht des Schweizerischen Zivilgesetzbuches*, 3rd Ed., Bern 2007, para. 10.81 et seq.

7 See e.g. §4.02(3) of the ALI-Principles (*Fn. 4.*), with comment on p. 648.

8 M. Antokolskaia, *(fn. 2)*, p. 480.

9 For a general overview of the matrimonial property systems found in Europe see D. Henrich, "Vermögensregelung bei Trennung und Scheidung im europäischen Vergleich", *Zeitschrift für das das gesamte Familienrecht 2000*, p. 6 et seq.; D. Henrich, "Zur Zukunft des Güterrechts in Europa", *Zeitschrift für das gesamte Familienrecht 2002*, p. 1521 et seq.

10 E.g. the United Kingdom.

11 E.g. Switzerland, France or Germany.

2. TWO DIFFERENT CONCEPTS: SWITZERLAND AND ENGLAND & WALES

2.1. SWITZERLAND

Switzerland[12] has opted for a system promising the utmost precision and predictability.[13] Under the statutory matrimonial property regime of '*Errungenschaftsbeteiligung*', the starting point is separate property, i.e. the position of ownership is not affected by this matrimonial property regime.[14] 'Property adjustment' merely takes place as financial adjustment,[15] without redistributing property rights.

First, the property of each spouse must be allocated to one of the following four 'property masses'. These are: the wife's matrimonial property, the wife's non-matrimonial property and the respective masses of the husband.[16] The matrimonial property consists of the assets attained in return for consideration, the most important example being one partner's income.[17] These are the assets that will be shared. The non-matrimonial property comprises personal property, inherited property, property that was already owned by one of the partners before marriage, and compensation for pain and suffering, as well as surrogate acquisitions of personal property.[18] If an asset has been purchased with means originating

---

12 For a general and brief overview of Swiss matrimonial property law see S. Sandoz, "Les regimes matrimoniaux en droit Suisse – Système actuel et perspectives de réforme", in: A. Bonomi/ M. Steiner, *Les Régimes Matrimoniaux en Droit Comparé et en Droit International Privé*, Genève 2006, p. 15 et seq.

13 Interestingly, however, maintenance between former spouses in Switzerland is not governed by a mathematically precise system (in contrast to, for instance, Germany, where maintenance is determined according to precise tables), but by a discretionary clause, followed by criteria which the court must take into account when fixing the amount of maintenance due. See Art. 125 Swiss Civil Code (Schweizerisches Zivilgesetzbuch vom 10. Dezember 1907, SR 210, hereafter the Swiss Civil Code). On the advantages of this discretionary clause see H. Hausheer, "Nachehelicher Unterhalt: Streitobjekt für die (verschiedenen) Experten des Bundesrates in der anstehenden Scheidungsrechtsrevision", *Zeitschrift des Bernischen Juristenvereins 1993*, p. 644 et seq., p. 645.

14 Th. Sutter-Somm/F. Kobel, "Ist das schweizerische Ehegüterrecht revisionsbedürftig?", *Die Praxis des Familienrechts 2004*, p. 776 et seq., p. 779; H. Hausheer/R. Reusser/Th. Geiser, *Berner Kommentar zum schweizerischen Privatrecht*, Bern 1992, Art. 196, para. 16. See also Arts 201 and 202 Swiss Civil Code.

15 A. Büchler/R. Vetterli, (*Fn. 4*), p. 58.

16 Arts 196 – 198 Swiss Civil Code; D. Steck, *FamKomm Scheidung*, 2nd Ed., Bern 2005, Art. 196, para. 1 et seq.

17 Art. 197 Swiss Civil Code; H. Hausheer, Art. 197, in: H. Honsell/N. P. Vogt/Th. Geiser, *Basler Kommentar zum Zivilgesetzbuch*, 2nd Ed., Basel 2002 (in the following cited as Ba-Komm/Author).

18 Art. 198 Swiss Civil Code.

from both masses, the major contribution decides to which mass the asset is allocated.[19]

In a next step, the contributions of one property mass to another have to be determined.[20] If, for example, the husband has bought a mountain bike – which would belong to the non-matrimonial property as it is a good for his sole personal use – with his salary (which belongs to the matrimonial property, as it was attained in return for consideration), the husband's matrimonial property has a compensation claim against his non-matrimonial property. If a painting is bought by the wife who pays 4/5 of the price with her earnings and 1/5 with money inherited by her husband, the painting would belong to the wife's matrimonial property, since it was primarily financed with means originating from the matrimonial property. However, the husband's non-matrimonial property would in this case have a compensation claim against the wife's matrimonial property.[21] In theory, all these calculations must not only be made once for each asset at the end of a marriage, but also at the beginning of the marriage, and they must be repeated every time an investment is made – e.g. if part of a mortgage is repaid, or if money is invested in renovating the family home.[22] One can only imagine the difficulties that arise if the spouses continuously repay their mortgage!

After having determined the value of each property mass in this way, the value of each spouse's matrimonial property is split in half. This amount is owed to the other partner. These respective claims are then set off, and the balance is paid as a lump sum.[23]

Considering the complexity of this regime, it is hardly surprising that Swiss legal scholars have suggested that Parliament must have envisaged a marriage between an accountant and a mathematics professor when designing this regime![24]

---

19 D. Steck, *FamKomm Scheidung*, (*Fn. 16*), Art. 197, para. 7.

20 Arts 206 and 209 Swiss Civil Code.

21 It is important to distinguish between compensation claims between one spouse's own property masses (e.g. a claim by the non-matrimonial property of the wife against her matrimonial property, Art. 206 Swiss Civil Code) and compensation claims by the property mass of one spouse against the property mass of the other spouse (Art. 209 Swiss Civil Code). In the latter case, the nominal value of the compensation claim is guaranteed, whereas in the first case the compensation claim may be reduced if the value of the asset diminishes. See in detail H. Hausheer/ Th. Geiser/R. Aebi-Müller, (*Fn. 6*), para. 12.75 et seq.

22 A. Büchler/R. Vetterli, (*Fn. 4*), p. 66 et seq.; H. Hausheer/Th. Geiser/R. Aebi-Müller, (*Fn. 6*), para. 12.136.

23 Art. 215 Swiss Civil Code.

24 Th. Sutter-Somm/F. Kobel, (*Fn. 6*), p. 790.

2.2. ENGLAND & WALES

The English system follows an altogether different approach. Rather than providing for distinct compensation mechanisms for maintenance, property adjustment and pension sharing, English law provides for a general financial adjustment upon divorce.[25]According to section 23 et seq. Matrimonial Causes Act 1973, the court has discretion not only in deciding which kind of order is the most adequate, i.e. whether to make an order for financial provision, for property adjustment or pension sharing; but also with regard to the content of the order (i.e. periodical payments or a lump-sum payment).

Section 25 then lists the criteria that the court should take into account when exercising its discretion. The court shall consider all the circumstances of the case, first consideration being given to the welfare of any minor child of the family. Subsequently, other relevant factors are specified. These include the financial resources of the parties, their respective contributions, their needs, the age of each party and the duration of the marriage. However, no criterion is given priority over the others. This system of financial relief has been summarised by *Lord Dennig* as follows: 'The court puts the rights and obligations of the parties all together and puts them into a mixed bag [...]. The court hands them out [...] according to what is the fairest provision for the future [...]'.[26]

Two fairly recent cases have particularly influenced the law of ancillary relief in the United Kingdom: The case of *White v White*[27] and the case of *Miller/McFarlane*.[28] Both cases concerned so-called big-money cases, i.e. cases where the available resources by far exceeded the needs of the parties. It is not my task to provide an in-depth account of the facts of these cases, so I will rather briefly highlight the core points of these decisions. In *White*, the House of Lords held that a marriage should be recognized as a common endeavour, in which the contributions of the wife and mother ought to be valued equally with the contributions of the breadwinner, regardless of whether they may be difficult to assess financially. Consequently, the result should finally be checked against the "yardstick" of equal sharing. However, the House of Lords rejected a presumption or a principle of equal sharing.

---

25 For an overview of the powers of the courts see N.-V. Lowe/G. Douglas, *Bromley's Family Law*, 10th Ed., Oxford 2007, p. 991 et seq.; S. Cretney/J. Masson/R. Bailey-Harris, *Principles of Family Law*, 7th Ed., London 2003, p. 330 et seq.

26 *Hanlon v The Law Society* [1981] A.C. 124, 146. For the historical background and a critical appraisal of this discretionary system see S. Cretney, "Trusting the Judges: Money After Divorce", *52 Current Legal Problems 1999*, p. 286 et seq.

27 *White v White*, [2000] 2 FLR 981.

28 *Miller v Miller*; *McFarlane v McFarlane*, [2006] UKHL 24.

In *Miller*, it was discussed whether the "yardstick of equality" should also apply in the case of a marriage of brief duration, and whether matrimonial property should be distinguished from non-matrimonial property. The House of Lords came to the conclusion that even if a substantial gain had resulted from assets acquired before the marriage, the other spouse could claim a share therein. However, in such a case there would be a reason to depart from the 'yardstick of equality', either because of the brief duration of the marriage or because the increased value of the assets had to be regarded as an exceptional contribution by the owner-spouse. There was disagreement, however, on how non-matrimonial property should be defined. The Lords agreed, however, that the importance of the source of the assets may diminish in time, in the sense that non-matrimonial property might initially be regarded as a contribution after a long marriage.[29]

In *McFarlane*, the court held that a career sacrifice could constitute a contribution to a spouse's increased earning capacity after the marriage. Therefore, the contributing spouse should be able to benefit from enhanced earning capacity after the divorce.

The case of *Miller/McFarlane* is further notable for its guidance on the rationale for ancillary relief in England and Wales. Baroness Hale identified the following three factors that should be considered when making an order for ancillary relief: (1) the needs of the parties, (2) compensation for contributions, and (3) equal sharing.[30] Finally, in the very recent decision of *Charman v Charman*[31], the Court of Appeal attempted to clarify the principles enunciated in *White* and *Miller/McFarlane*, stating that the 'yardstick of equality' amounted to a 'sharing princi-

---

29 *Miller v Miller*; *McFarlane v McFarlane*, [2006] UKHL 24, at para. 25 per Lord Nicholls and at para. 152 per Baroness Hale.

30 *Miller v Miller*; *McFarlane v McFarlane*, [2006] UKHL 24, at para. 144 per Baroness Hale. For a critical appraisal of these principles see S. Bridge, "Money, Marriage and Cohabitation", *Family Law 2006*, p. 641 et seq., p. 642.
Further, from a functional perspective, the 'needs' criterion may in certain respects be regarded as equivalent to the 'maintenance system' found in many continental European systems. One should therefore not place too much weight on the fact that also 'non-matrimonial property' may be used to satisfy one party's needs in England and Wales, because in continental European maintenance law the distinction between matrimonial and non-matrimonial property is also not decisive. In this respect, cf. also J. Scherpe, "Matrimonial Causes for Concern? A Comparative Analysis of Miller v Miller; McFarlane v McFarlane [2006] UKHL 24", *18 King's Law Journal 2007*, p. 348 et seq., p. 356. Also, some commentators have doubted the suitability of the English cases reported above to establish general principles, since they concern quite extraordinary "big-money cases". However, when comparing continental matrimonial property regimes with the English system on ancillary relief, it is only in this context that the pertinent questions arise. Also in continental legal systems, interesting problems with regard to matrimonial property law mainly arise in a big-money context.

31 *Charman v Charman*, [2007] EWCA Civ 503. See also A. Meehan, "Charman in the Court of Appeal", *Family Law 2007*, p. 601 et seq.

ple, meaning that property must be shared in equal proportions unless there is good reason to depart from such proportions.' A reason for such a departure may lie in extraordinary contributions on the part of one spouse.[32]

3. A COMPARISON WITH REGARD TO SELECTED ISSUES

3.1. OPERABILITY

When comparing the Swiss system of '*Errungenschaftsbeteiligung*' with the English system of ancillary relief, an important difference lies in the mathematical precision of the Swiss system, which leads to the impression that in Switzerland property adjustment is merely the result of a calculation with a certain outcome.

However, before calculations can be made, the assets have to be valued. This must not only be done at the beginning and end of the marriage, but also retrospectively, at various stages in between, whenever an investment – e.g. renovating the matrimonial home or repayments to a mortgage – has been made.[33] Since only very few couples periodically make an inventory, this task is nearly impossible in practice.[34] Another case where valuation proves difficult, if not impossible, is when there is a family business where the amount of goodwill or the value of the shares can be extremely difficult to calculate.[35] It is therefore not surprising that Swiss parties in a divorce often spend enormous amounts on expert fees in order to have their property valued. This reveals a hidden inadequacy in the Swiss system: the result can never be more precise than its basis. If the latter cannot be determined with sufficient certainty, the result will be nothing less than arbitrary.

---

32 Id., at para. 65 et seq.

33 H. Hausheer/Th. Geiser/R. Aebi-Müller, (*Fn. 6*), para. 12.136.

34 Th. Sutter-Somm/F. Kobel, (*Fn. 14*), p. 791 and p. 809; A. Büchler/R. Vetterli, (*Fn. 4*), p. 58.

35 In *D v D and another*, [2007] EWHC 278 (Fam), the Court stated that in such a situation, rather than just seeking to achieve a clean break, a 'creative solution' had to be found. For valuation issues see e.g. C. Horn, "Kriterien für den Goodwill bei Praxen von Freiberuflern", *Zeitschrift für das gesamte Familienrecht 2006*, p. 317 et seq.; cf. also R. Aebi-Müller/D. Trachsel, "Grundfragen der güterrechtlichen Auseinandersetzung", in: I. Schwenzer/A. Büchler (Eds.), *Dritte Schweizer Familienrechtstage 23./24. Februar in Basel*, Bern 2006, p. 223 et seq., p. 227, who address the question of how an additional value of a family business must be allocated according to Swiss law, taking into consideration the spouses' contributions. In this regard, see also the decision of the Swiss Federal Supreme Court, BGE 131 III 559.

Under the English system, the assets only have to be valued once at the end of marriage. Even then, the practice seems to be a rather broad assessment of the spouses' wealth,[36] as the courts do not calculate a cast-iron precise figure, but also have discretion – the parties' income, earning capacity, property and other financial resources are only some of the factors to be taken into account under section 25(a) Matrimonial Causes Act 1973. Additionally, the courts may also take into account resources which the parties are likely to acquire in the future[37] and which, in many cases, can only be estimated.

In conclusion, the Swiss system's apparent advantage of reaching a fair outcome by a mathematical calculation turns out to be a false promise, since the basis for the calculation can hardly ever be properly established, or would at least result in disproportionate costs.

3.2. SEPARATE COMPENSATION MECHANISMS AS OPPOSED TO GENERAL FINANCIAL RELIEF

Apart from the above-mentioned practical problems arising under Swiss law, which frequently prevent a state-of-the-art property division, another issue deserving a closer look is the separation of the various financial adjustment mechanisms under Swiss law – most importantly, between maintenance and property adjustment, as opposed to the general power of the courts to order financial relief in England & Wales.

The problems arising from the separation of the compensation regimes can be illustrated by the 'medical student syndrome'.[38] Here, one of the partners pays for the livelihood of both in order to allow the other spouse to enhance his career perspectives – the classical example being the nurse who finances her partner's medical studies. Less pronounced, this situation arises where one of the spouses gives up her career to take care of the home, and thereby enables her partner to successfully advance his/her own career.

The Swiss legislator even recognized this problem and enacted a provision according to which extraordinary contributions to maintenance expenses may be com-

36 A. Mainz/J. Walker/D. Wreford, "The Valuation of Assets Post-White", *Family Law 2001*, p. 221 et seq., p. 224.

37 Section 25(2)(a) Matrimonial Causes Act 1973.

38 See already I. Schwenzer, "'The Medical Student Syndrome' – Ausgleich von Karrierechancen nach Ehescheidung?", *Zeitschrift für das gesamte Familienrecht 1988*, p. 1114 et seq., who provides an overview of the possible solutions to this problem, particularly taking US law into account.

pensated.[39] However, this compensation claim would be allocated to the matrimonial property and, therefore, half of the sum would eventually have to be repaid to the other spouse.[40] This well-meaning provision cannot therefore solve the problem. Furthermore, the prospectively enhanced earning capacity of the other spouse is not taken into account for the division of property, since it does not constitute a tangible asset. It is only a factor to be considered when determining maintenance obligations. Since maintenance following divorce in Switzerland focuses predominantly on enabling the party in need to retain the standard of living which she enjoyed during the marriage[41] and not on sharing a marriage-related benefit, the contributing partner receives hardly any compensation for her sacrifices.

In other situations, the distinction between maintenance and property law may lead to arbitrary results. Swiss matrimonial property law only compensates contributions to assets which are present at the time of divorce. Maintenance expenses, in general, are not reimbursed; they fall outside the scope of property law. This entails the following consequences: In a case where the husband and wife have each inherited CHF 200,000, and the husband invests his money in the matrimonial home, whereas the wife's money is used to maintain a higher standard of living or maybe to finance a luxurious holiday, only the husband's non-matrimonial property has a compensation claim at the time of divorce, and even participates proportionally in an increase in the value of the matrimonial home. The wife is left empty-handed because her contributions have been used up without resulting in a tangible asset.[42]

Therefore, it would be preferable to have a flexible system, with financial compensation as a whole being governed by the same principles.

3.3. EQUAL SHARING

Matrimonial property law, however, is not only about compensating contributions – another of its functions is to share the matrimonial property. Today, many legal systems prescribe an equal sharing of benefits obtained during a marriage. This is the case in Switzerland where the matrimonial property is shared

---

39 Art. 165 Swiss Civil Code. See also Botschaft über die Änderung des Schweizerischen Zivilgesetzbuches (Wirkungen der Ehe im allgemeinen, Ehegüterrecht und Erbrecht), *Bundesblatt 131 (1979)*, p. 1191 et seq., p. 1254.

40 See also TH. SUTTER-SOMM/F. KOBEL (*Fn. 14*), p. 794.

41 In the case of a long marriage, cf. A. BÜCHLER/R.VETTERLI, (*Fn. 4*), p. 128.

42 Cf. TH. SUTTER-SOMM/F. KOBEL (*Fn. 14*), p. 793.

equally.[43] In England & Wales, by contrast, it is disputed whether there is a general presumption of equal sharing following *White v White*.[44] In this case, Lord Nicholls rejected the notion of an equal-sharing principle; however, he acknowledged that the court should finally check its result against the 'yardstick of equality'.[45]

The reason behind the concept of equal sharing lies in the recognition of non-financial contributions.[46] This legal assumption merits approval in so far as valuating these contributions as being equal either to the money lost due to a career sacrifice or the amount which would have to be spent on the market for similar services would neither be practical nor would it lead to a satisfactory result.[47]

It is submitted, however, that the presumption of equal sharing no longer corresponds to today's reality in matrimonial life. Increasingly, the traditional role model of the husband as the sole breadwinner and the wife as the homemaker is being replaced by a plurality of different family forms.[48] Take the case where both spouses continue to pursue their professional careers after their marriage, and where one spouse is significantly more successful. It is difficult to see why, in such

---

43 Art. 215 Swiss Civil Code.

44 E.g. R. Bailey-Harris, *54 Current Legal Problems 2001*, (*Fn. 3*), p. 539 et seq.; A. Mainz/ J. Walker/D. Wreford, *Family Law 2001*, (*Fn. 36*), p. 221; E. J. Da Costa, "The Continuing Impact of White", *Family Law 2001*, p. 742 et seq.; J. Eekelaar, "Back to Basics and Forward Into the Unknown", *Family Law 2001*, p. 30 et seq.; P. Duckworth/D. Hodson, "White v White – Bringing Section 25 Back to the People", *Family Law 2001*, p. 24 et seq.; E. Cooke, "Miller/McFarlane: Law in Search of Discrimination", *19 Child and Family Law Quarterly 2007*, p. 98 et seq., p. 100 et seq.

45 But see now the develpoments in *Charman v Charman*, [2007] EWCA Civ 503.

46 For Switzerland: H. Hausheer, "Eheliche Gemeinschaft, Partnerschaft und Vermögen im Europäischen Vergleich", in: D. Henrich/D. Schwab (Eds.), *Eheliche Gemeinschaft, Partnerschaft und Vermögen im europäischen Vergleich*, Bielefeld 1999, p. 223 et seq., p. 252; A. Büchler/R. Vetterli, (*Fn. 415*), p. 52; see also Botschaft über die Änderung des Schweizerischen Zivilgesetzbuches (Wirkungen der Ehe im allgemeinen, Ehegüterrecht und Erbrecht), *Bundesblatt 131 (1979)*, p. 1191 et seq., 1320. For England & Wales see *White v White*, [2000] 2 FLR 981, at p. 989 per Lord Nicholls; *Charman v Charman*, [2007] EWCA Civ 503 at para. 64; cf. also para. 80; G. Brasse, "It's Payback Time! Miller, McFarlane and the Compensation Culture", *Family Law 2006*, p. 647 et seq.; S. Cretney/J. Masson/R. Bailey-Harris, (*Fn. 25*), p. 369 et seq. Cf. also §4.09 of the ALI-Principles (*Fn. 4*), with comment c. on p. 735.

47 Cf. P. Parkinson, "Quantifying the Homemaker Contribution in Family Property Law", *31 Federal Law Review (2003)*, p. 1 et seq., with regard to the Australian controversy about the valuation of such non-financial contributions.

48 For Switzerland: B. Fux, *Eidgenössische Volkszählung 2000, Familale Lebensformen im Wandel*, Bundesamt für Statistik, Neuchâtel 2005, p. 14 and p. 41 et seq. For England & Wales: *The Law Commission Consultation Paper No. 179, Cohabitation: The Financial Consequences of Relationship Breakdown*, London 2006, p. 27. See already M. Rheinstein/M. A. Glendon, (*Fn. 2*), p. 181.

a case, the more successful spouse should have to share the benefits obtained during the marriage.[49]

In certain situations, the equal sharing model may even lead to manifestly inequitable results. Consider the case in which the spouses decide to separate after a relatively short marriage, but only obtain a divorce much later. If one spouse, after separation, makes exceptional efforts and consequently greatly increases her earnings, while the other spouse prefers a modest and stress-free life, there is no reason to support equal sharing. In such a situation, equal sharing would evidently be unfair.[50]

Equal sharing is not sufficiently flexible to adapt to the diversity of family forms which is present today. A satisfactory matrimonial property law must be adaptable to new role models. This goal is more likely to be achieved by a discretionary provision such as that under English law. Nevertheless, because a system under which the contributions have to be meticulously determined would presumably only lead to more argument in court, the principle of equal sharing may be a practical starting point, with the amount of the respective contributions only being considered where it would be inequitable to disregard them. As a minimum solution, at least an exception clause should be present for cases in which the result manifestly conflicts with the principle of fairness.

3.4. THE DISTINCTION BETWEEN MATRIMONIAL PROPERTY AND NON-MATRIMONIAL PROPERTY

Next, the distinction between matrimonial property and non-matrimonial property merits a closer look. Whereas Swiss law draws a rigid line between these

49 Interesting in this regard is the interpretation of Lord Mance's judgment in *Miller/McFarlane* in *Charman v Charman*, [2007] EWCA Civ 503 at para. 86, where some weight is attributed to the parties' agreement by 'word or conduct'.

50 Cf. I. Schwenzer/E. Freivogel, "Das fleissige Lieschen", *Die Praxis des Familienrechts 2007*, p. 318 et seq. On the possibility of denying an equal share see the obiter dictum in the Swiss Federal Supreme Court's decision 5C.224/2006 of 14 June 2007; see also Botschaft über die Änderung des Schweizerischen Zivilgesetzbuches (Wirkungen der Ehe im allgemeinen, Ehegüterrecht und Erbrecht), *Bundesblatt 131 (1979)*, p. 1191 et seq., p. 1321. In such a situation, the law should at least provide for an escape clause analoguos to §1381 German BGB. For a critical appraisal of §1381 BGB, its limitations and suggestions for reform see I. Gross, "§1381 BGB – Unbestimmtheit des Tatbestandes contra Ausweitung von Einzelfallkorrekturen", *Zeitschift für das gesamte Familienrecht 2007*, p. 175 et seq. With regard to English law, see *Rossi v Rossi*, [2006 EWHC] 1482 (Fam) and *S v S*, [2006] EWHC 2339 (Fam). In both cases it was important whether the increase in the assets had occurred as a result of one spouse's industry, or only by a passive economic growth in the assets already present at the time of separation: *Rossi v Rossi* at para. 24.2 and *S v S* at paras 110 and 111.

two kinds of property,[51] in England & Wales a lively debate has emerged following the cases of *Miller* and *McFarlane*.

Three criteria may be used to draw this distinction: The purpose of the goods in question, their origin and the time of acquisition.[52] Under Swiss law, all three criteria are relevant: Non-matrimonial property consists of both the goods for the personal use of one spouse and damages paid for pain and suffering (applying the first criterion), as well as existing and inherited property (applying the second and third criterion).

First, I will address the distinction according to the origin of the assets. This criterion gradually loses significance with time. Imagine the case where at the beginning of a long marriage the spouses have decided to start a common enterprise. The start-up capital is financed by the wife's inheritance.[53] Assuming that the spouses have always paid themselves an adequate salary, but have continually reinvested the remaining gains in the enterprise, is it then fair that after many years of common endeavour only the wife benefits from the increased value of the common enterprise? The same holds true for the family home. The concept of marriage as a common endeavour should prevail over an accounting approach. However, no rigid time-limit can aptly reflect this gradual process.[54]

The problems arising from the distinction according to the time of acquisition may be illustrated by the following case: The wife lends money to her husband in order to buy a family home before marriage, which he does in his own name. Because this contribution by the wife has taken place before the marriage, the house would belong to the husband's non-matrimonial property according to Swiss law. The wife's compensation claim would thus be reduced to the nominal value of the sum lent. Here again, only a discretionary approach will lead to a satisfactory result. [55]

Coming to the third distinction – defining matrimonial property according to its purpose –, this criterion merits full acceptance in principle. However, here again the time factor has to be taken into account, albeit the other way around. Whereas

51 Articles 197 and 198 Swiss Civil Code.

52 See also J. Eekelaar, (*Fn. 3*), p. 470.

53 Under Swiss law the business would therefore be allocated to the non-matrimonial property.

54 *Miller v Miller*; *McFarlane v McFarlane*, [2006] UKHL 24, para. 148 per Baroness Hale.

55 However, before the new Swiss marriage law entered into force on 1 January 2000 the Swiss Federal Supreme Court did not apply a rigid time-lime in order to separate matrimonial from non-matrimonial property in BGE 96 II 305 and BGE 109 II 92, due to the particular circumstances of these cases, in which the husband had used his fiancée's money to buy the future matrimonial home *before* the marriage.

the importance of the origin of an asset diminishes over time, the importance of the purpose of an asset increases with the passage of time, reflecting the development of marriage as a common endeavour.[56]

Therefore, a rigid distinction between property masses is hardly suitable for reflecting the flexible character of marriage.

3.5. ENCOURAGING A SETTLEMENT

As a final point, it will be examined how a system following a 'hard and fast rule' proves its value in the context of a settlement. With the liberalisation of divorce law in the 1960s, and the recognition of divorce by consent in many countries, the settlement of the financial consequences of divorce is often left to the parties.[57]

In Switzerland, the parties to a divorce may agree on the financial consequences of the divorce, the court only being able to exercise very limited control in the case of obvious inadequacies.[58] In England & Wales, although divorce by consent is formally not available (an irretrievable breakdown of the marriage must be established),[59] an agreement between the parties on the financial consequences of their divorce is encouraged.[60] The terms of the agreement will then be incorporated in a 'consent order' by the court, which – as in Switzerland – only exercises very limited control. If the parties are both represented by lawyers, the threshold for interference by the court is the violation of public policy.[61]

Sociological research has revealed that discretionary rules tend to disadvantage the 'weaker party', which in this context is the party with inferior economic

56 J. EEKELAAR, (*Fn. 3*), 472, recognises the importance of the duration of a marriage in this context. He proposes, however, to fix the proportions in which the matrimonial property should be divided for certain set periods.

57 See M. ANTOKOLSKAIA, (*Fn. 2*), p. 313 et seq.

58 Art. 140(2) Swiss Civil Code. See also M. LEUENBERGER/I. SCHWENZER, *FamKomm Scheidung*, 2nd Ed., Bern 2005, Art. 140, para. 17 et seq.; BA-KOMM/GLOOR, (*Fn. 17*), Art. 140, para. 5 et seq.

59 Section 1(1) Matrimonial Causes Act 1973. On how this is handled in practice (i.e. the 'special procedure' for undefended divorce cases) see N. V. LOWE/G. DOUGLAS, (*Fn. 25*), p. 279 et seq; for the historical background of the 'special procedure' see S. CRETNEY, *Family Law in the Twentieth Century – a History*, Oxford 2003, p. 381 et seq. For the reasons why divorce by consent was not provided for in the Divorce Reform Act 1969 see IBID., p. 333.

60 N. V. LOWE/G. DOUGLAS, (*Fn. 25*), p. 986 et seq. and p. 1008; F. ODERSKY, "Ehrecht in Grossbrittannien: England und Wales", in: R. SÜSS/G. RING (Eds.), *Eherecht in Europa*, Angelbachtal 2006, p. 623.

61 DEAN v DEAN [1978] Fam 161; BROCKWELL v BROCKWELL [1975] Court of Appeal Transcript 468, CA.

resources (in most cases the wife),[62] and that, therefore, rigid rules are preferable.[63] In general, this assertion may be true. However, if it is barely possible to determine the basis of the calculations, this seeming advantage may turn out to have a boomerang effect. If the 'weaker party' cannot prove which assets the other party owns or how much they are worth, she cannot benefit from a 'hard and fast rule' at all. By contrast, negotiations are likely to turn into prolonged haggling over valuation, with the economically stronger party benefiting from the uncertainty, or in the end forcing the economically weaker party to resort to the courts.

Additionally, it remains questionable whether a rigid rule in fact encourages a willingness to compromise which is indispensable for reaching a settlement. A rigid rule evokes the idea of being entitled to a certain outcome, whereas the uncertainty of the outcome might provide an incentive to reach a compromise preserving both parties' interests.[64]

Finally, the most important factor in encouraging a settlement is probably the allocation of the costs of a divorce. This incentive to negotiate may be decisive, possibly superseding the arguments on the structure of the legal regime.

4. CONCLUDING REMARKS AND PROSPECTS FOR COHABITEES

Is Swiss law merely an example of a particularly rigid system of seemingly precise calculation, or can the same conclusions be drawn for any system with a non-discretionary property regime?

Today, increasingly different forms of matrimonial cohabitation coexist – the married couple with children where one of the parents takes care of the home and

---

62 Taking into consideration sociological, psychological and economic factors, M. Courvoisier, *Voreheliche und eheliche Scheidungsfolgenvereinbarungen – Zulässigkeit und Grenzen*, Basel 2002, p. 200 et seq., concludes that women are regularly in an inferior position when negotiating a divorce settlement.

63 Cf. M. Binkert/K. Wyss, *Die Gleichstellung vom Frau und Mann im Ehescheidungsrecht*, Basel/Frankfurt a. M. 1997, p. 30 et seq. On the effect of rules and discretion on the bargaining framework in the context of reaching a settlement in divorce cases see: R. H. Mnookin/ L. Kornhauser, "Bargaining in the Shadow of the Law: The Case of Divorce", *88 Yale Law Journal (1978–1979)*, p. 950 et seq., p. 977 et seq.

64 Cf. J. Eekelaar, (*Fn. 3*), p. 469; cf. also J. Dewar, "Reducing Discretion in Family Law", *11 Australian Journal of Family Law 1997*, p. 309 et seq., p. 319, who finally prefers firmer rules to a discretionary approach.

family, while the other is the sole breadwinner; the couple where both spouses pursue a successful career without children; the couple where one of the spouses renders exceptional contributions to the family, e.g. cases in which the wife not only takes care of the household, but also has to take up employment in order to secure the family's standard of living; or, finally, couples who equally share the burden of homemaking and work. It is submitted that it is impossible to draft a rigid regime which leads to satisfactory results for every family form.

Having said that, how should the ideal matrimonial property law be drafted? While the English and the Swiss systems both represent extremes, a compromise may lie in a discretionary clause, prescribing that, in principle, marriage-related detriments and benefits ought to be shared equally, followed by a hierarchical list of criteria allowing a departure from this principle. Such a rule would embody the necessary flexibility, but would still provide sufficient guidance for both the courts and the parties.

Taking these thoughts one step further, and assuming a functional perspective, which takes the diminishing importance of status[65] in family law into account, this approach might equally lead to a satisfactory solution for cohabiting partners. Considering that in family law a key element should be the assumption of responsibility, the consequences of the breakdown of a relationship should not differ merely because of status. By contrast, consideration should be given to the behaviour of the partners. This should not be understood as the reintroduction of fault as a determining factor for financial relief, but as follows: If partners live in a relationship which in respect of commitment and reliance-inducing behaviour is comparable to the traditional concept of marriage, there is no reason why the law should differentiate between these two relationships.[66] A more flexible property regime[67] may therefore bring a solution to more than one controversially discussed topic in family law.

---

65 I. Schwenzer, "The Evolution of Family Law", *3 European Journal of Law Reform 2001*, p. 199 et seq., p. 201.

66 Cf. A. Büchler, "Family Law in Switzerland: Recent Reforms and Future Issues – an Overview", *3 European Journal of Law Reform 2001*, p. 275 et seq., p. 291.

67 Interesting in this regard is the system in New Zealand. See in this regard S. Aeschlimann, "Financial Compensation Upon the Ending of Informal Relationships – a Comparison of Different Approaches to Ensure the Protection of the Weaker Party", in: K. Boele-Woelki (ed.), *Common Core and Better Law*, Antwerp 2005, p. 243 et seq.

PROPERTY RELATIONS BETWEEN SPOUSES IN THE LEGISLATION OF THE CZECH REPUBLIC AND IN THAT OF SELECTED POST-COMMUNIST COUNTRIES

Anna Horínová

1. INTRODUCTION

Emotions and property form the background to any marriage.[1] Their role in society has always been subject to change depending on different factors. One of these factors is the political regime which could have a serious impact on property relationships through legislation.[2] Property was the major focus of the communist theory. The role of the communist regime in inter-spousal relationships and the further development of legislation in that respect can thus be considered as a specific situation. However, various communist countries differed in terms of their social, religious and political attitudes based on their historical backgrounds. The aim of this article is therefore to explore this model situation by using a comparative approach.

Countries whose legislation has been compared are: the Czech Republic and Slovakia (in other words, the former Czechoslovakia (the CSSR)), Poland and Bulgaria. The comparison covers the period from the 1950s until the present.

Due to the complexity of the topic, not all legal matters relating to the property relations between spouses have been considered. Questions of maintenance

1 Hrusakova, M., Fiala, J.: *Considering property relations between spouses* (In Czech: Několik úvah nad institutem majetkových vztahů mezi manžely). Právník 02/1991. p. 134.

2 "The form of the matrimonial property legislation chosen by the legislator is considerably influenced by a system of economic and property relations and is developing together with these relations." Hrusakova, M., Fiala, J.: *Considering property relations between spouses* (In Czech: Několik úvah nad institutem majetkových vztahů mezi manžely). Právník 02/1991, p. 134.

between spouses, the matrimonial home and inheritance have not been analyzed for the purposes of this study.

2. HISTORY

Due to the widespread political changes in the 1950s, the legal systems of the countries compared had to be harmonised according to the Russian pattern. A new concept of ownership and property relations had been introduced based on the official communist political doctrine. Therefore, collective ownership was strongly emphasized in contrast to personal property that was systematically suppressed.[3] In the communist ideology, property in general was regarded as a negative manifestation of consumption. These attitudes, along with the legal culture of the time, thus predetermined general as well as specific theoretical concepts of civil law.[4]

A new family policy was adopted at this time in order to achieve a so-called *socialist model* of the family. It was based on principles like gender equality, equality between legitimate and illegitimate children, solidarity and cooperation within the family. Such principles were rather advanced compared to the legal conditions of that time and they are also still useful today. Although they were reflected in the legal order, they were unfortunately not consistently respected and pursued in practice.[5] Nevertheless, some of these principles served to establish the Family Code.[6]

Due to the extraordinary character of family relations, their regulation was separated from the civil code and moved to newly constituted family codes.[7] Personal relations were considered to be of more value than property relations within the family. There was a substantial misunderstanding of the role of personal and property relations among family members. This led to a serious underestimation

3 Hrusakova, M., Kralickova, Z. *Czech Family Law* (In Czech: České rodinné právo). Second edition. Brno: Masaryk University. 2001, p. 83.

4 Explanatory note to the Civil Code draft. Zuklinova, M., Elias, K. *Civil Code Draft. Draft by The Preparatory Committee* (In Czech: Návrh občanského zákoníku. Návrh pracovní komise). Prague: Ministry of Justice of the Czech Republic. 2007, p. 2.

5 One of these principles was the principle of equality between the spouses. In spite of the fact that it sometimes resulted in more of a burden on women rather than equality, the legislation was consequently created according to this principle.

6 Hrusakova, M., Kralickova, Z. *Czech Family Law* (In Czech: České rodinné právo). Second edition. Brno: Masaryk University. 2001. p. 9.

7 Cizkovska, V. *Socialist Matrimonial Property Law. Comparative Study.* (In Czech: Socilaistické majetkové právo manželské). Prague: Universitas Carolina. 1971, p. 14.

of property within family relations. Due to this, the legislation on this issue was rigid and very brief.

A citation from the Explanatory note relating to the family code adopted in 1964 in the former CSSR can serve as an informative example:

> "Marriage should be separated from any speculation concerning property involvement. The prerequisites of its moral purity and stability have been defined, aiming to establish marriage as a harmonious and everlasting union between a man and a woman as a healthy basis for educating children."

3. AUTONOMOUS FREE WILL AND PROPERTY RELATIONS BETWEEN SPOUSES

An explanation of the communist attitude to intra-familial property relations is provided by Lasok:[8] "Community of property is said to promote the strength and cohesion of the socialist family." Since the concept of community of property (i.e. joint property of the spouses or a specific form of co-ownership) as the automatic legal consequence of marriage prevailed, the principle of autonomous free will was ignored. Poland remained the only country whose legislation always permitted a rather flexible conventional matrimonial regime.[9] The legal regime pertaining to a specific form of co-ownership of matrimonial property was of a subsidiary character in Poland.[10]

The fundamental conventional regime was also possible under the Czechoslovak Family Code of 1950 although it did not survive for long. On the other hand, private property was suppressed so much that it was almost impossible to own anything privately. Consequently, it was not important, in practical terms, whether there was a conventional regime or not. The situation changed after the recodification of the Civil and Family Code in 1964. The legislation on inter-spousal property relations, in contrast to the other countries compared, was moved from the Family Code to the newly constituted Civil Code in 1964. This fragmentation was justified by the extraordinary character of personal relations as regulated by the Family Code. Therefore, the Civil Code of the CSSR lost its original position as the *lex generalis* during the period between 1963 and 1965 and it was split

8 Lasok, D., *Polish Family Law.* No. 16, "Law in Eastern Europe. A series of publications issued by the Documentation Office for East European Law", University of Leyden. Leyden: A.W. Sijthoff. 1968, p. 90.

9 Idem p. 89–95.

10 Cizkovska, V., *Socialist Matrimonial Property Law. Comparative Study.* (In Czech: Socilaistické majetkové právo manželské). Prague: Universitas Carolina. 1971, p. 48.

between several branches of the law.[11] All of these steps aimed to fragment and weaken the role of privacy-related legislation in general. The Civil Code of 1964 led to a complete (material as well as formal) break from the European continental standards.[12] The objective of this *diversion* was to create a new civil law in terms of its content and form that would be absolutely opposite to *capitalist civil law*. The reason for this was that *capitalist law* would not match the specific conditions of a socialist society. One of the roles of civil law should be to provide the best conditions for the development of interpersonal property relations. Here, however, the Civil Code of 1964 primarily served to govern society and to protect the so-called "(social class) interests." The legal possibility of a conventional matrimonial regime was not reconsidered at this time.

In Bulgaria, the situation was very different until 1968. Here, a strictly separate property regime between the spouses was the legal matrimonial regime.[13] The legislation was changed principally due to the new Family Code of 1968 so that the only possible arrangement between the spouses was the legal regime of community of property, quite similar to the legal regulation in the other countries compared.

4. THE CONCEPT AND EXTENT OF MATRIMONIAL PROPERTY

The rigidity of the legal regulation was also supported by the fact that at this time any property rights and liabilities could not generally be part of community property. A legal community of property regime existed in a specific form of co-ownership called *undivided co-ownership between the spouses*. The underlying principle of this form of co-ownership is that: "Neither spouse has any definite or definable share in the common property, but each of them has equal rights in respect of the whole.".[14] Only movable and immovable property acquired during the marriage were covered by it. The situation was different in the Polish legislation and in the Czechoslovak legislation until 1964. Property rights and liabilities were included within the legal community of property regime as well. The

11 Labour Code, Commercial Code, Civil Code etc. The Family Code already existed.

12 Explanatory note to the Civil Code draft. Zuklinova, M., Elias, K., *Civil Code Draft. Draft of The Preparatory Committee* (In Czech: Návrh občanského zákoníku. Návrh pracovní komise). Prague: Ministry of Justice of the Czech Republic. 2007, p. 3.

13 Cizkovska, V., *Socialist Matrimonial Property Law. Comparative Study.* (In Czech: Socilaistické majetkové právo manželské). Prague: Universitas Carolina. 1971, p. 74.

14 Lasok, D., *Polish Family Law.* No. 16. *Law in Eastern Europe,* A series of publications issued by the Documentation Office for East European Law, University of Leyden. Leyden: A.W. Sijthoff. 1968, p. 90.

Bulgarian Family Code of 1985 was similar to the Czechoslovak regulation of 1964.[15]

The extent of the legal matrimonial regime depended on the concepts applied in a particular country. Usually, it was defined as a complex of assets (and liabilities) acquired by one of the spouses or by both during the marriage. The exceptions to this rule were gifts, inheritances, and personal property and chattels necessary for exercising their profession and which were acquired by one of the spouses during the marriage.

The legislation was based on mandatory (cogent) rules so that there was no way to avoid the legal consequences of marriage in the property sphere. As mentioned above, there were some ways to modify the legal matrimonial regime. According to the Polish and in certain cases also in the Czech legal system, there was a possibility to modify the extent of the legal system by an agreement between the spouses.

The legal regime of the Polish Family Code of 1964 was based on the community property of spouses as mentioned above, with emphasis on *ordinary household effects.* [16]

5. DISSOLUTION AND SETTLEMENT OF THE LEGAL MATRIMONIAL REGIME

Due to the predominant existence of *undivided co-ownership between the spouses* as the legal community property regime in the compared legislation, the shares of any of the spouses were not defined during the marriage. As a rule, the dissolution of the matrimonial regime was related to the dissolution of the marriage where the settlement of the community property was made. In serious cases,[17] the dissolution of the matrimonial regime was also admitted during the existence of the marriage through a judicial decision.

15 Cizkovska, V., *Socialist Matrimonial Property Law. Comparative Study.* (In Czech: Socilaistické majetkové právo manželské). Prague: Universitas Carolina. 1971, p. 74.

16 Lasok, D., *Polish Family Law.* No. 16, *Law in Eastern Europe.* A series of publications issued by the Documentation Office for East European Law, University of Leyden. Leyden: A.W. Sijthoff. 1968, p. 90.

17 Judicial practice speaks of, for example, drug or alcohol addiction.

There were two ways in which property could be settled: by an agreement (CSSR, Poland) between the spouses or settlement by a court decision. Settlement by agreement was not permitted by Bulgarian law.[18]

The principle of a refutable legal presumption established that the shares of each of spouses were equal. In order to modify these shares several legal criteria had to be taken into account. First, each of the spouses had to compensate assets that were excluded from the common property as his or her separate property. On the other hand, each of the spouses could request that what he or she had spent on the community property be reimbursed. Secondly, it was necessary to take into consideration and to respect the needs of the minor children. The contribution of each of the spouses to the community property had to be considered. The *contribution* was understood in its broader sense, not only in a strictly economic sense. The economic value of the wife´s work at home and of her caring for the children was legally recognized.[19]

6. PROTECTION OF A THIRD PERSON'S RIGHTS

One of the economic consequences of a marriage is the fact that spouses represent an independent economic unit.[20] Therefore it is necessary to protect the rights of third persons who come into legal contact with them. This fact had affected the legal construction of obligations in the compared legislation. Consequently, the contractual liability of spouses existed in a form of passive solidarity between debtors.

7. THE POST-COMMUNIST ERA

7.1. INTRODUCTION

Due to the fundamental social changes, new economic conditions were established. Legal orders consequently had to adapt based on the needs of the developing socio-economic situation. A complete substitution of the political as well as of the legal system cannot be a simple single-step procedure. Therefore, in certain areas, the legacy of the socialist legislation still remains a burden for all post-

18 Cizkovska, V., *Socialist Matrimonial Property Law. Comparative Study.* (In Czech: Socialistické majetkové právo manželské). Prague: Universitas Carolina. 1971, p. 75.

19 E.g. Polish Family Code 1964 art. 43. Czech Family Code 1964 §150.

20 Hrusakova, M., Kralickova, Z., *Czech Family Law* (In Czech: České rodinné právo). Second edition. Brno: Masaryk University. 2001, p. 13.

communist countries. In the first decade of this adaptation period, it was necessary to cope with fundamental problems related to the transformation of the whole social establishment. Questions relating to matrimonial property law were thus not dealt with.

Another important geopolitical change having an impact on the legal process was the splitting up of the former Czechoslovakia into two separate countries in 1993. Since then, the legal systems of the Czech Republic and Slovakia have followed their own path.

7.2. POLAND

As mentioned above, Poland was not considerably affected by socialist legal theory and the Soviet family pattern in the area of matrimonial property legislation. The Polish matrimonial property law included in the Family Code of 1964[21] always remained close to the legislation of Western European countries. Therefore, there was no specific need to introduce fundamental changes. Nowadays, it is the most liberal and the most sophisticated legislation on inter-spousal property relations among all the post-communist countries. Following tradition, it includes an extensive conventional regime while the legal community of property regime is of a subsidiary character.

7.3. BULGARIA

The Bulgarian legislation on inter-spousal property relations included in the Family Code of 1985 is based on the legal community of property regime.[22] It covers property as well as rights in property and bank deposits acquired by the spouses during the marriage. The Code also provides a list of what is the separate property of spouses. According to the Code, it is called the *personal property of spouses*. Except for all things acquired before the date of the marriage, the personal property can be made up of an inheritance, chattels for personal use and chattels which are necessary for exercising a profession. There is no legal possibility to amend such property.

The management and disposal of matrimonial community property is based on the equality of the spouses. In Article 23, affirming the matrimonial home as the personal property of one of the spouses is allowed. The termination of the

21 It is called *Matrimonial Community Property.*
22 Art. 19 of the Bulgarian Family Code.

matrimonial community property is related to the termination of the marriage. The matrimonial community property can be terminated even during the marriage, based on serious reasons that have to be carefully documented. A refutable legal presumption of equal shares between the spouses has been established. Determining a larger share must comply with several specific criteria. They are mainly based, as mentioned above, on the contribution of each of the spouses, regardless of whether it was a contribution in the form of work or raising children.

7.4. CZECHOSLOVAKIA

The State of Czechoslovakia existed until it was split up in 1993. The matrimonial property law of the former Czechoslovakia in general was of a rather fragmentary character. The problem was that some of its aspects were regulated by the Civil Code while others were covered by the Family Code. It is possible to say that inter-spousal property[23] relations were regulated by the Civil Code while personal inter-spousal relations were regulated by the Family Code.[24] By a Civil Code amendment in 1991, a fundamental conventional regime was adopted so that the rigidity of the legal system was reduced to some extent.

7.5. THE SLOVAK REPUBLIC

Unlike the Czech Republic, Slovakia left its original regulation of the legal community of property regime almost unchanged. The institution of *undivided co-ownership between the spouses* has been left in the Civil Code until now. Slovakia thus preserved the legislation on matrimonial property that does not respect the autonomous free will of the spouses and is still predominantly based upon mandatory rules.[25] This legal situation neither reflects the social and economic reality nor the present needs of the parties.

Slovakia is currently preparing an entirely new Civil Code. This is thus an important step, but we still lack any details concerning its contents.

---

23 Undivided co-ownership between the spouses, joint flat tenancy of the spouses, inheritances.

24 However, even this separation of the legal regulation of inter-spousal relations was not consistent. The regulation of maintenance between the spouses remained in the Family Code.

25 Pavelkova, B., *Matrimonial Law* (In Slovak: Manželské právo). Bratislava: Comenius University of Bratislava. 2004, p. 135 - 140

7.6. THE CZECH REPUBLIC

1998 was a year of substantial changes in the Czech legislation on inter-spousal property relations.[26] It was improved and the institution of *undivided co-ownership between the spouses* was transformed into the new *joint property of the spouses.* Property acquired by one of the spouses or by the spouses together during their marriage is now covered by the joint property of spouses according to the current legislation. Liabilities[27] as well as proprietary rights have been included. Primarily, the legal matrimonial regime now takes the form of *joint property of the spouses.* As an alternative to the legal regime, spouses/persons intending to marry can enter into an agreement[28] which modifies the legal joint property regime, but they cannot ignore it completely.[29] Any modifications can concern either an extension of the legal regime or its restriction. Spouses or persons intending to marry can exclude a particular form of property, a proprietary right or a particular liability[30] from the legally presumed extent of the community property. A third person‘s rights are protected, however. If a third party who comes into legal contact with the spouses is not aware of the content of such an agreement, the spouses cannot rely on it when considering its legal effects. The management and disposal of the *joint property of the spouses* is based on the principle of equality between the spouses. The other spouse is also protected when one of the spouses starts a business.[31]

It is possible to restrict the extent of the joint property of the spouses by means of a judicial decision when serious reasons have been documented.[32]

The termination of the joint property of the spouses is related to the termination of the marriage. If the marriage is terminated, a settlement of joint property has to be made. The legal presumption is that the shares of the spouses are equal, but that there are possibilities to modify these shares. If the spouses reach an agreement, they can make a settlement of their joint property according to their free

26 Dvorak, J., *Community Property of Spouses.* (In Czech: Majetkové společenství manželů). Praha: ASPI Publishing, 2004, p. 113.

27 ...with the exception of liabilities related to assets in the exclusive ownership of only one of the spouses and liabilities incurred without the approval of the other spouse if their extent exceeds a level commensurate to the means of the spouses. Hrusaková, M., *Czech Family Law.* Brno: Masaryk University, 2006, p. 32.

28 In the form of a notarial deed.

29 "... joint property of the spouses may only be reduced to the extent of the items forming part of the usual contents of the common household and no further." Hrusaková, M. *Czech Family Law.* Brno: Masaryk University, 2006, p. 32.

30 §143a of the Civil Code 1964.

31 §146, §148/2 of the Civil Code 1964.

32 §148 of the Civil Code 1964.

will and can therefore modify their shares. Otherwise, one of the spouses can instigate judicial proceedings and the court can consequently settle the property according to the criteria listed in §149 of the Civil Code of 1964.[33]

7.6.1. New Civil Code of the Czech Republic

Although some fundamental changes have been introduced, the regulation of matrimonial property law still remains very brief. It has been announced that this field will be dealt with in more detail during an early anticipated recodification. For the committee preparing a first draft of the anticipated recodification in the Czech Republic, the Government's proposal for the Civil Code of 1937, which aimed to update the ABGB, has been taken as the basic theoretical model.[34] The most important reason for this decision was to abolish the continuity with the communist legislation and to return to the tradition of the pre-World War II legislation. The primary objective of this recodification is to create a classical continental code. The sources of inspiration are quite broad.[35] However, not all of them can serve as a model for the new legislation on inter-spousal property relations. In general, the concept of autonomous free will has been adopted as the main notion and principle of the new legislation. This principle has thus also significantly influenced the regulation of inter-spousal relations. In contrast to the former regulations, much more attention has been paid to property problems that can arise between spouses and this question has been regulated in much more detail.

The recodification also anticipates that all of the so far separated legal branches will once again be covered by a single legislative act. Family Law will thus be Part II of the new Code.[36] The intention is that all matters related to intrafamiliar rela-

---

33 Each of the spouses has to compensate for assets that were taken from the common property for his or her separate account. On the other hand, each of the spouses could demand what he or she has spent on the community property. Secondly, it is necessary to take the needs of the minor children into account. The contribution of each of the spouses to establishing and developing the community property has to be considered, the wife working in the home and caring for children being included.

34 The ABGB from 1811 was applicable in Czechoslovakia until the political changes in 1950. The Government draft from 1937 was predominantly inspired by the German and Swiss civil codes.

35 Mainly the Austrian, Swiss and German Civil Codes. Further the Italian, Dutch, Polish, Québec and Russian Codes are mentioned as an inspiration. Explanatory note to the Civil Code draft. Zuklinova, M., Elias, K., *Civil Code Draft. Draft of The Preparatory Committee.* (In Czech: Návrh občanského zákoníku. Návrh pracovní komise). Prague: Ministry of Justice of the Czech Republic. 2007, p. 7.

36 As far as the internal organization of the Code is concerned, the Code civil du Québec, the BWB and Codice civil have been taken into account. The regulation of all family questions together was preferred.

tions[37] will be regulated within Part II.[38] The complete integration of family matters should express the fact that marriage is an emotional as well as a property unit and both of its aspects are equally important for its proper functioning.

7.6.2. New Regulation of Inter-Spousal Property Relations

As mentioned above, all of the issues dealing with inter-spousal property relations are covered by Part II of the Code. A special section (Section II) is dedicated to the so-called *matrimonial property law.*[39]

Two regimes (legal and/or modified) are possible according to the new regulation. The modified regime is based either upon an agreement between the spouses (or persons intending to marry) or upon a court decision.

The new Civil Code is very similar to the current legislation in terms of its terminology as well as the regulation of the legal regime. Therefore, the legal regime is supposed to exist in the form of *joint property of the spouses*. The scope of the joint property of the spouses has also remained almost unchanged.[40]

Unlike the current legal situation, there is wider legal protection for the spouse relating to the business activities of the other spouse.

Matrimonial property matters can be governed by an agreement between persons intending to marry or by an agreement between the spouses. Such an agreement can under certain circumstances ignore the legal consequences that would otherwise arise and can therefore establish a separate property regime or modify the legal regime under the Code. There is also a possibility to limit the joint property of spouses as from the day of the termination of the marriage. Specific agreements on the regulation of property relations between the spouses during the marriage as well as in the case of its termination can be made in specific situations.

---

37 Except for inheritance.

38 As mentioned above, the present situation can be characterized by fragmented regulation. Questions concerning the *joint property of the spouses* and the matrimonial home are governed by the present Civil Code while maintenance between the spouses and the personal rights and obligations of the spouses are regulated by the Family Code.

39 In Czech: *Manželské právo majetkové.*

40 It means: the rights and obligations assumed by one of the spouses or by spouses together during the marriage. As far as rights are concerned there are several exceptions: gratuitous legal actions or property for personal use. The extent of joint obligations has been somewhat modified. If one of the spouses assumes an obligation which is not intended for common family needs, joint liability does not arise.

The possibility of inter-spousal modifying agreements as anticipated by the Code[41] is a very useful tool in my view. Enhanced protection for the matrimonial home is another issue that I personally find very important. This problem seems to me to be rather underestimated in the current Civil Code from 1964.

It thus seems that in the Draft the conventional regime seems to include a broader, more flexible and more detailed concept.

8. CONCLUSIONS

The remnants of the so-called *socialist understanding* of family and family relations have persisted in the post-communist countries until the present. Among other things, it was the serious underestimation of property relations within the family that consequently led to the suppression of the autonomous free will of the spouses. According to certain representatives of the committee preparing the new Civil Code of the Czech Republic, the early communist *status quo* in civil law based on the *primitive materialism* did not basically change.[42] Despite the existence of many issues to be addressed in this context, this attitude is, in my opinion, rather extreme.

Nevertheless, the Civil Code of 1964 is for the moment the only applicable Civil Code in the Czech Republic. Although essential changes were subsequently introduced, its principles were established in 1960 and it is obvious that an entirely new Code is absolutely necessary.

This is one of the reasons why the recodification of the civil law in the Czech Republic is now at a terminal stage.

The Czech Republic as well as the other countries compared here are at a crossroads at this moment. Our legislation and legal cultures have been influenced by continuous European integration, on the one hand, and by different cultural and social backgrounds and by their recent history on the other.[43] Property relations in general can serve as an example. They have been strongly influenced by a systematic underestimation and deformation by socialist legal theory. It would seem that 18 years after the change of regime, the transformation has been completed

41 It is not yet clear which institution should retain evidence of such an agreement. There are a few suggestions like the Notarial Association or the courts.

42 Explanatory note to the Civil Code draft. Zuklinova, M., Elias, K., *Civil Code Draft. Draft of The Preparatory Committee* (In Czech: Návrh občanského zákoníku. Návrh pracovní komise). Prague: Ministry of Justice of the Czech Republic. 2007, p. 2.

43 The historical consequences are different from "Western Europe".

and that it is no longer necessary to remind ourselves of the communist era.[44] This is unfortunately not completely realistic. Despite a few articles being amended and adapted to the new political, economic and social conditions, the Civil and Family Codes of the 1960s are still in effect, they are the *laws in action*.[45] In contrast to, for example, German or Swiss matrimonial property laws, the sophisticated regulation of these matters is still lacking in these countries.[46]

We can agree with Hrusakova and Fiala that the stability of marriage, as a social institution, can be improved by suitable legislation.[47] Due to this fact, it is impossible to leave the legal *status quo* without substantial and systematic changes. The present legislation cannot cope with the variety of economic of inter-spousal relations. The crossroads concerning the Czech legislation means that partial amendments to the Family/Civil Codes are going be substituted by principally new documents and a comprehensive legal solution is going to be adopted. During the preparation of the Draft, legal experts have sought inspiration mainly in countries with a similar legal culture.[48] Based on the discussion of the Draft, changes are anticipated. Their importance is very straightforward: the future of inter-spousal property relationships in this country will be determined in the long term by the quality of the ongoing legal process.

44 There are slight differences from country to country.

45 Although changes to these Codes were introduced, the basic elements remained.

46 Poland remained quite resistant to socialist ideology so that its matrimonial property legislation was more elaborate than the legislation of the other compared countries.

47 Hrusakova, M., Fiala, J., Consideration over property relations between spouses (In Czech: Několik úvah nad institutem majetkových vztahů mezi manžely). Právník 02/1991. p. 134.

48 With regard to the legal culture before World War II.

PART FIVE
CROSS-BORDER FAMILY RELATIONSHIPS

THE SECOND REVISION OF THE BRUSSELS II REGULATION: JURISDICTION AND APPLICABLE LAW

Th. M. de Boer*

1. THE MYTH OF CERTAINTY AND PREDICTABILITY

I have been teaching private international law for more than thirty five years now, and I have been a part-time judge adjudicating conflicts cases for more than twenty. In all those years, I have seldom met anybody who was not a lawyer who was even aware of the problems conflicts law is meant to solve, let alone that they would have any idea of the way they are actually solved. I once conducted a little quiz among my non-lawyer friends explaining the problem of international divorce and asking them which law they thought would govern the judicial consequences of the breakdown of a marriage: divorce, maintenance, parental authority, matrimonial property, etc. Most of them assumed that courts can only apply their own law, and when I told them that occasionally they do apply foreign law as well, they were all agreed that, in that case, an international divorce should be governed by the law of the country 'under whose law the spouses were married', by which they obviously meant the *lex loci celebrationis*.

Given this unawareness of the general public of the problems and solutions of private international law, it never ceases to amaze me that so many of my colleagues apparently show much faith in concepts like legal certainty, predictability and uniformity of result. Private international law, they claim, should conform to the parties' justified expectations as to jurisdiction and applicable law. In my experience, particularly as a judge,[1] the parties in a divorce case have no

* The author is member of the Netherlands Standing Committee on Private International Law. I concluded my research on September 1, 2007.

1 In 1985, I was appointed as a part-time judge in the District Court of Alkmaar, where I was asked to deal with conflict-of-law cases only. The bulk of my case load – roughly estimated at 90% – involved divorce and ancillary matters (maintenance, matrimonial property and parental responsibility). Over the years that followed, I have adjudicated a few thousand of such cases. In only a few of them – less than a dozen perhaps – did the central issue focus on juris-

expectations at all other than being heard in a court in their own country and being treated with fairness, which usually means that they expect the court to support their point of view. That has nothing to do with expectations as to the law to be applied, but at best with notions of substantive justice.

That is why I cannot quite believe in the cogency of the harmonization of divorce choice of law, as professed by the European Commission in the explanatory memorandum accompanying its proposal for a second revision of the Brussels II Regulation: 'The great differences between, and complexity of national conflict-of-law rules make it very difficult for international couples to predict which law will apply to their matrimonial proceeding'.[2] I very much doubt that international couples ever cared about those complexities and differences before their lawyers explain the problem to them at the time they are contemplating divorce. That is why I do not have much faith in the added value of the provisions allowing choice-of-forum and choice-of-law agreements proposed by the Commission. As long as the spouses are still living in (pre-)marital bliss, very few of them will contemplate the consequences of a break-up, and fewer still will think of something abstruse as a choice of the court that will handle their divorce, or the law they want to be applied.[3] By the time divorce has become an inevitable reality, the spouses may be instructed by their lawyers on their freedom of choice, but at that stage their willingness to come to an agreement is probably slight.

Well, that is only to set the mood. I have much more to say about the Commission's proposal, and I intend to do so in an orderly way. First, I will give an overview of the changes the EU member states may expect with regard to international divorce if and when the revision of Brussels II-*bis* enters into force (2 and 3). After that, I should like to focus on the proposed conflict-of-law rules, particularly in light of the principles underlying contemporary choice of law. To that end,

diction or the applicable law. This experience also contradicts the Commission's assertion that, due to the lack of uniform conflict-of-law rules, forum-shopping frequently occurs.

2 COM (2006) 0399 final, 17 July 2006, at p. 3. Since then, the German Presidency and the (incoming) Portuguese Presidency – on the basis of meetings of the Committee on Civil Matters and the comments of the delegations – have published four more drafts: 5274/07 JUSTCIV 4, 12 January 2007; 6258/07 JUSTCIV 26, 13 February 2007; 7144/07 JUSTCIV 47, 9 March 2007; and 11295/07 JUSTCIV 183, 28 June 2007.

3 A relatively small number of future spouses may have the benefit of being advised by an attorney or notary public on the financial consequences of their marriage. After Brussels II-*ter* enters into force, their legal advisors would do well to address the issue of divorce as well, pointing out the possibilities for a choice of forum and a choice of law. However, if the fiancés are nationals of the same country and still have their habitual residence there at the time of marriage, their lawyers are likely to overlook the international complications that may present themselves after one of the spouses, or both of them, have moved abroad. In other words: in very few cases will the spouses be alerted to possible conflicts issues until they actually contemplate divorce.

I will have to make a few preliminary remarks on the objectives of modern conflicts law (4) and the policies expressed in the substantive divorce laws of the member states (5), so as to enable us to assess the methodological validity of the proposed choice-of-law rules (6). To end on a constructive note, I will come up with an alternative solution (7).

2. A BRIEF SURVEY OF THE PROPOSED RULES: JURISDICTION

In the field of jurisdiction, the revision of Brussels II-*bis* – the result of which is likely to be dubbed 'Brussels II-*ter*' – introduces two major innovations. First of all, it would seem that there will no longer be any room for recourse to national law, as allowed under the 'residual' standards of Article 7 Brussels II-bis.[4] This Article is going to be replaced by a provision on 'subsidiary jurisdiction'[5] for situations in which the spouses do not have a common EU nationality and neither of them is habitually resident in a member state. In such cases, jurisdiction is conferred (1) upon the national courts of either spouse and (2) on the courts of the member state in which the spouses had their habitual residence for at least three years before they moved elsewhere, as long as they did not move from that country more than three years before the court was seized. For instance: a Greek husband is married to a Swedish wife. They have been living for ten years in France, then move to the United States. Under Article 3 of Brussels II-bis, no court in the European Union would have jurisdiction. Under Article 7 of the revised version, a petition for divorce could be lodged with a court in Greece (being the *forum patriae* of the husband), in Sweden (*forum patriae* of the wife), or in France (as the member state where the spouses were habitually resident for more than three years) provided the parties did not leave France more than three years before the

4 In Brussels II-*bis*, Article 6 provides that the regulation's rules on divorce jurisdiction exclude recourse to national law if the respondent is either a resident or a national of a member state, while Article 7 stipulates that 'residual' jurisdiction shall be determined by national law 'where no court of a member state has jurisdiction pursuant to Articles 3, 4 and 5'. In Brussels II-*ter*, Article 6 will be deleted. In footnote 9 of the latest draft (of 28 June 2007, *supra*, note 3), it is suggested that 'a recital could clarify that the deletion of Article 6 does not change the exclusive nature of the provisions on jurisdiction'. The big difference, however, is the replacement of Article 7 by a provision that no longer allows the application of national rules of jurisdiction in extracommunity cases but directly confers jurisdiction on the courts of the member states if none of the conditions of Article 3 has been met.

5 Incomprehensibly, the Commission used the phrase 'residual jurisdiction' as a caption for a provision (Article 7 Brussels II-*ter*) that does not allow recourse to national law, but, instead, introduces additional jurisdictional grounds. In the draft of 12 January 2007, submitted by the German Presidency (*supra*, note 2), this heading was rightly rephrased as 'subsidiary jurisdiction'.

court was seized. According to the Explanatory Memorandum, the new version of Article 7 is meant to be a 'uniform and exhaustive rule', inspired by the fact that national rules on international jurisdiction 'do not always effectively ensure access to court for spouses although they may have a close connection with the Member State in question'.[6] That implies that, as far as divorce jurisdiction is concerned, the territorial scope of Brussels II-*ter* will be universal.

The second innovation in this field is the introduction of prorogation in matrimonial matters, as it already existed in Brussels II-bis with regard to parental authority.[7] In proceedings relating to divorce and legal separation, the spouses are allowed a choice of court. The choice is limited, however, to the fora listed in Article 3 and the fora introduced by the new version of Article 7. In other words: the parties may not select *any* forum within the European Union but only those with which they have some connection on account of the nationality or habitual residence of either spouse, their common nationality or their former common habitual residence. I do not quite see why such restrictions are necessary, and why the spouses are not allowed to choose any forum within the European Union, as I have argued in a comment on the *first* revision of the Brussels II Regulation:

> 'The reason for not allowing the spouses a choice of forum lies probably in the differences between the divorce laws in force in the various member states and between their choice-of-law rules for divorce. [...] One of the objectives of the European Commission to be achieved in the immediate future is the unification or harmonization of choice-of-law rules with regard to divorce. Once that mission has been accomplished, I cannot think of any reason why adult people would not be allowed to start divorce

6 COM (2006) 399, at p. 9 (Article 7). It could be argued that a court may resort to national criteria if jurisdiction cannot be based on Articles 3, 3a, 4, 5 or 7 of the proposed regulation. However, the Explanatory Memorandum makes it clear that Article 7 is an 'exhaustive' rule. Besides, it is hard to see on what (national) ground a court in a member state could reasonably assume jurisdiction if the case is not linked to the forum state by any of the connections listed in the regulation. In my opinion, the only useful forum missing from the regulation's jurisdictional catalogue is the *forum necessitatis*.

7 *Cf.* Art. 12(1) and Art. 12(3) Brussels II-*bis*. There is a curious discrepancy between the wording of these provisions and that of Article 3a Brussels II-*ter*. Where it says in Article 12 Brussels II-*bis* that 'the jurisdiction of the courts has been accepted expressly or otherwise in an unequivocal manner... at the time the court is seised', Article 3a Brussels II-*ter* evidently expects the spouses to behave in a proactive way: 'The spouses may agree that a court or the courts of a Member State shall have jurisdiction...'. It would seem that the emphasis in Article 12 is on (express or implied) acceptance by the respondent, while Article 3a requires an agreement explicitly endorsed by both spouses. However, Article 3a(5) also allows tacit submission to jurisdiction, without the requirement (laid down in Article 12) that it must be clear, at the time the court is seized, that the respondent will not object to its jurisdiction. In other words, under Article 3a(5) petitioner is not required to file some kind of statement that respondent is prepared to submit to the court's jurisdiction. Provided the respondent does not contest jurisdiction, entering an appearance suffices. I fail to see why this form of tacit submission would be unacceptable under Article 12. See also, *infra*, note 10 and accompanying text.

> proceedings before the court of their choice in any EU member state, as long as the Regulation guarantees that courts in all member states will arrive at the same choice-of-law result, while another Regulation, Brussels II, guarantees the mutual recognition of their decrees. If Article 12(1) Brussels II-*bis* allows the spouses to ask the *forum divortii* for a decision on parental responsibility for a child habitually resident in another member state, why could it not be the other way round? Why are they not allowed, then, to choose a *forum divortii* in the member state where their child is habitually resident?'[8]

Now that we have actually reached the stage of choice-of-law harmonization – or rather unification – I still cannot think of any reason why the spouses should not be allowed to choose any forum within the European Union, and why their freedom of choice should be limited to a number of options under the general motto that they have 'a substantial connection' with the forum state.[9] If the harmonization of conflict-of-law rules is thought to be an effective means to prevent forum-shopping, there cannot possibly be any objection to allowing the spouses to choose any court within EU territory as long as either of them has some connection with one of the member states, not necessarily the forum state.[10] Besides, if the European Union is to become one big '*espace juridique*', it would suffice to adopt one or more rules attributing jurisdiction on 'the courts of the EU member states' collectively, while the exact venue could be determined by a set of (non-mandatory) distributory rules. If we are prepared to experiment with the recognition and enforcement of sister-state judgments without the requirement of a 'special procedure' – to promote the free movement of judgments – I do not see why an adult couple who have access to the courts of one member state (for instance on the ground that the respondent is habitually resident in that state) may not sue one another, by mutual agreement, in the courts of an EU sister-state. Would that

8 Th.M. de Boer, Jurisdiction and Enforcement in International Family Law: A Labyrinth of European and International Legislation, *Netherlands International Law Review* 2002, p. 307–351, at p. 342/343.

9 Art. 3a(1) Brussels II-*ter*.

10 *Cf.* Art. 23 Brussels I Regulation, allowing the parties to choose any court within the EU as long as one of them is domiciled in a member state, not necessarily the forum state. The Commission's proposal for a regulation on international maintenance obligations COM (2005) 649, 15 December 2005, contained a similar provision. Unfortunately, however, this provision has been brought into line with the Brussels II-*ter* proposal. *Cf.* Article 4 of the latest draft, 11281/07 JUSTCIV 180, 28 June 2007: with regard to maintenance, the parties may choose one of the fora that would have jurisdiction if there had been no choice-of-court agreement, or the *forum patriae communis,* or the courts of the member state in which the (former) spouses had their last common habitual residence for a minimum length of time (one year? three years?). On the other hand, the maintenance proposal has retained the provision of Article 24 Brussels I (tacit submission to the jurisdiction of the court seized), while the Brussels II-*ter* proposal does not allow tacit submission unless the court seized 'would otherwise have jurisdiction under this Regulation': Art. 3a(5).

be a greater infringement upon the member states' sovereign power to adjudicate than the obligation to enforce sister-state judgments unconditionally?

The conditions laid down in the first two paragraphs of Article 3a(1) – one of the spouses should be a national of the forum state, or the spouses should have had their last common habitual residence in that state – should be met at the time the choice-of-court agreement is concluded. Thus, if a French/American couple agree to choose a divorce court in Paris, that court will have jurisdiction even if the French spouse subsequently lost his or her citizenship. There has been some debate on the time factor to be used if one of the fora listed in Article 3 is chosen, as allowed by the final paragraph of Article 3a(1). According to the latest draft, the jurisdiction of the chosen court should be measured against the time the court is seized rather than the time the agreement was concluded.[11] The choice between the two options reveals a basic flaw in the reference to jurisdictional grounds that were meant to be used in the *absence* of a choice-of-court agreement. If the spouses choose a forum before they actually contemplate a divorce, they have no way of knowing who is going to be the petitioner and who is going to be the respondent, both crucial data for the application of Article 3. If the conditions of Article 3 should be measured against the time of the agreement, the only foolproof criterion listed in that provision is the common residence of the spouses at that time.[12] All other factors that determine jurisdiction under Article 3 are unknown at the time the agreement is made. If, on the other hand, those factors should be measured against the time the court is actually seized, chances are that, since the date of the agreement, the circumstances have changed in such a way that the conditions of Article 3 are no longer satisfied.[13]

11 In the previous draft, the two options were still open to debate. In the draft of 28 June 2007, it is noted (in footnote 5) 'that the majority of Member States expressed a preference for this alternative'.

12 This is also true if they choose a forum in the member state of their common nationality: Article 3(1)(b). However, this alternative is redundant next to the first choice allowed in Article 3a: the court(s) of the member state of which *one* of the spouses is a national.

13 For instance: in their marriage contract, a Dutch husband (living in the Netherlands) and a Belgian wife (living in Belgium) have agreed that a German court should have jurisdiction in case of divorce, as the couple intend to take up residence in Germany after they are married. After two years in Germany, the marriage breaks down, the husband moves to Spain and the wife returns to Belgium. As agreed, the husband starts divorce proceedings in Germany. Under Article 3, a German court would have no jurisdiction, as neither spouse resides in Germany anymore, nor are they German nationals. If the choice-of-court agreement were to be measured against the conditions at the time the court is seized, it would therefore be invalid. If the date of conclusion were to be decisive, the agreement would also be invalid since neither husband nor wife were German residents or nationals at that time. If the parties had made their agreement at the time they were already living in Germany, it would be valid only if the date of agreement is deemed decisive, since, at that time, both spouses had their habitual residence in the (intended) forum state: Article 3(1)(a), first indent.

That is why I would have preferred a list of eligible fora rather than a reference to the fora of Article 3. Legal certainty demands that the time of the agreement rather than the time the court is actually seized determines the validity of the choice. Included in the list should be, in my opinion, all fora with which one or both of the spouses have a meaningful connection by virtue of (1) the nationality of either spouse, (2) the habitual residence of either spouse, and, arguably, (3) the habitual residence of any of the children for whom they share parental responsibility. Ideally, however, they should be allowed to choose any forum within the EU, as long as one of them is a EU citizen or resident at the time of the agreement.

3. A BRIEF SURVEY OF THE PROPOSED RULES: APPLICABLE LAW

A true novelty in the proposal for the revision of the Brussels II Regulation is the inclusion of a chapter on the applicable law in matters of divorce and separation. The plans for a so-called 'Rome III Regulation' have taken shape in Articles 20a and 20b of the 'Brussels II-*ter*' proposal. Basically, the Commission has suggested two conflicts rules, one allowing a limited form of party autonomy, the other designating the applicable law in the absence of. To start with the last one, Article 20b calls for the application of the law of the state where the spouses have their common habitual residence at the time the court is seized, or if they are by then living in different countries, the law of their last common habitual residence provided that one of them still resides there. If not, the law of their common nationality shall apply,[14] and if they do not have a common nationality, lex fori will fill the gap. To illustrate the operation of this set of rules: let us assume that an Irish couple have been living in the Netherlands until their marriage breaks down and the Irish wife decides to return to Ireland. The husband files for divorce in the Netherlands. The law to be applied is Dutch law, as the law of the couple's last common habitual residence. If the husband had moved from Holland to Belgium, and if he had filed for a divorce there, a Belgian court would have to apply Irish law as *lex patriae communis*. If either spouse had not been Irish, Belgian law would apply as lex fori.

Considering that quite a few member states have a strong preference for the application of their own law in matters of family law, including divorce, it is hardly surprising that, in the negotiations over Brussels II-*ter*, several attempts have been

14 There has been some debate on the order of Article 20b(1)(b) and (c). The French, it would seem, would rather give precedence to the *lex patriae communis* over the law of the last habitual residence of the spouses. See *infra*, text accompanying notes 17 and 18.

made to give the lex fori a more prominent role than that of a stopgap. One of those attempts has resulted in the adoption of a remedy for situations in which the applicable law 'does not provide for divorce'. In such cases, lex fori shall apply. According to the German Presidency, this provision not only covers cases where the applicable law does not know the concept of divorce at all, but also cases 'where the applicable law does not allow one of the spouses to lodge an application for divorce'.[15] Does the latter condition include situations in which the applicable divorce law is based on fault and 'does not provide for divorce' if the petitioner is the guilty party? Or did the Presidency only mean to refer to some (Muslim?) law that does not permit women to file for divorce? On the other hand, that situation already seems to be covered by an explanatory footnote accompanying the provision on Article 20e, where it is suggested that public policy could be invoked if 'the application of a foreign divorce law would discriminate one of the spouses, for example by not providing for the same rights for each spouse with respect to divorce or legal separation'.[16] It is to be hoped that the recital 'clarifying' this issue will be clearer than the Presidency's footnotes.

Another attempt to boost the role of lex fori in divorce proceedings was made by the French delegation. Based on the doctrine of facultative choice of law, their proposal would allow the courts to apply their own law as long as neither party requests the application of the (foreign) law designated by Article 20b. In the Netherlands, a similar approach has been widely supported since the early 1990s, when it was clear that under the International Divorce Act the courts were obliged to apply Dutch law in virtually all cases except those in which (one of) the spouses expressly requested the application of their common national law.[17] Unfortunately, the French proposal does not quite conform to the rule applied in Dutch

15 Footnote 7 in the draft of 9 March 2007 (= footnote 29 in the draft of 28 June 2007), in which it is suggested that a recital should clarify the meaning of the phrase 'does not provide for divorce'.

16 Footnote 35 of the draft of 28 June 2007.

17 Pursuant to Article 1 *Wet conflictenrecht echtscheiding* (International Divorce Act), the spouses may opt for the application of either Dutch law or the law their common nationality. Even a unilateral choice will be upheld if it remains uncontested (which is *eo ipso* the case in default proceedings). In the absence of a choice by (one of) the parties, the primary reference is to the *lex patriae communis*. If the spouses are nationals of different countries, or if one of them no longer has a 'true social connection' with his or her home country, the law of the spouses' common habitual residence will be applied, and failing that, the lex fori. Since jurisdiction usually hinges on the condition that one of the spouses is habitually resident in the Netherlands (*cf.* Art. 3 Brussels II-bis), the law of the spouses' common habitual residence is likely to be Dutch law. By the same token, it is readily assumed that the spouse residing in the Netherlands is not likely to have maintained a true social connection with his or her home country. The result is the application of Dutch law in all cases save those in which the spouses have a common nationality and both of them may be deemed to have retained a true social connection with their home country, or, if not, one of them has requested the application of their national law and the other one does not object.

judicial practice. First of all, lex fori may only be used as a point of departure if both parties have entered an appearance; in default proceedings, the applicable law is determined by the criteria listed in Article 20b. Secondly, this implies that lex fori can be displaced by foreign law on at least two counts; either because the spouses have a foreign common nationality, or because they had their last common habitual residence abroad.[18] The Dutch approach, on the other hand, also allows facultative choice of law in default proceedings – which implies the application of Dutch law unless the petitioner relies on foreign law – and there is no other choice-of-law alternative than the application of the spouses' common national law. In other words: the necessity of applying foreign law is considerably less than it will be if the French proposal were to be adopted.

In the latest draft of the Brussels II-ter proposal, the Presidency has included an 'escape clause' favouring the application of lex fori.[19] It appears that such a clause was deemed necessary, as it was feared that nationals of a divorce-friendly country returning home after the break-up of their marriage would be unable to get a simple divorce under the law of the couple's last habitual residence. As it stands now, the clause is meant to displace the law of the spouses' last common habitual residence in favor of lex fori, provided that (1) one of the spouses so requests; (2) their common residence abroad lasted less than three years, and (3) the requesting spouse has a 'substantial connection' with the forum state, either on account of his or her nationality, or because he or she was a resident of the forum state for at least ten years before departing to another country, provided that less than three years have elapsed between the date of departure and the moment the court is seized. As I see it, this exception to Article 20b(1)(b) tries to reconcile a policy-oriented approach (allowing the application of a divorce-friendly lex fori) with the principle of the closest connection. From a methodological point of view, such a compromise should be rejected, as it obscures the true nature of the escape clause. What it is meant to achieve is a quick and easy divorce under forum law, not an adjustment of the closest connection.

The other conflicts rule I mentioned, Article 20a, allows the spouses a choice between the law of their common habitual residence, the law of their last common

18 If jurisdiction is based on nationality – *cf.* Article 3(1)(b) and Article 7(b) – or, in extracommunity cases, on the fact that the spouses had their habitual residence in the forum state for at least three years – *cf.* Article 7(a) – foreign law may also be applicable as the law of the country were both spouses currently have their common habitual residence: Article 20b(1)(a).

19 Article 20b(1a). In a 'Presidency non-paper' of 21 March 2007, the following elements of such an escape are enumerated: (a) it should only be used to escape application of the law of the spouses' last habitual residence; (b) it should not be applied *ex officio* but only at the request of one of the spouses, provided that the requesting spouse has a 'significantly closer connection' with the forum state than with the state of their last habitual residence, and (c) the escape clause should specify the conditions determining a significantly closer connection.

habitual residence as long as one of them still resides there at the time of the designation, the national law of either spouse, or the law of the forum. In fact, the alternatives are hardly different from the laws that would apply under Article 20b,[20] but the main difference is that the parties may choose a law that would not be applicable under that provision, either because they have chosen an alternative that would not be the primary choice in the absence of an agreement, or because the circumstances at the time of their choice were different from those at the time of divorce. To illustrate this point, let us go back to the example I gave in the context of jurisdiction. A Greek husband and his Swedish wife had been living in France until they both moved to New York. The marriage breaks down, and the wife moves to California. Suppose that the husband wants to file for divorce in Europe. A French court would have jurisdiction under Article 7 if no more than three years have elapsed since the couple's departure from France, but the petition could also be filed in Greece or Sweden, both qualifying as *forum patriae*. Without a choice by the parties, these courts would have to apply New York law, as the law of the couple's last common habitual residence. If the spouses could reach an agreement on the law to be applied, they could rule out the application of New York law by choosing either Greek law or Swedish law, as the law of their respective nationalities, or, if the action is brought in France, French law as lex fori.[21]

Most of the debate over this provision, thus far, concerned the *form* of the choice-of-law agreement and the *time period* within which it should be concluded. Apparently, some member states are not satisfied with a formal requirement that calls for a written agreement that is dated and signed by both spouses. To meet their objections, the proposal now features an extra rule on form:[22] if, at the time the agreement is concluded, either of the spouses is habitually resident in a member state providing for stricter formal requirements (a notarial document? witnesses?) those requirements should be satisfied. If the agreement is part of a marriage contract, the formal requirements for such contracts apply.

With regard to the time factor, the proposal allows the parties to choose the applicable law at any time before the court is seized, and possibly even later. The draft of 28 June 2007 offers several options: at the latest, the agreement must have been

---

20 While Article 20b refers to the *common* national law of the spouses, Article 20a allows them to choose the national law of *either* spouse.

21 If the spouses had agreed on the applicable law while still living in France, or at a time when one of them was still living in that country, they could have chosen French law as *lex domicilii (communis)* under Article 20a(a) or 20a(b). The time of designation is decisive.

22 The same applies to the form of choice-of-forum agreements: Article 3a(3). In the draft of 13 February 2007, the additional rules on formalities were still couched as an option. In the later drafts, they are presented as a complement to the basic requirement of a written, dated and signed document.

concluded (1) at the time the court is seized, or (2) at the first court hearing, or (3) in the absence of a court hearing, in the course of the first exchange of writs or, in case of a joint application, in the writ of application. An alternative solution, mentioned in a footnote, would allow the spouses to designate the applicable law before the court in the course of the proceedings if the law of the forum so provides. Curiously, the debate has not focused on the period *before* the court is seized.[23] Allowing the parties to choose the applicable law – as well as the competent court – even before they are married would seem to be a bigger problem than allowing them to do so during the proceedings. How can they assess the consequences of an agreement that must be carried out, if at all, in a distant future they do not want to contemplate as yet, under circumstances they cannot possibly foresee? Can one of them later opt out of the agreement without the cooperation of the other? Which law governs issues of consent or the principle of *rebus sic stantibus* when raised during the divorce proceedings? Such questions are more difficult to answer, in my opinion, than the ones now under discussion in Brussels.

4. SOME REMARKS ON THE POINTS OF DEPARTURE OF MODERN CHOICE OF LAW

Before trying to assess the merits of the Commission's conflict-of-law rules, I should like to make a few brief remarks on the principles underlying modern choice of law as it has evolved in Europe since the 1960s. It is probably common knowledge that the choice-of-law process no longer depends on the principle of the closest connection alone.[24] There are at least three other principles supporting the application of the law of another country than the one with which the case may be deemed to be most closely connected in a geographical sense. First of all, we now acknowledge the *principle of party autonomy*, allowing the parties to choose the applicable law themselves, at least in areas of substantive law where social or economic policies do not hamper their freedom of disposition. Examples can be found in the area of contracts and torts, and, to some extent, in the field of matrimonial property, maintenance obligations, succession, and even divorce, as shown by Article 20a Brussels II-*ter*.

---

23 A proposal submitted by the Dutch delegation, only allowing the parties to choose the forum and/or the applicable law when divorce proceedings are imminent (six months before the court is seized at the earliest) has found little support.

24 See, generally, Th.M. de Boer, Facultative Choice of Law: The Procedural Status of Choice-of-Law Rules and Foreign Law, Chapter II: Methods and objectives of private international law, *Recueil des Cours* Vol. 257 (1996), p. 223–427, at p. 271–302. See also: Dieter Martiny, Objectives and Values of (Private) International Law in Family Law, in: *International Family Law for the European Union* (eds. Johan Meeusen *et al.*), Antwerp/Oxford, 2007, p. 69–99.

Furthermore, we have created conflicts rules that reflect the objectives of the corresponding substantive law rather than an abstracted conception of the closest connection. First of all, there are now choice-of-law rules based on the *function* of the corresponding substantive law. Where substantive law focuses on the protection of the weaker party, such as consumers, employees, children, or maintenance creditors, that focus is translated into a connecting factor referring to the law of the weaker party's daily environment, not necessarily the state with which the case is most closely connected in a geographical way.[25] Examples can be found in Article 4 of the Hague Maintenance Convention of 1973, duplicated in the Commission's proposal for a Regulation on Maintenance, or in the provisions on consumer transactions and employment contracts in the Rome Convention of 1980, duplicated in the 'Rome I' proposal. The principle underlying this type of conflicts rule is known as the *principle of functional allocation*.[26] Secondly, in most European systems of conflicts law, there are rules based on the so-called '*favor*' principle, offering a choice between various alternatives, where the choice is dictated by a predetermined substantive result.[27] Thus, we have choice-of-law rules supporting the *favor negotii* (pertaining to matters of form), or the *favor infantis* (pertaining to the position of illegitimate children), the *favor matrimonii* (a valid marriage is better than a marriage that is null an void), or the *favor divortii* (a law that supports the possibility of divorce is favoured over a law that does not). Another example can be found, again, in the Maintenance Convention 1973, where Articles 5 and 6 allow the application of the common national law or,

---

25 Under the heading 'Protection of the weaker party, child protection', MARTINY, *ibid.* at p. 93, acknowledges the emergence of a new type of conflicts rule: 'Often under national conflict of law rules the law of the nationality of the child is applied. However, today there is also a tendency to apply the law of the habitual residence of the child. This law generally best reflects the situation of the child. The application of the law of the creditor's habitual residence for maintenance claims also follows this concept.'

26 In the Netherlands, it is also known as the 'protection principle' (*beschermingsbeginsel*), as a conflicts rule of this type is meant to protect the weaker party. I am not altogether happy with this appellation, as it suggests that the law designated on the basis of this principle *eo ipso* affords protection to the weaker party. This is not true. Under Article 4 of the Hague Maintenance Convention 1973, for instance, maintenance creditors – even if Article 4 calls for the application of their domiciliary law – might not be entitled to maintenance if their domiciliary law does not provide for it. Similarly, Article 5(3) Rome Convention 1980 leaves a consumer empty-handed if he or she happens to live in a country where consumers are not entitled to protection. The best that could be said about the so-called 'protection principle' is that it achieves equal treatment of consumers, employees, maintenance creditors, children, etc., regardless of whether they are involved in an international or in a domestic relationship. Under Article 5(3) Rome Convention, for instance, all consumers living in the same country will be treated equally, whether their contractual partner is established abroad or not.

27 *Cf.* MARTINY, *supra*, note 24, p. 92: 'In some cases private international law cannot pretend not to be interested in the concrete result of a legal conflict. Instead it favours a certain result.' For an extensive treatment of alternative reference rules, see: HARALD BAUM, *Alternativanknüpfungen: Begriff, Funktion, Kritik*, Tübingen, 1985.

respectively, lex fori if the maintenance creditor would be left empty-handed under his or her domiciliary law.[28]

Apart from policy-oriented choice-of-law rules, there are all kinds of conflicts provisions expressing some kind of preference for lex fori. One example is the type of rule in which the applicable law is displaced if it does not meet the forum's minimum standards, as, for instance, a rule referring to the forum's own divorce law if divorce would not be possible under the applicable foreign law.[29] Finally, there are provisions, both in international conventions and in national conflicts laws, giving priority to 'overriding mandatory rules' of the forum state, also known as '*lois de police*', or '*Eingriffsnormen*', or '*norme di applicazione necessaria*'.

In other words, the designation of the applicable law no longer depends exclusively on the closest connection in a geographical sense. In some areas, the policies underlying substantive forum law have been translated into conflicts rules that are no longer blind to the final outcome. As a result, there is now less need for public policy and other corrective devices than there was in the days when mechanical and strictly neutral choice-of-law rules dictated results that were clearly inappropriate, the days when courts tried to bend the orthodox choice-of-law result to what they deemed just and fair by resorting to public policy, or to result-oriented characterization, selective application of the doctrines of renvoi, the incidental question, etc. The days, in short, in which private international law earned its reputation of being 'a dismal swamp, filled with quaking quagmires, and inhabited by learned but eccentric law professors.'[30]

5. THE POLICIES UNDERLYING SUBSTANTIVE DIVORCE LAW

After this methodological detour, let us focus again on divorce in the conflict of laws. Given that modern conflicts rules are based on various choice-of-law principles, we should ask ourselves whether the nature of substantive divorce law calls for a conflicts rule that, in some way, reflects the social policy with regard to

---

28 See also: Art. 13 of the proposal for a regulation on maintenance obligations, COM (2005) 649, 15 December 2005; latest draft: 11281/2007 JUSTCIV 180 of 28 June 2007.

29 *E.g.* Art. 17(1) German *Einführungsgesetz zum Bürgerlichen Gesetzbuche* (*EGBGB*); Art. 61(3) Swiss Statute on Private International Law of 1989. *Cf.* Article 20b(2) Brussels II-*ter* in all drafts following the Commission's proposal: 'Where the law applicable pursuant to paragraph 1(a), (b) or (c) does not provide for divorce, the law of the forum shall apply.' See also the text accompanying note 15.

30 W. Prosser, Interstate Publication, 51 *Mich. L.Rev.* 959, 971 (1953).

divorce a state or a group of states should like to further. Obviously, the states that have adopted the Rome Convention of 1980 all subscribe to a policy of protecting consumers and employees. Similarly, a state that supports a policy of equal treatment of legitimate and illegitimate children is likely to adopt a conflicts rule for the recognition of illegitimate children that calls for the application of a law favouring recognition. In areas of substantive law where the parties are not hampered in their freedom of disposition by rules of mandatory law – in other words: in areas where the substantive law does not express a distinct social policy – the conflicts rule is likely to be based on the principle of party autonomy or, in case the parties did not make use of their freedom of choice, by the principle of the closest connection.

So, the first question to be answered is whether the member states of the European Union want to further a distinct policy with regard to divorce, or could it be said that their position vis-à-vis divorce is completely neutral? Is divorce a facility that should be available to any spouse who no longer wants to be bound by the bonds of marriage, or should it be an *ultimum remedium* available only in the most desperate cases? Is divorce meant to offer an abused spouse an escape from an otherwise irrevocable contract? Should divorce be refused if there are still minor children to be raised? Or should it be seen as a right to which any married person is entitled, whatever the cause of their dissatisfaction with their present status?[31]

Having surveyed the grounds for divorce as listed on the websites of the Commission on European Family Law and the European Judicial Network, I came to the obvious conclusion that there are fundamental differences between the member states as to the objectives their divorce laws are meant to achieve. They range from the rigid position of Malta, where divorce is not allowed at all, to the liberal attitude of Spain, where divorce will be granted for no specific reason as long as the marriage has lasted at least three months.[32] In between, there is a wide variety of conditions, such as mutual consent, or in the absence of agreement, fault on the part of one of the spouses, or a de facto separation for at least six months in the Czech Republic to five years in Cyprus.[33] In quite a few member states, a divorce

31 On the values and objectives underlying various divorce laws, see, generally: Masha Antokolskaia, *Harmonisation of Family Law in Europe: A Historical Perspective*, Antwerp/Oxford, 2006, notably Chapter 14. A (no longer quite up-to-date) overview of the grounds for divorce in 22 European countries can be found in: *European Family Law in Action, Vol. I: Grounds for Divorce* (eds. Katharina Boele-Woelki *et al.*), Antwerp/Oxford/New York, 2003.

32 See Article 86 Spanish Civil Code, as amended by *Ley 15/2005 de 8 julio 2005*, *B.O.E.* no. 163, 9 July 2005, p. 24458 ff.

33 The five-year period applies to marriages concluded before the adoption of the 'Marriage Law of 2003' and to marriages concluded abroad. If the marriage is within the scope of the Marriage Law 2003, the separation period is four years rather than five, the same duration as prescribed by Irish or Greek law. In France, the separation period used to be six years. Since the

may be refused if it would be detrimental to the interests of the couple's minor children,[34] or if the financial support of the children and the other spouse cannot be warranted.[35] In other words: divorce can hardly be considered as a phenomenon in which the community to which the spouses belong, or have belonged, has no interest. On the contrary, most states display a very strong interest in the dissolution of a marriage, resulting in rather restrictive grounds for divorce. All in all, it can be concluded that some member states – and I think they are a minority – support a policy of allowing divorce by mutual consent or for non-specific reasons, while other states continue to adhere to a type of divorce which depends on fault or, at least, on a prolonged period of separation. The latter type reflects a strong public interest, while the former confirms a trend towards privatization.[36] In between are those systems that make an exception for divorce by mutual consent, but rely on specific grounds in the absence of an agreement.[37]

6. THE METHODOLOGICAL VALIDITY OF THE PROPOSED CHOICE-OF-LAW RULES

Which conclusions with respect to private international law can be drawn from these observations on substantive divorce law? In my view, the first conclusion is

enactment of *Loi no. 2004-439 du 26 mai 2004 relative au divorce*, it has been reduced to two years: Art. 238(1) *Code civil*.

34 See, *e.g.*, Article 1568 of the German Civil Code. According to the information available on the website of the European Judicial Network – which, with regard to the grounds for divorce of some member states, has proved to be not quite reliable – a divorce may be refused in Latvia 'in exceptional circumstances where the preservation of a marriage is necessary for specific reasons relating to the interests of a minor born within the marriage', a phrase that could have been copied from the German provision.

35 *Cf.* Article 5(1)(c) of the Irish Family Law (Divorce) Act 1996, and the conclusion by Geoffrey Shannon in his reply to question 4 of the CEFL 'Questionnaire on Grounds for Divorce and Maintenance between Former Spouses': 'The Irish court has the power to refuse to grant a decree of divorce in circumstances where it is not satisfied that proper financial arrangements have been put in place to ensure that the spouses and dependent family members have been catered for...': *European Family Law in Action, supra*, note 31, at p. 86/87. In answer to the same questionnaire (question 21), Andrzej Maczynski and Tomasz Sokolowski describe a similar exception in the divorce law of Poland: 'Grave financial or moral hardship to one spouse may exclude the divorce if the court finds it contrary to the principles of social intercourse'. *Ibid.*, at p. 268.

36 Even so, divorce brings about a change of personal status, which is usually considered a matter regarding public policy. That is why in most member states a divorce can only be granted by a court of law. On the other hand, an administrative divorce (granted by an administrative authority) is allowed in Denmark and Portugal. As a means to reduce the workload of the courts, it is now under discussion in some other member states, notably the Netherlands and the Czech Republic.

37 For instance: under Belgian law, a divorce may be granted on the ground of mutual consent, or, in the absence thereof, on the ground of fault (adultery, acts of violence, abuse, *injures graves*), or on the ground of a separation for at least two years.

this: the national views on divorce as a social phenomenon – or to put it differently: the social policies underlying the substantive divorce laws of the member states – are too divergent to support the unification of their conflicts rules on the basis of any other choice-of-law principle but the principle of the closest connection. The principle of party autonomy can hardly be reconciled with the notion that divorce cannot be granted on the ground of mutual consent, a view that still prevails in a number of member states. The principle, allowing a choice between alternative laws, is useless as long as we are not agreed on the result to be favoured: dissolution of the marriage at the mere request of either spouse, or preservation of the marital status as long as possible. The principle of functional allocation, calling for the application of the law of the weaker party's social environment, cannot be resorted to either, because it is impossible to mark either husband or wife as the weaker party.[38] That leaves us – at least as a basis for unification – with the neutral choice-of-law criterion of the closest connection.

My second conclusion is that the strong social policies expressed in the divorce laws of the various member states are likely to be ignored if a so-called 'neutral' conflicts rule is adopted, a rule which is blind to the result it achieves in terms of substantive law. In other words, an impartial, value-free rule based on the principle of the closest connection is unfit to designate the applicable law in an area in which the corresponding substantive laws reflect deeply ingrained cultural and perhaps religious attitudes of the communities concerned. This conclusion is confirmed by the inclusion, in the draft of 12 January 2007, of an exception allowing the application of lex fori where the applicable law 'does not provide for divorce'.[39] Whatever the proper interpretation of that phrase, it is clear that this provision introduces an alternative reference rule allowing a choice between *lex causae* and *lex fori* in favor of divorce. I consider this addition as an expression of a *European* policy, supporting divorce at least as an *ultimum remedium* that cannot be denied on the sole ground that it is not allowed in the state with which the spouses are supposed to be most closely connected. Yet, I am afraid that it does not solve the problems that are likely to arise under a choice-of-law approach that is still basically 'neutral'. The same is true of the proposed escape clause displacing the law of the last common habitual residence in favor of lex fori.[40] While it is obviously inspired by the *favor divortii* – what other motive could one have for requesting

---

38 At the CEFL conference in Oslo, someone suggested to me that a respondent opposing the divorce should be considered as the weaker party. I cannot quite see why a respondent in divorce proceedings would be more in need of protection than any other party acting as a defendant. Carried to its extreme, this suggestion implies that any lawsuit should be governed by the defendant's personal law.

39 *Supra*, note 15 and accompanying text.

40 *Supra*, note 19 and accompanying text.

the displacement of a foreign divorce law?[41] – its effect is reduced by the requirement that the spouses had their last common habitual residence abroad for less than three years.

My third conclusion follows from the other two. I think it is unwise to force the harmonization of choice-of-law rules in a sensitive area such as divorce, where the substantive laws of the member states are based on conflicting policies, and to do so on the neutral basis of the closest connection. Unless we assume that judges are robots, mindlessly applying the divorce law designated by the Regulation, it is to be expected that they will try to escape a choice-of-law result that does not sit well with the standards and values cherished in the forum state. If they are obliged to apply foreign law, chances are that they will find that law too liberal or too strict, depending on the prevailing attitude towards divorce in the forum state. Two examples may illustrate this view. Let us suppose that a Dutchman has been posted in Ireland to work there for a Dutch company for a period of five years. His wife has joined him, and the couple have lived in Ireland for just three years when the husband has an extramarital affair. The marriage breaks down, and the wife decides to go back to Holland. She files for divorce in the Netherlands, and unless she and her husband have chosen Dutch law, the Dutch court will have no alternative but to apply Irish law, as the spouses were last habitually resident in that country and the husband still resides there.[42] Under Irish law, a divorce can only be granted if there is no reasonable prospect of reconciliation and the spouses have been living apart for at least four years. As a judge, I would be inclined to manipulate the connecting factors. I could say, for instance, that the spouses were only temporarily in Ireland and that they thus retained their habitual residence in the Netherlands. Or I could refuse point-blank to apply Irish law, finding some reason why it would violate Dutch public policy. At any rate, I would be greatly

41 Assuming that the respondent is opposed to divorce, he or she may have an interest in requesting the application of lex fori if it is less divorce-friendly than the law of the spouses' last habitual residence. For instance: a Swedish husband and an Irish wife have been living in Sweden for less than three years when their marriage breaks down and the wife returns to Ireland. If the husband brings suit in Ireland, the court would have to apply Swedish law as the law of the couple's last common habitual residence, unless the wife requests the application of Irish law. Since the escape clause was meant to further the *favor divortii*, I think the right to request the application of lex fori should only be granted to petitioners. In the Presidency's 'non-paper' of 21 March 2007, the text of the escape clause still refers to a request by 'the applicant'. In the draft of 28 June 2007, the proposed text refers to 'one of the spouses'. If this text were to be adopted, petitioners should be advised to look for a divorce-friendly forum: in that case, the escape clause would be of no use to the respondent.

42 If an escape clause were to be adopted as phrased in the draft of 28 June 2007 (*supra*, note 40 and accompanying text) and the couple had been living together in Ireland for less than three years, the wife could request the application of the Dutch lex fori instead of Irish law. To be on the safe side, I have let my hypothetical couple live in Ireland for three years. Without the escape clause, this period could be much shorter.

frustrated by being unable to grant a divorce to a Dutch petitioner living in the Netherlands, on the sole ground that her Dutch husband still lives in Ireland, the country of the spouses' last habitual residence. If the respondent had moved to Sweden, I could have applied Dutch law as their common national law, and if he had been Irish and moved to Sweden, Dutch law would be applicable as lex fori. Thus, the Brussels II-*ter* proposal turns divorce choice of law into a lottery.

My second example illustrates the reverse situation. A Polish man, living in the Netherlands, marries an Irish woman in 2005. In a prenuptial agreement, they have chosen Dutch law as the law applicable to their divorce.[43] After one year in Holland, the couple move to Poland, where the wife acquires Polish citizenship. Ten years later, just after their second child is born, the marriage breaks down as a result of the husband's adultery. The husband wants to marry his new girlfriend and sues for divorce in Poland, claiming that Dutch law applies as the law chosen by the spouses in 2005. Under Dutch law, a divorce will be granted if the marriage has irretrievably broken down, which is automatically the case if one of the spouses petitions for divorce. Under Polish law, the court should take account of the effect the divorce may have on the welfare of the couple's minor children, and besides, an adulterous spouse has no right to ask for divorce anyhow. What would a Polish court be inclined to do? Under Brussels II-*ter*, it would be bound to apply Dutch law, but I have a feeling that it would be very much tempted to resort to some kind of escape device. It could argue, for instance, that this it not an international case, as both parties are Polish citizens and living in Poland. Or it could argue that a choice of Dutch law is only allowed if it is the law of the forum, or that Dutch conflicts law does not permit choice-of-law agreements when they are part of a marriage contract.[44] Or it could declare the liberal Dutch law to be in violation of Polish public policy.

43 Such a choice would be valid under Art. 20a(1)(a) Brussels II-*ter*. In a transitional provision – Article 1a of the draft of 28 June 2007, at p. 12 – agreements on choice of forum or choice of law in matters of divorce and legal separation are declared effective even when concluded before the Regulation enters into force, provided such an agreement fulfils the conditions of Art. 3a or, respectively, Art. 20a and is in accordance 'with the national law of a Member State'. The latter phrase apparently refers to the law of the member state whose court or, respectively, whose law was chosen by the parties. Under Dutch conflicts law, spouses have a right to choose Dutch law as the lex divortii: Art. 1(4) *Wet conflictenrecht echtscheiding*.

44 Actually, Dutch law does not expressly prohibit forum selection clauses or choice-of-law clauses laid down in prenuptial agreements. However, the Polish court might base its finding on the position the Dutch delegation has taken in the negotiations on Brussels II-*ter* with regard to the date when such agreements might be concluded at the earliest; see *supra*, note 23 and accompanying text.

7. ALTERNATIVE SOLUTIONS

In my view, the choice-of-law approach adopted in Article 20b of the Brussels II-*ter* proposal is methodologically unsound. Its main shortcoming is its focus on the closest connection as an overriding choice-of-law consideration in an area in which strong social policies determine the contents of the corresponding substantive law. The fact that those policies are largely incompatible does not justify a 'neutral' approach on the basis of the closest connection, as its results will prove to be unsatisfactory, not to say unacceptable, in cases in which the applicable foreign law is in direct conflict with lex fori. As a consequence, the courts will be tempted to resort to all kinds of escape devices for which modern conflicts law no longer has much use.

If the Commission's choice-of-law proposal should be rejected on these grounds, one might well ask: what are the alternatives? I think there are two, perhaps three. The first one is in line with the position the Dutch Parliament has taken in a letter to the European Commission,[45] in which the proposed harmonization of divorce choice of law was rejected as being contrary to the principles of subsidiarity and proportionality, and on the ground that there was no evidence that the Commission's proposal would further the proper functioning of the internal market, as required by Article 65 of the EC Treaty.[46] The conclusion was that the provisions on choice of law should be deleted from the proposal. Since I fully agree with this point of view, that would be my first alternative. However, the Commission was quick to reply[47] that it was not impressed by these objections, and I am told that very few member states – apart from the United Kingdom and Ireland – agreed with the Dutch view. So, to be realistic, let me suggest a more constructive alternative. It has the attraction of being simple, completely in line with the objectives of choice-of-law harmonization, and allowing the member states to preserve their own ideological views on divorce. The only conflicts rule that meets all these

---

45 Letter to the European Commission dated 26 September 2006; *Kamerstukken* 2006–2007, 30671, E and no. 5.

46 *Cf.* JOHAN MEEUSEN, System Shopping in European Private International Law in Family Matters, in: *International Family Law for the European Union, supra*, note 24, p. 239–278, at p. 270: 'Unfortunately, no satisfactory legal basis for Community harmonisation of private international law in family matters seems available at this moment.' *Id.*, Op weg naar een communautair internationaal familie(vermogens)recht? Enkele Europeesrechtelijke beschouwingen (Report for the 2006 meeting of the Netherlands International Law Association), *Mededelingen van de Nederlandse Vereniging voor Internationaal Recht* no. 33 (2006), p. 1–73, at p. 15 ff., p. 33 ff., suggesting that the proper legal basis for the harmonization of conflicts law should be found in the EU's general objective of offering its citizens an 'area of freedom, security and justice' rather than in Article 65 (at p. 41).

47 Letter to the Dutch Parliament dated 7 December 2006, *Kamerstukken* 2006–2007, no. 30671, F and no. 6.

conditions is the one referring to forum law. In other words, Article 20b(1) should be reduced to its final paragraph.

Let me explain why I think this is a reasonable alternative. First of all, no member state could have any objection to applying its own divorce law, so there would be no need for resorting to all kinds of twisted reasoning or the blunt axe of public policy to escape an unwelcome choice-of-law result. Second, the main objective of the harmonization of divorce choice of law, according to the Commission, is to further legal certainty and predictability. In international cases, spouses should know in advance which law will govern their separation or divorce. That kind of certainty and predictability, if you believe in it, can be achieved by a *lex fori in foro proprio* approach. No petitioner or respondent could be unduly surprised if a local court applies local law. In my own practice as a judge, I have noticed that foreign spouses naturally assumed I would apply Dutch law. The suggestion that their common national law might be applicable came as an unexpected and in many cases unwelcome surprise. A regulation requiring all member states to apply their own law in divorce cases unless the parties have chosen the applicable law themselves, puts an end to the discordance between the conflict-of-law rules of the member states. A choice-of-law rule referring to lex fori is no less a conflicts rule than the one referring to the (last) common residence or nationality of the spouses, and if the European Community is bent on harmonizing conflicts rules I do not see why its conflicts rule for divorce could not be modelled on a rule that, by a combination of jurisdiction and choice of law, is in effect more widespread in the member states than any other, and definitely more current than the rule under discussion.

Thirdly, in its reply to the Dutch Parliament the European Commission once more advanced the argument that harmonization of divorce choice of law would prevent a 'rush to the court'. Obviously, a lex fori approach does not solve the problem of forum-shopping. On the other hand, it has been emphasized in several comments that there is no evidence to support the suggestion that forum shopping frequently occurs. If it does, it has probably nothing to do with the divorce as such, but only with the parties' intention to swing the law applicable to maintenance obligations or, perhaps, matrimonial property.[48] Furthermore, I submit

---

48 It is hard to see why a spouse who does *not* want to be divorced should 'rush' to a court to start divorce proceedings. On the other hand, if both spouses want a divorce one of them might benefit from seizing a court that will grant the divorce, under the applicable law, on the ground of the respondent's fault. As a result, the respondent may be prevented from claiming maintenance. Conversely, a petitioner may benefit from seizing the court of a state where maintenance between ex-spouses is governed by the lex divortii (as prescribed by Art. 8 of the Hague Maintenance Convention 1973) and that law is more favourable to maintenance creditors than the one that would be applied by the courts of another state. Such benefits might justify the

that forum-shopping, if it is a real problem at all, had better be countered by a reduction of jurisdictional grounds than by a colourless uniform conflicts rule that invites judicial manipulation.

Finally, I should like to say something about the proposition that a uniform conflicts rule for divorce – or any other topic of family law for that matter – will promote the proper functioning of the internal market. In my view, the choice between lex fori and foreign law in matters of family law has no bearing on the internal market in general, or on the free movement of persons in particular. Whether or not a divorce will be granted, a maintenance claim upheld, an adoption allowed, a name changed, paternity established, etc., etc. – the application of law X or law Y *as such* does not affect the freedom of movement of the persons involved. That freedom can only be impeded if the status quo created in one member state, either by operation of law or by judicial decision, is not recognized in another. Choice of law has nothing to do with it. As long as all member states are obliged to recognize a divorce granted in an EU sister state, regardless of the applicable law and regardless of the substantive grounds for divorce, a uniform choice-of-law rule referring to the law of the forum cannot be an obstacle to the free movement of persons.

Even if I may have convinced most of my colleagues attending the CEFL Conference in Oslo,[49] where I presented my views as stated above, I do not have the illusion that my contribution will slow down the momentum of the legislative process in Brussels, which has already gone far beyond the stage of fundamental criticism and methodological objections. My best hope, then, is that major support will still come for the French proposal to apply lex fori if neither party raises the choice-of-law issue and insists on the application of foreign law. If, in the absence of a choice by the parties, an outright reference to lex fori is considered a bridge too far, facultative choice of law is probably the next best thing.

---

harmonization of choice of law with regard to maintenance, or the abolition of fault-based divorce, but a rush to the courts, if any, will not be prevented by uniform conflicts rules for divorce as such.

49 During the debate following my presentation, no speaker came forward to defend the Commission's proposal against my criticism. Instead, there was widespread support for a lex fori approach.

THE MAINTENANCE REGULATION: A CRITICAL ASSESSMENT OF THE COMMISSION'S PROPOSAL

Michael Hellner*

1. YET ANOTHER REGULATION

In December 2005 the Commission presented a proposal for a Regulation on Maintenance.[1] The proposed Regulation will, if adopted without substantial changes, have a very wide substantive scope and will cover all issues of private international law as well as including the harmonisation of certain matters of a procedural law nature.[2] There is, however, no shortage of international instruments regarding the recovery of maintenance claims. There are no less than four Hague Conventions: the two conventions on applicable law from 1956 and 1973 and the two conventions on recognition and enforcement from 1958 and 1973.[3] In addition, there is the 1956 New York Convention on administrative cooperation.[4] Maintenance claims also fall within the scope of the Brussels I Regulation and the

* The author is a member of the Swedish delegations to the Council working party considering the proposal (the Civil Law Committee) for a new Regulation and the ongoing work on a new Convention on maintenance at the Hague Conference for Private International Law. It should be underscored that the opinions expressed in this paper are those of the author and not necessarily those of the Swedish government.

1 Proposal for a Council Regulation on jurisdiction, applicable law, recognition and enforcement of decisions and cooperation in matters relating to maintenance obligations, OM(2005) 649 final, Brussels 15 December 2005.

2 In an earlier preliminary draft proposal (a "discussion paper") presented at an expert meeting on 12 May 2005, the Commission contemplated no less than three legal instruments: a Regulation on applicable law, a Regulation on recovery of maintenance claims and a Directive to improve the recovery of maintenance claims by establishing minimum common rules relating to access to information, decision making and enforcement of decisions.

3 Convention of 24 October 1956 on the law applicable to maintenance obligations towards children; Convention of 2 October 1973 on the law applicable to maintenance obligations; Convention of 15 April 1958 concerning the recognition and enforcement of decisions relating to maintenance obligations towards children; and the Convention of 2 October 1973 on the recognition and enforcement of decisions relating to maintenance obligations.

4 Convention of 20 June 1956 on the recovery abroad of maintenance, concluded at the United Nations.

Lugano Convention.[5] As if this were not enough, there are also several other bilateral or multilateral treaties that cover the area of maintenance.[6] Finally, work is ongoing at the Hague Conference for Private International Law to modernise the rules in the existing Conventions (including "taking over" the New York Convention). A diplomatic conference will be held in November 2007 and we can look forward to the birth of one or two further conventions (depending on what form will be given to the rules on the applicable law – an optional protocol has been discussed). This means that in an EU Member State there can be as many as a dozen or so international legal instruments applicable to a cross-border maintenance claim.

Given the work going on in The Hague to achieve a modernisation and given the plethora of existing instruments, the question that begs an answer is what the added value of the proposed Regulation would be. As late as in November 2000 the JHA Council stated in its "Action Programme" that "[a]lthough the guarantee of effective and rapid recovery of maintenance claims is indeed essential to the welfare of very large numbers of people in Europe, this does not necessarily imply that a separate legal instrument has to be drawn up. Maintenance creditors are already covered by provisions of the Brussels Convention and of the future Brussels I Regulation".[7] But in the 2004 "Hague Programme" the European Council urged the Commission to prepare a "draft instrument on the recognition and enforcement of decisions on maintenance, including precautionary measures and provisional enforcement".[8] The European Community has once on an earlier occasion attempted to adopt special rules for the recovery of maintenance claims, but the 1990 Rome Convention on Maintenance[9] was unsuccessful and never entered into force. It is our firm belief that that fate will not be shared by the present proposal. Something along the lines of what has been proposed will most likely be adopted.[10] The aim of this paper is to asses whether the Commission's

5 Council Regulation (EC) No. 44/2001 of 22 December 2000 on jurisdiction and the recognition and enforcement of judgments in civil and commercial matters, OJ L 12, 16 January 2001, p. 1 and the Convention of 16 September 1988 on jurisdiction and the enforcement of judgments in civil and commercial matters, OJ L 319, 25 November 1988, p. 9.

6 One example well known to this author is the Convention of 23 March 1962 between Sweden, Denmark, Finland, Iceland and Norway concerning the enforcement of maintenance claims (to our knowledge it has never been translated into English).

7 See the Draft programme of measures for the implementation of the principle of mutual recognition of decisions in civil and commercial matters (the Action Programme) adopted by the JHA Council on 30 November 2000, OJ C 12, 15 January 2001, p. 1 at p. 4.

8 Annex I to the Presidency Conclusions of the Brussels European Council 4/5 November 2005, p. 41.

9 Rome Convention of 6 November 1990 between the Member States of the European Communities on the Simplification of Procedures for the Recovery of Maintenance Payments.

10 However, the Council Working Party has suggested important amendments to the original proposal. We will return to those as we describe the proposal.

proposal is the answer to a real need, and in doing so inevitably providing the interested reader with a general description of the proposed Regulation.

In order to properly assess the proposal we need to identify what the problems with cross-border enforcement of maintenance claims are today.[11] There is, after all, something to be said for the proverb "if it ain't broke don't fix it!" It is submitted that the main problems with the cross-border enforcement of maintenance claims mainly concern the quality of enforcement and the administrative assistance offered.[12] Enforcement is slow and ineffective due to lengthy exequatur procedures and poor enforcement mechanisms in general in some states. Some Member States have poorly functioning and understaffed central authorities that are slow and provide only limited service. Moreover, a practical problem is that some states, notably France and Belgium, will not give any administrative assistance for the establishment of maintenance (inter alia on the location of the debtor and his assets) since it can be argued that the New York Convention only covers enforcement situations, and that some states, notably Germany and Austria, only provide administrative assistance to individuals and not to Central Authorities due to a literal interpretation of Article 1 of the New York Convention.[13]

Is the proposal aimed at solving these problems? The objective of the future Regulation is described as being "to eliminate all obstacles which still today prevent the recovery of maintenance within the European Union".[14] In this context the reader should bear in mind that the foremost purpose of the work in the area of judicial cooperation in civil matters is the mutual recognition of judicial decisions and judgments.[15] The "Action Programme" labels all measures as either directly affecting mutual recognition or as ancillary thereto.[16] This emphasis on mutual recognition is not clear from the present legal basis in the EC Treaty, *viz.*

---

11 A study of the functioning of the Hague Conventions and the New York Convention was made by the Deputy Secretary General of the Hague Conference, M. Pelichet, in 1995. See M. Pelichet, "Note on the operation of the Hague Conventions relating to maintenance obligations and of the New York Convention on the Recovery Abroad of Maintenance", available at http://hcch.e-vision.nl/index_en.php?act=publications.details&pid=2984&dtid=2.

12 Here the author would like to thank Ms Anna Svantesson, an expert at the Swedish Social Insurance Agency with more than 25 years of experience in working with cross-border enforcement of maintenance claims, for her input.

13 It should be noted that the Commission gives a slightly different problem description. See SEC(2005) 1629, Brussels 15 December 2005, Commission Staff Working Document annexed to the Proposal for a Council Regulation on jurisdiction, applicable law, recognition and enforcement of decisions and cooperation in matters relating to maintenance obligations, with an impact assessment, p. 19.

14 COM(2005) 649 final, p. 3.

15 See the Presidency Conclusions from the meeting of the European Council in Tampere 15–16 October 1999 (the Tampere Conclusions), paras 33–37.

16 See the Action Programme (*supra* note 7), p. 5.

Article 65, but is explicit in Article 69d of the EU Draft Reform Treaty (which seeks to pick up the pieces from the Treaty Establishing a Constitution for Europe).[17] Article 69d states in its *chapeau* that "The Union shall develop judicial cooperation in civil matters having cross-border implications, *based on the principle of mutual recognition* [emphasis added] of judgments and decisions in extra-judicial cases." The proposal must therefore in particular be judged on what its effects on cross-border enforcement can be expected to be.

2. AN ASSESSMENT OF THE REGULATION

The proposal is very ambitious and covers all aspects of private international law and several procedural law issues. It is 53 articles long and contains rules on the jurisdiction of courts (Chapter II); the applicable law (Chapter III); common procedural rules, which most notably includes rules on the service of documents and default judgments (Chapter IV); enforceability and enforcement of decisions, including the abolition of the exequatur procedure, direct enforceability of maintenance judgments, garnishment of salary, and the freezing of assets (Chapters V and VI); and administrative cooperation (Chapter VIII).

2.1. SUBSTANTIVE SCOPE

The proposed Regulation also has a very wide substantive scope in that it basically covers all kinds of maintenance arising from family relationships. This has caused concern in Member States that are not quite ready to abolish exequatur for all types of maintenance and would rather see a limitation to e.g. children, at least when it comes to the abolition of exequatur. However, negotiations have shown that these states constitute a small minority.

Nonetheless, it should be noted that since maintenance is a matter relating to family law, the co-decision procedure is not applicable, and the Regulation can be adopted by the Council alone, acting unanimously after consulting the European Parliament. (cf. Article 67(5) EC). The Commission has, due to "the hybrid nature of the concept of maintenance obligation – a family matter in origin but a pecuniary issue in its implementation, like any other claim", urged the Council to make use of the so-called "passerelle" in Article 67(2) EC and make the co-decision

[17] Article III-269 of the proposed Constitution for Europe contained the same wording.

procedure in Article 251 EC applicable.[18] The proposal does not appear to have met with favour from the Member States.

2.2. GEOGRAPHIC SCOPE

Quite unlike the case of the Brussels I and Brussels II bis Regulations,[19] there is no limitation in the geographic scope of the proposed Regulation. The Brussels I Regulation is limited in its scope to situations where the defendant has his habitual residence in a Member State (Article 3).[20] If such is not the case, an applicant may avail himself of the national rules on jurisdiction (Article 4). The Brussels II bis Regulation applies in divorce matters to situations where the respondent is either habitually resident in a Member State or is a national of a Member State (Article 6) or in matters concerning parental responsibility if the child has its habitual residence in a Member State (Article 8).[21] If this is not the case, the national rules on jurisdiction apply (Articles 7 and 14).

In the proposed Maintenance Regulation there is no room left for national law. The rules on jurisdiction are always applicable to courts in the Member States.[22] If none of the grounds of jurisdiction in Articles 3 to 5 are applicable, the Regulation gives residual jurisdiction to the courts of the Member State of the common nationality of the creditor and debtor or in cases of spousal maintenance to the courts of the Member State of the last common habitual residence of the spouses. Regardless of arguments concerning the possible lack of a legal basis for such a wide geographic scope (the required connection to the Internal Market can be questioned), this carries with it a practical problem.

---

18 COM(2005) 648 final, Brussels, 15 December 2005, Communication from the Commission to the Council calling on the Council to provide for measures relating to maintenance obligations taken under Article 65 of the Treaty establishing the European Community to be governed by the procedure laid down in Article 251 of that Treaty. For a quotation see p. 4. At an expert meeting in Brussels on 12 May 2005 the Commission even argued that the matter did not relate to family law in the sense of Article 65 EC. Practically nobody who was present agreed.

19 Council Regulation (EC) No. 2201/2003 of 27 November 2003 concerning jurisdiction and the recognition and enforcement of judgments in matrimonial matters and the matters of parental responsibility, repealing Regulation (EC) No. 1347/2000, OJ L 338, 23 December 2003, p. 1 (Brussels II bis Regulation).

20 With the exceptions given in Articles 22 and 23 for exclusive jurisdiction and prorogation agreements.

21 Subject to certain exceptions in Articles 9–13.

22 It is submitted that they are only applicable when there is a cross-border element. This would follow from the limitation of the legal basis of the Regulation in Article 65 EC to cross-border situations.

The following example will serve to illustrate the shortcomings of the proposed rule: A, the maintenance creditor, and B, the debtor, are both habitually resident in state X, that has no enforcement agreement with any of the Member States. B has no assets in state X but owns property in Sweden. Under Swedish national law, a foreign decision on maintenance is not enforceable unless there is an enforcement agreement with the country from which the judgment originates. Under Swedish national rules on jurisdiction A could bring an action for maintenance in a Swedish court on the basis that there are assets in Sweden.[23] The proposed Maintenance Regulation would preclude this pragmatic approach and the only way to gain access to the assets located in Sweden would be if the creditor could somehow obtain a judgment in a state party to one of the Hague Conventions.[24] The Commission's proposal should be amended so as either to include a subsidiary ground for jurisdiction based on the location of assets or preferably, as in Brussels I and Brussels II bis, to include a reference to national law. Some Member States might also be reluctant to give up the possibility of providing a forum for their nationals.

It should also be noted that the United Kingdom has not, whereas Ireland has, exercised its right to opt in to the proposal according to the 1997 Protocol to the EC and EU Treaties on the position of the United Kingdom and Ireland (agreed together with the Amsterdam Treaty). The UK does not have to give any formal reasons for this, but those informally given to us are an unwillingness to introduce rules on the applicable law and, following the "Lugano" opinion by the European Court of Justice, a reluctance to give up external competence.[25] The Regulation will also not apply to Denmark, which is exempt from EC judicial cooperation in civil matters.[26]

2.3. RULES ON JURISDICTION

Article 3 of the proposed Regulation gives jurisdiction to the following courts:

- the court of the defendant's habitual residence (cf. Article 2 Brussels I),
- the court of the creditor's habitual residence (cf. Article 5(2) Brussels I),

---

23 Ch. 10 §3 of the Swedish Procedural Code.

24 This is far-fetched but theoretically possible if the debtor does not contest jurisdiction. Such a judgment would be enforceable under the 1973 Hague Convention on enforcement, Article (3), and that Convention is applicable irrespective of the habitual residence or nationality of the parties, Art. 2.

25 Opinion 1/03 *Lugano Convention* 7.2.2006.

26 According to the 1997 Protocol on the position of Denmark, Denmark does not participate in the judicial cooperation in civil matters.

- a court having jurisdiction to determine the status of a person (typically proceedings establishing the parentage of a child or divorce proceedings) if the maintenance issue is ancillary, provided that the jurisdiction is not based solely on the nationality of one of the parties (cf. Article 5(2) Brussels I),
- a court having jurisdiction under the Brussels II bis Regulation in proceedings concerning parental responsibility.

The rules on jurisdiction have been copied from the Brussels I Regulation with the welcome addition of jurisdiction for a court having jurisdiction under the Brussels II bis Regulation[27] to determine parental responsibility. According to Article 8 of that Regulation the courts of the habitual residence *of the child* have jurisdiction – not those of the creditor or defendant. It should be noted that in some legal systems it may be a parent rather than the child itself that acts as the applicant in proceedings concerning child support. Nonetheless, it would be rather unusual for a child to have its habitual residence neither with the creditor nor with the defendant *and* still having a parent acting as the applicant (if the child itself is the creditor it can always sue at its own habitual residence). Rather, the added value of the provision lies in its reference to Articles 13 and 15 of the Brussels II bis Regulation. Article 13 gives jurisdiction to the courts of the country in which the child is present if the child's habitual residence cannot be determined or if the child is a refugee. Article 15 provides for a limited form of *forum non conveniens* that makes it possible to transfer a case to a court in another country with which the child has a close connection.[28]

The situation under the Brussels I Regulation is that parties are free to enter into choice of court agreements also in the area of maintenance, cf. Article 23. To our knowledge this freedom has not given rise to any problems. The proposal confirms this situation in Article 4 but introduces a limitation concerning children below the age of 18. This is not entirely justified and it should be borne in mind that a prorogation agreement could also be in the best interests of a child.[29] If a limitation is called for, the Regulation should at least allow for prorogation agreements giving a right to the child to bring proceedings in a court.

Nevertheless, in the Council several delegations have expressed their concerns against such unlimited freedom to chose a court and have insisted that the choice

---

27 Council Regulation (EC) No. 2201/2003 of 27 November 2003 concerning jurisdiction and the recognition and enforcement of judgments in matrimonial matters and the matters of parental responsibility, repealing Regulation (EC) No. 1347/2000, OJ L 338, 23 December 2003, p. 1.

28 Cf. Articles 8 and 9 of the Hague Convention of 19 October 1996 on Jurisdiction, Applicable Law, Recognition, Enforcement and Co-operation in respect of Parental Responsibility and Measures for the Protection of Children.

29 See *infra* 3.4.2 concerning restrictions to party autonomy in the field of applicable law.

should be limited to certain courts with which the situation has a close connection. In the latest Presidency text the choice is limited to 1) those courts that have jurisdiction if there had been no active choice; 2) the courts of a Member State the nationality of which the parties share; 3) in the case of spouses, the courts of the Member State of their last common habitual residence with a duration of at least one year. In addition, several delegations have expressed their disapproval of the idea of allowing for prorogation agreements with vulnerable adults.[30]

According to Article 48, in matters relating to maintenance obligations the proposed Regulation will replace the Brussels I Regulation. Since the UK has not opted in, and the Maintenance Regulation will not apply to Denmark, Article 5(2) of the Brussels I Regulation will not be repealed and maintenance claims will not be excluded from the scope of that Regulation.[31]

Strictly speaking, in order to achieve the purpose of the Regulation, common rules on jurisdiction are not necessary. For example, the two Hague Conventions only have indirect rules on jurisdiction, i.e. rules that indicate "approved" grounds of jurisdiction but do not directly prescribe certain rules. A contracting state can assume jurisdiction on any ground that it wishes, but only if an approved ground of jurisdiction has been used is the judgment enforceable in other states parties to the Convention. The same technique is foreseen for the 2007 Hague Convention. The disadvantage of not having common rules on jurisdiction is that not all judgments will be enforceable. In that sense common grounds on jurisdiction contribute to better enforcement. Nonetheless, it should be noted in this context that the 1962 Nordic Convention on the Enforcement of Maintenance Claims contains neither direct nor indirect rules on jurisdiction.[32] Having said this, we are fully aware that this is a discussion that was closed almost 40 years ago when the Brussels Convention was first concluded in 1968. It would be politically impossible to take such a significant step back from unification and it would be inconceivable not to include direct grounds of jurisdiction in a new Regulation on maintenance claims.

---

30 See *infra* note 31.

31 As stated above, Denmark does not participate in EC judicial cooperation in civil law matters and is therefore not automatically bound by the Brussels I Regulation. However, through an agreement between Denmark and the EC the provisions have been made applicable in and vis-à-vis Denmark. See the Agreement between the European Community and the Kingdom of Denmark on jurisdiction and the recognition and enforcement of judgments in civil and commercial matters, OJ L 299, 16 November 2005, p. 62.

32 See *supra* note 6.

2.4. APPLICABLE LAW

The proposed Regulation contains rules on the law applicable to maintenance obligations. This is a complete novelty since there are no rules on applicable law in the Brussels I Regulation. However, nine Member States are parties to the 1956 Hague Convention[33] and eleven Member States are parties to the 1973 Convention.[34] The parties to these Conventions are mainly EU Member States, and the only other states that have acceded to these Conventions are Japan, Switzerland and Turkey. In addition, Liechtenstein is a party to the 1956 Convention.

The present situation is that there is very little uniformity concerning the law applicable to maintenance obligations. As indicated, the two Hague Conventions have only been ratified by a minority of the Member States. What is more, in the common law countries, foreign law is not applied in maintenance cases[35] and it has been argued that doing so would create difficulties for the courts and additional costs to the parties.[36]

The great differences between the substantive laws in this area as well as the choice between different jurisdictions available to the creditor has prompted the Commission to introduce common rules on applicable law in its proposal in order to minimise the benefits of forum shopping. Although forum shopping could theoretically be quite lucrative in certain cases, it has not yet been shown that this constitutes a practical problem.

2.4.1. Relationship with the Future Hague Protocol

The work going on at the Hague Conference for Private International Law includes an overview of the choice of law rules[37] and the question of whether the EU should have its own rules or in one way or another accede to the future modernised Hague rules is still an open question. In Article 18 the proposed Regulation

33 *Supra* note 3. Those states are Austria, Belgium, France, Germany, Italy, Luxembourg, the Netherlands, Portugal, and Spain. Greece has signed but not ratified the Convention.

34 *Supra* note 3. Those states are Estonia, France, Germany, Greece, Italy, Lithuania, Luxembourg, the Netherlands, Poland, Portugal, and Spain. Belgium has signed but not ratified the Convention.

35 For the law of England and Wales see L. Collins (ed.), *Dicey, Morris and Collins on the Conflict of Laws*, 14th ed., Sweet & Maxwell, 2006, p. 1033 (para. 19–144).

36 *Response by the Family Law Bar Association of England and Wales to the European Commission Green Paper on Maintenance Obligations*, in particular para. 33 available at http://ec.europa.eu/civiljustice/maintenance_claim/maintenance_claim_ec_answer_bar_eng_en.pdf.

37 See Prel. Doc. No. 30 from June 2007 with a Preliminary Draft Protocol on the law applicable to maintenance obligations. See http://hcch.e-vision.nl/upload/wop/maint_pd30e.pdf. This author has been a member of the Hague working group drafting the new rules on applicable law.

foresees the universal application of its rules on applicable law. It would unnecessarily complicate things if there were to exist parallel systems for determining the applicable law – one set of rules from the Hague Conference and another from the EU. This area of the law is difficult enough as it is. One possible solution would therefore be to delete the rules on applicable law in the Regulation and have the EC accede to the Protocol (the EC became a member of the Hague Conference on 3 April 2007) or the EC and the Member States together – thus making the Protocol on applicable law a so-called mixed agreement.[38] However, this solution would require that the negotiations concerning a Hague Protocol on applicable law can be concluded within a reasonable time. There has to be something to mirror! Regrettably, there is reason to believe that the rules on applicable law might not be finished at the November 2007 diplomatic conference although this is at the moment of writing very much uncertain.

If there is to be an option through which the Hague Protocol will apply in lieu of rules in the future Regulation, experience tells us that deciding in which way to do this and then finally coming to a ratification could be a lengthy procedure involving the never-ending story of who has what external competence. The speediest way to achieve common rules would first be to "mirror" the Hague rules in the Regulation, thus giving the EC undisputed external competence to ratify the Hague Protocol.[39]

2.4.2. The Proposed Rules

The point of departure for the rules on applicable law are those of the 1973 Hague Convention. However, a welcome clarification is that Article 12 states that the law applicable to maintenance does not apply to the incidental question of e.g. the parentage of a child or the validity of a marriage. The two Hague Conventions are not clear on this issue.[40] In this context it should also be mentioned that there is no rule corresponding to the much criticised Article 8 of the 1973 Convention, according to which the law applied to the divorce shall govern the maintenance relation between the spouses and any later revisions.

Just as is the case in the 1973 Convention, the general rule in Article 13 is a "cascade rule", which gives the creditor several possibilities to obtain maintenance.

---

38 See for mixed agreements i.a. D. McGoldrick, *International Relations Law of the European Union*, Longman, 1997, pp. 78–88 with further references.

39 This follows from the doctrine of the "parallelism" of internal and external powers. See P. Koutrakos, *EU International Relations Law*, Hart, 2006, pp. 77 *et seq.*

40 See for the background and possible interpretation the explanatory report to the 1973 Convention by M. Verwilghen, paras. 124–128. The report is available at http://hcch.e-vision.nl/upload/expl23-24.pdf.

The cascade has three steps: 1) the law of the habitual residence of the creditor; 2) the law of the forum; 3) the law with which the situation has a close connection, in particular the country of a common nationality of the debtor and the creditor. If the creditor is unable to obtain maintenance according to the law indicated he may go one step further in the cascade and see if he is not able to obtain maintenance according to the law of that country. In addition, regardless of the cascade, the creditor has the option of asking for the application of the law of the forum, if the debtor is resident in that country. Article 13 differs from the rules in Articles 4–6 of the 1973 Hague Convention mainly in that the order in the cascade is reversed between the law of the common nationality and that of the forum. The opportunity to choose the law of the forum is not available in the Hague Conventions but is a welcome and pragmatic rule that has the potential of saving a lot of time and money.[41]

The Regulation does not make it clear which law applies to the question of determining who is the creditor – e.g. the child itself or the person exercising care of the child. Article 10 of the 1973 Hague Convention (as does Art. 10 of the Draft Protocol) includes the question of "who is entitled to institute maintenance proceedings" in the scope of the applicable law but no such wording is used in the corresponding Article 17 of the Regulation. In certain countries this is considered to be a matter of procedural law and thus subject to the *lex fori*.[42] The matter should be dealt with explicitly in a future Regulation, but even if such should not be the case it is submitted that an interpretation in line with the 1973 Hague Convention would be most practical and in line with the spirit of the Regulation. After all, Article 17 does not provide an exhaustive list of matters included within the scope of the applicable law.

A novelty in the area of maintenance is the possibility to choose the law applicable to maintenance. Such a possibility is not available under the Hague Conventions (but is foreseen in Article 8 of the draft Hague Protocol). The first Hague Convention to provide for party autonomy in the area of family law was the 1978 Hague Convention on matrimonial property regimes.[43] The proposal is in line with the general trend today, which is to give the parties more freedom to choose the

41 A version of this rule is to be found in Article 4(3) of the latest draft Hague Protocol on applicable law. See Prel. Doc. No. 30 with a Draft Protocol on the law applicable to maintenance obligations, available at http://hcch.e-vision.nl/upload/wop/maint_pd30e.pdf. A provisional explanatory report by Prof. A. Bonomi (as yet only in French) is available at http://hcch.e-vision.nl/upload/wop/expl_prot38f.pdf.

42 Se the Verwilghen report, (*supra* note 40), para. 172 quoting the explanatory report to the 1956 Convention by L.I. de Winter. *Actes et Documents de la Huitième session (1956)*, Vol. I, p. 311.

43 Convention of 14 March 1978 on the law applicable to matrimonial property regimes.

applicable law, also in the area of family law.[44] Given the ongoing shift from nationality to habitual residence as the deciding connecting factor[45] and the increased mobility in today's world, party autonomy provides people with a tool to prevent having the law applicable to their relationship changing with every relocation.[46] Even so, this presupposes an awareness of the law that is simply not there in most cases.

The typical situation in which the parties might want to make use of this possibility is in matters concerning matrimonial maintenance. This might be practical for a couple considering a longer sojourn in a foreign country who might want to retain, e.g., their national law as the law which is applicable to all marital matters – including maintenance. The proposal allows for such a choice of law so long as both parties are over 18 years of age and none of them is a "vulnerable adult", i.e. a person who by reason of impairment or insufficiency of his or her personal faculties is not in a position to protect his or her interests. Choice of law agreements with vulnerable adults and children can only be entered into in connexion with specific court proceedings, and only if they lead to the application of the law of the forum.

It is submitted that the exclusion of children and vulnerable adults from party autonomy is ill-conceived. The point of departure appears to be that all agreements entered into by children and vulnerable adults are somehow to their detriment, either through a failure of their legal representatives to protect their interests or through a conflict of interests, e.g. the legal representative is also the maintenance debtor. The truth is that a maintenance agreement may very well be favourable to a child or a vulnerable adult. However, instead of dealing with the problem of deceptive legal representatives, the proposal swats flies with a

---

44 See for the development in the areas of matrimonial property regimes and succession M. Jäntera-Jareborg, *Partsautonomi och efterlevande makes rättsställning*, Iustus, 1989, p. 69–179. Cf. also Art. 20a (to be inserted in the Brussels II bis Regulation) of the proposed Rome III Regulation, COM(2006) 399 final, Brussels 17 July 2006, Proposal for a Council Regulation amending Regulation (EC) No. 2201/2003 as regards jurisdiction and introducing rules concerning applicable law in matrimonial matters. Also in the area of divorce a limited degree of party autonomy is foreseen.

45 Admittedly, the relevant connecting factor in this area of the law has been habitual residence since 1956, which perhaps does not merit speaking of a shift. At least for those States parties to the 1956 Hague Convention.

46 Actually, Article 13 of the proposed Maintenance Regulation is silent on the issue of the effect of a change in habitual residence whereas Article 4 of the 1973 Hague Convention and Article 3(2) of the Hague Draft Protocol both explicitly state that a change of habitual residence shall immediately lead to the application of the law of the new habitual residence. An issue which remains unsettled in the 1973 Convention and in the Draft Protocol is what law applies to the maintenance claim of a person who does not have a habitual residence, e.g. a refugee. A literal interpretation of the text would point towards applying the law of the country of the last habitual residence, whereas a teleological interpretation would lead to the application of the law of the country in which the creditor is present.

sledgehammer and disposes of party autonomy altogether. What is more, the definition of a vulnerable adult stems from Article 1 of the 2000 Hague Convention for the protection of adults,[47] and that definition includes a person whose *physical* state prevents him from managing his personal or property interests.[48] Mentally he may be crystal clear and as able to decide on matters such as the law applicable to a maintenance agreement as any other adult.

The question of the validity of an agreement either because it is unfair to the maintenance creditor or because of disloyal representation is actually one of the law applicable to the material validity of the agreement. Probably all laws contain rules that would provide remedies in such situations. The proposed Regulation is silent on what law is applicable to the question of material validity, as is, e.g., the 1978 Hague Convention on the law applicable to matrimonial property regimes.[49] In the Draft Protocol Article 8(4) provides that "the law chosen shall not apply where the application of that law would lead to manifestly unfair or unreasonable consequences". That would probably suffice but a rule on material validity such as Article 8 of the Rome Convention could also be added for the sake of legal certainty.

The choice is limited to 1) the law of the parties' common nationality at the time of designation; 2) the law of the habitual residence of either party; and 3) in the case of a married couple, the law applicable to their matrimonial property regime at the time of designation. It should be noted that the proposed Rome III Regulation differs in the laws available to the parties.[50] For example, does the Rome III proposal (as does the Hague Draft Protocol) provide for a possibility for the parties to choose the law of a country in which they have resided for at least three years,[51] or the law of the nationality of *either* spouse. The argument for the differentiation remains to be made. The parties should have the possibility of choosing one and the same law for all aspects of a break up of a marriage. This is possible today, but it is a question of finding the least common denominator. Some synchronisation would be in order.

Since the "cascade" rule in Article 13 is very favourable to the creditor there is a need to protect the debtor. The technique used is the same as in Article 7 of the

47 Convention of 13 January 2000 on the International Protection of Adults.

48 See the explanatory report to the Convention drawn up by P. Lagarde, para. 10, available at http://hcch.e-vision.nl/upload/expl35e.pdf.

49 Convention of 14 March 1978 on the Law Applicable to Matrimonial Property Regimes. Note, however, Article 10 which deals with the matter of consent.

50 *Supra* note 44.

51 It should be noted that in the latest Presidency text this possibility has been deleted. See Council doc. 11295/07, JUSTCIV 183, 28 June 2007.

1973 Hague Convention. In that Convention, the creditor has the possibility to escape claims for maintenance from persons related collaterally or by affinity (e.g. siblings or parents-in-law) if there is no maintenance obligation under the law of their common nationality, or if there is none, under the law of the debtor's habitual residence. This rule was the result of a compromise between those that wanted to include maintenance between persons related collaterally or by affinity in the scope of the Convention and those that opposed this.[52]

In the proposed Regulation, Article 15 fulfils a similar function. The debtor can oppose a claim for maintenance if there is no such obligation under the law of the common nationality of the parties, or, if they do not share a nationality, the law of the habitual residence of the debtor. The rule is both wider and narrower in scope than that of the Hague Convention. It is wider in scope in that it covers also relatives in the descending or ascending line, but narrower in that it does not cover children or vulnerable adults even if they are related collaterally or through affinity.

In the case of maintenance obligations between spouses or ex-spouses, the debtor can oppose the claim if there is no such obligation under the law of a country to which the marriage has its closest connection, typically the country in which the parties had their last common habitual residence.

It is difficult to understand the exception to this rule for children and vulnerable adults. It is of course very easy to sympathize with children and vulnerable adults in need. But then there are other categories that can be just as impoverished and unable to support themselves, e.g. physically handicapped adults or victims of disaster. It should be noted that the similar defence rule in Article 6 of the Hague Draft Protocol excludes only obligations arising out of a parent-child relationship towards a child and spousal maintenance. The relevant question is not if the creditor is in need – a creditor is per definition in some need (with the exception of some varieties of spousal maintenance) – but rather whether it is fair and equitable that a particular person is designated to relieve this need. The question that should be answered is whether there is a close connection between *both* the creditor and the debtor and the country whose legal order prescribes the maintenance obligation. Such a close connection could arise if both parties had taken up habitual residence in that country for some time. The use of the common nationality is misplaced. Many people have the nationality of a country to which they have very little connection.

52 See the explanatory report to the 1973 Conventions by M. Verwilghen, (*supra* note 40), para. 146 *et seq*.

What comes as something of a surprise is that the defence rule appears to be applicable also in cases where the parties have chosen the applicable law in an agreement. In the Hague Draft Protocol the position of the rule on defence in Article 6, after the general rule but before the rules on party autonomy, would indicate that that defence is not available where the parties have agreed on the applicable law. That is only reasonable.

An example could best illustrate how the rules on party autonomy and defence in Article 15 would work (or rather not work). A is a Swedish citizen who has lived the greater part of his life in Portugal. His father has Portuguese nationality but his mother, who is now quite senile, has Swedish nationality (and her origins in that country). Both parents are poor and in need of financial support from their only son. A meets a Swedish woman and decides to go to Sweden and live with her. He is troubled by his conscience about leaving his parents and goes to a notary to have a contract drawn up which stipulates a monthly maintenance and that Portuguese law will be applied to the maintenance obligation.

After some time in Sweden he refuses to pay. As regards his mother, the contract is invalid since there is no party autonomy in relation to a vulnerable adult. According to the general rule Portuguese law applies but he can oppose the obligation on the ground that there is no obligation to pay maintenance to a parent under Swedish law, the law of their common nationality. The contract is valid in relation to his father but it would appear that nevertheless the rule on defence is applicable. Since father and son do not have a common nationality he can rely on the law of his new habitual residence, Sweden, to escape maintenance. In our opinion the result is both arbitrary and inequitable.

Quite surprisingly the proposal contains a rule on renvoi in Article 19. If the law of a non-Member State is applicable and the private international law rules of that State designate the law of another country, the law of the forum shall apply. According to the brief commentary that the Commission published after making the proposal "[i]t does not appear appropriate in a maintenance dispute in a court of a Member State to apply the law of a non-member country which would not apply it in an identical situation. However, to simplify this 'partial renvoi' technique, the lex fori is applied directly in such a case".[53]

It is difficult to understand why the Commission at this point in time presents a proposal containing a renvoi rule. Neither the 1956 nor the 1973 Hague

[53] COM(2006) 206 final, Brussels 12.5.2006, Commentary on the articles of the proposal for a Council Regulation on jurisdiction, applicable law, recognition and enforcement of decisions and cooperation in matters relating to maintenance obligations, p. 5.

Conventions do so. The general idea behind renvoi is that it should increase the international harmony of decisions. Nevertheless, that has not been the result of renvoi but rather that of strengthening the so-called homeward trend.[54] In its 1999 resolution on renvoi the Institut de Droit International, displaying a generally positive attitude to this phenomenon, gave a number of reasons why renvoi should be considered in certain situations: if the validity or uniform treatment of a transaction could be achieved, or if the parties had chosen a certain law including its private international law.[55] None of those reasons would be relevant in the case of the proposed rule.

The proposed rule on renvoi also does not make practical sense. Assume that a child living in and having the nationality of non-Member State X sues her father, who has the same nationality but lives in Belgium, for maintenance. If she for reasons of enforceability of judgments sues him in a Belgian court, that court will apply the law of the habitual residence of the child, state X. Assuming that that law designates the law of the common nationality as the one which is applicable, the Belgian court will apply Belgian law – the law of the debtor. It is difficult to see why and, in particular, it is difficult to see why only in relation to third States.

2.4.3. *Is There a Need for Rules on Applicable Law?*

The reason that the Commission gives for including choice-of-law rules in the proposed Regulation is to strengthen legal certainty. A harmonisation of the conflict-of-law rules would make it possible for creditors (nothing is said about debtors) "to act with full knowledge of the situation, without being subjected to the diversity of national [PIL] systems". Most importantly: "the decision is less problematic to accept if it is given in accordance with a law designated according to harmonised rules".[56]

---

54 F. Bouckaert, "Professio Juris dans le Code de Droit international privé belge", in: Deutsches Notarinstitut, *Étude de droit comparé sur les règles de conflits de juridictions et de conflits de lois relatives aux testaments et successions dans les Etats membres de l'Union Européenne*, p. 417–429 at p. 419, available at http://www.dnoti.de/eu_studie/eu_studie_en.htm; H. J. Sonnenberger, "Artikel 4 Rück- und Weiterverweisung; Rechtsspaltung", in: H. J. Sonnenberger, *Münchener Kommentar zum Bürgerlichen Gesetzbuch: Band 10 Einführungsgesetz zum Bürgerlichen Gesetzbuche (Art. 1–46) Internationales Privatrecht*, 4. Aufl., C. H. Beck, 2006, pp. 403–444 at p. 409 (para. 23).

55 Resolution of the Institut de Droit International, "Taking foreign private international law to account", available at http://www.idi-iil.org/idiE/resolutionsE/1999_ber_01_en.PDF.

56 COM(2005) 649 final, p. 5.

It must be admitted that the question of which law the foreign court has applied is sometimes relevant to the question of enforceability.[57] However, in most legal systems this is not relevant. Rather, the enforceability of the foreign judgment depends on what grounds the foreign court assumed jurisdiction and whether or not the judgment violates procedural or substantive public policy.[58] Both the 1958 and the 1973 Hague Conventions on the enforcement of maintenance decisions do without rules on the applicable law. A large number of States have joined these Conventions without also joining the 1956 and 1973 Conventions on applicable law. What is more, the Brussels I Regulation works well and the problems that exist relating to enforcement under this Regulation do not pertain to differences between national rules on applicable law. In analysing whether an action by the Community is proportional, it is necessary to determine whether it is necessary for the attainment of the aim.[59] It can hardly be said that the Commission has gone to any great lengths in trying to do so.

Moreover, the introduction of rules on applicable law in the Regulation might prove to be counterproductive. Today, several Member States will apply the law of the forum to maintenance obligations or at least only apply foreign law if a party so requests. If the choice-of-law rules are included in a Regulation, it is doubtful whether the principle of solidarity contained in Article 10 EC would not require that courts apply foreign law *ex officio*.[60] It is our experience that the application of foreign law will slow down a procedure by several months and increase costs. Since most maintenance claims concern a few tens or hundreds of euro per month it is extremely doubtful whether the application of foreign law is worth it. It has also not been proven, let alone argued, that forum shopping, another argument commonly used to support common choice-of-law rules, is a practical problem in the area of maintenance.

2.5. COMMON PROCEDURAL RULES

The rules in chapter IV containing common procedural rules mainly serve the purpose of avoiding a particular kind of procedural public policy pertaining to

---

57 See in this direction e.g. Ch. 2 §12 of the Swedish law on international succession (*Lag [1937:81] om internationella förhållanden rörande dödsbo*) that refuses recognition if the foreign decision was based on a law the provisions of which are contrary to those that would have been applicable under Swedish PIL; Art. 25 §1(3) of the Belgian PIL Code (*Loi portant le Code de droit international privé*), that in cases where there is no party autonomy, refuses recognition of a judgment if the sole reason for turning to the deciding court was to grant the application of the law of a certain country.

58 See e.g. Arts 25–27 of the Swiss PIL Code (*Bundesgesetz über das internationale Privatrecht*) or Art. 117 of the Bulgarian PIL Code (*Kodeks na mezhdunarodnoto chastno pravo*)

59 See case 66/82 *Fromançais SA v. FORMA* [1983] ECR 395, para. 8.

60 See M. Jänterä-Jareborg, "Foreign Law in National Courts: a Comparative Perspective", in: 304 (2003-IV) *Recueil des cours*, pp. 181–385 at p. 367 *et seq.*

poor or non-existent service of the defendant. According to Article 34(2) of the Brussels I Regulation the court entrusted with the granting of declarations of enforceability of a foreign judgment (the so-called exequatur procedure) *shall* refuse enforceability if a default judgment has been given against a person who was not served in sufficient time to prepare his defence unless he failed to challenge the judgment after having been made aware of it. Since the proposed Maintenance Regulation does away with the exequatur procedure, in the words of the Commission, "these rules constitute the essential accessory to the removal of the exequatur procedure".[61] The underlying idea is that if it is not possible to refuse enforceability, common rules on service of documents and the right for a review of a judgment are necessary.

2.5.1. Service of Documents

Article 22 contains common rules for the service of documents in maintenance proceedings. The main difference between Article 22 and the Service Regulation is that the latter is only applicable when a document has to be transmitted from one Member State to another (Art. 1).[62] The rules on service in the Maintenance Regulation are always applicable also in purely domestic situations. However, Article 23 on examination as to admissability (in particular para. 2) indicates that Article 22 is only applicable so long as the defendant is habitually resident in a Member State.

In the negotiations in the Council, the Commission has defended its position of full harmonisation by reminding delegations that it is impossible to know in advance if a creditor in a case that appears to be entirely domestic might not at a later stage seek enforcement in another Member State. Hence *all* cases potentially have a cross-border dimension. Even so, it is submitted that such a position is contrary to the requirement in Article 65 EC that there be a cross-border element present. That limitation of the legislative competence of the EC would be rendered utterly meaningless if the Commission's line of reasoning were accepted.

A difference between the rules on service in the Maintenance Regulation and those contained in the Regulation on a European Enforcement Order (EEO), another area in which the exequatur procedure has been abolished, is that the former fully harmonise the rules on service whereas the latter only states that a

---

61 COM(2006) 206 final, p. 5.

62 Council Regulation (EC) No. 1348/2000 of 29 May 2000 on the service in the Member States of judicial and extrajudicial documents in civil and commercial matters, OJ L 160, 30 June 2000, p. 37.

particular method of service is a prerequisite for enforcement (cf. Article 12).[63] The difference can be likened to the difference between direct and indirect rules on jurisdiction.

Article 22 mirrors Article 13 of the EEO, which contains rules on service with proof of receipt by the debtor. However, there is no rule corresponding to Article 14 of the EEO on service without proof of receipt by the debtor and Article 15 of the EEO on service on the debtor's representatives. Such methods of service include perfectly reasonable methods of service such as personal service to a person living or working at the debtor's household, personal service at the debtor's business premises on persons who are employed by the debtor, or service by e-mail and automatic confirmation of delivery, provided that the debtor has expressly accepted this method of service in advance. This is an unnecessarily restrictive attitude that will make it more difficult to serve debtors and obstruct the obtainment of maintenance judgments. What is striking is that this is not commented upon by the Commission in its commentary.[64]

2.5.2. Default Judgments and Review

Article 24 contains a proposal for the full harmonisation of the rules on when a court may deliver a default judgment if the defendant has not been properly served or prevented from entering a defence for reasons of *force majeure* etc. It may do so provided that the defendant is given a right to have the judgment reviewed and a time period in which to react of not less than 20 days from being properly informed about the decision.

2.5.3. Reaction in the Council

In the latest Presidency Proposal Article 22 has been deleted since Member States had serious doubts about the proportionality of full harmonisation.[65] Consequently, Article 23 on examination as to admissibility has been amended (and moved to the chapter on jurisdiction as a new Article 6–3). Article 24 has been moved to a new Chapter V bis on Application for Review, renumbered as Article 26a and supplemented inter alia with rules on the effect of an appeal and what actually happens if the review is granted or not granted. The result is that the entire Chapter IV on the harmonisation of procedural rules has been deleted.

---

63 Regulation (EC) No. 805/2004 of the European Parliament and of the Council of 21 April 2004 creating a European Enforcement Order for uncontested claims, OJ L 143, 30 April 2004, p. 15. According to its Article 48(1) the Maintenance Regulation will take precedence over the EEO.

64 Cf. COM(2006) 206 final, p. 5–6.

65 See *supra* note 51.

2.6. ENFORCEABILITY OF DECISIONS

One of the major changes that the proposed Regulation brings about in its Chapter V on enforceability of decisions is the abolition of the exequatur procedure. According to Article 25, a decision given in a Member State that is enforceable in that Member State shall be recognised and enforceable in another Member State without the need for a declaration of enforceability. According to the same Article there will also be no possibility of opposing its recognition.

2.6.1. Is the Abolition of Exequatur Proportional?

The abolition of the exequatur procedure is certainly a step forward in improving the mutual recognition of judgments. The time required to obtain a declaration of enforceability differs very much from country to country and from case to case, but the slowness of this procedure and abuse of the possibility to appeal is certainly a problem. One way of solving the problem is, of course, to abolish the exequatur procedure totally, but another way, that does not appear to have been considered by the Commission, would be to reform the exequatur procedure itself. This could have been done through introducing time-limits and limits on appeal. The proportionality of the measure is therefore questionable since the Commission appears to be proposing a measure that goes beyond what is necessary for the attainment of the aim. It is also submitted that the Commission has failed to fulfil its duty under the 1997 Protocol on the application of the principles of subsidiarity and proportionality.[66] That protocol requires that "[f]or any proposed Community legislation, the reasons on which it is based shall be stated with a view to justifying its compliance with the principles of subsidiarity and proportionality".[67] There is a token proportionality analysis, but never is the central issue of the abolition of exequatur discussed.[68] However, it must be admitted that Member States have already committed themselves to the abolition of exequatur in the Action Programme.[69] What is not yet decided is whether the abolition of exequatur should be limited to certain types of maintenance, such as child support.

2.6.2. Provisional Enforcement

Article 26 deals with provisional enforcement and stipulates that a decision shall be enforceable by operation of law notwithstanding any appeal. This entails a full

66 Annexed to the EC Treaty through the Treaty of Amsterdam. See OJ C 340, 10 November 1997, p. 105.
67 Para. 4.
68 See COM(2005) 649 final, p. 8 *et seq.*
69 *Supra* note 7, p. 4.

harmonisation of the laws of Member States since at present not all decisions from all Member States are provisionally enforceable. The Commission explains that "[a] similar measure has already been taken by the Community legislature as regards rights of access (second subparagraph of Article 41(1) of [the Brussels II bis Regulation])."[70] The provision is similar but not identical. An important difference is that in Brussels II bis the court of origin has a *possibility* of declaring a decision provisionally enforceable irrespective of whether national law provides for this or not. In the proposed Maintenance Regulation *all* decisions will *always* be provisionally enforceable regardless of whether there is a need for it or not.

2.6.3. *Reactions in the Council*

The outcome of the Council negotiations on this Article is uncertain. In the latest Presidency text it is proposed to either replace the text either with a rule identical to that of Brussels II bis or with a rule that enables a court to declare a judgment *not* provisionally enforceable if that is possible under its own law.[71]

2.7. ENFORCEMENT

The point of departure in Chapter VI on enforcement is, like in other EC instruments,[72] that enforcement takes place according to the law of the Member State of enforcement. However, where the Regulation harmonises procedure those rules shall apply. Below we will outline the major changes that the proposed Regulation would bring about.

2.7.1. *Translation*

An important change compared to the existing situation is that the applicant (or the Central Authority of the Member State of origin) will not have to pay for the translation of the original judgment, only for the translation of a standard form accompanying the judgment containing an extract of the decision. The provision has the potential of saving considerable time and money as translation is expensive and judgments often contain a great deal of "collateral" information concerning a divorce and questions of child custody. However, in the Presidency text certain additional requirements in order to safeguard the rights of the debtor have been introduced.[73] Firstly, it may be required that the standard form be translated

70 COM(2006) 206 final, p. 6.

71 *Supra* note 51.

72 See Article 47 of the Brussels II bis Regulation (*supra* note 19), Article 20 of the EEO (*supra* note 63).

73 *Supra* note 51.

into an official language of the Member State of enforcement and, secondly, if the debtor requests that enforcement be refused or suspended, the competent authorities of the Member State of enforcement *may* ask for a translation of the judgment.

2.7.2. Legal Aid and Costs

The proposal is conservative in the area of legal aid and costs. Article 29 on legal aid is virtually a cut and paste of Article 50 of the Brussels I Regulation.[74] It would be a great step forward if the Member States could agree on exempting the enforcement of child support from all enforcement costs (as is the case in e.g. Sweden). This should apply regardless of whether the creditor is a child or an authority that seeks reimbursement for advances or other benefits paid to the creditor. Since the EC has forwarded a proposal for free enforcement of child support at the negotiations for a new Hague Convention the Community should, regardless of the outcome in The Hague, be prepared to introduce such rules for intra-Community enforcement.[75]

2.7.3. Refusal or Suspension of Enforcement

Article 33 contains rules on the right of the debtor to ask for full or partial refusal or suspension of the enforcement. Such a request may be granted if: 1) the debtor states new or hitherto unknown circumstances, 2) the debtor has applied for review, 3) the debtor has already satisfied his debt, 4) the claim has been extinguished through prescription or limitation of actions, or 5) the decision of the court of origin is irreconcilable with a decision given in the Member State of enforcement.

The Article is a significant exception to the rule in Article 27 that enforcement takes place according to the law of the Member State of enforcement. What is more, as it is drafted it would appear to invite an unnecessary delay of the enforcement procedure. The first ground of refusal, new or hitherto unknown circumstances, would either belong in a court or be unnecessary. If the new circumstances pertain to the duty to pay maintenance as such, such as news about the parentage or information that the wife *also* had been unfaithful (thus affecting her right to "punitive" maintenance), it belongs in a court. The same would apply if the creditor had sufficiently improved his financial situation and was no longer

---

74 *Supra* note 5.

75 And not necessarily as stated in the Presidency text "consistent with the corresponding provision in the draft Hague Convention", see supra note 51, p. 24 note 1. See Article 14 bis of option 2 concerning effective access to procedures in the draft Convention, see *infra* note 86.

in need of maintenance. If, however, the debtor's financial situation had significantly deteriorated and he is no longer able to pay the maintenance ordered, there are already rules concerning non-attachable property and reserved income in the national enforcement rules and Article 27 suffices. There is no need to spell this out once again in Article 33.

The fifth ground of refusal, *viz.* that the decision of the court of origin is irreconcilable with a decision given in the Member State of enforcement, appears to give precedence to older judgments. If so, it should have been known to the Commission that the principle of *res judicata* does not apply in the area of maintenance where new circumstances are always relevant. Precedence should therefore be given to the newest judgment, regardless of whether it comes from the Member State of enforcement or from another Member State. In the latest Presidency text precedence will also be given to decisions from all Member States and, quite sensibly, to those from a third State which fulfils the conditions necessary for their recognition in the Member State of enforcement. What is somewhat surprising is that the requirement that the decision given priority is newer is still in square brackets (indicating a lack of consensus).[76]

2.7.4. *Garnishment*

Article 34 contains a novelty in that it empowers a court in one Member State to give an employer or a bank in another Member State a direct order for monthly payment without contacting any authority in the Member State of enforcement. There are two problems with this proposal. Firstly, it presupposes that courts are involved in enforcement and have a certain proficiency in the area. That is not so in those countries in which enforcement of judgments is entirely cut loose from the court that gave the judgment. Secondly, the proposal creates a problem of coordination. A European system of garnishment must avoid the risk of the garnishee having to pay twice.[77] As things stand, only the enforcement authority in the Member State of enforcement will have the overall picture of whether there are other parallel monthly payments from the debtor's salary or bank account and what the overall financial status of the debtor is. It will be most difficult for the court of origin to respect the applicable rules in the Member State of enforcement on reserved or non-attachable assets.

---

76 *Supra* note 51.

77 See B. Hess, *Study No. JAI/A3/2002/02 on making more efficient the enforcement of judicial decisions within the European Union: Transparency of a Debtor's Assets, Attachment of Bank Accounts, Provisional Enforcement and Protective Measures, Version of 2/18/2004*, p. 89. Available at http://ec.europa.eu/justice_home/doc_centre/civil/studies/doc/enforcement_judicial_decisions_180204_en.pdf

The rules on garnishment are an important exception to the rule that enforcement is carried out by the competent authorities in the Member State of enforcement. Although there are certain benefits in allowing for the universality of enforcement (as opposed to the territoriality principle) the problems are many and are not so easily overcome – cf. the Insolvency Regulation.[78] However, the problem of multi-country assets (and the benefits involved in universality) are probably considerably less in the area of maintenance than in insolvency. What is more, the Commission has not done its homework properly and more work is needed before rules such as Article 34 can be introduced.

2.7.5. *Freezing of Bank Accounts*

In order to prevent the debtor from escaping enforcement through quickly moving assets from one country to another, the Commission has proposed rules on the temporary freezing of bank accounts in Article 35. It is a rapid procedure for a provisional measure and for obvious reasons the debtor is not actively involved at the initial stage (para. 2).

Just like with garnishment, the freezing of bank accounts constitutes an anomaly within the proposed Regulation in that it is a court in the Member State of origin that decides on the freezing of a bank account in another Member State. This proposal has not passed without demur. The Member States have been reluctant to let go of their sovereignty and the proportionality of the proposal has been questioned. After all, the freezing of a bank account is not, and should not be, a common measure in the enforcement of *maintenance* claims. Most Member States have also felt that the freezing of bank accounts is a "horizontal" question that affects several other areas than maintenance and is best dealt with in connection with the Commission's Green Paper on the attachment of bank accounts.[79] In the latest text from the outgoing German and incoming Portuguese Presidencies, the Article has been deleted but "the Presidencies suggest that other possibilities for improving the enforcement of decisions should be considered on the basis of a working document that will be submitted later".[80] This working document is still awaited.

2.7.6. *Ranking of Maintenance Claims*

Article 36 of the proposal harmonises the enforcement law of the Member States in that maintenance claims are given priority over all other debts owed by the

78 Council Regulation (EC) No. 1346/2000 of 29 May 2000 on insolvency proceedings, OJ L 160, 30 June 2000, p. 1.

79 COM(2006) 618 final, Brussels 24.10.2006, Green Paper on improving the efficiency of the enforcement of judgments in the European Union: the attachment of bank accounts.

80 See *supra* note 51, p. 27 *et seq.*

debtor, including those that have arisen from his duty to pay the cost of enforcement. Most Member States give priority to maintenance claims over other claims when it comes to garnishment of the debtor's salary. However, the bluntness of the proposal is almost shocking. The Commission has completely failed to take into consideration the needs of the credit industry. As the proposal stands, maintenance claims would have preferential ranking in the attachment of a chattel sold with a retention of title clause (quite common in Europe, particularly in Germany) or have priority to the claim of a bank that has given a mortgage loan for the purchase of a house.

Quite rightly, the Article has been deleted in the latest Presidency text.[81]

2.8. AUTHENTIC INSTRUMENTS AND AGREEMENTS

Chapter VII deals with the enforcement of authentic instruments and agreements. Under the Brussels I Regulation only authentic instruments and court settlements are enforceable, see Article 57 *et seq*. Hence, the novelty lies in the enforceability of agreements. The terminology is far from clear since many agreements could also be characterised as authentic instruments. For example, an agreement that has been approved by an administrative authority would according to Article 57(2) of the Brussels I Regulation qualify as an authentic instrument.

The main issue is whether or not a purely private agreement that has neither been drawn up before nor been approved by any authority in the Member State of origin should be enforceable. Some countries require such control by a competent authority whereas others do not.[82] Such private agreements are currently not enforceable under the Brussels I Regulation or the 1973 Hague Convention but would appear to be enforceable under the proposed Maintenance Regulation.

According to Article 37 of the proposal "agreements between parties that are enforceable in a Member State" are enforceable to the same extent as decisions. The proposal is not clear as to whether *all* agreements that are enforceable in any one of the Member States are also enforceable in all the other Member States. Does the enforceability also include agreements from a third State which are enforceable in a Member State?

81 See *supra* note 51.

82 For a comparative overview regarding in particular spousal maintenance, see K. Boele-Woelki et al., *Principles of European Family Law Regarding Divorce and Maintenance between Former Spouses*, Intersentia, 2004, p. 130 *et seq*.

In the latest Presidency text agreements are enforceable if they are enforceable in the Member State of origin.[83] In the context of private agreements it can sometimes be difficult to find a Member State of origin. What is the Member State of origin of a maintenance agreement concluded at a distance between a man habitually resident in Sweden and a woman habitually resident in Finland? Under Swedish law it is sufficient that two people witness the signatures of the parties;[84] this does not exclude a distance contract. Under Finnish law, however, a maintenance agreement must be approved by the local social authorities.[85] What is the Member State of origin for such an agreement?[86] A rule governing the formal validity of agreements might prove to be necessary.[87]

The outcome in the matter of private agreements is very much dependent on the outcome of the negotiations in The Hague. In the draft Convention, private agreements are enforceable, see Article 26. This is, however, a contentious issue and will be decided at the diplomatic conference in November 2007. It is likely that the EC Regulation will take the same position towards private agreements as does the Hague Convention. It would at least not appear reasonable to be more restrictive than the Convention.

2.9. ADMINISTRATIVE COOPERATION

Chapter VIII of the proposed Maintenance Regulation contains rules on administrative co-operation. This is a novelty in comparison to the Brussels I Regulation and indeed also the 1973 Hague Convention, neither of which contain rules on administrative cooperation. The relevant rules on administrative cooperation today can be found in the 1956 New York Convention, which 22 Member States have ratified.[88] Under the New York Convention "receiving agencies" shall take, only on behalf of the claimant, "all appropriate steps for the recovery of

83 *Supra* note 51.

84 Ch. 3 §19 of the Swedish Enforcement Act.

85 §50 Finnish Marriage Act.

86 However, it should be noted that the latest draft Hague Convention also refers to a "state of origin" in its Article 26. See Prel. Doc. No. 29 of June 2007 with a revised preliminary draft convention on the international recovery of child support and other forms of family maintenance, available at http://hcch.e-vision.nl/upload/wop/maint_pd29e.pdf.

87 Cf. Article 9 of the 1980 Rome Convention on the law applicable to contractual obligations, OJ L 266, 9 October 1980, p. 1.

88 *Supra* note 4. Those States are: Austria, Belgium, Cyprus, the Czech Republic, Denmark, Estonia, Finland, France, Germany, Greece, Hungary, Ireland, Italy, Luxembourg, the Netherlands, Poland, Portugal, the Slovak Republic, Slovenia, Spain, Sweden, and the United Kingdom. I.e. all the EU Member States except for Bulgaria, Latvia, Lithuania, Malta and Romania.

maintenance". This includes working for a settlement, assistance in bringing an action for maintenance and the enforcement of decisions.

According to Article 40 the general functions of central authorities under the proposed Maintenance Regulation are to communicate information and work through the European Judicial Network in Civil and Commercial Matters.[89] The specific functions of central authorities that are given in Article 41 are quite similar to those under the 1956 New York Convention: *viz.* to collect and exchange information, provide assistance to creditors involved in proceedings, facilitate settlements, and also to represent creditors at the stages of establishment of maintenance and in enforcement.

The main difference in the functions of central authorities between the 1956 New York Convention and the proposed Maintenance Regulation lies in the exchange of information foreseen under the latter and, not to be underestimated, the fact that EU central authorities, according to Article 43, will all meet regularly. A perhaps slightly less important difference is that under the 1956 New York Convention the assistance of central authorities is available to all those that are present in a particular Contracting State whereas the proposed Regulation requires a creditor to turn to the central authority of the Member State in which he has habitual residence. Apart from the fact that not all people have a habitual residence it would have been useful to allow for requests for assistance from e.g. temporarily posted workers and others who stay for a considerable time in a foreign state but do not acquire a new habitual residence there.

Practically important, but also highly controversial in terms of protection of privacy and data protection is Article 44 on access to information. Central authorities are under an obligation to give information in order to locate the debtor, evaluate his assets, identify the debtor's employer, and the debtor's bank accounts. For this purpose the central authorities shall have access to public registers concerning taxes, social security, population registers, land registers, motor vehicle registers, and information held by central banks. The text does not say to whom central authorities shall give all this information and in the Presidency text it is made clear that this information is sent to other competent authorities and not directly to creditors.[90] What is more, a rule on proportionality has been added in Article 44(3) so that the access to information given shall not exceed what is necessary in order to achieve the objective of recovering the maintenance claim.

89 See Council Decision 2001/470/EC of 28 May 2001 establishing a European Judicial Network in civil and commercial matters, OJ L 174, 27 June 2001, p. 25.

90 *Supra* note 51.

According to Article 45(1), in order to make a request for information, the creditor has to first turn to the court for the place where he is habitually resident and that court in its turn shall send the application. The paragraph does not say to whom the request should be sent – to the central authority of the Member State of the court or the central authority of the state from which information is sought. Paragraph 4, which speaks of a requesting central authority, would indicate the former. It is difficult to understand why a court should be involved. It would make perfect sense if the creditor could turn directly to his central authority. Involving courts will only slow down the request.

The proposed rules are likely to improve administrative cooperation compared to the current situation (after all not all Member States have central authorities) but there are certain shortcomings. Nothing is done to improve the quality of service in those Member States with poorly functioning central authorities.[91] It would have been a good idea to introduce time-limits, cf. Article 12 of the draft Hague Convention.

In the case of administrative cooperation, it is actually just as interesting to consider what is not included in the proposal as what is. There is very little detail as to what the central authorities should actually do when they meet regularly (cf. Article 43). In its own impact assessment, the Commission speaks of "an EU wide peer learning forum to facilitate the development of best practice guidance on the case of cross-border claims".[92] It would be a good idea to dedicate the meetings of the central authorities inter alia to furthering this purpose. This might well happen, but the proposed Regulation is silent on the matter.

In most cases it will be the creditor that requests administrative assistance but the debtor might also require the help of a central authority. As the proposal stands, central authorities are not even under an obligation to answer simple questions from debtors. It should be borne in mind that maintenance debtors are very often on the verge of poverty themselves and a categorisation of creditors as the weaker party and of debtors as the stronger party is simply not correct. The normal situation is rather that both parties can be characterised as weak and the situation therefore calls for a minimum of equality of arms.

One aspect that makes the proposed EC Regulation different from the draft Hague Convention is that the latter fully recognises the crucial role played by central

---

91 A very poorly functioning central authority could of course in itself be seen as a violation of the Regulation specifically and in general against the requirement of efficient application of EC law. See for a general treatise on the requirements of EC law concerning national administration J. Reichel, *God förvaltning i EU och i Sverige*, Jure, 2006.

92 *Supra* note 13, p. 13.

authorities at all stages of the procedure from establishment to enforcement. In the draft Hague Convention it is recognised that a vast majority of all applications for recognition and enforcement, establishment or modification are made through a central authority and not directly by the creditor to a court or an enforcement agency in a foreign country. Chapter III in the draft Convention deals with "applications through central authorities" and only in Article 16(5) are so-called direct applications foreseen, and then only for recognition and enforcement. In the proposed Regulation this fact is not recognised.

Finally, the relationship between the rules on administrative cooperation in the future Hague Convention and those in the future Regulation must be clarified. The Commission has orally declared in meetings that the Regulation is intended to build upon the Convention and to take cooperation one step further. The problem is that the text in the proposed Regulation does not build on that of the Convention and add what is missing. This would of course also have been impossible unless the Commission had waited for the Convention to be concluded – which would in fact have been a good idea.[93] As the proposal stands the relationship between the two sets or rules on administrative cooperation is unclear. According to Article 49 of the proposed Regulation it takes precedence over the future Convention. The draft Hague Convention, in its Article 45(4), gives precedence to rules of EC law concerning the recognition and enforcement of decisions – not administrative cooperation. The draft Hague Convention also allows for the application of more effective rules concerning legal assistance (legal aid) than those provided for in the Convention.

Under Article 45(2) of the draft Convention "any Contracting State may conclude with one or more Contracting States agreements [reciprocity schemes and uniform laws based on special ties], which contain provisions on matters governed by this Convention, *with a view to improving the application of this Convention* [emphasis added] between or among themselves, provided that such agreements are consistent with the objects and purpose of this Convention". If this paragraph also covers EC law, diverging rules are only in conformity with the Convention if it takes administrative cooperation one step further. However, that is not what Article 49 of the proposed Regulation says. To conclude, the relationship between the two planned instruments is far from clear.

93 A similar argument against duplication of rules between the Brussels II bis Regulation and the 1996 Hague Children's Convention (*supra* note 28) is made in J. Pirrung, "Brüche zwischen internationaler und europäischer Rechtsvereinheitlichung – das Beispiel des internationalen Kindschaftsrechts in der Brüssel IIa-Verordnung", in: R. Freitag et al [eds.], *Internationales Familienrecht für das 21. Jahrhundert: Symposium zum 65. Geburtstag von Ulrich Spellenberg*, Sellier, 2006, pp. 89–101 at p. 100.

3. DOES THE PROPOSED REGULATION SOLVE ANY PROBLEMS?

Earlier we described the problems involved with cross-border enforcement of maintenance claims as mainly concerning the quality of enforcement and administrative cooperation in general and more specifically the lack of assistance in locating the debtor and his assets and the lack of cooperation between central authorities.[94] In its impact assessment the Commission identifies the problems of cross-border enforcement as the following:

- Problems in locating the debtor.
- Accessing information on the debtor's assets.
- Lack of provision of advice and legal aid to the creditor.
- Lack of cooperation between competent authorities.
- Lack of mutual recognition of judgments.
- Problems associated with intermediate measures.
- Administrative inefficiencies.[95]

There appears to be no major disagreement concerning the problems involved; it is more a question of how they are expressed. We will therefore accept the Commission's inventory and see to which extent the proposed measures constitute an adequate remedy for the problem. However, it is just as important to analyse whether the Commission also proposes measures that are not the answer to a problem.

3.1. REMEDIES FOR PROBLEMS?

A problem with the Commission's impact analysis is that it is not fully structured around the concrete problems that are identified. It is true that some problems are identified in the impact assessment and illustrated in some detail, but there are also several problems that are not described and then suddenly pop up in various tables describing the relative success of different policy options.[96] The impact assessment is structured around four policy options involving different levels of harmonisation available to reach certain objectives that are not connected to the problems initially identified. Not until the end of the impact analysis are all the actual concrete problems identified and then only as boxes in a table. This is

94 See *supra* 0.

95 See *supra* note 13, p. 19.

96 *Supra* note 13, pp. 4 and 18 *et seq.*

letting the tail wag the dog. An impact analysis should first identify the problems and then consider possible solutions, not the other way around.

3.1.1. *Problems in Locating the Debtor and His Assets*

The proposed Article 44 would contribute to the solution of this problem. However, the Article is unnecessarily limited to enforcement in that it speaks only of the "recovery of maintenance claims" and not of establishment. It does not solve the "Franco-Belgian problem" of the refusal to give administrative assistance to creditors seeking establishment. Admittedly, with the abolition of the exequatur the necessity for the creditor to sue anywhere else than at home diminishes and consequently also the need for administrative assistance at the stage of establishment. However, if, for example, the creditor lives in a country with a notoriously slow legal system he might be interested in suing abroad.

In addition, a Member State can only give information that it has. If there are poor public records concerning addresses etc. the information given will be just as poor. However, using mutual recognition of judgments as an argument to adopt EU-wide rules requiring Member States to improve their systems for national registration would be stretching the legal basis beyond reasonability (not to speak of proportionality).

3.1.2. *Lack of Provision of Advice and Legal Aid to the Creditor*

The Commission rates the level of the relative effectiveness of policy option 4 "complete mutual recognition" (which is the one chosen in its final proposal) as a 3 on a scale of 4.[97] Since the problem is not described more in detail it is difficult to draw independent conclusions on the effectiveness of the proposed Regulation.

The lack of provision of advice would appear to be a problem of general poor service of central authorities and/or legal aid in maintenance proceedings. As stated earlier the proposal does not really tackle the issue of poorly functioning and understaffed central authorities. The meetings of central authorities within the framework of the European Judicial Network could create pressure to improve services, but only indirectly so.

If the outcome of negotiations is that free legal assistance for child support applications is granted, as in Article 14 bis (option 2) in the draft Hague Convention, it would be a considerable step forward towards the solution of this problem.

---

97 *Supra* note 13, p. 21 *et seq.*

3.1.3. *Lack of Cooperation Between Competent Authorities*

According to the Commission's impact analysis, already option 2 "non-legislative action" involving the development of collaborative mechanisms between the competent authorities of Member States will reach a 4 on a scale of 4 in terms of relative effectiveness.[98] It is difficult to asses the accuracy of the Commission's rating but Article 43 on meetings will probably have a positive impact on the cooperation at least between central authorities. This largely depends on what content these meetings are given.

3.1.4. *Lack of Mutual Recognition of Judgments*

The abolition of the exequatur procedure also entails an end to the possibility to refuse enforcement of a judgment on the grounds of public policy. To our knowledge, it is extremely rare that a Member State will invoke public policy against a judgment from another Member State. The Commission points at the possibility to make a reservation under Article 26 of the 1973 Hague Convention as an obstacle to mutual recognition. Under that provision a Contracting State has the possibility to enter a reservation against the enforcement of maintenance to adults (except spouses), persons related collaterally or by affinity, and non-periodical payments. Of the 17 Member States that are parties to the 1973 Hague Convention, 15 have entered reservations that are distributed as follows:

Country	Adults	Collaterals	Affinity	Non-periodical
CZ		X	X	
DK	X	X	X	
EE		X	X	X
FI	X	X	X	
DE		X	X	
GR		X[99]	X	
IT				X[100]
LT	X	X	X	
LU		X	X	X
NL		X		

98 *Supra* note 13, pp. 13 and 21 *et seq.*
99 With the exception of maintenance between siblings.
100 With the exception of divorce settlements.

Country	Adults	Collaterals	Affinity	Non-periodical
PL				X
PT	X		X	
SK		X	X	
SE	X	X	X	
UK		X[101]	X[102]	X

In its analysis the Commission points at Article 71 of the Brussels I Regulation, which states that "this Regulation shall not affect any conventions to which the Member States are party and which in relation to particular matters, govern jurisdiction or the recognition or enforcement of judgments" and draws the conclusion that the reservations entered into are valid also between EU Member States. In the Commission's opinion this is unacceptable "within the European Union which has decided, at the highest political level, to favour the free movement of maintenance decisions". [103]

First of all, the initial analysis made by the Commission, *viz.* that the reservations stand, is not self-evident. Article 23 of the 1973 Hague Convention stipulates that "[t]his Convention shall not restrict the application of an international instrument in force between the Member State of origin and the State addressed or other law of the State for the purposes of obtaining recognition and enforcement of a decision or settlement". Making sense out of Article 71 of the Brussels I Regulation and Article 23 of the 1973 Hague Convention and the situation of "double subsidiarity" that arises is not easy. This paper is not the right place to solve this intricate legal problem but it should be said that Swedish courts do not make the same interpretation as the Commission and are quite ready to declare judgments concerning maintenance to, e.g., a parent enforceable under the Brussels I Regulation. A highly informal and unscientific survey of ours shows that this appears to be the case in several other Member States as well.

Secondly, the political conclusion that the Commission makes can also be questioned. If 15 out of 17 Member States have made some sort of reservation and if 12 out of those States have made reservations against the enforcement of maintenance between persons related collaterally or by affinity, that would rather indicate that there is a lack of political will to enforce such decisions and that the

101 Unless the creditor is a "child of the family" (England and Wales and Northern Ireland) or is a child of the maintenance creditor who has been accepted as a child of the family by the debtor (Scotland).
102 See *supra* note 101.
103 *Supra* note 1, p. 6.

abolition of exequatur should perhaps not be extended to all categories of maintenance.

Nevertheless, it has to be admitted that if one accepts the Commission's standpoint that the mutual recognition of judgments takes priority over other concerns, then the abolition of the exequatur procedure and the deletion of an Article corresponding to Article 71 of the Brussels I Regulation (cf. Article 49 of the proposed Regulation) are effective.

3.1.5. Problems Associated with Intermediate Measures

The exequatur procedure, which is a necessary intermediate stage in order to obtain a declaration of enforceability, produces delays. The procedure as such is slow, particularly in certain Member States, and the possibility to appeal against an exequatur decision as well as to suspend the proceedings if the debtor has, for example, questioned the parentage in new court proceedings, cause considerable delay. The elimination of the exequatur procedure practically eliminates this problem. Add to this the proposed Article 26 on provisional enforcement and we do have a very effective system of enforceability of judgments. The question is rather if it is not too effective. There is a risk that the measures proposed go beyond what is necessary for the attainment of the aim and that the interests of the debtor have been thrown out with the bathwater. On the other hand, the very liberal rules on the debtor's rights to have enforcement refused or suspended go too far in the other direction and would cause unnecessary delays in enforcement.

3.1.6. Administrative Inefficiencies

It is difficult to asses the success rate of the Commission's proposal in countering administrative inefficiencies as these are never properly identified in the impact assessment. It is one of those problems that pop up in the tables concerning the rating of the various policy options. In policy option 2 "non-legislative action", the success is described as "[g]reater cooperation and the sharing of best practice should improve inefficiencies, however will fall short if minimum common standards or deadlines are not enforced". Option 4 "complete mutual recognition" speaks of minimum common standards and mandatory standards on processing and enforcement.

The Commission's final proposal does not appear to fully go along with option 4. In the area of enforcement there are suggestions concerning garnishment of salaries and bank accounts and the freezing of bank accounts (that have been thrown out by the Council) but there are no proposals concerning, e.g., deadlines.

Administrative inefficiencies could also pertain to the work of central authorities and here the regular meetings, if they are made to further the use of best practices, could further the improvement of the services of central authorities.

It remains to be seen what the impact of the future Regulation will be but if there is future work to be done after some experience of the Regulation it will probably be in this area. This is, of course, not a problem which is unique to mutual recognition but a "horizontal" one. Several Member States lack the administrative capacity (the problems go beyond "basic" problems such as corruption) in one or many areas to correctly give effect to EC law.

3.2. REMEDIES FOR NON-PROBLEMS

It is highly questionable whether the rules on applicable law really solve more problems than they create. It is true that differences in the applicable law between the Member States create uncertainty – in particular since the choice-of-law rules in some Member States are not codified and case law is not settled.[104] However, not even the Commission lists this as a real problem; the unification of conflicts rules is listed as a "policy objective". Many Member States today either apply only the *lex fori* or only apply foreign law at the request of a party. The time and expense needed to establish the content of a particular foreign law would in many cases be prohibitively or disproportionately expensive and likely to lead to precisely the sort of delays which the proposed Regulation purports to combat. Now that the Commission has felt it necessary to include rules on applicable law, they should also have combined this with mechanisms to simplify and speed up the application of foreign law (admittedly this is also a "horizontal" problem).

3.3. DOES THE PROPOSED REGULATION HAVE ADDED VALUE?

There are a number of reasons to be critical vis-à-vis the Commission's proposed Maintenance Regulation. First of all, there is a lack of coordination with the ongoing Hague project for a revised Maintenance Convention. This is particularly evident in the area of administrative cooperation where the relationship between Hague and Brussels instruments is far from clear and the case for an additional set of rules applicable between the Member States of the European Union has not been made. It is also not clear to us why the Commission should have spent time and manpower on drafting rules on the applicable law when the same work is

104 Such is the case in Sweden.

being done in The Hague and there is widespread consensus that there should not be parallel systems for choice of law. The Commission appears to place a very high intrinsic value in Community legislation while the truth that the principle of subsidiarity in Article 5 of the EC Treaty tells us is that it should be a last resort![105]

Secondly, the Commission also appears to have taken the principle of proportionality, also contained in Article 5 of the EC Treaty, lightly. It would appear that in the eyes of the Commission, the introduction of conflict-of-law rules in lieu of harmonising the substantive law rules on maintenance is all that it takes to fulfil the requirements of proportionality.[106] As the proposal stands we have serious doubts about the proportionality of several aspects thereof, in particular the harmonisation of the rules on service, provisional enforcement, freezing of bank accounts, and the priority of maintenance claims.

Thirdly, there are certain shortcomings in terms of quality. As we have outlined above, there are some drafting errors that probably could have been avoided if the proposal had been prepared more thoroughly. The Commission had an expert meeting on 12 May 2005 upon which a preliminary draft proposal consisting of two Regulations and one Directive were presented. This proposal was much criticised. Only seven months later was there a final proposal for a Regulation. Given the internal bureaucracy of the Commission and the time needed for translations, the time available for redrafting cannot have been more than a month or two. The fact that the commentary to the proposal was not published until five months later indicates that there was considerable haste involved.[107]

Our initial analysis of the Commission's proposal for a Maintenance Regulation leaves us with mixed impressions. To be true, the Commission has identified a number of relevant problems and proposed solutions thereto. However, in our opinion the focus of the proposal is not sufficiently aimed at strengthening administrative cooperation and speeding up the work of authorities involved at all stages in the recovery of maintenance claims. Nevertheless, our overall impression is that on the day that the Maintenance Regulation enters into force the world will be a slightly better place to live in[108] – albeit also a more complicated one.

---

105 See for an appeal for legislative restraint M. Jänterä-Jareborg, "Unification of International Family Law in Europe – A Critical Perspective", in: K. Boele-Woelki (ed.), *Perspectives for the Unification and Harmonisation of Family Law in Europe*, Intersentia, 2003, pp. 194–216 at p. 212.

106 Cf. COM(2005) 649 final, p. 8.

107 See *supra* note 53. For a general critique of the lack of preparatory work by the Commission in the area of family law, see M. Jänterä-Jareborg, *supra* note 105, p. 213.

108 Given that the Regulation finally adopted bears resemblance to the original Commission proposal.

UNIFICATION OF CONFLICT OF LAWS IN EUROPE

– Matrimonial Property Regimes –

Kathrin Kroll

1. INTRODUCTION

International Family Law has long been regarded as law in the books and as a mere subject of academic research. After years of being disregarded, the European Union has finally taken note of the legal difficulties which "cross-border couples" have to deal with. Having already been mentioned in the 1998 Vienna Action Plan,[1] a European instrument on matrimonial property regimes has recently been prepared. On 7 July 2006, the European Commission presented a Green Paper on "the conflict of laws in matters concerning matrimonial property regimes, including the question of jurisdiction and mutual recognition"[2] intending to examine all property aspects of both married couples and other forms of unions. Thirty-four submissions[3] by national governments, parliaments and stakeholders in response to the Green Paper have been received in the aftermath dealing with the main aspects that are to be regulated by a future Community instrument. However, the Green Paper is only one part within a harmonisation process concerning conflict-of-law rules in family matters.[4] The European Commission has also presented proposals for Council Regulations concerning the law applicable to divorce and legal separation (the so-called Rome III proposal)[5] as well as to maintenance.[6]

1 OJC 19, 23 January 1999.

2 COM(2006) 400 final.

3 The responses are published on the internet at: http://ec.europa.eu/justice_home/news/consulting_public/news_consulting_public_en.htm.

4 Concerning succession law, see the Green Paper on succession and wills of 1 March 2005, COM(2005) 65 final.

5 Proposal for a Council Regulation amending Regulation (EC) No. 2201/2003 as regards jurisdiction and introducing rules concerning the applicable law in matrimonial matters of 17 July 2007, COM(2006) 399 final.

6 Proposal for a Council Regulation on jurisdiction, applicable law, recognition and enforcement of decisions and cooperation in matters relating to maintenance obligations of 15 December 2005, COM(2005), 649 final.

To date, international family law regarding property relations between spouses is very much national law. The 1978 Hague Convention on the law applicable to matrimonial property regimes[7] is still only in force in the Netherlands, France and Luxembourg. The question of how national conflict-of-law rules currently vary within the European Union will be the subject of the following analysis (2.). I will thereby focus on two main issues: the identification of the connecting factors and party autonomy. Due to space limitations, choice of law questions regarding registered partnerships and other forms of union will be omitted, thus focussing on matrimonial property regimes. A close look should be taken at the major changes which a future Community instrument is probably about to introduce (3.). The Green Paper as well as the responses that have been received thereon will be analysed. Finally, the present article will provide a critical discussion on both the connecting factors and the choice-of-law questions proposed (4.).

2. STATUS QUO

2.1. CONNECTING FACTORS

2.1.1. The Nationality Principle

Under a future Community instrument regarding harmonized conflict-of-law rules in matters of matrimonial property, the question of which connecting factor should be used to determine the applicable law is of particular importance. An overall view of the European status quo will lead to the following picture: Most European countries, such as, for example, Austria,[8] Denmark,[9] Germany,[10] Greece,[11] Poland,[12] Portugal[13] and Spain[14] take the common nationality of the spouses as the primary connecting factor. In the absence of a common nationality, the law of the place of the first habitual residence is applied followed by further

7 The English text of the Convention is available at http://hcch.e-vision.nl/index_fr.php?act=conventions.text&cid=87.

8 §§18, 19 para. 1 Austrian CPIL.

9 Denmark is the only European country that still applies the nationality of the husband; for details see J. Scherpe, in: A. Bergmann/M. Ferid/D. Henrich, *Internationales Ehe- und Kindschaftsrecht* (2003), Dänemark, p. 25.

10 Arts. 15 para. 1, 14 para. 1 no. 1 German ILCC.

11 Arts. 14 no. 1, 15 Greek Civil Code.

12 Art. 17 §1 Polish CPIL.

13 Arts. 52 para. 1, 53 para. 1 Portuguese Civil Code.

14 For a detailed comparative outline see *Study in comparative law on the rules governing conflicts of jurisdiction and laws on matrimonial property regimes and the implementation for property issues of the separation of unmarried couples in the Member States* of 30 April 2003, ASSER-UCL Consortium commissioned by the Commission, p. 124, available at http://europa.eu.int/comm/justice_home/doc_centre/civil/studies/doc_civil_studies_en.htm.

subsidiary factors such as, for example, the place of the matrimonial ceremony[15] or the law with which the spouses have the closest connection.[16] For reasons of legal certainty and stability the majority[17] of the national conflict-of-law systems provide for the determination of the applicable law at the moment when the marriage was celebrated.[18] That means that in the event of a modification in the connecting factors the applicable law does not change at all. Thus, if spouses change their common nationality or – more likely – their common habitual residence, the law applicable to their matrimonial property regime will still be the same as at the moment of the celebration of the marriage.

2.1.2. Habitual Residence

There are only a few states, in particular those which are members of the 1978 Hague Convention but also Belgium,[19] Latvia[20] and Denmark,[21] that determine the first common habitual residence of the spouses as the leading connecting factor.[22] Instead, Art. 7 para. 2 of the 1978 Hague Convention provides for mutability allowing the applicable law to change automatically when the spouses move to another country. However, according to this provision, the law of the "new" habitual residence of the spouses becomes applicable only if the nationality of that State is their common nationality or when, after marriage, that habitual residence has lasted for a period of at least ten years or when that habitual residence is established in cases where the matrimonial property regime was subject to the law of the state of the common nationality and the spouses did not establish their first habitual residence after marriage in the same state.[23]

---

15 *Lex loci celebrationis*, see e.g. Art. 9 para. 2 Spanish Civil Code.

16 See e.g. Art. 15 para. 2 no. 3 German ILCC; Art. 14 no. 3, 15 Greek Civil Code.

17 For a different solution see Art. 17 §1 al. 1 Polish CPIL that applies the law of the state of the common nationality of the spouses in the respective current version.

18 For a comparative overview see Study in comparative law, *op cit* (fn 14), pp. 126–127.

19 See Art. 51 para. 1 Belgian PIL that was approved on 16 July 2004. For details concerning the replacement of nationality by domicile see H. van Houtte, "Updating Private International Law? The Belgian Experiment", in: *Liber Memoralis Petar Šarčević* (2006), pp. 65 *et seq.*, at pp. 71–72; M. Pertegás, "The Belgian Code on Private International Law: a tour d'horizon", *Praxis des Internationalen Privat- und Verfahrensrechts* (IPRax) 2006, pp. 53 *et seq.*, at pp. 58 *et seq.*

20 Art. 13 para. 1 Latvian Civil Code.

21 Cf. Scherpe, *op cit* (fn 9) at p. 25.

22 For – different – comparative reports, see the Study in comparative law, *op cit* (fn 14) at p. 127; see also Document de travail des services de la Commission, Annexe au Livre Vert sur le règlement des conflits de lois en matière de régime matrimonial, traitant notamment de la question de la compétence judiciaire et de la reconnaissance mutuelle, COM(2006), 952, pp. 20–21.

23 For a critical view of Article 7 of the 1978 Hague Convention see Y. Requette, "Le droit international privé de la famille à l'épreuve des conventions internationales", *Recueil des Cours* 246 (1994 II), pp. 19 et *seq.*, at p. 167; P. Mayer/V. Heuzé, *Droit international privé* (2004), no. 791.

2.1.3. *The Common Law Approach*

A third group of countries must be mentioned separately as they do not really fit in the conflict-of-law systems mentioned so far, i.e. common law countries. Two particular premises have to be noted with regard to the law which is applicable to marital property: first, substantive family law does not provide for any matrimonial property regime at all but deals with the spouses' property during marriage separately. Marriage has no effect upon the assets of the spouses whether these were antenuptial or postnuptial.[24] And second: questions relating to the law applicable to matrimonial property therefore only arise when the marriage has broken down and property has to be divided. Under English law, the court exercises discretion while requiring one spouse to pay money or to transfer property to the other from his or her separate assets (financial relief).[25] Thus, under common law, there is no choice of law rule providing how to deal with foreign matrimonial property regimes. Take, for example, a German marrying an English domiciliary in Frankfurt without having contracted an antenuptial agreement.[26] The only question that interests an English court granting divorce in England & Wales would be which influence the German *Zugewinngemeinschaft* (deferred community property) would probably have on the property of the spouses.[27]

Concerning the applicable law, a general rule may be deduced as follows: an English court applies only English law to all matters of divorce, i.e. amongst other things financial relief and property distribution.[28] In cases where the question of proprietary ownership is concerned – and no contract has been concluded – movable property is governed by the law of the matrimonial domicile at the time of the celebration of the marriage.[29] Even though the legal situation is unclear regarding immovables, the majority opinion seems to prefer the application of the matrimonial domicile as well.[30] Under English law, one of the most controversial questions is whether the domicile approach leads to mutability or immutability regarding matrimonial property. It was a decision by the House of Lords in 1900[31] that is taken as an indicator for both positions. Despite the House of Lords' clear ruling that the matrimonial property regime applying to the parties was not affected by a change of the matrimonial domicile, some were of the opinion that

---

24 C.M.V. Clarkson/J. Hill, *The Conflict of Laws* (2006), p. 434.

25 For the various orders that may be made see N. Lowe/G. Douglas, *Bromley's Family Law* (2007), pp. 991 *et seq.*

26 Example taken from Clarkson/Hill, *op cit* (fn 24), p. 434.

27 Cf. F. Odersky, in: R. Süss/G. Ring, *Eherecht in Europa*, England und Wales (2004), at p. 22.

28 Cf. Clarkson/Hill, *op cit* (fn 24), at p. 435.

29 Cf. Dicey, Morris and Collins on the Conflict of Laws (2006), Rule 148, 28–007 to 28–019.

30 Cf. Dicey, Morris and Collins, *op cit* (fn 29), Rule 148, 28–020.

31 *De Nichols v. Culier* [1900] A.C. 21.

this could only be true assuming that the spouses had entered into an implied contract.[32] However, the majority opinion seems to follow the doctrine of immutability.[33]

2.2. THE ROLE OF PARTY AUTONOMY

With the exception of Greece[34] that totally ignores the principle of party autonomy, the vast majority of the Member States of the EC[35] allow spouses to choose the law which is applicable to their marital property.[36] This solution is known both in common law and civil law systems. Under English law, pre-nuptial agreements determining the proprietary consequences in the event of divorce have long been regarded as void and unenforceable.[37] Nevertheless, in recent cases[38] the courts have started suggesting that a court may give considerable effect to a pre-nuptial contract in the exercise of its discretion as provided in section 25 of the 1973 Matrimonial Causes Act. Due to this development, established case law on conflict of law rules regarding the validity and enforcement of antenuptial contracts does not exist.[39] It is uncertain, though, whether the law applicable to marriage contracts would also apply to modern pre-nuptial agreements.[40] As a general rule – that can be drawn from commercial contracts – the validity of a marriage contract is governed by its proper law, i.e. the law governing the contract.[41] The proper law of a marriage settlement is the law of the matrimonial domicile.[42] Even if spouses are given the freedom to choose the proper law by an express clause in the settlement, there is no reported case law supporting this

---

32 Cf. Dicey, Morris and Collins, *op cit* (fn 29), Rule 150, at 28–48 and 28–49 for further details.

33 Cf. Dicey, Morris and Collins, *op cit* (fn 29), Rule 150, at 28–049; Clarkson/Hill, *op cit* (fn 24), at p. 438.

34 Cf. Study in comparative law, *op cit* (fn 14) at p. 128.

35 Except Malta, Poland, Slovakia and Lithuania.

36 Cf. Study in comparative law, *op cit* (fn 14), at p. 128.

37 See *Hyman v Hyman* [1929] AC 601. For a historical and comparative perspective see J. Morley, "Enforceable Pre-nuptial Agreements: the World View", *IFLJ* 2006 (195), J. Scherpe, "A Comparative View of Pre-Nuptial Agreements", *IFLJ* 2007 (18).

38 See e.g. *Ella v Ella* [2007] EWCA Civ 99 (Court of Appeal); *K v K* [2003] 1 FLR 120; *M v. M* [2002] 1 FLR 654; *X v X* (Y and Z Intervening) [2002] 1 FLR 508; *S v S* [1997] 2 FLR 100. See also the proposal "A more certain future – Recognition of pre-marital agreements in England and Wales" (2004) by the Solicitors Family Law Association (Resolutions by the Law Reform Committee), suggesting the legal acceptance of pre-nuptial agreements, available at http://www.sfla.org.uk.

39 Cf. Clarkson/Hill, *op cit* (fn 24), p. 442.

40 Cf. Clarkson/Hill, *op cit* (fn 24), p. 442.

41 Cf. Dicey, Morris and Collins, *op cit* (fn 29), Rule 149, at 28–030.

42 Cf. Dicey, Morris and Collins, *op cit* (fn 29), Rule 149, at 28R-029.

proposition.[43] Party autonomy regarding marriage contracts therefore still seems to be a mere theoretical approach. Concerning pre-nuptial agreements, of significant note is the view of Charles J in *Ella v Ella*[44] stating that "... in England financial provisions of the agreement would not be enforced as a matter of contract". Should the English courts decide on the issue, it is to be doubted, however, that the validity and effect of a pre-nuptial agreement would be governed by the proper law of the contract.

In civil law countries, however, party autonomy is broadly accepted with regard to matrimonial property regimes. However, the spouses' freedom to choose the applicable law is mostly[45] limited to those laws that would be applicable in the absence of a choice, i.e. in particular common nationality and habitual residence of both or either spouse. This limited approach does not only apply to the majority of national conflict of law systems,[46] but also to the 1978 Hague Convention which in Article 3 para. 2 provides that the spouses may designate only the law of any state of which either spouse is a national at the time of designation or the law of the state in which one of them has his or her habitual residence at that time or, finally, the law of the state where one of the spouses establishes a new habitual residence after marriage.[47] As far as immovable property is concerned, Article 3 para. 2 of the 1978 Hague Convention, just like similar provisions under German[48] and Austrian[49] law, allows spouses to designate the law of the place where the immovables are situated, therefore applying the *lex situs*. As a consequence, the relevant connecting factor must not be the same for all aspects of the matrimonial property regime. Instead, different criteria may be used for different aspects although they result in a so-called *depeçage*. As an example, a German-French couple living in Germany while owing extensive real estate in France may choose French law to govern their immovable property according to Article 15 para. 2 no. 3 German ILCC. Nevertheless, the law applicable to their movable property is German law as provided in Articles 15 para. 1 and 14 para. 1 no. 2 German ILCC. The purpose of the law allowing for a *depeçage* is, first, to prevent conflicts arising from the application of mandatory rules of the *lex situs* and, second, to facilitate real estate transactions.[50] However, the majority of Member

43 Cf. DICEY, MORRIS and COLLINS, *op cit* (fn 29), Rule 149, at 28–032.
44 *Ella v Ella* [2007] EWCA Civ 99 (Court of Appeal) at para. 50.
45 For an exception see §19 Austrian CPIL that gives spouses a wide degree of freedom to choose the applicable law.
46 For a comparative review see the Study in comparative law, *op cit* (fn 14), pp. 118 *et seq*.
47 REQUETTE, *op cit* (fn 23), pp. 148–149 criticizes such "autonomie restreinte et renforcée".
48 Art. 15 para. 2 no. 3 German ILCC.
49 §19 Austrian CPIL.
50 For the German legal position compare STAUDINGER/P. MANKOWSKI, *Kommentar zum Bürgerlichen Gesetzbuch* (2003), Art. 15 EGBGB at 151 *et seq*.

States of the EC provide for a uniform solution thus using the same connecting factor for all aspects of the matrimonial property regime.[51]

Concerning formal requirements, several Member States of the EC, for example England & Wales,[52] Spain[53] and Portugal[54] require the parties' choice of law to be included in a marriage contract. Thus, the principle of *favor negotii* prevails, being destined to "save" the validity of the contract by multiplying different connecting factors as regards formalities.[55] Under Spanish law, for instance, the *lex loci contractus*, the *lex causae* or the law of the common nationality of the parties apply to the formal requirements of a marriage contract.[56] Other Member States, such as Austria[57] and Germany,[58] do not require that the choice-of-law clause is necessarily related to a marriage contract. However, as to the form, under German law a choice-of-law settlement is only valid if it complies with the formal requirements of a marriage contract prescribed by either the *lex loci actus* or the *lex causae*. If the agreement is concluded in Germany it has to be authorized by a notary public.[59] Article 11 of the 1978 Hague Convention may be called a compromise solution thus allowing the designation of the applicable law by express stipulation as well as by necessary implication from the provisions of a marriage contract. Even an express stipulation has to comply with the form prescribed for marriage contracts as required either by the *lex causae* or *lex fori*.[60] Furthermore, Article 12 provides that a marriage contract must at least be in writing, duly dated and signed by both spouses.

3. REVISION OF THE NATIONAL CONFLICT-OF-LAW RULES BY THE EUROPEAN COMMISSION

3.1. CHANGE TOWARDS HABITUAL RESIDENCE

To start with the connecting factors, a fundamental change in the current national solutions – as described above – is to be expected. There has been a trend among several respondents to the Green Paper on matrimonial property regimes towards

51 For a comparative survey see the Study in comparative law, *op cit* (fn 14), pp. 117–118.
52 Cf. Dicey, Morris and Collins, *op cit* (fn 29), Rule 149, at 28–030.
53 Art. 11 Spanish Civil Code.
54 Art. 53 para. 1 Portugese Civil Code.
55 Cf. the Study in comparative law, *op cit* (fn 14) at p. 121.
56 Art. 11 para. 1 Spanish Civil Code.
57 §19 Austrian CPIL.
58 Art. 15 para. 2 German ILCC.
59 Arts 15 para. 3, 14 para. 4 ILCC.
60 Art. 13 of the 1978 Hague Convention.

using the common habitual residence of the spouses as the first connecting factor.[61] Surprisingly, many of these responses emerged from those Member States which currently apply the law of the common nationality of the spouses, e.g. Germany.[62] The Green Paper itself tends to favour this solution while corresponding to the Commission's Rome III proposal on divorce and legal separation.[63] It not only cites considerable statistical data as to the significant increase in all forms of unions between nationals of different Member States or the presence of such couples in a Member State of which they do not have the nationality, but it also supports a more flexible approach.[64] Furthermore, in question 2 of the Green Paper the Commission proposes a certain order of priority as regards connecting factors starting with the first habitual residence of the spouses followed by their common nationality.[65] As the preliminary study commissioned by the Commission has already been proposed, the solution of the 1978 Hague Convention on matrimonial property regimes may be taken as a model approach.[66] The study prefers the first common habitual residence of the spouses as the primary connecting factor.[67] In the absence of a common habitual residence, the applicable law should be determined on the basis of subsidiary connecting factors, based in the first place on the common nationality of the spouses and, secondly, on the *lex loci celebrationis*.[68]

As to the question whether to allow an automatic change to the applicable law in the event of a change in the connecting factors,[69] the study speaks of a full doctrine of immutability.[70] Since the concept of mutability as provided in Article 7 is considered to be the weakest point in the 1978 Hague Convention and the reason for its scarce acceptance it is not taken as a model for a prospective Community instrument.[71] Instead, the authors of the study propose to apply the law of the first

61 See e.g. the reports of the French Authorities, the Austrian Ministry of Justice, the Federal Government of Germany, the Commission of the Bishops' Conference of the European Community (COMECE) and the Council of Bars and Law Societies of Europe (CCBE), *op cit* (fn 3).

62 There is a discrepancy between the report of the German Federal Government being in favour of the habitual residence approach, on the one hand, and that of the *Bundesrat* on the other; *op cit* (fn 3).

63 See Proposal, *op cit* (fn 5), Art. 20b, p. 13.

64 See Green Paper, *op cit* (fn 2), at p. 3.

65 See Green Paper, *op cit* (fn 2), Question 2 lit. a, p. 5.

66 Cf. the Study in comparative law, *op cit* (fn 14), at p. 164.

67 Study in comparative law, *op cit* (fn 14), at p. 164.

68 For further explanations of this proposal see the Study in comparative law, *op cit* (fn 14), pp. 164–165.

69 Question 4 of the Green Paper, *op cit* (fn 2) at p. 6.

70 Cf. the Study in comparative law, *op cit* (fn 14) at p. 167.

71 Study in comparative law, *op cit* (fn 14), at p. 167.

habitual residence of the spouses while allowing them to contract differently.[72] The majority[73] of the respondents to the Green Paper argue likewise.

3.2. PARTY AUTONOMY

The Green Paper does not support any substantial innovations regarding the principle of party autonomy. The freedom of the spouses to choose the law which is applicable to their marital property will be limited to a number of connecting factors with which they have a close connection, for example habitual residence or the nationality of one or both spouses.[74] Freedom of choice is merely deemed necessary to set off the defects of the connecting factors, especially the lack of flexibility arising from the doctrine of immutability. Accordingly, most of the respondents support such a limited approach.[75] Concerning a further choice of the *lex situs* for immovables, a narrow majority are also in favour of such a solution, thus accepting a *depeçage* as regards the law applicable to matrimonial property regimes.[76]

4. COMMENTS

4.1. THE METHOD CHOSEN BY THE COMMISSION

Developing separate Community instruments for different fields of family law, i.e. divorce, maintenance and matrimonial property regimes instead of creating one single code on conflict-of-law rules is the method chosen by the EU Commission. Such an approach can be strongly criticized. Not only general questions of private international law as regards, e.g., definitions, *renvoi*[77] or qualification are left unanimously unanswered. Concerning public policy, even if all Member States are subject to the European Convention on Human Rights,[78] uniform

---

72 Study in comparative law, *op cit* (fn 14), at p. 164.

73 For different opinions see e.g. the comments of the Ministry of Estonia, the Swiss Ministry of Justice and the International Academy of Matrimonial Lawyers; *op cit* (fn 3).

74 See Green Paper, *op cit* (fn 2), at p. 6.

75 Responses, *op cit* (fn 3).

76 Responses, *op cit* (fn 3).

77 For the doctrine of renvoi within the Community, see D. Martiny, "Objectives and values of (private) international law in family law", in: J. Meeusen/M. Pertegás/G. Straetmans/F. Swennen (eds.), *International Family Law for the European Union* (2007), pp. 69 *et seq.*, at p. 96.

78 For the role of Human Rights in developing EU family law see H. Stalford, "EU family law: A human rights perspective", in: Meeussen/Pertegás et al. (eds.), *op cit* (fn 77), pp. 101 *et seq.*, at pp. 107 *et seq.*; for controlling the Member States by the European legal system see S.

guidelines so as to apply public policy clauses that are part of prospective Community instruments are still lacking.[79] Moreover, the Commission artificially divides aspects that – under substantive law – depend on each other, such as divorce and maintenance or rather divorce and the division of marital property. Concerning the latter, the difficult question arises whether a Community instrument should apply to the property consequences of the marriage bond while the parties are still living together or only when they separate and the marriage is dissolved.[80] The large majority of the respondents to the Green Paper are in favour of a broad scope of the future instrument, thus proposing to include both the property consequences of the dissolution of marriage and those arising during its existence.[81] Indeed, given that the Commission will follow this proposal, one might expect further inconsistency in legislation as regards the provisions on applicable law in the Rome III proposal, on the one hand, and those in a future Community instrument on matrimonial property regimes on the other.

4.2. THE LAW APPLICABLE TO MATRIMONIAL PROPERTY

4.2.1. *The Habitual Residence Approach*

To start with the new trend towards applying the principle of habitual residence as the primary connecting factor, several advantages can be highlighted regarding this approach. First, in accordance with the Rome III proposal: As mentioned before, the Commission prefers to develop instruments for selected fields of family law. Balancing the connecting factors therefore seems to be at least an appropriate means to attain a minimum standard of harmonisation. Since, under substantive law, questions regarding the division of marital property mostly arise in cases of divorce it would be preferable if connecting factors in both Community instruments, i.e. on divorce and legal separation, on the one hand, and on matrimonial property regimes, on the other, were to be consistent with each other. Article 20e of the Rome III proposal provides for the application of the law of the State:

(a) where the spouses have their common habitual residence, or failing that,

Poillot Peruzzetto, "The exception of public policy in family law within the European legal system", in: Meeussen/Pertegás et al. (eds.), *op cit* (fn 77), pp. 279 *et seq.*, at pp. 285 *et seq.*

79 Cf. K. Kroll, "Scheidung auf europäisch? Die (derzeit) nicht scheidbare Ehe im IPR", *Das Standesamt* (StAZ) 2007 (forthcoming); for certain values of public policy as regards matrimonial matters see Martiny, *op cit* (fn 77), at p. 96.

80 See question 1 of the Green Paper, *op cit* (fn 2).

81 Responses, *op cit* (fn 3.).

(b) where the spouses had their last common habitual residence insofar as one of them still resides there, or failing that,
(c) of which both spouses are nationals, or, in the case of the United Kingdom and Ireland, both have their "domicile" there, or failing that,
(d) where the application is lodged.

Since the rule is based, in the first place, on the habitual residence of the spouses and, failing that, on their last habitual residence if one of them still resides there, it will result in the application of the law of the forum in the vast majority of cases thus providing for mutability.[82] Problems relating to the application of foreign law will therefore be scarce. Such a *lex fori*-oriented approach is, nevertheless, inefficient in those cases where foreign law provides for more reasonable results in view of the individual circumstances as this is particularly important in family matters.[83] If, as it seems likely, the Commission will accept the suggestion of the preliminary study and apply the doctrine of immutability as regards matrimonial property regimes, a full harmonisation of both instruments will not be realized.

Second, in accordance with the growing mobility of European citizens: Only the habitual residence approach is considered to be the right answer to the growing mobility of citizens within the European Union and the increasing number of spouses being of different nationalities.[84] There is no denying that the increased mobility of persons throughout the European Union reflects an increase in cross-border marriages, i.e. those between nationals of different states or the presence of such couples in a Member State of which they do not have the nationality.[85] To date, more than 5 million people are living in another Member State of the EC.[86] According to a study that has been carried out on behalf of the European Commission, 29.7% of EU migrants move for love or family matters whereas "work opportunities" have been mentioned by 25.2%.[87] In Germany alone approximately 20% of all parties contracting a marriage in 2005 were of different nationalities.[88] With these facts in mind, the current assumption that a person has the closest connection with the laws of his or her home country can no longer be said

82 See Proposal, *op cit* (fn 5), at p. 10.
83 For an economic analysis of the lex fori approach see G. Rühl, "Methods and Approaches in Choice of Law: An Economic Perspective", 24 *Berkeley J. Int.'L.* 801 (2006).
84 Cf. Martiny, *op cit* (fn 88) at pp. 88 *et seq.*
85 Green Paper, *op cit* (fn 2) at p. 3.
86 Cf. the Study in comparative law, *op cit* (fn 14) at p. 13.
87 Pioneers of European Integration "From Below": Mobility and the emergence of European Identity among National and Foreign Citizens in the EU (*PIONEUR*), 5th Framework Programme – European Commission (2006), p. 5 *et seq.*, available at http://www.obets.ua.es/pioneur/difusion/PioneurExecutiveSummary.pdf.
88 German Federal Bureau of Statistics, "Im Blickpunkt: Frauen in Deutschland" (2006) at p. 37.

to be true.[89] On the contrary, it is more likely that – if the marriage breaks up – the couple have the closest ties with the country where they are actually living.

Finally, in accordance with the parties' needs: The use of habitual residence as the primary connecting factor in many cases allows the courts to apply their own law and therefore helps to avoid a difficult and lengthy procedure for finding the applicable law.[90] However, this finding can only be accepted as true if jurisdiction and the applicable law match as is the case when the (last) common habitual residence of the spouses is applied. If, as it seems likely, a future Community instrument on the conflict of laws in matters concerning matrimonial property regimes were to take the *first* common habitual residence of the spouses as the primary connecting factor, thus allowing the law to be determined at the time of celebrating the marriage, the situation where the courts always apply the law of the forum would not be likely to happen. Conversely, given the increasing mobility of citizens within Europe, one might expect that most spouses will not file for divorce at the place of their first matrimonial residence. The court granting divorce will therefore often have to apply foreign law.

4.2.2. Dilemma

The principle of habitual residence faces a considerable dilemma: on the one hand, reflecting the increasing mobility within the Community would require the applicable law to change automatically every time the spouses change their residence. Only such a complete doctrine of mutability would allow the applicable law to "move" together with the spouses and would therefore correspond to their factual living conditions. On the other hand, the mutability of the law governing marital property regimes is certainly not an acceptable solution for the following reasons: First, due to the divergence in substantive family law, a couple's property could be subject to different marital property regimes in the case of marriage. In the case of divorce, the judge would therefore face the problem of reconstructing the moments of acquisition as well as the effects of common changes in the habitual residence – a task that is quite impossible. Second, as there are often third parties involved in property transactions a special need for stability regarding the

---

89 Martiny, *op cit* (fn 77), at pp. 86 *et seq.*; D. Martiny, "Ein internationals Scheidungsrecht für Europa – Konturen einer Rom III-Verordnung", in: *Symposium zum 65. Geburtstag von Ulrich Spellenberg* (2006), pp. 119 *et seq.*, at pp. 127 *et seq.* (concerning a Council Regulation on divorce and legal separation); D. Henrich, "Abschied vom Staatsangehörigkeitsprinzip?", in: *Festschrift für Hans Stoll* (2001), pp. 437 *et seq.*, at p. 449; for a different opinion see T. Rauscher, "Heimatlos in Europa – Gedanken gegen eine Aufgabe des Staatsangehörigkeitsprinzips im IPR", in: *Festschrift für Erik Jayme* (vol. 1), 2004, pp. 718 *et seq.*, at p. 738.

90 For a critical note see C. Kohler, "Einfluss der Globalisierung auf die Wahl der Anknüpfungsmomente", in: *Symposium Spellenberg*, *op cit* (fn 89), pp. 9 *et seq.*, at p. 13.

applicable law exists. Third, the parties themselves cannot be deemed interested in spending high information and transaction costs on determining the law which applies to their respective residence. Moreover, from a more general point of view, it may be questioned whether the exclusive application of the law of the common habitual residence collides with the freedom of movement as provided in Article 18 of the EC Treaty.[91] In this regard, it may be that the party who prefers to have the law of the country of nationality applied will argue that his or her right to free movement is negatively affected.[92] Finally, referring to the first habitual residence of the spouses seems to correspond to the common law notion of matrimonial domicile,[93] that being a factor that cannot be said to have served as a substantive approach regarding choice of law.

4.3. FREEDOM TO CHOOSE THE APPLICABLE LAW

The question is whether and how party autonomy may serve as a way out of this dilemma. Allowing spouses to choose the applicable law is the only solution that takes account of the legitimate interests of cross-border couples. It grants spouses the possibility to reconcile the applicable law with their individual circumstances and therefore enhances legal certainty and predictability. From an economic perspective, it can be assumed that before choosing the relevant law spouses are aware of the effects that different substantive law rules may have on their matrimonial property regime. Relevant costs have therefore been calculated.[94] Taking these aspects in mind, one might ask whether the Commission's approach towards limited party autonomy is still an appropriate means to enhance the flexibility of cross-border couples. If, as we have seen, not one of the connecting factors provides for a reasonable solution, why not take freedom of choice as the cornerstone of harmonised conflict-of-law rules in matters of marital property? Even if a future Community instrument – as the Rome III proposal eventually does – takes party autonomy as the primary connecting factor, thus increasing flexibility and legal certainty, it would continue to apply a mere limited approach. Unlike the parties in cross-border contracts who are traditionally given almost unlimited autonomy under Article 3 para. 1 of the Rome Convention[95] the spouses' freedom

---

91 For the use of habitual residence as a connecting factor in view of the EC Treaty see M. Bogdan, "The EC Treaty and the use of nationality and habitual residence as connecting factors in international family law", in: Meeusen/Pertegás et al. (eds.), *op cit* (fn 77), pp. 303 *et seq.*, at p. 315.

92 Bogdan, *op cit* (fn 91), at p. 317.

93 Kohler, *op cit* (fn 90), at p. 13.

94 E. O'Hara/L.E. Ribstein, "From Politics to Efficiency in Choice of Law", 67 *U. Ch. L. Rev.* 1151 (2000).

95 According to the Proposal for a Regulation of the European Parliament and the Council on the law applicable to contractual obligations (Rome I) of 15 December 2005, COM(2005) 650 final,

to choose the law which is applicable to their marital property has always been limited to those laws with which they have an actual link. Party autonomy therefore merely acts as a makeshift solution. But, one can imagine that spouses might also be interested in choosing a law which is different from that of their nationality or habitual residence. Take, for example, a childless English couple living in the Netherlands and neither wants the Dutch system of community property[96] nor the English system of separate property[97] to apply to their marital assets. Instead, they prefer a law that basically treats property during marriage separately, but also provides for equalisation in case of divorce. They might therefore be interested in choosing German law,[98] for instance. Why not allow spouses to choose whatever law they deem appropriate?[99]

Nevertheless, serious doubts have to be taken into account regarding such an extended approach. Not only the rights of third persons who were involved in proprietary transactions have to be protected. Also the applicable law should not run the risk of giving rise to unreasonable results. As parties are not likely to impair their own economic interests no irrational choice of "exotic" laws is to be expected. Instead, opting for religious laws of a Third State that ignores the spouses' equal rights, for instance, could be a problem that should be taken seriously. However, it is to be expected that the exception of public policy will serve as a mechanism to apply European standards against a Third State, thereby avoiding results that clash with Human Rights.[100] Finally, one has to make sure that the financially weaker party – still mostly women – is adequately protected against any "law shopping" by the other.[101] It seems at least necessary – as most of the respondents to the Green Paper proposed – to require the agreement to be expressed in writing and be signed by both spouses.

Article 3 para. 1 of the Rome Convention will be adopted.

96 Art. 1:93 Dutch Civil Code.

97 For the property consequences of a marriage see LOWE/DOUGLAS, *op cit* (fn 25), pp. 127 *et seq.*

98 For the German system of deferred community property see A. LÜDERITZ/N. DETHLOFF, *Familienrecht* (2007), §5 at 56 *et seq.*

99 G.-R. DE GROOT favours such a broad understanding of party autonomy with regard to the Member States of the European Union, see "Auf dem Weg zu einem europäischen (internationalen) Familienrecht", *Zeitschrift für Europäisches Privatrecht* (ZEuP), 2001, pp. 618 et *seq.*, at p. 624.

100 For this notion of public policy see POILLOT PERUZZETTO, *op cit* (fn 78), pp. 297 *et seq.*

101 For the protection of the weaker party, especially children, in other fields of family law see MARTINY, *op cit* (fn 77), at p. 93.

5. CONCLUSION

The European Commission has demonstrated considerable efforts in unifying conflict-of-law rules in Europe. Apart from those fields of law, e.g. contractual obligations, that directly relate to the "proper functioning of the internal market" as provided in Article 65 EC, the Commission is increasingly dealing with matters of family law that, to date, have rarely been subject to harmonization. Due to the existence of the 1978 Hague Convention, the law applicable to matrimonial property regimes has always been exceptional. However, to date, only three Member States of the European Union have adopted the Convention. Nevertheless, the Convention was recently taken by the preliminary study as a model for the development of a Community instrument on conflict of law rules as regards matrimonial property regimes. It is in particular the habitual residence approach as used in the Convention as the primary connecting factor that seems to be convincing. Only this approach is considered to be the right answer to the growing mobility of citizens within the European Union and the increasing number of spouses being of different nationalities. One might expect further attempts by the Commission to use the common habitual residence of the spouses as the primary connecting factor, thus potentially instigating a change towards this approach in conflict of laws in matters concerning matrimonial property regimes.

As diverging national conflict of law rules in family law can be obstacles to the free movement of persons as provided under Article 18 EC the efforts of the European Commission to unify conflict-of-law rules on matrimonial property regimes are certainly to be welcomed. Strengthening legal certainty and predictability as well as allowing more flexible solutions within European Private International Law are steps that are overdue. It is to be greatly regretted, however, that the Green Paper on the law applicable to matrimonial property regimes provides no fundamental rethinking of the doctrine of immutability or of weighing the possible connecting factors in family law. It is also the function of party autonomy, in particular its limitation, that calls for further discussion. Also further proposals such as, e.g., that of developing uniform substantive rules in terms of a "Matrimonium Europaeum",[102] should appear on the agenda. The European Commission would be well advised to take the necessary time to decide on basic problems of Private International Family Law. Ongoing discussions on a Community instrument regarding contractual obligations demonstrate that the harmonisation process might be long and complicated. The same is true for the unification of conflict of laws with regard to family law. Difficult questions should not be left out.

---

[102] For a detailed illustration see N. DETHLOFF, "Europäische Vereinheitlichung des Familienrechts", *Archiv für die civilistische Praxis* (AcP) 204 (2004), pp. 544 *et seq.*, at pp. 564 *et seq.*

THE DISSOLUTION OF THE MATRIMONIAL PROPERTY REGIME AND THE SUCCESSION RIGHTS OF THE SURVIVING SPOUSE IN PRIVATE INTERNATIONAL LAW

Maria Álvarez Torné

1. INTRODUCTION

These pages are addressed to examining the problems arising from the regulation of the dissolution of the matrimonial property regime upon the death of one of the spouses in relation to the determination of the succession rights of the surviving spouse in Private International Law (*hereafter*, PIL). I will specifically try to analyse the conciliation difficulties between what is stipulated in each relevant field after the death of one of the spouses. The surviving spouse's situation often depends on the simultaneous effect of the matrimonial property regime and also of Succession Law. In fact, this study deals with a classical problem of PIL which has been subject to recent innovative interpretations and has acquired a new importance.

My research also includes the treatment of succession rights in cases of homosexual and heterosexual civil partnerships. It is mainly focussed on the German and the Spanish PIL systems, but I will also refer occasionally to the legal systems of other EU Member States.

2. GENERAL PIL QUESTIONS

Firstly, when we are faced with a PIL case, the elements establishing international jurisdiction have to be examined, given that the adaptation difficulties referred to above, which are centred in the field of applicable law, appear as a result of the choice of law rules of the forum, and the determination of the competent court always takes place first. In this sense, it is worth highlighting the absence of international conventions concerning international succession in the field of jurisdiction, except for some bilateral conventions and a Nordic multilateral convention. The private international law of succession in each jurisdiction is essentially based on national sources. Nevertheless, the "Hague Convention of 1 August 1989 on the Law Applicable to Succession to the Estates of Deceased Persons" has been signed by a few countries and is not yet in force, although it has already been ratified by the Netherlands.[1]

When a conflict of law system has different rules on succession and matrimonial property it may be the case that different laws apply at the same time. This may result in allowing the widow or widower to obtain either more or less than would be available under each of the two national systems concerned. This means that the widow or widower can be economically advantaged if both statutes grant him or her succession rights. On the contrary, she or he will be unfairly neglected when each applied legal system provides that the widow or widower has no succession rights. An additional difficulty is that some legal systems, like the French one, adopt the principle of the scission of the succession only in relation to the succession statute and not to the matrimonial property regime. This means that we could find a case of renvoi only regarding, for example, the succession to an immovable.

We can start tackling the difficulty of this kind of international case by referring to a practical case commented upon by Droz in the *Hague Conference Acts and Documents of the Twelfth Session*:[2] "A person dies domiciled in the Netherlands. Together with his or her Dutch goods, the decedent leaves a building in England, a bank account in France and a trunk in a Swiss bank. The Dutch court may have jurisdiction on the basis of the decedent's domicile. Jurisdiction may be exercised regarding the entire succession, while an English judge probably has jurisdiction only concerning the liquidation of the English building. In France, a judge could take a decision because of the nationality of one of the parties…" The complexity of this example may increase if this decedent dies leaving a surviving spouse or partner, whose succession rights have to be determined, often by a judge who can choose between applying a conflict of laws rule on succession or a rule on matrimonial property.

A European instrument unifying PIL rules on the law applicable to succession and wills is still not available, awaiting legislative development after the adoption

1 With regard to the text of the Convention, see P. Lagarde, "La nouvelle Convention de La Haye sur la loi applicable aux successions", *Rev. Crit.*, 1989, pp. 249 ff. Concerning the ratification of the Convention by the Netherlands, see A. Borrás, "La ratificación por Holanda del Convenio de La Haya de 1 de agosto de 1989 sobre ley aplicable a las sucesiones por causa de muerte", *Revista Española de Derecho Internacional*, 1996, pp. 363 f.

2 G. Droz, in "Actes et Documents de la Douzième session", 1972, t. II, p. 16.

of the Green Paper on Succession Law in 2005.[3] As a consequence, each autonomous PIL system handles the conciliation difficulties between the law applicable to the succession and the law applicable to the effects of marriage in its own way. Therefore, the national judge has to resolve the possibly incongruous results generated by the application of different laws to closely linked aspects in accordance with her or his own PIL system.

3. DETERMINATION OF THE SUCCESSION RIGHTS OF THE WIDOWED SPOUSE FROM A PIL PERSPECTIVE

Historically we can see a trend in European substantive laws consisting of strengthening the succession rights of the surviving spouse, which of course involves a loss of succession rights for other family members, such as children.[4] In general, EU legal systems coincide in holding that in order to determine the precise amount of the decedent's estate, it is necessary, first, to divide the matrimonial property of the spouses.[5] However, it may be the case that a certain PIL system applies different rules to the dissolution of the matrimonial property regime and the law governing succession, so that characterisation problems between the succession and the matrimonial property statute can arise because their regulation is not subjected to the same legal system. European PIL systems in general have no specific PIL rule clarifying unequivocally how to define the succession rights of the surviving spouse. Consequently, the ways of resolving this problem vary according to each particular legal system.

For instance, the conflict of laws system in England & Wales differs from continental legal systems with respect to sources, and also regarding the fact that when an English judge decides that he has international jurisdiction, he will often apply domestic law. In the field of the effects of marriage on property, rights obtained by the husband or the wife dealing with movable property are determined by the law of the matrimonial domicile when there is no specific contract or settlement. It is not clear if this rule also applies to immovables, because although some decisions of the House of Lords adopt a unitary view applying both to movables and

3 Concerning the need for harmonization in the field of conflict of laws concerning Succession within the European Union, see the study by DNotI/H. Dörner/P. Lagarde, "Les Successions Internationales dans l'UE: Perspectives pour une Harmonisation", German Notary Institute, Brussels, 2004.

4 W. Pintens, "Europäisierung des Erbrechts", *ZEuP 2001*, pp. 632 f.

5 K.H. Neumayer, "The surviving spouse" in K. H. Neumayer (ed), *International Encyclopedia of Comparative Law, Volume V Succession*, co-published by Mohr Siebeck, Tübingen, and Martinus Nijhoff Publishers, Dordrecht/Boston/Lancaster, 2002, p. 45.

immovables, other decisions consider that the latter depend on the *lex situs*. Changes in the matrimonial domicile, which is also a controversial concept, do not necessarily carry with them alterations in the matrimonial property regime. Coordination disadjustments between matrimonial property law and succession law will derive from this fact.[6] As can also be noted in general in the continental PIL systems, a specific rule establishing the succession rights of the surviving spouse in intestate succession does not exist in English PIL, and the need to reconcile the protection granted as a result of the dissolution of the matrimonial property regime and that conferred by the law of succession is also subject to debate. In the legal literature, it is difficult to give a satisfactory answer to this problem given the current configuration of the English rules on the conflict of laws. It has been suggested in this sense that the law of succession in the field of substantive law (as distinct from the rules on conflict of laws) should be changed so as to subject the succession rights of the widowed spouse to matrimonial property law.[7]

3.1. THE PARTICULAR CASE OF THE SPANISH PIL SOLUTION: THE PROS AND CONS

3.1.1. The Formulation of Article 9.8 of the Spanish Civil Code

In Spanish PIL there are different conflicts rules on succession and the matrimonial property regime. It should also be recalled that Spanish private law is not unified and that we therefore have many conflict situations in cases where there is no international element. Article 9.8 of the Spanish Civil Code (CC) applies to both international and internal situations. The final sentence of the conflict of laws rule contained in Article 9.8 CC,[8] which contains the conflict of laws rule on succession, seeks, however, to avoid the problem of reconciling the law applicable to matrimonial property and the law applicable to the succession rights of the

6 A.V. Dicey/J.H.C. Morris/L. Collins, *The conflict of laws*, Sweet & Maxwell, London, 2006, p. 1299.

7 A.V. Dicey/J.H.C. Morris/L. Collins, *The conflict of laws*, Sweet & Maxwell, London, 2006, p. 1300.

8 Article 9.8 Spanish Civil Code determines: Succession by reason of death will be governed by the national law of the deceased at the moment of his death, whatever the nature of the property and whichever country it is in. However, dispositions in the will and successory agreements which are in accordance with the national law of the testator or of the disponent at the moment of their being executed will conserve their validity, although another law may govern the succession, and any legally reserved portions will be in accordance with the latter. The rights that by law are attributed to the surviving spouse will be governed by the same law that regulates the effects of the marriage, save in respect of the legally reserved portions of the descendants.

surviving spouse. This involves, as we have seen, an important exception to the general outlook of the European PIL systems. Article 9.8 CC provides that the succession claim of the surviving spouse is governed by the law applicable to the effects of the marriage under Article 9.2 CC, unless there has been a will, not including the legally reserved portions of the descendants. Contractual or testate succession will not be governed by this remission of Article 9.8, but rather by the testator's national law or the disponent's national law at the moment of the grant.

This final section of Article 9.8 CC was introduced by Law 11/1990 of 15 October, which modified some articles of the Spanish Civil Code. It is a conflictual solution, instead of working on the substantive laws in question by way of adaptation. This solution seeks to be a preventive mechanism, rather than a corrective one.[9] This article has chosen the so-called formula of "indirect adaptation". For a long time, Spanish legal literature has criticized this adaptation model, insofar as it operates without taking into account whether it is really necessary or not. As result of this point of view, this sector of Spanish legal literature prefers the technique of direct adaptation, which works on the correction of the material rules when an effective disadjustment is confirmed.[10] Before the modification of Law 11/1990 of 15 October was introduced, the Spanish courts resolved the cases we are examining without unified criteria, sometimes by means of not very technical criteria in order to find a theoretical equity.[11] That is why different legal systems were sometimes applied cumulatively or the application of a particular legal system was ruled out without justification.

An attempt is made to overcome the apparent split in the law of succession produced by the wording of Article 9.8 CC by adding the final words "not including the legally reserved portions of the descendants". Nevertheless, in the legal literature these final words have been criticized, because in certain situations they could adulterate the reach of the succession rights of the widowed spouse, specifically when these cover the descendants' legally reserved portions, although these portions are governed by a law of succession which does not allow them to be affected.[12] In this sense, the final words of Article 9.8 CC have been branded as excessively inflexible and unconnected with the *favor viduitatis*. Besides, in the

9 M.E. Zabalo Escudero, *La situación jurídica del cónyuge viudo: Estudio en el Derecho internacional privado y Derecho interregional*, Aranzadi, Pamplona, 1993, p. 107.

10 N. Bouza Vidal, *Problemas de adaptación en Derecho internacional privado e interregional*, Tecnos, Madrid, 1977, p. 92.

11 A.L. Calvo Caravaca/J. Carrascosa González/E. Castellanos Ruíz, *Derecho de familia internacional*, Colex, Madrid, 2005, p. 307.

12 M.E. Zabalo Escudero, *La situación jurídica del cónyuge viudo: Estudio en el Derecho internacional privado y Derecho interregional*, Aranzadi, Pamplona, 1993, p. 212.

legal literature it has also been argued that a solution like the one contained in Article 16.2 CC, relating to the widowhood right regulated in the Compilation of Aragón, would have been more suitable.[13] This right resorts to the compensation of succession rights[14] in order to avoid an excessive benefit or damage for the widowed spouse.

3.1.2. *Conflictive Interpretations and the Characterization Dilemma*

Although the aforementioned rule apparently clarifies the situation of how to regulate the succession rights of the widowed spouse, there have been certain decisions by the General Directorate of Registries and Notaries (*from now on*, DGRN), an administrative body within the Spanish Ministry of Justice, which have held that when referring to the succession rights of the widow or widower not all succession rights are meant.[15] From this perspective, only certain personal rights, such as the year of mourning, the domestic trosseau and some advantages under local law follow the law applicable to matrimonial property. In both cases it was intended to designate the law applicable to the succession rights of a widow within the framework of an intestate succession in Interregional Law in which the decedent had Catalan civil law status but the spouses' joint earnings were governed by Spanish Civil Law. Both resolutions of the DGRN were clearly shaped in favour of applying Catalan Civil Law as *lex successionis* to determine the succession rights of the surviving spouse instead of Spanish Civil Law, which governed matrimonial property. This was confirmation of the notaries′ opinion against the one of the registrars, who refused to register the deeds of acceptance and the partition of inheritance, and sought a more favourable regime for the widow or widower.

This solution pleases the Civil law academics more than their PIL counterparts, given that the former consider that these decisions of the DGRN are more in line with the principle of *favor viduitatis* and the preferential application of the autonomous regional legal systems before the Civil Code.[16]

---

13 A. Borrás Rodríguez, "No discriminación por razón de sexo: Derecho internacional privado español", *Anuario de Derecho Civil*, 1991, p. 242.

14 Article 16.2 CC specifically determines that: "The widowhood right regulated in the Compilation of Aragon corresponds to spouses who come under the matrimonial property regime of this Compilation, even if their civil law status has changed later, excluding in that case the legally reserved portion established by the law of succession. (…)" and, in its last section: "The widow's usufruct also corresponds to the widowed spouse when the dead spouse had Aragonese civil law status at the moment of death".

15 Resolution of the DGRN of 11 March 2003 (BOE num. 100 of 26 April 2003) and Resolution of the DGRN of 18 June of 2003 (BOE num. 181 of 30 July 2003).

16 E. Corral García, *Los derechos sucesorios del cónyuge viudo en el Derecho civil común y autonómico*, Bosch, Barcelona, 2007, p. 240.

In the context of Spanish Interregional Law, it is frequent that a court has to examine a case which covers aspects depending on different legal systems. At that point, the court will face characterization problems and it will have to decide if it is necessary to opt for a *lex fori* characterization, or more precisely a *lex judicii* characterization, or for a characterization of the law governing the merits of the case or a *lex civilis litis* characterization.[17] In the opinion of the authors who support the last kind of characterization, only this makes the uniformity of decisions possible, because its results would not depend on the diverging characterization of each competent court,[18] but on the characterization carried out by the *lex civilis litis*, which would be the same irrespective of the competent court applying the conflict of laws rule. In both cases resolved by the DGRN, intestate successions governed by the Catalan Law of Succession were analyzed, and the conclusion was reached by means of a *lex causae* or more precisely a *lex civilis litis* characterization, which allowed the widow's usufruct to be obtained over the whole inheritance. It is a *mortis causa* right shaped from the perspective of Catalan Civil Law.

Other authors point out that the problem of accepting this kind of *lex civilis litis* characterization in cases of Interregional Law is that it could protect the case-by-case nature of decisions,[19] given that they will depend on what is established in each Spanish legal system, a fact which could go against the Article 9.8 CC objective of avoiding this characterization problem. In this sense, these authors do not argue for a *lex judicii* characterization, but for a characterization according to the system of Interregional Law, i.e. based on the conception contained in its rules.[20] This sector of the legal literature believes that the characterization procedure has to be closely connected with the interpretation and the delimitation of the conflict of laws rules, without separating the characterization from the rules of the Interregional Law system.[21] In this case, it would be necessary to characterize what is

---

17 Terminology proposed in Spanish legal literature in the field of Spanish Interregional Law by A. Borrás Rodríguez, *Calificación, reenvío y orden público en el Derecho interregional español*, Servicio de Publicaciones de la Universidad Autónoma de Barcelona, Bellaterra, 1984, p. 34. Also arguing for a *lex civilis litis* characterization in this context is A. Borrás Rodríguez, "Los conflictos internos en materia civil a la luz de la legislación actualmente vigente" in *Conflictos de leyes en el desarrollo del Derecho civil vasco*, Real Sociedad Bascongada de Amigos del País (Comisión de Bizkaia), Bilbao, 1999, p. 80.

18 A. Borrás Rodríguez, *Calificación, reenvío y orden público en el Derecho interregional español*, Servicio de Publicaciones de la Universidad Autónoma de Barcelona, Bellaterra, 1984, p. 33.

19 A. Font i Segura, "Comentario a la Resolución DGRN de 18 de junio de 2003", *Revista Española de Derecho Internacional*, 2003, pp. 994 f.

20 A. Font i Segura, "Comentario a la Resolución DGRN de 18 de junio de 2003", *Revista Española de Derecho Internacional*, 2003, p. 995.

21 S. Álvarez González, "Derecho interregional: claves para una reforma", *Anuario Español de Derecho Internacional Privado*, 2003, p. 52.

established in Article 9.8 CC, the obvious purpose of which is to avoid these difficulties by means of a remittal to Article 9.2 CC. Whatever the case may be, the observation indicating that the competent court should choose a matrimonial or a successory characterization according to what is more favourable for the surviving spouse[22] could also be appropriate, although the more favourable law should also be the limit of the obtainable rights.

On the other hand, although the scope of the rights referred to in article 9.8 CC has been debated for a long time, it has been generally admitted that it includes all the rights which are attributed by law to the widowed spouse when he or she has not been designated as the inheritor by his or her spouse, in order to guarantee the continuity of the standard of living enjoyed until the decedent's death.[23] Consequently, these rights would not only be personal rights. Nevertheless, it is worthwhile paying attention to the criticism underlined in the legal literature regarding the formulation of Article 9.8 CC remitting to Article 9.2 CC.[24] When Article 9.2 CC refers to the effects of the marriage, it has to be recalled that Article 9.3 CC is the rule which specifically refers to matrimonial property regime agreements, and this Article 9.3 CC remits to Article 9.2 CC as a first possible point of connection for the conflict of laws rule. Consequently, if the spouses opt for a matrimonial property regime which differs from the one contemplated by the applicable law for the effects of the marriage under Article 9.2 CC, the aim of Article 9.8 CC will absolutely fail: the conflict between the rights granted to the widowed spouse by the *lex successionis* and the law applicable to the effects of the marriage will appear once again. It has been proposed to avoid this inconvenience by adopting an interpretation determining that the law applicable to the effects of the marriage has to be understood as the law which effectively governs the matrimonial property regime.

In both decisions analyzed of the DGRN, the application of the remittal in Article 9.8 CC to Article 9.2 CC was avoided, justifying this decision as a harmonizing interpretation of both articles in order to preserve the unity of the succession contained in Spanish Succession Law, which could be theoretically threatened if various aspects of the succession depend on different laws.

In the same sense, S. Álvarez González, *Estudios de Derecho interregional*, Servizo de Publicacións da Universidade de Santiago de Compostela, 2007, p. 102.

22 F. Boulanger, *Droit international des successions*, Economica, 2004, p. 142.

23 M.E. Ginebra Molins, "Els conflictes de lleis derivats de la coexistència de diversos ordenaments jurídics civils a l'Estat Espanyol", *La Notaría 4*, 1996, web edition.

24 S. Álvarez González, "Dos cuestiones de actualidad en el reciente Derecho internacional privado" in *Estudios de Derecho civil: Homenaje al Profesor Francisco Javier Serrano García*, Secretariado de Publicaciones e Intercambio Editorial de la Universidad de Valladolid, Valladolid, 2005, p. 142.

Nevertheless, the aforementioned reason does not seem to be enough to reject the exceptional fragmentation of the succession against the principles of the unity and universality of the succession upheld in the Spanish PIL, as is admitted by Article 9.8 CC, in order to avoid adaptation problems.[25] However, the DGRN has kept defending the aforementioned point of view in the analyzed decisions in other recent decisions.[26]

3.2. THE GERMAN ANSWER TO THESE COORDINATION DIFFICULTIES

The aforementioned problem of an unequal sharing of the estate may also take place in German PIL through the application of Article 15 EGBGB concerning the law applicable to matrimonial property and Article 25 regarding the law of succession. The goal is that the widow or widower does not obtain less than what she or he would obtain if only one legal system were applicable. German PIL tries to resolve the possible incompatibility between statutes through the mechanism of adaptation (*Angleichung* or *Anpassung*), which, however, entails legal insecurity and possible unjust results.

The characterization dilemma also appears in German PIL. §1371.1 BGB assigns the surviving spouse, in cases where the spouses lived under the German statutory marital property regime of deferred community (*Zugewinngemeinschaft*), an automatic increase in his or her statutory share of one quarter of the estate. A doubt arises concerning the characterization of the increase as successory or as a matter falling under the matrimonial property regime.[27] If we opt for a successory characterization, it is doubtful whether it is possible to grant this right when the succession is governed by a foreign legal system. The same problem arises with characterization as a question falling under the matrimonial property regime when the law applicable to the matrimonial property regime is a foreign law.

According to the theory of double characterization (it is called *double* because it means a simultaneous characterization as successory and as a matter falling under the matrimonial property regime), it is not possible to grant this right in

---

25 J.C. Fernández Rozas/S. Sánchez Lorenzo, "Derecho internacional privado", *Thomson-Civitas*, 3rd ed., Madrid, 2004, p. 432.

26 RDGRN of 5 February 2005 (BOE num. 82 of 6 April 2005): "This article (9.8 CC) leads to the decedent's national law at the moment of death, and including in its field of application, as has been established by this Directorate, the succession rights of the surviving spouse."

27 M.E. Völkl, "Kommentar zu Art. 25 EGBGB" in Deutsche Gesellschaft für Erbrechtskunde (ed), *Deutscher Erbrechtskommentar*, Carl Heymanns Verlag KG, Köln/Berlin/München, 2003, p. 1477.

such international cases because the rule only operates if both succession and the matrimonial property regime follow German law in order to prevent adaptation problems.[28] Nonetheless, according to both the majority of the legal literature and the case law, §1371.1 BGB may also apply if the succession follows a foreign legal system, appealing to the mechanisms of *Angleichung* or *Anpassung*. This will not be possible if the matrimonial property regime is governed by a foreign law, given that §1371.1 BGB is originally a German material rule which is only applicable if German Law governs the matrimonial property regime.[29] This perspective is in line with a characterization as a matter falling under the matrimonial property regime.

During the process of reforming the German PIL, the Spanish solution was taken into consideration but was finally rejected. One of the reasons was that the law applicable to testamentary dispositions would be pending at the time of drawing up one's will,[30] since the matrimonial property regime can change until the death of one of the spouses. It would make no sense for the succession of the surviving spouse to follow a matrimonial property regime which was changed after the will was drawn up.

3.3. PROPOSALS MADE TO SOLVE THIS PROBLEM

It has been proposed to admit *professio iuris* to determine the *lex hereditatis*, as was provided by Article 5 of the Hague Convention of 1 August 1989 on the Law Applicable to Succession to the Estates of Deceased Persons. This would enable a testator to choose the law of a state as the applicable law, whenever this person holds the nationality of that state or has her or his habitual residence therein at the moment of the choice or at the moment of death. With this possibility of election, it would be easier to coordinate the law applicable to the matrimonial property regime and the law applicable to succession,[31] thereby avoiding the necessity of later adjustments.

---

28 P. Mankowski, "Kommentar zu §1371.1 BGB" in J. von Staudingers *Kommentar zum Bürgerlichen Gesetzbuch mit Einführungsgesetz und Nebengesetzen*, Sellier-de Gruyter, Berlin, 2003, Rn. 343 f.

29 K. Siehr, "Kommentar zu §1371 BGB, Güterstand" in K. Rebmann, F.J. Säcker and R. Rixecker (eds.), *Münchener Kommentar zum Bürgerlichen Gesetzbuch*, Band 10, C.H. Beck, Münich, 2006, Art. 15, Rn. 114 ff.

30 Article 26 EGBGB (on the form of testamentary dispositions) applies to Article 25 EGBG concerning the content of the will: "(5) Notwithstanding the foregoing provisions the validity of the testamentary disposition and the binding effect of such a disposition underlies the law applicable to successions. (…)".

31 M. Revillard, "Note à la decisión de la Cour d'appel de Versailles, première chambre, 20 décembre 1990", *JDI (Clunet) 1*, 1992, p. 113.

However, there are also critical voices against the possibility of electing the applicable law by the *de cujus*.[32] In this sense, it is maintained that the essential difference between the possibility of electing the applicable law in the matrimonial property regime field and in the field of succession consists of the fact that in the former the spouses dispose solely in relation to the interests of both of them. On the contrary, the election of the applicable law by the decedent can affect others who have an interest in the inheritance.

Notwithstanding this, more recent opinions in legal literature[33] rightly point out that it would be enough to protect the potential inheritors who could be harmed to formulate a rule similar to Article 24 1 d) of the Hague Convention of 1 August 1989 on the Law Applicable to Succession to the Estates of Deceased Persons, which establishes:

> "Any State may, at the time of signature, ratification, acceptance, approval or accession, make any of the following reservations – (...)
>
> that it will not recognize a designation made under Article 5, if all of the following conditions are met – (...)
>
> – the application of the law designated under Article 5 would totally or very substantially deprive the spouse or a child of the deceased of an inheritance or family provision to which the spouse or child would have been entitled under the mandatory rules of the law of the State making this reservation,"

Without entering into further discussions on the convenience of admitting the *professio iuris* in the field of international succession, the criticism does not seem to be a sufficiently well-founded reason against the election, at least, of the law applicable to the succession rights of the widowed spouse, because there are certain ways to protect the interests of other potential inheritors.

In fact, Finnish PIL already allows that when a married person draws up a will, she or he can establish that the succession rights of his or her spouse are governed by the law applicable to matrimonial property. According to Chapter 26 Section 6 of the Finnish Code of Inheritance the deceased may designate the law applicable to inheritance with some limitations. Paragraph 3 of Chapter 26 establishes: "Moreover, if the decedent is married at the time of the designation, it may be

---

32 M. GORÉ, "De la mode... dans les successions internationales: contre les prétensions de la professio iuris" in *L'internationalisation du droit, Mélanges en l'honneur de Yvon Loussouarn*, Dalloz, Paris, 1994, p. 196.

33 E. VASSILAKAKIS, "La professio iuris dans les successions internationales" in *Le droit international privé : esprit et méthodes*, Dalloz, Paris, 2005, p. 814.

provided that the applicable law is the law of the state applicable to matrimonial property matters." However, this solution does not guarantee coordination, because it depends on good legal advice in each specific case.

In this sense, German legal literature has been emphasising for a long time that the formulation of an election clause avoiding friction problems between the matrimonial property regime and the law of succession could be shaped, thereby easily avoiding the aforementioned difficulties.[34] It would mean choosing the law applicable to the matrimonial property regime of the couple by using the same law which will govern the succession of the decedent. The election would have retrospective effect to the day before the spouse's death, and the settlement of the matrimonial property regime would be governed by the new matrimonial property regime, avoiding the well-known adjustment problems.

4. THE SITUATION IN CASES OF NON-MARRIED COUPLES: A QUICK LOOK AT EUROPE

Only Spain, Belgium, South Africa, the Netherlands, Canada and the state of Massachusetts in the USA recognize same-sex marriages. In these systems, the widowed spouse enjoys the same succession rights regardless of whether the marriage is between a couple of the same or a different sex. When marriage is not available to same-sex couples, some legal systems establish civil partnerships which may or may not grant succession rights to the surviving partner. Consequently, the protection level for the surviving partner can be very limited, which different States have tried to avoid by adopting regulations which are more and more assimilated to the ones governing married couples.

For PIL the main problem is that the succession rights of a same-sex spouse, a registered partner or a cohabitee are not universally known. This entails important problems in the recognition and enforcement of foreign judgments.

In Germany, with the entry into force of the Law on civil partnerships (*Lebenspartnerschaftsgesetz*) for same-sex couples, a new PIL rule was adopted with Article 17b EGBGB. Civil partnerships are governed by the law of the state of registry. The succession rights of the surviving partner are however determined by the general rule which is applicable to succession according to the national law of the deceased in Article 25 EGBGB. With this reference it is intended to preserve

34 P. Mankowski/W. Osthaus, "Gestaltungsmöglichkeiten durch Rechtswahl beim Erbrecht des überlebenden Ehegatten in internationalen Fällen", *Deutsche Notar-Zeitschrift 1*, 1997, pp. 26 f.

the interests of third parties who could demand inheritance rights.[35] The conflict with the widowed spouse's interests appears once again. However, Article 17b EGBGB provides that if the surviving partner does not obtain succession rights through the connecting factor of Article 25 EGBGB, the law of the place of registry will apply. It is a reference to the material rules (a so-called *Sachnorm-verweisung*), which tries to avoid subsequent renvois. It has to be emphasized that resorting to the law of the place of registry only operates when the law applicable to succession does not recognize succession rights for civil partnerships in general or when it does not provide them in the case at hand.[36] At this point, the extent of the obtainable rights for the surviving partner remains unclear. It will be necessary to resort, for the time being, to the aforementioned mechanisms of *Angleichung* or *Anpassung* in order to look for a reasonable balance of interests.

German legal literature has also considered the difficulties which can arise from cases in which a German couple dissolve their union abroad by means of a private act or a marriage, without any judgment. In these cases preliminary questions may arise, which concern how to deal with the coexistence of claims for succession rights of both the widowed spouse and the partner, if the subsistence of the partnership created in Germany is admitted. Should only the widowed spouse or only the partner inherit? It is not clear whether these preliminary questions have to be solved by means of the *lex causae* or the *lex fori*.

On the other hand, it is doubtful whether an unmarried couple registered in a foreign country could be governed by the material rules of the German *Lebenspartnerschaftsgesetz* in order to determine the succession rights of the partner. In principle, this would depend on the possibility of replacing the concept of the foreign couple with the German one with the same value. This substitution would be problematic if the foreign law does not provide for succession rights for the partner.[37]

As another example of legal provisions in these cases, the PIL system in Belgium also provides that if the surviving partner does not obtain succession rights through the law applicable to non-marital registered partnerships, the *lex loci registrationis* should be applied.[38] On the other hand, the Netherlands has chosen another way to avoid these possible imbalances when such cases arise, which

---

35 R. Wagner, "Das neue Internationale Privat- und Verfahrensrecht zur eingetragenen Lebenspartnerschaft", *IPRax 2001*, p. 291.

36 M. Forkert, *Eingetragene Lebenspartnerschaften im deutschen IPR: Art. 17b EGBGB*, Mohr Siebeck, Tübingen, 2003, p. 230.

37 D. Henrich, "Kollisionsrechtliche Fragen der eingetragenen Lebenspartnerschaft", *FamRZ 3*, 2002, p. 143.

38 Article 60(3), second sentence, Belgian Code of Private International Law.

involve the concurrence of various legal systems. Instead of applying PIL rules, the Dutch authorities aim to provide good legal advice to couples who intend to register in order to convince them of the advantages of drawing up a will. This written will would certainly prevent problems by determining the applicable law. France, on the other hand, does not have PIL rules to define the succession rights of registered partners, and there are different possibilities which the judge has to examine in different ways.[39] In this way, the solution will not be the same when the *lex successionis* does not recognize succession rights for the surviving partner but the law of registration does or vice versa, or when the *lex successionis* recognizes these succession rights but the *lex fori* does not. Faced with each specific situation, the French competent judge will have to resort to different resolution techniques, from the adaptation mechanisms of the material laws to the replacement of foreign legal concepts in order to check if they can be assimilated with the French ones.

In Sweden, the Registered Partnership Act, which regulates same-sex couples as well as those of a different sex, in its Preamble assigns to the Swedish judge the function of applying any foreign rules providing succession rights to maintain the surviving partner if foreign Succession Law is applicable when the decedent dies and it does not provide for these succession rights.[40] It has to be recalled that the Swedish Registered Partnership Act was enacted in 1995 when the Scandinavian countries were pioneers in legislating in the field of civil partnerships. Since then, new forms of coexistence, like cohabitation, have appeared, which would not fit the Swedish solutions for models similar to married couples.[41]

Denmark was the first country in the world to regulate civil unions in 1989 by introducing a law on registered partnership for persons of the same sex, also called the Registered Partnership Act. Apart from a few exceptions, the conditions are precisely the same as for heterosexual marriages, so this would include the succession rights of surviving partners. Nevertheless, no PIL rules are provided in this act, so international cases like the ones we have analyzed would not receive uniform treatment under the Danish legal system.

In Spain there are different partnership laws in different Autonomous Regions. The Catalan statute on unmarried couples, which came into force in 1998, grants succession rights to homosexual couples, but not to heterosexual ones. From a

---

39 G. Kessler, *Les partenariats enregistrés en droit international privé*, Librairie Générale de Droit et de Jurisprudence, Paris, 2004, p. 347.

40 M. Bodgan, *IPR-Aspekte der schwedischen Eingetragenen Partnerschaft für Homosexuelle*, IPRax 1995, p. 57.

41 C. González Beilfuss, *Parejas de hecho y matrimonios del mismo sexo en la Unión Europea*, Marcial Pons, Barcelona, 2004, p. 181.

PIL perspective, specific rules are lacking. In the legal literature, the German solution has been favoured. In this sense, a flexible interpretation of Article 9.8 CC has been suggested.[42] It would make it possible to consider that the effects of the registered partnership (instead of the "effects of the marriage" mentioned in Article 9.8 CC) have to be governed by the law of registration, which would also determine the succession rights of the surviving partner. In this way, the succession rights of the surviving partner would be clearly set, entailing the same treatment as that given to a widowed spouse.

It has to be underlined that in the aforementioned European process for the adoption of a European instrument relating to successions, account has been taken of the possibility of having to resolve as a preliminary question the validity not only of a marriage but also of a non-marital registered partnership.[43] The law which is applicable to these incidental questions will have to be determined.

In general, from a PIL perspective, we can highlight the difficulty of classifying a non-marital registered partnership when, as is frequently the case, there is no available specific conflict of laws rule for this purpose. This generates obvious legal uncertainty. Some authors opt for considering these couples as personal relationships, which justifies giving them the same treatment as married ones. Other authors in legal literature think that they are patrimonial relationships to be placed in the law of obligations in PIL. However, specialized treatment of this complex subject recommends conferring a special dimension on these couples by combining personal and patrimonial elements.[44] In this way, when nowadays specific rules in this field are lacking, although having them is always the best solution and the aim to which we should aspire, it will be necessary to combine different PIL techniques to solve each particular case. Sometimes, the law of the country with which the case is most closely connected shall be applied, on other occasions an analogical application of conflict of laws rules could be necessary and, ultimately, an adaptation in the field stipulated by the material rules could be suitable.

---

42 C. González Beilfuss, *Parejas de hecho y matrimonios del mismo sexo en la Unión Europea*, Marcial Pons, Barcelona, 2004, p. 185.

43 I. Curry-Sumner, *All's well that ends registered? The Substantive and Private International Law Aspects of Non-Marital Registered Relationships in Europe*, Intersentia, Antwerp-Oxford, 2005, p. 493.

44 O. Van Caillie, *La protection du partenaire survivant dans le cadre des lois européennes sur la cohabitation non-maritale*, Schulthess, Geneva, 2005, p. 190.

5. CONCLUSIONS

Adjustment problems between succession and matrimonial property when dealing with succession rights of widowed spouses should be dealt with in the future European instrument, which intends to unify the law applicable to succession. Despite the widespread acceptance of the proposal to include the *professio iuris* in order to allow a choice of the law governing matrimonial property as the law applicable to the succession rights of the surviving spouse or partner, this does not solve the problems which arise in the majority of cases when parties are unaware of this kind of difficulty and do not foresee this necessity of making an election.

A conflict of laws rule similar to the one contained in Article 9.8 of the Spanish Civil Code (CC), which would directly point to the law which is applicable in this field, could avoid the analyzed problems. Nevertheless, as we have seen, the formulation of Article 9.8 CC is neither the object of unanimous interpretation, nor a flawless solution. That is why a better formulation of such a rule would be desirable. In this sense a clear determination of which specific law is expected to govern the succession rights of the widowed spouse would be necessary, without allowing any misunderstandings and subsequent adjustments, which always run the risk of being arbitrary.

Regarding the situation of the surviving non-married partner, we have to take into account that the regulation of non-marital forms of coexistence has just begun to be developed in most EU countries. Consequently, the determination of the succession rights of the surviving partner has to overcome extra difficulties compared to the widowed spouse, because of the lack of a universal acknowledgment of their existence.

It would be suitable to include the legitimate expectations of the surviving non-married partner in the aforementioned rule of the future European instrument, providing a specific clause for all those States which, for the time being, do not admit the legal existence of alternative models of families beyond the traditional forms. The reason for this admission of exceptions is that an instrument on Succession Law is not the appropriate setting to urge the evident necessity of regulating new relationship forms, a challenge which other EU projects should overcome successfully.

At least, it deserves further consideration.

CONCLUDING REMARKS

EUROPEAN CHALLENGES IN CONTEMPORARY FAMILY LAW: SOME FINAL OBSERVATIONS

Katharina Boele-Woelki

1. DETERMINING THE STRUCTURE

This book contains twenty contributions which were delivered at CEFL's 3rd conference that was held in Oslo from 7–9 June 2007. More than half of the authors were selected by the organizers upon a call for papers. They belong to the young researchers who presented their papers in three parallel working groups. Their presentation skills were striking. Most of them had prepared a power point presentation, which is undoubtedly a supportive element today, but who had no problem at all in continuing after the beamer and the computer suddenly malfunctioned. The other half of the authors were selected by the organizers. They presented their papers in plenary sessions. The conference structure has not been followed in this book. Instead a thematic approach has been chosen and all contributions have been integrated into five selected themes: (1) The Harmonisation of Family Law; (2) Children and their Parents; (3) Irregular Marriages and the Influence of Multiculturalism; (4) (Property) Relations between Spouses and Cohabitants; and (5) Cross-border Family Relationships. This structure has been adapted in these concluding remarks. They are primarily restricted to some aspects of the plenary session contributions which caught the author's interest.[1]

[1] By way of an apology: The closing remarks at CEFL's third conference on European Challenges in Contemporary Family Law have been written by someone who was partly involved in the organization of this conference, in particular in the selection of the topics to be discussed and the selection of the speakers. In addition, a contribution by this author is included in this volume. Initially, she was not supposed to provide the overall conclusions which by their nature are always based on a personal perspective. Such a task should primarily be carried out by someone who as an outside observer can distance oneself from the organization, its programme, its speakers and their presentations/contributions in order to guarantee a critical assessment. Due to the fact that the author is strongly involved in the CEFL, this requirement has not been fulfilled in respect of the activities of this commission. However, pressing personal circumstances involving a colleague who was asked to summarize and to comment unfortunately prevented him from doing so. Therefore, the general rules of impartiality and non-involvement concerning the person providing the concluding remarks were not adhered to.

2. THE HARMONISATION OF FAMILY LAW

Different approaches and areas in the harmonization and unification process of family law are represented in the first part. First of all, a clarification of the terminology is essential. It is regrettable that not only in the field of (international) family law the terms "unification" and "harmonisation" of the law are often used incorrectly. The "unification" of the law leads to the application of identical rules. These uniform rules are to be applied, for instance, in all national systems which are bound by either the international or the regional instrument which contains these rules. Consequently, the future instruments in the field of European Private International Law (PIL) are instruments that will make uniform and not only harmonize the PIL rules in Europe. The same rules are to be applied in all member states, at least in those which will be bound by the regulations. In contrast, the "harmonisation" of the law is less far-reaching. Similar rules indicate that the laws of the legal systems in a specific area are in harmony with each other. The differences are reduced to a minimum. Peter Lødrup pays attention to this terminological issue. In his view the term unification better captures the aims and results of the Nordic cooperation in the field of family law. When one argues for or against harmonisation in the Scandinavian countries – he continues – it is more a discussion for or against a higher degree of unification. At the CEFL's 1st conference in 2002, Esin Örücü posed the question whether the Nordic cooperation was either a success or a failure. She could not provide an answer. At the Oslo conference, Peter Lødrup could.[2] He clearly explains why the work of the Nordic Council is to be considered of great importance. He favours the unification of certain areas of family law. As an outside observer this author wonders about the following: Given the fact that three Scandinavian countries also belong to the EU the question arises whether the unification of Nordic family law is the best way to proceed. The answer should undoubtedly be provided by our Nordic colleagues and Peter Lødrup is also aware of this aspect when he states that for the Nordic countries the days of harmonization and even unification are not over, but, of course, European integration will add an uncertain element in considering the future. In this respect it is worth mentioning that recently Thomas Eeg[3] from the University of Bergen has critically assessed the future of the Nordic cooperation by referring in particular to the results of the CEFL. He even argues that the Nordic cooperation should be given a lower priority than the harmonization of family law within Europe. Within the CEFL, which is no more than an academic

---

2 See also Lund-Andersen, I., Approximation of Nordic Family Law within the Framework of Nordic Cooperation, in: Antokolskaia, M., *Convergence and Divergence of Family Law in Europe*, European Family Law Series no. 18, p. 51–61.

3 Eeg, T., Bør nordisk familieformuerett harmoniseres? In: T. Frantzen, J. Giertsen, G. Cordero Moss (eds.), *Rett og toleranse - Festskrift til Helge Johan Thue 70 år*, Gyldendal akademisk Forlag, Oslo (2007) p. 60–76.

initiative, the desirability and feasibility of the harmonization of family law in Europe has always been discussed intensively. However, the results of the CEFL, its Principles on European Family Law, are only aimed at contributing to this process. CEFL has to wait and see whether its models will be used as a source of inspiration by those who, for instance, have competence to legislate.

However, the process of harmonizing family law in Europe has undeniably been and will continue to be further influenced by human rights and in this process the ECHR and the decisions of the European Court in Strasbourg play central roles. Dagmar Coester-Waltjen makes a very successful and original attempt to draw a demarcation line between human rights as such and other rights and values. She raises the question whether the term marriage may be used if we speak about the formalization of a same-sex relationship. Dagmar Coester-Waltjen holds the view that this term should be reserved to different sex couples. However, she admits that the rights and duties of a formalized relationship might be completely identical to the consequences of marriage and only the indication of such a relationship as a marriage is not possible. Well, what's in a name if there are no differences between the legal consequences? How can one justify that relationship A is called A and relationship B is called B only because the gender of the couples differs? In this author's opinion there are hardly any convincing arguments that justify the difference in terminology. In the Netherlands, Belgium, and Spain – probably Sweden will join the club – no problems have arisen in this respect. However, there is an argument also in favour of Dagmar Coester-Waltjen's approach. The legal recognition of same-sex relationships is a political question. In more socialist and liberal systems it turned out to be possible to introduce either new institutions which are similar or identical to marriage or to open up marriage to same-sex couples. More conservative governments oppose or heavily argue against any legal recognition. Compromises have been reached. In many countries in Europe new institutions have been introduced in addition to marriage. The English civil partnership, for instance, is identical to the institution of marriage. The introduction of new institutions was the only alternative which was finally accepted. If this distinction would not have been made homosexual couples would not have received the legal recognition which they deserve. The introduction of a new and differently labelled institution is a compromise for the time being. New countries will opt for this distinction, while others will immediately or at a later stage open up marriage to these couples. The Dutch situation demonstrates that homosexual couples only had to wait for three years before they could transform their registered partnership into a marriage. 'Marriage is a wonderful institution, but who wants to live in an institution?' This well-known quote originates from Groucho Marx. It reminds us of the symbolic meaning of marriage. Homosexual couples do want and they do have the right to live in an institution that is called marriage. The symbolism is of great importance for them. Why should they be derived of its symbolic meaning?

In the discussion on the harmonization of family law in Europe, the American view should always be included. Where does the United States stand on the harmonization process concerning its family laws? In comparison with Europe, are similar developments discernable? ROBIN FRETWELL WILSON provides some interesting answers. She illustrates that there are still huge differences among the 51 federal states when it comes to family law. The American Law Institute promotes the simplification and clarification of the law by providing model regulations. Five years after the publication of the ALI Principles of the Law of Family Dissolution which contains recommendations as to how the law in this field could be harmonized, the differences remain, however. To date, they have not been introduced in any state. Besides, they have been partly critically received. ROBIN FRETWELL WILSON perfectly demonstrates how controversial cases are solved if the ALI Principles are taken into account. Her overall assessment of the ALI Principles carries a negative tone. Are all her views shared by everyone? To this author's knowledge and awareness the scientific discourse also includes family law scholars in the United States who take a more positive view of the ALI Principles.[4] At any rate, a comparison between these Principles and the CEFL Principles would be an interesting project also in respect of the harmonization of family law from a global perspective. They are comparable.

In conclusion it is submitted that the comparison of the harmonization of family law in the United States, the Nordic countries and in Europe reveals that different stages have been reached. Both the United States and the Nordic cooperation have, however, one big advantage, admittedly the Nordic cooperation to a lesser extent: The harmonization process is not hindered by so many different languages. In Europe, we first have to agree on the terminology in a language which for many is first not their native language and, second, is different from the language in which one's legal education has been received and the law is practised. These terminological problems are extremely difficult. They are, for instance, currently being again experienced by the CEFL in its drafting of the questionnaire on property relations between spouses.

4 See for instance: BARTLETT, K.T., 'Preference, Presumption, Predisposition, and Common Sense: From Traditional Custody Doctrines to the American Law Institute's Family Dissolution Project,' 36 *Fam.L.Q.* 11 (2002) pp. 11–12, who discusses well-known U.S. family law scholars ROBERT LEVY, IRA ELLMAN, HERMA HILL KAY, GARY SKOLOFF and JOHN GREGORY, who were involved in drafting the ALI Principles; SCHEPARD, A.I., *The Unfinished Business of Modern Court Reform: Reflections on Children, Courts and Custody*, 2004; COOMBS, M., 'Insiders and Outsiders: What the American Law Institute Has Done for Gay and Lesbian Families', 8 *Duke J. Gender L.& Pol'y* (2001), p. 88.

3. CHILDREN AND THEIR PARENTS

This part of the book contains six contributions. The concluding remarks mainly focus on the eloquent contribution by LUCY SMITH on recent developments in child law, in particular the rights of the child. The most important instrument here is the Convention on the Rights of the Child (CRC). This author completely agrees with most of her views, especially with her interpretation of the best interest principle. In respect of two aspects, however, a different view can be held.

First, she argues that the *travaux préparatoires* of the CRC are not of any great assistance. The drafters were an open-ended working group who held different opinions on many important issues, and the final draft in many ways represented a compromise. This is a more general aspect of how to interpret international instruments. In this respect it is commonly acknowledged that explanatory reports to international conventions are one of the most important sources of information regarding the issues addressed in conventional rules. How should they be interpreted? What were the objectives of the drafters? What is the rationale of the different provisions? It goes without saying that international instruments are living instruments and social developments should be taken into account, but explanatory reports which are at our disposal in the case of international instruments remain important. This can be illustrated by the second aspect which is also debatable.

According to LUCY SMITH the wording of Article 7 CRC does not support the understanding that it gives the child a right to information about its biological parents because it would not have been the intention of the drafters to say anything about the identity of the biological father in cases of sperm donation. In particular, this restrictive interpretation provides food for thought. It intrigues this author who at Utrecht University is supervising RICHARD BLAUWHOFF's comparative PhD research which addresses 'The Right of the Child to Know his Origins'. In his view the following arguments should be taken into account. Whereas the *travaux préparatoires* with respect to Article 7 CRC do not indicate that the States Parties had contemplated a prohibition or limitation of donor anonymity, it cannot be concluded either that most States Parties expressly wished to exclude such an extensive interpretation. In fact, the General Guidelines call on States Parties to specify the measures they have taken to enable the child to know her or his 'parents'. In addition, Article 7 CRC is multi-interpretable because of the absence of a definition of the term '*parent*' coupled with the insertion of the words '*as far as possible*'. Article 8 CRC, proposed by the Argentine delegation, refers to the child's right to preserve her or his identity. In an extensive interpretation of identity, that latter provision may therefore also be regarded as a basis for the right to know one's origins. Thus, the original Argentine proposal conceptualised the child's identity as something deeper and more encompassing than the protection of cornerstones of the child's legal identity (name, nationality and legal parentage) with reference to the '*inalienable right to retain his true and genuine personal, legal and family identity.*' When deprived of important elements of identity, Argentina added that '*in particular, this obligation of the State includes restoring the child to his blood-relations to be brought up.*' On the basis of country reports of the Committee on the Rights of the Child, Hodgkin and Newell hold that it is reasonable to assume that the child's right to know within the meaning of Article 7 CRC encompasses three forms of parentage: the genetic parents, the birth parents and the psychological parents.[5] In view of expected problems with the practice of secret adoption, the words '*as far as possible*' were proposed by Germany and the United States, even though the latter has not ratified the Convention. For the same reason Poland also objected to a more absolute definition. The Czech Republic expressed reservations with respect to both artificial insemination and secret adoption. Only the insertion of the words 'as far as possible' proved acceptable to all States Parties, although some states perceived that their inclusion could lead to arbitrary limitations to the right to know. Furthermore, it seems significant that in relation to the Norwegian report, the Committee on the Rights of the Child mentioned the '*possible contradiction*' between '*the right to know his or her genetic origins*' and the policies of State Parties '*in relation to artificial insemination namely in keeping the identity of donors secret*'.[6] In addition, in relation to the French practice of permitting mothers to give birth anonymously, the Committee has tentatively voiced the criticism that this '*might not fully reflect the provisions of the Convention, particularly its general principles*'.[7] From such comments it may be inferred that the right contained in Articles 7 and 8 may indeed very well include knowledge of *genetic* parentage and that the words '*as far as possible*' as contained in Article 7 CRC should be interpreted as requiring a significant effort on the part of States Parties to enable children to have access to such information, regardless of the way in which they have been conceived, the circumstances under which they have been born or the form of their legal parents' relationship.

The common point of departure of the other contributions belonging to this part has not been equality between parents regarding their children, but equality between all children in respect of their parents. This line has been drawn by Balázs Somfai, Mariel Dimsey, David Hill and Machteld Vonk in respect

5 Hodgkin R./Newell P., *Implementation Handbook for the Convention on the Rights of the Child* (2002), p. 105.

6 Ibid, p. 107.

7 France IRCO, Add. 20, par. 14.

of the legal position of children in different-sex and same-sex relationships. The idea of strengthening their position is generally supported. Due to the fact that a third party is involved the new term 'multi-parent families' has been created. Further, what should be the meaning of 'intention' as a legal basis of parenthood? The views differ; however, it is important that the differences in the legal status of the parents should not be decisive but only the need to protect children. This is also the primary consideration of the CEFL Principles on Parental Responsibilities which in this part of the book are introduced and explained by this author.

4. IRREGULAR MARRIAGES AND THE INFLUENCE OF MULTICULTURALISM

Three contributions belong to this part. In discussing the decision of the ECHR on 13 September 2005 in the Case of B. and L. v. the United Kingdom where the Court decided that the prohibition on parents-in-law marrying children-in-law under United Kingdom law constitutes a violation of Article 12 ECHR, Maebh Harding addresses the issue of prohibited degrees of affinity as a restriction on the right to marry. In his comparative study which includes Irish, English and French law the author critically analyses the law on marriage within prohibited degrees of affinity whereby the historical development of the respective rules plays an important role. In many other European countries these bars on marriage were lifted some years ago as serving no purpose.[8] According to Maebh Harding it is clear that the prohibitions on marriage between those related by affinity have changed from being a universally understood element of marriage itself to being a restriction on marriage. He concludes that this change is yet another example of how the right to marry is growing stronger and the restrictions on the right to marry are constantly being eroded.

The other two contributions address the influence and meaning of Islamic law within Western society. During the last 30 years many European countries have experienced through immigration a considerable enlargement of the Muslim population. The clash of cultures often causes legal problems. Mosa Sayed explores the question of how the Islamic *mahr* should be qualified within a European jurisdiction. He makes special reference to the Swedish situation where the categorization of the Muslim dower has caused considerable difficulties. The author argues that the *mahr* should be qualified as a special agreement of its own separated from both maintenance and the spouses' matrimonial property regime.

8 See in general on the influence of the decisions of the ECHR on national family law, Van Grunderbeeck D., *Beginselen van personen- en familierecht. Een mensenrechtelijke benadering*, 2003.

When it comes to cross-border relationships he favours the application of the *lex loci contractus* rule.

Aspasia Tsaoussi and Eleni Zervogianni remind us that multiculturalism is a very clever term to use when trying to explain religious and cultural differences – but it does not hold up well when trying to account for weak or non-existent rights. They demonstrate – by taking Greece as an example – that in Islamic subcultures living in countries of the West, freedom of religion has become the legitimate excuse for Muslim women's inferior legal and social status in relation to men. According to this author's opinion their general conclusion that Muslim women are twice disadvantaged: once as members of a religious minority (as Muslims) and twice as members of a social minority (as women) does not only apply to the situation in Greece but to many other European countries. If Muslim women were free to choose, they would no doubt choose the legal system that would offer them greater guarantees for the protection of their rights. This author agrees that the State must choose for Muslim women and secure their access to any and all mechanisms of legal redress because they are not free to choose.

5. (PROPERTY) RELATIONS BETWEEN SPOUSES AND COHABITANTS

Due to its increased importance the non-formalized relationship is a highly debated legal issue. Crucial are the following questions: When does cohabitation start and when does it end? Should a financial relief system be introduced? Göran Lind provides a global comparative overview of the different legal constructions which are currently applied. He suggests making a compromise between the need for protection on the one side, and the freedom of the parties to choose, on the other. Legislation should only provide basic minimum protection and parties, in order to obtain more extensive protection, should themselves actively take legal measures by entering into a contract, drafting a will or marrying. In addition to Göran Lind's comprehensive overview Jo Miles explores the different European approaches (including other common law jurisdictions outside the EU) to cohabitation, whereby she includes the legislative measures that have recently been taken in order to improve the legal relationship of same-sex couples. She addresses three interrelated sets of questions: (1) Should cohabitants simply be subject to the same laws as spouses in the relevant jurisdiction? If not, (2) what sort of regime or remedy should be adopted for cohabitants? And finally (3) on what principles should that regime or remedy be based? By taking in particular both recent Scottish legislation and the report of the English Law Commission, which in July 2007 reported on cohabitation and its financial consequences when a relationship breaks down, into account the author argues that the opt-out model is the better option in the particular context of financial relief upon the breakdown of a relationship. This model has been adopted within Europe, for example by Sweden and Scotland, and has recently been recommended for Ireland and for England and Wales. Consequently, a default regime is to be provided by the national legislator. In this respect it is striking that Jo Miles refers to recent judicial decisions emanating from English courts. These decisions (*White v. White, Miller v. Miller, McFarlane v. McFarlane* and *Charman v Charman*) have already gained a great deal of attention also outside the United Kingdom. In Anne-Florence Bock's contribution, for instance, they are extensively discussed and compared to the Swiss matrimonial property regime. According to Jo Miles the three principles that have been identified to guide the court's assessment of what is "fair" in divorce also provide a useful menu to be considered when devising a new scheme for cohabitants in all European jurisdictions. These principles are: (1) sharing or partnership; (2) compensation for an economic disadvantage which has arisen as a result of the parties' contributions to the relationship, for example, as a result of one spouse giving up paid employment in order to care for children; and (3) the needs of both parties. The proposal raises many interesting questions at different levels. Not only on the national level is it to be considered whether cohabitants should be treated like spouses, e.g. that the matrimonial property regime should also apply to non-formalised relationships. Here a choice is to be made between an opt-in or opt-out model as earlier discussed. When we enter the European level it becomes more difficult. The drafting of a new scheme for cohabitants in all European jurisdictions will very much depend on whether a European matrimonial property scheme can and will be established. At this level the comparative perspective reveals that within Europe several completely different regimes are to be taken into account, such as Community of property, Community of accrued gains, Participation in acquisitions, a Deferred community of property, the Separation of property and the Separation of property together with distribution by the competent authority. Given this great variety of solutions it will be impossible to draft one single European matrimonial property regime. Instead, the devising of two systems is more feasible, one based on community and the other based on separation. Subsequently, the following question to be answered is whether the European matrimonial property regimes are also suitable as a European scheme for cohabitants or whether we should follow Jo Miles' proposal which is more oriented towards the adoption of national principles – in her case English law. Anyhow, these questions undoubtedly belong to the most important European challenges in today's family law. Furthermore, it should be noted that both contributions in this book on the legal position of cohabitants clearly demonstrate that non-formalised relationships are always compared with formalized relationships, predominately with marriage. This was finally the decisive argument why the CEFL did not continue its work in the field of cohabitation. First, a European framework which addresses the property relationship of spouses is needed. CEFL's provisional planning in this respect is as follows: The questionnaire on property relations between spouses which contains a total of 201 questions was finalised in December 2007. The national reports are to be submitted in the summer of 2008, a first investigation of the issues that should be addressed in the Principles on Property Relations between Spouses will take place at the end of 2008 whereas the final result is only scheduled for the end of 2010. In the drafting process of the CEFL Principles the already mentioned contribution by ANNE-FLORENCE BOCK and the one by ANNA HORÍNOVÁ on property relations between spouses in the legislation of the Czech Republic and in that of selected post-communist countries will prove to be useful.

6. CROSS-BORDER FAMILY RELATIONSHIPS

The current private international law aspects of cross-border family relations have been systematically and thoroughly addressed. In particular, TED DE BOER and MICHAEL HELLNER are very critical about the proposals of the European Commission in the field of divorce and maintenance law which are currently under discussion. Mainly the subsidiarity and proportionality of the new instruments give rise to considerable doubts. Also in this author's opinion the proposed amendment of the Brussels II bis Regulation should determine the applicability of the *lex fori* as the default rule when the spouses have not chosen the applicable divorce law. This is the Scandinavian proposal which has so far been rejected. However, every effort should still be undertaken to achieve this result. The final version of the amendment of Brussels II bis is expected to be published in the first half of 2008.

Apart from this principal concern regarding the conflict of law rules, according to this author's opinion the abbreviations of the new and amended instruments are a matter of concern. Uniform terminology is needed. Reference to *Rome III, IV* and *V* or *Brussels II ter* apparently becomes preposterous. In fact they do not say anything and become misleading. The amendment of *Brussels II bis* or *Brussels II a* or *Brussels II revised* will also contain conflict of law rules whereas the name *Brussels* so far only refers to international procedural law. How can this problem be resolved? According to this author's view it is desirable to only have one Private International Law regulation for cross-border family matters. This instrument should include rules on jurisdiction, conflict of law, recognition and enforcement and cooperation between central authorities. By the way, in addition to such a regulation on family matters the European legislator might also compile the *Brussels I*, the *Rome I* and the *Rome II* regulations and put them together into one European instrument: the Private International Law Regulation in Civil and Commercial Matters. All this should be based on a common European Private International Law methodology which should be established.

Private international law issues with regard to the Green Paper on the conflict of laws in matters concerning matrimonial property regimes including the question of jurisdiction and mutual recognition are critically analysed by Kathrin Kroll. Her guiding principles are certainty and predictability. It is to be expected that the future EU instrument in this field will introduce party autonomy. However, the parties are often not aware of the possibility to make a choice. How can relevant and correct information in this respect be provided? Should notaries and civil registrars be involved? Dutch practice, for instance, shows that even for a specialist in private international law it is very difficult to understand the content of the leaflets which are widely distributed in the Netherlands. Finally, Maria Álvarez Torné addresses the dissolution of the matrimonial property regime and the succession rights of the surviving spouse in private international law. She concludes that adjustment problems between succession and matrimonial property when dealing with succession rights of widowed spouses should be dealt with in the future European instrument, which intends to unify the law applicable to succession. Also in her contribution the information provided to spouses and partners about their possibility to select the applicable matrimonial property law and succession law plays an important role.

7. CEFL'S NEXT CHALLENGE: ITS 4TH CONFERENCE

Editing the conference proceedings and contributing to its content has been highly enjoyable. In addition, the conference itself was again another stimulating, well-organised and interesting event. Hence, there is every reason to continue the successful organisation of CEFL conferences in the field of European Family Law. Therefore, CEFL's 4th conference will be organised along the same lines as its predecessors. It will take place in Cambridge in 2010 in co-operation with Jo Miles and Jens Scherpe.

European Family Law Series

1. *Legal Recognition of Same-Sex Couples in Europe*, K. Boele-Woelki and A. Fuchs (eds.)
2. *European Family Law in Action Volume I: Grounds for divorce*, K. Boele-Woelki, B. Braat and I. Sumner (eds.)
3. European Family Law in Action Volume II: Maintenance Between Former Spouses, K. Boele-Woelki, B. Braat and I. Sumner (eds.)
4. *Perspectives for the Unification and Harmonisation of Family Law in Europe*, K. Boele-Woelki (ed.)
5. *Family Law Legislation of the Netherlands*, I. Sumner and H. Warendorf
6. *Indépendance et interdépendance patrimoniales des époux dans le régime matrimonial légal des droits néerlandais, français et suisse*, B. Braat
7. *Principles of European Family Law Regarding Divorce and Maintenance Between Former Spouses*, K. Boele-Woelki, F. Ferrand, C. González Beilfuss, M. Jänterä-Jareborg, N. Lowe, D. Martiny and W. Pintens
8. *Inheritance Law Legislation of the Netherlands*, I. Sumner and H. Warendorf
9. *European Family Law in Action Volume III: Parental Responsibilities*, K. Boele-Woelki, B. Braat and I. Curry Sumner (eds.)
10. *Common Core and Better Law in European Family Law*, K. Boele-Woelki (ed.)
11. *All's well that ends registered?*, I. Curry-Sumner
12. *Model Family Code – From a global perspective*, I. Schwenzer and M. Dimsey
13. *Harmonisation of Family Law in Europe. A Historical Perspective*, M. Antokolskaia
14. *Brussels II bis: Its Impact and Application in the Member States*, Katharina Boele-Woelki and Cristina González Beilfuss (eds.)
15. *Tensions between Legal, Biological and Social Conceptions of Parentage*, I. Schwenzer (ed.)
16. *Principles of European Family Law Regarding Parental Responsibilities*, K. Boele-Woelki, F. Ferrand, C. González Beilfuss, M. Jänterä-Jareborg, N. Lowe, D. Martiny and W. Pintens (eds.)
17. *Juxtaposing Legal Systems and the Principles of European Family Law on Divorce and Maintenance*, E. Örücü and J. Mair (eds.)
18. *Convergence and Divergence of Family Law in Europe*, M. Antokolskaia (ed.)
19. *European Challenges in Contemporary Family Law*, K. Boele-Woelki and T. Sverdrup (eds.)
20. *Children and their parents*, M. Vonk

www.ingramcontent.com/pod-product-compliance
Ingram Content Group UK Ltd.
Pitfield, Milton Keynes, MK11 3LW, UK
UKHW051925100926
8556IPUK00022B/1373

9 789050 956925